Guide to College Reading

Guide to College Reading

SIXTH EDITION

Kathleen T. McWhorter

Niagara County Community College

New York   San Francisco   Boston
London   Toronto   Sydney   Tokyo   Singapore   Madrid
Mexico City   Munich   Paris   Cape Town   Hong Kong   Montreal

VICE PRESIDENT AND EDITOR-IN-CHIEF	Joseph Terry
SENIOR ACQUISITIONS EDITOR	Steven Rigolosi
DEVELOPMENT EDITOR	Leslie Taggart
SENIOR MARKETING MANAGER	Melanie Craig
SUPPLEMENTS EDITOR	Donna Campion
MEDIA SUPPLEMENTS EDITOR	Nancy Garcia
PRODUCTION MANAGER	Donna DeBenedictis
PROJECT COORDINATION, TEXT DESIGN, AND ELECTRONIC PAGE MAKEUP	Elm Street Publishing Services, Inc.
COVER DESIGN MANAGER	John Callahan
COVER DESIGNER	Kay Petronio
COVER PHOTOS	PhotoDisc, Inc.
PHOTO RESEARCHER	Julie Tesser
MANUFACTURING BUYER	Al Dorsey
PRINTER AND BINDER	RR Donnelley & Sons Company/ Harrisonburg
COVER PRINTER	Phoenix Color Corp.

For permission to use copyrighted material, grateful acknowledgment is made to the copyright holders on pp. 595–599, which are hereby made part of this copyright page.

Library of Congress Cataloging-in-Publication Data

McWhorter, Kathleen T.
    Guide to college reading / Kathleen T. McWhorter.—6th ed.
        p.; cm.
    Includes bibliographical references and index.
    ISBN 0-321-08862-X (alk. paper)
        1. Reading (Higher education) 2. Development reading. 3. College reading. I. Title.

LB2395.3 .M386 2003
428.4'071'1—dc21

2002276820

Please visit our website at http://www.ablongman.com/mcwhorter

ISBN 0-321-08862-X (Student Edition)
ISBN 0-321-08863-8 (Annotated Instructor's Edition)

5 6 7 8 9 10—DOH—05 04

Brief Contents

Detailed Contents

CHAPTER 7   Understanding Paragraphs: Topics, Stated Main Ideas, and Implied Main Ideas   180

CHAPTER 8   Understanding Paragraphs: Supporting Details and Transitions   222

CHAPTER 9   Following the Author's Thought Patterns   259

CHAPTER 14   Evaluating: Asking Critical Questions   471

Part Five: A Fiction Mini Reader   507

Reading and Interpreting Short Stories   507

Part Six: Reading Selections   533

To the Instructor

The influx of nontraditional students into both two- and four-year colleges has enriched the educational scene; at the same time, it has made the preparation of these students for academic success an institutional priority. *Guide to College Reading*, Sixth Edition, is written to equip students of widely different backgrounds with the basic reading and critical thinking skills needed to cope with the demands of academic work. This Sixth Edition offers students new and expanded material on self-assessment of reading skills, stated and implied main ideas, supporting details and transitions, summarizing, and reading fiction. Two new mastery tests have been added to each chapter as well. Vocabulary development is integrated throughout the book to provide ongoing reinforcement and review.

THE PURPOSE OF THIS TEXT

Guide to College Reading addresses the learning characteristics, attitudes, and motivational levels of reading students. It is intended to equip students with the skills they need to handle the diverse reading demands of college courses. Specifically, the book guides students in becoming active learners and critical thinkers. This text adopts an encouraging, supportive, nonthreatening voice and an unassuming attitude toward learning. The text provides a variety of everyday examples and extensive exercises to encourage students to become involved and to apply the skills presented.

The chapters are divided into numerous sections; exercises are frequent but brief and explicit. The language and style are simple and direct; explanations are clear and often presented in step-by-step form. Reading topics and materials have been chosen carefully to relate to the students' interests and background, while exhibiting potential for broadening their range of experience. Many students have compensated for poor reading skills with alternate learning styles; they have become visual and auditory learners. To capitalize on this adaptation, a visual approach to learning, including drawings, diagrams, and visual aids to illustrate concepts, is used throughout.

CONTENT OVERVIEW

The text is organized into six major sections, following the logical progression of skill development from words to sentences and then to paragraphs, articles, essays, and chapters. It also proceeds logically from literal comprehension to critical interpretation and response. An opening chapter focuses on student success strategies, including such topics as attitudes toward college, concentration, learning styles, and comprehension monitoring.

- **Part One teaches students basic approaches to vocabulary development.** It includes contextual aids, analysis of word parts, pronunciation, and the use of the dictionary and other reference sources.
- **Part Two helps students develop literal comprehension skills.** It emphasizes prereading techniques that prepare and enable the student to comprehend and to recall content. Previewing, activating background knowledge, and using guide questions are emphasized. The unit provides extensive instruction and practice with sentence and paragraph comprehension and recognition of thought patterns. An entire chapter is now devoted to stated and implied main ideas; another entire chapter focuses on supporting details and transitions.
- **Part Three teaches students textbook reading skills.** Topics include textbook learning aids, chapter organization, ways to read graphics and technical material, and methods of organizing and retaining course content.
- **Part Four introduces critical reading and thinking skills.** It presents skills that enable students to interact with and evaluate written material, including material on the Internet. Topics include making inferences, identifying the author's purpose, recognizing assumptions, and distinguishing fact and opinion.
- **Part Five, "A Fiction Mini Reader," offers a brief introduction to reading fiction.** An introductory section discusses the essential elements of a short story, using Chopin's "The Story of An Hour" as a demonstration. Four additional short stories with accompanying apparatus are also included.
- **Part Six, "Reading Selections," contains eight additional articles, essays, and textbook excerpts.** Each selection was chosen on the basis of interest and applicability to the skills taught in the text and is prefaced by an interest-catching introduction, a vocabulary preview, and a previewing question. Literal and critical questions as well as a words-in-context exercise, vocabulary review, and a writing exercise follow each selection.

SPECIAL FEATURES

The following features enhance the text's effectiveness and directly contribute to students' success:

- **Integration of Reading and Writing.** The text integrates reading and writing skills. Students respond to exercises by writing sentences and paragraphs. Answers to most questions for each reading selection also require composition. A writing exercise accompanies each reading selection.
- **Reading as Thinking.** Reading is approached as a thinking process—a process in which the student interacts with textual material and sorts, evaluates, and reacts to its organization and content. For example, students are shown how to define their purpose for reading, ask questions, identify and use organization and structure as a guide to understanding, make inferences, and interpret and evaluate what they read.
- **Comprehension Monitoring.** Comprehension monitoring is also addressed within the text. Through a variety of techniques, students are encouraged to be aware of and to evaluate and control their levels of comprehension of the material they read.
- **Skill Application.** Chapters 2 through 14 conclude with four mastery tests that enable students to apply the skills taught in each chapter and to evaluate their learning.

NEW TO THE SIXTH EDITION

Numerous changes and additions have been made in this Sixth Edition to offer more frequent opportunities for monitoring skill development through additional mastery tests. There is expanded coverage of main ideas and supporting details through the creation of a separate chapter for each, reinforcement of summary writing skills, and new coverage of skills for reading fiction.

- **Reading Self-Assessment, "How Do You READ?"** A new four-part self-assessment has been added at the beginning of the book. The questions guide students in rating their attitudes toward learning, evaluating their reading habits, assessing their skills, and deciding how they learn best.
- **Mastery Tests.** Two new mastery tests in a multiple-choice format have been added to Chapters 2–14, making four in all. The first mastery test with questions based on sentences or small units of prose, applies chapter content at the most elemental level. The second, with questions usually based on single paragraphs, measures chapter skills as applied to paragraph level material. Two other mastery tests were carried over from the previous edition; the third mastery test is based on a passage while the fourth includes a complete reading selection.
- **A Separate Chapter on Stated and Implied Main Ideas.** In the previous edition, main ideas and details were covered in a single chapter. The Sixth Edition includes a separate chapter for each skill. The new chapter on main ideas offers expanded coverage of general vs. specific ideas and of implied main ideas. Extensive new practice exercises have also been added.
- **A Separate Chapter on Supporting Details and Transitions.** This new chapter takes a strong visual approach, using maps to show relationships

among main ideas, major supporting details, and minor details. Many additional practice exercises have been added.

- **Fiction Mini Reader.** Comprising a new Part Five of the book, a fiction mini reader offers an introduction to reading short stories, including the key elements of setting, tone, plot, characterization, and theme. Chopin's "The Story of An Hour" is used as a model. Four additional short stories with accompanying multiple-choice and discussion questions are included. Students read an African folk tale and works by Poe, John Collier, and Frank Stockton.

- **Summarizing.** A new exercise on summarizing has been added to each reading in Part Six, "Reading Selections." For the first four readings, the exercises provide an incomplete summary and students are asked to supply missing information. As the section progresses, these exercises provide diminishing cues, requiring students to supply more information and demonstrate greater mastery of summarizing skills. The summary exercises for the last four readings ask students to write their own summaries.

- **New Reading Selections.** Eight new reading selections have been added to the book, replacing outdated selections in the previous edition.

BOOK-SPECIFIC ANCILLARY MATERIALS

- **Annotated Instructor's Edition**
  The Annotated Instructor's Edition is identical to the student text but includes all answers printed directly on the pages where questions, exercises, or activities occur. 0-321-08863-8

- **Instructor's Manual**
  An Instructor's Manual, including an Answer Key, accompanies the text. The manual describes in detail the basic features of the text and offers suggestions for structuring the course, for teaching nontraditional students, and for approaching each section of the text. 0-321-08864-6

- **Test Bank**
  This new supplement features two sets of chapter quizzes and a mastery test for each chapter. It is printed in an 8½ x 11 format that allows for easy photocopying and distribution. 0-321-08865-4

- **PowerPoint Presentations**
  For the lab or electronic classroom, a PowerPoint Presentation is available for each chapter of *Guide to College Reading*. Each chapter's presentation consists of approximately 15–20 slides highlighting key concepts from the text, as well as additional activities. Download the presentations from our Website at **http://www.ablongman.com/mcwhorter.**

- **Companion Website**
  We are proud to offer a complete Website to accompany *Guide to College Reading*. Visit this site for additional quizzes, readings, and Web-based activities for each chapter of the text. **http://www.ablongman.com/ mcwhorter.**

THE LONGMAN BASIC SKILLS PACKAGE

In addition to the book-specific supplements discussed above, a series of other skills-based supplements is available for both instructors and students. All of these supplements are available either free or at greatly reduced prices.

Electronic and Online Offerings

[NEW WEB VERSION] Longman Reading Road Trip Multimedia Software, CD Version and Web Version. This innovative and exciting multimedia reading software is available either on CD-ROM or on the Web. The package takes students on a tour of 15 cities and landmarks throughout the United States. Each of the 15 modules corresponds to a reading or study skill (for example, finding the main idea, understanding patterns of organization, and thinking critically). All modules contain a tour of the location, instruction and tutorial, exercises, interactive feedback, and mastery tests. To shrinkwrap the CD or the access code to the Website with this textbook, please consult your Longman sales representative.

[NEW] Longman Vocabulary Website. For additional vocabulary-related resources, visit our free vocabulary Website at **http://www.ablongman.com/vocabulary.**

The Longman English Pages Website. Both students and instructors can visit our free content-rich Website for additional reading selections and writing exercises. From the Longman English pages, visitors can conduct a simulated Web search, learn how to write a resume and cover letter, or try their hand at poetry writing. Stop by and visit us at **http://www.ablongman.com/englishpages.**

The Longman Electronic Newsletter. Twice a month during the spring and fall, instructors who have subscribed receive a free copy of the Longman Developmental English Newsletter in their e-mailbox. Written by experienced classroom instructors, the newsletter offers teaching tips, classroom activities, book reviews, and more. To subscribe, visit the Longman Basic Skills Website at **http://www.ablongman.com/basicskills,** or send an e-mail to **Basic Skills@ablongman.com.**

For Additional Reading and Reference

The Dictionary Deal. Two dictionaries can be shrinkwrapped with *Guide to College Reading* at a nominal fee. *The New American Webster Handy College*

Dictionary is a paperback reference text with more than 100,000 entries. *Merriam Webster's Collegiate Dictionary,* Tenth Edition, is a hardback reference with a citation file of more than 14.5 million examples of English words drawn from actual use. For more information on how to shrinkwrap a dictionary with your text, please contact your Longman sales representative.

Penguin Quality Paperback Titles. A series of Penguin paperbacks is available at a significant discount when shrinkwrapped with any Longman Basic Skills title. Some titles available are Toni Morrison's *Beloved,* Julia Alvarez's *How the Garcia Girls Lost Their Accents,* Mark Twain's *Huckleberry Finn, Narrative of the Life of Frederick Douglass,* Harriet Beecher Stowe's *Uncle Tom's Cabin,* Dr. Martin Luther King, Jr.'s *Why We Can't Wait,* and plays by Shakespeare, Miller, and Albee. For a complete list of titles or more information, please contact your Longman sales consultant.

The Pocket Reader **and** *The Brief Pocket Reader.* These inexpensive volumes contain 80 brief readings and 50 readings, respectively. Each reading is brief (1–3 pages each). The readers are theme-based: writers on writing, nature, women and men, customs and habits, politics, rights and obligations, and coming of age. Also included is an alternate rhetorical table of contents.

The Longman Textbook Reader. This supplement, for use in developmental reading courses, offers five complete chapters from Addison-Wesley/Longman textbooks: computer science, biology, psychology, communications, and business. Each chapter includes additional comprehensive quizzes, critical thinking questions, and group activities. Available FREE with the adoption of this Longman text. For information on how to bundle *The Longman Textbook Reader* with your text, please contact your Longman sales representative. Available in two formats: with answers and without answers.

Newsweek **Alliance.** Instructors may choose to shrinkwrap a 12-week subscription to *Newsweek* with any Longman text. The price of the subscription is 57 cents per issue (a total of $6.84 for the subscription). Available with the subscription is a free "Interactive Guide to *Newsweek*"—a workbook for students who are using the text. In addition, *Newsweek* provides a wide variety of instructor supplements free to teachers, including maps, Skills Builders, and weekly quizzes. For more information on the *Newsweek* program, please contact your Longman sales representative.

For Instructors

[NEW] Electronic Test Bank for Reading. This electronic test bank offers more than 3,000 questions in all areas of reading, including vocabulary, main idea, supporting details, patterns of organization, language, critical thinking, analytical reasoning, inference, point of view, visual aids, and textbook reading. With this easy-to-use CD-ROM, instructors simply choose questions from the electronic test bank, then print out the completed test for distribution. CD-ROM: 0-321-08179-X Print version: 0-321-08596-5

CLAST Test Package, Fourth Edition. These two 40-item objective tests evaluate students' readiness for the CLAST exams. Strategies for teaching CLAST preparedness are included. Free with any Longman English title. Reproducible sheets: 0-321-01950-4 Computerized IBM version: 0-321-01982-2 Computerized Mac version: 0-321-01983-0

TASP Test Package, Third Edition. These 12 practice pre-tests and post-tests assess the same reading and writing skills covered in the TASP examination. Free with any Longman English title. Reproducible sheets: 0-321-01959-8 Computerized IBM version: 0-321-01985-7 Computerized Mac version: 0-321-01984-9

Teaching Online: Internet Research, Conversation, and Composition, Second Edition. Ideal for instructors who have never surfed the Net, this easy-to-follow guide offers basic definitions, numerous examples, and step-by-step information about finding and using Internet sources. Free to adopters. 0-321-01957-1

[NEW] The Longman Guide to Classroom Management. Written by Joannis Flatley of St. Philip's College, this is the first in a series of monographs for developmental educators. It focuses on issues of classroom etiquette, providing guidance on dealing with unruly, unengaged, disruptive, or uncooperative students. 0-321-09246-5

[NEW] The Longman Instructor's Planner. This is an all-in-one resource for instructors. It includes monthly and weekly planning sheets, to-do lists, student contact forms, attendance rosters, a gradebook, an address/phone book, and a mini almanac. It is free upon request. 0-321-09247-3

For Students

[NEW] The Longman Reader's Journal, by Kathleen T. McWhorter. This reader's journal offers students a space to record their questions about, reactions to, and summaries of materials they've read. Also included is a personal vocabulary log, as well as ample space for free writing. For an examination copy, contact your Longman sales consultant. 0-321-08843-3

[NEW] The Longman Reader's Portfolio. This unique supplement provides students with a space to plan, think about, and present their work. The portfolio includes a diagnostic area (including a learning style questionnaire), a working area (including calendars, vocabulary logs, reading response sheets, book club tips, and other valuable materials), and a display area (including a progress chart, a final table of contents, and a final assessment). Ask your Longman sales representative for ISBN 0-321-10766-7

***Researching Online,* Sixth Edition.** A perfect companion for a new age, this indispensable new supplement helps students navigate the Internet. Adapted from *Teaching Online,* the instructor's Internet guide, *Researching Online* speaks directly to students, giving them detailed, step-by-step instructions for performing electronic searches. Available free when shrinkwrapped with this text. 0-321-11733-6

Ten Practices of Highly Successful Students. This popular supplement helps student learn crucial study skills, offering concise tips for a successful career in college. Topics include time management, test-taking, reading critically, stress, and motivation. 0-205-30769-8

[For Florida Adopters] *Thinking Through the Test,* by D. J. Henry. This special workbook, prepared specially for students in Florida, offers ample skill and practice exercises to help students prep for the Florida State Exit Exam. To shrinkwrap this workbook free with your textbook, please contact your Longman sales representative. Available in two versions: with answers and without answers. Also available are two laminated grids (one for reading, one for writing) that can serve as handy references for students preparing for the Florida State Exit Exam.

The Longman Planner. This free planner helps students organize a busy life. Ask your Longman sales representative for an examination copy. 0-321-04573-4

ACKNOWLEDGMENTS

I wish to express my gratitude to my reviewers for their excellent ideas, suggestions, and advice on this and previous editions of this text:

Dorothy Booher, Florida Community College at Jacksonville, Kent Campus
Diane Bosco, Suffolk County Community College
Shirley Hall, Middle Georgia College
Kevin Hayes, Essex County College
Peggy Hopper, Walters State Community College
Arlene Jellinek, Palm Beach Community College

Jeanne Keefe, Belleville Area College
Jackie Stahlecker, St. Phillips College
Mary Wolting, Indiana University—Purdue University at Indianapolis
Danica Hubbard, College of DuPage
Suzanne E. Hughes, Florida Community College at Jacksonville
Patti Levine-Brown, Florida Community College at Jacksonville
Catherine Packard, Southeastern Illinois College
Kathy Purswell, Frank Phillips College
Diane Schellack, Burlington County College
Nora Yaeger, Cedar Valley College

I am particularly indebted to Leslie Taggart, my developmental editor, for her energetic guidance and valuable advice and to Steven Rigolosi, Senior Acquisitions Editor, for his enthusiastic support of this project.

                                                    Kathleen T. McWhorter

Quick Guide to the Book

Guide to College Reading offers students careful, step-by-step instruction and practice in crucial discrete reading skills, such as identifying the main idea, learning the SQ3R approach to reading, and using textbook learning aids. At the same time, the text builds reading and thinking skills by integrating instruction and assessment throughout the book in important areas such as vocabulary development, methods for improving comprehension, and techniques for students with different learning styles.

READING COMPREHENSION (See also Main Ideas and Details and Transitions, below)

MAIN IDEAS

DETAILS AND TRANSITIONS

VOCABULARY DEVELOPMENT

CRITICAL READING, THINKING, AND WRITING

LEARNING STYLE ANALYSIS AND TIPS

READING ELECTRONIC SOURCES

READING SHORT FICTION

ASSESSMENT AND EVALUATION

To the Student

- Do you find reading difficult or boring?
- Do you find yourself daydreaming as you read?
- Do you sometimes read an entire page and remember very little of what you read?
- As you read, do you often meet words you don't know or cannot pronounce?

HOW THIS BOOK CAN HELP YOU

If you answered "yes" to any of the above questions, this book can help you find a new, more successful approach to reading. This text is designed to make you a more successful college student by improving your ability to grasp and remember what you read. This book will also show you how to learn as you read and how to think clearly and critically about what you read. You will learn how to complete a reading assignment with little pain and much gain! The following sections describe the book and tell you how to get the most out of it.

HOW THE BOOK IS ORGANIZED

The book is divided into six parts:

Part One: Vocabulary
Part Two: Comprehension Skills
Part Three: Textbook Reading Skills
Part Four: Critical Reading
Part Five: A Fiction Mini Reader
Part Six: Reading Selections

The chapters in Parts One through Five offer you new techniques and methods for building your skills. Part Six contains eight reading selections that give you an opportunity to practice the skills you have learned in the text. Each reading contains a brief introduction, a vocabulary preview, a prereading question, the reading itself, questions that check your comprehension, questions that ask you to think critically, two vocabulary exercises, exercises for writing summaries, and writing exercises.

HOW EACH CHAPTER IS ORGANIZED

Each chapter has numerous features to help you learn. As you read through the following features, choose a chapter, locate each feature in it, and then place a checkmark in the box to the left of its name.

This Chapter Will Show You How To

Each chapter begins with a list of skills you will learn in the chapter.

> **THIS CHAPTER WILL SHOW YOU HOW TO**
>
> 1. **Start with a positive attitude**
> 2. **Build your concentration**
> 3. **Analyze your learning style**
> 4. **Strengthen your comprehension**

Before you read the chapter, read through the list of skills; you will then know what to expect in the chapter and will avoid any surprises. After you have read the chapter, you can use the list as a quick self-test. Turn each item in the list into a question and try to answer it without looking in the chapter itself. For example, the item "Pick out the key details" becomes "How do I pick out the key details?"

Skill Instruction

Each chapter offers clear, step-by-step instructions for mastering each skill, usually followed by one or more examples.

> ### Contrast Clues
>
> It is sometimes possible to determine the meaning of an unknown word from a word or phrase in the context that has an opposite meaning. If a single word provides a clue, it is often an **antonym**—a word opposite in meaning of the unknown word. Notice, in the following sentence, how a word opposite in meaning from the boldfaced word provides a clue to its meaning:
>
> One of the dinner guests **succumbed** to the temptation to have a second piece of cake, but the others resisted.

As you read these instructional sections, highlight important information. When you have finished a chapter, review your highlighting before closing your book.

Exercises

After you have learned a skill, you immediately practice it in the numerous exercises contained in the chapter.

> **EXERCISE 2-3**   **Directions:** Read each sentence and write a definition or synonym for each boldfaced word. Use the contrast clue to help you determine meaning.
>
> 1. Some city dwellers are **affluent**; others live in or near poverty.

Mastering Vocabulary

Each chapter contains one or more vocabulary exercises that help you learn difficult words presented in the chapter.

> ### MASTERING VOCABULARY
>
> **Directions:** Match each word in Column A with its meaning in Column B. Determine the meaning from its context in this chapter, its word parts, or use a dictionary, if necessary.
>
> | | Column A | | Column B |
> |---|---|---|---|
> | _____ | 1. imitating (p. 152) | a. | changes in tune or rhythm |
> | _____ | 2. evidence (p. 156) | b. | data, information |
> | _____ | 3. inhabited (p. 156) | c. | possible, capable of happening |
> | _____ | 4. interpretation (p. 159) | d. | current, modern |
> | _____ | 5. norms (p. 159) | e. | following the example of |
> | _____ | 6. variations (p. 161) | f. | spreading, enlarging |
> | _____ | 7. distinction (p. 163) | g. | explanation of meaning |
> | _____ | 8. potential (p. 164) | h. | standards |
> | _____ | 9. contemporary (p. 164) | i. | difference |
> | _____ | 10. expansion (p. 165) | j. | lived in |

To learn these words, choose a method that works best for you: create a separate section of your notebook, open a computer file for vocabulary, or start a file of index cards. Enter words and meanings that you want to learn. Study and review your list frequently.

☐ Learning Style Tip

In Chapter 1 you will complete a questionnaire (pp. 11–5) that will help you discover five aspects of how you learn, known as your learning style. You will find out, for example, whether you are a creative learner or a practical, systematic learner. Each chapter contains a box that offers suggestions for how to learn or apply skills taught in the chapter for one or more aspects of your learning style.

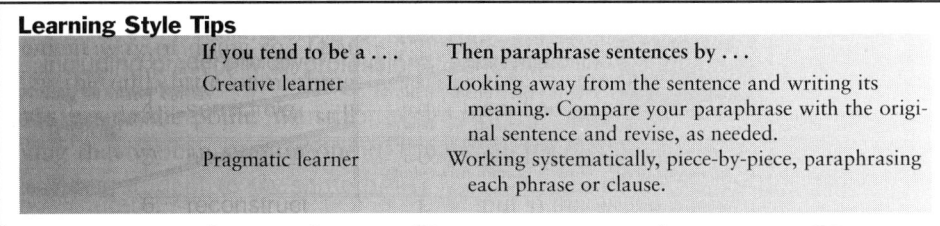

Learning Style Tips

If you tend to be a . . .	Then paraphrase sentences by . . .
Creative learner	Looking away from the sentence and writing its meaning. Compare your paraphrase with the original sentence and revise, as needed.
Pragmatic learner	Working systematically, piece-by-piece, paraphrasing each phrase or clause.

Be sure to try out each suggestion. Don't hesitate to experiment. You might also try suggestions for learning styles other than your own.

☐ Summary

After you finish a chapter, use the summary to test yourself. Good students always test themselves before their instructor does.

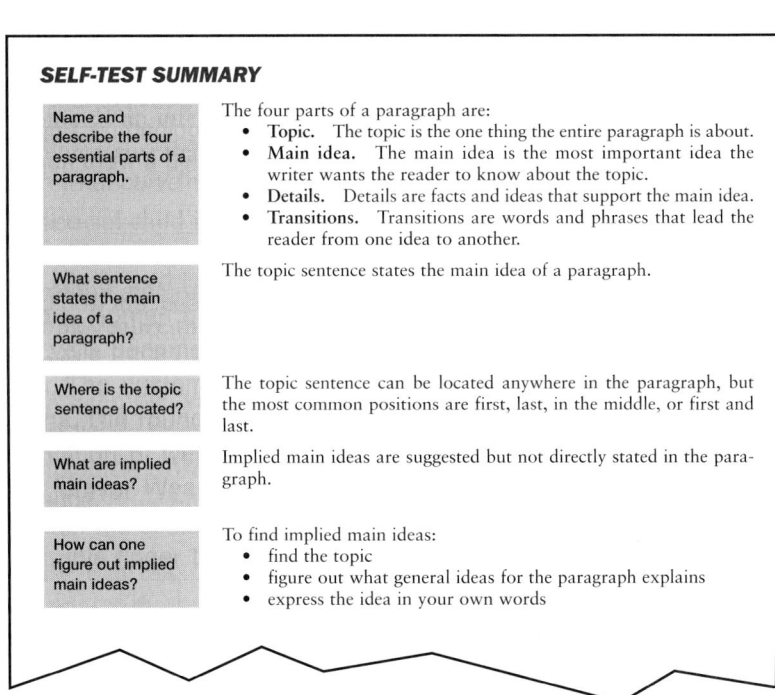

SELF-TEST SUMMARY

Name and describe the four essential parts of a paragraph.	The four parts of a paragraph are: • **Topic.** The topic is the one thing the entire paragraph is about. • **Main idea.** The main idea is the most important idea the writer wants the reader to know about the topic. • **Details.** Details are facts and ideas that support the main idea. • **Transitions.** Transitions are words and phrases that lead the reader from one idea to another.
What sentence states the main idea of a paragraph?	The topic sentence states the main idea of a paragraph.
Where is the topic sentence located?	The topic sentence can be located anywhere in the paragraph, but the most common positions are first, last, in the middle, or first and last.
What are implied main ideas?	Implied main ideas are suggested but not directly stated in the paragraph.
How can one figure out implied main ideas?	To find implied main ideas: • find the topic • figure out what general ideas for the paragraph explains • express the idea in your own words

Mastery Tests 1, 2, and 3: Applying Your Skills

Each chapter concludes with three mastery tests designed to help you find out if you have learned and can apply the skills taught in the chapter. The first tests usually involve sentences and the later tests ask you to work on paragraphs.

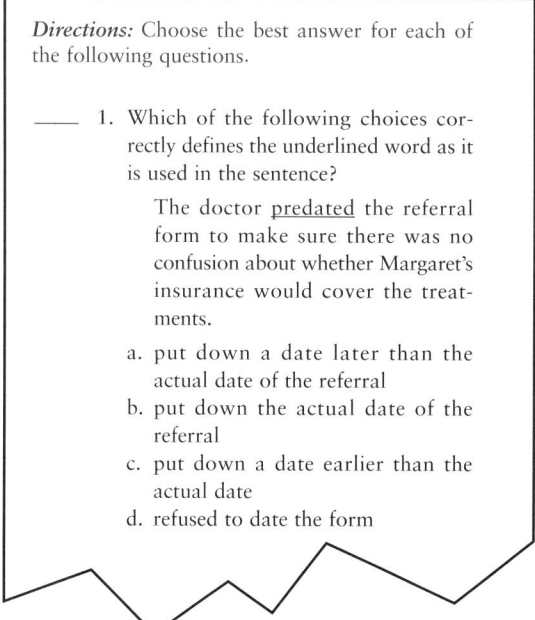

Directions: Choose the best answer for each of the following questions.

_____ 1. Which of the following choices correctly defines the underlined word as it is used in the sentence?

The doctor <u>predated</u> the referral form to make sure there was no confusion about whether Margaret's insurance would cover the treatments.

a. put down a date later than the actual date of the referral
b. put down the actual date of the referral
c. put down a date earlier than the actual date
d. refused to date the form

To do your best on mastery tests, review the chapter and use the summary as a self-test before beginning the mastery tests.

Chapter Reading with Mastery Test 4

A reading selection chosen from a book, article, or essay, along with questions appears at the end of each chapter.

Right Place, Wrong Face

Alton Fitzgerald White

In this selection, the author describes what it was like to be treated as a criminal on the basis of nothing more than having the "wrong face."

Vocabulary Preview

ovation (par. 3) enthusiastic, prolonged applause

overt (par. 4) not secret, obvious

splurged (par. 5) indulged in a luxury

vestibule (par. 5) a small entrance hall or passage into the interior of a building

residue (par. 9) something that remains after a substance is taken away

violation (par. 14) the condition of being treated unfairly or offended

1   As the youngest of five girls and two boys growing up in Cincinnati, I was raised to believe that if I worked hard, was a good person, and always told the truth, the world would be my oyster. I was raised to be a gentleman and learned that these qualities would bring me respect.

2   While one has to earn respect, consideration is something owed to every human being. On Friday, June 16, 1999, when I was wrongfully arrested at my Harlem apartment building, my perception of everything I had learned as a young man was forever changed—not only because I wasn't given even a second to use the manners my parents taught me, but mostly because the police, whom I'd always naively thought were sup-

posed to serve and protect me, were actually hunting me.

3   I had planned a pleasant day. The night before was payday, plus I had received a standing ovation after portraying the starring role of Coalhouse Walker Jr. in the Broadway musical *Ragtime*. It is a role that requires not only talent but also an honest emotional investment of the morals and lessons I learned as a child.

4   Coalhouse Walker Jr. is a victim (an often misused word, but in this case true) of overt racism. His story is every black man's nightmare. He is hard-working, successful, talented, charismatic, friendly, and polite. Perfect prey for someone with authority and not even a fraction of those qualities. On that Friday afternoon, I became a real-life Coalhouse Walker. Nothing could have prepared me for it. Not even stories told to me

Each reading contains a brief introduction, a vocabulary preview, and ten multiple-choice questions that check your comprehension and ask you to apply skills taught in the chapter. As you work through each reading selection make a conscious effort to apply the skills taught in the chapter, as well as those from previous chapters you have already learned. Record your score on the Progress Charts on pp. 585–586.

HOW TO MAKE RAPID PROGRESS

To improve your reading skills you will need a lot of practice—even more than this book provides. The more you practice, the more quickly your skills will improve. Here are a few sources of additional practice.

- **Textbooks for your other courses.** Take time to apply each skill you learn to all reading assignments you complete for each of your other college courses.
- **The Longman English Pages. http://www.ablongman.com/englishpages.** This is an Internet site sponsored by the publisher of this book. It contains useful exercises that you can complete for further practice. You may need to ask your instructor for a password in order to use the site. You may also access this book's Website at **http://www.ablongman. com/mcwhorter.**
- **Your college's Skills Center or tutoring program.** Many colleges have Academic Skills Centers and tutoring programs where you can obtain additional assistance in improving your skills.
- **Books, newspapers, and magazines.** One of the best ways to improve your reading skills is to read widely. Read a variety of materials; read anything that interests you, that looks like fun, or that will keep you informed about current news and issues.

The opportunity of college lies ahead of you. The skills this text provides, along with plenty of hard work, will make your college experience a meaningful and valuable one.

Kathleen T. McWhorter

How Do You READ?

R Rate your attitudes
E Evaluate your habits
A Assess your skills
D Decide how to learn

> **Directions:** Rate how accurately each of the following statements describes you using a scale of 1 to 4, with 1 being Highly Accurate and 4 being Very Inaccurate.

R—Rate Your Attitudes	Highly Accurate	Somewhat Accurate	Somewhat Inaccurate	Very Inaccurate
1. I will become a successful student.	1	2	3	4
2. I have academic and career goals for the next several years.	1	2	3	4
3. I know it is up to me to learn what is needed in each of my courses.	1	2	3	4
4. I can visualize myself passing exams and earning good grades.	1	2	3	4

E—Evaluate Your Habits				
5. I enjoy spending my free time reading.	1	2	3	4
6. I expect reading assignments to be time-consuming and am committed to spending the time necessary to complete them.	1	2	3	4
7. I have little or no difficulty concentrating.	1	2	3	4
8. As I read textbooks, I try to decide what is important to learn.	1	2	3	4

A—Assess Your Skills	Highly Accurate	Somewhat Accurate	Somewhat Inaccurate	Very Inaccurate
9. When I read, I seldom meet words I don't know.	1	2	3	4
10. When I read, I look for main ideas and details that explain them.	1	2	3	4
11. I can usually remember what I read.	1	2	3	4
12. When I read, I question what I read and analyze the author's ideas.	1	2	3	4

D—Decide How You Learn

	Highly Accurate	Somewhat Accurate	Somewhat Inaccurate	Very Inaccurate
13. I know my strengths and weaknesses as a learner.	1	2	3	4
14. I decide how to best learn something before I begin.	1	2	3	4
15. I use different study methods for different assignments.	1	2	3	4
16. I can describe my learning style.	1	2	3	4

If you checked one or more Somewhat Inaccurate or Very Inaccurate boxes in any section, then you will find Chapter 1 of this book especially useful in improving how you READ. The remaining chapters will focus on specific skills for strengthening your vocabulary, comprehension, and critical thinking skills.

1

Successful Attitudes toward Reading and Learning

THIS CHAPTER WILL SHOW YOU HOW TO

1. **Start with a positive attitude**
2. **Build your concentration**
3. **Analyze your learning style**
4. **Strengthen your comprehension**

College is very different from any other type of educational experience. It is different from high school, job training programs, adult education, or technical training programs. New and different types of learning are demanded, and you need new skills and techniques to meet these demands. This chapter offers you ways to become a successful student. You will discover what is expected of you in college, learn how to improve your concentration, analyze how you learn, and strengthen your comprehension.

Following is a list of statements about college. Treat them like a quiz, if you wish. Decide whether each statement is true or false, and write *T* for True or *F* for False in the space provided. Each statement will make you think about the reading and study demands of college. Check your answers by reading the paragraph following each item. As you work through this quiz, you will find out a little about what is expected of you in college. You will see whether or not you have an accurate picture of what college work involves. You will also see how this text will help you to become a better, more successful student.

_____   1. For every hour I spend in class, I should spend one hour studying outside of class.

False. Many students feel that even one hour for each class (or 15 hours per week for students carrying a 15 credit-hour load) is a lot. Actually, the rule of thumb used by many instructors is two hours of study for each class hour. So you can see that you are expected to do a great deal of reading, studying, and learning on your own time. The purpose of this text is to help you read and learn in the easiest and best way for you.

_____   2. I should expect to read about 80 textbook pages per week in each of my courses.

True. A survey of freshman courses at one college indicated that the average course assignment was roughly 80 pages per week. This may seem like a lot of reading—and it is. You will need to build your reading skills to handle this task. To help you do this, techniques for understanding and remembering what you read, improving your concentration, and handling difficult reading assignments will be suggested throughout this book.

_____   3. There are a lot of words I don't know, but my vocabulary is about as good as it needs to be.

False. For each college course you take, there will be new words to learn. Some will be everyday words; others will be specialized or technical. Part One of this book will show you how to develop your vocabulary by learning new words, figuring out words you don't know, and using reference sources.

_____   4. College instructors will tell me exactly what to learn for each exam.

False. College instructors seldom tell you exactly what to learn or review. They expect you to decide what is important and to learn that information. In Part Two of this text you will learn how to identify what is important in sentences and paragraphs and how to follow authors' thought patterns.

_____   5. The more facts I memorize, the higher my exam grades will be.

False. Learning a large number of facts is no guarantee of a high grade in a course. Some instructors and the exams they give are concerned with your ability to see how facts and ideas fit together, or to evaluate ideas, make comparisons, and recognize trends. Parts Two and Three of this text will help you to do this by showing you how to read textbook chapters, use graphic aids, and organize and remember information.

_____ 6. The only assignments that instructors give are readings in the textbook.

False. Instructors often assign readings in a variety of sources including periodicals, newspapers, reference and library books, and Internet sources. These readings are intended to add to the information presented in your text and by your instructor. The ten reading selections contained in Part Six will give you the opportunity to practice and apply your skills to readings taken from a variety of sources. These selections are similar to the outside readings your instructors will assign.

_____ 7. Rereading a textbook chapter is the best way to prepare for an exam on that chapter.

False. Rereading is actually one of the poorest ways to review. Besides, it's often dull and time-consuming. In Chapter 12, you will learn about four more effective alternatives: highlighting and marking, outlining, mapping, and summarizing.

_____ 8. College instructors expect me to react to, evaluate, and criticize what I read.

True. Beyond understanding the content of textbooks, articles, and essays, instructors also want their students to be able to criticize and evaluate ideas. To help you read and think critically, Part Four of this text will show you how to interpret what you read, find the author's purpose, and ask critical questions.

_____ 9. The best way to read a textbook assignment is to turn to the correct page, start reading, and continue until you reach the end of the assignment.

False. There are numerous things you can do before you read, while you read, and after you read that can improve your comprehension and retention. These techniques for improving your comprehension and recall are presented throughout this text. For example, later in this chapter you will learn techniques for building your concentration. In Chapter 5 you will be shown how to preview, think about what you will read, and use questions to guide your reading. Chapter 12 will focus on techniques to use after you read to strengthen comprehension and recall.

_____ 10. You can never know whether you have understood a textbook reading assignment until you take an exam on the chapter.

False. As you read, it is possible and important to keep track of and evaluate your level of understanding. You will learn how to keep track of your comprehension, recognize comprehension signals, and strengthen your comprehension.

By analyzing the above statements and the correct responses, you can see that college is a lot of work, much of which you must do on your own. However, college is also a new, exciting experience that will acquaint you with new ideas and opportunities.

This text will help you to get the most out of college and to take advantage of the opportunities it offers. Its purpose is to equip you with the reading and learning skills necessary for academic success.

The opportunity of college lies ahead of you. The skills you are about to learn, along with plenty of hard work, will make your college experience a meaningful and valuable one. The remainder of this chapter will help you take four important steps to becoming a successful student. You will learn to develop a positive attitude, control your concentration, strengthen your comprehension, and analyze how you learn.

START WITH A POSITIVE ATTITUDE

Reading and studying are keys to college success and, later, to success on the job. In fact, many employers identify reading, thinking, and communicating as three essential skills for the workplace. Here are a few approaches that will help you become a successful college student.

1. **Be confident: send yourself positive messages.** Tell yourself that college is something you want and can do. Negative messages such as "I might not be able to do this" or "What if I fail?" will only get in the way. In fact, there is substantial evidence to suggest that negative thinking interferes with performance. In other words, you may be limiting your success by thinking negatively. Instead, send yourself positive messages such as "I can do this" or "I've studied hard and I'm going to pass this test."

2. **Accept responsibility for your own learning.** Think of your instructors as guides. Fishing guides take you to where you are likely to catch fish, but they do not catch them for you. Similarly, your college instructors will

lead you to the information you need to learn, but they will not learn for you. You must choose the strategies and techniques to learn from your textbooks and college lectures.

3. **Visualize success.** Close your eyes and imagine yourself completing a long or difficult assignment or passing an upcoming exam. Just as athletes prepare for a competition by visualizing themselves finishing a marathon in record time or completing a difficult ski run, you should visualize yourself successfully working through challenging tasks.

4. **Set long-term goals for yourself.** You will feel more like working on assignments if you have things you are working toward. Goals such as "To get my own apartment," "Be able to quit my job at Kmart," or "To become a registered nurse" will help you focus and stick with daily tasks.

Reading can open up worlds of new ideas, show you different ways of looking at things, and provide a welcome escape from day-to-day problems. It is an opportunity to visit new places, meet new people and ideas, and broaden your experience. You will spend a great deal of time in college reading your textbooks and other assignments. Think of reading in a positive way. Here are a few approaches that will make reading work for you:

1. **Stick with a reading assignment.** If an assignment is troublesome, experiment with different methods of completing it. Consider highlighting, outlining, testing yourself, preparing vocabulary cards, or drawing diagrams, for example. You will learn these methods in later chapters.

2. **Plan on spending time.** Reading is not something you can rush through. The time you invest will pay off in increased comprehension.

3. **Actively search for key ideas as you read.** Try to connect these ideas with what your instructor is discussing in class. Think of reading as a way of sifting and sorting out what you need to learn from the less important information.

4. **Think of reading as a way of unlocking the writer's message to you, the reader.** Look for clues about the writer's personality, attitudes, opinions, and beliefs. This will put you in touch with the writer as a person and help you understand his or her message. Part Four of this book will offer suggestions to help you do this.

BUILD YOUR CONCENTRATION

Do you have difficulty concentrating? If so, you are like many other college students who say that concentration is the main reason they cannot read or study effectively. Building concentration involves two steps: (1) controlling your surroundings and (2) focusing your attention.

Controlling Your Surroundings

Poor concentration is often the result of distractions caused by the time and place you have chosen to study. Here are a few ideas to help you overcome poor concentration.

1. **Choose a place to read where you will not be interrupted.** If people interrupt you at home or in the dormitory, try the campus library.

2. **Find a place that is relatively free of distractions and temptations.** Avoid places with outside noise, friends, a television set, or an interesting project close at hand.

3. **Read in the same place each day.** Eventually you will get in the habit of reading there and concentration will become easier, almost automatic.

4. **Do not read where you are too comfortable.** It is easy to lose concentration, become drowsy, or fall asleep when you are too relaxed.

5. **Choose a time of day when you are mentally alert.** Concentration is easier if you are not tired, hungry, or drowsy.

Focusing Your Attention

Even if you follow these suggestions, you may still find it difficult to become organized and stick with your reading. This takes self-discipline, but the following suggestions may help.

1. **Set goals and time limits for yourself.** Before you begin a reading assignment, decide how long it should take, and check to see that you stay on schedule. Before you start an evening of homework, write down what you plan to do and how long each assignment should take. Sample goals for an evening are shown in Figure 1-1 below.

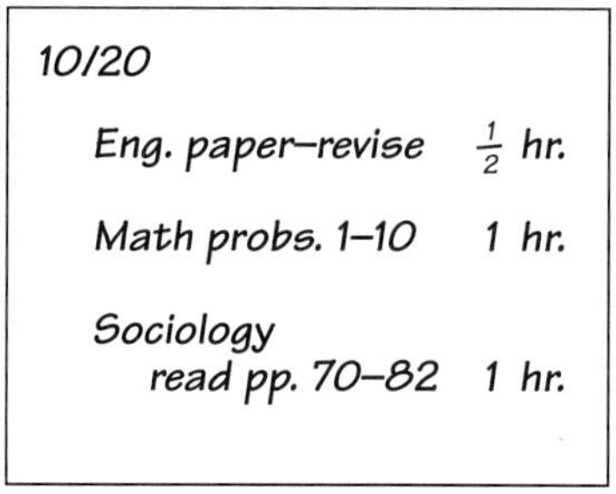

```
10/20

Eng. paper–revise      ½ hr.

Math probs. 1–10      1 hr.

Sociology
   read pp. 70–82    1 hr.
```

Figure 1-1 Goals and time limits

2. **Choose and reserve blocks of time each day for reading and study.** Write down what you will study in each time block each day or evening. Working at the same time each day establishes a routine and makes concentration a bit easier.

3. **Vary your reading.** For instance, instead of spending an entire evening on one subject, work for one hour on each of three subjects.

4. **Reward yourself for accomplishing things as planned.** Delay entertainment until after you have finished studying. Use such things as ordering a pizza, calling a friend, or watching TV as rewards after you have completed several assignments.

5. **Plan frequent breaks.** Do this at sensible points in your reading—between chapters or after major chapter divisions.

6. **Keep physically as well as mentally active.** Try highlighting, underlining, or making summary notes as you read (see Chapter 12). These activities will focus your attention on the assignment.

EXERCISE 1-1

Directions: Answer each of the following questions as honestly as you can. They will help you analyze problems with concentration. You may want to discuss your answers with others in your class.

1. Where do you read and study? _____

   What interruptions, if any, occur there? _____

2. Do you need to find a better place? _____

   If so, list a few alternatives. _____

3. What is the best time of day for you to read? (If you don't know, experiment with different times until you begin to see a pattern.)

   _____

4. How long do you normally read without a break?

   _____

5. What type of distraction bothers you the most?

   _____

6. On average, how many different assignments do you work on in one evening?

_____

7. What types of rewards might work for you?

_____

EXERCISE 1-2

Directions: As you read your next textbook assignment, either for this course or another, be alert for distractions. Each time your mind wanders, try to identify the source of distraction. List in the space provided the cause of each break in your concentration and a way to eliminate each, if possible.

_____

_____

_____

EXERCISE 1-3

Directions: Before you begin your next study session, make a list in the space provided of what you intend to accomplish and how long you should spend on each task.

Assignment   **Time**

1. _____   _____

2. _____   _____

3. _____   _____

ANALYZE YOUR LEARNING STYLE

Reading assignments are the primary focus of many college classes. Instructors make daily or weekly textbook assignments. You are expected to read the material, learn it, and pass tests on it. Class lectures and discussions are often based on textbook assignments. An important part of many college classes, then, is completing reading assignments. So far in this chapter you have learned how to monitor and strengthen your understanding of an assignment.

Reading and understanding an assignment, however, does not mean you have learned it. In fact, if you have read an assignment once, you probably have *not* learned it. You need to do more than read to learn an assignment. Your question, then, is "What else should I do?" The answer is not a simple one.

Not everyone learns in the same way. In fact, everyone has his or her own individual way of learning, which is called *learning style*. The following section contains a brief Learning Style Questionnaire that will help you analyze how you learn and how to prepare an action plan for learning what you read.

LEARNING STYLE QUESTIONNAIRE

Directions: Each item presents two choices. Select the alternative that best describes you. In cases in which neither choice suits you, select the one that is closer to your preference. Write the letter of your choice in the space provided.

Part One

B 1. I would prefer to follow a set of
   a. oral directions.
   b. written directions.

A 2. I would prefer to
   a. attend a lecture given by a famous psychologist.
   b. read an article written by the psychologist.

B 3. When I am introduced to someone, it is easier for me to remember the person's
   a. name.
   b. face.

B 4. I find it easier to learn new information using
   a. language (words).
   b. images (pictures).

B 5. I prefer classes in which the instructor
   a. lectures and answers questions.
   b. uses films and videos.

B 6. To follow current events, I would prefer to
   a. listen to the news on the radio.
   b. read the newspaper.

A 7. To learn how to operate a fax machine, I would prefer to
   a. listen to a friend's explanation.
   b. watch a demonstration.

Part Two

_A_   8. I prefer to
    a. work with facts and details.
    b. construct theories and ideas.

_A_   9. I would prefer a job involving
    a. following specific instructions.
    b. reading, writing, and analyzing.

_A_   10. I prefer to
    a. solve math problems using a formula.
    b. discover why the formula works.

_A_   11. I would prefer to write a term paper explaining
    a. how a process works.
    b. a theory.

_A_   12. I prefer tasks that require me to
    a. follow careful, detailed instructions.
    b. use reasoning and critical analysis.

_A_ 13. For a criminal justice course, I would prefer to
    a. discover how and when a law can be used.
    b. learn how and why it became law.

_A_   14. To learn more about the operation of a high-speed computer printer, I would prefer to
    a. work with several types of printers.
    b. understand the principles on which they operate.

Part Three

_B_   15. To solve a math problem, I would prefer to
    a. draw or visualize the problem.
    b. study a sample problem and use it as a model.

 _B_   16. To best remember something, I
    a. create a mental picture.
    b. write it down.

_A_ 17. Assembling a bicycle from a diagram would be
   a. easy.
   b. challenging.

_A_ 18. I prefer classes in which I
   a. handle equipment or work with models.
   b. participate in a class discussion.

_B_ 19. To understand and remember how a machine works, I would
   a. draw a diagram.
   b. write notes.

_A_ 20. I enjoy
   a. drawing or working with my hands.
   b. speaking, writing, and listening.

_B_ 21. If I were trying to locate an office on an unfamiliar campus, I would prefer
   a. a map.
   b. written directions.

Part Four

_B_ 22. For a grade in biology lab, I would prefer to
   a. work with a lab partner.
   b. work alone.

_B_ 23. When faced with a difficult personal problem I prefer to
   a. discuss it with others.
   b. resolve it myself.

_B_ 24. Many instructors could improve their classes by
   a. including more discussion and group activities.
   b. allowing students to work on their own more frequently.

_B_ 25. When listening to a lecturer or speaker, I respond more to the
   a. person presenting the idea.
   b. ideas themselves.

_B_ 26. When on a team project, I prefer to
   a. work with several team members.
   b. divide the tasks and complete those assigned to me.

_A_ 27. I prefer to shop and do errands
     a. with friends.
     b. by myself.

_B_ 28. A job in a busy office is
     a. more appealing than working alone.
     b. less appealing than working alone.

Part Five

_A_ 29. To make decisions I rely on
     a. my experiences and gut feelings.
     b. facts and objective data.

_A_ 30. To complete a task, I
     a. can use whatever is available to get the job done.
     b. must have everything I need at hand.

_A_ 31. I prefer to express my ideas and feelings through
     a. music, song, or poetry.
     b. direct, concise language.

_A_ 32. I prefer instructors who
     a. allow students to be guided by their own interests.
     b. make their expectations clear and explicit.

_B_ 33. I tend to
     a. challenge and question what I hear and read.
     b. accept what I hear and read.

_B_ 34. I prefer
     a. essay exams.
     b. objective exams.

_B_ 35. In completing an assignment, I prefer to
     a. figure out my own approach.
     b. be told exactly what to do.

To score your questionnaire, record the total number of _a_'s you selected and the total number of _b_'s for each part of the questionnaire. Record your totals in the scoring grid provided below.

Scoring Grid

Parts	Choice A Total	Choice B Total
Part One	_2_	_5_
	Auditory	Visual
Part Two	_7_	_0_
	Applied	Conceptual
Part Three	_3_	_4_
	Spatial	Verbal
Part Four	_1_	_6_
	Social	Independent
Part Five	_4_	_3_
	Creative	Pragmatic

Now, circle your higher score for each part of the questionnaire. The word below the score you circled indicates a strength of your learning style. The next section explains how to interpret your scores.

Interpreting Your Scores

The questionnaire was divided into five parts; each part identifies one aspect of your learning style. Each of these five aspects is explained below.

Part One: Auditory or Visual Learners This score indicates whether you learn better by listening (auditory) or by seeing (visual). If you have a higher score on auditory than visual, you tend to be an auditory learner. That is, you tend to learn more easily by hearing than by reading. A higher score in visual suggests strengths with visual modes of learning—reading, studying pictures, reading diagrams, and so forth.

Part Two: Applied or Conceptual Learners This score describes the types of learning tasks and learning situations you prefer and find easiest to handle. If you are an applied learner, you prefer tasks that involve real objects and situations. Practical, real-life examples are ideal for you. If you are a conceptual learner, you prefer to work with language and ideas; you do not need practical applications for understanding.

Part Three: Spatial or Verbal (Nonspatial) Learners This score reveals your ability to work with spatial relationships. Spatial learners are able to visualize or mentally see how things work or how they are positioned in space. Their strengths may include drawing, assembling, or repairing things. Verbal learners lack skills in positioning things in space. Instead they rely on verbal or language skills.

Part Four: Social or Independent Learners This score reveals whether you like to work alone or with others. If you are a social learner, you prefer to work with others—both classmates and instructors—closely and directly. You tend to be people-oriented and enjoy personal interaction. If you are an independent learner, you prefer to work alone and study alone. You tend to be self-directed or self-motivated and are often goal-oriented.

Part Five: Creative or Pragmatic Learners This score describes the approach you prefer to take toward learning tasks. Creative learners are imaginative and innovative. They prefer to learn through discovery or experimentation. They are comfortable taking risks and following hunches. Pragmatic learners are practical, logical, and systematic. They seek order and are comfortable following rules.

If you disagree with any part of the Learning Style Questionnaire, go with your own instincts rather than the questionnaire results. The questionnaire is just a quick assessment; trust your knowledge of yourself in areas of dispute.

Developing a Learning Action Plan

Now that you know more about *how* you learn, you are ready to develop an action plan for learning what you read. Suppose you discovered that you are an auditory learner. You still have to read your assignments, which is a visual task. However, to learn the assignment you should translate the material into an auditory form. For example, you could repeat aloud, using your own words, information that you want to remember, or you could tape-record key information and play it back. If you also are a social learner, you could work with a classmate, testing each other out loud.

Table 1-1 on page 17 lists each aspect of learning style and offers suggestions for how to learn from a reading assignment. To use the table:

1. **Circle the five aspects of your learning style in which you received higher scores.** Disregard the others.
2. **Read through the suggestions that apply to you.**
3. **Place a checkmark in front of suggestions that you think will work for you.** Choose at least one from each category.
4. **List the suggestions that you chose in the box labeled Action Plan for Learning on page 18.**

TABLE 1-1   Learning Styles and Reading/Learning Strategies

If your learning style is ...	Then the reading/learning strategies to use are ...
Auditory	• discuss/study with friends • talk aloud when studying • tape-record self-testing questions and answers
Visual	• draw diagrams, charts, tables (Chapter 11) • try to visualize events • use films and videos, when available • use computer-assisted instruction, if available
Applied	• think of practical situations to which learning applies • associate ideas with their application • use case studies, examples, and applications to cue your learning
Conceptual	• organize materials that lack order • use outlining (Chapter 12) • focus on organizational patterns (Chapter 9)
Spatial	• use mapping (Chapter 12) • use outlining (Chapter 12) • draw diagrams, make charts and sketches • use visualization
Verbal (Nonspatial)	• translate diagrams and drawings into language • record steps, processes, procedures in words • write summaries (Chapter 12) • write your interpretation next to textbook drawings, maps, graphics
Social	• form study groups • find a study partner • interact with instructor • work with a tutor
Independent	• use computer-assisted instruction, if available • purchase review workbooks or study guides, if available
Creative	• ask and answer questions • record your own ideas in margins of textbooks
Pragmatic	• study in an organized environment • write lists of steps, procedures, and processes • paraphrase difficult material (Chapter 6)

In the Action Plan for Learning box you listed four or more suggestions to help you learn what you read. The next step is to experiment with these techniques, one at a time. (You may need to refer to chapters listed in parentheses in Table 1-1 to learn or review how a certain technique works.) Use one technique for a while, then move to the next. Continue using the techniques that seem to work; work on revising or modifying those that do not. Do not hesitate to experiment with other techniques listed in the table as well. You may find other techniques that work well for you.

Action Plan for Learning

Learning Strategy 1 _____

_____

Learning Strategy 2 _____

_____

Learning Strategy 3 _____

_____

Learning Strategy 4 _____

_____

Learning Strategy 5 _____

_____

Learning Strategy 6 _____

_____

Developing Strategies to Overcome Limitations

You should also work on developing styles in which you are weak. Your learning style is not fixed or unchanging. You can improve areas in which you
scored lower. Although you may be weak in auditory learning, for example,
many of your professors will lecture and expect you to take notes. If you work
on improving your listening and note-taking skills, you can learn to handle lectures effectively. Make a conscious effort to work on improving areas of weakness as well as taking advantage of your strengths.

EXERCISE 1-4	**Directions:** For each learning strategy you listed in your Action Plan for Learning, write a brief evaluation of the strategy. Explain which worked; which, if any, did not; and what changes you have noticed in your ability to learn from reading.

PAY ATTENTION TO COMPREHENSION SIGNALS

Think for a moment about how you feel when you read material you can easily understand. Now compare that to what happens when you read something difficult and complicated. When you read easy material, does it seem that everything "clicks"? That is, do ideas seem to fit together and make sense? Is that "click" noticeably absent in difficult reading?

Read each of the following paragraphs. As you read, be aware of how well you understand each of them.

Paragraph 1

The **spinal cord** is actually an extension of the brain. It runs from the base of the brain down the center of the back, protected by a column of bones. The cord acts as a sort of bridge between the brain and the parts of the body below the neck. But the spinal cord is not merely a bridge. It also produces some behaviors on its own, without any help from the brain. These behaviors, called spinal **reflexes**, are automatic, requiring no conscious effort. For example, if you accidentally touch a hot iron, you will immediately pull your hand away, even before the brain has had a chance to register what has happened. Nerve impulses bring a message to the spinal cord (HOT!), and the spinal cord immediately sends out a command via other nerve impulses, telling muscles in your arm to contract and pull your hand away from the iron. (Reflexes above the neck, such as sneezing and blinking, involve the lower part of the brain rather than the spinal cord.)[1]

Paragraph 2

In an isolated antiworld, antipeople would go about their lives the same as we do. When an antiperson flipped an antiswitch, antiatoms in the antilightbulb would give off the same kind of light that you are using to read these words. There would be no annihilation going on, because there would be no ordinary matter involved. If, however, you happened to be transported to this antiworld, and tried to shake hands with your antiself, the two of you would disappear in a titanic explosion. In that explosion your bodies would be converted almost entirely into pure energy; all that would be left would be electromagnetic radiation and a thin cloud of particles.[2]

Did you feel comfortable and confident as you read Paragraph 1? Did ideas seem to lead from one to another and make sense? How did you feel while reading Paragraph 2? Most likely you sensed its difficulty and felt confused. Some words were unfamiliar, and you could not follow the flow of ideas.

As you read Paragraph 2, did you know that you were not understanding it? Did you feel lost and confused? Table 1-2 lists and compares some common signals that are useful in monitoring your comprehension. Not all signals appear at the same time, and not all signals work for everyone. As you study the list, identify those positive signals you sensed as you read Paragraph 1 on the spinal cord. Then identify those negative signals that you sensed when reading about the antiworld.

Once you are able to recognize negative signals while reading, the next step is to take action to correct the problem. Specific techniques are given in the last section of this chapter.

TABLE 1-2   Comprehension Signals

Positive Signals	Negative Signal
Everything seems to fit and make sense; ideas flow logically from one to another.	Some pieces do not seem to belong; the ideas do not fit together or make sense.
You are able to understand what the author is saying.	You feel as if you are struggling to stay with the author.
You can see where the author is leading.	You cannot think ahead or predict what will come next.
You are able to make connections among ideas.	You are unable to see how ideas connect.
You read at a regular comfortable pace.	You often slow down or lose your place.
You understand why the material was assigned.	You do not know why the material was assigned and cannot explain why it is important.
You can understand after reading the material once.	You need to reread sentences or paragraphs frequently.
You recognize most words or can figure them out from context.	Many words are unfamiliar.
You can express the key ideas in your own words.	You must reread and use the author's language to explain an idea.
You feel comfortable with the topic; you have some background knowledge.	The topic is unfamiliar; you know nothing about it.

EXERCISE 1-5

Directions: Read the following excerpt from a biology textbook on the theory of continental drift. It is intended to be difficult, so do not be discouraged. As you read, monitor your comprehension. After reading, answer the questions that follow.

In 1912, Alfred Wegener published a paper that was triggered by the common observation of the good fit between South America's east coast and Africa's west coast. Could these great continents ever have been joined? Wegener coordinated this jigsaw-puzzle analysis with other ecological and climatological data and proposed the theory of continental drift. He suggested that about 200 million years ago, all of the earth's continents were joined together into one enormous land mass, which he called Pangaea. In the ensuing millennia, according to Wegener's idea, Pangaea broke apart, and the fragments began to drift northward (by today's compass orientation) to their present location.

Wegener's idea received rough treatment in his lifetime. His geologist contemporaries attacked his naivete as well as his supporting data, and his theory was neglected until about 1960. At that time, a new generation of geologists revived the idea and subjected it to new scrutiny based on recent findings.

The most useful data have been based on magnetism in ancient lava flows. When a lava flow cools, metallic elements in the lava are oriented in a way that provides permanent evidence of the direction of the earth's magnetic field at the time, recording for future geologists both its north-south orientation and its latitude. From such maps, it is possible to determine the ancient positions of today's continents. We now believe that not only has continental drift occurred, as Wegener hypothesized, but that it continues to occur today. . . .

The disruption of Pangaea began some 230 million years ago in the Paleozoic era. By the Mesozoic era, the Eurasian land mass (called Laurasia) had moved away to form the northernmost continent. Gondwanaland, the mass that included India and the southern continents, had just begun to divide. Finally, during the late Mesozoic era, after South America and Africa were well divided, what was to be the last continental separation began, with Australia and Antarctica drifting apart. Both the North and South Atlantic oceans would continue to widen considerably up to the Cenozoic era, a trend that is continuing today. So we see that although the bumper sticker "Reunite Gondwanaland" has a third-world, trendy ring to it, it's an unlikely proposition.[3]

1. How would you rate your overall comprehension? What positive signals did you sense? Did you feel any negative signals?

2. Test the accuracy of your rating in Question 1 by answering the following questions based on the material you read.
   a. Explain Wegener's theory of continental drift.
   b. Which two continents led Wegener to develop his theory?
   c. What recent findings have supported Wegener's theory?
   d. Describe the way in which Pangaea broke up and drifted to become the continents we know today.
3. In which sections was your comprehension strongest?
4. Did you feel at any time that you had lost, or were about to lose, comprehension? If so, go back to that paragraph now. What made that paragraph difficult to read?
5. Would it have been useful to refer to a world map?
6. Underline any difficult words that interfered with your comprehension.

WORK ON IMPROVING YOUR COMPREHENSION

At times, you will realize that your comprehension is poor or incomplete. When this occurs, take immediate action. Identify as specifically as possible the cause of the problem. Do this by answering the following question: "Why is this not making sense?" Determine if it is your lack of concentration, difficult words, complex ideas, or organization that is bothering you. Next, make changes in your reading to correct or compensate for the problem. Table 1-3 on page 24 lists common problems and offers strategies to correct them.

EXERCISE 1-6	**Directions:** Read each of the following difficult paragraphs, monitoring your comprehension as you do so. After reading each passage, identify and describe any problems you experienced. Then indicate what strategies you would use to correct these.

A. A word about food—in the simplest of terms, there are two kinds of organisms: those that make their own food, usually by photosynthesis (autotrophs, "self-feeders") and those that depend upon an outside-the-cell food source (heterotrophs, "other-feeders"). The autotrophs include a few kinds of bacteria, some one-celled eukaryotes (protistans), and all green plants. The heterotrophs encompass most bacteria, many protistans, all fungi, and all animals. Because this chapter is about animal nutrition, attention first will be given to examining the nature of food, then to how food is made available to cells.[4]

• Problem: _____

• Strategies: _____

B. The vestibular apparatus in the inner ear has two distinct components: the semicircular canals (three mutually perpendicular, fluid-filled tubes that contain hair cells connected to nerve fibers), which are sensitive to angular acceleration of the head; and the otolith organs (two sacs filled with calcium carbonate crystals embedded in a gel), which respond to linear acceleration. Because movement of the crystals in the otoliths generates the signal of acceleration to the brain and because the laws of physics relate that acceleration to a net force, gravity is always implicit in the signal. Thus, the otoliths have been referred to as gravity receptors. They are not the only ones. Mechanical receptors in the muscles, tendons and joints—as well as pressure receptors in the skin, particularly on the bottom of the feet—respond to the weight of limb segments and other body parts.[5]

- Problem: _____

- Strategies: _____

C. The objective of some tariffs is to protect an industry that produces goods vital to a nation's defense. In the case of a strategic industry, productive efficiency relative to that of other nations may not be an important consideration. The domestic industry—oil, natural gas, shipping, or steel, for example—may require protection because of its importance to national defense. Without protection, such industries might be weakened by foreign competition. Then, in an international crisis, the nation might find itself in short supply of products essential to national defense.[6]

- Problem: _____

- Strategies: _____

TABLE 1-3   How to Improve Your Comprehension

Problems	Strategies
Poor concentration	1. Take limited breaks. 2. Tackle difficult material when your mind is fresh and alert. 3. Choose an appropriate place to study. 4. Focus your attention.
Words are difficult or unfamiliar	1. Use context and analyze word parts. 2. Skim through material before reading. Mark and look up meanings of difficult words. Jot meanings in the margin. 3. Refer to the vocabulary preview list, footnotes, or glossary.
Sentences are long or confusing	1. Read aloud. 2. Locate the key idea(s). 3. Check difficult words. 4. Express each sentence in your own words.
Ideas are hard to understand, complicated	1. Rephrase or explain each in your own words. 2. Make notes. 3. Locate a more basic text that explains ideas in simpler form. 4. Study with a classmate; discuss difficult ideas.
Ideas are new and unfamiliar; you have little or no knowledge about the topic and the writer assumes you do	1. Make sure you didn't miss or skip introductory information. 2. Get background information by referring to a. an earlier section or chapter in the book. b. an encyclopedia. c. a more basic text.
The material seems disorganized or poorly organized	1. Pay more attention to headings. 2. Read the summary, if available. 3. Try to discover organization by writing an outline or drawing a map as you read (see Chapter 12).
You don't know what is and is not important	1. Preview 2. Ask and answer guide questions. 3. Locate and underline topic sentences (see Chapter 7).

Learning Style Tips

If you are a(n) . . .	Then improve your comprehension by . . .
Auditory learner	Reading aloud
Visual learner	Visualizing paragraph organization
Applied learner	Thinking of real-life situations that illustrate ideas in the passage
Conceptual learner	Asking questions

WORKING TOGETHER

Directions: Bring to class a difficult paragraph or brief excerpt. Working in groups, each group member reads each piece and then together (1) discuss why the material was difficult and (2) compare negative and positive signals they received (refer to Table 1-2). Each student then selects strategies to overcome the difficulties.

SELF-TEST SUMMARY

How can you develop a positive attitude toward reading?

You can begin to develop a positive attitude if you think of reading as an active process of looking for important ideas and unlocking a writer's message and if you realize to do this successfully you cannot rush through it.

What can you do to control your concentration?

Building concentration involves two steps:

1. Control your surroundings by wisely choosing your time and place of study and avoiding distractions.
2. Focus your attention on the assignment by setting goals and rewarding yourself for achieving them by working in planned, small time blocks with frequent breaks, and by getting actively involved in the assignment.

What is learning style?

Learning style refers to your profile of relative strengths as a learner. Its five components are:

1. Auditory or visual learner
2. Applied or conceptual learner
3. Spatial or verbal learner
4. Social or independent learner
5. Creative or pragmatic learner

How can knowing your learning style make you a better student?

Discovering what type of learner you are can help you find out what strategies work best for you in reading and studying. It will also help you to recognize your limitations so that you can work on overcoming them.

What can you do to be sure that you understand your reading assignments?

First, you should pay attention to whether you sense positive or negative signals while reading. Next, if the signals are mostly negative, you should determine what is causing your poor comprehension—your concentration, the words, the ideas, or the organization. Finally, you should make changes in your reading methods to correct the problem.

**CHAPTER 1
MASTERY TEST 1:**
Reading Selection

Name _____

Section _____ Date _____

Number right _____ x 10 points = Score _____

ASSESSMENT READING SELECTION

This reading and the questions that follow are intended to help you assess your current level of skill. Read the article then answer the questions that measure your comprehension. You may refer back to the reading in order to answer them. Compute your score by filling in the scoring box above.

Primary Colors

Kim McLarin

This essay, originally published in the *New York Times Magazine,* describes a mother's response to her interracial child.

Vocabulary Preview

retrospect (par. 5) reviewing the past

eccentricities (par. 6) oddities

abduction (par. 9) kidnapping

disconcerting (par. 10) upsetting

condemnation (par. 12) strong criticism or disapproval

allegiances (par. 13) loyalties

denounce (par. 13) to criticize openly

align (par. 14) join with others

1   A few weeks after my daughter was born, I took her to a new pediatrician for an exam. The doctor took one look at Samantha and exclaimed: "Wow! She's so light!" I explained that my husband is white, but it didn't seem to help. The doctor commented on Sam's skin color so often that I finally asked what was on her mind.

2   "I'm thinking albino," she said.

3   The doctor, who is white, claimed she had seen the offspring of many interracial couples, but never a child this fair. "They're usually a darker, coffee-with-cream color. Some of them are this light at birth, but by 72 hours you can tell they have a black parent."

4   To prove her point, she held her arm next to Samantha's stomach. "I mean, this could be my child!"

5   It's funny now, in retrospect. But at the time, with my hormones still raging from childbirth, the incident sent me into a panic. Any fool could see that Samantha wasn't an albino*—she had black hair and dark blue eyes. It must be a trick. The doctor, who had

*person lacking skin pigmentation resulting in abnormally white hair or skin

left the room, probably suspected me of kidnapping this "white" child and was outside calling the police. By the time she returned I was ready to fight.

6   Fortunately, her partner dismissed the albino theory, and we escaped and found a new pediatrician, one who knows a little more about genetic eccentricities. But the incident stayed with me because, in the months since, other white people have assumed Samantha is not my child. This is curious to me, this inability to connect across skin tones, especially since Samantha has my full lips and broad nose. I'll admit that I myself didn't expect Sam to be quite so pale, so much closer to her father's Nordic* coloring than my own umber tones. My husband is a blue-eyed strawberry blond; I figured that my genes would take his genes in the first round.

7   Wrong.

8   Needless to say, I love Sam just as she is. She is amazingly, heartbreakingly beautiful to me in the way that babies are to their parents. She sweeps me away with her mischievous grin and her belly laugh, with the coy way she tilts her head after flinging the cup from her highchair. When we are alone and I look at Samantha, I see Samantha, not the color of her skin.

9   And yet I admit that I wouldn't mind if she were darker, dark enough so that white people would know she was mine and black people wouldn't give her a hard time. I know a black guy who, while crossing into Canada, was suspected of having kidnapped his fair-skinned son. So far no one has accused me of child abduction, but I have

been mistaken for Samantha's nanny. It has happened so often that I've considered going into business as a nanny spy. I could sit in the park and take notes on your child-care worker. Better than hiding a video camera in the living room.

10   In a way it's disconcerting, my being mistaken for a nanny. Because, to be blunt, I don't like seeing black women caring for white children. It may be because I grew up in the South, where black women once had no choice but to leave their own children and suckle the offspring of others. The weight of that past, the whiff of a power imbalance, still stains such pairings for me. That's unfair, I know, to the professional, hard-working (mostly Caribbean) black nannies of New York. But there you are.

11   On the flip side, I think being darker wouldn't hurt Samantha with black people, either. A few weeks ago, in my beauty shop, I overheard a woman trashing a friend for "slathering" his light-skinned children with sunscreen during the summer.

12   "Maybe he doesn't want them getting skin cancer," suggested the listener. But my girl was having none of that.

13   "He doesn't want them getting black!" she said, as full of righteous condemnation as only a black woman in a beauty shop can be. Now, maybe the woman was right about her friend's motivation. Or maybe she was 100 percent wrong. Maybe because she herself is the color of butterscotch she felt she had to declare her allegiances loudly, had to place herself prominently high on the unofficial black scale and denounce anyone caught not doing the same. Either way, I know it means grief for Sam.

14   I think that as time goes on my daughter will probably align with black people

*characteristic of Scandinavian people—light-skinned, blond-haired people

anyway, regardless of the relative fairness of her skin. My husband is fine with that, as long as it doesn't mean denying him or his family.

15   The bottom line is that society has a deep need to categorize people, to classify and, yes, to stereotype. Race is still the easiest, most convenient way of doing so. That race tells you, in the end, little or nothing about a person is beside the point. We still feel safer believing that we can sum up one another at a glance.

CHECKING YOUR COMPREHENSION

Directions: Select the best answer for each of the following questions.

_____ 1. The main point of this selection is that
   a. people classify others on the basis of skin color because it is what they notice first.
   b. being the mother of an interracial child has more negative than positive moments.
   c. having an interracial child is easier in the North than in the South.
   d. although people are still aware of race, most people realize that race is not important.

_____ 2. The main idea of paragraph 9 is that
   a. having people think she is not the mother has several advantages.
   b. people usually think a dark-skinned adult is not the parent of a light-skinned child.
   c. white people have more difficulty than black people in accepting skin tone differences in a parent and child.
   d. having a light-skinned child is easier for the author than having a dark-skinned child.

_____ 3. The main idea of paragraph 10 is that
   a. the author has negative feelings about black women caring for white children.
   b. black women have always cared for white children.
   c. Caribbean nannies are hardworking professionals.
   d. because the author grew up in the South, she is used to seeing nannies.

_____ 4. Samantha has
   a. blond hair.
   b. brown eyes.
   c. coffee-with-cream skin coloring.
   d. full lips.

_____ 5. One reason the author wishes her daughter were darker is that she
   a. wants Sam to identify more with her father's family.
   b. doesn't want Sam to have to use sunscreen.
   c. wants to travel to Canada with Sam.
   d. doesn't want black people to criticize Sam.

_____ 6. The term "retrospect" in paragraph 5 means
a. analysis.
b. looking back.
c. expectation.
d. commentary.

_____ 7. The incident at the pediatrician's office upset the author because she was afraid that
a. her daughter might have a serious disease.
b. the doctor thought Samantha was not her child.
c. her child might have been switched at birth.
d. the doctor would harm Samantha.

_____ 8. The main idea of paragraph 8 is that
a. Sam is a beautiful, teasing child.
b. the author is most aware of Sam's skin tone when she is with other people.
c. skin color does not come between the author and Sam.
d. the author feels guilty for wishing Sam were darker.

_____ 9. The author finds a new pediatrician because the first one
a. calls in her partner to help her.
b. has never examined an interracial child.
c. offended her and seemed to have incorrect ideas about genetics.
d. accuses the author of kidnapping a child.

_____ 10. The term "slathering" in paragraph 11 means
a. rubbing in thoroughly.
b. artificially coloring.
c. insisting on applying.
d. covering thickly.

Go Electronic!
For additional readings, exercises, and Internet activities, visit this book's Web Companion site at:

http://www.ablongman.com/mcwhorter

If you need a user name and password, please see your instructor.

Take a Road Trip to Mount Rushmore!
Visit the Time Management, Memorization, and Concentration module in your Reading Road Trip CD-ROM—or on the Reading Road Trip Web site—for multimedia tutorials, exercises, and tests.

2

Using Context Clues

THIS CHAPTER WILL SHOW YOU HOW TO

1. Figure out the meanings of words from their use in a sentence
2. Use four types of context clues

WHAT IS CONTEXT?

Read the following brief paragraph. Several words are missing. Try to figure out the missing words and write them in the blanks.

Most Americans can speak only one _____. Europeans, however, _____ several. As a result, Europeans think _____ are unfriendly and unwilling to communicate with them.

Did you insert the word *language* in the first blank, *speak* or *know* in the second blank, and *Americans* in the third blank? Most likely, you correctly identified all three missing words. You could tell from the sentence which word to put in. The words around the missing words—the sentence context—gave you clues as to which word would fit and make sense. Such clues are called **context clues**.

While you probably won't find missing words on a printed page, you will often find words that you do not know. Context clues can help you to figure out the meanings of unfamiliar words.

Example:

Phobias, such as fear of heights, water, or confined spaces, are difficult to eliminate.

From the sentence, you can tell that *phobia* means "fear of specific objects or situations."

Here's another example:

The couple finally **secured** a table at the popular, crowded restaurant.

You can figure out that *secured* means "got or took ownership of" the table.

TYPES OF CONTEXT CLUES

There are four types of context clues to look for: (1) definition, (2) example, (3) contrast, and (4) inference.

Definition Clues

Many times a writer defines a word immediately following its use. The writer may directly define a word by giving a brief definition or a synonym (a word that has the same meaning). Such words and phrases as *means, is, refers to,* and *can be defined* as are often used. Here are some examples:

Corona refers to *the outermost part of the sun's atmosphere.*

A **soliloquy** is *a speech made by a character in a play that reveals his or her thoughts to the audience.*

At other times, rather than formally define the word, a writer may provide clues or synonyms. Punctuation is often used to signal that a definition clue to a word's meaning is to follow. Punctuation also separates the meaning clue from the rest of the sentence. Three types of punctuation are used in this way. In the examples below, notice that the meaning clue is separated from the rest of the sentence by punctuation.

1. Commas

   An **oligopoly**, *control of a product by a small number of companies,* exists in the long-distance phone market.

   Equity, *general principles of fairness and justice,* is used in law when existing laws do not apply or are inadequate.

2. Parentheses

A leading cause of heart disease is a diet with too much **cholesterol** (*a fatty substance made of carbon, hydrogen and oxygen*).

3. Dashes

Ancient Egyptians wrote in **hieroglyphics**—*pictures used to represent words.*

Facets—*small flat surfaces at different angles*—bring out the beauty of a diamond.

EXERCISE 2-1	**Directions:** Read each sentence and write a definition or synonym for each boldfaced word or phrase. Use the definition context clue to help you determine word meaning.

1. **Glog**, a Swedish hot punch, is often served at holiday parties.

   _____

2. The judge's **candor**—his sharp, open frankness—shocked the jury.

   _____

3. A **chemical bond** is a strong attractive force that holds two or more atoms together.

   _____

4. **Lithium** (an alkali metal) is so soft it can be cut with a knife.

   _____

5. Hearing, technically known as **audition**, begins when a sound wave reaches the outer ear.

   _____

6. Five-line rhyming poems, or **limericks**, are among the simplest forms of poetry.

   _____

7. Our country's **gross national product**—the total market value of its national output of goods and services—is increasing steadily.

   _____

8. A **species** is a group of animals or plants that share similar characteristics and are able to interbreed.

_____

_____

9. Broad, flat noodles that are served covered with sauce or butter are called **fettucine**.

_____

10. Many diseases have **latent periods**, periods of time between the infection and the first appearance of a symptom.

_____

Example Clues

Writers often include examples that help to explain or clarify a word. Suppose you do not know the meaning of the word *toxic,* and you find it used in the following sentence:

> **Toxic** materials, such as arsenic, asbestos, pesticides, and lead, can cause bodily damage.

This sentence gives four examples of toxic materials. From the examples given, which are all poisonous substances, you could conclude that *toxic* means "poisonous."

Examples:

Forest floors are frequently covered with **fungi**—molds, mushrooms, and mildews.

Legumes, such as peas and beans, produce pods.

Arachnids, including tarantulas, black widow spiders, and ticks, often have segmented bodies.

Newsmagazines, like *Time* or *Newsweek,* provide more details about news events than newspapers because they focus on only a few stories.

Directions: Read each sentence and write a definition or synonym for each boldfaced word or phrase. Use the example context clue to help you determine meaning.

1. Many **pharmaceuticals**, including morphine and penicillin, are not readily available in some countries.

   Morphine and penicillin

2. The child was **reticent** in every respect; she would not speak, refused to answer questions, and avoided looking at anyone.

   not speak, refused to answer questions and avoid looking at anyone.

3. Most **condiments**, such as pepper, mustard, and catsup, are used to improve the flavor of foods.

   pepper, mustard, and catsup

4. Instructors provide their students with **feedback** through test grades and comments on papers.

   Test grades, comments on papers

5. **Physiological needs**—hunger, thirst, and sex—promote survival of the human species.

   hunger, thirst, and sex

6. Clothing is available in a variety of **fabrics**, including cotton, wool, polyester, and linen.

   cotton, wool, polyester and linen

7. In the past month, we have had almost every type of **precipitation**—rain, snow, sleet, and hail.

   rain, snow, sleet, and hail.

8. **Involuntary reflexes**, like breathing and beating of the heart, are easily measured.

   breathing and beating of the heart

9. The student had a difficult time distinguishing between **homonyms**— words such as *see* and *sea, wore* and *war,* and *deer* and *dear.*

   see and sea, wore and war, deer and dear

10. Abstract paintings often include such **geometrics** as squares, cubes, and triangles.

<u>_Squares, cubes, and triangles_</u>

Contrast Clues

It is sometimes possible to determine the meaning of an unknown word from a word or phrase in the context that has an opposite meaning. If a single word provides a clue, it is often an **antonym**—a word opposite in meaning of the unknown word. Notice, in the following sentence, how a word opposite in meaning from the boldfaced word provides a clue to its meaning:

> One of the dinner guests **succumbed** to the temptation to have a second piece of cake, but the others resisted.

Although you may not know the meaning of *succumbed*, you know that the one guest who succumbed was different from the others who resisted. The word *but* suggests this. Since the others resisted a second dessert, you can tell that one guest gave in and had a piece. Thus, *succumbed* means the opposite of *resist*; that is, to give in to.

Examples:

> The professor **advocates** testing on animals, *but* many of her students feel it is cruel.

> Most of the graduates were **elated**, *though* a few felt sad and depressed.

> The old man acted **morosely**, *whereas* his grandson was very lively.

> The gentleman was quite **portly**, *but* his wife was thin.

EXERCISE 2-3

Directions: Read each sentence and write a definition or synonym for each boldfaced word. Use the contrast clue to help you determine meaning.

1. Some city dwellers are **affluent**; others live in or near poverty.

<u>_poverty   Rich_</u>

2. I am certain that the hotel will hold our reservation; however, if you are **dubious**, call to make sure.

<u>_reservation   unsure_</u>

3. Although most experts **concurred** with the research findings, several strongly disagreed.

   Strongly disagreed

4. The speaker **denounced** certain legal changes while praising other reforms.

   praising accuse

5. The woman's parents **thwarted** her marriage plans though they liked her fiancé.

   Ruined

6. In medieval Europe, **peasants** led difficult lives, whereas the wealthy landowners lived in luxury.

7. When the couple moved into their new home they **revamped** the kitchen and bathroom but did not change the rest of the rooms.

8. The young nurse was **bewildered** by the patient's symptoms, but the doctor realized she was suffering from a rare form of leukemia.

9. Despite my husband's **pessimism** about my chances of winning the lottery, I was certain I would win.

10. The mayoral candidate praised the town council, while the mayor **deprecated** it.

Inference Clues

Many times you can figure out the meaning of an unknown word by using logic and reasoning skills. For instance, look at the following sentence:

Bob is quite **versatile;** he is a good student, a top athlete, an excellent car mechanic, and a gourmet cook.

You can see that Bob is successful at many different types of activities, and you could reason that *versatile* means "capable of doing many things competently."

Examples:

When the customer tried to pay with Mexican **pesos,** the clerk explained that the store accepted only U.S. dollars.

The potato salad looked so plain that I decided to **garnish** it with parsley and paprika to give it some color.

We had to leave the car and walk up because the **incline** was too steep to drive.

Since Reginald was nervous, he brought his rabbit's foot **talisman** with him to the exam.

EXERCISE 2-4

Directions: Read each sentence and write a definition or synonym for each boldfaced word. Try to reason out the meaning of each word using information provided in the context.

1. The **wallabies** at the zoo looked like kangaroos.

_____

2. The foreign students quickly **assimilated** many aspects of American culture.

_____

3. On hot, humid summer afternoons, I often feel **languid**.

_____

4. Some physical fitness experts recommend jogging or weight lifting to overcome the effects of a **sedentary** job.

_____

5. The legal aid clinic was **subsidized** by city and county funds.

_____

6. When the bank robber reached his **haven**, he breathed a sigh of relief and began to count his money.

_____

7. The teenager was **intimidated** by the presence of a police officer walking the beat and decided not to spray-paint the school wall.

_____

8. The vase must have been **jostled** in shipment because it arrived with several chips in it.

_____

9. Although she had visited the fortune teller several times, she was not sure she believed in the **occult**.

_____

10. If the plan did not work, the colonel had a **contingency** plan ready.

_____

EXERCISE 2-5

Directions: Read each sentence and write a definition or synonym for each boldfaced word. Use the context clue to help you determine meaning.

1. The economy was in a state of continual **flux**; inflation increased one month and decreased the next.

Confusion

2. The grand jury **exonerated** the police officer of any possible misconduct or involvement in illegal activity.

questioned

3. Art is always talkative, but Ed is usually **taciturn**.

quiet

4. Many **debilities** of old age, including poor eyesight and loss of hearing, can be treated medically.

   _____ *illnesses* _____

5. Police **interrogation**, or questioning, can be a frightening experience.

   _____ *hearing* _____

6. The soap opera contained numerous **morbid** events: the death of a young child, the suicide of her father, and the murder of his older brother.

   _____ *sad* _____

7. After long hours of practice, Peter finally learned to type; Sam's efforts, however, were **futile**.

   _____ *poor* _____

8. Although the farm appeared **derelict**, we discovered that an elderly man lived there.

   _____ *abandoned* _____

9. The newspaper's error was **inadvertent**; the editor did not intend to include the victim's name.

   _____ *mistake* _____

10. To save money, we have decided to **curtail** the number of tapes we buy each month.

    _____ *record* _____

11. Steam from the hot radiator **scalded** the mechanic's hand.

    _____ *burned* _____

12. The businesswoman's **itinerary** outlined her trip and listed Cleveland as her next stop.

    _____ *(ticket) schedule* _____

13. **Theologies**, such as Catholicism, Buddhism, and Hinduism, are discussed at great length in the class.

    _____ *Religions* _____

14. Steven had very good **rapport** with his father, but was unable to get along well with his mother.

_____

15. The duchess had a way of **flaunting** her jewels so that everyone could see and envy them.

_____

EXERCISE 2-6

Directions: Read each of the following passages and use context clues to figure out the meaning of each boldfaced word or phrase. Write a synonym or brief definition for each in the space provided.

A. Can looking at a color affect your behavior or **alter** your mood? Some researchers are **skeptical**, but others believe color can influence how you act and feel. A number of experiments have been conducted that **demonstrate** the effects of color. In 1979 a psychologist named Schauss **evaluated** the effect of the color pink. He found that the color relaxed the subjects so much that they could not perform simple strength tests as well as they did when looking at other **hues**. The officer in charge of a U.S. Navy **brig** in Washington noticed Schauss's findings and allowed Schauss to test his calm-color **hypothesis** on inmates. Today, many **institutions**, such as jails, juvenile correction facilities, and holding centers, put individuals in pink rooms when their tempers **flare**.

No one is certain how color affects behavior. Schauss **conjectures** that a person's response to color is determined in the brain's **reticular formation**, a relay station for millions of the body's nerve impulses. Another researcher **speculates** that **perception** of color by the eye **spurs** the release of important chemicals in the body.[1]

1. alter

Change

2. skeptical

don't believe ; doubtful

3. demonstrate

explanations ; to show clearly

4. evaluated

to exam; to study

5. hues

classification of colors ; shades

6. brig

a naval ship jail

7. hypothesis

Educated guess

8. institutions

collection facilities

9. flare

a sudden anger

10. conjectures

to guess

11. reticular formation

nerve impulses

12. speculates

thinks; believes ; wonder

13. perception

seeing ; awarness

14. spurs

increase

B. The most important set of symbols is language. **Language,** among humans, refers to the systemized use of speech and hearing to convey or express feelings and ideas. It is through language that our ideas, values, beliefs, and knowledge are **transmitted**, expressed, and shared. Other

media such as music, art, and dance are also important means of communication, but language is uniquely flexible and precise. It permits us to share our experiences in the past and present, to **convey** our hopes for the future, and to describe dreams and fantasies that may bear little **resemblance** to reality. Some scientists have questioned whether thought is even possible without language. Although language can be used **imprecisely** and may seem hard to understand, it is the chief factor in our ability to transmit culture.[2]

1. language

_____

2. transmitted

_____

3. media

_____

4. convey

_____

5. resemblance

_____

6. imprecisely

_____

C. Social norms are another element of culture. **Norms** are rules of conduct or social expectations for behavior. These rules and social expectations **specify** how people should and should not behave in various social situations. They are both **prescriptive** (they tell people what they should do) and **proscriptive** (they tell people what they should not do). . . .

An early American sociologist, William G. Sumner (1840–1910), identified two types of norms, which he labeled "folkways" and "mores." They are **distinguished** not by their content, but by the degree to which group members are **compelled** to conform to them, by their degree of importance, by the **severity** of punishment if they are violated, or by the intensity of feeling associated with adherence to them. Folkways are customs or conventions. They are norms in that they provide rules for conduct, but **violations** of folkways bring only mild censure.[3]

1. norms

   _____

2. specify

   _____

3. prescriptive

   _____

4. proscriptive

   _____

5. distinguished

   _____

6. compelled

   _____

7. severity

   _____

8. violations

   _____

THE LIMITATIONS OF CONTEXT CLUES

There are two limitations to the use of context clues. First, context clues seldom lead to a complete definition. Second, sometimes a sentence does not contain clues to a word's meaning. In these cases you will need to draw on other vocabulary skills. Chapters 3 and 4 will help you with these skills.

WORKING TOGETHER

Directions: Bring a brief textbook excerpt, editorial, or magazine article that contains difficult vocabulary to class. Working in pairs with another student, locate and underline at least three words in your article that your partner can define by using context clues. Work together in reasoning out each word, checking a dictionary to verify meanings.

Learning Style Tips

If you tend to be a(n) . . .	Then use context by . . .
Auditory learner	Reading the context aloud
Visual learner	Visualizing the context

SELF-TEST SUMMARY

What are context clues used for?	They are used to figure out the meaning of an unknown word used in a sentence or paragraph.
What are the four types of context clues?	The four types of context clues are:

- Definition—a brief definition of or synonym for a word
- Example—specific instances or examples that clarify a word's meaning
- Contrast—a word or phrase of opposite meaning
- Inference—the use of reasoning skills to figure out word meanings

Name _____
Section _____ Date _____
Number right _____ x 10 points = Score _____

Directions: Each of the following sentences contains a word whose meaning can be determined from context. Select the choice that most nearly states the meaning of the underlined word as it is used in the sentence.

_____ 1. The new zoo project will be <u>subsidized</u> by city, county, state, and federal funds.
a. prevented
b. forgotten
c. replaced
d. financed

_____ 2. The burglar was so <u>intimidated</u> by the bright lights and barking dogs that he left hastily.
a. frightened
b. assisted
c. excited
d. encouraged

_____ 3. I explained to him that I would take care of his problem later, but he was not <u>appeased</u>.
a. satisfied
b. angry
c. present
d. frightened

_____ 4. Embassies typically follow well-established <u>protocols</u>, or accepted procedures, for seating guests at a government dinner.
a. sets of rules
b. scientific plans
c. list of invitations
d. preferences of leaders

_____ 5. He seemed quite free and easy with a few friends, but at large parties he was quite <u>inhibited</u>.
a. occupied
b. controlled
c. breathless
d. expressive

_____ 6. He was <u>prone</u> to taking a nap in the afternoon as he had done every day for most of his life.
a. not going
b. trying
c. likely
d. anxious

_____ 7. Cracking passwords is the most prevalent method of <u>illicit</u> entry to computer systems.
a. illegal
b. permitted
c. regular
d. senseless

_____ 8. She <u>disrupted</u> the entire performance by coughing during the most important part.
a. showed she appreciated
b. participated in
c. enjoyed
d. upset

_____ 9. You can <u>confirm</u> that your test results are correct by checking the answer key.
a. not know
b. make sure
c. apply
d. guess   *(continued)*

_____ 10. Rather than staying together, the group <u>dispersed</u>, and many became lost.
a. sat down
b. laughed
c. scattered
d. arranged itself

Name _____

Section _____ Date _____

Number right _____ x 20 points = Score _____

Directions: For each of the following statements, select the answer that correctly defines the underlined word.

_____ 1. In the past two hundred years, many species of whales have been hunted almost to the point of extinction. In response to worldwide concern over whales, the International Whaling Commission (IWC) declared a <u>moratorium</u> on commercial whaling in 1986.
a. promotion
b. proposition
c. stopping of activity
d. competition

_____ 2. Despite the example of athletic, attractive young women such as soccer star Mia Hamm, many teenage girls believe "the thinner the better." Fashion magazines featuring rail-thin models only <u>perpetuate</u> this belief, leading some teenagers to develop unrealistic and often unhealthy perceptions about their bodies.
a. continue
b. distort
c. prevent
d. correct

_____ 3. Although Lillian was 94 years old, she was healthy and mentally sharp. As she had done for most of her life, she insisted on living in her own apartment, buying her own groceries and paying her own bills, taking care of herself and making her own decisions—it was clear that she valued her <u>autonomy</u> above all else.
a. social life
b. family support
c. loneliness
d. independence

_____ 4. Our idea of the perfect vacation includes first-class airline tickets, a deluxe hotel room, and 24-hour room service, whereas Anne and Neil prefer something much more <u>rustic</u>. The last place they stayed didn't even have indoor plumbing!
a. elegant
b. simple
c. comfortable
d. active

_____ 5. The third-grade teacher marveled at the physical <u>disparities</u> among her students. Some were the size of kindergartners while others were almost as tall as she was.
a. dislikes
b. attitudes
c. differences
d. appearances

Name _____

Section _____ Date _____

Number right _____ x 20 points = Score _____

Directions: Read the following passage and choose the answer that best defines each bold-faced word from the passage.

1   *Worms* and *viruses* are rather unpleasant terms that have entered the **jargon** of the computer industry to describe some of the ways that computer systems can be invaded.

2   A worm can be defined as a program that transfers itself from computer to computer over a network and plants itself as a separate file on the target computer's disks. One worm was **injected** into an electronic mail network where it multiplied uncontrollably and clogged the memories of thousands of computers until they could no longer function.

3   A virus is a set of illicit instructions that passes itself on to other programs or documents with which it comes in contact. It can change or delete files, display words or obscene messages, or produce bizarre screen effects. In its most **vindictive** form, a virus can slowly **sabotage** a computer system and remain undetected for months, contaminating data or wiping out an entire hard drive. A virus can be dealt with using a vaccine, or antivirus, which is a computer program that stops the virus from spreading and often **eradicates** it.[4]

_____ 1. jargon
  a. language
  b. system
  c. confusion
  d. security

_____ 2. injected
  a. avoided
  b. introduced
  c. removed
  d. discussed

_____ 3. vindictive
  a. creative
  b. simple
  c. harmful
  d. typical

_____ 4. sabotage
  a. prevent
  b. destroy
  c. transfer
  d. produce

_____ 5. eradicates
  a. eliminates
  b. allows
  c. repeats
  d. produces

Name _____

Section _____ Date _____

Number right _____ x 10 points = Score _____

Climbing Mount Everest

Seaborn "Beck" Weathers

This essay, taken from a book titled *Everest: Mountain Without Mercy*, describes one man's attempt to climb Mt. Everest, the highest mountain in the world.

Vocabulary Preview

constrict (par. 1) to make smaller

dilated (par. 5) expanded

disembodied (par. 9) separated from the body

halting (par. 11) slow and uncertain, hesitant

remote (par. 12) distant, far away

primitive (par. 17) primary, basic

1   As I approached the Southeast Ridge of Mt. Everest shortly before sunrise, I was feeling strong, but my eyes simply weren't focusing. Fortunately, I didn't really need to see the route, because deep steps had been kicked ahead of me. The traverse at the bottom of the Southeast Ridge required more vision, however, and I had great difficulty feeling my way along it. When we reached the Balcony, I had to tell Rob Hall that I wouldn't be able to continue climbing—for the moment. In the brightness of the sun perhaps my pupils would constrict and I could follow later, I told him optimistically.

2   "Only if you're able to leave here within the next 30 minutes," Rob told me.

3   "Well, if I can't, then I'll just head back down the mountain."

4   But Rob didn't like the idea of not knowing whether I had made it down safely or not, so he made me promise to stay put until he returned.

5   I was still waiting there for Rob when the evening light started to fade. My vision again deteriorated when my pupils dilated. I now regretted my promise to Hall, especially because some hours earlier, around 1 p.m., others on our team had abandoned their summit attempt and offered to help me down.

6   Jon Krakauer, a teammate, was the first climber to return from the summit. He didn't mention having seen a storm coming, though in one of his accounts he reported that when high on the mountain he noticed that to the south a blanket of clouds had quickly replaced clear skies. I told Jon that I really couldn't see very well and that I needed to descend, and might need him to downclimb close enough to be my eyes.

7   Jon was willing to descend with me, but he reminded me that he was not a guide and that Mike Groom was coming 20 minutes behind him. Mike had a radio, and could let Hall know that I was heading down with him.

8   When Mike descended, he was assisting Yasuko Namba, who was badly exhausted. Neal Beidleman also came, with clients from Scott Fischer's group. Mike turned Yasuko over to Neal, then short-roped me down the Triangular Face.

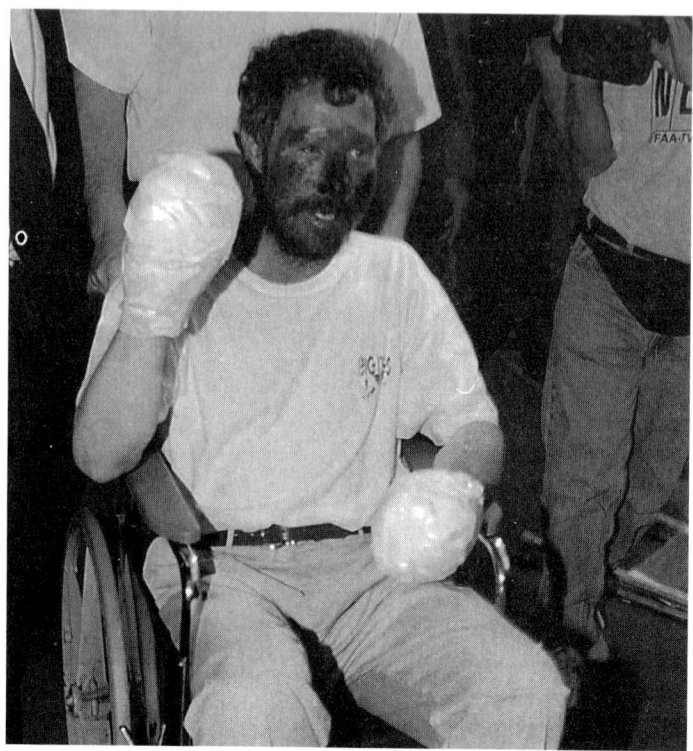

A severely frostbitten Beck Weathers receives much needed fluids.

9   From the face we climbed onto the South Col, and were there for only a few minutes when the storm came up—very quickly. I was cold but not particularly tired, and held onto Groom's coat sleeve. Visibility went to zip, and in the blowing snow and gathering darkness the other climbers became nothing more than fuzzy, disembodied headlamps. Totally lost, we were a pod of people following, like kids playing soccer, whoever was the current leader. We came to a standstill within feet of the sheer drop-off of the Kangshung Face, on the eastern edge of the South Col, and formed a huddle.

10   All of our oxygen had run out, and we rubbed and pounded on each others' backs, trying to keep every muscle in our bodies moving in order to generate heat and stay awake. I removed my right mitten, while leaving on the expedition-weight polypropylene glove liner, in order to place my hand inside my parka to warm it. The skin on my arm instantly froze. In that instant the wind blew my mitten away, and suddenly I was unable to zip up my parka. The spare pair of gloves in my pack might as well have been on the face of the moon, and I couldn't have opened my pack anyway.

11   After a few hours, some stars shone through a hole in the clouds, and we had a halting discussion about how to proceed. Some of us were barely able to walk, and I couldn't see. Groom and Beidleman decided to strike out in search of the camp, to send people back for us. This seemed reasonable.

12   Gradually, the whole scene became more remote. I had a sensation of floating, and didn't feel cold anymore. That must have been when I drifted off. I was not conscious when Anatoli Boukreev returned for the others.

13   Some time the next afternoon, I found myself alone on the ice. I was not terribly uncomfortable, and was convinced I was dreaming: The hardest part was coming to grips with the fact that my situation was real, and serious. I rolled over and looked at my right hand, which appeared like an unnatural, plastic, twisted gray thing attached to the end of my arm—not at all the hand that I knew. I banged it on the ice and it made a hollow sound, a sickening thunk.

14   This focused my attention. I could see my family there in front of my eyes, and managed to sit up, realizing that if I didn't get moving, I was going to lie there for eternity. None of our group was there; either they had left or I had become separated from them. It was clear that help wouldn't show up now.

15   I dumped my pack and ice ax, figuring this was a one-shot deal: I would either find camp or lose my last remnant of energy and sit down to wait for the end. For about an hour and a half I wandered in different directions, unable to orient myself, hoping I'd recognize something.

16   Then I remembered that during the night someone had said that the wind blows over the South Col from the Western Cwm, from the west. Camp had to be upwind. So I turned into the wind, put my head down, and figured I'd either walk into camp or off the edge of the mountain.

17   I was propelled by a primitive desire to survive. My oxygen-starved brain wasn't working, but I was certain of one thing: that I would die, that very soon I would sit down in the snow and wait for exhaustion and the cold to overcome me. I began to hallucinate. The landscape was moving and the rocks changed shape and crawled around on me, but I accepted this and continued wandering. It was not at all frightening. I was in a very calm state, except for a feeling of sadness that I would be unable to say some of the things I wanted to to my family. I knew that I could accept death.

18   But I had a heck of a lot to live for, and wasn't going down easy. My family, standing there before me, became an enormous driving force. The changing, uneven surface of ice and rocks caused me to lose my balance and fall several times. I knew not to fall on my hands, so I rolled as I went down—which was exhausting in itself.

19   And then a miracle happened. A couple of soft, bluish rocks appeared in front of me, and their smoothness led me to think they might be tents. But right away I caught myself indulging this thought, knowing I would only be disappointed, which would affect my will to continue. I steered toward them anyway, preparing to walk right past them.

20   Suddenly, someone was standing there, and it was Todd Burleson. He took one look

at me, got me by the arm, and led me to
camp. Pete Athans and Todd were sure that I
was going to die, too, but I'm glad they didn't
tell me. When a middle-aged guy like me can
survive that, it gives truth to the possibility
that this kind of strength resides in each of us.

Directions: Select the best answer for each of
the following questions.

CHECKING YOUR COMPREHENSION

_____ 1. The main point of the reading is that
  a. climbing Mt. Everest should only
     be attempted by young men with
     good eyesight.
  b. when facing death, it is harder to
     give up than to keep fighting to
     live.
  c. staying together is the key to sur-
     vival in dangerous situations.
  d. most people have more inner
     strength than they realize.

_____ 2. Paragraph 10 is primarily about
  a. how cold the temperature was.
  b. the group's efforts to stay awake.
  c. why the author's arm was frozen.
  d. the oxygen supply.

_____ 3. Which of the following best expresses
   the main idea of paragraph 17?
  a. The author is not afraid to die.
  b. The moving landscape was confus-
     ing.
  c. Hallucinations are a way of know-
     ing when death is near.
  d. Exhaustion is the result of lack of
     oxygen to breathe.

_____ 4. At the time others were rescued, the
   author was
  a. unwilling to leave.
  b. in severe pain.
  c. unconscious.
  d. crying.

_____ 5. At first the author abandoned his
   attempt to climb Everest because
  a. a snowstorm came up.
  b. he got separated from his guide.
  c. night came.
  d. his vision deteriorated.

APPLYING YOUR SKILLS

_____ 6. In paragraph 5, the word "deteriorated" means
  a. worsened.
  b. removed.
  c. cleared.
  d. settled.

_____ 7. In paragraph 9, the word "zip" means
  a. close.
  b. vigorous movement.
  c. energy.
  d. nothing.

_____ 8. In paragraph 15, the word "remnant"
   means
  a. leftover piece.
  b. important group.
  c. destroyed piece.
  d. expression.

_____ 9. In paragraph 16, the word "upwind" means
 a. over the top of a mountain.
 b. into the wind.
 c. away from the wind.
 d. toward the edge of a mountain.

_____ 10. In the sentence "I told Jon that I really couldn't see very well and that I needed to descend, and might need him to downclimb close enough to be my eyes," the word "descend" has which of the following types of context clue?
 a. synonym
 b. example
 c. contrast
 d. inference

Go Electronic!
For additional readings, exercises, and Internet activities, visit this book's Web site at:

http://www.ablongman.com/mcwhorter

If you need a user name and password, please see your instructor.
Take a Road Trip to the Library of Congress!
Be sure to visit the Vocabulary module in your Reading Road Trip CD-ROM for multimedia tutorials, exercises, and tests.

3

Learning Word Parts

THIS CHAPTER WILL SHOW YOU HOW TO

1. Figure out the meaning of unfamiliar words
2. Use prefixes, roots, and suffixes

Many students build their vocabulary word by word: if they study ten new words, then they have learned ten new words. If they study 30 words, they can recall 30 meanings. Would you like a better and faster way to build your vocabulary?

This chapter will show you how to make a dramatic difference in how many words you know by studying word parts. By learning the meaning of the parts that make up a word, you will be able to figure out the meanings of many more words. For example, if you learn that *pre-* means *before*, then you can begin to figure out hundreds of words that begin with *pre* (premarital, premix, preemployment).

In this chapter you will learn about compound words and about the beginnings, middles, and endings of words called prefixes, roots, and suffixes.

FINDING MEANINGS IN COMPOUND WORDS

A new word formed by two words that are put together is called a compound word. For example, the word *paperwork* is formed from the words *paper* and *work*. The meanings of the two words will lead you to the meaning of the compound word: *work done on paper*. On the next page are a few more examples of compound words:

waterproof	water + proof
horseshoe	horse + shoe
endpoint	end + point
checklist	check + list
outcome	out + come

Some words appear frequently in compound words. The word *under*, for example, is common:

undertow

underage

underachiever

undergo

undercover

A first step, then, when you meet an unfamiliar word, is to look for words you recognize within it. *Underachiever*, for example, means someone who achieves or performs under or below average.

EXERCISE 3-1	**Directions:** Select five additional compound words and show your understanding of them by writing a sentence using each word.

LEARNING PREFIXES, ROOTS, AND SUFFIXES

Suppose that you came across the following sentence in a human anatomy textbook:

> Trichromatic plates are used frequently in the text to illustrate the position of body organs.

If you did not know the meaning of *trichromatic*, how could you determine it? There are no clues in the sentence context. One solution is to look up the word in a dictionary. An easier and faster way is to break the word into parts and analyze the meaning of each part. Many words in the English language are made up of word parts called **prefixes, roots,** and **suffixes.** These word parts have specific meanings that, when added together, can help you determine the meaning of the word as a whole.

The word *trichromatic* can be divided into three parts: its prefix, root, and suffix.

- Prefix—tri- ("three")
- Root—chrome ("color")
- Suffix—atic ("characteristic of")

You can see from this analysis that *trichromatic* means "having three colors."

Here are a few other examples of words that you can figure out by using prefixes, roots, and suffixes:

The parents thought the child was **unteachable.**

un- = not

teach = help someone learn

-able = able to do something

unteachable = not able to be taught

The student was a **nonconformist.**

non- = not

conform = go along with others

-ist = one who does something

nonconformist = someone who does not go along with others

The first step in using the prefix-root-suffix method is to become familiar with the most commonly used word parts. The prefixes and roots listed in Tables 3-1 and 3-2 (pages 58–59) will give you a good start in determining the meanings of thousands of words without looking them up in the dictionary. For instance, more than 10,000 words can begin with the prefix *non-*. Not all these words are listed in a collegiate dictionary, but they would appear in an unabridged dictionary (see Chapter 4). Another common prefix, *pseudo-*, is used in more than 400 words. A small amount of time spent learning word parts can yield a large payoff in new words learned.

Before you begin to use word parts to figure out new words, there are a few things you need to know:

1. In most cases, a word is built upon at least one root.
2. Words can have more than one prefix, root, or suffix.
   a. Words can be made up of two or more roots (geo/logy).
   b. Some words have two prefixes (in/sub/ordination).
   c. Some words have two suffixes (beauti/ful/ly).
3. Words do not always have a prefix and a suffix.
   a. Some words have neither a prefix nor a suffix (read).
   b. Others have a suffix but no prefix (read/ing).
   c. Others have a prefix but no suffix (pre/read).
4. The spelling of roots may change as they are combined with suffixes. Some common variations are included in Table 3-2.
5. Different prefixes, roots, or suffixes may have the same meaning. For example, the prefixes *bi-*, *di-*, and *duo-* all mean "two."
6. Sometimes you may identify a group of letters as a prefix or root but find that it does not carry the meaning of that prefix or root. For example, the letters *mis* in the word *missile* are part of the root and are not the prefix *mis-*, which means "wrong; bad."

PREFIXES

Prefixes appear at the beginnings of many English words. They alter the meaning of the root to which they are connected. For example, if you add the prefix *re-* to the word *read*, the word *reread* is formed, meaning to read again. If *pre-* is added to the word *reading*, the word *prereading* formed, meaning before reading. If the prefix *post-* is added, the word *postreading* is formed, meaning after reading. In Table 3-1, 40 common prefixes are grouped according to meaning.

TABLE 3-1 Common Prefixes

Prefix	Meaning	Sample Word
Prefixes referring to amount or number		
mono/uni	one	monocle/unicycle
bi/di/du	two	bimonthly/divorce/duet
tri	three	triangle
quad	four	quadrant
quint/pent	five	quintet/pentagon
deci	ten	decimal
centi	hundred	centigrade
milli	thousand	milligram
micro	small	microscope
multi/poly	many	multipurpose/polygon
semi	half	semicircle
equi	equal	equidistant
Prefixes meaning "not" (negative)		
a	not	asymmetrical
anti	against	antiwar
contra	against, opposite	contradict
dis	apart, away, not	disagree
in/il/ir/im	not	incorrect/illogical/irreversible/impossible
mis	wrongly	misunderstand
non	not	nonfiction
pseudo	false	pseudopregnancy
un	not	unpopular
pseudo	false	pseudoscientific
Prefixes giving direction, location, or placement		
ab	away	absent
ad	toward	adhesive
ante/pre	before	antecedent/premarital
circum/peri	around	circumference/perimeter
com/col/con	with, together	compile/collide/convene
de	away, from	depart
dia	through	diameter
ex/extra	from, out of, former	ex-wife/extramarital
hyper	over, excessive	hyperactive
inter	between	interpersonal
intro/intra	within, into, in	introduction
post	after	posttest
re	back, again	review
retro	backward	retrospect
sub	under, below	submarine
super	above, extra	supercharge
tele	far	telescope
trans	across, over	transcontinental

TABLE 3-2 Common Roots

Common Root	Meaning	Sample Word
aud/audit	hear	audible
aster/astro	star	astronaut
bene	good, well	benefit
bio	life	biology
cap	take, seize	captive
chron(o)	time	chronology
cog	to learn	cognitive
corp	body	corpse
cred	believe	incredible
dict/dic	tell, say	predict
duc/duct	lead	introduce
fact/fac	make, do	factory
graph	write	telegraph
geo	earth	geophysics
log/logo/logy	study, thought	psychology
mit/miss	send	permit/dismiss
mort/mor	die, death	immortal
path	feeling	sympathy
phono	sound, voice	telephone
photo	light	photosensitive
port	carry	transport
scop	seeing	microscope
scrib/script	write	inscription
sen/sent	feel	insensitive
spec/spic/spect	look, see	retrospect
tend/tent/tens	stretch or strain	tension
terr/terre	land, earth	territory
theo	god	theology
ven/vent	come	convention
vert/vers	turn	invert
vis/vid	see	invisible/video
voc	call	vocation

EXERCISE 3-2	**Directions:** Using the list of common prefixes in Table 3-1, match each word in Column A with its meaning from Column B. Write the letter of your choice in the space provided.

	Column A		**Column B**
_f_	1. misplaced	a.	half of a circle
_d_	2. postgraduate	b.	build again
_i_	3. dehumidify	c.	tiny duplicate of printed material
_a_	4. semicircle	d.	continuing studies past graduation
_h_	5. nonprofit	e.	not fully developed
_b_	6. reconstruct	f.	put in the wrong position
_j_	7. triathlete	g.	build up electrical power again
_c_	8. microcopy	h.	not for making money
_g_	9. recharge	i.	to remove moisture from
_e_	10. immature	j.	one who participates in three-part sporting events

EXERCISE 3-3	**Directions:** Use the list of common prefixes in Table 3-1 to determine the meaning of each of the following words. Write a brief definition or synonym for each. If you are unfamiliar with the root, you may need to check a dictionary.

1. interoffice _between offices_

2. supernatural _above natural_

3. nonsense _no sense_

4. introspection _within sight_

5. prearrange _arrange before_

6. reset _start over_ (set)

7. subtopic _under topic_

8. transmit _Carry over across_

9. multidimensional _many dimensions_

10. imperfect _not perfect_

EXERCISE 3-4

Directions: Write a synonym for each word in boldface type.

1. an **atypical** child _____

2. to **hyperventilate** _____

3. an **extraordinary** request _____

4. **semisoft** cheese _____

5. **antisocial** behavior _____

6. to **circumnavigate** the globe _____

7. a **triweekly** delivery _____

_____

8. an **uneventful** weekend _____

9. a **disfigured** face _____

10. to **exhale** smoke _____

EXERCISE 3-5

Directions: Read each of the following sentences. Use your knowledge of prefixes to fill in the blank and complete the word.

1. A person who speaks two languages is _bi_**lingual**.

2. A letter or number written beneath a line of print is called a _sub_**script**.

3. The new sweater had a snag, and I returned it to the store because it was
unim **perfect**.

4. The flood damage was permanent and _unir_ **reversible**.

5. I was not given the correct date and time; I was _unmis_ **informed**.

6. People who speak several different languages are _bimicro_ **lingual**.

7. A musical _inter_ **lude** was played between the events in the ceremony.

8. I decided the magazine was uninteresting, so I _dis_ **continued** my
subscription.

9. Merchandise that does not pass factory inspection is considered _sub_ **standard** and sold at a discount.

10. The tuition refund policy approved this week will apply to last year's tuition as well;
the policy will be _retro HA_ **active** to January 1 of last year.

11. The elements were _re_ **acting** with each other when they began to bubble
and their temperature rose.

12. _Contra_ **ceptives** are widely used to prevent unwanted pregnancies.

13. All of the waitresses were required to wear the restaurant's _uni_ **form**.

14. The _inter_ **viewer** asked the presidential candidates unexpected questions
about important issues.

15. The draperies were _mis_ **colored** from long exposure to the sun.

EXERCISE 3-6	**Directions:** Use your knowledge of prefixes to supply the missing word in each sentence. Write the word in the space provided.

1. Our house is a duplex. The one next door with three apartments is a _triplex_.

2. A preparation applied to the skin to reduce or prevent perspiration is called an
antiperprisant

3. A person who cannot read or write is _illiterate_.

4. I did not use my real name; instead I gave a _pseudonym_

5. If someone seems to have greater powers than do normal humans, he or she might be called _super human_.

6. A friend who criticizes you too often is (disrespectful) _hypercritical_

7. If you plan to continue to take college courses after you graduate, you will be taking _post graduate_ courses.

8. Substances that fight bacteria are known as _anti bacterial_ drugs.

9. The branch of biology that deals with very small living organisms is _microbiology_

10. In the metric system a _centimeter_ is one one-hundredth of a meter.

11. One one-thousandth of a second is called a _millisecond_.

12. The tape showed an instant _replay_ of the touchdown.

13. A disabling physical handicap is often called a _disability_.

EXERCISE 3-7

Directions: Working with a classmate, list as many words as you can think of for two of the following prefixes: **multi-, mis-, trans-, com-, inter-**. Then share your lists with the class.

ROOTS

Roots carry the basic or core meaning of a word. Hundreds of root words are used to build words in the English language. Thirty-two of the most common and most useful are listed in Table 3-2. Knowledge of the meanings of these roots will enable you to unlock the meanings of many words. For example, if you know that the root *dic/dict* means "tell or say," then you would have a clue to the meanings of such words as *dictate* (to speak for someone to write down), *diction* (wording or manner of speaking), or *dictionary* (book that "tells" what words mean).

EXERCISE 3-8 **Directions:** Using the list of common roots in Table 3-2, match each word in Column A with its meaning from Column B. Write the letter of your choice in the space provided.

Column A

___G___ 1. benediction
___i___ 2. audible
___h___ 3. missive
___J___ 4. telecommunicate
___A___ 5. mortician
___D___ 6. intervene
___B___ 7. reverted
___e___ 8. aqueduct
___C___ 9. photoactive
___f___ 10. vocalize

Column B

a. undertaker
b. went back
c. able to respond to light
d. come between two things
e. channel or pipe that brings water from a distance
f. use the voice
g. blessing
h. letter or message
i. can be heard
j. send and receive messages over long distances

EXERCISE 3-9 **Directions:** Use the list of common roots in Table 3-2 to determine the meanings of the following words. Write a brief definition or synonym for each, checking a dictionary if necessary.

1. dictaphone _____
2. biomedicine _____
3. photocopy _____
4. porter _____
5. visibility _____
6. credentials _____
7. speculate _____

8. terrain _____

9. audition _____

10. sentiment _____

11. astrophysics _____

12. capacity _____

13. chronicle _____

14. corporation _____

15. facile _____

16. autograph _____

17. sociology _____

18. phonometer _____

19. sensation _____

20. vocal _____

EXERCISE	**Directions:** Complete each of the following sentences with one of the words listed
3-10	below.

apathetic	dictated	graphic	scriptures	tendon
captivated	extensive	phonics	spectators	verdict
deduce	extraterrestrial	prescribed	synchronized	visualize

1. The jury brought in its _verdict_ after one hour of deliberation.

2. Religious or holy writings are called _scriptures_.

3. She closed her eyes and tried to _visualize_ the license plate number.

4. The _spectators_ watching the football game were tense.

5. The doctor _prescribed_ two types of medication.

6. The list of toys the child wanted for his birthday was _extensive_.

7. The criminal appeared _apathetic_ when the judge pronounced sentence.

8. The runners _synchronized_ their watches before beginning the race.

9. The textbook contained numerous _graphic_ aids, including maps, charts, and diagrams.

10. The study of the way different parts of words sound is called _phonics_.

11. The athlete strained a(n) _tendon_ and was unable to continue training.

12. The movie was about a(n) _extraterrestrial_, a creature not from earth.

13. The district manager _dictated_ a letter to her secretary, who then typed it.

14. Through his attention-grabbing performance, he _captivated_ the audience.

15. By putting together the clues, the detective was finally able to _deduce_ who committed the crime.

EXERCISE 3-11	**Directions:** List two words for each of the following roots: **dict/dic, spec/spic/spect, fact/fac, phono, scrib/script.**

SUFFIXES

Suffixes are word endings that often change the part of speech of a word. For example, adding the suffix *y* to the noun *cloud* forms the adjective *cloudy*. Accompanying the change in part of speech is a shift in meaning (*cloudy* means "resembling clouds; overcast with clouds; dimmed or dulled as if by clouds").

Often, several different words can be formed from a single root word by adding different suffixes.

Examples:

> **Root:** class
>
> root + suffix = class/ify, class/ification, class/ic
>
> **Root:** right
>
> root + suffix = right/ly, right/ful, right/ist, right/eous

If you know the meaning of the root word and the ways in which different suffixes affect the meaning of the root word, you will be able to figure out a word's meaning when a suffix is added. A list of common suffixes and their meanings appears in Table 3-3 on page 68.

You can expand your vocabulary by learning the variations in meaning that occur when suffixes are added to words you already know. When you find a word that you do not know, look for the root. Then, using the sentence the word is in (its context; see Chapter 2), figure out what the word means with the suffix added. Occasionally you may find that the spelling of the root word has been changed. For instance, a final *e* may be dropped, a final consonant may be doubled, or a final *y* may be changed to *i*. Consider the possibility of such changes when trying to identify the root word.

Examples:

> The article was a **compilation** of facts.
>
> root + suffix
>
> compil(e) + -ation = something that has been compiled, or put together into an orderly form
>
> We were concerned with the **legality** of our decision to change addresses.
>
> root + suffix
>
> legal + -ity = pertaining to legal matters
>
> Our college is one of the most **prestigious** in the state.
>
> root + suffix
>
> prestig(e) + -ious = having prestige or distinction

TABLE 3-3   Common Suffixes

Suffix	Sample Word
Suffixes that refer to a state, condition, or quality	
able	touchable
ance	assistance
ation	confrontation
ence	reference
ible	tangible
ion	discussion
ity	superiority
ive	permissive
ment	amazement
ness	kindness
ous	jealous
ty	loyalty
y	creamy
Suffixes that mean "one who"	
an	Italian
ant	participant
ee	referee
eer	engineer
ent	resident
er	teacher
ist	activist
or	advisor
Suffixes that mean "pertaining to or referring to"	
al	autumnal
ship	friendship
hood	brotherhood
ward	homeward

EXERCISE 3-12

Directions: For each suffix shown in Table 3-3 write another example of a word you know that has that suffix.

**EXERCISE
3-13**

Directions: For each of the words listed, add a suffix so that the word will complete the sentence. Write the new word in the space provided. Check a dictionary if you are unsure of the spelling.

1. converse

    Our phone _____ lasted ten minutes.

2. assist

    The medical _____ labeled the patient's blood samples.

3. qualify

    The job applicant outlined his _____ to the interviewer.

4. intern

    The doctor completed her _____ at Memorial Medical Center.

5. eat

    We did not realize that the blossoms of the plant could be _____.

6. audio

    She spoke so softly that her voice was not _____.

7. season

    It is usually very dry in July, but this year it has rained constantly. The weather isn't

    very _____.

8. permit

    The professor granted her _____ to miss class.

9. instruct

    The lecture on Freud was very_____.

10. remember

    The wealthy businessman donated the building in_____ of his deceased

    father.

11. mortal

    The _____ rate in Ethiopia is very high.

12. president

    The _____ race held many surprises.

13. feminine

    She called herself a _____, although she never actively supported the

    movement for equal rights for women.

14. hazard

    The presence of toxic waste in the lake is _____ to health.

15. destine

    The young man felt it was his _____ to become a priest.

EXERCISE 3-14	**Directions:** For each word listed below, write as many new words as you can create by adding suffixes.

1. compare _____

2. adapt _____

3. right _____

4. identify _____

5. will _____

6. prefer _____

7. notice _____

8. like _____

9. pay _____

10. promote _____

HOW TO USE WORD PARTS

Think of roots as being at the root or core of a word's meaning. There are many more roots than are listed in Table 3-2. You already know many of these, because they are used in everyday speech. Think of prefixes as word parts that are added before the root to qualify or change its meaning. Think of suffixes as add-ons that make the word fit grammatically into the sentence in which it is used.

When you come upon a word you do not know, keep the following pointers in mind:

1. **First, look for the root.** Think of this as looking for a word inside a larger word. Often a letter or two will be missing.

   Examples:

   un/utter/able   defens/ible
   inter/colleg/iate   re/popular/ize
   post/operat/ive   non/adapt/able
   im/measur/ability   non/commit/tal

2. **If you do not recognize the root, then you will probably not be able to figure out the word.** The next step is to check its meaning in a dictionary. For tips on locating words in a dictionary rapidly and easily, see Chapter 4.

3. **If you did recognize the root word, look for a prefix.** If there is one, determine how it changes the meaning of the word.

   Examples:

   un/utterable   un- = not
   post/operative   post- = after

4. **Locate the suffix.** Determine how it further adds to or changes the meaning of the root word.

Examples:

unutter/able   -able = able to
postoperat/ive   -ive = state or condition

5. **Next, try out the meaning in the sentence in which the word was used.** Substitute your meaning for the word and see whether the sentence makes sense.

Examples:

Some of the victim's thoughts were **unutterable** at the time of the crime. unutterable = that which cannot be spoken

My sister was worried about the cost of **postoperative** care. postoperative = state or condition after an operation

EXERCISE **3-15**	**Directions:** Use the steps listed previously to determine the meaning of each bold-faced word. Underline the root in each word and then write a brief definition of the word that fits its use in the sentence.

1. The doctor felt the results of the X rays were **indisputable**.

_____

2. The **dissimilarity** among the three brothers was surprising.

_____

3. The **extortionist** demanded two payments of $10,000 each.

_____

4. It is **permissible** to camp in most state parks.

_____

5. The student had **retentive** abilities.

_____

6. The **traumatic** event changed the child's attitude toward animals.

_____

7. We were surprised by her **insincerity**.

_____

8. The child's **hypersensitivity** worried his parents.

_____

9. The English instructor told Peter that he had written a **creditable** paper.

_____

10. The rock group's agent hoped to **repopularize** their first hit song.

_____

11. The gambler was filled with **uncertainty** about the horse race.

_____

12. The **nonenforcement** of the speed limit led to many deaths.

_____

13. The effects of the disease were **irreversible**.

_____

14. The mysterious music seemed to **foretell** the murder of the movie's heroine.

_____

15. The **polyphony** filled the concert hall.

_____

16. Sailors used to think the North Sea **unnavigable**.

_____

17. She received a **dishonorable** discharge from the Marines.

_____

18. The criminal was **unapologetic** to the judge about the crimes he had committed.

_____

19. A systems analysis revealed that the factory was **underproductive**.

_____

20. He rotated the dial **counterclockwise**.

_____

EXERCISE 3-16	**Directions:** Read each of the following paragraphs and determine the meaning of each boldfaced word. Write a brief definition for each in the space provided.

A. Exercising in hot weather can create stress on the circulatory system due to the high **production** of body heat. In hot weather the **distention** of blood vessels in the skin **diverts** increased quantities of blood to the body surfaces, where heat is released. As the body heats, skin heat evaporates the sweat, cooking the skin and the blood **circulating** near the skin.[1]

1. production _____

2. distention _____

3. diverts _____

4. circulating _____

B. In addition to being **irreversible**, interpersonal communication is also **unrepeatable**. The reason is simple: Everyone and everything are constantly changing. As a result, you can never **recapture** the exact same situation, frame of mind, or relationship that defined a previous interpersonal act. For example, you can never repeat meeting someone for the first time, comforting a grieving friend, or resolving a specific conflict.[2]

1. irreversible_____

2. unrepeatable _____

3. recapture _____

C. People with positive emotional **wellness** can function **independently**. They can think for themselves, make decisions, plan their lives, and follow through with their plans. **Conversely**, people who have difficulty making decisions are often immature and **insecure**. They are afraid to face the consequences of the decisions they make, so they make as few decisions as possible. Growth involves making **mistakes** as well as achieving success. Our mistakes are best viewed as learning experiences. We must take some risks in order to live our lives most fully.[3]

1. wellness _____

2. independently _____

3. conversely _____

4. insecure _____

5. mistakes _____

   D. We could probably greatly reduce the risks associated with nuclear power by simply exercising more care and common sense. There are a **multitude** of published accounts that attest to our carelessness, however. For example, it has been revealed that the Diablo Canyon nuclear power plant in California was built on an earthquake fault line. Of course it was girded for that risk. **Incredibly**, however, the blueprints were somehow **reversed** and the earthquake supports were put in backwards. Furthermore, the mistake was not noticed for four years. At the Comanche Peak Plant in Texas, supports were **constructed** 45 degrees out of line. At the Marble Hill in Indiana, the concrete surrounding the core was found to be full of air bubbles. At the WNP-2 plant in Washington state, the concrete contained air bubbles and pockets of water as well as shields that had been **incorrectly** welded. At the San Onofre plant in California, a 420-ton reactor vessel was installed backwards and the error was not detected for months.[4]

1. multitude _____

2. incredibly _____

3. reversed _____

4. constructed _____

5. incorrectly _____

WORKING TOGETHER

Directions: Your instructor will choose a reading selection from Part 5 and form groups. Locate and underline at least five words in the selection not included in its Vocabulary Preview or Words in Context that other group members can define by analyzing word parts. Work together with group members to determine the meaning of each word, checking a dictionary to verify meanings.

Learning Style Tips

If you tend to be a(n) . . .	Then learn word parts by . . .
Social learner	Studying with a group of classmates
Independent learner	Making up review tests, or asking a friend to do so, and practice taking the tests

SELF-TEST SUMMARY

When you can't figure out an unknown word by using context clues, what should you do?	Break the word into word parts and use your knowledge of prefixes, root words, and suffixes to figure out the word.
What are prefixes, roots, and suffixes?	Prefixes are beginnings of words, roots are middles of words, suffixes are endings of words.
Why is it useful to learn prefixes, roots, and suffixes?	They unlock the meaning of thousands of English words

Name _____

Section _____ Date _____

Number right _____ x 10 points = Score _____

Directions: Each of the following words contains a root and a prefix and/or suffix. Select the answer that correctly divides the word into its parts.

Example: bo/tan/i/cal

_____ 1. teleconference
     a. tel/e/con/ference
     b. te/le/con/fer/ence
     c. tele/confer/ence
     d. tele/conference

_____ 2. intangible
     a. in/tan/gi/ble
     b. in/tang/ible
     c. in/ta/ngi/ble
     d. in/tangi/ble

_____ 3. avocation
     a. a/voc/ation
     b. avo/ca/tion
     c. av/o/cation
     d. a/vo/cation

_____ 4. biographer
     a. bio/graph/er
     b. bi/og/ra/pher
     c. bio/grapher
     d. bi/ograph/er

Directions: Each of the following underlined words contains a root and a prefix and/or suffix. Using your knowledge of roots, prefixes, and suffixes, select the best definition for each word.

B 5. The <u>antiwar</u> movement of the 1960s helped bring about U.S. withdrawal from Vietnam.
     a. before war
     b. against war
     c. in favor of war
     d. during war

D 6. If you use spaces instead of tabs in your computer document, your columns will <u>misalign</u>.
     a. be against one line
     b. skip a line
     c. form a small line
     d. line up wrong

B 7. The coroner prepared a <u>postmortem</u> report on the drowning victim.
     a. before life
     b. after death
     c. written again
     d. confused

B 8. The Supreme Court's decisions are <u>irreversible</u>.
     a. capable of great injury
     b. not able to be turned around
     c. unacceptable
     d. flawless

(continued)

C 9. The congressman pledged to put an end
to <u>substandard</u> wages in his district.
a. illegal
b. under investigation
c. below normal
d. dishonest

A 10. The <u>economist</u> predicted that unemployment will increase.
a. person who studies economics
b. theories of economics
c. former studies of the economy
d. the quality of the economy

Name _____

Section _____ Date _____

Number right _____ x 20 points = Score _____

Directions: For each of the following statements, select the answer that provides the correct prefix, root, or suffix in the blank next to the boldfaced word.

C 1. Students who attend ethnically diverse schools are often exposed to a variety of foreign languages. One suburban Atlanta elementary school, for instance, has students whose native languages are Spanish, Vietnamese, Romanian, and Sudanese. Parents and school administrators in this school speak in glowing terms about their _____**lingual** student population.
   a. mono
   b. tri
   c. multi
   d. semi

B 2. Samuel L. Clemens was born in 1835 in Hannibal, Missouri. Using the _____**nym** Mark Twain, he drew upon his childhood experiences along the Mississippi River to write *Tom Sawyer* and *The Adventures of Huckleberry Finn.*
   a. anti
   b. pseudo
   c. poly
   d. retro

d 3. Melanie's father and grandfather are both police officers so it was not surprising that she decided to pursue a career in law enforcement. She has already enrolled at the community college where she plans to major in criminal justice and take classes in **crimino**_____ in order to learn more about crime, criminals, and criminal behavior.
   a. graphy
   b. scopy
   c. pathy
   d. logy

A 4. The portion of the earth that is inhabited by living things is known as the earth's _____**sphere**. It includes the atmosphere and the oceans to specified heights and depths, as well as lakes and rivers.
   a. bio
   b. astro
   c. geo
   d. chrono

C 5. Our composition instructor always asked us to exchange our essays with each other in class in order to get another person's feedback on our work. He only allowed us to make **construct**_____ criticism, encouraging us to keep in mind how we would want our own work to be reviewed.
   a. ent
   b. ible
   c. ive
   d. or

CHAPTER 3
MASTERY TEST 3:
Vocabulary Skills

Name _____

Section _____ Date _____

Number right _____ x 20 points = Score _____

Directions: Using your knowledge of roots, prefixes, and suffixes, choose the correct definition for each of the following boldfaced words from the passage.

1   Concerns about being overweight are based on more than vanity. Too much weight is harmful to your health and may significantly increase your risk for **hypertension,** cancer, stroke, heart disease, and adult-onset diabetes.

2   There is also a **relationship** between weight and the length of a hospital stay. Researchers have found that extremely overweight patients had average hospital stays 35 percent longer than patients of normal weight. One possible reason that obese patients stay in the hospital longer is an increased incidence of **postoperative** wound infections.

3   In many respects, underweight represents as serious a health threat as **obesity.** Even thin men and women who are well have higher **mortality** rates than do well men and women of average weight.[5]

_B_ 1. hypertension
   a. low blood pressure
   b. high blood pressure
   c. normal blood pressure
   d. absence of blood pressure

_B_ 2. relationship
   a. difference
   b. connection
   c. cause
   d. performance

_C_ 3. postoperative
   a. before a surgical operation
   b. during a surgical operation
   c. after a surgical operation
   d. between surgical operations

_B_ 4. obesity
   a. one who is obese
   b. the condition of being obese
   c. not obese
   d. unrelated to obesity

_BC_ 5. mortality
   a. sickness
   b. health
   c. death
   d. body

Name _____

Section _____ Date _____

Number right _____ x 10 points = Score _____

The Dolphin Affair

Dan Greenburg

In this article, first printed in the magazine *Modern Maturity,* Greenburg vividly describes his experiences swimming with dolphins.

Vocabulary Preview

linguistic (par. 1) having to do with language

compulsive (par. 1) driven by an inner force

relentlessly (par. 3) over and over again

apprehension (par. 3) fear or anxiety that something unpleasant will happen

ominous (par. 4) threatening, unfavorable

bravado (par. 18) display of courage

caveats (par. 21) rules, warnings

1   I have always been fascinated by dolphins. By their intelligence, their playfulness, their kindness to humans. I'd heard that dolphins become alarmed if you're upright in the water and will do anything, including pushing you with their beaks and whapping you with their tails, to get you into a horizontal position. I'd heard that dolphins use their sonar to examine you for signs of distress. That's like having a radiologist friend x-ray you when you come over for dinner. I had a picture of dolphins as helpful, protective, concerned, worried, compulsive, some-

what controlling creatures—Jewish mothers of the sea—and I wanted to meet some. So I made plans to swim with them in Florida, then join an experimental program in Hawaii that tests their intelligence and linguistic skills.

2   Dolphins Plus in Key Largo, Florida, studies interaction between dolphins and humans and conducts dolphin-assisted therapy for people with disabilities. It houses a huge dolphin pool and lecture hall and allows small groups of visitors to swim with its dolphins.

3   I'm accompanied by my fiancée, Judith, my 13-year-old son, Zack, and local photographer Stephen Frink, a dead ringer for movie star Chuck Norris. We're taken to an 80 × 120-foot partially fenced-off section of a canal that leads into the ocean. Seven dolphins, all females, swim around in the murky water. I've been told relentlessly that they're safe to swim with, but I'm uneasy. My apprehension grows when an instructor named Christy enters and gives us our preswim briefing. "The dolphins are not trained to allow people to touch them in this program—in other programs you can—so whatever you do, don't touch them. Don't reach out to them either. They might interpret that as threatening. In fact," she says, "don't swim with your hands at all—trail

Dolphins mate 365 days a year—no wonder they're always smiling.

them at your sides or clasp them behind your back."

4   I find it frustrating not being allowed to touch them. I find it ominous not being allowed to swim with my hands. But the implication seems to be that if I use them now, I might not be able to use them afterwards.

5   "If a dolphin looks at you," says Christy, "break eye contact immediately. That's how they challenge each other." They challenge each other? Is she saying that adorable Flipper, the Lassie of the sea, has attitude?

6   "Also, stay ten feet away from any other human in the water," she continues.

"Dolphins consider us toys, and they don't like sharing them. Most important, don't jerk your head." Head-jerks, she explains, are tantamount to saying rude things about a dolphin's mother. We're then told that dolphins are eight to ten feet long, weigh more than 350 pounds, and can swim up to 40 miles per hour. We're told that dolphins will mate 365 days a year. We're told that dolphins like kids best, women second, and men least.

7   "Okay," says Christy, "get into the water."

8   Getting into the water is the last thing I want to do right now, but I see Judith and Zack slip into the pool, so I follow.

Underwater, I peer warily at the dolphins. They're off in a corner, like girls at a mixer, too shy to come over and say hi.

9 Suddenly, one of them screws up her courage and zooms across the pool—toward me—missing me by millimeters. Another dolphin decides this is amusing and whizzes toward me at what seems like double the speed. I freeze, wondering what it's like to be rammed by more than 300 pounds of speeding mammal, but she misses me by the diameter of a hair. The girls retreat to the far side of the pool and snigger. And that's it. They make no more advances, show no more interest, not even in Zack or Judith.

10 Stephen says he's not getting the shots he needs and asks us to attract the dolphins by making sounds. Attracting the dolphins toward me again is not something I'm eager to do, but I know we need the pictures. Judith hums sea chanteys. I do flawless imitations of whale song.

11 "Dad, why are you doing sad puppy sounds?" Zack asks. "Are you trying to guilt them into coming over?"

12 Christy suggests we swim across the pool on our bellies in a sort of Busby Berkeley water ballet. I ask what this is for and she says it's for the girls' amusement. Ah. Well, I do hope they're amused, but they no longer seem to notice.

13 Unable to get the pictures he wants from the deck, Stephen enters the pool. He's wearing a black and purple wet suit with neon-colored accessories and is carrying several shiny underwater cameras and lights. The girls come to life, race across the pool, and

converge on him like high school sophomores around Brad Pitt.

14 I'm a tad disappointed. No, let's be frank. I am speechless with jealousy. Your buddy begs you to let him tag along to this great party, and when you get there the women ignore you but hang onto him like lint on a black suit. I find the Dolphins Plus girls surprisingly shallow, being less impressed by a writer with a good personality than by a Chuck Norris look-alike in flashy clothing. I hope for better luck in Hawaii. . . .

15 The dolphins at the Kewalo Basin Marine Mammal Laboratory have been taught to respond to approximately 150 sign-language gestures and several thousand combinations thereof. One of these is truly amazing. Give them a list of commands, then slip the sign for ERASE anywhere into your list. The dolphins will automatically delete every command before ERASE and do all the others.

16 Their most impressive maneuver, though, is called TANDEM-CREATIVE and requires two dolphins. The TANDEM-CREATIVE sign means "Okay guys, do whatever you like, but discuss it first, do it together, and do it now." No sooner does the trainer give the sign than they're off, whistling and clicking. They race around the pool, leap into the air, and do three backward somersaults in perfect synchrony. I naively suggest that they probably just do the same trick each time. She gives me a "Watch this" look and repeats the command. This time they leap into the air, touch flippers, then swim on their backs while touching pectoral fins. Hmm. Most of

my friends couldn't even get past choosing the activity.

17   I've been learning to sign at KBMML and have mastered roughly three dozen commands. Today I'm to perform my first "local," or one-on-one, with Elele (whom the staff call Ellie). I think of it as our first date. I am nervous. For one thing, there was the rejection by the fickle hussies at Key Largo. For another, there's the language barrier. Will I "speak" gracefully or will I utter pidgin dolphin?. . .

18   With a bravado more feigned than felt, I ascend the stand and flash PRESENT BELLY. Ellie considers this a moment, and then . . . complies! She rolls over submissively and presents her belly. I stroke it avidly. Touching a dolphin's skin is a pleasant surprise, like smooth rubber. Judith dubbed them big rubber puppies, which is as good a description as I've heard.

19   Without thinking, I flash OPEN MOUTH. She does. Uh-oh! I am now expected to stick my hand and forearm into the mouth of a creature that weighs over 350 pounds, has approximately 100 sharp teeth, and has a tail and a dorsal fin like a shark's. I poke my hand and forearm tentatively inside. The skin of my hand grazes her teeth and tongue. If she closes her jaws now, I will return as Captain Hook.

20   She doesn't. In fact, she presents all of her body parts. After thoroughly inspecting Ellie's body, which I've rarely been able to get away with on most first dates, I reward her with a dead smelt (on dates I always provide dinner).

21   The tryst ends sweetly with a HUG and a KISS. But before I do, my trainer-chaperone warns me: (1) don't hug too long, (2) don't pet below the "waist" (beneath the dorsal fin on the back or beneath the navel on the belly), and (3) keep kisses chastely close-mouthed (a needless directive). Her caveats are not whimsical. Dolphins are highly sexual and harbor no stuffy biases against inter-species romance. Indeed, women who have swum with dolphins have reported behavior more commonly associated with former Senator Packwood.

22   I flash HUG (bend forward, arms in a circle) and Ellie rises into them and rests her head on my shoulder. Awww. Then KISS (two fingers on my mouth) and she rises to touch her beak to my lips. Prigs keep their fingers between their mouths and the dolphin's. I am not a prig.

23   At the end of the week, it's time to finally say good-bye. Farewells are bittersweet. I wave my hand. Ellie waves a flipper. We hug. We kiss. I don't suggest we correspond. I suspect we both know this was just a summer fling.

CHECKING YOUR COMPREHENSION

Directions: Select the letter of the best answer for each of the following questions.

_____ 1. The main point of this selection is that
   a. dolphin research centers differ in what they allow visitors to do with the dolphins.
   b. after swimming together, a human and a dolphin will create a lifetime bond.
   c. learning to swim and communicate with dolphins is a difficult but rewarding experience.
   d. dolphins are more like humans than was ever imagined.

_____ 2. The main idea of paragraph 16 is that dolphins can
   a. communicate and make up their own tricks.
   b. touch flippers in the air.
   c. diagnose human illnesses with their sonar.
   d. perform only if they are told what to do.

_____ 3. The main point of paragraph 17 is that the author
   a. has learned three dozen commands.
   b. was rejected by dolphins in Key Largo.
   c. is afraid of Ellie's sharp teeth.
   d. is nervous about his "date" with Ellie.

_____ 4. According to the passage, which of the following is true of dolphins?
   a. They weigh about 100 pounds.
   b. They swim up to 40 mph.
   c. They usually obey spoken commands from humans.
   d. They like men best among humans.

_____ 5. When the author got into the pool with Ellie, she
   a. followed all of his commands.
   b. hid at the other end of the pool.
   c. leapt into the air and did a back flip.
   d. knocked him over.

_____ 6. In paragraph 13, the word "converge" means
   a. communicate.
   b. make gestures.
   c. come together.
   d. become interested.

APPLYING YOUR SKILLS

Directions: Using your knowledge of roots, prefixes, and suffixes, choose the correct definition for each of the following words from the passage. Circle the letter of your choice.

_____ 7. radiologist (par. 1)
   a. one who takes x-rays
   b. having a specific quality of voice
   c. pertaining to the study of x-rays
   d. to say again

(continued)

_____ 8. preswim (par. 3)
   a. small swim
   b. while swimming
   c. before swimming
   d. swim again

_____ 9. flawless (par. 10)
   a. making no sense
   b. quiet
   c. helpless
   d. without any faults

_____ 10. synchrony (par. 16)
   a. one who studies light
   b. at the same time
   c. using extra space
   d. in a quick way

 **Go Electronic!**
For additional readings, exercises, and Internet activities, visit this book's Web site at:

http://www.ablongman.com/mcwhorter

If you need a user name and password, please see your instructor.

Take a Road Trip to the Library of Congress!
Be sure to visit the Vocabulary module in your Reading Road Trip CD-ROM for multimedia tutorials, exercises, and tests.

4

Learning New Words

THIS CHAPTER WILL SHOW YOU HOW TO

1. Use the dictionary and the thesaurus
2. Pronounce unfamiliar words
3. Develop a system for learning new words

Most people think they have just one level of vocabulary and that this can be characterized as large or small, strong or weak. Actually, everyone has at least four levels of vocabulary, and each varies in strength:

1. Words you use in everyday speech or writing

   Examples: decide, death, daughter, damp, date

2. Words you know but seldom or never use in your own speech or writing

   Examples: document, disregard, destination, demon, dense

3. Words you've heard or seen before but cannot fully define

   Examples: denounce, deficit, decadent, deductive, decisive

4. Words you've never heard or seen before

   Examples: doggerel, dogma, denigrate, deleterious, diatropism

In the spaces provided, list five words that fall under each of these four categories. It will be easy to think of words for Category 1. Words for Categories 2–4 may be taken from the list on the next page:

contort	connive	fraught
continuous	congruent	gastronome
credible	demean	havoc
activate	liberate	impertinent
deletion	heroic	delicacy
focus	voluntary	impartial
manual	resistance	delve
garbanzo	alien	attentive
logic	meditate	osmosis

Category 1	Category 2	Category 3	Category 4
_____	_____	_____	_____
_____	_____	_____	_____
_____	_____	_____	_____
_____	_____	_____	_____
_____	_____	_____	_____

To build your vocabulary, try to shift as many words as possible from a less familiar to a more familiar category. This task is not easy. You start by noticing words. Then you question, check, and remember their meanings. Finally, and most important, you use these new words often in your speech and writing.

This chapter will help you improve your word awareness by (1) discussing the use of reference sources, (2) showing you how to pronounce difficult words, and (3) presenting an index card system for learning new words.

WORD INFORMATION SOURCES

Three written sources are most useful in improving one's vocabulary: (1) the dictionary, (2) subject area dictionaries, and (3) the thesaurus.

The Dictionary

The Collegiate Dictionary The dictionary is an essential tool. If you do not already own a collegiate dictionary, buy one as soon as possible. You will need it to complete the exercises in this chapter.

Inexpensive paperback editions of the collegiate dictionary are available and recommended. Do not buy a condensed pocket dictionary. These do not contain enough words and will not give you enough information to suit your needs. Most college bookstores stock several collegiate dictionaries. Among the most widely used are *The American Heritage Dictionary of the English Language, Webster's New Collegiate Dictionary,* and *Webster's New World Dictionary of the American Language.*

The Unabridged Dictionary Libraries own large, complete dictionaries, called unabridged dictionaries. These often have thousands of pages. They contain much more information about each word than collegiate dictionaries. You may need to refer to an unabridged dictionary to find an unusual word, an unusual meaning of a word, or to check the various prefixes or suffixes that can be used with a particular word.

Subject Area Dictionaries

Many subject areas have specialized dictionaries that list most of the important words used in that field. These dictionaries give specialized meanings for words and suggest how and when to use them. For the field of nursing, for instance, there is *Taber's Cyclopedic Medical Dictionary.* Other subject area dictionaries include *A Dictionary of Anthropology, The New Grove Dictionary of Music and Musicians,* and *A Dictionary of Economics.*

Find out whether there is a subject area dictionary for the subjects you are studying. Most such dictionaries are available only in hardback and are likely to be expensive. However, many students find them worth the initial investment. You might find less expensive copies on sale at a used-book store. Most libraries have copies of specialized dictionaries in the reference section.

EXERCISE 4-1	**Directions:** Find the name of a subject area dictionary for each of the fields listed below.

1. psychology _____

2. law _____

3. statistics _____

The Thesaurus

A thesaurus is a dictionary of synonyms. It groups words with similar meanings together. A thesaurus is particularly useful when you want to do the following:

- locate the precise term to fit a particular situation
- find an appropriate descriptive word
- replace an overused or unclear word
- convey a more specific shade of meaning

Suppose you are looking for a more precise word for the expression *will tell us about* in the following sentence:

In class today, our chemistry instructor **will tell us about** our next assignment.

The thesaurus lists the following synonyms for "tell–explain":

10 **explain, explicate, expound,** exposit; **give the meaning,** tell the meaning of; **spell out,** unfold; **account for,** give reason for; **clarify, elucidate,** clear up; **make clear,** make plain; **simplify,** popularize; **illuminate,** enlighten, **shed** *or* **throw light upon;** rationalize, euhemerize, demythologize, allegorize; tell *or* show how, show the way; **demonstrate, show, illustrate,** exemplify; decipher, crack, unlock, find the key to, unravel, **solve;** explain oneself; explain away.

11 **comment upon,** commentate, remark upon; **annotate,** gloss; **edit,** make an edition.

12 **translate, render,** transcribe, transliterate, put *or* turn into, transfuse the sense of; construe; English.

13 **paraphrase, rephrase, reword, restate,** rehash; give a free *or* loose translation.

Read the above entry and underline words or phrases that you think would be more descriptive than *tell about.* You might underline words and phrases such as *comment upon, illustrate, demonstrate,* and *spell out.*

The most widely used thesaurus is *Roget's Thesaurus.* Inexpensive paperback editions are available in most bookstores.

When you first consult a thesaurus, you will need to familiarize yourself with its format and learn how to use it. The following is a step-by-step approach:

1. **Start with the extensive index in the back to locate the word you are trying to replace.** Following the word, you will find the number(s) of the section(s) in the main part of the thesaurus that list the synonyms of that word.
2. **Turn to those sections, scanning each list and jotting down all the words you think might work.**

3. **Test each of the words you selected in the sentence in which you will use it.** The word should fit the context of the sentence.
4. **Select the word that best expresses what you are trying to say.**
5. **Choose only words whose shades of meaning you know.** Check unfamiliar words in a dictionary before using them. Remember, misusing a word is often a more serious error than choosing an overused or general one.

EXERCISE 4-2	**Directions:** Using a thesaurus, replace the boldfaced word or phrase in each sentence with a more precise or descriptive word. Write the word in the space provided. Rephrase the sentence, if necessary.

1. Although the movie was **good,** it lasted only an hour.

   _____

2. The judge **looked at** the criminal as she pronounced the sentence.

   _____

3. The accident victim was awarded a **big** cash settlement.

   _____

4. The lottery winner was **happy** to win the $100,000 prize, but he was surprised to learn that a sizable portion had already been deducted for taxes.

   _____

5. On the first day of class, the instructor **talked to** the class about course requirements.

   _____

USING YOUR DICTIONARY

The first step in using your dictionary is to become familiar with the kinds of information it provides. In the sample entry on the next page, each kind of information is marked:

Pronunciation

Etymology

Restrictive meanings

Meanings

Parts of speech

Spelling of other forms
of the entry word

Synonyms

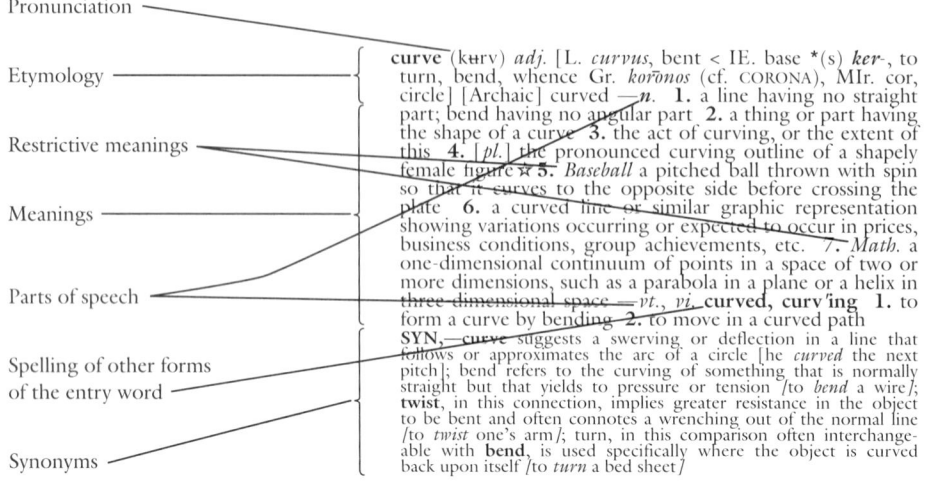

curve (kʉrv) *adj.* [L. *curvus*, bent < IE. base *(s) *ker-*, to turn, bend, whence Gr. *korōnos* (cf. CORONA), MIr. cor, circle] [Archaic] curved —*n.* **1.** a line having no straight part; bend having no angular part **2.** a thing or part having the shape of a curve **3.** the act of curving, or the extent of this **4.** [*pl.*] the pronounced curving outline of a shapely female figure ☆ **5.** *Baseball* a pitched ball thrown with spin so that it curves to the opposite side before crossing the plate **6.** a curved line or similar graphic representation showing variations occurring or expected to occur in prices, business conditions, group achievements, etc. **7.** *Math.* a one-dimensional continuum of points in a space of two or more dimensions, such as a parabola in a plane or a helix in three-dimensional space —*vt., vi.* curved, curv′ing **1.** to form a curve by bending **2.** to move in a curved path **SYN.**—*curve* suggests a swerving or deflection in a line that follows or approximates the arc of a circle [he *curved* the next pitch]; *bend* refers to the curving of something that is normally straight but that yields to pressure or tension [to *bend* a wire]; *twist*, in this connection, implies greater resistance in the object to be bent and often connotes a wrenching out of the normal line [to *twist* one's arm]; *turn*, in this comparison often interchangeable with **bend**, is used specifically where the object is curved back upon itself [to *turn* a bed sheet]

You can see that a dictionary entry provides much more than the definition of a word. Information about the word's pronunciation, part of speech, history, and special uses can also be found.

| **EXERCISE 4-3** | **Directions:** Use the sample dictionary entry above to complete the following items. |

1. Find three meanings for *curve* and write a sentence using each.

   _____

2. Explain what *curve* means when used in baseball.

   _____

3. Explain how the meaning of *curve* differs from the meaning of the word *bend*.

   _____

EXERCISE 4-4

Directions: Find each of the following words in your dictionary and in the space provided list all the different parts of speech it can be.

1. that _____

2. except _____

3. clear _____

4. fancy _____

5. record _____

In the past, you may have found parts of the dictionary confusing or difficult to use. Many students complain about the numerous symbols and abbreviations. Actually, once you are familiar with its format, you will see that the dictionary is systematic and highly organized. It provides a great deal of information about each word. The following is a brief review of the parts of a dictionary entry most often found confusing.

Abbreviations

All dictionaries provide a key to abbreviations used in the entry itself as well as some commonly used in other printed material. Most often this key appears on the inside front cover or on the first few pages of the dictionary.

EXERCISE 4-5

Directions: Find the meaning of each of the following symbols and abbreviations in a dictionary and write it in the space provided.

1. v.t. _____

2. < _____

3. c. _____

4. Obs. _____

5. Fr. _____

6. pl. _____

Word Pronunciation

After each word entry, the pronunciation of the word is given in parentheses.

Examples:

helmet (hĕl′mĭt)   connection (kə-nĕk′shən)

apologize (ə-pŏl′ə-jīz)   orchestra (ôr′kĭ-strə)

This part of the entry shows how to pronounce a word by spelling it the way it sounds. Different symbols are used to indicate certain sounds. Until you become familiar with this symbol system, you will need to refer to the pronunciation key. Most dictionaries include a pronunciation key at the bottom of every or every other page. Here is a sample key from the *American Heritage Dictionary:*

ă pat/ā pay/â care/ä father/b **bib**/ch **church**/d **deed**/ĕ pet/ē be/f **fife**/g **gag**/h hat/hw **which**/ĭ pit/i pie/îr pier/j **judge**/k **kick**/l lid, needle/m **mum**/n no, sudden/ng thing/ŏ not/ō toe/ô paw, for/oi noise/ou **out**/ŏŏ took/ōō boot/p **pop**/r roar/s sauce/sh **ship**, dish/t tight/th thin, path/*th* this, bathe/ŭ cut/ûr urge/v valve/w with/y yes/z **zebra**, size/zh vision/ə about, item, edible, gallop, circus/

The key shows the sound the symbol stands for in a word you already know how to pronounce. For example, suppose you are trying to pronounce the word *helix* (hē′lĭks). The key shows that the letter *e* in the first part of the word sounds the same as the *e* in the word *be*. The *i* in *helix* is pronounced the same way as the *i* in *pit*. To pronounce a word correctly, you must also accent (or put stress on) the appropriate part of the word. In a dictionary respelling, an accent mark (′) usually follows the syllable, or part of the word, that is stressed most heavily.

Examples:

audience   ō′de-əns

football   fŏŏt′bôl

literacy   lĭt′ər-ə-sē

juror   jŏŏr′ər

immediate   ĭ-mē′dē-ĭt

Some words have two accents—a primary stress and a secondary stress. The primary one is stressed more heavily and is printed in darker type than the secondary accent.

Examples:

interstate	in′ter-stāt′
homicide	hôm′i-sīd′

Try to pronounce each of the following dictionary respellings, using the pronunciation key:

dĭ-vûr′sə-fī′	bŏosh′əl
chăl′ənj	bär′bĭ-kyoo′

EXERCISE 4-6	**Directions:** Use the pronunciation key above to sound out each of the following words. Write the word, spelled correctly, in the space provided.

1. kə-mĭt′ _____

2. kăp′chər _____

3. bə-röm′ĭ-tər _____

4. skĕj′ool _____

5. ī-den′te-fĭ-kā′shən _____

6. ĭn-dĭf′ər-əns _____

7. lûr′nĭd _____

8. lĭk′wĭd _____

9. noo′səns _____

10. fär′mə-sē _____

Etymology

Many dictionaries include information on each words **etymology**—its origin and development. A words etymology is its history, traced back as far as possible to its earliest use, often in another language. The sample dictionary entry on p. 92 shows that the word "curve" was derived from the Latin word *curvus* and the Greek word *koronos*.

EXERCISE 4-7	**Directions:** Find the origin of each of the following words in a dictionary and write it in the space provided.

1. Ginger _____

_____

_____

2. Tint _____

3. Calculate _____

4. Fantastic _____

_____

5. Authentic _____

_____

Restrictive Meanings

Many dictionaries include restrictive meanings of words. These are definitions that apply only when the word is being used with respect to a specific topic or field of study. The sample entry on p. 92 gives two restrictive meanings for the word "curve"—one for baseball and another for math.

EXERCISE 4-8

Directions: Locate the following words in your dictionary and find the restrictive meaning for the field of study given in parentheses beside each word. Write the definitions in the space provided.

1. Trust (Law)

   _____

   _____

2. Induction (Logic)

   _____

   _____

3. Compound (Chemistry)

   _____

   _____

4. Primary (Government)

   _____

   _____

5. Journal (Accounting)

   _____

   _____

Multiple Meanings

Most words have more than one meaning. When you look up the meaning of a new word, you must choose the meaning that fits the way the word is used in the sentence context. On the next page, the sample entry for the word *green* contains many meanings for the word.

MEANINGS
GROUPED BY
PARTS OF SPEECH

11 Adjectives

8 Nouns

1 Verb

green (grēn) *adj.* [ME. *grene* < OE., akin to G. *grün*, Du. *groen:* for IE. base see GRASS] **1.** of the color that is characteristic of growing grass **2.** overspread with or characterized by green plants or foliage /a *green* field/ **3.** keeping the green grass of summer; snowless; a mild /a *green* December/ **4.** sickly or bilious, as from illness, fear, etc. **5.** *a)* flourishing; active /to keep someone's memory *green*/ *b)* of the time of one's youth /the *green* years/ **6.** not mature; unripe /*green* bananas/ **7.** not trained; inexperienced **8.** easily led or deceived; simple; naive **9.** not dried, seasoned, or cured; unprocessed /*green* lumber/ **10.** fresh; new **11.** [cf. GREEN-EYED] [Colloq.] jealous —*n.* **1.** the color of growing grass; any color between blue and yellow in the spectrum: green can be produced by blending blue and yellow pigments **2.** any green pigment or dye **3.** anything colored green as clothing **4.** [*pl.*] green leaves, branches, sprigs, etc., used for ornamentation **5.** [*pl.*] green leafy plants or vegetables eaten cooked or raw, as spinach, turnip tops, lettuce, etc. **6.** an area of smooth turf set aside for special purposes /a village *green*, a bowling *green*/ ★**7.** [Slang] money, esp. paper money: chiefly in **long green, folding green** **8.** *Golf a)* the plot of carefully tended turf immediately surrounding each of the holes to facilitate putting *b)* an entire golf course —*vt., vi.* to make or become green —**green with envy** very envious —**green′ish** *adj.* —**green′ly** *adv.* —**green′ness** *n.*

MANY DIFFERENT
MEANINGS

Unripe fruit
Inexperienced person

Type of vegetable

Part of golf course

The meanings are grouped by part of speech and are numbered consecutively in each group. Generally, the most common meanings of the word are listed first, with more specialized, less common meanings appearing toward the end of the entry. Now find the meaning that fits the use of the word *green* in the following sentence.

> The local veterans' organization held its annual fund-raising picnic on the village **green**.

In this sentence, *green* refers to "an area of grass used for special purposes." Since this is a specialized meaning of the word, it appears toward the end of the entry.

Here are a few suggestions for choosing the correct meaning from among those listed in an entry:

1. **If you are familiar with the parts of speech, try to use these to locate the correct meaning.** For instance, if you are looking up the meaning of a word that names a person, place, or thing you can save time by reading only those entries given after *n* (noun).

2. **For most types of college reading, you can skip definitions that give slang and colloquial (abbreviated colloq.) meanings.** Colloquial meanings refer to informal or spoken language.

3. **If you are not sure of the part of speech, read each meaning until you find a definition that seems correct.** Skip over restrictive meanings that are inappropriate.

4. **Test your choice by substituting the meaning in the sentence with which you are working.** Substitute the definition for the word and see whether it makes sense in the context (see Chapter 2).

Suppose you are looking up the word *oblique* to find its meaning in this sentence:

My sister's **oblique** answers to my questions made me suspicious.

Oblique is used in the above sentence as an adjective. Looking at the entries listed after *adj.* (adjective), you can skip over the definition under the heading *Geometry,* as it wouldn't apply here. Definition 2 (indirect, evasive) best fits the way *oblique* is used in the sentence.

> o•blique (ō-blēk´, ə; *Military* ō-blīk´, ə) *adj. Abbr.* obl. **1. a.** Having a slanting or sloping direction, course, or position; inclined. **b.** *Geometry.* Designating lines or planes that are neither parallel nor perpendicular. **2.** Indirect or evasive in execution, meaning, or expression; not straightforward. **3.** Devious, misleading, or dishonest; *oblique answers.* **4.** Not direct in descent; collateral. **5.** *Botany.* Having sides of unequal length or form: *an oblique leaf.* **6.** *Grammar.* Designating any noun case except the nominative or the vocative. **7.** *Rhetoric.* **Indirect** (*see*).—*n.* **1.** An oblique thing, such as a line, direction, or muscle. **2.** *Nautical.* The act of changing course by less than 90 degrees.—*adv. Military.* At an angle of 45 degrees: *Right oblique, march!* [Middle English *oblike,* from *Latin obliquus.*]—o•blique´ly *adv.*—o•blique´ness *n.*

EXERCISE 4-9	**Directions:** The following words have two or more meanings. Look them up in your dictionary and write two sentences with different meanings for each word.

1. culture

    _____

    _____

2. perch

    _____

    _____

3. surge

_____

_____

4. apron

_____

_____

5. irregular

_____

_____

EXERCISE 4-10	**Directions:** Use the dictionary to help you find an appropriate meaning for the bold-faced word in each of the following sentences.

1. The last contestant did not have a **ghost** of a chance.

    _____

2. The race car driver won the first **heat.**

    _____

3. The police took all possible **measures** to protect the witness.

    _____

4. The orchestra played the first **movement** of the symphony.

    _____

5. The plane stalled on the **apron.**

    _____

Spelling

The entry gives the correct spelling of a word. It also shows how the spelling changes when a word is made plural or endings (suffixes—see Chapter 3) are added, as in the following examples.

Word	Word + Ending
budget	budgetary
	budgeter
exhibit	exhibitor
	exhibition
fancy	fancily
	fanciness
	fancier

Entries may also include alternative spellings of words when there are two acceptable ways to spell the word. If you see the word *also* or *or* following the entry word, you will know that either is acceptable:

medieval also **mediaeval**

archaeology or **archeology**

Each entry shows how the word is divided into syllables, so you know how to hyphenate a word when it appears at the end of a line of print (hyphens are placed only between syllables).

liv-a-ble   mil-li-me-ter   ob-li-ga-tion

For verbs, each entry contains the verb's principal parts: past tense, past participle, present participle (if different from the past), and third person singular present tense.

go	went, gone, going, goes
feed	fed, feeding, feeds

EXERCISE 4-11	**Directions:** Use your dictionary to answer the following questions. Write your answers in the spaces provided.

1. What is the plural form of *crisis?*

   _____

2. What is the alternate spelling of *judgment?*

   _____

3. If you had to hyphenate *surprise* at the end of a line, where would you divide it?

   _____

4. What is the past form of *burst?*

   _____

5. What is the adverb form of *criminal?*

   _____

Usage Notes

Collegiate dictionaries contain a Usage Note or Synonym section of the definition for words that are close in meaning to others. For example, a usage note for the word *indifferent* may explain how it differs in meaning from *unconcerned, detached,* and *uninterested.*

EXERCISE 4-12	**Directions:** Use your dictionary to answer the differences in meaning between the following pairs of words. Write your explanations in the spaces provided.

1. petite, diminutive

   _____

   _____

2. careless, thoughtless

_____

_____

3. odor, aroma

_____

_____

4. grin, smirk

_____

_____

_____

5. hurt, damage

_____

_____

_____

Idioms

An idiom is a phrase that has a meaning other than what the common meanings of the words in the phrase mean. For example, the phrase "wipe the slate clean" is not about slates. It means "to start over." Most idiomatic expressions are not used in academic writing because they are trite or overused.

EXERCISE 4-13   **Directions:** Use your dictionary to help you explain the meanings of the following underlined idiomatic expressions. Write your explanations in the space provided.

1. One thousand dollars is nothing to <u>sneeze at</u>.

_____

2. The home team <u>kicked off</u> the season with an easy win.

   _____

3. I intend to <u>turn over a new leaf</u> and work harder next semester.

   _____

4. The lake is two miles from here <u>as the crow flies</u>.

   _____

5. The owner's incompetent nephew was <u>kicked upstairs</u> rather than fired.

   _____

Other Aids

Many dictionaries (especially hardback editions) also contain numerous useful lists and tables. These are usually printed at the back of the dictionary. Frequently included are tables of weights and measures and of periodic elements in chemistry, biographical listings for famous people, a pronouncing gazetteer (a geographical dictionary), and lists of standard abbreviations, colleges, and signs and symbols.

EXERCISE 4-14	**Directions:** Use a dictionary to answer each of the following items. Write your answer in the space provided.

1. What parts of speech can the word *interior* be used as?

   _____

2. How is the word *exacerbate* pronounced? Record its phonetic spelling.

   _____

3. Which part of the word *opinion* is stressed (accented)?

   _____

4. How many different meanings can you think of for the word *pitch?* Write as many as you can think of. Then check to see how many meanings are given in the dictionary.

Locating Words Rapidly

Most dictionaries include guide words to help you locate words rapidly. At the top of each dictionary page are two words in bold print, one on the left corner and one on the right. The guide word on the left is the first entry on that page. The right-hand guide word is the last entry. All the words on that page come between the two guide words in alphabetical order.

To check quickly whether a word is on a certain page, look at the guide words. If the word you are looking for falls alphabetically between the two guide words on the page, scan that page until you find the word. If the word does not come between those guide words, you need not look at that page at all.

Suppose you are looking up the word *loathsome.* The guide words on a particular page are *livid* and *lobster.* You know that the word *loathsome* will be on that page because, alphabetically, *loathsome* comes after *livid* and before *lobster.*

EXERCISE 4-15

Directions: Read each entry word and the pair of guide words that follows it. Decide whether the entry word would be found on the dictionary page with those guide words. Write *yes* or *no* in the space provided.

Entry Word	Guide Words	
1. grotesque	gritty—ground	_____
2. stargaze	standard—starfish	_____
3. ridicule	ridgepole—rigid	_____
4. exponent	expletive—express	_____
5. dissident	displease—dissidence	_____

PRONOUNCING UNFAMILIAR WORDS

At one time or another, each of us comes across words that we are unable to pronounce. To pronounce an unfamiliar word, sound it out syllable by syllable. Here are a few simple rules for dividing words into syllables:

1. **Divide compound words between the individual words that form the compound word.**

   Examples:

   house/broken   house/hold   space/craft
   green/house   news/paper   sword/fish

2. **Divide words between prefixes (word beginnings) and roots (base words) and/or between roots and suffixes (word endings).**

   Examples:

   Prefix + Root

   pre/read   post/pone   anti/war

   Root + Suffix

   sex/ist   agree/ment   list/ing

   (For a more complete discussion of prefixes, roots, and suffixes, see Chapter 3.)

3. **Each syllable is a separate, distinct speech sound.** Pronounce the following words and try to hear the number of syllables in each.

   Examples:

   expensive   ex/pen/sive = 3 syllables
   recognize   rec/og/nize = 3 syllables
   punctuate   punc/tu/ate = 3 syllables
   complicated   com/pli/cat/ed = 4 syllables

4. **Each syllable has at least one vowel and usually one or more consonants.** (The letters a, e, i, o, u, and sometimes y are vowels. All other letters are consonants.)

   Examples:

   as/sign   re/act   cou/pon   gen/er/al

5. **Divide words before a single consonant, unless the consonant is the letter r.**

   Examples:

   hu/mid   pa/tron   re/tail   fa/vor   mor/on

6. Divide words between two consonants appearing together.

Examples:

pen/cil   lit/ter   lum/ber   sur/vive

7. Divide words between two vowel sounds that appear together.

Examples:

te/di/ous   ex/tra/ne/ous

These rules will prove helpful but, as you no doubt already know, there will always be exceptions.

EXERCISE 4-16   **Directions:** Use slash marks (/) to divide each of the following words into syllables.

1. polka	6. innovative	11. tangelo	16. tenacity
2. pollute	7. obtuse	12. symmetry	17. mesmerize
3. ordinal	8. germicide	13. telepathy	18. intrusive
4. hallow	9. futile	14. organic	19. infallible
5. judicature	10. extoll	15. hideous	20. fanaticism

A SYSTEM FOR LEARNING NEW WORDS

As you read textbook assignments and reference sources and while listening to your instructors' class presentations, you are constantly exposed to new words. Unless you make a deliberate effort to remember and use these words, many of them will probably fade from your memory. One of the most practical and easy-to-use systems for expanding your vocabulary is the index card system. It works like this:

1. **Whenever you hear or read a new word that you intend to learn, jot it down in the margin of your notes or mark it some way in the material you are reading.**
2. **Later, write the word on the front of an index card.** Then look up its meaning and write it on the back of the card. Also, record a phonetic key for the word's pronunciation, its part of speech, other forms the word may take, and a sample sentence or example of how the word is used. Your cards should look like the one in Figure 4-1.

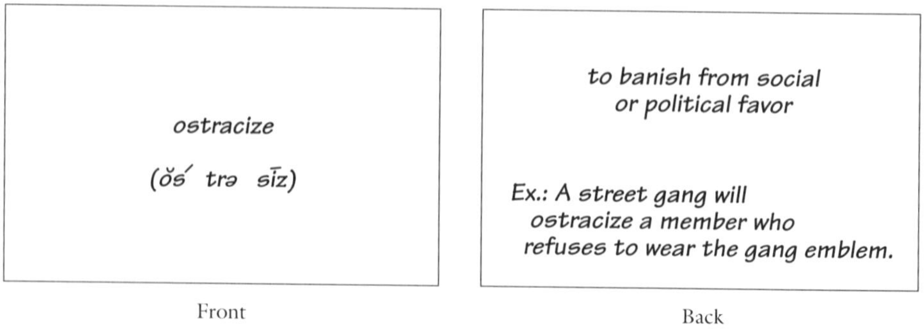

Figure 4-1 Sample Index Card

3. **Once a day, take a few minutes to go through your pack of index cards.** For each card, look at the word on the front and try to recall its meaning on the back. Then check the back of the card to see whether you were correct. If you were unable to recall the meaning or if you confused the word with another word, retest yourself. Shuffle the cards after each use.

4. **After you have gone through your pack of cards several times, sort the cards into two piles—words you know and words you have not learned.** Then, putting the known words aside, concentrate on the words still to be learned.

5. **Once you have learned the entire pack of words, review them often to refresh your memory.**

This index card system is effective for several reasons. First, it can be reviewed in the spare time that is often wasted waiting for a class to begin, riding a bus, and so on. Second, the system enables you to spend time learning what you do *not* know rather than wasting time studying what you already know. Finally, the system overcomes a major problem that exists in learning information that appears in list form. If the material to be learned is presented in a fixed order, you tend to learn it in that order and may be unable to recall individual items when they appear alone or out of order. By shuffling the cards, you scramble the order of the words and thus avoid this problem.

EXERCISE 4-17

Directions: Make a set of at least 20 word cards, choosing words from one of your textbooks or from one of the reading selections in Part Five of this book. Then study the cards using the method described in this chapter.

WORKING TOGETHER

Directions: Locate ten words that you find difficult to pronounce. Sources may be a dictionary, a textbook, or one of the more difficult reading selections in Part 6 of this book. Write each of the ten words on a separate index card and then establish a list of the words and how they are pronounced. Your instructor will form groups. Pass the cards around the group. Each student attempts a pronunciation. The student who pronounces the word correctly keeps the card. Make a note of words that you were unable to pronounce; check their pronunciation in your dictionary.

Learning Style Tips

If you tend to be a . . .	Then strengthen your vocabulary by . . .
Creative learner	Experimenting with new words in both speech and writing
Pragmatic learner	Creating lists or computer files of words you need to learn and use

SELF-TEST SUMMARY

What reference sources are useful in building a strong vocabulary?	Collegiate and unabridged dictionaries, subject area dictionaries, and the thesaurus are all useful.
How do you pronounce unfamiliar words?	To pronounce unfamiliar words, use the pronunciation key in the dictionary and apply the seven rules listed in this chapter.
Explain the index card system.	The index card system is a method of learning vocabulary. Write a word on the front of an index card and its meaning on the back. Study the cards by sorting the cards into two piles—known and unknown words.

CHAPTER 4
MASTERY TEST 1:
Dictionary Skills

Name _____

Section _____ Date _____

Number right _____ x 20 points = Score _____

Directions: Use the dictionary entry below to answer the following questions.

ar•tic•u•late (är-tĭk′yə-lĭt) *adj.* **1.** Endowed with the power of speech. **2.** Composed of distinct, meaningful syllables or words, as human speech. **3.** Expressing oneself easily in clear and effective language: *an articulate speaker.* **4.** Characterized by the use of clear, expressive language: *an articulate essay.* **5.** *Anatomy.* Consisting of sections united by joints; jointed.—**articulate** (är-tĭk′yə-lāt) *v.* **lat•ed, -lat•ing, -lates.**—*tr.* **1.** To pronounce distinctly and carefully; enunciate. **2.** To utter (a speech sound) by making the necessary movements of the speech organs. **3.** To express in coherent verbal form; give words to: *couldn't articulate my fears.* **4.** To fit together into a coherent whole; unify: *articulate statewide nursing programs.* **5.** *Anatomy.* To unite by forming a joint or joints. —*intr.* **1.** To speak clearly and distinctly. **2.** To utter a speech sound. **3.** *Anatomy.* To form a joint; be jointed: *The thighbone articulates with the bones of the hip.* [Latin *articulātus,* past participle of *articulāre,* to divide into joints, utter distinctly, from *articulus,* small joint. See ARTICLE.] —**ar•tic′u•late•ly** *adv.* —**ar•tic′u•late•ness, ar•tic′u•la•cy** *n.*[1]

_____ **1.** The origin of **articulate** is
   a. Middle English.
   b. Latin.
   c. French.
   d. Greek.

_____ **2.** For the adjective form of **articulate,** the dictionary provides
   a. 4 meanings.
   b. 5 meanings.
   c. 10 meanings.
   d. 13 meanings.

_____ **3.** For the verb form of **articulate,** the most accurate phonetic spelling is
   a. are tick you lit.
   b. are tick uh lit.
   c. are tick you late.
   d. are tick uh late.

_____ **4.** The restrictive meanings for **articulate** refer to the field of
   a. law.
   b. music.
   c. computer science.
   d. anatomy.

_____ **5.** The adverb form of **articulate** is
   a. articulately.
   b. articulated.
   c. articulateness.
   d. articulacy.

Name _____

Section _____ Date _____

Number right _____ x 20 points = Score _____

Directions: Each numbered sentence below is followed by a dictionary entry for the boldfaced word. Use this entry to select the choice that best fits the meaning of the word as it is used in the sentence.

_____ 1. At the entrance to the international exhibition hall, visitors are greeted by a **panoply** of flags representing every nation in the world.

pan•o•ply (păn′ə-plē) *n., pl.* **-plies. 1.** A splendid or striking array: *a panoply of colorful flags.* See Synonyms at **display. 2.** Ceremonial attire with all accessories: *a portrait of the general in full panoply.* **3.** Something that covers and protects: *a porcupine's panoply of quills.* **4.** The complete arms and armor of a warrior. [Greek *panoplia* : *pan-*, pan- + *hopla*, arms, armor, pl. of *hoplon*, weapon.][2]

    a. the complete arms and armor of a warrior

    b. ceremonial attire with all accessories

    c. something that covers and protects

    d. a splendid and striking array

_____ 2. At the town meeting, several citizens **ventilated** their concerns about the proposed increase in property taxes.

ven•ti•late (věn′tl-āt) *tr.v.* **-lat•ed, -lat•ing, -lates. 1.** To admit fresh air into (a mine, for example) to replace stale or noxious air. **2.** To circulate through and freshen: *A sea breeze ventilated the rooms.* **3.** To provide with a vent, as for airing. **4.** To expose (a substance) to the circulation of fresh air, as to retard spoilage. **5.** To expose to public discussion or examination: *The*

students ventilated their grievances. **6.** To aerate or oxygenate (blood). [Middle English *ventilaten*, to blow away, from Latin *ventilāre, ventilāt-*, to fan, from *ventulus*, diminutive of *ventus*, wind. See **wē** in Appendix. —**ven′ti•la′tion** *n.*[3]

    a. to admit fresh air in order to replace stale or noxious air

    b. to circulate through and freshen

    c. to expose to the circulation of fresh air, as to retard spoilage

    d. to expose to public discussion or examination

_____ 3. Many people with coronary artery disease do not **manifest** symptoms until they have their first heart attack.

man•i•fest (măn′ə-fěst′) *adj.* Clearly apparent to the sight or understanding; obvious. See Synonyms at **apparent. —manifest** *tr.v.* **-fest•ed, -fest•ing, -fests. 1.** To show or demonstrate plainly; reveal: *"Mercedes . . . manifested the chaotic abandonment of hysteria"* (Jack London). **2.** To be evidence of; prove. **3.a.** To record in a ship's manifest. **b.** To display or present a manifest of (cargo). —**manifest** *n.* **1.** A list of cargo or passengers carried on a ship or plane. **2.** An invoice of goods carried on a truck or train. **3.** A list of railroad cars according to owner and location. [Middle East *manifeste*, from Old French, from Latin *manufestus, manifestsus*, caught in the act, blatant, obvious. See **gʷhedh-** in Appendix.] — **man′i•fest′ly** *adv.* [4]

    a. clearly apparent to the sight or understanding; obvious

    b. to show or demonstrate plainly; reveal

    c. to be evidence of; prove

    d. to record in a ship's manifest

_____ 4. After moving halfway across the country for his new job, Kerry was **besieged** by rumors that the company was going out of business.

be•siege (bĭ-sēj′) *tr.v.* -sieged, -sieg•ing, -sieg•es. **1.** To surround with hostile forces. **2.** To crowd around; hem in. **3.** To harass or importune, as with requests: *Reporters besieged the winner for interviews.* **4.** To cause to feel distressed or worried: *She was besieged by problems.* [Middle English *besegen*, probably (with substitution of *bi-*, be-) from *assegen*, from Old French *assegier*, from Vulgar Latin *as sedicāre*: Latin *ad-*, ad- + Vulgar Latin *sedicāre*, to sit (from Latin *sedēre*; see SIEGE).] —**be•siege′ment** *n.*—**be•sieg′er** *n.*

Synonyms: *besiege, beleaguer, blockade, invest, siege.* The central meaning shared by these verbs is "to surround with hostile forces": *besiege a walled city: a beleaguered settlement; blockaded the harbor; investing a fortress; a castle sieged by foot soldiers and cavalry.*[5]

a. to cause to feel distressed or worried

b. to crowd around; hem in

c. to harass or importune, as with requests

d. to surround with hostile forces

_____ 5. The student task force obviously did not spend much time considering the problem of the limited number of parking spaces on campus; its **facile** solution to the problem disappointed all of us.

fac•ile (făs′əl) *adj.* **1.** Done or achieved with little effort or difficulty; easy. See Synonyms at **easy**. **2.** Working, acting, or speaking with effortless ease and fluency. See Synonyms at **nimble**. **3.** Arrived at without due care, effort, or examination; superficial: *proposed a facile solution to a complex problem.* **4.** Readily manifested, together with an aura of insincerity and lack of depth: *a facile slogan devise by politicans.* **5.** *Archaic.* Pleasingly mild, as in disposition or manner. [Middle English, from Old French, with Latin *facilis.* See **dhē-** in Appendix.] —**fac′ ile•ly** *adv.* —**fac′ ile•ness** *n.* [6]

a. done or achieved with little effort or difficulty; easy

b. working, acting, or speaking with effortless ease and fluency

c. arrived at without due care, effort, or examination; superficial

d. pleasingly mild, as in disposition or manner

Copyright © 2003 by Kathleen T. McWhorter

Name _____

Section _____ Date _____

Number right _____ x 10 points = Score _____

Directions: Use a dictionary to answer the following questions. Select the best answer.

_____ 1. The definition of the word "ligature" is
a. legal suit
b. relief
c. coal
d. bond

_____ 2. The most accurate phonetic spelling for the word "neuropathy" is
a. nyu ro path e
b. nyur o path e
c. nyu rop a the
d. nyu rop a te

_____ 3. What part of speech is the word "tole"?
a. noun
b. verb
c. adjective
d. adverb

_____ 4. What is the origin of the word "hirsute"?
a. French
b. German
c. Latin
d. Middle English

_____ 5. The noun form of the word "infallible" is
a. infallibility
b. infallibly
c. infallibleness
d. infallible

_____ 6. The correct syllabication of the word "marsupial" is
a. mar sup i al
b. mar su pi al
c. mars up ial
d. mar su pial

_____ 7. What syllable or part of the word "developer" is stressed?
a. de
b. vel
c. op
d. er

Directions: Use *Roget's Thesaurus* to answer the following questions. Select the best answer.

_____ 8. Which of the following is a synonym for "gross"?
a. net
b. chaste
c. total
d. fumble

_____ 9. Which of the following is a synonym for "droll"?
a. boring
b. eccentric
c. elf
d. confused

_____ 10. Which of the following is a synonym for "grip"?
a. suitcase
b. lost
c. repel
d. protest

CHAPTER 4
MASTERY TEST 4:
Reading Selection

Name _____
Section _____ Date _____
Number right _____ x 10 points = Score _____

She Said Yes! She Said Yes! She Said Yes!

Michael Kernan

This humorous essay taken from the *Smithsonian* magazine describes unusual marriage proposals.

Vocabulary Preview

enlightenment (par. 2) awareness; use of reason

amorous (par. 3) having to do with love or courtship

insouciance (par. 4) carefree feeling

ingenuity (par. 6) cleverness

1   Not so very long ago, according to the cartoons of my youth, a guy who wanted to get married would hit his girl with a club, grab her by the hair and drag her into his cave.

2   But a time came when it was discovered that you should *ask* for a woman's hand. You asked her father, of course, and he put a price on her, whether in cattle, gold or debentures.* Eventually what passes for enlightenment set in. Nowadays you can ask the girl herself. Or she can ask you.

3   Today, many amorous couples jump the gun, so to speak, draining a certain significance from a proposal. Perhaps as a result, an odd thing has happened: the proposal has gone public.

. . .

4   This may be the influence of our advertising-besotted age and the possibility that we have to see something on TV in order to believe it. Or it may be that, beneath our hard insouciance, we are still romantics. In any case, Americans are popping the question on talk shows, on billboards and even on the concert stage. Love-struck males hire planes to fly banners over stadiums with messages like "Ethel, Will You Marry Me?" We broadcast our marital message at supermarkets, in airports and almost anywhere where there is a public to be impressed.

5   Things have gotten to such a pass that one interested party down in Texas has proposed the establishment of an official Proposal Day to occur twice a year at the equinoxes, thus symbolizing the equality of men and women. It is aimed at the people who keep putting it off and putting it off. And there are a lot of them: baby boom women now in their 30s and 40s are roughly three times less likely to marry than were women that age a generation ago.

6   Inevitably, a lot of ingenuity goes into proposals nowadays, even by those who don't make a public spectacle of themselves. Consider Neil Nathanson and Leslie Hamilton. They met in Palo Alto, California, where they had separate apartments in one of those wonderful old shingled houses. Neil was studying law at

*short-term bonds

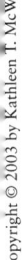

Stanford. Leslie had just got her degree in city planning.

7   They soon discovered that they loved doing crosswords. On Sunday mornings they would hang out together working on the *San Francisco Examiner* puzzle. One Sunday Leslie noticed that many of the puzzle answers struck close to home. "State or quarterback" turned out to be MONTANA, which is where she came from. "Instrument" was CELLO, which she plays. There were references to weddings and marriage, and when she came to "Astronaut Armstrong," which could only be NEIL, she did a double take.

8   "I was about halfway through the puzzle," she remembers, "when I figured out that a string of letters running across the middle of the puzzle said 'DEAR—WILL YOU MARRY ME NEIL.' The missing clue was 'Actress Caron.' I didn't know who that was, it could have been Lauren for all I knew, so I began on the Down clues. Sure enough, it was LESLIE."

9   She was stunned. She looked up, found him staring at her, and said, "Yes." What else?

10   It seems Neil had talked to Merl Reagle, the *Examiner* puzzle maker and a genius of sorts, and they had worked on the project for four months. Neil and Leslie have been married four years and now have a daughter. What did the other puzzle solvers think? For them it was just a neat crossword on the theme of weddings.

11   Oh, and they invited Reagle to the wedding, in Great Falls, Montana.

12   "I never did finish the puzzle," she says.

13   That proposal was relatively private, though attended by millions of readers. Sportscaster Ahmad Rashad proposed to *The Cosby Show* star Phylicia Ayers-Allen live on a pregame TV show. And not too long ago singer Anita Baker, during a Radio City Music Hall concert, handed the mike to a young man who had come up from the audience by prearrangement. In ringing, amplified tones he asked, "Mitzi, will you marry me?" The audience gave the couple a standing ovation.

14   But what if the girl says no?

15   Tony Ferrante of Richmond, Virginia, had this great idea: he would lure his friend, Kathryn Webber, to a mall at Christmastime and get her to sit on Santa's lap for a gag photograph. Then Santa would hand her the usual little gift, only the gift would turn out to be an engagement ring.

16   Unfortunately, Kathryn had just finished her college finals and was tired, hungry and cross. Tony finally persuaded her to see Santa, but the ring hadn't arrived yet. So Tony had to drag her around the mall for another half-hour while a friend fetched the ring. At last Kathryn was sweet-talked into sitting on Santa's lap a second time. Santa gave her a tiny box.

17   Tony had to tell her to open it. She was so shaken that she couldn't give him an answer; they had never discussed marriage before. He thought he was a goner. But finally, seven hours later at dinner, she took pity on him. "I don't think I ever answered your question," she said. "Yes, I will."

. . .

18   Romantic is as romantic does. Randi Reese was not the kind of girl that anyone could surprise, or so her parents told Mark Roger. When they attended a performance of *Grandma Sylvia's Funeral*, an Off Broadway play in which the audience takes part, Mark arranged for one of the actors to approach him in his seat and say these lines from the script: "Grandma wanted to will you her engagement ring as long as you have someone you love to give it to."

19   At this point Mark jumped up, turned to Randi next to him, and said, for all the audience to hear, "Yes, I do! I would like to give this ring to Randi Reese, if she would marry me."

20   Randi was surprised.

21   They invited all the cast members to the wedding.

. . .

22   Here's a classic: it seems this Yale law school student kept staring at a certain girl in a civil liberties course. She had Coke-bottle glasses, no makeup and out-of-control hair. When he saw her again in the law library and started gawking, she got up and approached him. "If you're going to keep looking at me and I'm going to keep looking at you, we ought to at least know each other."

23   They dated, became close, moved to Fayetteville, Arkansas, where he was to teach law at the University of Arkansas. Despite offers from law firms in Washington, D.C., New York and Chicago, she stayed in Fayetteville. "I loved him," she says. "I had to stay."

24   Then he ran for office and lost, though he later won a big one. She started teaching

law at the university, too. They did some dreaming. There was a particular brick house she loved. But she needed time before making any commitments, so she went home to Illinois to think things over.

25   When she returned, he met her at the airport. "I bought that house you like," he said, "so you better marry me because I can't live in it by myself."

26   They were married in the house. She took off her glasses for the occasion.

• • •

27   We take you now from Paris to the Steel Valley School District in western Pennsylvania. Michael Bujdos, then a first-grade teacher at Barrett Elementary, called Jean Kabo, his high school sweetheart from Serra Catholic High in McKeesport. "Jean," he said, "I'm having some volunteers come in to read stories to the class. Would you like to help me out?"

28   Sure, she replied. When she got to the school, Michael said the kids had an art project they wanted to show her before she read the story. In the classroom, first-graders were lined up at the blackboard with their hands behind them. She thought something was going on, because the kids were awfully serious. But giggling. While she stood there, more than somewhat bemused, Michael told the children, "All right, boys and girls. Show the lady what we made in art class."

29   At that, the children proudly held up sheets of paper that spelled the words, "Will You Marry Mr. B?"

30   "I sort of looked at it," she said recently from their home in Munhall, Pennsylvania. "I was in shock. It was really funny. I didn't notice a colleague of his

videotaping the whole thing from the back of the room."

31   For a long moment everyone stood there, the kids watching her, mouths open, Michael holding his breath.

32   "And I said yes. And the kids loved it. And they were laughing and jumping up and down and shouting, 'She said yes! She said yes! She said yes!'"

CHECKING YOUR COMPREHENSION

Directions: Select the letter of the choice that best answers each of the following questions.

_____ 1. The main point of this reading is that
   a. most people have unusual stories about their marriage proposals.
   b. some people are making their marriage proposals in public rather than in private.
   c. although people often turn down public proposals, only the positive answers make the news.
   d. people usually say "yes" to a public proposal, even if they are reluctant to marry.

_____ 2. The main idea of paragraph 2 is that
   a. a woman proposing to a man is common now.
   b. dowries for brides should be brought back.
   c. men need to ask women to marry them.
   d. ways of arranging a marriage have changed.

(continued)

_____ 3. The main point of paragraph 6 is that
   a. apartment houses are good places to meet your mate.
   b. private proposals are usually not very interesting.
   c. a creative proposal does not have to be a public one.
   d. a public proposal requires a crowd.

_____ 4. The official Proposal Day in Texas was suggested to
   a. give women a chance to propose to men.
   b. make women and men equal under the law.
   c. encourage people to propose.
   d. set a world record for the most proposals.

_____ 5. Mark Rodgers was able to propose at _Grandma Sylvia's Funeral_ because
   a. he was a cast member in the play.
   b. he had arranged it ahead of time with Anita Baker.
   c. Randi's parents knew the director of the play.
   d. the audience routinely participates in the play.

_____ 6. In paragraph 5, the word "equinoxes" refers to
   a. the days of the year when night and day are equal.
   b. the longest days of the year.
   c. the first and last days of the year.
   d. holidays common to all religions.

APPLYING YOUR SKILLS

Directions: Use a dictionary to answer the following questions. Select the letter of the best answer.

_____ 7. Which of the following is the correct phonetic spelling for the word "debenture" from paragraph 2?
   a. di ben chur
   b. deb in chur
   c. dab un chur
   d. de ban chur

_____ 8. What is the origin of the word "insouciance" in paragraph 4?
   a. Middle English
   b. German
   c. French
   d. Italian

_____ 9. What is the best definition of the word "bemused" as it is used in paragraph 28?
   a. absent-minded
   b. entertained
   c. distracted
   d. confused

Directions: Use *Roget's Thesaurus* to help you answer the following question. Select the best answer.

_____ 10. Which of the following is the best synonym for the word "neat" in the following sentence from paragraph 10? "For them it was just a neat crossword on the theme of weddings."
   a. orderly
   b. imaginative
   c. methodical
   d. straight

Go Electronic!

For additional readings, exercises, and Internet activities, visit this book's Web site at:

http://www.ablongman.com/mcwhorter

If you need a user name and password, please see your instructor.

Take a Road Trip to the Library of Congress!

Be sure to visit the Vocabulary module in your Reading Road Trip CD-ROM for multimedia tutorials, exercises, and tests.

5

Reading as Thinking

THIS CHAPTER WILL SHOW YOU HOW TO

1. **Preview before reading**
2. **Develop questions to guide your reading**
3. **Review after you read**

Rhonda is taking an anatomy and physiology course, one required in nursing. She reads all the assignments and spends long hours studying. She rereads the assignments, and rereads them before each quiz. When the instructor returns the weekly quiz, Rhonda is always surprised and disappointed. She thinks she has done well, but receives a failing grade. She cannot understand why she fails the quizzes, since she has read the material.

Rhonda decides to visit the college's learning center. The first thing the instructor asks her to do is to locate the correct answer to each quiz item in her textbook. When Rhonda has difficulty doing this, the instructor questions her on portions of the textbook. The instructor realizes that Rhonda has not thought about what she read so he asks Rhonda several questions about how she read the chapters and discovers that she simply reads and rereads. Rhonda did nothing before beginning to read a chapter to sharpen her mind and make reading easier. She read mechanically, from beginning to end, and she did not check her understanding of the material. She did not realize her comprehension was poor or incomplete and she did not review what she had read. She was reading, but she wasn't thinking about what she was reading. The instructor then suggests five strategies to help Rhonda get involved with what she is reading, and shows her how to keep track of her level of comprehension.

In this chapter you will learn to approach reading as a thinking process. You will learn five strategies that, when combined, lead to a systematic, effective method of reading called SQ3R. You will also learn how to keep track of your level of understanding and what to do if it is poor or incomplete.

PREVIEW

Would you cross a city street without checking for traffic first? Would you pay to see a movie you had never heard of and knew nothing about? Would you buy a car without test driving it or checking its mechanical condition?

Most likely you answered "no" to each of these questions. Now answer a related question, one that applies to reading: Should you read an article or textbook chapter without knowing what it is about or how it is organized? You can probably guess that the answer is "no." This section explains a technique called previewing.

Previewing is a way of quickly familiarizing yourself with the organization and content of written material *before* beginning to read it. It is an easy method to use and will make a dramatic difference in how effectively you read.

How to Preview

When you preview, try to (1) find only the most important ideas in the material, and (2) note how they are organized. To do this, look only at the parts that state these important ideas and skip the rest. Previewing is a fairly rapid technique. Take only a few minutes to preview a 15- to 20-page textbook chapter. The parts to look at in previewing a textbook chapter are listed here.

1. **The Title and Subtitle** The title is a label that tells what the chapter is about. The subtitle, if there is one, suggests how the author approaches the subject. For example, an article titled "Brazil" might be subtitled "The World's Next Superpower." In this instance, the subtitle tells which aspects of Brazil the article discusses.

2. **Chapter Introduction** Read the entire chapter introduction if it is brief. If it is lengthy, read only the first few paragraphs.

3. **The First Paragraph** The first paragraph, or introduction, of each section of the chapter may provide an overview of the section and/or offer clues about its organization.

4. **Boldfaced Headings** Headings, like titles, serve as labels and identify the topic of the material. By reading each heading, you will be reading a list of the important topics the chapter covers. Together, the headings form a mini-outline of the chapter.

5. **The First Sentence under Each Heading** The first sentence following the heading often further explains the heading. It may also state the central thought of the entire selection. If the first sentence is purely introductory, read the second as well.

6. **Typographical Aids** Typographical aids are those features of a page that help to highlight and organize information. These include *italics*, **bold-faced type**, marginal notes, colored ink, <u>underlining</u>, and enumeration (listing). A writer frequently uses typographical aids to call attention to important key words, definitions, and facts.

7. **Graphs, Charts, and Pictures** Graphs, charts, and pictures will point you toward the most important information. Glance at these to determine quickly what information is being emphasized or clarified.

8. **The Final Paragraph or Summary** The final paragraph or summary will give a condensed view of the chapter and help you identify key ideas. Often, a summary outlines the key points of the chapter.

9. **End-of-Chapter Material** Glance through any study or discussion questions, vocabulary lists, or outlines that appear at the end of the chapter. These will help you decide what in the chapter is important.

Demonstration of Previewing

The following article was taken from a chapter of a communications textbook on nonverbal messages. It discusses four major functions of eye communication and has been included to demonstrate previewing. Everything that you should look at or read has been shaded. Preview this excerpt now, reading only the shaded portions.

Functions of Eye Communication

From Ben Jonson's poetic observation "Drink to me only with thine eyes, and I will pledge with mine" to the scientific observations of contemporary researchers, the eyes are regarded as the most important nonverbal message system. Researchers note four major functions of eye communication.

To Seek Feedback

You frequently use your eyes to seek feedback from others. In talking with someone, you look at her or him intently, as if to say, "Well, what do you think?" As you might predict, listeners gaze at speakers more than speakers gaze at listeners. Research shows that the percentage of interaction time spent gazing while listening was between 62 and 75 percent. However, the percentage of time spent gazing while talking was between 38 and 41 percent.

Women make eye contact more and maintain it longer (both in speaking and in listening) than do men. This holds true whether the woman is interacting with other women or with men. This difference in eye behavior may result from women's tendency to display their emotions more than men; eye contact is one of the most effective ways of communicating emotions. Another possible explanation is that women have been conditioned more than men to seek positive feedback from others. Women may thus use eye contact in seeking this visual feedback.

To Regulate the Conversation

A second function of eye contact is to regulate the conversation and particularly to pass the speaking turn from one person to another. You use eye contact, for example, to tell the listener that you are finished with your thought and that you would now like to assume the role of listener and hear what the other person has to say. Or, by maintaining a steady eye contact while you plan your next sentence, you tell the other person that although you are now silent, you don't want to give up your speaking turn. You also see this in the college classroom when the instructor asks a question and then locks eyes with a student—without saying anything, the instructor clearly communicates the desire for that student to say something.

To Signal the Nature of the Relationship

Eye contact is also used to signal the nature of the relationship between two people—for example, a focused attentive glance indicates a positive relationship, but avoiding eye contact shows one of negative regard. You may also signal status relationships with your eyes. This is particularly interesting because the same movements of the eyes may signal either subordination or superiority. The superior individual, for example, may stare at the subordinate or may glance away. Similarly, the subordinate may look directly at the superior or perhaps at the floor.

Eye movements may also signal whether the relationship between two people is amorous, hostile, or indifferent. Because some of the eye movements expressing these different relationships are so similar, you often use information from other areas, particularly the rest of the face, to decode the message before making any final judgments.

To Compensate for Increased Physical Distance

Last, eye movements may compensate for increased physical distance. By making eye contact you overcome psychologically the physical distance between you and the other individual. When you catch someone's eye at a party, for example, you become psychologically close even though separated by a large physical distance. Not surprisingly, eye contact and other expressions of psychological closeness, such as self-disclosure, are positively related; as one increases, so does the other.

Although you may not realize it, you have gained a substantial amount of information from the minute or so that you spent previewing. You have become familiar with the key ideas in this section. To demonstrate, read each of the following statements and mark them *T* for "True" or *F* for "False" based on what you learned by previewing.

_____ 1. The most important nonverbal message system involves the eyes.

_____ 2. We can obtain feedback from others by using just our eyes.

_____ 3. Eye movements cannot compensate for physical distances.

_____ 4. The relationship between two people can be signaled through eye contact.

_____ 5. Eye contact regulates conversations.

This quiz tested your recall of some of the more important ideas in the article. Check your answers by referring back to the article. Did you get most or all of the above items correct? You can see, then, that previewing acquaints you with the major ideas contained in the material before you read it.

EXERCISE 5-1

Directions: Preview Chapter 6 in this book. After you have previewed it, complete the items below.

1. What is the subject of Chapter 6?

   Reading as Thinking Understanding Sentences

2. List the four major topics Chapter 6 covers.

   a. *Locating Key Ideas*

   b. *Studying Modifiers*

   c. *Checking Unfamiliar Vocabulary*

   d. *Paraphrasing*

EXERCISE 5-2	**Directions:** Preview a chapter from one of your other textbooks. After you have previewed it, complete the items below.

1. What is the chapter title?

   _____

2. What subject does the chapter cover?

   _____

3. List some of the major topics covered.

   _____

Previewing Articles and Essays

Previewing works on articles and essays, as well as textbook chapters. However, you may have to make a few changes in the steps listed on pages 122 and 123. Here are some guidelines:

1. **Check the author's name.** If you recognize the author's name, you may have an idea of what to expect in the article or essay. For example, you would expect humor from an article by Dave Barry but more serious material from an article written by the governor of your state.

2. **Check the source of the article.** Where was it originally published? The source may suggest something about the content or slant of the article. (For more about sources see Chapter 14.)

3. **If there is no heading, read the first sentence of a few paragraphs throughout the essay.** These sentences will usually give you a sense of what the paragraph is about.

EXERCISE 5-3	**Directions:** Preview the article that appears at the end of this chapter, "Body Piercing and Tattooing." Then answer the questions on the next page.

1. What is the purpose of the article?

   _____

2. The article offers advice to those considering tattoos or body piercing. Which can you recall?

   _____

Learning Style Tips

If you tend to be a(n) . . .	Then strengthen your prereading skills by . . .
Auditory learner	Asking and answering guide questions aloud or tape-recording them
Visual learner	Writing guide questions and their answers

Discover What You Already Know

After you have previewed an assignment, take a moment to discover what you already know about the topic. Regardless of the topic, you probably know *something* about it. We will call this your **background knowledge.** Here is an example.

A student was about to read an article entitled "Growing Urban Problems" for a sociology class. At first she thought she knew very little about urban problems since she lived in a small town. Then she began thinking about her recent trip to a nearby city. She remembered seeing homeless people and overcrowded housing. Then she recalled reading about drug problems, drive-by shootings, and muggings.

Now let's take a sample chapter from a business textbook, titled *Small Business Management.* The headings are listed below. Spend a moment thinking about each one; then make a list of things you already know about each.

- Characteristics of Small Businesses
- Small-Business Administration
- Advantages and Disadvantages of Small Businesses
- Problems of Small Businesses

Discovering what you already know is useful for three important reasons. First, it makes reading easier because you have already thought about the topic. Second, the material is easier to remember because you can connect the new information with what you already know. Third, topics become more interesting if you can link them to your own experiences. You can discover what you know by using one or more of the following techniques.

1. **Ask questions and try to answer them.** For the above business textbook headings, you might ask and try to answer questions such as: Would or wouldn't I want to own a small business? What problems could I expect?

2. **Draw upon your own experience.** For example, if a chapter in your business textbook is titled "Advertising: Its Purpose and Design," you might think of several ads you have seen on television, in magazines, and in newspapers and analyze the purpose of each and how it was constructed.

3. **Brainstorm.** On a scrap sheet of paper, jot down everything that comes to mind about the topic. For example, suppose you are about to read a chapter on domestic violence in your sociology textbook. You might list types of violence—child abuse, rape, and so on. You could write questions such as: "What causes child abuse?" or "How can it be prevented?" Or you might list incidents of domestic violence you have heard or read about. Any of these approaches will help to make the topic interesting.

EXERCISE 5-4	**Directions:** Assume you have just previewed a chapter in your American government text on freedom of speech. Discover what you already know about freedom of speech by using each of the techniques suggested above. Then answer the questions below.

1. Did you discover you knew more about freedom of speech than you initially thought?
2. Which technique worked best? Why?

EXERCISE 5-5	**Directions:** For the essay "Body Piercing and Tattooing" at the end of the chapter, preview it and discover what you already know about the health risks of tattooing or body piercing by using one of three techniques described in this section.

DEVELOP QUESTIONS TO GUIDE YOUR READING

Did you ever read an entire page or more and not remember anything you read? Have you found yourself going from paragraph to paragraph without really thinking about what the writer is saying? Most likely you are not looking for anything in particular as you read. As a result, you do not notice or remember anything specific, either. The solution is a relatively simple technique that takes just a few seconds: Develop questions that will guide your reading and hold your attention.

How to Ask Guide Questions

Here are a few useful suggestions to help you form questions to guide your reading:

1. **Preview before you try to ask questions.** Previewing will give you an idea of what is important and indicate which questions you should ask.
2. **Turn each major heading into a series of questions.** The questions should ask something that you feel is important to know.
3. **As you read the section, look for the answers to your questions.** Highlight the answers as you find them.
4. **When you finish reading a section, stop and check to see whether you can recall the answers.** Place check marks by those you cannot recall.
5. **Avoid asking questions that have one-word answers.** Questions that begin with *what, why,* or *how* are more useful.

Here are a few headings and some examples of questions you could ask:

Heading	Questions
1. Reducing Prejudice	1. How can prejudice be reduced? What type of prejudice is discussed?
2. The Deepening Recession	2. What is a recession? Why is it deepening?
3. Newton's First Law of Motion	3. Who is or was Newton? What is his First Law of Motion?

EXERCISE 5-6	**Directions:** Write at least one question for each of the following headings.

Heading   **Questions**

1. World War II and Black Protest   1. _____

                                                            _____

2. Foreign Policy under Reagan   2. _____

                                                            _____

3. The Increase of Single-Parent   3. _____
   Families
                                                            _____

4. Changes in Optical Telescopes   4. _____

                                                            _____

5. Causes of Violent Behavior   5. _____

                                                            _____

EXERCISE 5-7	**Directions:** Preview Chapter 9 of this book. Then write a question for each major heading.

_____

_____

_____

_____

_____

_____

_____

EXERCISE 5-8	**Directions:** Turn back to the textbook excerpt on pp. 123–124. You have already previewed it. Without reading the article, write four important questions to be answered after finishing it. Then read the article and answer your questions.

_____

_____

_____

_____

EXERCISE 5-9	**Directions:** Select a textbook from one of your other courses. Preview a five-page portion of a chapter that you have not yet read. Then write questions for each heading.

_____

_____

_____

_____

READ FOR MEANING

Once you have previewed an assignment and written guide questions to focus your attention, you are ready to begin reading. Read to answer your guide questions. Each time you find an answer to one of your guide questions, highlight it. Also, highlight what is important in each paragraph. In Chapter 7 you will learn more about how to discover what is important in a paragraph; in Chapter 12 you will learn specific strategies for highlighting.

Learning Style Tips

If you are a(n) . . .	Then improve your comprehension by . . .
Applied learner	Thinking of real-life situations that illustrate ideas in the passage
Conceptual learner	Asking questions

TEST YOUR RECALL AS YOU READ

Many students read an assignment from beginning to end without stopping. Usually, this is a mistake. Instead, it is best to stop frequently to test yourself to see if you are remembering what you are reading. You can do this easily by using your guide questions. If you write your guide questions in the textbook margin next to the section to which it corresponds, you can easily use them as test questions after you have read the section. Cover the textbook section and try to recall the answer. If you cannot, reread the section. You have not yet learned the material. Depending on your learning style, you might either repeat the answer aloud (auditory style) or write it (verbal).

REVIEW AFTER YOU READ

Once you have finished reading, it is tempting to close the book, take a break, and move on to your next assignment. If you want to be sure that you remember what you have just read, take a few moments to go back through the material, looking things over one more time.

You can review using some or all of the same steps as you followed to preview (see pages 122–126). Instead of viewing the assignment *before* reading, you are viewing it again *after* reading. Think of it as a "re-view." Review will help you pull ideas together as well as help you retain them for later use on a quiz or exam.

BUILDING A SYSTEM: SQ3R

Each of the five techniques presented in this chapter, (1) previewing, (2) asking guide questions, (3) reading for meaning, (4) testing yourself, and (5) reviewing will make a difference in how well you comprehend and remember what you read. While each of these makes a difference by itself, when you use all five together you will discover a much bigger difference. Because these five techniques do work together, numerous researchers and psychologists have put them together into a reading-learning system. One of the most popular systems is called SQ3R. The steps in the system are listed below. You will see that the steps are just other names for what you have already learned in this chapter.

SQ3R

S	Survey	(Preview)
Q	Question	(Ask Guide Questions)
R	Read	(Read for Meaning)
R	Recite	(Test Yourself)
R	Review	(Review after You Read)

Be sure to use SQ3R on all your textbook assignments. You will find that it makes an important difference in the amount of information you can learn and remember.

EXERCISE 5-10

Directions: Read the following excerpt from a chapter on food additives in a nutrition textbook (pages 134–136), following the steps listed.

---

1. Preread the excerpt. Write a sentence describing what the chapter will be about.

   _____

   _____

2. Form several questions that you want to answer as you read. Write them in the space provided.

   _____

   _____

3. Read the excerpt, and on a separate sheet, answer your guide questions.

   _____

   _____

4. Review the excerpt immediately after you finish reading. Write a brief list of the major points covered in the reading.

   _____

   _____

Food Additives

Why Do We Use Additives?

1. *City living:* We live in cities and suburbs, not on farms. We shop infrequently, sometimes only once a week. Since food is produced far from the consumption point and must be kept fresh and wholesome until it reaches the consumer, added preservatives are often required.
2. *Modern lifestyle:* The need and desire for refined foods and lower caloric intake require some foods to be fortified with nutritional additives to assure adequate vitamin and mineral intake.
3. *New knowledge of the relationship of food to disease*—most significantly, of saturated fats and cholesterol to heart disease—has created a need and demand for new man-made foods, which require additives to make them acceptable.
4. *High-speed processing of foods* often requires additives to make the processing economical, or even possible.
5. *More women than ever are working*, creating an enormous demand for convenience foods: prepared, ready-to-eat, or heat-and-eat foods. Additives preserve the flavor, texture, appearance, and safety of these products.
6. *Snacking* has become a national pastime. Many snacks are man-made—with additives required to make them.

What Additives Do

A food additive has been defined by the Food Protection Committee as "a substance or mixture of substances, other than a basic foodstuff, which is present in food as a result of any aspect of production, processing, storage or packaging. This term does not include chance contaminants."

Substances are added to foods in order to accomplish one or more of the following things:

1. To preserve the product; that is, to prevent its deterioration from any cause.
2. To improve the texture of the food.
3. To improve the flavor, taste, or appearance of the food.
4. To improve the nutritional quality of the food.
5. To minimize the loss of quality during processing itself.
6. To protect the food during its growth, harvest, and storage. These are the incidental, rather than the deliberate, materials, such as pesticides.

How Additives Work

Let's take a closer look at the different types of food additives and how they work.

Preservatives function to slow down or prevent the growth of bacteria, yeasts, or molds. These microorganisms may merely spoil the flavor and texture of the food or may actually produce an end product that is dangerous for human consumption. Some of the more common preservatives used are sodium benzoate, sorbic acid (or potassium sorbate), and sodium nitrate.

Antioxidants slow down or prevent the reaction of components of a food with the oxygen in the air. Such reaction can produce undesirable flavors, such as rancidity in fats; unpleasant colors; and loss of vitamin value.

Emulsifiers are used for smooth blending of liquids or batters. Mono- and diglycerides are commonly used emulsifiers.

Stabilizers are often added to obtain a certain texture or to preserve a food's texture or its physical condition. For example, stabilizers are used to keep a liquid thick, to slow down the melting of ice cream, to prevent the fluid in a cheese from running off like water. Algin, xanthan gum, and other gums are stabilizers.

Sequestrants combine with trace amounts of metals that may be present in a product and prevent those metals from reacting with the foods to produce undesirable flavors or physical changes (to sequester means to keep in isolation). EDTA (ethylenediaminetetraacetic acid, a synthetically produced chemical) is a sequestrant.

Acids, alkalies, and buffers regulate the acidity of a food. We all know the difference between a tart cooking apple and a less tart (but still slightly acid) eating apple. In addition to its effect on taste, however, acidity is also very important to the preservation of food. Harmful bacteria usually do not grow in foods that are acid enough. Vitamins, including the natural vitamins present in food, tend to resist destruction more in foods that are acid, especially during the cooking process. In many foods, the preservation of the ideal flavor and color is helped by maintaining a specific acidity in the food. For these purposes, the acids make foods more acid, the alkalies make them less acid, and the buffers prevent change in acidity during storage. Citric acid is a typical acid, sodium citrate is a typical and common buffer, and sodium bicarbonate is a typical alkali.

Nutritional additives are the vitamins, minerals, and amino acids added to food either to enhance its nutritional value or to replace nutrients that might have been removed during processing. Some confusion has arisen now that vitamins are referred to by their chemical names rather than as vitamins in the ingredient list. It's unfortunate, but the listings of vitamins on the food label sometimes sound horrifying because their precise chemical names are given. "Vitamin B_1" is a lot more reassuring than "thiamine mononitrate."

Colors and flavors are added to make the food more appealing in appearance, smell, and taste.

Bleaching or maturing agents serve to oxidize wheat flour. While many foods must be protected against oxidation in order to preserve their quality, wheat flour used for baking must be oxidized in order to achieve the necessary quality.[1]

EXERCISE 5-11

Directions: Choose a chapter from one of your textbooks, or use a later chapter in this book. Complete each of the following steps.

---

1. Preview the chapter. Write a sentence describing what the chapter will be about.

   _____

   _____

2. Form several questions that you want to answer as you read. Write them in the space provided.

   _____

   _____

3. Read the first section (major heading) of the chapter and highlight the important information.

4. Review the section immediately after you finish reading and highlighting.

5. On a separate sheet, write a brief outline or draw a map of the major ideas in the section of the chapter that you read.

WORKING TOGETHER

Directions: Bring two brief magazine or newspaper articles or two two-page textbook excerpts on interesting subjects to class. You should preview and then read both articles before class. Working in pairs with another student, exchange and preview each other's articles. Take turns predicting each article's content and organization. The student who has read the article verifies or rejects the predictions. Alternately, the "reader" may ask the "previewer" about the article's content or organization. Then work together to generate a list of guide questions that could be used when reading the material.

MASTERING VOCABULARY

Directions: Determine the meaning of each of the following words used in this chapter. Then insert each one in the sentence in which it makes most sense.

intently (p. 123)

tendency (p. 123)

attentive (p. 124)

hostile (p. 124)

consumption (p. 134)

fortified (p. 134)

aspect (p. 134)

deterioration (p. 134)

enhance (p. 135)

precise (p. 135)

1. He has a _____ to snack too much.

2. The audience became loud and _____ when it was announced that the concert was being cancelled.

3. The physician gave the patient _____ instructions to speed her part-operative recovery.

4. Without proper care, _____ came quickly to the old house.

5. It is wise to reduce your _____ of fatty foods.

6. The children listened _____ to the story their teacher was reading.

7. Which _____ of the plan appeals to you most?

8. They were very _____ to the guests at their party.

9. That green blouse will _____ the color of your eyes.

10. She _____ herself for a busy afternoon by taking a short nap.

SELF-TEST SUMMARY

What techniques can you use *before* reading to read efficiently?	There are three techniques you can use *before* you even begin to read which will help you to read more efficiently. These three techniques are: 1. Preview. Become familiar with the material before you read it. Bring to mind what you already know about a topic. 2. Activate your background knowledge. Bring to mind what you already know about the topic. 3. Use Guide Questions. Formulate a series of questions that you expect to answer as you read. These questions guide your reading and increase your recall.
How can you read for meaning?	Highlight answers to your guide questions. Also, highlight important information in each paragraph.
How can you test your recall as you read?	Cover the text and try to recall answers to each of your guide questions.
How can you review after you read?	Use the steps you followed to preview the assignment.
What is the SQ3R system?	SQ3R is a system that enables you to learn as you read (Survey, Question, Read, Recite, and Review).

Name _____

Section _____ Date _____

Number right _____ x 20 points = Score _____

Directions: For each of the following headings, choose the most effective guide question.

_____ 1. Stress and Disease (Psychology)
   a. Are stress and disease related?
   b. How are stress and disease related?
   c. Who first studied the connection between stress and disease?
   d. In what year was the connection between stress and disease first identified?

_____ 2. Human Digestive System (Biology)
   a. In what part of the body does digestion begin?
   b. Does most digestion take place in the stomach?
   c. How does the human digestive system work?
   d. Is the esophagus part of the digestive system?

_____ 3. Types of Visual Aids (Public Speaking)
   a. Are graphs considered visual aids?
   b. What are the various types of visual aids?
   c. Can you use more than one visual aid at a time?
   d. Should a visual aid be used every time you give a speech?

_____ 4. Internal Influences on Consumer Decisions (Marketing)
   a. Are consumers affected by internal influences?
   b. Is personality an internal influence on consumer decisions?
   c. Are consumer decisions influenced by external factors also?
   d. How do internal factors influence consumer decisions?

_____ 5. Internment of the Japanese (American History)
   a. When were Japanese-Americans interned?
   b. Why were Japanese-Americans interned?
   c. Where were the Japanese-American internment camps?
   d. Were German-Americans also sent to internment camps?

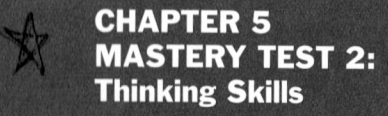

Name _____
Section _____ Date _____
Number right _____ x 20 points = Score _____

Indoor Air Pollution

1   Combating the problems associated with air pollution begins at home. Indoor air can be 10 to 40 times more hazardous than outdoor air. There are between 20 and 100 potentially dangerous chemical compounds in the average American home. Indoor air pollution comes primarily from six sources: woodstoves, furnaces, asbestos, formaldehyde, radon, and household chemicals.

Woodstove Smoke

2   Woodstoves emit significant levels of particulates and carbon monoxide in addition to other pollutants, such as sulfur dioxide. If you rely on wood for heating, you should make sure that your stove is properly installed, vented, and maintained. Burning properly seasoned wood reduces the amount of particulates released into the air.

Furnace Emissions

3   People who rely on oil- or gas-fired furnaces also need to make sure that these appliances are properly installed, ventilated, and maintained. Inadequate cleaning and maintenance can lead to a buildup of carbon monoxide in the home, which can be deadly.

Asbestos

4   Asbestos is another indoor air pollutant that poses serious threats to human health. Asbestos is a mineral that was commonly used in insulating materials in buildings constructed before 1970. When bonded to other materials, asbestos is relatively harmless, but if its tiny fibers become loosened and air-borne, they can embed themselves in the lungs and cannot be expelled. Their presence leads to cancer of the lungs, stomach, and chest lining, and is the cause of a fatal lung disease called mesothelioma.

Formaldehyde

5   Formaldehyde is a colorless, strong-smelling gas present in some carpets, draperies, furniture, particle board, plywood, wood paneling, countertops, and many adhesives. It is released into the air in a process called outgassing. Outgassing is highest in new products, but the process can continue for many years.

Exposure to formaldehyde can cause respiratory problems dizziness, fatigue, nausea, and rashes. Long-term exposure can lead to central nervous system disorders and cancer.

Radon

6   Radon is one of the most serious forms of indoor air pollution. This odorless, colorless gas is the natural by-product of the decay of uranium and radium in the soil. Radon penetrates homes through cracks, pipes, sump pits, and other openings in the foundation. An estimated 30,000 cancer deaths per year have been attributed to radon, making it second only to smoking as the leading cause of lung cancer.

Household Chemicals

7   When you use cleansers and other cleaning products, do so in a well-ventilated room, and be conservative in their use. All other caustic chemicals that zap mildew, grease, and other household annoyances cause a

major risk to water and the environment. Avoid buildup. Regular cleanings will reduce the need to use potentially harmful substances. Cut down on dry cleaning, as the chemicals used by many cleaners can cause cancer. If your newly cleaned clothes smell of dry-cleaning chemicals, either return them to the cleaner or hang them in the open air until the smell is gone. Avoid the use of household air freshener products containing the carcinogenic agent *dichlorobenzene*.[2]

Directions: Select the correct answer.

_a_ 1. The typographical aids in this passage include
  a. boldfaced headings.
  b. italics.
  c. underlined phrases.
  d. a and b only.

_B_ 2. The most useful guide question for the first heading would be
  a. How are woodstoves constructed?
  b. How do woodstoves contribute to indoor pollution?
  c. What types of wood produce the most heat?
  d. How is woodstove smoke different from furnace emissions?

_B_ 3. The most useful guide question for the last heading would be
  a. Which household chemicals cause indoor pollution?
  b. Why do people use household chemicals?
  c. How are household chemicals manufactured?
  d. Which household chemicals are safest for children?

_D_ 4. Which sentence in the first paragraph best describes what the remainder of the passage will discuss?
  a. Sentence 1
  b. Sentence 2
  c. Sentence 3
  d. Sentence 4

_D_ 5. The best way to review this passage would be to
  a. brainstorm about the topic.
  b. reread the entire pasage.
  c. reread the first and last paragraphs only.
  d. reread the headings.

Name _____
Section _____ Date _____
Number right _____ x 10 points = Score _____

The Real World: Bilingual Children

Conger and Galambos

Directions: Preview the following article by reading only the title, first paragraph, headings, first sentence of each paragraph, and the last paragraph. Do not read the entire article.

1   What happens to children who are exposed to two or more languages from the beginning? How confusing is this for a child? And how can parents ease the process? At least two important practical questions surround this issue of bilingualism:

- Should parents who speak different native languages try to expose their children to both, or will that only confuse the child and make any kind of language learning harder? What's the best way to do this?
- If a child arrives at school age without speaking the dominant language of schooling, what is the best way for the child to acquire that second language?

Learning Two Languages at the Same Time

2   Parents should have no fears about exposing their child to two or more languages from the very beginning. Such simultaneous exposure does seem to result in slightly slower early steps in word learning and sentence construction, and the child will initially "mix" words or grammar from the two languages in individual sentences. But bilin-gual children catch up rapidly to their monolingual peers.

3   The experts agree that the best way to help a child to learn two languages fluently is to speak both languages to the child from the beginning, *especially* if the two languages come at the child from different sources. For example, if Mom's native language is English and Dad's is Italian, Mom should speak only English to the infant/toddler and Dad should speak only Italian. If both parents speak both languages to the child or mix them up in their own speech, this is a much more difficult situation for the child and language learning will be delayed. It will also work if one language is always spoken at home and the other is spoken in a day-care center, with playmates, or in some other outside situation.

Bilingual Education

4   For many children, the need to be bilingual does not begin in the home, but only at school age. In the United States today, there are 2.5 million school-age children for whom English is not the primary language of the home. Many of those children arrive at school with little or no facility in English. Educators have had to grapple with the task of teaching children a second language at the same time that they are trying to teach them subject matter such as reading and mathematics. The problem for the schools has been

to figure out the best way to do this. Should the child learn basic academic skills in his native language and only later learn English as a second language? Or will some combination of the two work?

5   The research findings are messy. Still, one thread does run through it all: Neither full immersion nor English-as-a-second-language programs are as effective as truly bilingual programs in which the child is given at least some of her basic instruction in subject matter in her native language in the first year or two of school but is also exposed to the second language in the same classroom. After several years of such combined instruction, the child makes a rapid transition to full use of the second language for all instruction. Interestingly, in her analysis of this research, Ann Willig has found that the ideal arrangement is very much like what works best at home with toddlers: If some subjects are always taught in one language and other subjects in the other language, children learn the second language most easily. But if each sentence is translated, children do not learn the new language as quickly or as well.

Directions: Choose the best answer for each of the following questions.

_____ 1. The title of the article is
   a. "How to Teach Two Languages to Children"
   b. "Teaching Bilingual Children"
   c. "The Real World: Bilingual Children"
   d. "Children Who Learn Two Languages"

_____ 2. The article focuses *mostly* on what issue?
   a. The best way to teach two languages to children.
   b. Children who know several languages.
   c. Research findings on the academic performance of children.
   d. Whether parents should teach their children a foreign language.

_____ 3. What is the author's view on whether parents should expose their children to two languages?
   a. It is better to teach a child only one language at a time.
   b. Children can be expected to learn a second language only after they've mastered the first.
   c. Teachers should teach a second language to a child if that language is spoken in the home.
   d. Parents should not be afraid to expose their children to two or more languages.

_____ 4. In the author's view, the *best* way to help a child learn two languages fluently is to
   a. speak a second language to the child once she is fluent in the first.
   b. speak both languages to the child from the beginning.
   c. speak both languages to a child but wait until the child is at least school age.
   d. speak only one language to the child, otherwise confusion arises.

(continued)

_____ 5. According to the article, the need to be bilingual (for many children) begins
   a. at school age.
   b. at home.
   c. during the preschool years.
   d. as soon as the child develops language.

_____ 6. According to the article, research findings on this topic are
   a. in agreement.
   b. plentiful.
   c. messy.
   d. rare.

_____ 7. Research shows that the best way to teach bilingual children is through
   a. full immersion programs.
   b. English as a second language (ESL) programs.
   c. truly bilingual programs or combined instruction.
   d. the same methods as monolingual children.

_____ 8. The best guide question for the heading that follows paragraph 1 is
   a. What is learning two languages at the same time?
   b. How should children learn two languages at the same time?
   c. Can all students learn languages equally well?
   d. What should be done about children who cannot learn two languages at the same time?

_____ 9. The best guide question for the heading that follows paragraph 3 is
   a. What is bilingual education in the schools?
   b. Who should teach bilingual students?
   c. Should we eliminate bilingual education in the United States?
   d. What is the best way for the schools to find out who is bilingual?

_____ 10. The author's purpose in writing this article is to
   a. criticize.
   b. entertain.
   c. persuade.
   d. inform.

Body Piercing and Tattooing: Risks to Health

Rebecca J. Donatelle

Tattoos and body piercings are showing up almost everywhere these days. This selection discusses the growing popularity of "body art" as well as the health risks associated with it.

Vocabulary Preview

enclaves (par. 1) distinct group or community

medium (par. 2) a means of conveying something

elitism (par. 2) a perceived superiority

transmitters (par. 5) something that carries or spreads germs

exacerbates (par. 6) makes worse

adverse (par. 6) unfavorable

1   One look around college campuses and other enclaves for young people reveals a trend that, while not necessarily new, has been growing in recent years. We're talking, of course, about body piercing and tattooing, also referred to as "body art." For decades, tattoos appeared to be worn only by motorcyclists, military guys, and general roughnecks; and in many people's eyes, they represented the rougher, seedier part of society. Body piercing, on the other hand, was virtually nonexistent in our culture except for pierced ears, which didn't really appear until the latter part of the twentieth century. Even then, pierced ears were limited, for the most part, to women.

2   Various forms of body art, however, can be traced throughout human history when people "dressed themselves up" to attract attention or be viewed as acceptable by their peers. Examinations of cultures throughout the world, both historical and contemporary, provide evidence of the use of body art as a medium of self- and cultural expression. Ancient cultures often used body piercing as a mark of royalty or elitism. Egyptian pharoahs underwent rites of passage by piercing their navels. Roman soldiers demonstrated manhood by piercing their nipples.

The Popularity of Body Art

3   But why the surge in popularity of body art in current society, particularly among young people? Today, young and old alike are getting their ears and bodies pierced in record numbers, in such places as the eyebrows, tongues, kips, noses, navels, nipples, genitals, and just about any place possible. Many people view the trend as a fulfillment of a desire for self-expression, as this University of Wisconsin—Madison student points out:

> The nipple [ring] was one of those things that I did as a kind of empowerment, claiming my body as my own and refuting the stereotypes that people have about me . . . The tattoo was kind

of a lark and came along the same lines and I like it too . . . [T]they both give me a secret smile.

4   Whatever the reason, tattoo artists are doing a booming business in both their traditional artistry of tattooing as well as in the "art" of body piercing. Amidst the "oohing" and "aahing" over the latest artistic additions, however, the concerns over health risks from these procedures have been largely ignored. Despite warnings from local health officials and federal agencies, the popularity of piercings and tattoos has grown.

Common Health Risks

5   The most common health-related problems associated with tattoos and body piercing include skin reactions, infections, and scarring. The average healing times for piercings depend on the size of the insert, location, and the person's overall health. Facial and tongue piercings tend to heal more quickly than piercings of areas not commonly exposed to open air or light and which are often teeming with bacteria, such as the genitals. Because the hands are great germ transmitters, "fingering" of pierced areas poses a significant risk for infection.

6   Of greater concern, however, is the potential transmission of dangerous pathogens that any puncture of the human body exacerbates. The use of unsterile needles—which can cause serious infections and can transmit HIV, hepatitis B and C, tetanus, and a host of other diseases—poses a very real risk. Body piercing and tattooing are performed by body artists, unlicensed "pro-

fessionals" who generally have learned their trade from other body artists. Laws and policies regulating body piercing and tattooing vary greatly by state. While some states don't allow tattoo and body-piercing parlors, others may regulate them carefully, and still others provide few regulations and standards by which parlors have to abide. Standards for safety usually include minimum age of use, standards of sanitation, use of aseptic techniques, sterilization of equipment, informed risks, instructions for skin care, record keeping, and recommendations for dealing with adverse reactions. Because of this varying degree of standards regulating the business and the potential for transmission of dangerous pathogens, anyone who receives a tattoo, body piercing, or permanent makeup tattoo cannot donate blood for one year.

Important Advice

7   Anyone who does opt for tattooing or body piercing should remember the following points:

- Look for clean, well-lit work areas, and ask about sterilization procedures.
- Before having the work done, watch the artist at work. Tattoo removal is expensive and often undoable. Make sure the tattoo is one you can live with.
- Right before piercing or tattooing, the body area should be carefully sterilized and the artist should wear new latex gloves and touch nothing else while working.
- Packaged, sterilized needles should be used only once and then discarded. A

piercing gun should not be used because it cannot be sterilized properly.

- Only jewelry made of noncorrosive metal, such as surgical stainless steel, niobium, or solid 14-karat gold, is safe for new piercing.
- Leftover tattoo ink should be discarded after each procedure.
- If any signs of pus, swelling, redness, or discoloration persist, remove the piercing object and contact a physician.

Directions: Choose the best answer for each of the following questions.

CHECKING YOUR COMPREHENSION

_____ 1. The primary purpose of this selection is to
   a. discuss the use of body art throughout history.
   b. promote the use of body art as a form of self-expression.
   c. explain the popularity of body art.
   d. describe the health risks associated with body art.

_____ 2. The selection focuses on the trend in body piercing and tattooing among
   a. women.
   b. ancient cultures.
   c. young people.
   d. people in the military.

_____ 3. According to the selection, anyone who has received a tattoo or body piercing must wait a year before
   a. donating blood.
   b. getting another tattoo.
   c. getting another piercing.
   d. having a tattoo removed.

_____ 4. One of the greatest health risks from body piercing and tattooing results from
   a. leftover ink.
   b. unsterile needles.
   c. allergic reactions.
   d. overexposure to air or light.

_____ 5. The laws and policies regulating body piercing and tattooing can best be described as
   a. strict in every state.
   b. moderate in every state.
   c. completely nonexistent.
   d. varying from state to state.

_____ 6. The best synonym for the word "pathogens" in paragraph 6 is
   a. methods.
   b. standards.
   c. risks.
   d. germs.

(continued)

APPLYING YOUR SKILLS

_____ 7. The only typographical aid used in this selection is
   a. italics to emphasize key terms.
   b. boldfaced type to announce important ideas.
   c. listing of key points.
   d. underlining of key ideas.

_____ 8. The most useful guide question for this selection would be
   a. What does "body art" mean?
   b. What are the health risks of body piercing and tattooing?
   c. Which is more popular among young people, body piercing or tattooing?
   d. What is the average healing time for piercings?

_____ 9. Which of the following techniques would be most helpful in connecting the reading to your own experience?
   a. reread the reading
   b. think of people you know who have tattoos or body piercing
   c. highlight key information in the reading
   d. locate and read another article on the same topic

_____ 10. In previewing this article, you should read all of the following except
   a. the title.
   b. the first paragraph.
   c. the entire second paragraph.
   d. the first sentence of each paragraph.

Go Electronic!
For additional readings, exercises, and Internet activities, visit this book's Web site at:

http://www.ablongman.com/mcwhorter

If you need a user name and password, please see your instructor.

Take a Road Trip to New Orleans!
Be sure to visit the Active Reading module in your Reading Road Trip CD-ROM (or the Reading Road Trip Web site) for multimedia tutorials, exercises, and tests.

6

Understanding Sentences

THIS CHAPTER WILL SHOW YOU HOW TO

1. Identify the parts of a sentence that express its basic meaning
2. Recognize sentences that combine ideas
3. Read complicated sentences

Suppose you read the following sentence in a U.S. government textbook:

> The president is the party's leader, not by any authority of the Constitution, whose authors abhorred parties, but by strong tradition and practical necessity.

Try to explain what this sentence means. The real test of whether you understand an idea is whether you can express it in your own words.

Basically, the sentence explains why the president is the leader of his or her political party. Although less important, the sentence also explains that this is not a rule stated in the Constitution. Finally, the sentence contains the additional information that the authors of the Constitution abhorred, or hated, political parties.

Now let us look at how you might have arrived at this meaning. Answer each of the following questions:

1. Did you search for the most important information in the sentence?
2. Did you try to discover how various parts of the sentence were connected?
3. Did you check the meaning of any unfamiliar words such as *abhorred*?
4. Did you put the meaning of the sentence in your own words?

If you answered "yes" to each of these questions, you are well on your way to reading sentences effectively. Together, these questions suggest a four-step approach to sentence reading:

Step 1: Locate the key ideas

Step 2: Study the modifiers

Step 3: Check unknown words

Step 4: Paraphrase, or use your own words to express ideas

This chapter will show you how to find important information in sentences, sort or sift out less important ideas, see how ideas are connected, and paraphrase sentences.

STEP 1: LOCATING KEY IDEAS

Every sentence expresses at least one key idea, or main point. This main idea is a statement about someone or something. You can identify the main point by finding the subject and the predicate. Both are discussed in more detail below.

Finding the Subject and Predicate

Every sentence is made up of at least two parts, a subject and a predicate. The **subject**, often a noun, identifies the person or object the sentence is about. The main part of the predicate—the verb—tells what the person or object is doing or has done. Usually a sentence contains additional information about the subject and/or the predicate.

Example:

The <u>average</u> <u>American</u> consumed six gallons of beer last year.

The key idea of this sentence is "American consumed." It is expressed by the subject and predicate. The simple subject of this sentence is *American*; it explains who the sentence is about. The words *the* and *average* give more information about the subject, American, by explaining which one. The main part of the predicate is the verb *consumed;* this tells what the average American did. The rest of the sentence gives more information about the verb by telling what (beer) and how much (six gallons last year) was consumed. Here are a few more examples:

The <u>ship</u> <u>entered</u> the harbor early this morning.

<u>Lilacs</u> <u>bloom</u> in the spring.

<u>Jeff</u> <u>cooks</u> dinner for the family every night.

In many long and complicated sentences, the key idea is not as obvious as in the previous examples. To find the key idea, ask these questions:

1. Who or what is the sentence about?
2. What is happening in the sentence?

Here is an example of a complicated sentence that might be found in a psychology textbook:

Intelligence, as measured by IQ, depends on the kind of test given, the skill of the examiner, and the cooperation of the subject.

In this sentence, the answer to the question, "Who or what is the sentence about?" is *intelligence*. The verb is *depends*, and the remainder of the sentence explains the factors upon which intelligence depends. Let us look at a few more examples:

<u>William James</u>, often thought of as the father of American psychology, <u>tested</u> whether memory could be improved by exercising it.

<u>Violence</u> in sports, both at amateur and professional levels, <u>has increased</u> dramatically over the past ten years.

Some sentences may have more than one subject and/or more than one verb in the predicate.

Examples:

Poor <u>diet</u> and <u>lack</u> of exercise can cause weight gain.

My brother always <u>worries</u> and <u>complains</u> about his job.

Many <u>homes</u> and <u>businesses</u> are <u>burglarized</u> or <u>vandalized</u> each year.

The angry <u>customer</u> was <u>screaming</u>, <u>cursing</u>, and <u>shouting</u>.

Directions: Find the key idea in each of the following sentences. Draw one line under the subject and two lines under the verb.

Example: The instructor assigned a fifteen-page article to read.

1. Every summer my parents travel to the eastern seacoast.

2. Children learn how to behave by imitating adults.

3. William Faulkner, a popular American author, wrote about life in the South.

4. Psychologists are interested in studying human behavior in many different situations.

5. Terminally ill patients may refuse to take their prescribed medication.

6. The use of cocaine, although illegal, is apparently increasing.

7. The most accurate method we have of estimating the age of the earth is based on our knowledge of radioactivity.

8. Elements exist either as compounds or as free elements.

9. Attention may be defined as a focusing of perception.

10. The specific instructions in a computer program are written in a computer language.

Finding Combined Ideas within a Sentence

Sentences always express at least one complete idea. However, a sentence may combine several ideas. Two common types of sentences combine ideas:

1. Sentences with Two Important Ideas (Coordinate Sentences)
2. Sentences with One Important Idea and One Less Important Idea (Subordinate Sentences)

Each type gives you clues about how the ideas are connected and whether one is more important than the other.

Sentences with Two Important Ideas Coordinate sentences express ideas that are equally important. They got that name because they coordinate, or tie together, two or more ideas. This is done for three reasons: (1) to emphasize the relationship between ideas, (2) to indicate their equal importance, and/or (3) to make the material more concise and easier to read. In the following example notice how two related ideas can be combined.

Two related ideas:

1. Marlene was in obvious danger.
2. Joe quickly pulled Marlene from the street.

Combined sentence:

Marlene was in obvious danger, and Joe quickly pulled her from the street.

In this case the combined sentence establishes that the two equally important events are parts of a single incident.

As you read coordinate sentences, be sure to locate both subjects and predicates. If you do not read carefully or if you are reading too fast, you might miss the second idea. Often you can recognize a sentence that combines two or more ideas by its structure and punctuation. Coordinate ideas are combined in one of two ways:

1. **With a semicolon.**

   The union members wanted to strike; the company did nothing to discourage them.

2. **With a comma and one of the following joining words:** *and, or, but, nor, so, for, yet.* These words are called coordinating conjunctions. See Table 6-1 (page 154) for the meaning clues each provides.

   Some students decided to take the final exam, *and* others chose to rely on their semester average.

   The students wanted the instructor to cancel the class, *but* the instructor decided to reschedule it.

Sentences with One Important Idea and One Less Important Idea
Subordinate sentences contain one key idea and one or more less important, or

Table 6-1   Words That Join Two Important Ideas (Coordinating Conjunctions)

Joining Words	Meaning Clues	Example
and	links similar and equally important ideas	Jim is in my biology class, <u>and</u> Pierce is in my psychology class.
but, yet	connects opposite ideas or indicates a change in thought	Professor Clark gave a homework assignment, <u>yet</u> she did not collect it.
for, so	indicates reasons or shows that one thing is causing another	Most English majors in our college take a foreign language, <u>for</u> it is a requirement.
or, nor	suggests choice or options	We could make a fire in the fireplace, <u>or</u> we could get out some extra blankets.

subordinate, ideas that explain the key idea. These less important ideas each have their own subject and predicate, but they depend on the main sentence to complete their meaning. For example, in the following sentence you cannot understand fully the meaning of the underlined portion until you read the entire sentence.

<u>Because Stewart forgot to make a payment</u>, he had to pay a late charge on his loan.

In this sentence, the more important idea is that Stewart had to pay a late charge since that portion of the sentence could stand alone as a complete sentence. The reason for the late charge is presented as background information that amplifies and further explains the basic message.

As you read subordinate sentences, be sure to notice the relationship between the two ideas. The less important idea may describe or explain a condition, cause, reason, purpose, time, or place set out in the more important idea. Here are a few additional examples of sentences that relate two or more ideas. In each the base idea is underlined and the function of the less important idea is indicated in brackets above it.

description
My <u>grandfather</u>, who is eighty years old, <u>collects stamps</u>.

time
<u>American foreign policy changed</u> when we entered the Vietnam War.

condition
<u>I'll be late for my dental appointment</u> unless my class is dismissed early.

reason
Since I failed my last history exam, <u>I decided to drop the course</u>.

Notice that if the subordinate idea comes first in the sentence, a comma follows it. If the key, complete idea comes first, a comma is not used.

TABLE 6-2 **Words That Join an Important Idea with a Less Important Idea (Subordinating Conjunctions)**

Joining Words	Meaning Clues	Example
before, after, while, during, until, when, once	indicates time	<u>After</u> taking the test, Leon felt relieved.
because, since, so that	gives reasons	<u>Because</u> I was working, I was unable to go bowling.
if, unless, whether, even if	explains conditions	<u>Unless</u> I leave work early, I'll miss class.
although, as far as, in order to, however	explains circumstance	<u>Although</u> I used a dictionary, I still did not fully understand the word.

As you read subordinate sentences, pay attention to the connecting word used. It should signal the relationship of ideas. You must be sure to pick up the signal. You should know *why* the two ideas have been combined and *what* they have to do with each other. Table 6-2 lists some common connecting words, called subordinating conjunctions, and tells you what each signals.

**EXERCISE
6-2**

Directions: Read each of the following sentences. In the space provided describe *how* the underlined idea is related to the rest of the sentence. For example, does it indicate time, give reasons, or explain a condition or circumstance?

---

1. <u>Although I broke my leg</u>, I am still able to drive a car.

   _____

2. Peter will become a truck driver, <u>unless he decides to go back to school for further training</u>.

   _____

3. She always picks up her mail <u>after she eats lunch</u>.

   _____

4. <u>Because violence is regularly shown on television</u>, children accept it as an ordinary part of life.

_____

5. <u>Since comparison shopping is a necessary part of the buying process</u>, wise consumers look for differences in quality as well as price.

_____

EXERCISE 6-3	**Directions:** Read each of the following and decide whether it is a coordinate or a subordinate sentence. Mark *C* in the space to the left if the sentence is coordinate and underline both sets of subjects and predicates. Mark *S* if it is subordinate, and underline the more important idea.

_____ 1. The personnel office eagerly accepted my application for a job, and I expect to receive an offer next week.

_____ 2. Computers have become part of our daily lives, but their role in today's college classrooms has not yet been fully explored.

_____ 3. As far as we can tell from historical evidence, humankind has inhabited this earth for several million years.

_____ 4. Because sugar is Cuba's main export, the Cuban economy depends upon the worldwide demand for sugar.

_____ 5. We never learn anything in a vacuum; we are always having other experiences before and after we learn new material.

STEP 2: STUDYING MODIFIERS

After you have identified the key ideas, the next step in understanding a sentence is to see how the modifiers affect its meaning. **Modifiers** are words that change, describe, qualify, or limit the meaning of another word or sentence part. Most modifiers either add to or change the meaning of the key idea.

Usually they answer such questions about the subject or predicate as what, where, which, when, how, or why. For example:

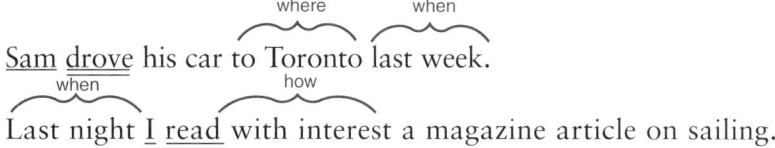

Sam drove his car to Toronto last week.

Last night I read with interest a magazine article on sailing.

As you read a sentence, be sure to notice how the details change, limit, or add to the meaning of the key idea. Decide, for each of the following examples, how the underlined portion affects the meaning of the key idea.

Maria took her dog to the pond <u>yesterday</u>.

Recently, I selected <u>with great care</u> a wedding gift for my sister.

The older Cadillac <u>with the convertible top</u> belongs to my husband.

In the first example, the underlined detail explains *when* Maria took her dog to the pond. In the second example, the underlined words tell *how* the gift was selected. In the last example, the underlined phrase indicates *which* Cadillac.

EXERCISE 6-4	**Directions:** Read each of the following sentences. Circle the subject and predicate, and decide what the underlined part of the sentence tells about the key idea. Write *which, when, where, how,* or *why* in the space provided.

1. You can relieve tension <u>through exercise</u>. _____

2. Many students <u>in computer science courses</u> can use the computer terminals only late at night. _____

3. Many shoppers clip coupons <u>to reduce their grocery bills</u>. _____

4. <u>After class</u> I am going to talk to my instructor. _____

5. The world's oil supply is concentrated <u>in only a few places around the globe</u>.

_____

STEP 3: CHECKING UNFAMILIAR VOCABULARY

If a word (or words) interferes with your comprehension of the sentence, you will need to figure out its meaning. Try the following steps until you have figured out the word's meaning.

1. **Pronounce it.** Often hearing the word will help you recognize it and recall its meaning.

2. **Use context.** Try to figure out the meaning of the word from the way it is used in a sentence (see Chapter 2 for specific techniques). In the following sentence, you can figure out the meaning of *nonverbal communication* from context.

   Nonverbal communication, or communication using the body rather than words, can be easily misinterpreted.

   Here nonverbal means "communication using the body rather than words."

3. **Analyze word parts.** Look for prefixes, roots, and suffixes that you are familiar with (refer to Chapter 3). In the following sentence word parts can help you figure out the meaning of *misdiagnosis.*

   The lawsuit was based on the doctor's misdiagnosis of the patient's symptoms.

   mis = wrong
   diagnose = to identify a disease
   misdiagnosis = incorrect identification of a disease

4. **Check the glossary.** Many textbooks include glossaries to define words used in that particular subject matter.

5. **Check the dictionary.** Some words do have several meanings. Be sure to find the meaning that fits the way the word is used in the sentence you are working with.

| EXERCISE 6-5 | **Directions:** Read each of the following paragraphs and determine the meaning of each underlined word. Write a brief definition or synonym in the space provided. |

A. A <u>rumor</u> is an <u>unverified</u> story that is spread from one person to another. As the story is <u>circulating</u>, each person <u>distort</u>s the account by dropping some items and adding his or her own interpretation. But a rumor is not necessarily false. It may turn out to be true. It is unverified *not* because it is necessarily a <u>distortion</u> but because people do not bother to check it against facts.[1]

1. rumor _____

2. unverified _____

3. circulating _____

4. distorts _____

5. distortion _____

B. Compared with crowds, fashions are more subject to traditional norms. Practically all aspects of human life—clothes, hairstyles, architecture, philosophy, and the arts—are influenced by fashions. A <u>fashion</u> is a great though brief enthusiasm among a relatively large number of people for a particular <u>innovation</u>. Because their <u>novelty</u> wears off quickly, fashions are very short-lived. Most are related to clothes, but as long as there is something new about any <u>artifact</u> that strikes many people's fancy, it can become a fashion.[2]

1. fashion _____

2. innovation _____

3. novelty _____

4. artifact _____

STEP 4: PARAPHRASING

Paraphrasing means putting an author's thoughts in your own words. Paraphrasing is the true test of whether you have understood an author's ideas. It provides a useful way to figure out what difficult and confusing sentences mean and it helps you remember what you read. By taking time with and thinking through an idea in order to paraphrase it, you'll find you'll be able to remember it.

Paraphrasing involves two skills:

1. Using synonyms (words that mean the same thing) to replace the author's words
2. Rearranging the order of ideas

Substituting Synonyms

A **synonym** is a word that has the same general meaning as another word. The following pairs of words are synonyms:

ruin—destroy   rich—affluent

rough—harsh   repeat—reiterate

real—actual   quibble—nit-pick

Now, let's try substituting synonyms in a sentence from the U.S. Constitution:

The Congress shall have power to . . . regulate commerce with foreign nations, and among the several States and with the Indian tribes. . . .

Notice how the following underlined synonyms have been substituted.

Congress is <u>allowed</u> to <u>control trade</u> with foreign <u>countries</u>, among states, and with Indian tribes.

When selecting synonyms use the following guidelines.

1. **Choose words close in meaning to the original.**

   Prehistoric people worshipped *animate* objects.

   The words *living, alive,* and *vital* are synonyms for *animate,* but in the previous sentence, *living* is closest in meaning to *animate.*

2. **Make sure the synonym you choose fits the context (overall meaning) of the sentence.**

   The physician attempted to *neutralize* the effects of the drug overdose.

   All the following words are synonyms for *neutralize: negate, nullify, counteract.* However, *counteract* fits the context, while *negate* and *nullify* do not. *Negate* and *nullify* suggest the ability to cancel, and a drug over-dose, once taken, cannot be canceled. It can, however, be *counteracted*.

3. **Use a dictionary, if necessary.** If you get stuck, check a dictionary. You don't have to replace every word in a sentence with a synonym. Often, the word the author used is the clearest or most accurate word choice.

   A riot is an extended outbreak of *violent behavior.*

   The phrase *violent behavior* clearly and accurately describes what happens in a riot, so it's fine to use that phrase in your paraphrase.

   A riot involves frequent and long-lasting occurrences of violent behavior.

4. **When the author is introducing or defining a new term, be sure to use that term in your paraphrase.** Specialized terminology is the basic language of a course, and it is often the best and most concise word to use.

   Sentence:
   A *panic* is characterized by a massive flight from something that is feared.[3]

   Paraphrase:
   A panic occurs when people run away from something they fear.

EXERCISE 6-6	**Directions:** Write synonyms above each of the underlined words.

1. Homeless people are in <u>desperate</u> need of <u>sustenance</u>.

2. The Constitution <u>limits</u> the presidential <u>term</u> of office to four years.

3. The politician's speech, which was full of <u>witticisms</u>, <u>elicited</u> much laughter from the audience.

4. The <u>convivial</u> group of business leaders agreed to <u>establish</u> a <u>consortium</u> to <u>regulate</u> international trade agreements.

5. The musician <u>performed</u> a <u>complex</u> set of musical |variations.|

Rearranging Sentence Parts

In a paraphrase you often change or rearrange the order of ideas to make the ideas clearer or simpler. On the next page are a few obvious rearrangements without the use of synonyms:

Last night a robbery occurred.
A robbery occurred last night.

Because the first set of results was inconclusive, the researcher repeated
  the experiment.
The researcher repeated the experiment because the first set of results
  was inconclusive.

When rearranging sentence parts, use the following guidelines:

1. **Split lengthy, complicated sentences into two or more shorter sentences.**

   Lengthy:
   Especially since the rise of television, modern presidents have enhanced
   their power to shape public opinion, as Reagan did in mobilizing support
   for his tax and budget cuts in 1981, as Kennedy did when he dramatically
   called up the reserves during the Berlin crisis in 1961, and as Bush did in
   building support for the Persian Gulf War.[4]

   Split Paraphrase:
   a. Television has increased the ability of modern presidents to influence
      public opinion.
   b. Examples of this influence include Reagan building public support for
      tax and budget reductions in 1981, Kennedy calling up the reserves in
      1961 during the Berlin crisis, and Bush shaping public opinion during
      the Persian Gulf War.

2. **Identify the author's key ideas and related ideas; emphasize these in your
   paraphrase.**

   Sentence:
   Some analysts argue that the federal government should provide money
   to deal with urban problems, because a national solution is possible for
   such nationwide problems.[5]

   Incomplete paraphrase:
   The federal government should pay for urban problems.

   Correct paraphrase:
   The federal government should pay for urban problems, since national
   solutions may help such widespread problems.

   The incomplete paraphrase does not include the reason *why* (a related
   idea) the federal government should pay for them.

Sentence:
Fads—temporary, highly imitated outbreaks of unconventional behavior—are particularly common in popular music, where the desire to be "different" continually fosters the emergence of new looks and sounds.[6]

Incorrect paraphrase:
Fads are occurrences of nontraditional behaviors that are imitated by others, especially in the field of music.

Correct paraphrase:
Fads are occurrences of nontraditional behavior. Fads are especially common in popular music because the need to set oneself apart from others encourages the development of new looks and sounds.

The incorrect paraphrase does not convey fully the idea of popular music creating fads.

EXERCISE 6-7	**Directions:** Read each of the following sentences. Using the procedure suggested in this chapter, paraphrase each sentence.

1. There has been an increase in female sports participation since the early 1970s.

   _____

   _____

   _____

2. A distinction still exists between what are traditionally considered to be male and female sports.

   _____

   _____

   _____

3. Two primary motivations for shoplifting are being poor or unemployed and desiring fashionable clothes like those worn by peers.

   _____

   _____

   _____

4. The right of citizens of the United States, who are 18 years of age or older, to vote shall not be denied or abridged by the United States or any state on account of age. (Amendment XXIV to the U.S. Constitution)

   _____

   _____

   _____

5. In armed robberies, potential violence—violence that is rarely carried out—enables the robber to achieve his or her material goal, usually money.

   _____

   _____

   _____

6. There are two opposing views of what constitutes mental illness. The medical view holds that mental illness is biological, similar to a physical disease, while the psychosocial view defines mental illness as an emotional problem.

   _____

   _____

   _____

7. In trying to identify the causes of problem drinking, some researchers have stressed the role of genetic factors, while others have viewed it as an inability to adjust to the stress of life.

   _____

   _____

   _____

8. Much of the progress has been effected by the Supreme Court, but the Court has mainly done this, we have found, when it was pushed by popular pressures: elections, public opinion, civil liberties and civil rights organizations, and social movements.

   _____

   _____

   _____

   _____

9. Organized crime is not unique to contemporary America: in the last [nineteenth] century, there were already a number of criminal groups in other parts of the world, including the Thugs of India, who were well known for killing travelers for possessions, and the Assassins in the Middle East, who held a reputation for murdering Christians.[7]

   _____

   _____

   _____

10. American history has witnessed an expansion of the boundaries of rights and liberties, especially during the present [twentieth] century, though much remains to be achieved.

_____

_____

_____

WORKING TOGETHER

Directions: Bring a difficult sentence to class. Working in groups, each group member should write a statement to paraphrase each sentence.

Learning Style Tips

If you tend to be a . . .	Then paraphrase sentences by . . .
Creative learner	Looking away from the sentence and writing its meaning. Compare your paraphrase with the original sentence and revise, as needed.
Pragmatic learner	Working systematically, piece-by-piece, paraphrasing each phrase or clause.

MASTERING VOCABULARY

Directions: Match each word in Column A with its meaning in Column B. Determine the meaning from its context in this chapter, its word parts, or use a dictionary, if necessary.

	Column A	Column B
_____	1. imitating (p. 152)	a. changes in tune or rhythm
_____	2. evidence (p. 156)	b. data, information
_____	3. inhabited (p. 156)	c. possible, capable of happening
_____	4. interpretation (p. 159)	d. current, modern
_____	5. norms (p. 159)	e. following the example of
_____	6. variations (p. 161)	f. spreading, enlarging
_____	7. distinction (p. 163)	g. explanation of meaning
_____	8. potential (p. 164)	h. standards
_____	9. contemporary (p. 165)	i. difference
_____	10. expansion (p. 165)	j. lived in

SELF-TEST SUMMARY

What are the four steps in understanding complicated sentences?	Understanding difficult sentences involves four steps: Step 1: Locate key ideas Step 2: Study the modifiers Step 3: Check unknown words Step 4: Paraphrase
Explain the terms *subject* and *predicate*.	The *subject* of a sentence is usually a noun that identifies the person or object that the sentence is about. The *predicate* of a sentence tells what the person or object is doing, has done, or will do.
Explain the two common types of sentences that combine ideas. How are the ideas connected?	Coordinate sentences express two ideas that are equally important. They are connected by using a semicolon or a comma and a coordinating conjunction. Subordinate sentences contain one key idea and at least one less important subordinate idea. They are connected with a comma if the subordinating idea appears first in the sentence.
What steps should you follow in figuring out the meaning of an unknown word?	1. Pronounce it. 2. Use context. 3. Analyze word parts. 4. Check the glossary. 5. Check the dictionary.
How do you paraphrase a sentence?	1. Substitute synonyms (words that have the same general meaning as another word). 2. Rearrange sentence parts, if needed. Split lengthy sentences into two or more shorter sentences. Identify the author's key ideas and related ideas and emphasize these in your paraphrase.

CHAPTER 6
MASTERY TEST 1:
Sentence Skills

Name _____

Section _____ Date _____

Number right _____ x 10 points = Score _____

Directions: Choose the best answer for each of the following questions

_____ 1. Which of the following choices correctly defines the underlined word as it is used in the sentence?

The doctor <u>predated</u> the referral form to make sure there was no confusion about whether Margaret's insurance would cover the treatments.

a. put down a date later than the actual date of the referral

b. put down the actual date of the referral

c. put down a date earlier than the actual date

d. refused to date the form

_____ 2. Which of the following choices correctly defines the underlined word as it is used in the sentence?

When he turned the corner, James saw the source of the <u>malodor</u>.

a. bad smell

b. loud noise

c. fight

d. man's fear

_____ 3. What does the underlined part of the following sentence tell about the main idea?

Many students <u>who work full time</u> can use the library only at night.

a. where students work

b. which students can use the library

c. when students work

d. why students work

_____ 4. What does the underlined part of the following sentence tell about the main idea?

Professor Rodriquez expects students to submit two copies of their papers <u>so that she can keep one for her files</u>.

a. which papers to submit the two copies

b. where to submit the papers

c. when to submit the papers

d. why students should submit two copies

_____ 5. Which of the choices below expresses the following two equally important ideas?

We will go get ice cream.
You must finish your homework.

a. Before we go get ice cream, you must finish your homework.

b. We will go get ice cream, and you must finish your homework.

c. You must finish your homework because we will go get ice cream.

d. Although we will go get ice cream, you must finish your homework.

_____ 6. Which statement is the main idea of the following sentence?

Although Maria wanted a new job and she was willing to take a pay cut, she was afraid the change would be too stressful for her.

a. Maria wanted a new job.

b. She was willing to take a pay cut.

c. Changes can create stress.

d. She was afraid the change would be too stressful.

_____ 7. Which choice is the main idea of the following sentence?

Because Robert wanted more money, he frequently worked in the evenings, even though his family asked him to spend time with them.

a. Robert frequently worked in the evenings.

b. Robert's family asked him to spend time with them.

c. Robert did not want to spend time with his family.

d. Robert wanted more money.

_____ 8. Which choice is the best paraphrase of the following sentence?

Although Susan finished gardening work, we discovered that she only did it because she wanted to get a tan, because her friends helped her out, and because her parents paid her to do it.

a. We thought Susan liked gardening, but she actually hates it.

b. Susan finished the gardening work because she likes working outside.

c. The gardening work has been completed. We found out she did the work because she wanted a tan, her friends helped out, and her parents paid her.

d. Although Susan doesn't really like gardening, some of the gardening work has been done.

_____ 9. Which choice is the best paraphrase of the following sentence?

When classifying the drugs, the volunteer arranged them by color and shape, which confused the doctor who expected them to be arranged in alphabetical order or grouped by what they treated.

a. The volunteer arranged the medicine by color and shape rather than by what they treated.

b. The volunteer arranged the drugs by color and shape. The doctor was confused because she expected them to be arranged in alphabetical order or by what they treated.

c. The doctor was confused by the arrangement of the drugs.

d. The volunteer confused the doctor when he didn't arrange the medicine alphabetically.

(continued)

_____ 10. Which choice is the best paraphrase of the following sentence?

> Although it comes as a surprise to most Americans, the murder rate in the 20th century was lower than it was in the 19th century: in San Francisco, for example, the murder rate was four times higher in the 1880s than in the 1980s.

a. Most Americans are surprised to learn that the murder rate was lower in the 20th century than it was in the 19th century. For example, the murder rate in San Francisco was four times higher in the 1880s than in the 1980s.

b. The murder rate in San Francisco was lower in the 1880s than in the 1980s.

c. In San Francisco, the murder rate in 1980 was one fourth of what it was 100 years later.

d. In San Francisco, the murder rate in 1980 was one fourth of the rate in 1880. This proves that the murder rate in America is lower now than it was in the 19th century.

Name _____

Section _____ Date _____

Number right _____ x 20 points = Score _____

Directions: Select the correct answer.

[1]Botanical gardens are another important part of the tourism attraction mix for many communities. [2]Some botanical gardens are renowned for their magnificent displays, and they draw visitors from all over the world. [3]The oldest botanical garden was established at the University of Pisa in Italy in 1544. [4]The Royal Botanical Gardens in Edinburgh, the Munich Botanical Gardens, The Montreal Botanical Gardens, and the Missouri Botanical Gardens in St. Louis are just a few of some of the more popular and frequently visited botanical gardens.[8]

_____ 1. In sentence 1, the subject is
    a. botanical gardens.
    b. communities.
    c. the Royald Botanical Gardens.
    d. tourism attraction mix.

_____ 2. In sentence 3, the verb is
    a. botanical gardens.
    b. was established.
    c. in Italy.
    d. at the University.

_____ 3. Which of the following sentences contains two equally important related ideas?
    a. Sentence 1.
    b. Sentence 2.
    c. Sentence 3.
    d. Sentence 4.

_____ 4. Which of the following sentences contains more than one subject?
    a. Sentence 1.
    b. Sentence 2.
    c. Sentence 3.
    d. Sentence 4.

_____ 5. In sentence 2, the word *renowned* means
    a. criticized.
    b. deficient.
    c. well known.
    d. challenged.

**CHAPTER 6
MASTERY TEST 3:
Sentence Skills**

Name _____

Section _____ Date _____

Number right _____ x 20 points = Score _____

Directions: Choose the answer that gives the best paraphrase for each of the following sentences.

_____ 1. The accommodations segment of the tourism industry consists of many popular alternatives such as bed and breakfasts, condominiums, time-shares, conference centers, hotels and motels as well as recreational vehicle parks and campgrounds.[9]

    a. There are many options for tourists to choose from when they are deciding on accommodations, depending upon what their recreational needs are and where they want to be located.

    b. The tourism industry offers many options for lodgings, including hotels, motels, bed and breakfasts, time-shares and condominiums, and campgrounds and parks for recreational vehicles.

    c. Hotels are just one of the many accommodations options offered by the tourism industry.

    d. Bed and breakfasts are a popular alternative to the hotels and motels typically offered by the tourism industry.

_____ 2. Proponents of a plan to extend the city's mass transit system to the suburbs cited several reasons for the proposed extension, including the dramatic population growth in the suburbs in the past ten years and the corresponding increase in commuters to downtown businesses.

    a. The city's mass transit system should be extended to the suburbs.

    b. In the past ten years, the number of people living in the suburbs and commuting to downtown businesses has increased dramatically, while the population of the city has been gradually declining over the same period.

    c. Supporters of a proposal to extend the mass transit system from the city to the suburbs justified it by noting the substantial increase in suburban commuters that has accompanied the population growth in the suburbs in the past decade.

    d. Supporters of mass transit say that it is the best way to cope with the increasing number of suburbanites who commute to work downtown.

_____ 3. The most prominent view emerging from the debate over rehabilitation during the 1970s was that while prison is the proper place for custody, the community is the proper place for correction and rehabilitation.[10]

   a. During the 1970s a debate took place over whether the proper place for rehabilitation was in prison or in the community.

   b. Community-based rehabilitation is better than rehabilitation that takes place in prison.

   c. The debate over rehabilitation indicated that prisoners who cannot be rehabilitated belong in prison, not in the community where they would be free to carry out further criminal activity.

   d. The most important theory that came out of the rehabilitation debate of the 1970s was that the right place for correction and rehabilitation is in the community, whereas the right place for custody is in prison.

_____ 4. After additional funds were allocated by the school board for the renovation of the elementary school, the architect was called in to amend the original plan. The revised plan featured a more comprehensive renovation, with a media center and computer lab to be located adjacent to the auditorium.

   a. When the school board designated more money for the elementary school renovation, the architect enlarged and improved upon the first plan by including a media center and computer lab next to the auditorium.

   b. After more money was allowed for the school renovation, the architect came up with a more extensive plan.

   c. The additional money for the elementary school renovation was provided by the school board.

   d. The new architectural plan for the school renovation included a media center next to the auditorium, which was paid for by funds from the school board.

_____ 5. The young girl who witnessed the bank robbery was able to foil the crime by using her fingernail to scratch the license plate number of the robber's car on a piece of cardboard.

   a. The bank robbery was thwarted when a child wrote down the robber's license plate number as he sped from the scene of the crime.

   b. The bank robber was prevented from getting away with the crime by a young girl who wrote the robber's license plate number on a scrap of cardboard with her fingernail.

   c. A young girl helped police identify the suspect in the bank robbery.

   d. The child who wrote down the robber's license plate number was a witness to the bank robbery.

Name _____
Section _____ Date _____
Number right _____ x 10 points = Score _____

How to Manage Your Doctor

Diane Cyr

Have you ever been displeased with the care you received from a doctor? In this essay Cyr offers advice on how to make sure you get quality health care from your physician.

Vocabulary Preview

mythological (par. 3) imaginary, beyond belief

savants (par. 3) scholars, learned people

empathy (par. 3) understanding of another's situation

demeanor (par. 4) the way a person behaves

caveat (par. 11) rule, warning

coyness (par. 18) shyness, bashfulness

1   Maybe all that a person really needs out of life is for Dr. C. Everett Koop to tell them they're okay.

2   Just look at the man: admiral-straight, shoulders squared, bow-tie perpendicular to the famously tufted chin. With his stony brow and compressed expression, the former U.S. surgeon general is not the sort of person you would want to see across your plate of chili fries. He is, however, exactly the sort— confident, knowledgeable, full of authority— you would want to see across the examining table. "As a pediatric surgeon," he says, "the thing I got the greatest kick out of was when I could send the child's parents out feeling they were in the right place and with the

right doctor and it was all going to be okay. It was being able to find their anxiety spot and settle it for them."

3   Would that all physicians today could do the same. In fact, doctors like Koop seem almost mythological. It's not hard to find the Body-by-Jake type doctors, reassuring but sketchily informative. Nor is it hard to find respected medical savants high on knowledge but low on empathy.

4   But just try to find someone with Koop's demeanor and stamina. At age 81, the founder of Shape Up America is still scarily fit, frequently putting in 90-hour work weeks that include chairing Dartmouth's C. Everett Koop Institute, the National Safe Kids Campaign, Personal Medical Records, Inc., and a host of other causes. He is blunt, calling the United States an "obese nation," and noting aloud that achieving quality of life means saying no to that extra slice of pizza. He is respected, knowledgeable, informed, and passionate. You would believe Koop was the type of person to practice surgical knots at age 8, which he did.

5   So when Koop tells a listener, as he does in his Time-Life medical video series, "You'll not only be healthier, but you'll also look and feel better," you believe it. Just one problem: How do you find other doctors who can do the same for you?

6   Not easy, says Koop, who is fluent in doctor-patient statistics. "Seventy percent of doctors, by poll, think they have not been properly trained in how to talk to patients," he says. According to another 5-year-old study, he notes, "only one in 52 patients leaves an interview with their doctor telling them what needs to be told."

7   It's not just the doctor with the problem. Since few patients know how their bodies operate (can you define "triglyceride"?), they often treat health-care professionals like car mechanics, giving them unearned authority. They're reluctant to converse, ask "stupid" questions, or take up the doctor's time. As a result, they never know if they're getting the best treatment, or even if the best person is treating them. So they take the prescription, the bill, and the occasional doubts, and they're out of there.

8   Picking a good doctor, then, is really a dual issue. The best doctors, of course, know what they're talking about—but it's the best patients who know how to get the information out of them. The bottom line is this: "Doctors like to take care of patients who are knowledgeable." It's the familiar Koop hard line: Be responsible. "Under the present health system," he says, "you had better take charge of your health because no one else is going to do it."

9   Here's where to start.

10   **1 Know your body.** Yes, body-conscious baby boomers do have a health advantage. Most at least know what their body parts should look like, and when something hurts that shouldn't. "Baby boomers are so much more understanding of their bodies than their parents were," says Koop. "Doctors find that easier to deal with." Better, boomers also like to hang out on the World Wide Web, which has a site for nearly every symptom, malady, and diagnosis that exists. Once you've got a diagnosis, "the Internet is great for understanding what you have," says Koop.

11   One caveat, though: Bad health information can be worse than no information.

So pay attention to brand. "If you're looking something up from the University of Minnesota, or the Mayo Clinic, you have reason to believe those people know what they're talking about," Koop says. "But if you find a farmer in West Virginia who says, 'I put cobwebs in my ears,' that's probably not reliable."

12   **2 Don't go in cold.** More Koop statistics: Male doctors, on average, interrupt their patients within 18 seconds of asking, "What's wrong?" (Female doctors wait almost a minute.) In a typical 20-minute interview, most doctors spend just one minute teaching their patients about their diagnosis.

13   The solution isn't necessarily to find a chatty doctor. It's to make your doctor tell you what you need to know. "Sit down and write out the questions you want answered three to five days before your visit," Koop says. "The day before, cross off the ones that aren't pertinent. Then don't leave until your questions are answered."

14   Start with the basics: What do I want to talk about? What do these symptoms usually mean? What else might they mean? How can I find out? What are my treatment choices? What are the advantages and disadvantages? Bring a tape recorder and take down what's said, and ask a nurse to write out a layperson's description.

15   Better to put a doctor on the spot than on a pedestal. "He *has* to be put on the spot," says Koop. "Even if he is at the point of having his hand on the doorknob, you say, 'You haven't answered my questions.'" Which means . . .

16   **3 Act on your behalf.** Among Koop's medical anecdotes, there's one about the doctor who diagnosed a child with a Wilm's kidney tumor. Just before surgery by the doctor's recommended urologist, the child's father discovered that a nearby hospital—not under the plan—was actually the center of excellence for the procedure. The father took the child there, sued to have the procedure covered, and won.

17   It pays, in other words, to play hardball with your health. "If a doctor says, 'I take out lots of kidneys,' you can say, 'How many children with tumors of the kidney do you see every year?'" Koop notes. "If he says one, say goodbye. If there's the slightest doubt, see another physician. Insurance companies are easy in payment with this because they want to be sure there's no unnecessary surgery, either."

18   It also pays to be assertive in bringing up uncomfortable health topics, like incontinence, impotence, or mental illness. You should mention alternative therapies you've tried, like over-the-counter herbs or therapeutic massages. Coyness doesn't pay in either case. First off, self-treatment might contradict or antagonize a doctor's prescribed treatment. Second, the more willing you are to discuss awkward issues, the more productive you can make the discussion. (Remember, doctors may not like talking, either.)

19   **4 Follow your instincts.** Once you've got a health concern, make sure first of all that you find a doctor who's knowledgeable in the specific area you're dealing with. From there, see if you're comfortable discussing "stupid" questions or embarrassing issues. Listen to whether your questions are answered or merely brushed aside. If you're not getting the right "vibe," trust your instincts and move on.

20 And don't rush your choice. If you're running a 102-degree temperature, you're probably not in the best frame of mind to begin choosing your primary-care physician. Instead, you can first try calling a nurse, nurse practitioner, or physician's assistant. They can either get the attention of a health provider, or even save you a trip by offering you practical, helpful advice over the phone.

21 Other tips: If you have a diagnosis, find an accredited specialist in that particular field. Call a local county medical office to discover any nearby medical centers of excellence. Check "best doctor" reference guides. Even if you've got managed care, it's likely that you have an ample range of physician choices, so use them. "You can request a change if you don't get along," says Koop. "Personally, I choose doctors I know, who are expert in what they do to me, but who are also people who can be empathetic to me and my family."

22 And if you've had a bad experience, Koop says, let the managed-care company know about it, along with your employer. "The human resources person should be sensitive to what employees like and don't like about the system," says Koop.

23 **5 Then follow the directions.** Getting the best medical advice is one thing. Taking it is another. Any proven weight-loss treatment won't work if you keep stuffing yourself, and if you're prescribed two weeks of bed rest, don't get up after one. In matters of health, it pays to follow the rules. And it pays to understand what you're doing and why. "There's no doubt in my mind," says Koop, "one of the most valuable messages you can

hear today is that you must take charge of your health."

24 In a perfect world, in fact, perhaps the ultimate health-care solution might simply be to be Dr. C. Everett Koop. Blessed as he is with inhuman energy and decent habits, he is further endowed with two other gifts: He not only can diagnose himself, but also is old enough to get Medicare to cover it. "I always know what I have, so if I know it's my heart, I pick out a cardiologist; if I'm having arrhythmia, I go to someone whose specialty is heart rhythm," he says.

Directions: Choose the best answer for each of the following questions.

CHECKING YOUR COMPREHENSION

_____ 1. The main purpose of this article is to
  a. interview C. Everett Koop about his health habits.
  b. push for changes in the health care system.
  c. tell readers how to choose and interact with a doctor.
  d. describe the characteristics of a good doctor.

_____ 2. The main idea of paragraph 7 is that
  a. doctors are like car mechanics.
  b. patients ask stupid questions.
  c. patients do not know how to discuss things with their doctors.
  d. patients usually take medicine without knowing why.

(continued)

_____ 3. The main idea of paragraph 11 is that
   a. where you get medical information is important.
   b. people in Minnesota are smarter than people in West Virginia.
   c. the brand of medicine you take is important.
   d. getting good information is hard.

_____ 4. How much time does the author suggest that male doctors spend explaining an illness to a patient?
   a. 18 seconds
   b. 1 minute
   c. 5 minutes
   d. 20 minutes

_____ 5. Which of the following is described as a good source of information about symptoms and illnesses?
   a. your health insurance company
   b. the World Wide Web
   c. your county medical office
   d. the telephone book

_____ 6. In paragraph 13, the word "pertinent" means
   a. reliable.
   b. answerable.
   c. hard.
   d. important.

APPLYING YOUR SKILLS

_____ 7. Which of the following is a synonym for the word "malady" in paragraph 10?
   a. treatment
   b. body type
   c. intelligence
   d. illness

_____ 8. In the last sentence of paragraph 20, the phrase "by offering you practical, helpful advice over the phone" describes which of the following about the main idea?
   a. how
   b. which
   c. where
   d. when

9. Which of the following is the best paraphrase for the second sentence of paragraph 4?
   a. Koop is busy with Shape Up America, Dartmouth's C. Everett Koop Institute, the National Safe Kids Campaign, and Personal Medical Records.
   b. Koop is age 81 and the founder of Shape Up America. He often works 90 hours a week at many causes, including Dartmouth's C. Everett Koop Institute, the National Safe Kids Campaign, and Personal Medical Records.
   c. Koop spends 90 hours a week at his job. He also works out and creates new organizations like Shape Up America.
   d. Koop founded Shape Up America, Dartmouth's C. Everett Koop Institute, the National Safe Kids Campaign, and Personal Medical Records at the age of 81. He keeps in shape by working 90 hours a week.

10. Which of the following is the best paraphrase of the last sentence of paragraph 17?
   a. Insurance companies will pay for a visit to another doctor because they want to make sure surgery is necessary.
   b. Insurance companies do not want to pay for unnecessary surgery.
   c. Insurance companies are easy to talk with about visiting another doctor.
   d. Insurance companies do not require as much paperwork or documentation from the second doctor who performs the surgery.

Go Electronic!
For additional readings, exercises, and Internet activities, visit this book's Web site at:

http://www.ablongman.com/mcwhorter

If you need a user name and password, please see your instructor.
Take a Road Trip to Spring Break in Florida!
Be sure to visit the Paraphrasing section of the Outlining module, and Summarizing, Mapping, and Paraphrasing module in your Reading Road Trip CD-ROM for multimedia tutorials, exercises, and tests.

7

Understanding Paragraphs: Topics, Stated Main Ideas, and Implied Main Ideas

THIS CHAPTER WILL SHOW YOU HOW TO

1. Identify topics
2. Identify main ideas in paragraphs
3. Recognize topic sentences
4. Understand implied main ideas

When you plan to go to see a movie, the first thing you ask is: "What is it about?" As the movie begins, various characters interact. To understand this interaction, you have to know who the characters are and understand what they are saying. Then you have to note how the characters relate to one another. To grasp the point the film is making, you have to realize what all the conversations and action, taken together, mean.

Understanding a paragraph is similar. The first thing you need to know is what the paragraph is about. Then you have to understand each of the sentences and what each one is saying. Next, you have to see how the sentences relate to one another. Finally, to understand the main point of the paragraph, you have to consider what all the sentences, taken together, mean.

The one subject the whole paragraph is about is called the **topic**. The point that the whole paragraph makes is called the **main idea**. The sentences that explain the main idea are called **details**. To connect their ideas, writers use words and phrases known as **transitions**.

A paragraph, then, is a group of related sentences about a single topic. It has four essential parts: (1) topic, (2) main idea, (3) details, and (4) transitions. To read paragraphs most efficiently, you will need to become familiar with each part of a paragraph and be able to identify and use these parts as you read.

This chapter concentrates on understanding main ideas, both stated and implied. The next chapter, Chapter 8, focuses on supporting details, transitions, and expressing paragraph ideas in your own words.

GENERAL AND SPECIFIC IDEAS

To identify topics and main ideas in paragraphs, it will help you to understand the difference between **general** and **specific**. A general idea is a broad idea that applies to a large number of individual items. The term *clothing* is general because it refers to a large collection of individual items—pants, suits, blouses, shirts, scarves, and so on. A specific idea or term is more detailed or particular. It refers to an individual item. The word *scarf,* for example, is a particular term. The phrase *red plaid scarf* is even more specific.

Examples:

General: pies
Specific: chocolate cream
apple
cherry

General: countries
Specific: Great Britain
Finland
Brazil

General: fruit
Specific: grapes
lemons
pineapples

General: types of context clues
Specific: definition
example
contrast

General: word parts
Specific: prefix
root
suffix

Directions: Read each of the following items and decide what term(s) will complete the group. Write the word(s) in the spaces provided.

1. General: college courses

   Specific: math

   _____

   _____

   _____

2. General: _____

   Specific: roses
   tulips
   narcissus

3. General: musical groups

   Specific: _____

   _____

   _____

4. General: art

   Specific: sculpture

   _____

   _____

   _____

5. General: types of movies

   Specific: comedies

   _____

   _____

EXERCISE 7-2	**Directions:** For each set of specifics, select the general idea that describes it.

1. Specific ideas: Martha Washington, Hillary Clinton, Jacqueline Kennedy
   a. famous twentieth century women
   b. famous American parents
   c. wives of American presidents
   d. famous wives

2. Specific ideas: touchdown, homerun, 3-pointer, 5 under par
   a. types of errors in sports
   b. types of activities
   c. types of scoring in sports
   d. types of sports

3. Specific ideas: for companionship, to play with, because you love animals
   a. reasons to visit the zoo
   b. reasons to feed your cat
   c. reasons to get a pet
   d. ways to solve problems

4. Specific ideas: taking a hot bath, going for a walk, watching a video, listening to music
   a. ways to relax
   b. ways to help others
   c. ways to listen
   d. ways to solve problems

_B_ 5. Specific ideas: listen, be helpful, be generous, be forgiving
   a. ways to get a job
   b. ways to keep a friend
   c. ways to learn
   d. ways to appreciate a movie

EXERCISE 7-3	**Directions:** Underline the most general term in each group of words.

1. pounds, ounces, kilograms, weights

2. soda, coffee, beverage, wine

3. soap operas, news, TV programs, sports special

4. home furnishings, carpeting, drapes, wall hangings

5. sociology, social sciences, anthropology, psychology

Applying General and Specific to Paragraphs

Now we will apply the idea of general and specific to paragraphs. The main idea is the most general statement the writer makes about the topic. Pick out the most general statement among the following sentences:

1. People differ according to height.
2. Hair color distinguishes some people from others.
3. People differ in a number of ways.
4. Each person has his or her own personality.

Did you choose item 3 as the most general statement? Now we will change this list into a paragraph by rearranging the sentences and adding a few facts.

> People differ in numerous ways. They differ according to physical characteristics, such as height, weight, and hair color. They also differ in personality. Some people are friendly and easygoing. Others are more reserved and formal.

In this brief paragraph, the main idea is expressed in the first sentence. This sentence is the most general statement expressed in the paragraph. All the other statements are specific details that explain this main idea.

EXERCISE 7-4

Directions: For each of the following groups of sentences, select the most general statement the writer makes about the topic.

 1. a. Brightly-colored annuals, such as pansies and petunias, are often used as seasonal accents in a garden.
   b. Most gardens feature a mix of perennials and annuals.
   c. Some perennials prefer shade, while others thrive in full sun.
   d. Butterfly bushes are a popular perennial.

2. a. Hiring a housepainter is not as simple as it sounds.
   b. You should try to obtain a cost estimate from at least three painters.
   c. Each painter should be able to provide reliable references from past painting jobs.
   d. The painter must be able to work within the time frame you desire.

 3. a. Flaxseed is an herbal treatment for constipation.
   b. Some people use Kava to treat depression.
   c. Gingko biloba is a popular remedy for memory loss.
   d. A growing number of consumers are turning to herbal remedies to treat certain ailments.

 4. a. Many students choose to live off-campus in apartments or rental houses.
   b. Most colleges and universities offer a variety of student housing options.
   c. Sororities and fraternities typically allow members to live in their organization's house.
   d. On-campus dormitories provide a convenient place for students to live.

 5. a. Try to set exercise goals that are challenging but realistic.
   b. Increase the difficulty of your workout gradually.
   c. Several techniques contribute to success when beginning an exercise program.
   d. Reduce soreness by gently stretching your muscles before you exercise.

IDENTIFYING THE TOPIC

The **topic** is the subject of the entire paragraph. Every sentence in a paragraph in some way discusses or explains this topic. If you had to choose a title for a paragraph, the one or two words you would choose are the topic.

To find the topic of a paragraph, ask yourself: What is the one thing the author is discussing throughout the paragraph?

Now read the following paragraph with that question in mind:

> Nutrition is the process of taking in and using food for growth, repair, and maintenance of the body. The science of nutrition is the study of foods and how the body uses them. Many North Americans define nutrition as eating a healthful diet. But what is healthful? Our food choices may be influenced by fads, advertising, or convenience. We may reflect on the meaning of nutrition while pushing a cart down a supermarket aisle, or while making a selection from a restaurant menu.[1]

In this example, the author is discussing one topic—nutrition—throughout the paragraph. Notice that the word *nutrition* is used several times. Often the repeated use of a word can serve as a clue to the topic.

Directions: Read each of the following paragraphs and then select the topic of the paragraph from the choices given.

A 1. Sometimes religious groups develop around a particular charismatic leader and have little or nothing in common with conventional religious traditions. These groups are called cults. Usually, cult members disavow the broader society because they view it as degenerate, and they further believe that each person must establish better relations with the spiritual. To accomplish these ends, cults sometimes require members to live together in group quarters or to move into communes.[2]

    a. religion
    b. spirituality
    c. cults
    d. communes

B 2. Solar energy—energy derived directly from the Sun—offers the best potential for providing the world's energy needs in future centuries. The Sun is a non-polluting and virtually perpetual source of energy. At present, solar energy is used in two principal ways: thermal energy and photovoltaic electricity production. Solar thermal energy is heat collected form sunshine. Photovoltaic electric production is a direct conversion of solar energy to electricity. Solar energy is likely to become more attractive as other energy sources become more expensive.[3]

    a. sources of energy
    b. solar energy
    c. thermal energy
    d. photovoltaic electricity

A 3. Because the mission of the Central Intelligence Agency (CIA) is to develop foreign intelligence and conduct counterintelligence activities to protect national security, it is not generally considered part of America's criminal justice system. However, it does engage in many of the same kinds of activities that are associated with domestic law enforcement, particularly the gathering of intelligence and the investigation of suspicious activities. The CIA employs thousands of people in a wide variety of jobs, from psychologists, engineers, computer scientists, and military analysts to statisticians, language instructors, attorneys, and theatrical effects specialists. Perhaps its most glamorous job is that of spy, referred to as the Clandestine Service.[4]

    a. the CIA
    b. national security
    c. America's criminal justice system
    d. domestic law enforcement

_____ 4. Daydreaming is a form of consciousness involving fantasy, occurring while you are awake. Almost all people daydream, although the frequency drops as we get older. Most daydreams are spontaneous images or thoughts that pop into our mind for a brief time and are then forgotten. We can, however, become adept at using daydreams to solve problems, to rehearse a sequence of events, or to find new ideas. Some daydreams are deliberate attempts to deal with situations like a boring job by providing some internal stimulation. Nevertheless, the content of most daydreams is related to such everyday events as paying bills or selecting clothes to wear.[5]

   a. consciousness
   b. fantasy
   c. internal stimulation
   d. daydreaming

_____ 5. The issue of inheritance is a controversial one in some families and should be resolved before the person dies in order to reduce both conflict and needless expense. Unfortunately, many people are so intimidated by the thought of making a will that they never do so and die intestate (without a will). This is tragic, especially because the procedure involved in establishing a legal will is relatively simple and inexpensive. In addition, if you don't make up a will before you die, the courts (as directed by state laws) will make up a will for you. Legal issues, rather than your wishes, will preside.[6]

   a. death
   b. inheritances
   c. wills
   d. state laws

EXERCISE 7-6

Directions: Read each of the following paragraphs and then select the topic of the paragraph from the choices given.

A. Discrimination doesn't go away: it just aims at whatever group appears to be out of fashion at any given moment. One expert feels that _age_ is the major factor in employment discrimination today, although studies have shown older workers may be more reliable than young workers and just as productive. The Age Discrimination in Employment Act gives protection to the worker between forty and sixty-five. If you're in this age range, your employer must prove that you have performed unsatisfactorily before he can legally fire you. This act also prohibits age discrimination in hiring, wages, and benefits. To report age discrimination, call your local office of the Wage and Hours Division of the U.S. Labor Department, or the Human Relations Commission in your state. If local offices are unable to help, try the national Equal Employment Opportunity Commission, Washington, D.C. 20460.[7]

Topic: _Discrimination_

B. Traditionally for men, and increasingly for women, one's job or career is tied in intimately with the way one regards oneself. Thus, loss of job becomes in part a loss of identity, and in part a seeming criticism of oneself as a total being, not merely as a worker. Even people who have lost jobs in mass layoffs through no fault of their own often feel guilty, especially if they are in the role of provider and no longer feel competent in fulfilling that role.[8]

Topic: _Job loss & Self Esteem_

C. The words "effortless exercise" are a contradiction in terms. Muscles grow in strength only when subjected to overload. Flexibility is developed only by extending the normal range of body motion. Endurance is developed only through exercise that raises the pulse rate enough to achieve a training effect on the heart, lungs, and circulatory system. In all cases, the benefits from exercise come from extending the body beyond its normal activity range. What this requires is, precisely, effort.[9]

Topic: _Benefits from (exercising and efforts)_

D. Mental illness is usually diagnosed from abnormal behavior. A woman is asked the time of day, and she begins to rub her arms and recite the Apostles' Creed. A man is so convinced that someone is "out to get him" that he refuses to leave his apartment. Unusual behaviors like these are taken as evidence that the mental apparatus is not working quite right, and mental illness is proclaimed .[10]

Topic: _Unusual behaviors - mental illness_

E. How, exactly, does sleep replenish your body's fund of energy? Despite much interesting recent research on sleep, we still don't know. Certainly the metabolic rate slows during sleep (down to a level of about one met). Respiration, heartbeat, and other body functions slow down; muscular and digestive systems slow or cease their activity, allowing time for tissue repair. But the precise mechanisms by which sleep restores and refreshes us remain a mystery.[11]

Topic: _Sleep_

FINDING THE STATED MAIN IDEA

The main idea of a paragraph is the most important idea; it is the idea that the whole paragraph explains or supports. Usually it is expressed in one sentence called the **topic sentence**. To find the main idea, use the following suggestions.

Locate the Topic

You have learned that the topic is the subject of a paragraph. The main idea is the most important thing the author wants you to know about the topic. To find the main idea, ask yourself, "What is the one most important thing to know about the topic?" Read the following paragraph and then answer this question.

> The earth's water environments may be classified roughly as fresh water or marine, although not all bodies of water fall neatly into one category or the other. For example, Lake Pontchartrain, near New Orleans, is brackish, or a mixture of salt and fresh water. So are estuaries, the places where rivers flow into seas. Fresh water has about 0.1 percent salt; seawater has about 3.5 percent salt; and, as we will see, each has its importance in the earth's drama.[12]

In this example, the topic is water classification. The most important point the author is making is that water can be classified as either fresh or marine, although exceptions do exist.

Locate the Most General Sentence

The most general sentence in the paragraph expresses the main idea. This sentence is called the topic sentence. This sentence must be broad enough to include or cover all the other ideas (details) in the paragraph. In the above paragraph, the first sentence makes a general statement about the earth's water—that most of it can be classified as fresh or marine. The rest of the sentences provide specifics about this classification.

Study the Rest of the Paragraph

The main idea must connect, draw together, and make the rest of the paragraph meaningful. You might think of the main idea as the one that all the details, taken together, add up to, explain, or support. In the above paragraph, sentences 2, 3, and 4 each give details about water classification. Sentences 2 and 3 give examples of exceptions to the fresh/marine categories. Sentence 4 defines the salt content of each category.

IDENTIFYING TOPIC SENTENCES

The topic sentence can be located anywhere in the paragraph. However, there are several positions where it is most likely to be found.

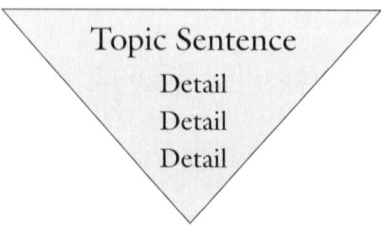

Topic Sentence First

Most often the topic sentence is placed first in the paragraph. In this type of paragraph, the author first states his or her main point and then explains it.

> <u>D. W. Griffith, among the first "star" directors, paved the way for future filmmakers</u>. Griffith refined many of the narrative techniques that are still used, including varied camera distances, close-up shots, multiple story lines, fast-paced editing, and symbolic imagery. His major work, *Birth of a Nation* (1915), was a controversial three-hour Civil War epic. Although considered a technical masterpiece, the film naively glorified the Ku Klux Klan and stereotyped southern blacks. It is nevertheless the movie that triggered Hollywood's eighty-year fascination with long narrative movies. By 1915, more than 20 percent of films were feature-length (around two hours), and *Birth of a Nation,* which cost a filmgoer a record $2 admission to see, ran for a year on Broadway.[13]

Here the writer first states that D. W. Griffith paved the way for future filmmakers. The rest of the paragraph explains how he did this.

Topic Sentence Last

The second most likely place for a topic sentence to appear is last in the paragraph. When using this arrangement, a writer leads up to the main point and then directly states it at the end.

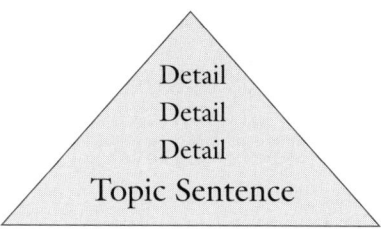

Fast foods tend to be short on fresh fruits and vegetables, and are low in calcium, although calcium can be obtained in shakes and milk. Pizza is a fast-food exception. It contains grains, meat, vegetables, and cheese, which represent four of the food groups. Pizza is often only about 25 percent fat, most of which comes from the crust. <u>Overall, studies have shown pizza to be highly nutritious.</u>[14]

This paragraph first states what nutrients fast foods usually lack. Then it explains how pizza is an exception. The paragraph ends with a general statement about the contents of pizza—that studies have shown it to be highly nutritious.

Topic Sentence in the Middle

If it is placed neither first nor last, then the topic sentence appears somewhere in the middle of the paragraph. In this arrangement, the sentences before the topic sentence lead up to or introduce the main idea. Those that follow the main idea explain or describe it.

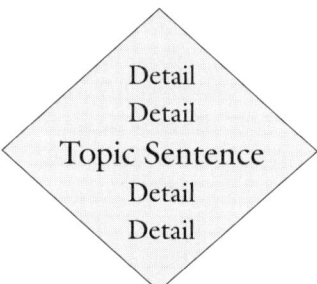

You could be the greatest mechanical genius since Thomas Edison, but if no one knows about your talent or is in a position to judge it, you're wasting your time. Being in the right field is important. <u>But within that field, it's also a good idea to maintain a high degree of visibility</u>. If you've got the potential to be a brilliant corporate strategist, you may be wasting your time working for a small company employing a dozen or so workers. You'd be better off working for a large corporation where you have the opportunity to take off in any number of directions, learn how the different departments interface, and thus have a larger arena to test your skills.[15]

In this paragraph, the writer begins with an example using Thomas Edison. He then states his main point and continues with examples that illustrate the importance of visibility in career advancement.

Topic Sentence First and Last

Occasionally the main idea will appear at the beginning of a paragraph and again at the end. Writers may use this organization to emphasize an important idea or to explain an idea that needs clarification.

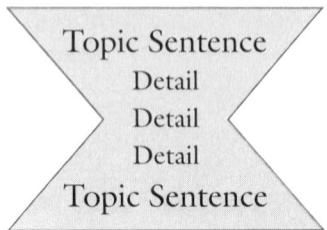

Burger King Corporation offers both a service and a product to its customers. Its service is the convenience it offers the consumer—the location of its restaurants and its fast food service—in catering to his or her lifestyle. Its product, in essence, is *the total Burger King experience,* which starts from the time you drive into the restaurant's parking lot and ends when you drive out. It includes the speed of service, the food you order, the price you pay, the friendliness and courtesy you are shown, the intangible feeling of satisfaction—in short, an experience. Burger King, then, is marketing a positive experience, as promised by its advertising and promotional efforts and delivered by its product.[16]

The first and last sentences both state, in slightly different ways, that Burger King provides a desirable product and service that result in a positive experience.

EXERCISE 7-7	**Directions:** Underline the topic sentence in each of the following paragraphs.

A. Leadership can assume any one of three basic styles: authoritarian, democratic, and laissez-faire. *Authoritarian* leaders give orders and direct activities with minimal input from followers. In extreme cases, they may be said to rule with an iron fist that crushes all dissent. In cultures where it is customary for authoritarian leaders to make decisions in both the political and domestic spheres, this leadership style may be preferred. In egalitarian societies, authoritarian leaders may be tolerated, but members of small groups typically prefer *democratic* leaders, who attempt to involve others in the decision-making process. *Laissez-faire* leaders take a "hands-off" approach; they neither set the agenda nor try to direct followers in any obvious way. Instead, they allow group members the freedom to choose whatever direction they think is best.[17]

B. Dirty words are often used by teenagers in telling off-color stories and this can be considered part of their sex education. As their bodies grow and change, both boys and girls wonder and worry. To keep from being overwhelmed by these fears, they turn them into jokes or dirty-word stories. By telling and retelling off-color stories, they gain a little information, more misinformation, and a lot of reassurance. They learn that they aren't the only ones in the group disturbed about their future roles in courtship and marriage. Using dirty words and stories to laugh at sexual doubts and fears may diminish their importance and make them less frightening.[18]

C. Deciding to buy a product or service takes preparation. Since time has already been spent to gather information and compare what is available, money managers should spend a little more time prior to arriving at a final decision. In this respect it is best if prospective buyers go home before making a selection. At home it is easier to evaluate all of the accumulated information while not under any sales or time pressure to make a purchase. In addition, at home it is possible to take a final look at financial plans to be sure the purchase will mesh with these plans.[19]

D. It is important to realize that the 1950s were to most Americans a time of great security. After World War II, the people prospered in ways they had never known before. Our involvement in the Korean War was thought to be successful from the point of view of national image. We saw ourselves as *the* world power, who had led the fight for democracy. When Dwight D. Eisenhower was elected president, we entered a period in American history where everything was all right, everyone was getting richer, and tomorrow would always be better than today.[20]

E. The other day a good friend, senior executive of a large company and in his early forties, dropped by for a visit. He told me he had been thinking of divorce after sixteen years of marriage. The couple have a boy, twelve, and two girls, one of whom is ten, the other eight. "We've grown apart over the years, and we have nothing in common left anymore other than the children. There are at least twenty years of enjoying life still ahead of me. I was worried about the children until we discussed it with them. So many of their schoolmates have had divorced parents or parents who had remarried, they are accustomed to the idea. It's part of life. Of course, if the older ones need help, I want them to see a good psychiatrist while we go through with this. My wife is still a good-looking woman, younger than I, and probably will remarry. I'm not thinking of it now, but I'll probably remarry someday." This situation illustrates an attitude and the climate of the times. Divorce has become as much an institution as marriage.[21]

F. If you have ever seen someone hooked up to an oxygen tank and struggling to breathe while climbing a flight of stairs or listened to someone gasping for air for no apparent reason, you have probably witnessed an emphysemic episode. Emphysema involves the gradual destruction of the alveoli (tiny air sacs) of the lungs. As the alveoli are destroyed, the affected person finds it more and more difficult to exhale. The victim typically struggles to take in a fresh supply of air before the air held in the lungs has been expended. What we all take for granted—the easy, rhythmic flow of air in and out of our lungs—becomes a continuous struggle for people with emphysema.[22]

G. Cultures can be classified in terms of their masculinity and femininity. **Masculine cultures** emphasize success and socialize their people to be assertive, ambitious, and competitive. Members of masculine cultures are thus more likely to confront conflicts directly and to competitively fight out any differences; they're more likely to emphasize win-lose conflict strategies. **Feminine cultures** emphasize the quality of life and socialize their people to be modest and to emphasize close inter-personal relationships. Members of feminine cultures are thus more likely to empha-size compromise and negotiation in resolving conflicts; they're more likely to seek win-win solutions.[23]

H. Large collections of animals, which were originally called menageries, have served as magnets for visitors since the times of the ancient Chinese, Egyptians, Babylonians, and Aztecs. Modern zoos (sometimes called zoological parks) now come in many sizes and can be found throughout the world. The Philadelphia Zoo was the first (1859) location in the United States dedicated to the large-scale col-lection and display of animals. While this facility is still of great importance, it has been eclipsed by more spectacular zoos such as the Bronx Zoo and the San Diego Zoo. Other notable zoos around the world can be found in Montreal, Vancouver, Frankfurt, London, Paris, Moscow, New Delhi, Tokyo, and Sydney.[24]

I. The lower courts are usually very busy places. If you visit one on a typical morning you will discover a crowded courtroom with all sorts of people milling around. Some are lawyers, some are victims, a few are unlookers and relatives of defendants, and there may be a police officer or two. But most are defendants waiting for their case to be called. At the front of the courtroom it is not uncommon to see the judge engaged in three or four conversations at once. People come and go constantly, and there is a lot of talking going on around the room. A plea of "Order in the court!" would probably be unheard, and court bailiffs have learned to overlook the apparent disor-der so long as the day's business gets done.[25]

J. You will periodically see warnings on the Internet about e-mail messages car-rying computer viruses. They typically tell you never to read anything with a specific subject header (like "Good Times" or "Pen Pal Greetings"), and then they tell you to be sure to pass this warning along to everyone you know. These warnings are all hoaxes. You cannot get a computer virus from reading a plain text mail message. If you see such a virus warning and suspect that it's a hoax, you can visit the Computer Virus Myths Web site to see if it is a known hoax. Whatever you do, don't forward the message to all your friends and coworkers. If there is a real virus on the loose, leave it to the professionals in technical support to distribute appropriate warnings.[26]

Learning Style Tips

If you tend to be a . . .	Then find topic sentences by . . .
Creative learner	Looking away from the paragraph and state its main point in your own words. Find a sentence that matches your statement.
Pragmatic learner	Reading through the paragraph, sentence-by-sentence, evaluating each sentence.

IMPLIED MAIN IDEAS

When you imply something, you suggest an idea, but you do not state it outright. Study the cartoon below. The point the cartoonist is making is clear—relationships change quickly. Notice, however, that this point is not stated directly. To get the cartoonist's point, you had to study the details and read the signs in the cartoon, and then reason out what the cartoonist is trying to say. You need to use the same reasoning process when reading paragraphs that lack a topic sentence. You have to study the details and figure out what all the details mean when considered together. This chapter will show you how to figure out main ideas that are suggested (implied) but not directly stated in a paragraph.

© The New Yorker Collection 1979 Mischa Richter from cartoonbank.com. All Rights Reserved.

What Does Implied Mean?

Suppose your favorite shirt is missing from your closet and you know that your roommate often borrows your clothes. You say to your roommate, "If that blue plaid shirt is back in my closet by noon, I'll forget that it was missing." Now, you did not directly accuse your roommate of borrowing your shirt, but your message was clear—Return my shirt! Your statement implied or suggested that your roommate had borrowed it and should return it. Your roommate, if he understood your message, inferred (reasoned out) that you suspected that he had borrowed your shirt and that you want it back.

Speakers and writers imply ideas. Listeners and readers must make inferences in order to understand them. Here are two important terms you need to know:

Imply   means   **to suggest an idea but not state it directly.**

Infer   means   **to reason out something based on what has been said.**

Here is another statement; what is the writer implying?

I wouldn't feed that cake to my dog.

No doubt you inferred that the writer dislikes the cake and considers it inedible, but notice that the writer did not say that.

EXERCISE 7-8

Directions: For each of the following statements, indicate which choice best explains what the writer in implying, but has not directly stated.

_____ 1. Jane's hair looked as if she just came out of a wind tunnel.
a. Jane's hair needs rearranging.
b. Jane's hair is messy.
c. Jane's hair needs styling.
d. Jane's hair needs coloring.

_____ 2. I would not recommend Professor Wright's class to my worst enemy.
a. The writer likes Professor Wright's class.
b. The writer dislikes Professor Wright's class.
c. Professor Wright's class is popular.
d. Professor Wright's class is unpopular.

_____ 3. The steak was overcooked and tough; the mashed potatoes were cold; the green beans were withered, and the chocolate pie was mushy.
   a. The dinner was tasty.
   b. The dinner was prepared poorly.
   c. The dinner was nutritious.
   d. The dinner was served carelessly.

_____ 4. Professor Rodriguez assigns three 5-page papers, gives weekly quizzes, and requires both a midterm and final exam. In addition to weekly assigned chapters in the text, we must read three to four journal articles each week. It is difficult to keep up.
   a. Professor Rodriguez' course is demanding.
   b. Professor Rodriguez is not a good teacher.
   c. Professor Rodriguez likes to give homework.
   d. Professor Rodriguez' course is unpopular.

_____ 5. It was my favorite time of year. The lilacs were blooming—finally!—and even though we still wore sweaters, the breeze held the promise of warm days to come.
   a. It was autumn.
   b. It was springtime.
   c. It was summertime.
   d. There was a storm coming.

_____ 6. When Alton got the estimate for repairing his car, he knew he had a tough decision to make.
   a. Alton was going to repair his own car.
   b. Alton would have to find another car repair shop.
   c. Alton's car repairs were going to be inexpensive.
   d. Alton would have to decide whether to repair the car or to buy a different one.

_____ 7. Charlie limped over to the couch and lay down. He put his foot up on a pillow and carefully placed the ice pack on his ankle.
   a. Charlie is getting ready to take a nap.
   b. Charlie has an injured ankle.
   c. Charlie has the flu.
   d. Charlie has been running.

_____ 8. After the girls' sleepover party last Saturday, it looked like a bomb had gone off in the basement.
   a. The sleepover party was too loud.
   b. The electricity went out during the sleepover party.
   c. There was an explosion in the basement after the sleepover party.
   d. The girls made a mess in the basement.

_____ 9. When it was Kei's turn to give her speech, her stomach did a flip and her face felt as if it were on fire.
   a. Kei looked forward to giving her speech.
   b. Kei was experienced at giving speeches.
   c. Kei was nervous about giving her speech.
   d. Kei enjoyed giving speeches.

_____ 10. People filed out of the movie theater slowly and quietly; many of them wiped their eyes and noses with tissues as they walked to their cars.
   a. The movie was sad.
   b. The movie was funny.
   c. The theater was cold.
   d. The moviegoers were disappointed.

Figuring Out Implied Main Ideas

Implied main ideas, when they appear in paragraphs, are usually larger, more important ideas than the details. You might think of implied ideas as general ideas that are suggested by specifics.

   What larger, more important idea do these details point to?

The wind was blowing at 35 mph.

The wind chill was 5 degrees below zero.

Snow was falling at the rate of 3 inches per hour.

Together these three details suggests that a snowstorm or blizzard was occurring. You might visualize this as follows:

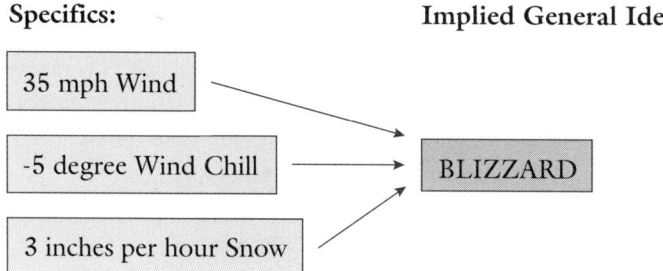

   Now what idea does the following set of specifics suggest?

Specifics: Implied General Idea:

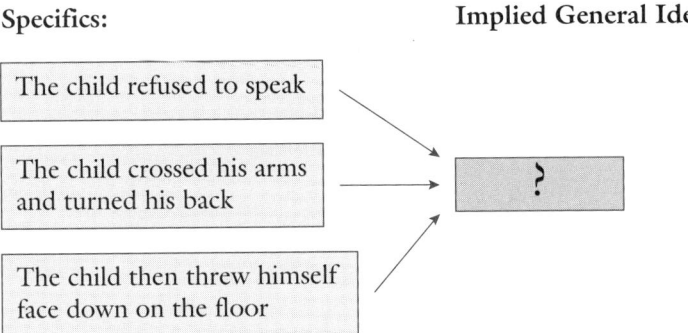

You probably determined that the child was angry or having a temper tantrum.

<table>
<tr><td>**EXERCISE**
7-9</td><td>**Directions:** Find a word from the list below that describes the larger idea or situation each set of specifics suggests. Each will require you to infer a general idea.</td></tr>
</table>

tonsillitis	closed	dying	flu	accident
power outage	accident	a burglary	going to fast	

1. The child has a headache

   The child has a queasy stomach.

   The child a mild fever.

   General Idea: The child had the _____.

2. The plant's leaves were withered.

   The blossoms had dropped.

   Its stem was drooping.

   General Idea: The plant is _____.

3. The windshield of the car was shattered.

   The door panel was dented.

   The bumper was crumpled.

   General Idea: The car had been in a(an) _____.

4. The lights went out.

The clock radio flashed.

The refrigerator stopped running.

   General Idea: There was a _____.

5. The supermarket door was locked.

The parking lot was nearly empty.

A few remaining customers were checking out.

   General Idea: The supermarket was _____.

Implied Ideas in Paragraphs

In paragraphs, writers sometimes leave their main idea unstated. The paragraph contains only details. It is up to you, the reader, to infer the writer's main point. You can visualize this type of paragraph as follows:

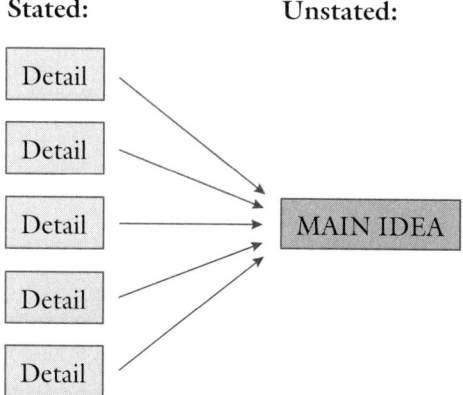

The details, when taken together, all point to a larger, more important idea. Think of the paragraph as a list of facts that you must add up or put together to determine the meaning of the paragraph as a whole. Use the following steps as a guide to find implied main ideas:

1. **Find the topic.** Ask yourself, "What is the one thing the author is discussing throughout the paragraph?"
2. **Decide what the writer wants you to know about that topic.** Look at each detail and decide what larger general idea each explains.
3. **Express this idea in your own words.** Make sure the main idea is a reasonable one. Ask yourself, "Does it apply to all the details in the paragraphs?"

Read the following paragraph; then follow the three steps listed above.

> Some advertisers rely on star power. Commercials may use celebrities to encourage consumers to purchase a product. Other commercials may use an "everyone's buying it" approach that argues that thousands of consumers could not possibly be wrong in their choice, so the product must be worthwhile. Still other commercials may use visual appeal to catch the consumers' interest and persuade them to make purchases.

The topic of this paragraph is commercials. More specifically it is about devices advertisers use to build commercials. Three details are given: use of star power, an everybody's-buying-it approach, and visual appeal. Each of the three details is a different persuasive device. The main point the writer is trying to make, then, is that commercials use various persuasive devices to appeal to consumers. Notice that no single sentence states this idea clearly.

You can visualize this paragraph as follows:

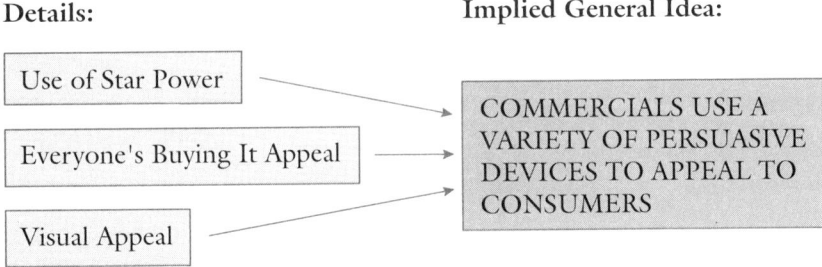

Details:

Use of Star Power

Everyone's Buying It Appeal

Visual Appeal

Implied General Idea:

COMMERCIALS USE A VARIETY OF PERSUASIVE DEVICES TO APPEAL TO CONSUMERS

Here is another paragraph. Read it and then fill in the diagram that follows:

> Yellow is a bright, cheery color; it is often associated with spring and hopefulness. Green, since it is a color that appears frequently in nature (trees, grass, plants), has come to suggest growth and rebirth. Blue, the color of the sky, may suggest eternity or endless beauty. Red, the color of both blood and fire, is often connected with strong feelings such as courage, lust, and rage.

Topic: <u>Colors</u>

Details: Implied General Idea:

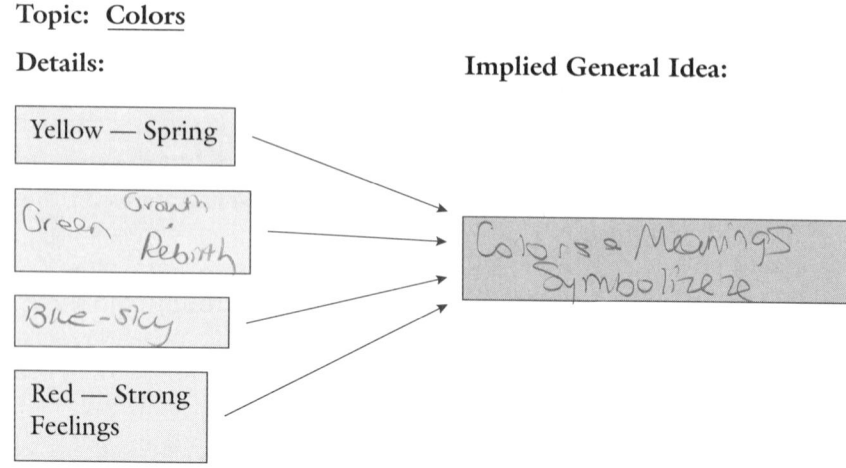

How to Know if You Have Made a Reasonable Inference

There is a test you can do to discover if you inferred a reasonable main idea. The idea you infer to be the main idea should be broad enough so that every sentence in the paragraph explains the idea you have chosen. Work through the paragraph, sentence by sentence. Check to see that each sentence explains or gives more information about the idea you have chosen. If some sentences do not explain your chosen idea, your main idea probably is not broad enough. Work on expanding your idea and making it more general.

EXERCISE 7-10	**Directions:** Read each of the following paragraphs and complete the diagram that follows.

A. Workers in the **primary sector** of an economy extract resources directly from Earth. Most workers in this sector are usually in agriculture, but the sector also includes fishing, forestry, and mining. Workers in the **secondary sector** transform raw materials produced by the primary sector into manufactured goods. Construction is included in this sector. All other jobs in an economy are within the **tertiary sector**, sometimes called the **service sector**. The tertiary sector includes a great range of occupations, from a store clerk to a surgeon, from a movie ticket seller to a nuclear physicist, from a dancer to a political leader.[27]

Details: Implied General Idea:

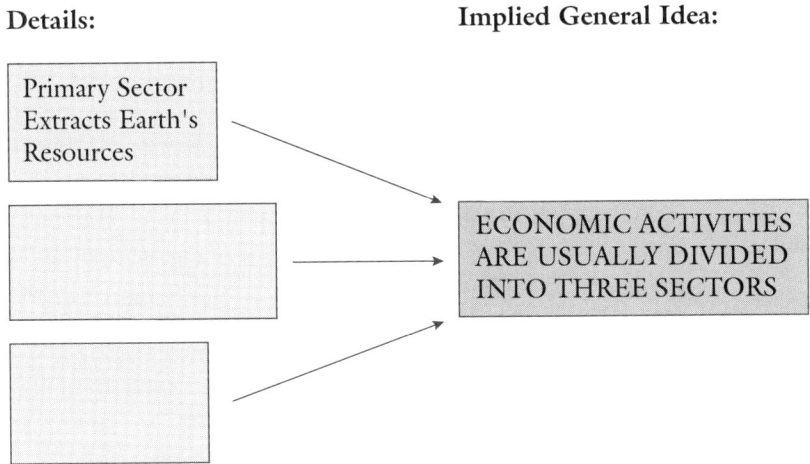

B. Among many other activities, urban gangs fight among themselves and prey on the weak and vulnerable. They delight in demonstrating ownership and control of their "turf," and they sometimes turn neighborhoods into war zones in defense of it. Once gangs form, their graffiti soon adorn buildings and alleyways, and membership is displayed through hand signs, clothing, and special colors. As a newly formed gang grows in reputation and confidence, it soon finds itself attracting those who would like to be members in order to reap the benefits: safety, or girlfriends, or a reputation for toughness.[28]

Details: Implied Main Idea:

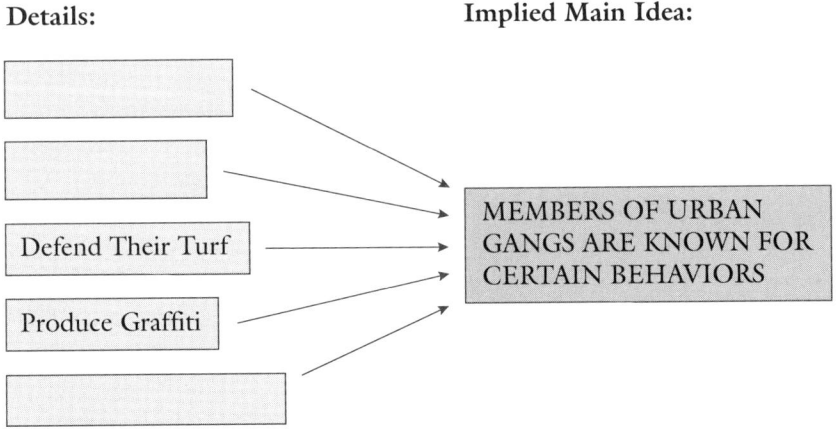

C. For many smokers, the road to quitting is too rough to travel alone. Some smokers turn to nontobacco products to help them quit; products such as nicotine chewing gum and the nicotine patch replace depleted levels of nicotine in the bloodstream and ease the process of quitting. Aversion therapy techniques attempt to reduce smoking by pairing the act of smoking with some sort of noxious stimulus so that smoking itself is perceived as unpleasant. For example, the technique of rapid smoking instructs patients to smoke rapidly and continuously until they exceed their tolerance for cigarette smoke, producing unpleasant sensations. Proponents of self-control strategies view smoking as a learned habit associated with specific situations. Therapy is aimed at identifying these situations and teaching smokers the skills necessary to resist smoking.[29]

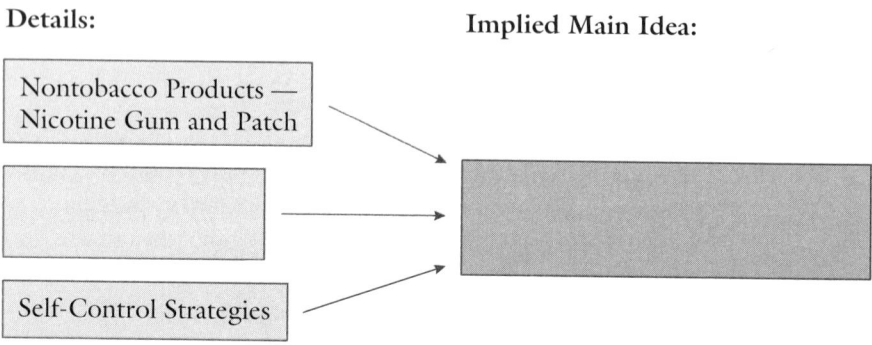

Details:

Nontobacco Products — Nicotine Gum and Patch

Self-Control Strategies

Implied Main Idea:

D. How should you present your speech? Let's consider your options. An **impromptu speech** is delivered on the spur of the moment, without preparation. The ability to speak off the cuff is useful in an emergency, but impromptu speeches produce unpredictable outcomes. It's certainly not a good idea to rely on impromptu speaking in place of solid preparation. Another option is a **memorized speech**. Speakers who use memorized presentations are usually most effective when they write their speeches to sound like informal and conversational speech rather than formal, written essays. A **manuscript speech** is written out beforehand and then read from a manuscript or TelePrompTer. When extremely careful wording is required (for example, when the president addresses Congress), the manuscript speech is appropriate. However, most speeches that you'll deliver will be extemporaneous. An **extemporaneous speech** is one that is prepared in advance and presented from abbreviated notes. Extemporaneous speeches are nearly as polished as memorized ones, but they are more vigorous, flexible, and spontaneous.[30]

Details: **Implied Main Idea:**

| Impromptu —
No Preparation |

| Memorized |

E. In order to measure social class standing, sociologists may use the *objective* method, which ranks individuals into classes on the basis of measures such as education, income, and occupational prestige. Sociologists may also use the *reputational* method, which places people into various social classes on the basis of reputation in the community (Warner 1960). A third method, *self-identification,* allows people to place themselves in a social class. Although people can readily place themselves in a class, the results are often difficult to interpret. People might be hesitant to call themselves upper-class for fear of appearing snobbish, but at the same time they might be reluctant to call themselves lower-class for fear of being stigmatized. The net result is that the method of self-identification substantially overestimates the middle portion of the class system.[31]

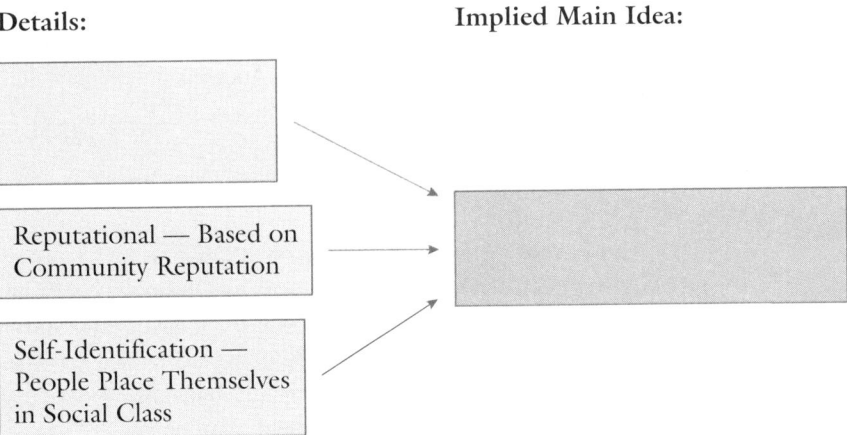

Details: **Implied Main Idea:**

EXERCISE 7-11

Directions: Read each of the following paragraphs and answer the questions that follow.

A. Thanks to the Internet, you can shop 24 hours a day without leaving home, you can read today's newspaper without getting drenched picking up a hard copy in a rainstorm, and you don't have to wait for the 6:00 news to find out what the weather will be like tomorrow—at home or around the globe. And, with the increasing use of handheld devices and wireless communications, you can get that same information—from stock quotes to the weather—even when you're away from your computer.[32]

1. What is the topic? *Internet*

2. What is the implied main idea? *you can use 24 hours a day*

B. Watch a nursery school teacher talk to preschool children and you'll see how age gaps of twenty years or more can be overcome. Nursery school teachers know that they must adapt to their young listeners or risk chaos. They adapt partly by simplifying their vocabulary and shortening their sentences. If you've ever read a story to a child, you know another secret to engaging youngsters. If you talk like a wizard or a teapot or a mouse, you can see children's eyes widen.[33]

1. What is the topic? _____

2. What is the implied main idea? _____

_____

C. The Federal Trade Commission has taken action against several infomercial producers when it decided their programs had the potential to be deceptive because viewers might believe the infomercial is a *bona fide* show. Some viewers have sued TV stations for losses when they were deceived by the advertisers. To avoid these problems, some infomercial producers and television stations voluntarily include a disclaimer to avoid lawsuits claiming deception or FTC actions. But because people tend to change channels frequently they may miss the disclaimer and thus be unaware of the true nature of the infomercial.[34]

1. What is the topic? _____

2. What is the implied main idea? _____

_____

D. Sleep conserves body energy so that we are rested and ready to perform during high-performance daylight hours. Sleep also restores the neurotransmitters that have been depleted during the waking hours. This process clears the brain of unimportant details as a means of preparing for a new day. Getting enough sleep to feel ready to meet daily challenges is a key factor in maintaining optimal physical and psychological status.[35]

1. What is the topic? _____

2. What is the implied main idea? _____

_____

E. Research suggests that women who are considered attractive are more effective in changing attitudes than are women thought to be less attractive. In addition, more attractive individuals are often considered to be more credible than less attractive people. They are also perceived to be happier, more popular, more sociable, and more successful than are those rated as being less attractive. With respect to shape and body size, people with fat, round silhouettes are consistently rated as older, more old-fashioned, less good-looking, more talkative, and more good-natured. Athletic, muscular people are rated as more mature, better looking, taller, and more adventurous. Tall and thin people are rated as more ambitious, more suspicious of others, more tense and nervous, more pessimistic, and quieter.[36]

1. What is the topic? _____

2. What is the implied main idea? _____

_____

EXERCISE 7-12	**Directions:** None of the following paragraphs has a topic sentence. Read each paragraph and, in the space provided, write a sentence that expresses the main idea.

A. Immigration has contributed to the dramatic population growth of the United States over the past 150 years. It has also contributed to the country's shift from a rural to an urban economy. Immigrants provided inexpensive labor which allowed industries to flourish. Native-born children of immigrants, benefitting from education, moved into professional and white collar jobs, creating a new middle class. Immigration also increased the U.S. mortality rate. Due to crowded housing and unhealthy living conditions, disease and fatal illness were common.[37]

Implied Main Idea: _Immigration   Contributions_

B. Jack Schultz and Ian Baldwin found last summer that trees under attack by insects or animals will release an unidentified chemical into the air as a distress signal. Upon receiving the signal, nearby trees step up their production of tannin—a poison in the leaves that gives insects indigestion. The team learned, too, that production of the poison is in proportion to the duration and intensity of the attack.[38]

Implied Main Idea: _Production of unidentified_
chemicals in the air

C. When President Lincoln was shot, the word was communicated by telegraph to most parts of the United States, but because we had no links to England, it was five days before London heard of the event. When President Reagan was shot, journalist Henry Fairlie, working at his typewriter within a block of the shooting, got word of it by telephone from his editor at the Spectator in London, who had seen a rerun of the assassination attempt on television shortly after it occurred.[39]

Implied Main Idea: _Speed of communication_
has changed

D. Suppose you wanted to teach your pet chimpanzee the English language. How would you go about it? Two psychologists raised Gua, a female chimpanzee, at home with their son, Donald. Both boy and chimp were encouraged to speak, but only Donald did. Gua indicated she could comprehend some language, for she could respond appropriately to about 70 different utterances, but she never produced a single word. A second attempt involved more intensive training in speech, and Viki, another chimpanzee, was eventually able to pronounce three recognizable words: "Mama," "Papa," and "cup."[40]

Implied Main Idea: _Learning chimpanzees how_
to talk the English language

E. Traffic is directed by color. Pilot instrument panels, landing strips, road and water crossings are regulated by many colored lights and signs. Factories use colors to distinguish between thoroughfares and work areas. Danger zones are painted in special colors. Lubrication points and removable parts are accentuated by color. Pipes for transporting water, steam, oil, chemicals, and compressed air are designated by different colors. Electrical wires and resistances are color coded.[41]

Implied Main Idea: _Distinguishing and regulations of lights and signs._

F. The Grand Canyon and the Colorado River and its banks are deteriorating due to the ever-increasing numbers of visitors descending into the Canyon and the thousands each year who enjoy its river-rafting thrills. Likewise, Banff National Park, Canada's oldest national park, continues to suffer from the millions of visitors it receives annually. Many places in its tundra wilderness have been severely trampled by hikers. In Yosemite National Park, the increase in vehicle traffic through the park causes the very air pollution that visitors try to escape by fleeing to national parks.[42]

Implied Main Idea: _Increasing populations in National Parks_

G. As the effects of caffeine begin to wear off, users may feel let down, mentally or physically depressed, exhausted, and weak. To counteract these effects, people commonly choose to drink another cup of coffee. But before you say yes to another cup of coffee, consider this. Although you would have to drink between 67 and 100 cups of coffee in a day to produce a fatal overdose of caffeine, you may experience sensory disturbances after consuming only 10 cups of coffee within a 24-hour period. These symptoms include tinnitus (ringing in the ears), spots before the eyes, numbness in arms and legs, poor circulation, and visual hallucinations. Because 10 cups of coffee is not an extraordinary amount for many people to drink within a 24-hour period, caffeine use is clearly something to think about.[43]

Implied Main Idea: _Symptoms on overdose of caffeine._

H. In 1947, the Levitt Company was finishing up Levittown. Practically overnight, what was formerly a Long Island potato field 25 miles east of Manhattan became one of America's newest suburbs, changing the way homes were built. The land was bulldozed and the trees removed, and then trucks dropped building materials at precise 60-foot intervals. Construction was divided into 27 distinct steps. At the peak of production, the company constructed 30 new single-family homes each day.[44]

Implied Main Idea: *Causes of America's newest suburbs.*

I. Pathogens, also known as disease carrying agents, may be transmitted by direct contact between infected persons, such as sexual relations, kissing, or touching. Pathogens may also be spread by indirect contact, such as touching an object the infected person has had contact with. The hands are probably the greatest source of infectious disease transmission. For example, you may touch the handle of a drinking fountain that was just touched by a person whose hands were contaminated by a recent sneeze. You may also autoinoculate yourself, or transmit a pathogen from one part of your body to another. For example, you may touch a sore on your lip that is teeming with the viral herpes and then transmit the virus to your eye when you subsequently scratch your itchy eyelid.[45]

Implied Main Idea: *Pathogens - Causes and Effects.*

H. *Turn-requesting cues* tell the speaker that you, as a listener, would like to take a turn as speaker; you might transmit these cues by using some vocalized "er" or "um" that tells the speaker that you would now like to speak, by opening your eyes and mouth as if to say something, by beginning to gesture with a hand, or by leaning forward.

Through *turn-denying cues* you indicate your reluctance to assume the role of speaker by, for example, intoning a slurred "I don't know"; giving the speaker some brief grunt that signals you have nothing to say; avoiding eye contact with the speaker who wishes you now to take on the role of speaker; or engaging in some behavior that is incompatible with speaking—for example, coughing or blowing your nose.

Through *backchanneling cues* you communicate various meanings back to the speaker—but without assuming the role of the speaker. For example, you can indicate your *agreement* or *disagreement* with the speaker through smiles or frowns, nods of approval or disapproval; brief comments such as "right," "exactly," or "never"; or vocalizations such as "uh-huh" or "uh-uh."

Implied Main Idea: *Types of speakers*

WORKING TOGETHER

Directions: Separate into groups. Using a reading selection from Part Six of this book, work with your group to identify and underline the topic sentence of each paragraph. If any of the main ideas are unstated, write a sentence that states the main idea. When all the groups have completed the task, the class will compare the findings of the various groups.

MASTERING VOCABULARY

Directions: Select the answer that best provides the meaning of each word as it was used in this chapter. Use context clues, word parts, and a dictionary, if necessary.

_____ 1. prohibits (p. 187)
   a. recognizes
   b. forbids
   c. encourages
   d. identifies

_____ 2. proclaimed (p. 188)
   a. unstated
   b. ignored
   c. declared
   d. generated

_____ 3. precise (p. 188)
   a. exact
   b. speedy
   c. general
   d. slow

_____ 4. dissent (p. 192)
   a. crime
   b. disagreement
   c. people
   d. harmony

_____ 5. accumulated (p. 193)
   a. intellectual
   b. collected
   c. specific
   d. practical

_____ 6. prospered (p. 193)
   a. progressed
   b. worked
   c. communicated
   d. joked

_____ 7. dramatic (p. 207)
   a. limiting
   b. simultaneous
   c. impressive
   d. blunt

_____ 8. duration (p. 208)
   a. heaviness
   b. harshness
   c. difficulty
   d. length of time

_____ 9. intensive (p. 208)
   a. objective
   b. subtle
   c. simple
   d. concentrated

_____ 10. accentuated (p. 209)
   a. highlighted
   b. hidden
   c. negatively perceived
   d. made duller

SELF-TEST SUMMARY

Name and describe the four essential parts of a paragraph.	The four parts of a paragraph are: • **Topic.** The topic is the one thing the entire paragraph is about. • **Main idea.** The main idea is the most important idea the writer wants the reader to know about the topic. • **Details.** Details are facts and ideas that support the main idea. • **Transitions.** Transitions are words and phrases that lead the reader from one idea to another.
What sentence states the main idea of a paragraph?	The topic sentence states the main idea of a paragraph.
Where is the topic sentence located?	The topic sentence can be located anywhere in the paragraph, but the most common positions are first, last, in the middle, or first and last.
What are implied main ideas?	Implied main ideas are suggested but not directly stated in the paragraph.
How can one figure out implied main ideas?	To find implied main ideas: • find the topic • figure out what general ideas for the paragraph explains • express the idea in your own words

Name _____

Section _____ Date _____

Number right _____ x 20 points = Score _____

Directions: For each of the following situations, indicate which choice best explains what the writer is implying.

_D_ 1. Muttering angrily to himself, Edgar stomped into his office and packed all of his belongings in a cardboard box. Mrs. Chen, the personnel director, soon arrived at his door and escorted him out of the building.
  a. Edgar was going home sick.
  b. The building was being evacuated.
  c. Mrs. Chen wanted to talk to him about his job.
  d. Edgar had been fired.

_B_ 2. We felt relaxed and happy. No telephone, no fax machine, no traffic jam at the end of the day. Just the wide open beach and all the seafood we could eat.
  a. The writer was on a business trip.
  b. The writer was on vacation.
  c. The writer was at a party.
  d. The writer was working at a restaurant.

_A_ 3. The entire classroom was silent except for the sound of Professor Seiquist's footsteps as he walked up and down the aisles. Everywhere he looked, students were writing busily on the papers in front of them, some pausing briefly to look into space with expressions of intense concentration before continuing to write.

  a. Professor Seiquist's class was taking a test.
  b. Professor Seiquist was conducting an experiment.
  c. The class was writing an evaluation of Professor Seiquist.
  d. The class was taking a break from studying.

_B_ 4. Even though it was just past noon, the sky was growing dark. Heavy clouds were moving along the horizon. The air felt thick and all of the birds seemed to be holding their breath.
  a. It was summertime.
  b. A storm was coming.
  c. A solar eclipse was taking place.
  d. A storm had just passed.

_C_ 5. Rosa stood up, wiping the dirt from her hands and the knees of her jeans before picking up the trowel and going inside. As she gulped a cold drink, she hoped that her hard work today would pay off later in the summer.
  a. Rosa was painting her house.
  b. Rosa was doing repairs around the house.
  c. Rosa was planting a garden.
  d. Rosa was helping a friend do yard work.

Name _____

Section _____ Date _____

Number right _____ x 20 points = Score _____

Directions: Read each of the following paragraphs and select the answer that correctly identifies the paragraph's main idea.

 B 1. Many "everyday" consumers have become entrepreneurs by participating in **virtual auctions**. Millions of consumers log on to eBay.com and other auction sites to bid on an enormous variety of new and used items offered by both businesses and individuals. From an economic standpoint, auctions offer savvy consumers the opportunity to buy overruns or excess inventories of new items at discounted prices much as they would in bricks-and-mortar discount stores. For many, however, the auctions also have become a form of entertainment. Players in the auction game spend hours a day on the auction sites, buying and selling collectibles or other items of (assumed?) value.[47]

a. Millions of consumers use eBay.com to buy and sell a wide variety of items.

b. Virtual auctions offer consumers the chance to buy and sell items and to be entertained.

c. Virtual auctions provide the same service as traditional discount stores.

d. Most consumers view virtual auctions as a form of entertainment.

 2. Pollutants have diverse sources. Some come from a *point source*—they enter a stream at a specific location, such as a wastewater discharge pipe. Others may come from a *nonpoint source*—they come from a large diffuse area, as happens when organic matter or fertilizer washes from a field during a storm. Point-source pollutants are usually smaller in quantity and much easier to control. Nonpoint sources usually pollute in greater quantities and are much harder to control.[48]

a. Point sources of pollution include wastewater discharge pipes.

b. Nonpoint sources of pollution are worse for the environment than point sources.

c. Nonpoint-source pollutants come from a widespread area, whereas point-source pollutants come from a specific location.

d. Pollutants can come from point or nonpoint sources.

_C_ 3. Much as feedback contains information about messages already sent, **feedforward** is information about messages before you send them. Opening comments such as "Wait until you hear this" or "Don't get me wrong, but . . ." are examples of feedforward. These messages tell the listener something about the messages to come or about the way you'd like the listener to respond. Nonverbally, feedforward is given by your facial expression, eye contact, and physical posture, for example; with these nonverbal messages you tell the other person something about the messages you'll be sending.[49]

a. Feedback is the opposite of feedforward.
b. Feedforward consists primarily of nonverbal messages.
c. Feedforward describes information that comes before a message is sent.
d. Feedback and feedforward are both necessary to communication.

_X_ 4. Support groups are an important part of stress management. Friends, family members, and co-workers can provide us with emotional and physical support. Although the ideal support group differs for each of us, you should have one or two close friends in whom you are able to confide and neighbors with whom you can trade favors. You should take the opportunity to participate in community activities at least once a week. A healthy, committed relationship can also provide vital support.[50]

a. Support groups are important in managing stress.
b. Support groups consist of friends and family.
c. Participation in community activities is one way of managing stress.
d. The ideal support group is different for each person.

_____ 5. Nowhere in the world is the love affair with the automobile stronger than in North America. Much of the credit for this attraction goes to the pioneering genius of Henry Ford, who ushered in the age of mass automobile travel with his famous Model T. Between 1908 and 1923, 15 million of these affordable cars were produced. The car is now more than simply transportation for most Americans; it is a symbol of freedom and individualized lifestyles.[51]

a. Henry Ford popularized mass automobile travel with his Model T.
b. Fifteen million Model T cars were produced between 1908 and 1923.
c. Americans love their cars.
d. Cars represent freedom and independence to Americans.

**CHAPTER 7
MASTERY TEST 3:
Paragraph Skills**

Name _____
Section _____ Date _____
Number right _____ x 10 points = Score _____

Directions: Read the following selection from a communications textbook and select the letter of the answer that best completes each statement.

1   The messages communicated by the eyes vary depending on the duration, direction, and quality of the eye behavior. In every culture, there are rather strict, though unstated, rules for the proper duration for eye contact. In much of England and the United States, for example, the average length of gaze is 2.95 seconds. The average length of mutual gaze (two persons gazing at each other) is 1.18 seconds. When eye contact falls short of this amount, you may think the person in uninterested, shy, or preoccupied. When the appropriate amount of time is exceeded, you may perceive this as showing high interest.

2   In much of the United States direct eye contact is considered an expression of honesty and forthrightness. But, the Japanese often view this as a lack of respect. The Japanese will glance at the other person's face rarely and then only for very short periods. In many Hispanic cultures direct eye contact signifies a certain equality and so should be avoided by, say, children when speaking to a person in authority. Try visualizing the potential misunderstandings that eye communication alone could create when people from Tokyo, San Francisco, and San Juan try to communicate.

3   The direction of the eye also communicates. Generally, in communicating with another person, you would glance alternatively at the other person's face, then away, then again at the face, and so on. When these directional rules are broken, different mean-

ings are communicated—abnormally high or low interest, self-consciousness, or nervousness over the interaction. The quality—how wide or how narrow your eyes get during interaction—also communicates meaning, especially interest level and such emotions as surprise, fear, and disgust.

4   On average we blink about 15 times a minute, in part to lubricate and protect the eye. You may increase blinking if you're uncomfortable or under lots of stress. For example, you would probably increase your blinking rate if you were being interrogated by the police. Excess blinking is one of the cues people use to detect lying and so it may communicate a kind of nervousness over telling a lie. In actual fact, however, it may be due to dry eyes.

 1. The topic of paragraph 1 is
   a. gazes.
   b. eye contact.
   c. cultures.
   d. time.

 2. The topic sentence of paragraph 1 is expressed in the
   a. first sentence.
   b. second sentence.
   c. fifth sentence.
   d. sixth sentence.

3. Which of the following is the topic of paragraph 2?
   a. direct eye contact
   b. honesty
   c. correcting misunderstandings
   d. Hispanic cultures

 4. Which of the following sentences in paragraph 2 does *not* add information on what different cultures think about eye contact?
   a. first
   b. second
   c. third
   d. fourth

 5. Which of the following sentences best states the implied main idea of paragraph 2?
   a. Talking to a person from another culture is difficult.
   b. Different cultures have different rules about making direct eye contact.
   c. The Japanese have the most strict rules about eye contact.
   d. Direct eye contact should be avoided except in the United States.

6. The topic of paragraph 3 is expressed in the
   a. first sentence.
   b. second sentence.
   c. third sentence.
   d. last sentence.

 7. The topic of paragraph 3 is
   a. glancing compared to staring.
   b. nervousness and fear.
   c. self-consciousness.
   d. the direction and quality of eye contact.

 8. The topic of paragraph 4 is
   a. dry eyes.
   b. lubrication.
   c. detecting lying.
   d. blinking.

 9. Which of the following sentences best expresses the implied main idea of paragraph 4?
   a. Nervous people have dry eyes.
   b. The primary purpose of blinking is to protect the eyes.
   c. Blinking a lot proves one is lying.
   d. Blinking increases under stress or discomfort.

 10. The purpose of the last sentence in paragraph 4 is to show that
   a. blinking may not be a sign of lying.
   b. people get nervous when they have dry eyes.
   c. lying is due to dry eyes.
   d. blinking causes dry eyes.

<table>
<tr><td>**CHAPTER 7**
MASTERY TEST 4:
Reading Selection</td><td>Name _____
Section _____ Date _____
Number right _____ x 10 point = Score _____</td></tr>
</table>

"Don't Ask"

Deborah Tannen

Men and women differ in many ways, including how they communicate. You'll probably recognize some of the differences Tannen describes in this excerpt taken from her book, *You Just Don't Understand*.

Vocabulary Preview

asymmetries (par. 1) lack of harmony and balance

status (par. 1) position or rank; one's standing in relation to others

paradox (par. 4) a situation that may seem to be contradictory, but in fact is or may be true

metamessages (par. 4) meanings that appear beneath the surface; hidden meanings

framed (par. 5) placed within a context

implicit (par. 6) not directly stated

theoretically (par. 6) based on theory, hypothetical

1   Talking about troubles is just one of many conversational tasks that women and men view differently, and that consequently causes trouble in talk between them. Another is asking for information. And this difference too is traceable to the asymmetries of status and connection.

2   A man and a woman were standing beside the information booth at the Washington Folk Life Festival, a sprawling complex of booths and displays. "You ask," the man was saying to the woman. "I don't ask."

3   Sitting in the front seat of the car beside Harold, Sybil is fuming. They have been driving around for half an hour looking for a street he is sure is close by. Sybil is angry not because Harold does not know the way, but because he insists on trying to find it himself rather than stopping and asking someone. Her anger stems from viewing his behavior through the lens of her own: If she were driving, she would have asked directions as soon as she realized she didn't know which way to go, and they'd now be comfortably ensconced in their friends' living room instead of driving in circles, as the hour gets later and later. Since asking directions does not make Sybil uncomfortable, refusing to ask makes no sense to her. But in Harold's world, driving around until he finds his way is the reasonable thing to do, since asking for help makes him uncomfortable. He's avoiding that discomfort and trying to maintain his sense of himself as a self-sufficient person.

4   Why do many men resist asking for directions and other kinds of information? And, it is just as reasonable to ask, why is it that many women don't? By the paradox of independence and intimacy, there are two simultaneous and different metamessages implied in asking for and giving information. Many men tend to focus on one, many women on the other.

5   When you offer information, the information itself is the message. But the fact that you have the information, and the person you are speaking to doesn't, also sends a

metamessage of superiority. If relations are inherently hierarchical, then the one who has more information is framed as higher up on the ladder, by virtue of being more knowledgeable and competent. From this perspective, finding one's own way is an essential part of the independence that men perceive to be a prerequisite for self-respect. If self-respect is bought at the cost of a few extra minutes of travel time, it is well worth the price.

6   Because they are implicit, metamessages are hard to talk about. When Sybil begs to know why Harold won't just ask someone for directions, he answers in terms of the message, the information: He says there's no point in asking, because anyone he asks may not know and may give him wrong directions. This is theoretically reasonable. There are many countries, such as, for example,

Mexico, where it is standard procedure for people to make up directions rather than refuse to give requested information. But this explanation frustrates Sybil, because it doesn't make sense to her. Although she realizes that someone might give faulty directions, she believes this is relatively unlikely, and surely it cannot happen every time. Even if it did happen, they would be in no worse shape than they are in now anyway.

7   Part of the reason for their different approaches is that Sybil believes that a person who doesn't know the answer will say so, because it is easy to say, "I don't know." But Harold believes that saying "I don't know" is humiliating, so people might well take a wild guess. Because of their different assumptions, and the invisibility of framing, Harold and Sybil can never get to the bottom of this difference; they can only get more

frustrated with each other. Keeping talk on the message level is common, because it is the level we are most clearly aware of. But it is unlikely to resolve confusion since our true motivations lie elsewhere.

8   To the extent that giving information, directions, or help is of use to another, it reinforces bonds between people. But to the extent that it is asymmetrical, it creates hierarchy: Insofar as giving information frames one as the expert, superior in knowledge, and the other as uninformed, inferior in knowledge, it is a move in the negotiation of status.

9   It is easy to see that there are many situations where those who give information are higher in status. For example, parents explain things to children and answer their questions, just as teachers give information to students. An awareness of this dynamic underlies one requirement for proper behavior at Japanese dinner entertainment, according to anthropologist Harumi Befu. In order to help the highest-status member of the party to dominate the conversation, others at the dinner are expected to ask him questions that they know he can answer with authority.

10   Because of this potential for asymmetry, some men resist receiving information from others, especially women, and some women are cautious about stating information that they know, especially to men. For example, a man with whom I discussed these dynamics later told me that my perspective clarified a comment made by his wife. They had gotten into their car and were about to go to a destination that she knew well but he did not know at all. Consciously resisting an impulse to just drive off and find his own way, he began by asking his wife if she had any advice about the best way to get there. She

told him the way, then added, "But I don't know. That's how I would go, but there might be a better way." Her comment was a move to redress the imbalance of power created by her knowing something he didn't know. She was also saving face in advance, in case he decided not to take her advice. Furthermore, she was reframing her directions as "just a suggestion" rather than "giving instructions."

Directions: Choose the best answer for each of the following questions.

CHECKING YOUR COMPREHENSION

_____ 1. The main point of the passage is
   a. men and women differ on asking for information because of how they think about relationships.
   b. men and women ask for directions in different ways.
   c. women are willing to ask for help because they are bad at remembering directions.
   d. you shouldn't give information to others because you will embarrass them.

_____ 2. The main idea of paragraph 5 is
   a. men have a fragile sense of self-respect.
   b. answers to questions are more important than the metamessages.
   c. men seem to need to retain their sense of superiority in relationships.
   d. because relations are based on gender, being competent is not important.

_____ 3. The main point of paragraph 7 is that
   a. information is more important than what motivates Harold and Sybil.
   b. Harold and Sybil have unspoken beliefs about what motivates people.
   c. Harold and Sybil know they have different approaches to asking for information.
   d. Harold and Sybil can never understand each other.

_____ 4. According to Harold's reasoning, when asked for directions, most people will
   a. try to embarrass him for having asked for help.
   b. be uncomfortable and avoid his question.
   c. lead him to his destination.
   d. give wrong directions rather than say "I don't know."

_____ 5. According to the passage, the wife said she wasn't sure her directions were the best because
   a. she has forgotten how to reach their destination.
   b. she was being considerate of how her husband would feel.
   c. she would prefer to ask for directions along the way.
   d. she wanted to confuse her husband with unclear advice.

_____ 6. In paragraph 5, the word "hierarchical" means
   a. formal or stylized.
   b. powerless.
   c. arranged in a set order.
   d. not directly stated.

APPLYING YOUR SKILLS

_____ 7. Which of the following sentences best states the implied main idea of paragraph 3?
   a. Sybil is angry.
   b. Harold is driving around in circles.
   c. Sybil does not understand Harold.
   d. Sybil is comfortable asking for directions, but Harold is uncomfortable.

_____ 8. Which sentence in paragraph 9 is the topic sentence?
   a. first sentence
   b. second sentence
   c. third sentence
   d. fourth sentence

_____ 9. Which of the following sentences best states the implied main idea of paragraph 8?
   a. Giving directions and information is helpful, but it also creates hierarchy.
   b. Negotiation of status depends on hierarchy.
   c. Direction-giving reinforces bonds between people.
   d. Giving directions creates a superior and an inferior position.

_____ 10. Which of the following sentences expresses the main idea of paragraph 10?
   a. first sentence
   b. second sentence
   c. fourth sentence
   d. last sentence

8

Understanding Paragraphs: Supporting Details and Transitions

THIS CHAPTER WILL SHOW YOU HOW TO

1. Recognize supporting details
2. Identify types of supporting details
3. Use transitions to guide your reading
4. Paraphrase paragraphs

Suppose you read the following sentence in a communication textbook. It appears as the opening sentence of a paragraph.

Men and women communicate differently in their nonverbal messages.

After reading this sentence you are probably wondering how the nonverbal communication, also known as body language, differs between the sexes.

Only poor writers make statements without supporting them. So you expect, then, that in the remainder of the paragraph the author will support his statement about gender differences in nonverbal communication. Here is the full paragraph.

Men and women communicate differently in their nonverbal messages. You may have observed some or all of these differences in your daily interactions. Women smile more than men. Women stand closer to each other than men do.

When they speak, both men and women look at men more than at women. Women both touch and are touched more than men. Men extend their bodies, taking up greater areas of space, than women.[1]

In this paragraph, the author explained his statement by giving examples of gender differences. The first sentence expresses the main idea; the remaining sentences are supporting details. You will recall from Chapter 7 that a paragraph has four essential elements.

- **Topic**—the one thing the whole paragraph is about
- **Main idea**—the broad, general idea the whole paragraph is concerned with
- **Supporting details**—the ideas that explain or support the main idea
- **Transitions**—the words or phrases that link ideas together

This chapter will focus on how to recognize supporting details and how to use transitions to guide your reading. You will also learn how to paraphrase paragraphs and longer pieces of writing.

RECOGNIZING SUPPORTING DETAILS

Supporting details are those facts and ideas that prove or explain the main idea of a paragraph. While all the details in a paragraph do support the main idea, not all details are equally important. As you read, try to identify and pay attention to the most important details. Pay less attention to details of lesser importance. The **key details** directly explain the main idea. Other **minor details** may provide additional information, offer an example, or further explain one of the key details.

The diagram in Figure 8-1 shows how details relate to the main idea and how details range in degree of importance. In the diagram, less important details appear below the important details they explain.

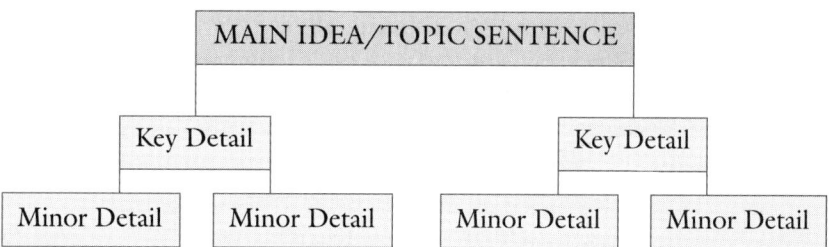

Figure 8-1

Read the following paragraph and study the diagram that follows.

The skin of the human body has several functions. First, it serves as a protective covering. In doing so, it accounts for 17 percent of the body weight. Skin also protects the organs within the body from damage or harm. The skin serves as a regulator of body functions. It controls body temperature and water loss. Finally, the skin serves as a receiver. It is sensitive to touch and temperature.

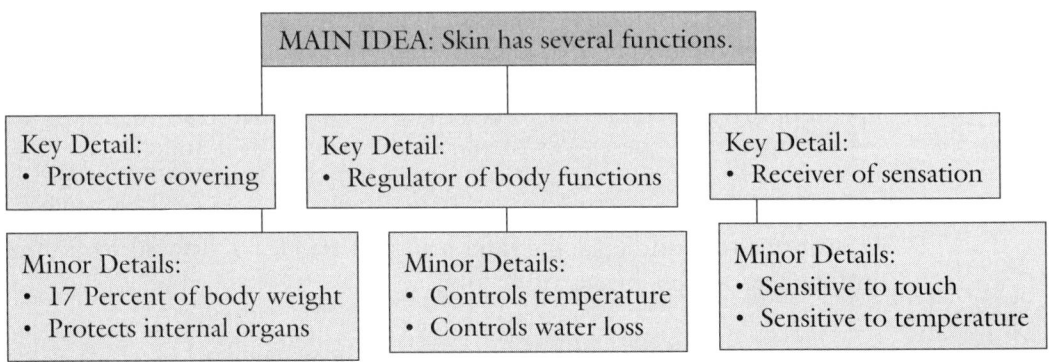

Figure 8-2

From the diagram in Figure 8-2 you can see that the details that state the three functions of skin are the key details. Other details, such as "protects internal organs," provide further information and are at a lower level of importance.

Read the following paragraph and try to pick out the more important details.

Communication occurs with words and gestures but did you know it also occurs through the sense of smell? Odor can communicate at least four types of messages. First, odor can signal attraction. Animals give off scents to attract members of the opposite sex. Humans use fragrances to make themselves more appealing or attractive. Smell also communicates information about tastes. The smell of popcorn popping stimulates the appetite. If you smell a chicken roasting you can anticipate its taste. A third type of smell communication is through memory. A smell can help you recall an event that occurred months or even years ago, especially if the event was an emotional one. Finally, smell can communicate by creating an identity or image for a person or product. For example, a woman may wear only one brand of perfume. Or a brand of shaving cream may have a distinct fragrance, which allows users to recognize it. [2]

This paragraph could be diagrammed as follows:

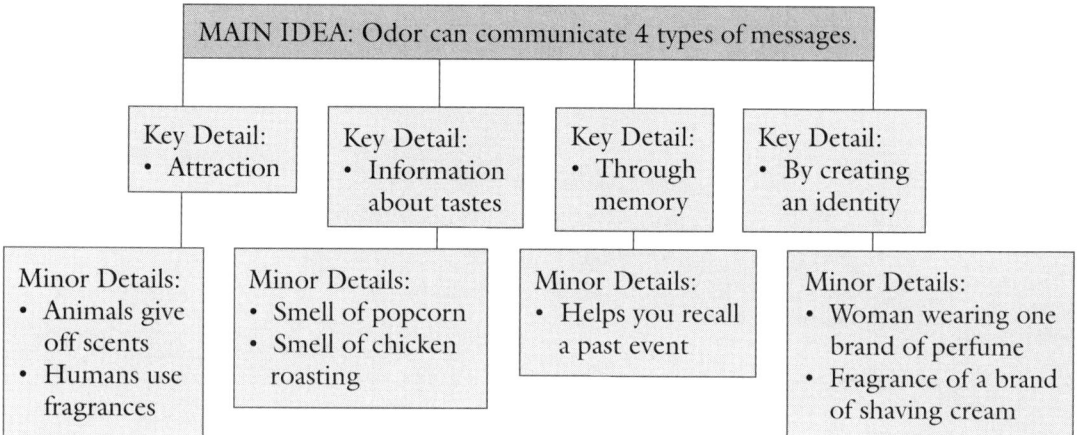

EXERCISE 8-1

Directions: Read each of the following paragraphs and then answer the multiple choice questions that complete the diagram that follows.

Paragraph 1. Don't be fooled by words that sound impressive but mean little. Doublespeak is language that fails to communicate; it comes in four basic forms. **Euphemisms** make the negative and unpleasant appear positive and appealing, for example, calling the firing of 200 workers "downsizing" or "reallocation of resources." **Jargon** is the specialized language of a professional class (for example, the computer language of the hacker); it becomes doublespeak when used to communicate with people who aren't members of the group and who don't know this specialized language. **Gobbledygook** is overly complex language that overwhelms the listener instead of communicating meaning. **Inflated language** makes the mundane seem extraordinary, the common exotic ("take the vacation of a lifetime; explore unsurpassed vistas"). All four forms can be useful in some situations, but, when spoken or listened to mindlessly, they may obscure meaning and distort perceptions.[3]

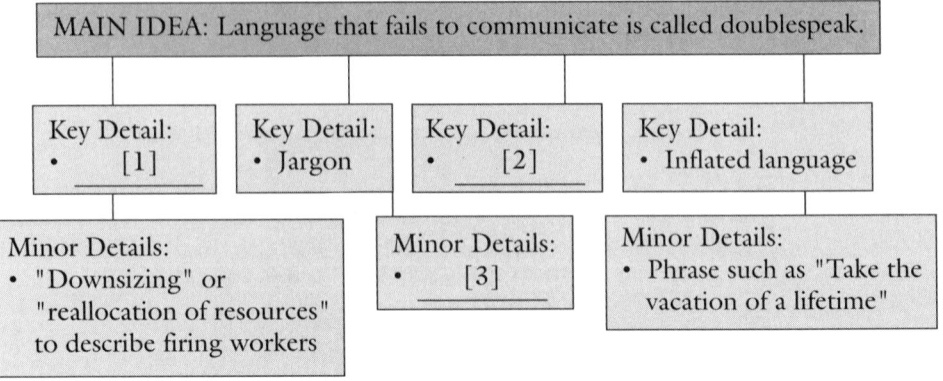

_____ 1. The correct word to fill in the blank labeled [1] is
    a. doublespeak.
    b. euphemisms.
    c. negative.
    d. positive.

_____ 2. The correct word or phrase to fill in the blank labeled [2] is
    a. complex language.
    b. specialized language.
    c. gobbledygook.
    d. mundane.

_____ 3. The correct phrase to fill in the blank labeled [3] is
    a. obscure meanings.
    b. distort perceptions.
    c. a professional class.
    d. the computer language of the hacker.

* * * * *

Paragraph 2. The risks associated with the consumption of alcohol are determined in part by how much an individual drinks. An **occasional drinker** is a person who drinks an alcoholic beverage once in a while. The occasional drinker seldom becomes intoxicated, and such drinking presents little or no threat to the health of the individual. A **social drinker** is someone who drinks regularly in social settings but seldom consumes enough alcohol to become intoxicated. Social drinking, like occasional drinking, does not necessarily increase health risks. **Binge drinking** is defined as having five drinks in a row for men or four in a row for women. Binge drinking can cause significant health and social problems. In comparison to nonbinge drinkers, binge drinkers are much more likely to have unprotected sex, to drive after drinking, and to fall behind in school.[4]

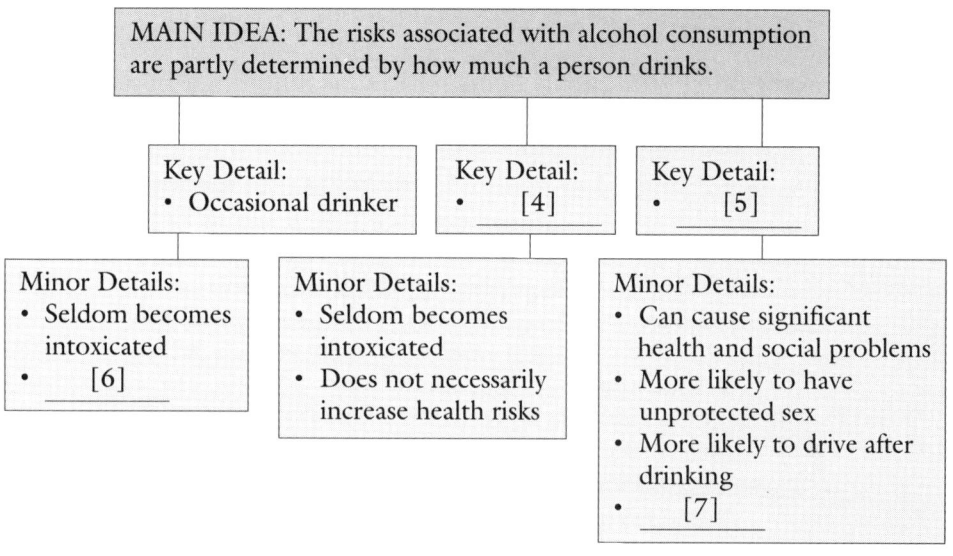

MAIN IDEA: The risks associated with alcohol consumption are partly determined by how much a person drinks.

Key Detail:
• Occasional drinker

Key Detail:
• _____[4]_____

Key Detail:
• _____[5]_____

Minor Details:
• Seldom becomes intoxicated
• _____[6]_____

Minor Details:
• Seldom becomes intoxicated
• Does not necessarily increase health risks

Minor Details:
• Can cause significant health and social problems
• More likely to have unprotected sex
• More likely to drive after drinking
• _____[7]_____

_____ 4. The correct phrase to fill in the blank labeled [4] is
   a. binge drinking.
   b. alcohol consumption.
   c. health risks.
   d. social drinker.

_____ 5. The correct phrase to fill in the blank labeled [5] is
   a. social drinker.
   b. binge drinking.
   c. health problems.
   d. social problems.

_____ 6. The correct phrase to fill in the blank labeled [6] is
   a. occasional drinker.
   b. social drinker.
   c. little or no health threat.
   d. drinks regularly in social settings.

_____ 7. The correct phrase to fill in the blank labeled [7] is
   a. more likely to fall behind in school.
   b. more likely to have health problems.
   c. little or no health threat.
   d. four or five drinks in a row.

* * * * *

Paragraph 3. There are four different dimensions of an arrest: legal, behavioral, subjective, and official (Erez, 1984; Walker, 1992). In **legal** terms, an arrest is made when someone lawfully deprives another person of liberty; in other words, that person is not free to go. The actual word *arrest* need not be uttered, but the other person must be brought under the control of the arresting individual. The **behavioral** element in arrests is often nothing more than the phrase "You're under arrest." However, that statement is usually backed up by a tight grip on the arm or collar, or the drawing of an officer's handgun, or the use of handcuffs. The **subjective** dimension of arrest refers to whenever people believe they are not free to leave; to all intents and purposes, they are under arrest. In any case, the arrest lasts only as long as the person is in custody, which might be a matter of a few minutes or many hours. Many people are briefly detained on the street and then released. **Official** arrests are those detentions that the police record in an administrative record. When a suspect is "booked" at the police station, a record is made of the arrest.[5]

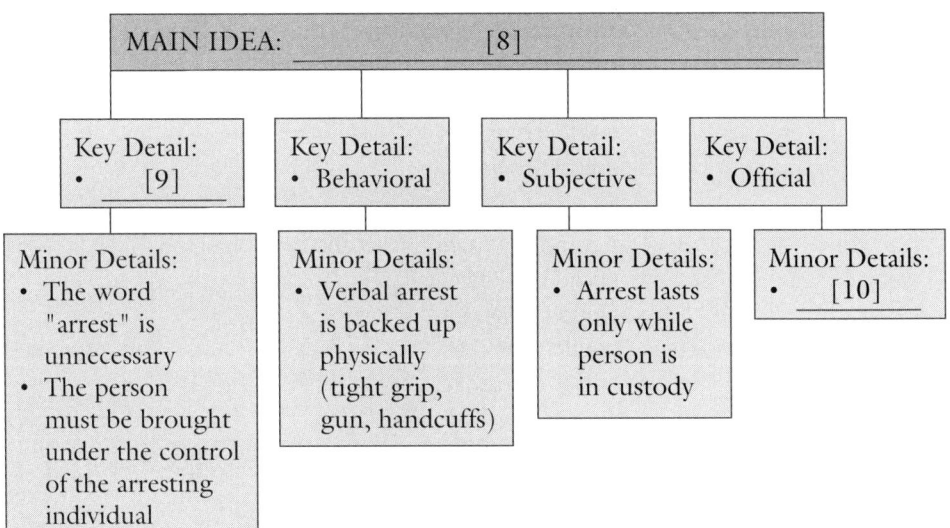

_____ 8. The correct sentence to fill in the blank labeled [8] is
    a. When a person is lawfully deprived of their freedom, it is not necessary to use the word _arrest_.
    b. The four different dimensions of an arrest are legal, behavioral, subjective, and official.
    c. People can be subjectively under arrest even when they are not officially under arrest.
    d. The only official arrests are those that are recorded at the police station.

_____ 9. The correct word or phrase to fill in the blank labeled [9] is
    a. dimensions.
    b. liberty.
    c. not free to go.
    d. legal.

_____ 10. The correct word or phrase to fill in the blank labeled [10] is
    a. arrest is recorded at police station.
    b. detentions.
    c. briefly detained.
    d. booked.

EXERCISE 8-2	**Directions:** Each of the following topic sentences states the main idea of a paragraph. After each topic sentence are sentences containing details that may or may not support the topic sentence. Read each sentence and put a "K" beside those that contain **key details** that support the topic sentence.

1. _Topic sentence:_ Many dramatic physical changes occur during adolescence between the ages of 13 and 15.

   Details:

   _____ a. Voice changes in boys begin to occur at age 13 or 14.

   _____ b. Facial proportions may change during adolescence.

   _____ c. Adolescents, especially boys, gain several inches in height.

   _____ d. Many teenagers do not know how to react to these changes.

   _____ e. Primary sex characteristics begin to develop for both boys and girls.

2. *Topic sentence:* The development of speech in infants follows a definite sequence or pattern of development.

Details:

_____   a. By the time an infant is six months old, he or she can make twelve different speech sounds.

_____   b. Mindy, who is only three months old, is unable to produce any recognizable syllables.

_____   c. During the first year, the number of vowel sounds a child can produce is greater than the number of consonant sounds he or she can make.

_____   d. Between six and twelve months, the number of consonant sounds a child can produce continues to increase.

_____   e. Parents often reward the first recognizable word a child produces by smiling or speaking to the child.

3. *Topic sentence:* The main motives for attending a play are the desire for recreation, the need for relaxation, and the desire for intellectual stimulation.

Details:

_____   a. By becoming involved with the actors and their problems, members of the audience temporarily forget about their personal cares and concerns and are able to relax.

_____   b. In America today, the success of a play is judged by its ability to attract a large audience.

_____   c. Almost everyone who attends a play expects to be entertained.

_____   d. Even theater critics are often able to relax and enjoy a good play.

_____   e. There is a smaller audience that looks to theater for intellectual stimulation.

4. *Topic sentence:* Licorice is used in tobacco products because it has specific characteristics that cannot be found in any other single ingredient.

Details:

_____ a. McAdams & Co. is the largest importer and processor of licorice root.

_____ b. Licorice blends with tobacco and provides added mildness.

_____ c. Licorice provides a unique flavor and sweetens many types of tobacco.

_____ d. The extract of licorice is present in relatively small amounts in most types of pipe tobacco.

_____ e. Licorice helps tobacco retain the correct amount of moisture during storage.

5. *Topic sentence:* An oligopoly is a market structure in which only a few companies sell a certain product.

Details:

_____ a. The automobile industry is a good example of an oligopoly, even though it gives the appearance of being highly competitive.

_____ b. The breakfast cereal, soap, and cigarette industries, although basic to our economy, operate as oligopolies.

_____ c. Monopolies refer to market structures in which only one industry produces a particular product.

_____ d. Monopolies are able to exert more control and price fixing than oligopolies.

_____ e. In the oil industry there are only a few producers, so each producer has a fairly large share of the sales.

EXERCISE 8-3

Directions: Read each of the following paragraphs and write the number of the sentences that contain only the most important key details.

Paragraph 1. [1]*Physical dependence* is what was formerly called addiction. [2]It is characterized by *tolerance* and *withdrawal.* [3]*Tolerance* means that more and more of the drug must be taken to achieve the same effect, as use continues. [4]*Withdrawal* means that if use is discontinued, the person experiences unpleasant symptoms. [5]When I quit smoking cigarettes, for example, I went through about five days of irritability, depression, and restlessness. [6]Withdrawal from heroin and other narcotics is much more painful, involving violent cramps, vomiting, diarrhea, and other symptoms that continue for at least two or three days. [7]With some drugs, especially barbiturates, cold-turkey (sudden and total) quitting can result in death, so severe is the withdrawal.[6]

Key Details: _____

Paragraph 2. [1]The two most common drugs that are legal and do not require a prescription are caffeine and nicotine. [2]*Caffeine* is the active ingredient in coffee, tea, and many cola drinks. [3]It stimulates the central nervous system and heart and therefore is often used to stay awake. [4]Heavy use—say, seven to ten cups of coffee per day—has toxic effects, that is, it acts like a mild poison. [5]Prolonged heavy use appears to be addicting. [6]*Nicotine* is the active ingredient in tobacco. [7]One of the most addicting of all drugs and one of the most dangerous, at least when obtained by smoking, it has been implicated in lung cancer, emphysema, and heart disease.[7]

Key Details: _____

Paragraph 3. [1]Hypnosis today is used for a number of purposes, primarily in psychotherapy or to reduce pain, and it is an acceptable technique in both medicine and psychology. [2]In psychotherapy, it is most often used to eliminate bad habits and annoying symptoms. [3]Cigarette smoking can be treated, for example, by the suggestion that the person will feel nauseated whenever he or she thinks of smoking. [4]Sufferers of migraine headaches treated with hypnotic suggestions to relax showed a much greater tendency to improve than sufferers treated with drugs; 44 percent were headache-free after 12 months of treatment, compared to 12 percent of their drug-treated counterparts.[8]

Key Details: _____

Paragraph 4. [1]There are four main types of sunglasses. [2]The traditional *absorptive* glasses soak up all the harmful sun rays. [3]*Polarizing* sunglasses account for half the market. [4]They're the best buy for knocking out glare, and reflections from snow and water, but they may admit more light rays than other sunglasses. [5]*Coated* sunglasses usually have a metallic covering that itself reflects light. [6]They are often quite absorptive, but a cheap pair of coated glasses may have an uneven or nondurable coating that could rub off after a short period of time. [7]New on the market are the somewhat more expensive *photochromatic* sunglasses. [8]Their chemical composition causes them to change color according to the brightness of the light: in the sun, they darken; in the shade, they lighten. [9]This type of sunglasses responds to ultraviolet light only, and will not screen out infrared rays, so they're not the best bet for continual exposure to bright sun.[9]

Key Details: _____

Paragraph 5. [1]How is a President chosen? [2]First, a candidate campaigns within his party for nomination at a national convention. [3]After the convention comes a period of competition with the nominee of the other major party and perhaps the nominees of minor parties. [4]The showdown arrives on Election Day; the candidate must win more votes than any other nominee in enough states and the District of Columbia to give him a majority of the electoral votes. [5]If he does all these things, he has won the right to the office of President of the United States.[10]

Key Details: _____

TYPES OF SUPPORTING DETAILS

There are many types of details that a writer can use to explain or support a main idea. As you read, be sure you know *how* or what types of detail a writer uses to support his or her main idea. As you will see in later chapters, the way a writer explains and supports an idea may influence how readily you accept or agree with it. The most common types of supporting details are (1) examples, (2) facts or statistics, (3) reasons, (4) descriptions, and (5) steps or procedures. Each will be briefly discussed here.

Examples

One way a writer may support an idea is by using examples. Examples make ideas and concepts real and understandable. In the following paragraph, an example is used to explain instantaneous speed.

The speed that a body has at any one instant is called instantaneous speed. It is the speed registered by the speedometer of a car. When we say that the speed of a car at some particular instant is 60 kilometers per hour, we are specifying its instantaneous speed, and we mean that if the car continued moving as fast for an hour, it would travel 60 kilometers. So the instantaneous speed, or speed at a particular instant, is often quite different from average speed.[11]

In this paragraph the author uses the speed of a car to explain instantaneous speed. As you read illustrations and examples, try to see the relationship between the example and the concept or idea it illustrates.

Facts and Statistics

Another way a writer supports an idea is by including facts and/or statistics. The facts and statistics may provide evidence that the main idea is correct. Or the facts may further explain the main idea. For example, to prove that the divorce rate is high, the author may give statistics about the divorce rate and percentage of the population that is divorced. Notice how, in the following paragraph, the main idea stated in the first sentence is explained using statistics.

> An increasing number of minority workers will join the work force by the year 2000. The United States Bureau of Labor Statistics estimates that white males, who have dominated the work force for several generations, will make up only 15 percent of the new entrants into the labor force between 1990 and 2000. Meanwhile, women, African Americans, Hispanics, and Asians will account for about 84 percent of the new entrants into the world of work. Of these categories, women, many of whom will be members of racial and ethnic minorities, will represent the largest proportion of new workers, accounting for approximately 64 percent.[12]

In this paragraph, the main idea that the number of minority workers will increase by the year 2000 is supported using statistics.

Reasons

A writer may support an idea by giving reasons *why* a main idea is correct. A writer might explain *why* nuclear power is dangerous or give reasons *why* a new speed limit law should be passed by Congress. In the following paragraph, the author explains why warm air rises.

> We all know that warm air rises. From our study of buoyancy we can understand why this is so. Warm air expands and becomes less dense than the surrounding air and is buoyed upward like a balloon. The buoyancy is in an upward direction because the air pressure below a region of warmed air is greater than the air pressure above. And the warmed air rises because the buoyant force is greater than its weight.[13]

Descriptions

When the topic of a paragraph is a person, object, place, or process, the writer may develop the paragraph by describing the object. Descriptions are details that help you create a mental picture of the object. In the following paragraph, the author describes a sacred book of the Islamic religion by telling what it contains.

> The Koran is the sacred book of the Islamic religion. It was written during the lifetime of Mohammed (570–632) during the years in which he recorded divine revelations. The Koran includes rules for family relationships, including marriage and divorce. Rules for inheritance of wealth and property are specified. The status of women as subordinate to men is well defined.

Steps or Procedures

When a paragraph explains how to do something, the paragraph details are often lists of steps or procedures to be followed. For example, if the main idea of a paragraph is how to prepare an outline for a speech, then the details would list or explain the steps in preparing an outline. In the following paragraph the author explains how fog is produced.

> Warm breezes blow over the ocean. When the moist air moves from warmer to cooler waters or from warm water to cool land, it chills. As it chills, water vapor molecules begin coalescing rather than bouncing off one another upon glancing collisions. Condensation takes place, and we have fog.[14]

EXERCISE 8-4	**Directions:** Each topic sentence is followed by a list of possible details that could be used to support it. Label each detail as example, fact/statistic, reasons, description, or steps/procedures.

1. *Topic sentence:* People make inferences about you by the way you dress.

   _____ First, they size you up from head to toe.

   _____ College students assume casually dressed instructors are friendly and flexible.

_____ Robert Molloy wrote a book called *Dress for Success* in which he discusses appropriate business attire.

2. *Topic sentence:* Many retailers with traditional stores have decided to market their products through Web sites as well.

_____ The Gap promotes its Web site in its stores by displaying the slogan *surf.shop.ship* on cash registers and store windows.

_____ Retailers are pushing e-commerce because the Internet can boost sales by luring nontraditional shoppers who don't usually visit their stores.

_____ The Gap's online sales tripled between 1999 and 2000 and are now estimated at $50–100 million, still only a fraction of the company's $9 billion in annual sales.[15]

3. *Topic sentence:* Every April 15th, millions of Americans make their way to the post office to mail their income tax forms.

_____ Corporate taxes account for about 10 cents of every federal revenue dollar, compared with 48 cents from individual income taxes.

_____ This year, the Burnette family filed a return that entitles them to a substantial refund on their state income taxes.

_____ In order to submit an income tax return, you must first obtain the proper forms.[16]

4. *Topic sentence:* Schizophrenia is one of the most difficult psychological disorders to understand.

_____ Diagnosis is difficult due to the lack of physical tests for schizophrenia; researchers do not know if schizophrenia results from a single process or several processes.

_____ Although the rate of schizophrenia is approximately equal in men and women, it strikes men earlier and with greater severity.

_____ After spending time in mental hospitals and home-less shelters, Greg was finally diagnosed with schizophrenia; he has responded well to medication and now lives in a group home.

_____ Schizophrenia involves a range of symptoms, including disturbances in perception, language, thinking, and emotional expression.[17]

5. *Topic sentence:* Many Americans are obsessed with losing weight.

_____ Weight loss obsession is often triggered by major events looming in the near future, such as a high school reunion or a "milestone" birthday.

_____ The two ways to lose weight are to lower caloric intake (through improved eating habits) and to increase exercise (expending more calories).

_____ Studies show that on any given day in America, nearly 40 percent of women and 24 percent of men over the age of 20 are trying to lose weight.

_____ Orlando, a college freshman from Raleigh, admits that he has been struggling with a weight problem since he reached puberty. [18]

6. *Topic sentence:* In the 1920s, many young American writers and artists left their country behind and became expatriates.

_____ One of the most talented of the expatriates was Ernest Hemingway.

_____ The expatriates flocked to Rome, Berlin, and Paris, in order to live cheaply and escape what seemed to them the "conspiracy against the individual" in America.

_____ Some earned a living as journalists, translators, and editors, or made a few dollars by selling a poem to an American magazine or a painting to a tourist.[19]

7. *Topic sentence:* Historical and cultural attractions can be found in a variety of shapes, sizes, and locations throughout the world.

   _____ In Europe, for every museum that existed in 1950, there are now more than four.

   _____ Living History Farms, located near Des Moines, Iowa, is an attraction that offers a "hands-on" experience for visitors.

   _____ More and more communities and countries are taking action to preserve historical sites because they attract visitors and generate income for local residents.[20]

8. *Topic sentence:* Knitting has become a popular hobby for many young career women.

   _____ Typically, aspiring knitters begin by visiting a yarn shop and then enrolling in a knitting class.

   _____ Knitting is popular because it provides a relaxing outlet and an opportunity to create something beautiful as well as useful.

   _____ Far from the image of the grandmotherly knitter, today's devoted knitters include a wide range of women, from Wall Street stockbrokers to movie stars like Julia Roberts.

9. *Topic sentence:* Using a search engine is an effective, though not perfect, method of searching the Internet.

   _____ Each time you begin a Web search, start with a simple query to see how many responses, or hits, you get.

   _____ In May 1998, the largest search engines reportedly indexed no more than 140 million documents, or less than 75 percent of those on the Web.

   _____ Used correctly, a search engine is efficient because it minimizes the time it takes to locate the information you're looking for.[21]

10. *Topic sentence:* The Anasazi Indians are best known for their artistic, architectural, and technological achievements.

_____ The Anasazi used all of the available materials to build their settlements; with wood, mud, and stone, they erected cliff dwellings and the equivalent of terraced apartment houses.

_____ The Anasazi built one structure with 500 living units; it was the largest residential building in North America until the completion of an apartment house in New York in 1882.

_____ One example of their technological genius was their use of irrigation: they constructed sand dunes at the base of hills to hold the runoff from the sometimes torrential rains.

_____ The Anasazi produced pottery that could rank in beauty with any in the world.[22]

| EXERCISE 8-5 | **Directions:** For each paragraph listed in Exercise 8-3 on pages 231–233, identify the type or types of details used to support the main idea. Write your answers below. |

1. Type of details: _____

2. Type of details: _____

3. Type of details: _____

4. Type of details: _____

5. Type of details: _____

TRANSITIONS

Transitions are linking words or phrases used to lead the reader from one idea to another. If you get in the habit of recognizing transitions, you will see that they often guide you through a paragraph, helping you to read it more easily.

In the following paragraph, notice how the underlined transitions lead you from one important detail to the next.

The principle of rhythm and line also contributes to the overall unity of the landscape design. This principle is responsible for the sense of continuity between different areas of the landscape. <u>One</u> way in which this continuity can be developed is by extending planting beds from one area to another. <u>For example</u>, shrub beds developed around the entrance to the house can be continued around the sides and into the backyard. Such an arrangement helps to tie the front and rear areas of the property together. <u>Another</u> means by which rhythm is given to a design is to repeat shapes, angles, or lines between various areas and elements of the design.[23]

Not all paragraphs contain such obvious transitions, and not all transitions serve as such clear markers of major details. Transitions may be used to alert you to what will come next in the paragraph. If you see the phrase *for instance* at the beginning of a sentence, then you know that an example will follow. When you see the phrase *on the other hand,* you can predict that a different, opposing idea will follow. Table 8-1 lists some of the most common transitions used within a paragraph and indicates what they tell you.

TABLE 8-1   Common Transitions

Type of Transition	Example	What They Tell the Reader
Time-Sequence	first, later, next, finally	The author is arranging ideas in the order in which they happened.
Example	for example, for instance, to illustrate, such as	An example will follow.
Enumeration	first, second, third, last, one, another, next	The author is marking or identifying each major point (sometimes these may be used to suggest order of importance).
Continuation	also, in addition, and, further, another	The author is continuing with the same idea and is going to provide additional information.
Contrast	on the other hand, in contrast, however	The author is switching to a different, opposite, or contrasting idea than previously discussed.
Comparison	like, likewise, similarly	The writer will show how the previous idea is similar to what follows.
Cause-Effect	Because, thus, therefore, since, consequently	The writer will show a connection between two or more things, how one thing caused another, or how something happened as a result of something else.
Summation	to sum up, in conclusion	The writer will draw his or her ideas together.

EXERCISE **8-6**	**Directions:** Match each transition in Column A with a transition of similar meaning in Column B. Write the letter of your choice in the space provided.

	Column A		Column B
_____	1. Because	a.	Therefore
_____	2. In contrast	b.	Also
_____	3. For instance	c.	Likewise
_____	4. Thus	d.	After that
_____	5. First	e.	Since
_____	6. One way	f.	In conclusion
_____	7. Similarly	g.	On the other hand
_____	8. Next	h.	One approach
_____	9. In addition	i.	In the beginning
_____	10. To sum up	j.	For example

EXERCISE **8-7**	**Directions:** Use the list below to identify the type of transition that appears in the following sentences. Note that B (Example) and E (Contrast) are each used twice.

a. Time-sequence
b. Example (2)
c. Enumeration
d. Continuation
e. Contrast (2)
f. Comparison
g. Cause-effect
h. Summation

_____ 1. The first step in the listening process involves receiving, or hearing, the message.

_____ 2. Some people consider computer games a purely passive activity. However, many games actually involve strategy, mathematical skills, and memorization.

_____ 3. On election day, several television stations reported a clear winner in the presidential race. Later, those stations were forced to retract their statements and wait—along with the rest of the nation—for a final tally.

_____ 4. In conclusion, proper soil preparation is essential to a successful garden.

_____ 5. There are many kinds of service dogs. For instance, there are dogs that are trained specifically to assist blind or deaf people as well as therapy dogs that are part of physical rehabilitation programs.

_____ 6. Always apply sunscreen before going out in the sun. In addition, a hat and protective clothing are recommended at high altitudes and near water.

_____ 7. In contrast to carnivores, _herbivores_ eat only plants.

_____ 8. Vegetarians typically do not have to worry about elevated cholesterol because cholesterol is found only in animal products.

_____ 9. Like Samuel Clemens, who became famous writing under the pen name Mark Twain, Mary Ann Evans found fame as the writer George Eliot.

_____ 10. In some communities, judges sentence offenders to community service programs instead of jail time. For example, in one Chicago program, offenders trade a "day for a day"—every day they would have spent in jail equals a day spent doing community service work.

EXERCISE 8-8	**Directions:** Read each of the following sentences. In each blank, choose a transitional word or phrase from the box below that makes sense in the sentence.

next	however	For example	another	consequently
because	similarly	Such as	to sum up	in addition

1. After a heart attack, the heart muscle is permanently weakened; _____,
its ability to pump blood throughout the body may be reduced.

2. Some metals, _____ gold and silver, are represented by symbols derived from their Latin names.

3. In order to sight-read music, you should begin by scanning it. _____, you should identify the key and tempo.

4. The *Oxford English Dictionary,* by giving all present and past definitions of words, shows how word definitions have changed with time. _____, it gives the date and written source where each word appears to have first been used.

5. Some scientists believe intelligence to be determined equally by heredity and environment. _____, other scientists believe heredity to account for about sixty percent of intelligence and environment for the other forty percent.

6. Tigers tend to grow listless and unhappy in captivity. _____, pandas grow listless and have a difficult time reproducing in captivity.

7. _____, the most important ways to prevent heat stress are to (1) allow yourself time to get used to the heat, (2) wear the proper clothing, and (3) drink plenty of water.

8. Many people who are dissatisfied with the public school system send their children to private schools. _____ option that is gaining in popularity is home-schooling.

9. Studies have shown that it is important to "exercise" our brains as we age. _____, crossword puzzles are a good way to keep mentally fit.

10. Buying smaller-sized clothing generally will not give an overweight person the incentive to lose weight. People with weight problems tend to eat when they're upset or disturbed, and _____ wearing smaller clothing is frustrating and upsetting, overweight people will generally gain weight by doing so.

EXERCISE 8-9

Directions: Each of the beginnings of paragraphs on the next page uses a transitional word or phrase to tell the reader what will follow in the paragraph. Read each, paying particular attention to the underlined word or phrase. Then, in the space provided, describe as specifically as you can what you would expect to find next in the paragraph.

---

1. Price is not the only factor to consider in choosing a pharmacy. Many provide valuable services that should be considered. <u>For instance</u> . . .

   _____

2. There are a number of things you can do to prevent a home burglary. <u>First,</u> . . .

   _____

3. Most mail order businesses are reliable and honest. <u>However,</u> . . .

   _____

4. One advantage of a compact stereo system is that all the components are built into the unit. <u>Another</u> . . .

   _____

5. Taking medication can have an effect on your hormonal balance. <u>Consequently,</u> . . .

   _____

   _____

6. To select the presidential candidate you will vote for, you should examine his or her philosophy of government. <u>Next</u> . . .

   _____

7. Eating solely vegetables drastically reduces caloric and fat intake, two things on which most people overindulge. <u>On the other hand</u> . . .

   _____

8. Asbestos, a common material found in many older buildings in which people have worked for decades, has been shown to cause cancer. <u>Consequently,</u> . . .

   _____

9. Cars and trucks are not designed randomly. They are designed individually for specific purposes. <u>For instance</u> . . .

   _____

10. Jupiter is a planet surrounded by several moons. <u>Likewise</u> . . .

Copyright © 2003 by Kathleen T. McWhorter

EXERCISE 8-10	**Directions:** Turn back to Exercise 8-3 on pp. 231–233. Reread each paragraph and underline any transitions that you find.

PARAPHRASING PARAGRAPHS

Paraphrasing paragraphs is a useful technique for both building and checking your comprehension. By taking a paragraph apart sentence by sentence, you are forced to understand the meaning of each sentence and see how ideas relate to one another. Paraphrasing paragraphs is similar to paraphrasing sentences. It involves the same two steps:

1. Substituting synonyms
2. Rearranging sentence parts

Refer to Chapter 6, pp. 160–163, for a review of these two steps.
Here are some additional guidelines for paraphrasing paragraphs.

1. Concentrate on maintaining the author's focus and emphasis. Ideas that seem most important in the paragraph should appear as most important in your paraphrase.
2. Work sentence-by-sentence, paraphrasing the ideas in the order in which they appear in the paragraph.

Here are two sample paraphrases of a paragraph. One is a good paraphrase; the other is poor and unacceptable.

Paragraph

For the most part, the American media share one overriding goal: to make a profit. But they are also the main instruments for manipulating public opinion. Politicians want to win our hearts and minds, and businesses want to win our dollars. Both use the media to try to gain mass support by manipulating public opinion. In other words, they generate **propaganda**—communication tailored to influence opinion. Propaganda may be true or false. What sets it apart from other communications is the intent to change opinion.[24]

Good Paraphrase

American media (newspapers, TV, and radio) have one common purpose, which is to make money. Media are also vehicles for controlling how the public thinks. Politicians want us to like them; businesses want our money. Both use media to get support by controlling how people think. Both use propaganda. Propaganda is words and ideas that are used to affect how people think. Propaganda can be either true or false. It is different from other forms of communication because its purpose is to change how we think.

Poor and Unacceptable Paraphrase

In general, the media only wants to control people. But the media also manipulates public opinion. Both politicians and businesses want our money and they use the media to try to get it. To do that, they generate propaganda, which is communication tailored to influence opinion. What sets propaganda apart from other communications is whether it is true or false, and how well it changes people's opinions.

The above paraphrase is unacceptable because it is inaccurate and incomplete.

EXERCISE 8-11	**Directions:** Write a paraphrase of paragraphs 1, 2, and 3 in Exercise 8-3 on pp. 231–233.

WORKING TOGETHER

Directions: Separate into groups. Using a reading selection from Part Five of this book, work with your group to identify and underline the topic sentence of each paragraph. Try to identify key supporting details and/or type of supporting details. When all the groups have completed the task, the class will compare the findings of the various groups.

MASTERING VOCABULARY

Directions: Select the choice that best provides the meaning of each word as it is used in this chapter. Use context clues, word parts, and a dictionary, if necessary.

_____ 1. gestures (p. 224)
  a. comments
  b. movements
  c. emotions
  d. gifts

_____ 2. distinct (p. 224)
  a. similar
  b. mysterious
  c. unique
  d. powerful

_____ 3. depression (p. 232)
  a. gloominess
  b. concern
  c. weakness
  d. disagreement

_____ 4. toxic (p. 232)
  a. clean
  b. alcoholic
  c. distasteful
  a. poisonous

_____ 5. prolonged (p. 232)
  a. long-term
  b. brief
  c. temporary
  d. permanent

_____ 6. psychotherapy (p. 232)
  a. physical treatment
  b. physical disability
  c. mental treatment
  d. mental disability

_____ 7. nondurable (p. 232)
  a. inexpensive
  b. sturdy
  c. flexible
  d. not returnable

_____ 8. dominated (p. 234)
  a. created
  b. contributed
  c. discouraged
  d. controlled

_____ 9. subordinate (p. 235)
  a. greater
  b. powerful
  c. inferior
  d. equal

_____ 10. continuity (p. 239)
  a. separation
  b. connection
  c. difference
  d. change

SELF-TEST SUMMARY

Name and describe the four essential parts of a paragraph.	The four parts of a paragraph are: 1. **Topic.** The topic is the one thing the entire paragraph is about. 2. **Main idea.** The main idea is the most important idea the writer wants the reader to know about the topic. 3. **Details.** Details are facts and ideas that support the main idea. 4. **Transitions.** Transitions are words and phrases that lead the reader from one idea to another.
What is the difference between key details and minor details?	Key details directly explain the main idea; minor details provide additional information or explain further a key detail.
What are the five types of details used to support the main idea?	The types of details are examples, facts or statistics, reasons, descriptions, and steps or procedures.
What are transitions, and what information do they give the reader?	Transitions are linking words and phrases that lead the reader from one idea to another. They suggest time/sequence, exemplification, enumeration, continuation, contrast, comparison, cause/effect, and summation.
What two steps are involved in paraphrasing paragraphs?	Paraphrasing paragraphs involves: 1. substituting synonyms 2. rearranging sentence parts

Name _____
Section _____ Date _____
Number right _____ x 20 points = Score _____

Directions: For each of the following sentences, choose the correct transition to fill in the blank.

_____ 1. College freshmen typically take a variety of courses their first semester. _____, freshman courses might include introductory biology, world history, sociology, English, and speech.
a. In contrast
b. For example
c. Such as
d. Similarly

_____ 2. Year-round schools offer the advantage of relatively uninterrupted learning throughout the year. _____, many teachers look forward to the traditional summer vacation as a time for traveling and studying.
a. In addition
b. Therefore
c. On the other hand
d. Second

_____ 3. It can be devastating to lose several hours of computer work because of a system failure. _____, be sure to save your documents frequently on a diskette as well as on the hard drive.
a. Another
b. Next
c. To illustrate
d. Therefore

_____ 4. There are several points to consider when planting a tree in your yard. _____, select a site.
a. First
b. Further
c. However
d. Consequently

_____ 5. Most of the actors in community playhouses are employed in 9-to-5 jobs during the day. _____, the children who act in community playhouse productions are typically full-time students.
a. For instance
b. Likewise
c. In conclusion
d. Thus

**CHAPTER 8
MASTERY TEST 2:
Paragraph Skills**

Name _____

Section _____ Date _____

Number right _____ x 20 points = Score _____

Directions: Read each of the following paragraphs, then choose the answer that correctly identifies the type of details used in the paragraph.

_____ 1. Many people do not know what to look for when considering the type of skin cancer called melanoma. A simple *ABCD* rule outlines the warning signals of melanoma: *A* is for asymmetry. One half of the mole does not match the other half. *B* is for border irregularity. The edges are ragged, notched, or blurred. *C* is for color. The pigmentation is not uniform. *D* is for diameter greater than 6 millimeters. Any or all of these symptoms should cause you to visit a physician.[25]
   a. statistics
   b. reasons
   c. descriptions
   d. procedures

_____ 2. In the second week of May, 1940 the German armies overran neutral Holland, Belgium, and Luxembourg. The next week they went into Northern France and to the English Channel. Designated as an open city by the French in order to spare its destruction, Paris fell on June 14. As the German advance continued, the members of the French government who wanted to continue resistance were voted down. Marshall Philippe Pétain, an 84-year-old World War I hero, became premier. He immediately asked Hitler for an armistice. On June 22, 1940, in the same dining car in which the French had imposed armistice terms on the Germans in 1918, the Nazis and French signed another peace agreement. The Germans had gained revenge for their shame in 1918.[26]
   a. facts
   b. reasons
   c. descriptions
   d. examples

_____ 3. Ethnic minority group members in the United States have a much higher dropout rate for psychotherapy than do white clients. Among the reasons ethnic clients terminate treatment so early are a lack of bilingual therapists and therapists' stereotypes about ethnic clients. The single most important reason may be that therapists do not provide culturally responsive forms of therapy. They may be unaware of values and customs within a culture that would help in understanding and treating certain behaviors. Therapy should be undertaken with an understanding of cultural values.[27]
   a. steps
   b. procedures
   c. facts
   d. reasons

_____ 4. Festivals celebrate a variety of special occasions and holidays. Some are derived from religious observances, such as New Orleans' or Rio de Janeiro's huge Mardi Gras festivals. Other festivals focus on activities as peaceful as ballooning (the Albuquerque Balloon Festival) or as terrifying as the running of the bulls in Pamplona, Spain. Often, festivals center on the cultural heritage of an area, such as the clan festivals that are prominent in the North Atlantic province of Nova Scotia. More recently, food has become the center of attention at locations such as the National Cherry Festival in Traverse City, Michigan, or the Garlic Festival in Gilroy, California.[28]

a. statistics

b. examples

c. facts

d. procedures

_____ 5. The **dissolution** stage, in both friendship and romance, is the cutting of the bonds tying you together. At first it usually takes the form of _interpersonal separation,_ in which you may not see each other anymore. If you live together, you move into separate apartments and begin to lead lives apart from each other. If this relationship is a marriage, you make seek a legal separation. If this separation period proves workable and if the original relationship is not repaired, you may enter the phase of _social or public separation._ If this is a marriage, this phase corresponds to divorce. Avoidance of each other and a return to being "single" are among the primary identifiable features of dissolution. In some cases, however, the former partners change the definition of their relationship; for example, ex-lovers become friends, or ex-friends become "just" business partners. This final, "goodbye," phase of dissolution is the point at which you become an ex-lover or ex-friend. In some cases this is a stage of relief and relaxation; finally it's over. In other cases this is a stage of anxiety and frustration, of guilt and regret, of resentment over time ill spent and now lost. In more materialistic terms, the goodbye phase is the stage when property is divided and when legal battles may ensue over who should get what.[29]

a. examples

b. reasons

c. descriptions

d. stages

**CHAPTER 8
MASTERY TEST 3:
Paragraph Skills**

Name _____

Section _____ Date _____

Number right _____ x 10 points = Score _____

Directions: Read the passage below and choose the letter that best answers each of the questions that follow.

1   A **punishment** is an unpleasant experience that occurs as a result of an undesirable behavior. Punishment is most effective if it has these three characteristics. First, punishment should be swift, occurring immediately after the undesired behavior. The old threat "Wait till you get home!" undermines the effectiveness of the punishment. Second, punishment must be consistent. The undesired behavior must be punished each and every time it occurs. Finally, the punishment should be sufficiently unpleasant without being overly unpleasant. For instance, if a child doesn't mind being alone in her room, then being sent there for pushing her brother won't be a very effective punishment.

2   Although punishment may decrease the frequency of a behavior, it doesn't eliminate the ability to perform that behavior. For example, your little sister may learn not to push you because your mother will punish her, but she may continue to push her classmates at school because the behavior has not been punished in that context. She may also figure out that if she hits you, but then apologizes, she will not get punished.

3   Furthermore, physical punishment, such as spanking, should be avoided. It may actually increase aggressive behavior in the person on the receiving end. In addition, the one being punished may come to live in fear of the one doing the punishing, even if the punishment is infrequent.

4   Overall, punishment alone hasn't been found to be an effective way of controlling behavior. This is because punishment doesn't convey information about what behavior should be exhibited in place of the undesired, punished behavior. That is, the person being punished knows what they should not do, but the person does not know what he or she should do.[30]

_____ 1. The primary purpose of the selection is to
a. describe the concept of punishment.
b. discourage the use of physical punishment.
c. identify behaviors that require punishment.
d. discuss alternative methods of discipline

_____ 2. The main type of transition used in paragraph 1 is
a. time-sequence.
b. enumeration.
c. continuation.
d. summation.

_____ 3. The transition word or phrase in paragraph 1 that indicates an example will follow is
a. first.
b. second.
c. finally.
d. for instance.

_____ 4. The main idea of paragraph 1 is that
   a. punishment must be consistent.
   b. punishment must be unpleasant.
   c. punishment has three qualities.
   d. punishment is targeted toward undesired behavior.

_____ 5. The main idea of paragraph 2 is supported by
   a. examples.
   b. facts.
   c. reasons.
   d. description.

_____ 6. The main idea of paragraph 2 is that
   a. punishment decreases the frequency of a behavior.
   b. a behavior that is punished at home may not be punished elsewhere.
   c. punishment doesn't eliminate a person's ability to engage in a behavior.
   d. a child may learn to avoid punishment by apologizing for a behavior.

_____ 7. The transition words in paragraph 3 that indicate a continuation of the same idea are
   a. actually.
   b. such as.
   c. even if.
   d. in addition.

_____ 8. A key detail in paragraph 3 that directly supports the main idea is
   a. spanking harms children.
   b. physical punishment may increase aggression in the person giving the punishment.
   c. physical punishment may increase aggression in the person receiving the punishment.
   d. physical punishment may become addictive.

_____ 9. The word or phrase that indicates a cause-effect transition in paragraph 4 is
   a. because.
   b. alone.
   c. in combination with.
   d. in place of.

_____ 10. The best paraphrase of paragraph 4 is:
   a. Punishment alone is not an effective means of controlling behavior. Punishment doesn't convey information about what behavior should take the place of the undesired, punished behavior.
   b. Combining punishment and reinforcement is more effective than using punishment by itself. Punishment quickly lets people know what behaviors are not desirable.
   c. Punishment should never be used because it does not demonstrate desirable behavior.
   d. Punishment doesn't give information about what behavior should replace the undesired, punished behavior.

Name _____

Section _____ Date _____

Number right _____ x 10 points = Score _____

The Game of Life

Mark Harris

Do you remember how to play? In this selection, the author argues that play isn't just for children—it's important that adults know how to play, too.

Vocabulary Preview

chaos (par. 5) a condition of complete disorder

epidemic (par. 6) a rapid, widespread development

frivolous (par. 9) not worth taking seriously

transcendent (par. 10) going beyond ordinary limits

drudgery (par. 13) difficult or boring work

seamless (par. 15) without interruption

tussle (par. 16) a struggle or scuffle

1   I have traveled to downstate Illinois recently to visit a friend and her 8-year-old daughter, Lillian. Early one morning, Lillian and I were sitting in the living room as she waited for her mother to drive her to school.

2   Lillian asked me if I was planning to stay another night. I said I wasn't sure. "Why?" I asked. "Do you have plans for later?" Lillian scrunched up her face. "I'm a kid," she blurted out. "Do you think I have plans?" Then she added, as if to emphasize what really goes on in her household, "My mother has plans."

3   Like most children, Lillian does not have a day planner or a Rolodex. Her life is lived in the moment, filled with adventure and imagination, silliness and laughter, curiosity and learning. Despite rules, responsibilities, and motherly planning, a child's world is usually simmering with fun, ready to bubble up at a moment's notice.

4   Children are the masters of play. It's what they do. It's also the way they learn, how they acquire cognitive and motor skills. As adults we still play, but less spontaneously. We tend to schedule our play time. When, that is, we can find time to schedule.

5   In fact, leisure time has dramatically eroded in recent decades, down to about 16.5 hours a week, reported the editors of the *Harvard Health Letter*. This is in part because of a rise in single-parent and two-wage-earner families, with all their attendance chaos. But it's also because a lot of us are working more—about a month more per year than was the norm in the 1960s.

6   Fifty years ago, commentators wondered what we were going to do with all the extra leisure time generated by the "automation revolution." But the technological good life has instead fostered a national epidemic of overwork, stress, and too little rest. As many as 30 percent of Americans say they experience great stress almost daily. Sleep disorders

and exhaustion have become all too common.

Hurry Up and Play

7   Not surprisingly, the rush of modern life has begun to spill over, even into the ways we play. I thought about this recently on a leisurely bike ride along the Evanston lakefront. Around me zoomed bikers hunched over sleek machines, dressed like Flash Gordon. I imagined they were officially playing while simultaneously getting in their prescribed 30 minutes of three-times-weekly aerobic exercise. No wasting the day here.

8   Later, as I drove down to Chicago's North Side, I passed a storefront window of men and women running on treadmills in a space that looked like it once might have been home to a dry cleaner or a restaurant. I admired their efforts but couldn't help wondering whether a judge had sentenced them to grimly sweat it out in public.

9   It's hard to blame people. Our high-tech life combined with the accelerated pace and insecurity of the modern workplace have fostered a culture that seems to be always working, always rushed, always (at least electronically) connected. In this environment play becomes frivolous. Yet we do manage to play. Being human, we just can't help it. Lenore Terr, a psychiatrist at the University of California, San Francisco, and author of *Beyond Love and Work: Why Adults Need to Play*, argues that play is crucial at every stage of life. In play, we discover pleasure, cultivate feelings of accomplishment, and acquire a sense of belonging. When we play, we learn and mature and—no small matter—

find an outlet for stress. "Play is a lost key," Terr writes. "It unlocks the door to ourselves."

10   When we're in a state of intense play, our cares and worries tend to vanish. Kayaking down a river, playing golf, or thoroughly engrossed in a good novel, we feel pleasurably alive, lighthearted. But play can also take us to new heights of conscious awareness. Athletes refer to moments when they're in "the zone," when body, mind and spirit acquire a kind of transcendent rhythm and performance is at a peak. Essayist Diane Ackerman, borrowing a phrase from 18th-century philosopher Jeremy Bentham, describes such moments in terms of "deep play," when, "levered by ecstasy, one springs out of one's mind."

11   In the zone of deep, transcendent play there is a calm but also focused readiness. Emotions are primed and ready for release. It is a state not unlike a kind of simulated anxiety attack, say researchers, but without the adrenaline and endocrine responses that normally accompany a real emergency.

12   Such moments of heightened awareness represent what University of Chicago researcher Mihaly Csikszentmihalyi has described as a state of "flow," when a person becomes so involved in an activity that nothing else seems to matter. Awareness of the task at hand acquires a kind of meditative brilliance. Mindfulness zeroes in like a laser beam. Everything feels in harmony. In the flow, we feel satisfied.

13   But the benefits of play are not limited to moments of peak performance. We can find satisfaction in subtle, everyday routine as

well. In her book, *Deep Play*, Ackerman describes the rapture of standing among a "vast city-state" of emperor penguins in Antarctica. Yet, she also discovers a transcendent, if not quite so exotic, pleasure in bicycling through her neighborhood or gardening in the back yard. Play is infinitely open-ended in its expression; one person's drudgery can be another's ecstasy. In *Flow: The Psychology of Optimal Experience*, Csikszentmihalyi tells the story of a 60-year-old factory worker named Joe who lived in Chicago's South Side. Joe built railroad cars in a huge hangar. Conditions there were harsh, unprotected as it was from Chicago's extremes of weather. And Joe, who had only a fourth-grade education, was on the low rung of the factory.

14 Yet, Csikszentmihalyi notes, Joe was one of the happiest people he had ever met. At work he was exactly where he wanted to be. He had no desire to be a foreman because he only wanted to fix the machinery, which he did better than anyone else. In fact, the word around the plant was that if Joe retired, they might as well close up shop because he kept everything going.

15 Joe's passion for fixing things didn't end at work. At home he had built a rock garden with an underground sprinkler and a lighting system that created rainbows in the mist. In the evenings, Joe and his wife could sit on their porch surrounded by rainbows. He had made of his life one seamless expression of a particular passion—building and fixing things. He was completely absorbed in his interests. In his living and in his working,

Csikszentmihalyi concludes, Joe was a man who knew how to play.

Let's Pretend

16 I once watched Lillian and her friend Krissy play with dolls and a large wooden doll house. Each of them alternately introduced a theme, such as "Pretend we're baking a pie for your brother's birthday, but he hasn't come home yet, and I'm the mother and I'm worried." A few minutes of this scenario would follow, eventually to be punctuated by the two words that signaled time for a change, "Pretend that . . ." and after some tussle negotiating the details, they'd be off on a new scenario of fun and fantasy.

17 I was struck by how thoroughly engaged they were—and how I envied them. If, as it is said, children think heaven is being an adult and adults think heaven is being a child, then in that moment their world seemed like heaven to me. The way they played was so natural, so complete.

17 I say, let's pretend we've created a world where we all work reasonable schedules with plenty of time to laugh and play and just enjoy each other. Let's pretend we've let go of our worries about money and power or whatever we think we want that we don't have. Let's pretend we've created a less strife-torn world, one in which we've learned to relax more and mistreat each other less.

18 I say, let's pretend, let's rediscover what any child knows about the truth of living in the moment. And how wonderful it is to be fully human, fully alive. Who knows? If we

play it for all it's worth, we might just make it happen.

Directions: Choose the letter that best answers each of the following questions.

CHECKING YOUR COMPREHENSION

_____ 1. The main purpose of this selection is to
   a. encourage adults to experience the benefits of play.
   b. review several recent books on the value of play.
   c. compare the play methods of children and adults.
   d. describe playful ways that adults can cope with stress.

_____ 2. The main idea of paragraph 3 is that
   a. Lillian is disorganized.
   b. Lillian's mother tries to plan her daughter's day too much.
   c. most children are usually eager and ready to play at any time.
   d. children have a difficult time learning rules and responsibilities.

_____ 3. The main idea of paragraph 6 is that
   a. people had more leisure time 50 years ago.
   b. technology has contributed to overwork, stress, and lack of rest.
   c. 30 percent of Americans experience stress every day.
   d. sleep disorders and exhaustion are common problems.

_____ 4. The main idea of paragraph 9 is that play
   a. is unimportant in the work environment.
   b. is important and inevitable for humans.
   c. offers an outlet for stress.
   d. provides a sense of belonging.

_____ 5. When athletes refer to "the zone," they are talking about
   a. the physical and mental preparation leading up to a competition.
   b. the joy of winning a competition.
   c. anxiety attacks that sometimes occur after injuries.
   d. moments of peak performance when body, mind, and spirit are in harmony.

_____ 6. In paragraph 5, the word "eroded" means
   a. somewhat altered.
   b. gradually diminished.
   c. slightly increased.
   d. slowly transformed.

APPLYING YOUR SKILLS

_____ 7. All of the following types of supporting details are used in this selection *except*
   a. examples.
   b. statistics.
   c. reasons.
   d. procedures.

(continued)

_____ 8. A time-sequence transition is indicated in paragraph 8 by the word
   a. later.
   b. passed.
   c. but.
   d. whether.

_____ 9. In paragraph 10 which of the following is a minor detail?
   a. We feel pleasurably alive kayaking down a river.
   b. During play, our cares and worries disappear.
   c. We are often in a state of intense play.
   d. Play can take us to new levels of awareness.

_____ 10. Which of the following is the most important detail in paragraph 13?
   a. Ackerman wrote the book _Deep Play._
   b. Csikszernmihalyi is a factory worker.
   c. There is a "vast city-state" of penguins in Antarctica.
   d. Play is open-ended and is unique among individuals.

Go Electronic!
For additional readings and exercises, and Internet activities, visit the book's Web site at:

http://www.ablongman.com/mcwhorter

If you need a username and password, please see your instructor.

Take a Road Trip to New Orleans!
Be sure to visit the Active Reading module in your Reading Road Trip CD-ROM for multimedia tutorials, exercises, and tests.

9

Following the Author's Thought Patterns

THIS CHAPTER WILL SHOW YOU HOW TO

1. Improve your understanding and recall by recognizing thought patterns
2. Identify commonly used thought patterns
3. Learn transitional words and phrases that signal thought patterns

As a way of beginning to think about authors' thought patterns, complete each of the following steps:

1. Study each of the drawings on page 260 for a few seconds (count to ten as you look at each one).
2. Cover up the drawings and try to draw each from memory.
3. Check to see how many you had exactly correct.

Most likely you drew all but the fourth correctly. Why did you get that one wrong? How does it differ from the others?

Drawings 1, 2, 3, and 5 have patterns. Drawing 4, however, has no pattern; it is just a group of randomly arranged lines.

From this experiment you can see that it is easier to remember drawings that have a pattern, some understandable form of organization. The same is true of written material. If you can see how a paragraph is organized, it will be easier

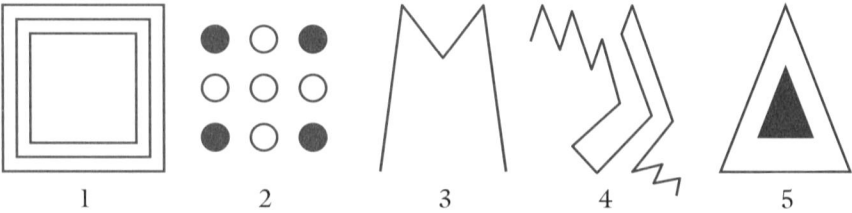

to understand and remember. Writers often present their ideas in a recognizable order. Once you can recognize the organizational pattern, you will remember more of what you read.

SIX COMMON THOUGHT PATTERNS

This chapter discusses six of the more common thought patterns that writers use and shows how to recognize them: (1) illustration/example, (2) definition, (3) comparison/contrast, (4) cause/effect, (5) classification, and (6) chronological order/process. A brief review of other useful patterns is provided in the section that follows.

Illustration/Example

One of the clearest, most practical, and most obvious ways to explain something is to give an example. Suppose you had to explain what anthropology is. You might give examples of the topics you study. By using examples, such as the study of apes and early humans, and the development of modern humans, you would give a fairly good idea of what anthropology is all about. When a subject is unfamiliar, an example often makes it easier to understand.

Usually a writer will state the idea first and then follow with examples. Several examples may be given in one paragraph, or a separate paragraph may be used for each example. It may help to visualize the illustration/example pattern this way:

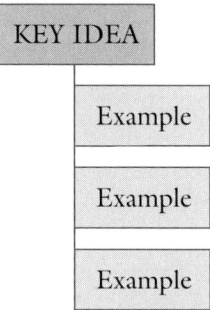

Notice how this thought pattern is developed in the following passage.

> Electricity is all around us. We see it in lightning. We receive electric shocks
> when we walk on a nylon rug on a dry day and then touch something (or someone).
> We can see sparks fly from a cat's fur when we pet it in the dark. We can rub a bal-
> loon on a sweater and make the balloon stick to the wall or the ceiling. Our clothes
> cling together when we take them from the dryer.
>
> These are all examples of *static electricity.* They happen because there is a
> buildup of one of the two kinds of electrical charge, either positive or negative. . . .[1]

In the preceding passage, the concept of static electricity was explained
through the use of everyday examples. You could visualize the selection as follows:

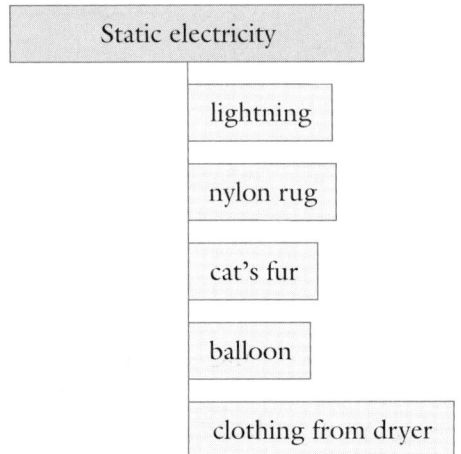

Here is another passage in which the main idea is explained through
example:

> It is a common observation that all bodies do not fall with equal accelerations. A
> leaf, a feather, or a sheet of paper, for example, may flutter to the ground slowly. That
> the air is the factor responsible for these different accelerations can be shown very
> nicely with a closed glass tube containing a light and heavy object, a feather and a
> coin, for example. In the presence of air, the feather and coin fall with quite unequal
> accelerations. But if the air in the tube is evacuated by means of a vacuum pump, and
> the tube is quickly inverted, the feather and coin fall with the same acceleration. . . .
> Although air resistance appreciably alters the motion of falling feathers and the like,
> the motion of heavier objects like stones and baseballs is not appreciably affected by

the air. The relationships $v = gt$ and $d = \frac{1}{2}gl^2$ can be used to a very good approximation for most objects falling in air.[2]

The author explains that objects do not fall at equal rates by using the examples of a leaf, a feather, and a sheet of paper.

Paragraphs and passages organized using illustration/example often use transitional words and phrases to connect ideas. Examples of such words and phrases include:

for example	for instance	to illustrate

EXERCISE 9-1   **Directions:** For each of the following paragraphs, underline the topic sentence and list the examples used to explain it.

TS   1. Perception is the process of gathering information and giving it meaning. You see a movie and you give meaning to it: "It's one of the best I've seen." You come away from class after the third week and you give meaning to it: "It finally makes sense." We gather information from what our senses see, hear, touch, taste, and smell, and we give meaning to that information. Although the information may come to us in a variety of forms, it is all processed, or *perceived,* in the mind.[3]

Examples: We gather info. from sense see hear, touch, taste and smell.

TS   2. The action and reaction forces make up a *pair* of forces. Forces always occur in pairs. There is never a single force in any situation. For example, in walking across the floor, we push against the floor, and the floor in turn pushes against us. Likewise, the tires of a car push against the pavement, and the pavement pushes back on the tires. When we swim, we push the water backward, and the water pushes us forward. The reaction forces, those acting in the direction of our resulting accelerations, are what account for our motion in these cases. These forces depend on friction; a person or car on ice, for example, may not be able to exert the action force to produce the needed reaction force by the ice.[4]

Examples: In walking across the floor, we push against the floor, and the floor in turn pushes against us.

3. Have you ever noticed that some foods remain hotter much longer than others? Boiled onions and squash on a hot dish, for example, are often too hot to eat when mashed potatoes may be eaten comfortably. The filling of hot apple pie can burn your tongue while the crust will not, even when the pie has just been taken out of the oven. And the aluminum covering on a frozen dinner can be peeled off with your bare fingers as soon as it is removed from the oven. A piece of toast may be comfortably eaten a few seconds after coming from the hot toaster, but we must wait several minutes before eating soup from a stove no hotter than the toaster. Evidently, different substances have different **capacities** for storing internal energy.[5]

Examples: _____

_____

_____

EXERCISE 9-2	**Directions:** Choose one of the following topics. On a separate sheet, write a paragraph in which you use illustration/example to organize and express your ideas on the topic. Then draw a diagram showing the organization of your paragraph.

1. Parents or friends are helpful (or not helpful) in making decisions.
2. Attending college has (has not) made a major change in my life.

Definition

Another way to provide an explanation is to offer a definition. Let's say that you see an opossum while driving in the country. You mention this to a friend. Since your friend does not know what an opossum is, you have to give a definition. Your definition should describe an opossum's characteristics or features. The definition should have two parts: (1) tell what general group or class an opossum belongs to—in this case, animals; and (2) explain how an opossum is different or distinguishable from other items in the group. For the term *opossum*, you would need to describe features of an opossum that would help someone tell the difference between it and other animals, such as dogs, raccoons, and squirrels. Thus, you could define an opossum as follows:

An opossum is an animal with a ratlike tail that lives in trees. It carries its young in a pouch. It is active at night and pretends to be dead when trapped.

This definition can be diagrammed as follows:

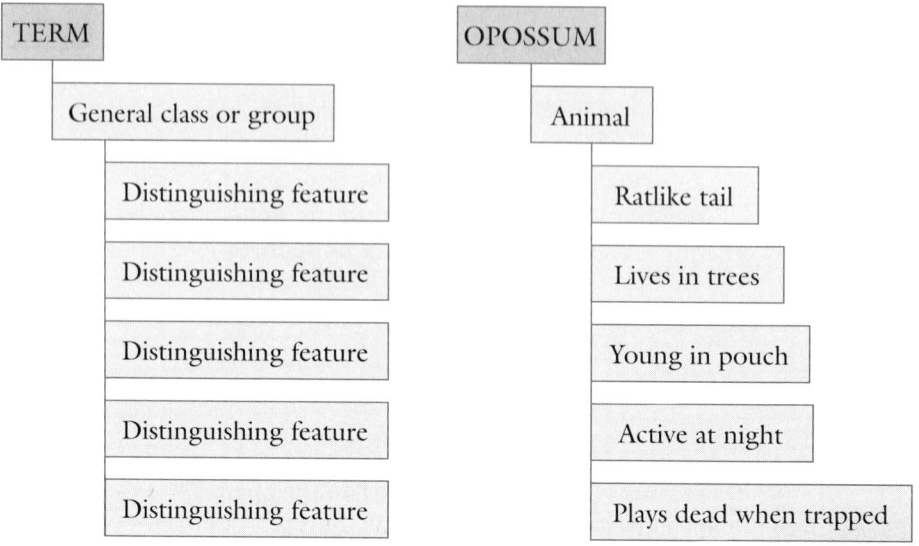

The following passage was written to define the term *ragtime music.*

> Ragtime music is a piano style that developed at the turn of the twentieth century. Ragtime music usually has four themes. The themes are divided into four musical sections of equal length. In playing ragtime music, the left hand plays chords and the right hand plays the melody. There is an uneven accenting between the two hands.

The thought pattern of this passage might be diagrammed as follows:

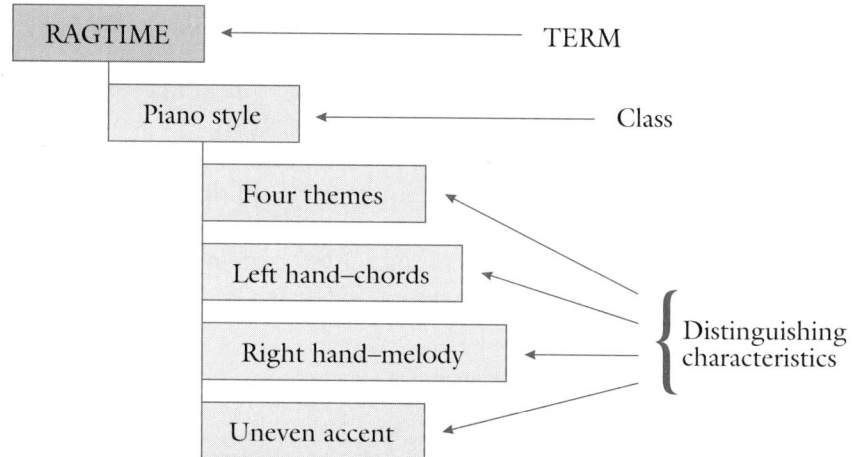

As you read passages that use the definition pattern, keep these questions in mind:

1. What is being defined?
2. What general group or class does it belong to?
3. What makes it different from others in the group?

Read the following passage and apply the above questions.

> Nez Perce Indians are a tribe that lives in north-central Idaho. The rich farmlands and forests in the area form the basis for the tribe's chief industries—agriculture and lumber.
>
> The name *Nez Perce* means *pierced nose*, but few of the Indians ever pierced their noses. In 1805, a French interpreter gave the name to the tribe after seeing some members wearing shells in their noses as decorations.
>
> The Nez Perce originally lived in the region where the borders of Idaho, Oregon, and Washington meet. Prospectors overran the Nez Perce reservation after discovering gold there in the 1860's.
>
> Part of the tribe resisted the efforts of the government to move them to a smaller reservation. In 1877, fighting broke out between the Nez Perce and U.S. troops. Joseph, a Nez Perce chief, tried to lead a band of the Indians into Canada. But he surrendered near the United States-Canadian border.[6]

This passage was written to define the Nez Perce. The general group or category is "Indian tribe." The distinguishing characteristics include their original location, their fight against relocation, and the source of their name.

EXERCISE 9-3   **Directions:** Read each of the following paragraphs. Then identify the term being defined, its general class, and its distinguishing features.

---

1. The partnership, like the sole proprietorship, is a form of ownership used primarily in small business firms. Two or more owners comprise a partnership. The structure of a partnership may be established with an almost endless variation of features. The partners establish the conditions of the partnership, contribution of each partner to the business, and division of profits. They also decide on the amount of authority, duties, and liability each will have.[7]

Term: _____

General Class: _____

Distinguishing features: _____

_____

2. A language is a complex system of symbols with conventional meanings, used by members of a society for communication. The term *language* is often thought to include only the spoken word, but in its broadest sense language contains verbal, nonverbal, and written symbols. Whereas complex cultures employ all three kinds of symbols in communication, simple and preliterate cultures typically lack written symbols.[8]

Term: *Language*

General Class: (Society * System of symbols * for Communication)

Distinguishing features: Verbal, nonverbal, and written symbols.

3. The Small Business Administration (SBA) is an independent agency of the federal government that was created by Congress when it passed the Small Business Act in 1953. Its administrator is appointed by and reports to the President. Purposes of the SBA are to assist people in getting into business, to help them stay in business, to help small firms win federal procurement contracts, and to act as a strong advocate for small business.[9]

Term: _____

General Class: _____

Distinguishing features: _____

_____

_____

Paragraphs and passages that are organized using definition oft sitional words and phrases to connect ideas. Examples of theses words and phrases include:

can be defined as	consists of	involves
is	is called	is characterized by
means	refers to	

**EXERCISE
9-4**

Directions: Choose one of the topics listed below. On a separate sheet, write a paragraph in which you define the topic. Be sure to include both the general group and what makes the item different from other items in the same group. Then draw a diagram showing the organization of your paragraph.

---

1. A type of music
2. Soap operas
3. Junk food

Comparison/Contrast

Often a writer will explain something by using **comparison** or **contrast**—that is, by showing how it is similar to or different from a familiar object or idea. Comparison treats similarities, while contrast emphasizes differences. For example, an article comparing two car models might mention these common, overlapping features: radial tires, clock, radio, power steering, and power brakes. The cars may differ in gas mileage, body shape, engine power, braking distance, and so forth. When comparing the two models, the writer would focus on shared features. When contrasting the two cars the writer would focus on individual differences. Such an article might be diagrammed as follows:

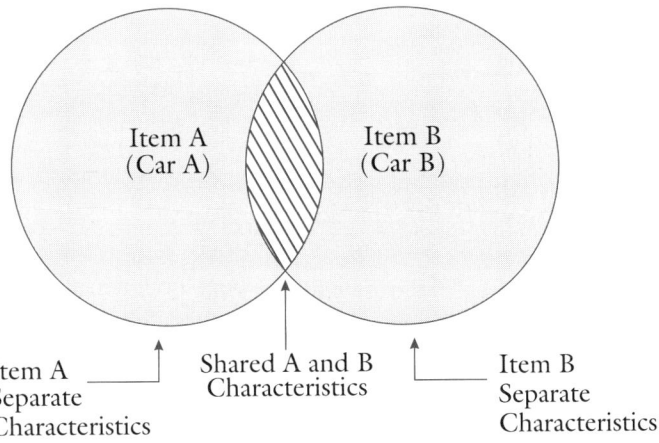

In this diagram, Items A and B are different except where they overlap and share the same characteristics.

In most articles that use the comparison/contrast method, you will find some passages that only compare, some that only contrast, and others that both compare and contrast. To read each type of passage effectively, you must follow the pattern of ideas. Passages that show comparison and/or contrast can be organized in a number of different ways. The organization depends on the author's purpose.

Comparison

If a writer is concerned only with similarities, he or she may identify the items to be compared and then list the ways in which they are alike. The following paragraph shows how chemistry and physics are similar.

> Although physics and chemistry are considered separate fields of study, they have much in common. First, both are physical sciences and are concerned with studying and explaining physical occurrences. To study and record these occurrences, each field has developed a precise set of signs and symbols. These might be considered a specialized language. Finally, both fields are closely tied to the field of mathematics and use mathematics in predicting and explaining physical occurrences.[10]

Such a pattern can be diagrammed as follows:

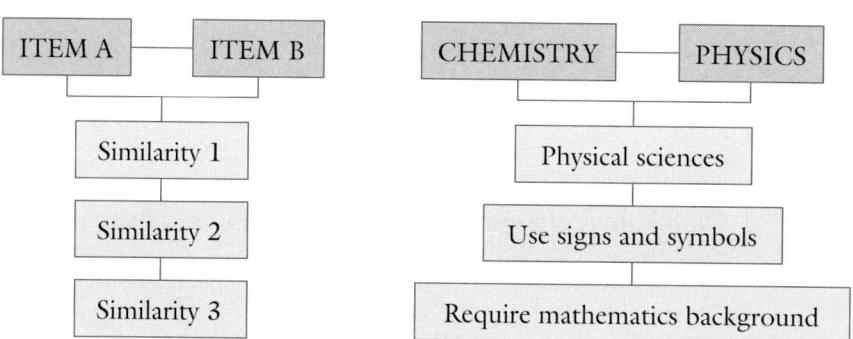

Contrast

A writer concerned only with the differences between sociology and psychology might write the following paragraph:

> Sociology and psychology, although both social sciences, are very different fields of study. Sociology is concerned with the structure, organization, and behavior of groups. Psychology, on the other hand, focuses on individual behavior. While

a sociologist would study characteristics of groups of people, a psychologist would study the individual motivation and behavior of each group member. Psychology and sociology also differ in the manner in which research is conducted. Sociologists obtain data and information through observation and survey. Psychologists obtain data through carefully designed experimentation.

Such a pattern can be diagrammed as follows:

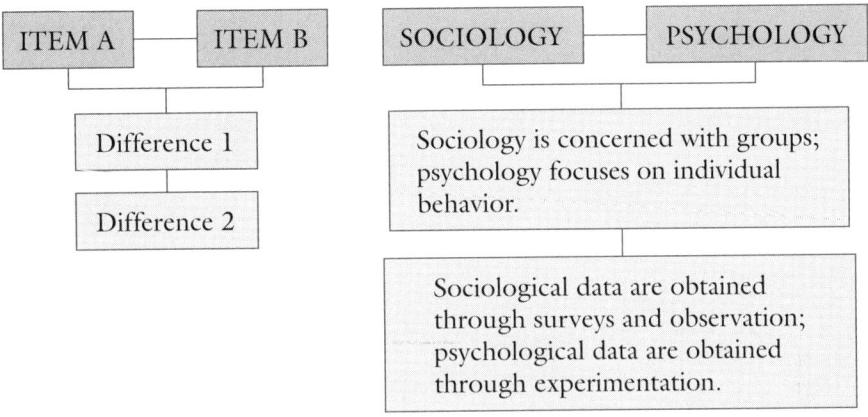

Comparison and Contrast

In many passages, writers discuss both similarities and differences. Suppose you wanted to write a paragraph discussing the similarities and differences between sociology and psychology. You could organize the paragraph in several different ways.

1. You could list all the similarities and then all the differences, as shown in this diagram:

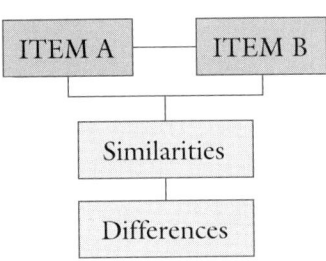

2. You could discuss Item A first, presenting both similarities and differences, and then do the same for Item B. Such a pattern would look like this:

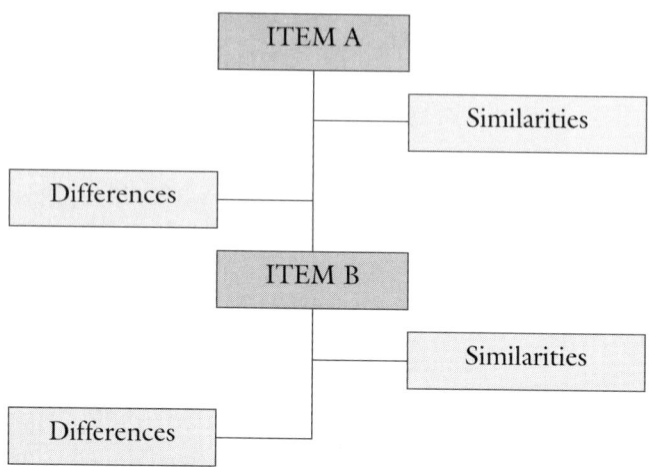

The following paragraph discusses housing in New York City. As you read it, try to visualize its pattern.

Housing in New York City differs in several ways from that in most other cities of the United States. About 65 percent of New York's families live in apartment buildings or hotels. In other cities, most people live in one- or two-family houses. About 70 percent of the families in New York rent their homes. In other U.S. cities, most families own their homes. About half of the housing in New York City was built before 1940. Most other cities in the United States have a far larger percentage of newer housing.[11]

Did you visualize the pattern like this?

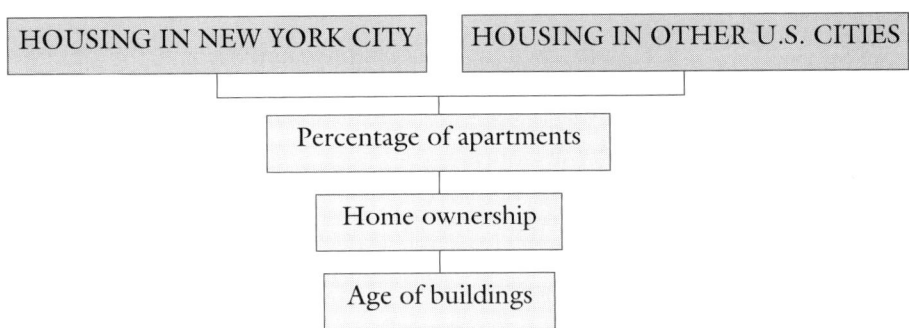

Now read the following passage and decide whether it discusses similarities, differences, or both.

> A program must be written in a form that a computer can understand. Every instruction must be prepared according to specific rules. The rules form a language that we use to instruct the computer. Humans use *natural languages* such as English and Spanish to communicate with each other. When we communicate with a computer we use a *computer programming language.*
>
> To write a sentence in a natural human language, we form words and phrases from letters and other symbols. The construction of the sentence is determined by the grammar rules of the language. The meaning of the sentence depends on what words are used and how they are organized. A computer programming language also has rules that describe how to form valid instructions. These rules are called the *syntax* of the language. The meanings or effects of the instructions are called the *semantics* of the language.[12]

This passage *compares* natural language with computer programming language. Both are means of communication and both are based on sets of rules.

Paragraphs and passages that use comparison/contrast often contain transitional words and phrases that guide readers through the material. These include:

Comparison	Contrast
both, in comparison, in the same way, likewise, similarly, to compare	as opposed to, differs from, however, in contrast, instead, on the other hand, unlike

EXERCISE 9-5

Directions: Read each of the following passages and identify the items being compared or contrasted. Then describe the author's approach to the items. Are they compared, contrasted, or both compared and contrasted?

1. Perhaps it will be easier to understand the nature and function of empathic listening if we contrast it to deliberative listening. When we make a definite "deliberate" attempt to hear information, analyze it, recall it at a later time and draw conclusions from it, we are listening deliberatively. This is the way most of us listen because this is the way we have been trained. This type of listening is appropriate in a lecture-based education system where the first priority is to critically analyze the speaker's content.

In empathic listening the objective is also understanding, but the first priority is different. Because empathic listening is transactional, the listener's first priority is to understand the communicator. We listen to what is being communicated not just by the words but by the other person's facial expressions, tone of voice, gestures, posture, and body motion.[13]

Items Compared or Contrasted: _Empathic listening + Deliberative listening_

Approach: _____

2. The term primary group, coined by Charles H. Cooley (1909), is used to refer to small, informal groups who interact in a personal, direct and intimate way. . . . A secondary group is a group whose members interact in an impersonal manner, have few emotional ties, and come together for a specific purpose. Like primary groups, they are usually small and involve face-to-face contacts. Although the interactions may be cordial or friendly, they are more formal than primary group interactions. Sociologically, however, they are just as important. Most of our time is spent in secondary groups—committees, professional groups, sales-related groups, classroom groups, or neighborhood groups. The key difference between primary and secondary groups is in the quality of the relationships and the extent of personal intimacy and involvement. Primary groups are person-oriented, whereas secondary groups tend to be goal-oriented.[14]

Items Compared or Contrasted: _Primary groups, Secondary groups_

Approach: _____

3. The differences in the lifestyles of the city and the suburbs should be thought of as differences of degree, not kind. Suburban residents tend to be more family-oriented and more concerned about the quality of education their children receive than city dwellers. On the other hand, because the suburbs consist largely of single-family homes, most young and single people prefer city life. Suburbanites are usually more affluent than city residents and more apt to have stable career or occupational patterns. As a result, they seem to be more hardworking and achievement-oriented than city residents. They may also seem to be unduly concerned with consumption, since they often buy goods and services that offer visible evidence of their financial success.[15]

Items Compared or Contrasted: *Lifestyles of the city + Suburbs*

Approach: _____

EXERCISE 9-6

Directions: Choose one of the topics listed below. On a separate sheet, write a paragraph in which you compare and/or contrast the two items. Then draw a diagram showing the organization of your paragraph.

1. Two restaurants
2. Two friends
3. Two musical groups

Cause/Effect

The **cause/effect** pattern is used to describe an event or action that is caused by another event or action. A cause/effect passage explains why or how something happened. For example, a description of an automobile accident would probably follow a cause/effect pattern. You would tell what caused the accident and what happened as a result. Basically, this pattern describes four types of relationships:

1. Single cause/single effect

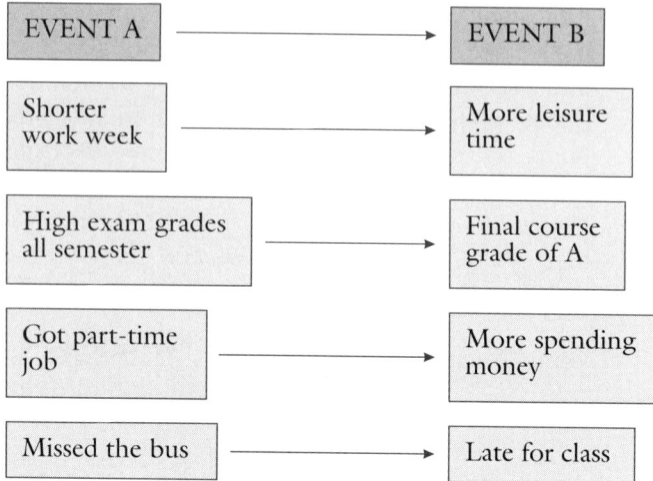

2. Single cause/multiple effects

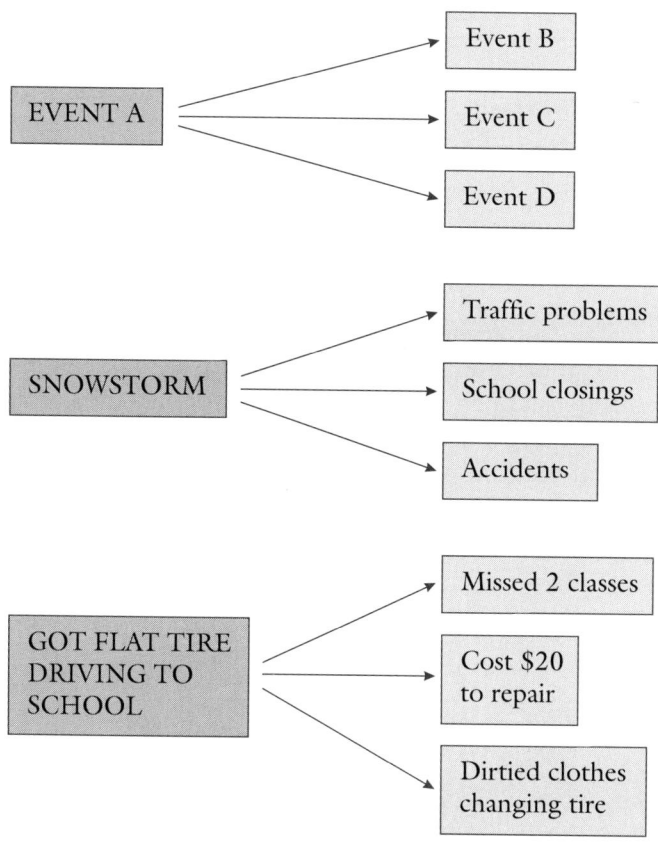

3. Multiple cause/single effect

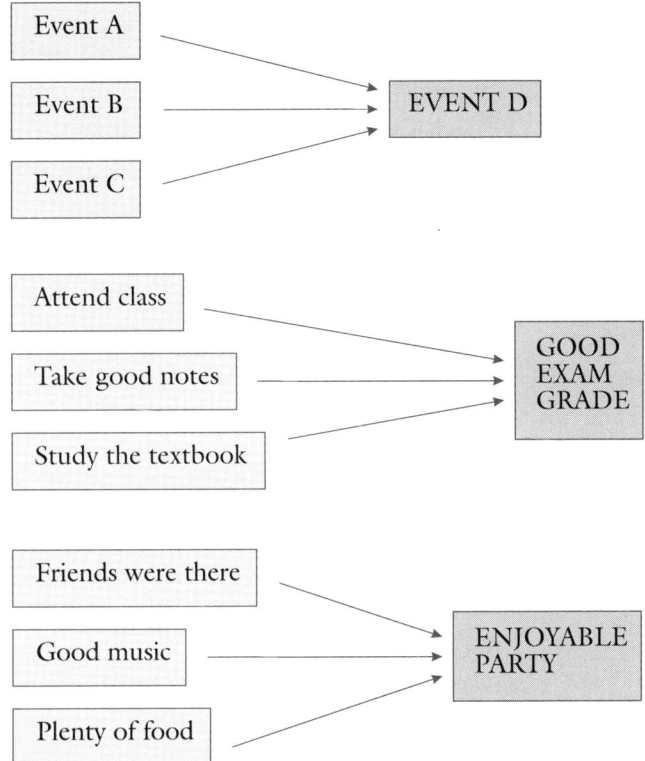

4. Multiple causes/multiple effects

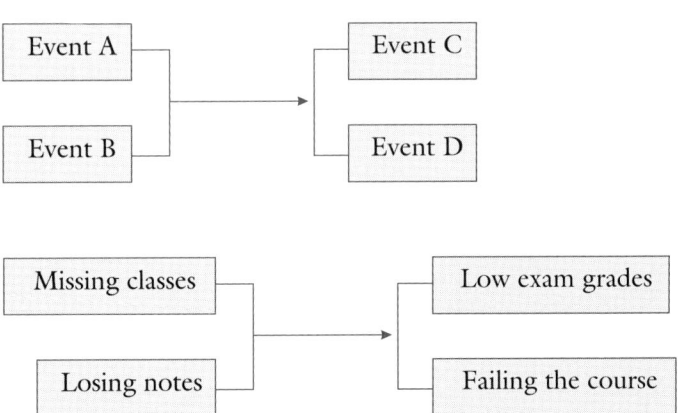

Read the following paragraph and determine which of the previous four relationships it describes.

> Research has shown that mental illnesses have various causes, but the causes are not fully understood. Some mental disorders are due to physical changes in the brain resulting from illness or injury. Chemical imbalances in the brain may cause other mental illnesses. Still other disorders are mainly due to conditions in the environment that affect a person's mental state. These conditions include unpleasant childhood experiences and severe emotional stress. In addition, many cases of mental illness probably result from a combination of two or more of these causes.

In this paragraph a single effect (mental illness) is stated as having multiple causes (chemical and metabolic changes, psychological problems).

To read paragraphs that explain cause/effect relationships, pay close attention to the topic sentence. It usually states the cause/effect relationship that is detailed in the remainder of the paragraph. Then look for connections between causes and effects. What event happened as the result of a previous action? How did one event cause the other to happen?

Look for the development of the cause/effect relationship in the following paragraph about racial conflict.

> Racial conflicts in New York City have had many causes. A major cause has been discrimination against blacks, Puerto Ricans, and other minority groups in jobs and housing. Many minority group members have had trouble obtaining well-paying jobs. Many also have had difficulty moving out of segregated neighborhoods and into neighborhoods where most of the people are white and of European ancestry. When members of a minority group have begun moving into such a neighborhood, the white residents often have begun moving out. In this way, segregated housing patterns have continued, and the chances for conflicts between the groups have increased.[16]

This paragraph explains why conflicts occur. It can be diagrammed as follows:

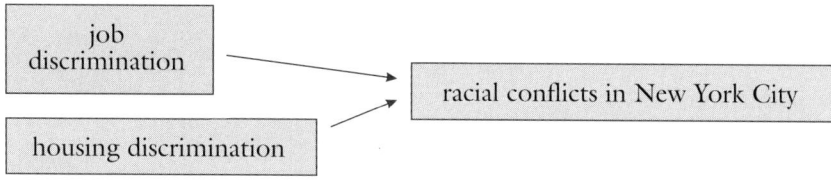

Within this paragraph, a second cause/effect relationship is introduced:

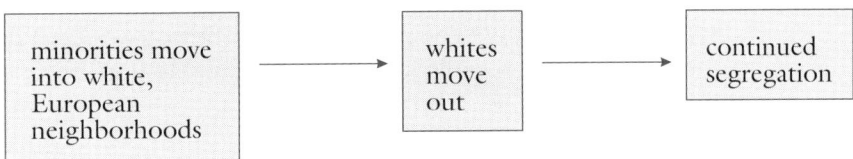

Paragraphs and passage that are organized using cause/effect often use transitional words and phrases to guide the reader. These include:

as a result	because	because of	causes	consequently	contributes
due to	leads to	since	therefore	thus	

EXERCISE 9-7

Directions: Read each of the following paragraphs and describe the cause/effect relationship in each.

1. By far the major cause of all business failure is inadequate management. As the Dun & Bradstreet data show, nearly 92 percent of all business failures are attributed to this one cause. What contributes to inadequate management? We see that causes of inadequate management include a lack of experience, unbalanced business experience, and incompetence.[17]

Cause: _Business Failure_

Effect: _Indaquate management_
Business Failure

2. If a light is directed into one eye, the pupils of both eyes normally constrict. The decrease in pupil size is caused by contraction of the sphincter muscles of the iris. Constriction of the pupil in the eye in which the light was directed is known as the direct light reflex. Whereas, constriction of the pupil in the other eye is called the consensual light reflex. Both light reflexes have the typical reflex components: a sensory pathway, a motor pathway, and a central nervous system integration center.[18]

Cause: _Light_

Effect: _Pupil contractions_

3. Snow is a poor conductor and hence is popularly said to keep the earth warm. Its flakes are formed of crystals, which collect feathery masses,

imprisoning air and thereby interfering with the escape of heat from the earth's surface. The winter dwellings of the Eskimos are shielded from the cold by their snow covering. Animals in the forest find shelter from the cold in snowbanks and in holes in the snow. The snow doesn't provide them with heat; it simply prevents the heat they generate from escaping.[19]

Cause: _____

Effect: _____

EXERCISE 9-8 | **Directions:** Choose one of the topics listed below. On a separate sheet, write a paragraph using one of the four cause/effect patterns described above to explain the topic. Then draw a diagram showing the organization of your paragraph.

1. Why you are attending college
2. Why you chose the college you are attending
3. How a particularly frightening or tragic event happened

Classification

A common way to explain something is to divide the topic into parts and explain each part. For example, you might explain how a home computer works by describing what each major component does. You would explain the functions of the monitor (screen), the disc drives, and the central processing unit. Or you might explain the kinds of courses taken in college by dividing the courses into such categories as electives, required basic courses, courses required for a specific major, and so on, and then describing each category.

Textbook writers use the classification pattern to explain a topic that can easily be divided into parts. These parts are selected on the basis of common characteristics. For example, a psychology textbook writer might explain human needs by classifying them into two categories, primary and secondary. Or in a chemistry textbook, various compounds may be grouped or classified according to common characteristics, such as the presence of hydrogen or oxygen.

The following paragraph explains horticulture. As you read, try to identify the categories into which the topic of horticulture is divided.

Horticulture, the study and cultivation of garden plants, is a large industry. Recently it has become a popular area of study. The horticulture field consists of four major divisions. First, there is pomology, the science and practice of growing and handling fruit trees. Then there is olericulture, which is concerned with growing and storing vegetables. A third field, floriculture, is the science of growing, storing, and designing flowering plants. The last category, ornamental and landscape horticulture, is concerned with using grasses, plants, and shrubs in landscaping.

This paragraph approaches the topic of horticulture by describing its four areas or fields of study. You could diagram the paragraph as follows:

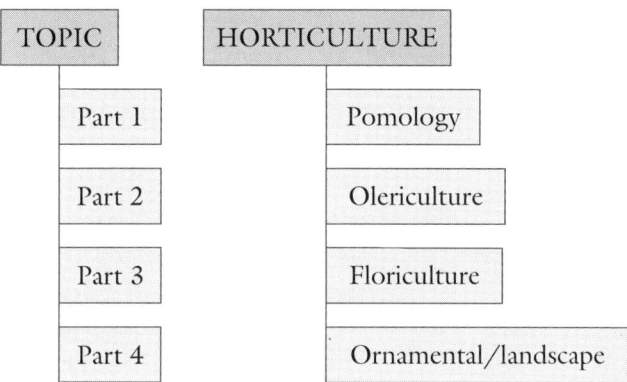

When reading textbook material that uses the classification pattern, be sure you understand *how* and *why* the topic was divided as it was. This technique will help you remember the most important parts of the topic.

Here is another example of the classification pattern:

A newspaper is published primarily to present current news and information. For large city newspapers, more than 2,000 people may be involved in the distribution of this information. The staff of large city papers, headed by a publisher, is organized into departments: editorial, business, and mechanical. The editorial department, headed by an editor-in-chief, is responsible for the collection of news and preparation of written copy. The business department, headed by a business manager, handles circulation, sales, and advertising. The mechanical department is run by a production manager. This department deals with the actual production of the paper, including typesetting, layout, and printing.

You could diagram this paragraph as follows:

LARGE CITY NEWSPAPERS

Editorial

Business

Mechanical

Paragraphs and passages that are organized using classification frequently use transitional words and phrases to guide the reader. These include:

another   another kind   classified as   include   is composed of   one   types of

EXERCISE 9-9   **Directions:** Read each of the following passages. Then identify the topic and the parts into which each passage is divided.

1. The peripheral nervous system is divided into two parts: the somatic (bodily) nervous system and the autonomic (self-governing) nervous system. The somatic nervous system, sometimes called the skeletal nervous system, controls the skeletal muscles of the body and permits voluntary action. When you turn off a light or write your name, your somatic system is active. The autonomic nervous system regulates blood vessels, glands, and internal (visceral) organs like the bladder, stomach, and heart. When you happen upon the secret object of your desire and your heart starts to pound, your hands get sweaty, and your cheeks feel hot, you can blame your autonomic nervous system.[20]

Topics: _Peripheral Nervous System_

Parts: _Somatic Nervous System_
      Autonomic Nervous System.

2. When we communicate with others we use either verbal messages, nonverbal messages, or a combination of the two. Verbal messages are either sent or not sent, just as a light switch is either on or off. They have an all-or-nothing feature built in. Nonverbal cues are not as clear-cut.

Nonverbal communication includes such behaviors as facial expressions, posture, gestures, voice inflection, and the sequence and rhythm of the words themselves. Just as a dimmer switch on the light can be used to adjust, nonverbal cues often reveal shades or degrees of meaning. You may say, for example, "I am very upset" but *how* upset you are will be conveyed more by your facial expressions and gestures than by the actual words.[21]

Topics: _Nonverbal Communication_

Parts: _Behaviors - facial expression, posture, gesture, voice inflection, sequence and rhythm of the word._

3. The word *script* is used in this concept to mean a habitual pattern of behavior. Thomas Harris defines scripts as decisions about how life should be lived. Muriel James and Dorothy Jongeward suggest that there are various levels of scripts: (1) cultural, which are dictated by society; (2) subcultural defined by geographical location, ethnic background, religious beliefs, sex, education, age and other common bonds; (3) family, the identifiable traditions and expectations for family members; and (4) psychological, people's compulsion to perform in a certain way, to live up to a specific identity, or to fulfill a destiny.[22]

Topics: _____

Parts: _____

EXERCISE 9-10

Directions: Choose one of the topics listed below. On a separate sheet, write a paragraph explaining the topic, using the classification pattern. Then draw a diagram showing the organization of your paragraph.

1. Advertising
2. Colleges
3. Entertainment

Chronological Order/Process

The terms **chronological order** and **process** both refer to the order in which something is done. Chronological order, also called sequence of events, is one of the most obvious patterns. In a paragraph organized by chronology, the details are presented in the order in which they occur. That is, the event that happened first, or earliest in time, appears first in the paragraph, and so on. Process refers to the steps or stages in which something is done. You might expect to read a description of the events in a World War II battle presented in the order in which they happened—in chronological order. Similarly, in a computer programming manual, the steps to follow to locate an error in a computer program would be described in the order in which you should do them.

Both chronological order and process patterns can be diagrammed as follows:

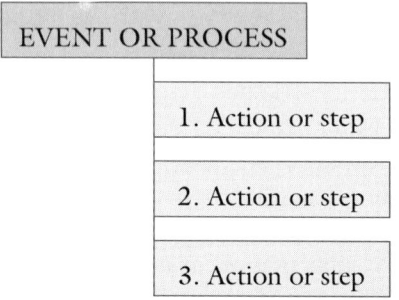

Read the following paragraph, paying particular attention to the order of the actions or steps.

> In the early 1930s, the newly established Federal Bureau of Narcotics took on a crucial role in the fight against marijuana. Under the directorship of Harry J. Anslinger, a rigorous campaign was waged against the drug and those using it. By 1937 many states had adopted a standard bill making marijuana illegal. In that same year, the federal government stepped in with the Marijuana Tax Act, a bill modeled after the Harrison "Narcotics" Act. Repressive legislation continued, and by the 1950s severe penalties were imposed on those convicted of possessing, buying, selling, or cultivating the drug.[23]

This paragraph traces the history of actions taken to limit the use of marijuana. These actions are described in chronological order, beginning with the earliest event and concluding with the most recent.

When reading text material that uses the chronological order/process pattern, pay particular attention to the order of the information presented. Both chronological order and process are concerned with the sequence of events in time.

Paragraphs and passages that use chronological order/process to organize ideas often contain transitional words and phrases to guide the reader. They include:

after	before	by the time	during	finally	first	later
meanwhile	on	second	then	until	when	while

EXERCISE 9-11	**Directions:** Read each of the following paragraphs. Identify the topic and write a list of the actions, steps, or events described in each period.

1. These benefits of good listening occur only when the cues we give back to a speaker allow that person to know how we receive the message, permitting the speaker to adjust the message as needed. This important process is known as *feedback*. Feedback is not a simple, one-step process. First, it involves monitoring the impact or the influence of our messages on the other person. Second, it involves evaluating why the reaction or response occurred as it did. Third and finally, it involves adjustment or modification. The adjustment of our future messages reveals the process-oriented nature of communication, and, too, the impact the receiver has on the communication cycle. Feedback can provide reinforcement for the speaker if it shows if he or she is being clear, accepted, or understood.[24]

Topics: _____ Feedback _____

Steps: _____

2. A geyser is a periodically erupting pressure cooker. It consists of a long, narrow, vertical hole into which underground streams seep. The column of water is heated by volcanic heat below to temperatures exceeding 100°C. This is because the vertical column of water exerts pressure on the deeper water, thereby increasing the boiling point. The narrowness of the shaft shuts off convection currents, which allows the deeper portions to become considerably hotter than the water surface. Water at the surface, of course, will boil at 100°C. The water is heated from below, so a temperature high enough to permit boiling is reached near the bottom before it is at the top. Boiling therefore begins near the bottom, the rising bubbles push out the column of water above, and the eruption starts. As the water gushes out, pressure and the remaining water is reduced. It then rapidly boils and erupts with great force.[25]

Topics: _____

Steps: _____

3. In spite of varied protests, the nineteenth century saw the admission of girls into elementary schools and eventually into secondary schools. In 1883, feminine education scored a victory when Oberlin College admitted women as well as men. In 1837, Mount Holyoke Seminary for Girls was established in Massachusetts, thanks to the pioneering efforts of Mary Lyon. Vassar College opened its doors in 1865, followed by Smith in 1871, Wellesley in 1877, and Bryn Mawr in 1880. The University of Michigan meanwhile had admitted women in 1870, and by the turn of the century coeducational colleges and universities were becoming commonplace. Today the great majority of the more than 2000 institutions of higher learning in the United States are coeducational, including practically all professional schools.[26]

Topics: _____

Steps: _____

EXERCISE 9-12

Directions: On a separate sheet, write a paragraph explaining how to do something that you do well or often, such as cross-country ski, change a tire, or use a VCR to tape a TV show. Use the chronological order/process pattern. Then draw a diagram showing the organization of your paragraph.

EXERCISE 9-13

Directions: Read each of the following selections and identify the thought pattern used. Write the name of the pattern in the space provided. Choose from among these patterns: illustration/example, definition, comparison/contrast, cause/effect, classification, chronological order/process. Next, write a sentence explaining your choice. Then draw a diagram that shows the organization of each selection.

---

1. Many wedding customs have been popular since ancient times. For example, Roman brides probably wore veils more than 2,000 years ago. Bridal veils became popular in Britain and the New World during the late 1700's. The custom of giving a wedding ring dates back to the ancient Romans. The roundness of the ring probably represents eternity, and the presentation of wedding rings symbolizes that the man and woman are united forever. Wearing the wedding ring on the ring finger of the left hand is another old custom. People once thought that a vein or nerve ran directly from this finger to the heart. An old superstition says that a bride can

ensure good luck by wearing "something old, something new, something borrowed, and something blue." Another superstition is that it is bad luck for a bride and groom to see each other before the ceremony on their wedding day.[27]

Pattern: _Illustration / Examples_

Reason: _Explains wedding customs_

Diagram:

2. Muscle is the tough, elastic tissue that makes body parts move. All animals except the simplest kinds have some type of muscle.

People use muscles to make various movements, such as walking, jumping, or throwing. Muscles also help in performing activities necessary for growth and for maintaining a strong, healthy body. For example, people use muscles in the jaw to chew food. Other muscles help move food through the stomach and intestines, and aid in digestion. Muscles in the heart and blood vessels force the blood to circulate. Muscles in the chest make breathing possible.

Muscles are found throughout the body. As a person grows, the muscles also get bigger. Muscle makes up nearly half the body weight of an adult.[28]

Pattern: _Illustration/ Example   Definition_

Reason: _Explains muscles_

Diagram:

3. Unless they were employed as servants, colonial women had little occupational opportunity. Even during the early 1800s, after certain types of jobs had been opened to women, female wage earners continued to be stigmatized by inferior social status.

The first large-scale influx of female workers took place in the New England factories. Most of the workers were unmarried farm girls, some hardly more than children. They were welcomed, nevertheless, because they not only were conscientious employees but would work for low wages.

During the Civil War an increasing number of occupations were opened to women, a phenomenon that was to be repeated in the First and Second World Wars. During World War II, women were employed as welders, mechanics, machinists, taxi drivers, and streetcar operators; in fact, with the exception of heavy-duty laboring jobs, females could be found in virtually every branch of industry. Also, because of their excellent record, women were made a permanent part of the armed forces.

Today there are more than 52 million women in the work force. Of those not in the labor force, the great majority are retired or have home responsibilities. From the sociological perspective it is important to note that currently even mothers with small children are likely to be employed outside the home. "Regardless of marital status or the presence of young children, labor force participation has become the norm for women." Since 1986, more than half of all women with children under three years of age have been in the labor force.[29]

Chronological Order.

Pattern: _Compare/ Contrast_

Reason: _Different years._

Diagram:

4. Mimosa is the name of a group of trees, shrubs, and herbs that have featherlike leaves. Mimosas grow chiefly in warm and tropical regions. In the United States, they are found from Maryland to Florida and west to Texas. The seeds of mimosas grow in flat pods. The small flowers may be white, pink, lavendar, or purple. The *silver wattle*, a shrub with silvery-gray leaves, is widely sold by florists as mimosa. It is closely related to mimosas.[30]

Pattern: _Classification Definition_

Reason: _Classifies Mimosa_

Diagram:

5. Morphine makes severe pain bearable and moderate pain disappear. The drug also stops coughing and diarrhea, checks bleeding, and may help bring sleep. Doctors give patients morphine only if other medicines fail. Besides being addictive, it interferes with breathing and heart action and may cause vomiting. Small doses of morphine leave the mind fairly clear. Larger doses cloud the mind and make the user feel extremely lazy. Most morphine users feel little hunger, anger, sadness, or worry, and their sex drive is greatly reduced. Most people with mental or social problems feel happy after using morphine, even though their problems have not really been solved.[31]

Pattern: _____

Reason: _____

Diagram:

6. Personality disorders are character traits that create difficulties in personal relationships. For example, antisocial *personality disorder* is characterized by aggressive and harmful behavior that first occurs before the age of 15. Such behavior includes lying, stealing, fighting, and resisting authority. During adulthood, people with this disorder often have difficulty keeping a job or accepting other responsibilities.

Individuals with *paranoid personality disorder* are overly suspicious, cautious, and secretive. They may have delusions that people are watching them or talking about them. They often criticize others but have difficulty accepting criticism.

People who suffer from *compulsive personality disorder* attach great importance to organization. They strive for efficiency and may spend a great deal of time making lists and schedules. But they are also indecisive and seldom accomplish anything they set out to do. They often make unreasonable demands on other people and have difficulty expressing emotions.[32]

Pattern: _____

Reason: _____

Diagram:

7. Only female mosquitoes "bite," and only the females of a few species attack human beings and animals. They sip the victim's blood, which they need for the development of the eggs inside their bodies. Mosquitoes do not really bite because they cannot open their jaws. When a mosquito "bites," it stabs through the victim's skin with six needlelike parts called *stylets,* which form the center of the proboscis. The stylets are covered and protected by the insect's lower lip, called the *labium.* As the stylets enter the skin, the labium bends and slides upward out of the way. Then saliva flows into the wound through channels formed by the stylets. The mosquito can easily sip the blood because the saliva keeps it from clotting. Most persons are allergic to the saliva, and an itchy welt called a "mosquito bite" forms on the skin. After the mosquito has sipped enough blood, it slowly pulls the stylets out of the wound, and the labium slips into place over them. Then the insect flies away.[33]

Pattern: _____

Reason: _____

Diagram:

8. To understand the organization of long-term memory, then, we need to understand what kinds of information can be stored there. Most theories distinguish skills or habits ("knowing how") from abstract or representational knowledge ("knowing that"). Procedural memories are memories of knowing how—for example, knowing how to comb your hair, use a pencil, or swim. Declarative memories are memories of "knowing that." Declarative memories, in turn, come in two varieties. Semantic memories are internal representations of the world, independent of any particular context. They include facts, rules, and concepts. On the basis of your semantic memory of the concept *cat,* you can describe a cat as a small, furry mammal that typically spends its time eating, sleeping, and staring into space, even though a cat may not be present when you give this description and you probably won't know how or when you learned it. Episodic memories, on the other hand, are internal representations of personally experienced events. They allow you to "travel back" in time. When you remember how your furry feline once surprised you in the middle of the night by pouncing on your face as you slept, you are retrieving an episodic memory.[34]

Pattern: _____

Reason: _____

Diagram:

9. People turn to magic chiefly as a form of insurance—that is, they use it along with actions that actually bring results. For example, hunters may use a hunting charm. But they also use their hunting skills and knowledge of animals. The charm may give hunters the extra confidence they need to hunt even more successfully than they would without it. If they shoot a lot of game, they credit the charm for their success. Many events occur naturally without magic. Crops grow without it, and sick people get well without it. But if people use magic to bring a good harvest or to cure a patient, they may believe the magic was responsible. People also tend to forget magic's failures and to be impressed by its apparent successes. They may consider magic successful if it appears to work only 10 percent of the time. Even when magic fails, people often explain the failure without doubting the power of the magic. They may say that the magician made a mistake in reciting the spell or that another magician cast a more powerful spell against the magician.

Many anthropologists believe that people have faith in magic because they feel a need to believe in it. People may turn to magic to reduce their fear and uncertainty if they feel they have no control over the outcome of a situation. For example, farmers use knowledge and skill when they plant their fields. But they know that weather, insects, or diseases might ruin the crops. So farmers in some societies may also plant a charm or perform a magic rite to ensure a good harvest.[35]

Pattern: _____

Reason: _____

Diagram:

10. Almost all companies realize the tremendous value of mathematics in research and planning. Many major industrial firms employ trained mathematicians. Mathematics has great importance in all engineering projects. For example, the design of a superhighway requires extensive use of mathematics. The construction of a giant dam would be impossible without first filling reams of paper with mathematical formulas and calculations. The large number of courses an engineering student must take in mathematics shows the importance of mathematics in this field.[36]

Pattern: _____

Reason: _____

Diagram:

OTHER USEFUL PATTERNS OF ORGANIZATION

The patterns presented in the previous section are the most common. Table 9-1 (page 294) presents a brief review of those patterns and their corresponding transitional words. However, writers do not limit themselves to these six patterns. Especially in academic writing, you may find one or more of the patterns listed in Table 9-2 (page 295), as well. Here is a brief review of each of these additional patterns.

Statement and Clarification

Many writers make a statement of fact and then proceed to clarify or explain that statement. For instance, a writer may open a paragraph by stating that "The best education for you may not be the best education for someone else." The remainder of the paragraph would then discuss that statement and make its meaning clear by explaining how educational needs are individual and based on one's talents, skills, and goals. Transitional words associated with this pattern are listed in Table 9-2.

Summary

A summary is a condensed statement that provides the key points of a larger idea or piece of writing. The summaries at the end of each chapter of this text provide a quick review of the chapter's contents. Often writers summarize what they have already said or what someone else has said. For example, in a psychology textbook you will find many summaries of research. Instead of asking you to read an entire research study, the textbook author will summarize the study's findings. Other times a writer may repeat in condensed form what he or she has already said as a means of emphasis or clarification. Transitional words associated with this pattern are listed in Table 9-2.

Addition

Writers often introduce an idea or make a statement and then supply additional information about that idea or statement. For instance, an education textbook may introduce the concept of home schooling and then provide in-depth information about its benefits. This pattern is often used to expand, elaborate, or discuss an idea in greater detail. Transitional words associated with this pattern are listed in Table 9-2.

TABLE 9-1 A Review of Patterns and Transitional Words

Pattern	Characteristics	Transitional Words
Chronological Order	Describes events, processes, procedures	after, as soon as, before, during, finally, first, following, in, last, later, meanwhile, next, on, second, then, until, when
Definition	Explains the meaning of a word or phrase	are those that, can be defined as, consists of, corresponds to, entails, involves, is, is a term that, is called, is characterized, is literally, means, occurs when, refers to
Classification	Divides a topic into parts based on shared characteristics	another, classified as, different groups that, different stages of, finally, first, includes, is composed of, is comprised of, last, one, second, several varieties of
Comparison-Contrast	Discusses similarities and/or differences among ideas, theories, concepts, objects, or persons	*Similarities*: both, also, similarly, like, likewise, too, as well as, resembles, correspondingly, in the same way, to compare, in comparison, share *Differences*: unlike, differs from, in contrast, on the other hand, instead, despite, nevertheless, however, in spite of, whereas, as opposed to
Cause-Effect	Describes how one or more things cause or are related to another	*Causes*: because, because of, for, since, stems from, one cause is, one reason is, leads to, causes, creates, yields, produces, due to, breeds, for this reason *Effects*: consequently, results in, one result is, therefore, thus, as a result, hence
Enumeration/Simple listing	Organizes lists of information: characteristics, features, parts, or categories	the following, several, for example, for instance, one, another, also, too, in other words, first, second, the numerals (1, 2), letters (a, b), most importantly, largest, the least, finally, importantly

TABLE 9-2 A Review of Additional Patterns and Transitional Words

Pattern	Characteristics	Transitional Words
Statement and Clarification	Indicates that information explaining an idea or concept will follow	clearly, evidently, in fact, in other words, obviously
Summary	Indicates that a condensed review of a idea or piece of writing will follow	in brief, in conclusion, in short, in summary, on the whole, to summarize, to sum up
Addition	Indicates that additional information will follow	additionally, again, also, besides, further, furthermore, in addition, moreover
Spatial Order	Describes physical location or position in space	above, behind, below, besides, in front of, inside, nearby next to, opposite, outside, within

Spatial Order

Spatial order is concerned with the physical location or position in space. Spatial order is used in disciplines in which physical descriptions are important. A photography textbook may use spatial order to describe the parts of a camera. An automotive technology textbook may use spatial order to describe disk brake operation. Transitional words associated with this pattern are listed in Table 9-2.

EXERCISE 9-14

Directions: For each of the following statements, identify the pattern that is evident and write its name in the space provided. Choose from among the following patterns:

a. statement and clarification
b. summary
c. generalization and example
d. addition
e. spatial order

_____ 1. Short fibers, dendrites, branch out around the cell body and a single long fiber, the axon, extends from the cell body.

_____ 2. Aspirin is not as harmless as people think. It may cause allergic reactions and stomach irritation. In addition, aspirin has been linked to a fatal condition known as Reye's disease.

_____ 3. If our criminal justice system works, the recidivism rate—the percentage of people released from prison who return—should decrease. In other words, in a successful system, there should be a decrease in the number of criminals who are released from prison and then become repeat offenders.

_____ 4. Students who are informed about drugs tend to use them in greater moderation. Furthermore, they tend to help educate others.

_____ 5. A successful drug addiction treatment program would offer free or very cheap drugs to addicts. Heroin addicts, for example, could be prescribed heroin when under a physician's care.

_____ 6. In conclusion, it is safe to say that crime by women is likely to increase as greater numbers of women assume roles traditionally held by men.

_____ 7. The pollutants we have just discussed all involve chemicals; we can conclude that they threaten our environment and our well-being.

_____ 8. A residual check valve that maintains slight pressure on the hydraulic system is located in the master cylinder at the outlet for the drum brakes.

_____ 9. Sociologists study how we are socialized into sex roles—the attitudes expected of males and females. Sex roles, in fact, identify some activities and behaviors as clearly male and others as clearly female.

_____ 10. Patients often consult a lay referral network to discuss their medical problems. Cancer patients, for instance, can access Internet discussion groups that provide both information and support.

Using Transitional Words

As you learned earlier in the chapter, transitional words can help you identify organizational patterns. These words are called _transitional words_ because they help you make the transition or connection between ideas. They may also be called _clue words_ or _directional words_ because they provide readers with clues about what is to follow.

Transitional words are also helpful in discovering or clarifying relationships between and among ideas in any piece of writing. Specifically, transitional words help you grasp connections between and within sentences. Transitional words can help you predict what is to come next within a paragraph. For instance, if you are reading along and come upon the phrase *in conclusion,* you know that the writer will soon present a summary. If you encounter the word *furthermore,* you know that the writer is about to present additional information about the subject at hand. If you encounter the word *consequently* in the middle of a sentence (The law was repealed; consequently, . . .), you know that the writer is about to explain what happened as a result of the repeal. Tables 9-1 and 9-2 on pages 294 and 295 list the directional words that correspond to the patterns discussed in this chapter.

EXERCISE 9-15

Directions: Each of the following beginnings of paragraphs uses a transitional word or phrase to tell the reader what will follow in the paragraph. Read each, paying particular attention to the underlined transitional word or phrase. Then, in the space provided, describe as specifically as you can what you would expect to find next in the paragraph.

1. Many Web sites on the Internet are reliable and trustworthy. <u>However,</u> . . .

   _____

2. One advantage of using a computer to take notes is that you can rearrange information easily. <u>Another</u> . . .

   _____

3. There are a number of ways to avoid catching the cold virus. <u>First of all,</u> . . .

   _____

4. Some pet owners care for their animals responsibly. <u>However, others</u> . . .

   _____

5. When planning a speech, you should choose a topic that is familiar or that you are knowledgeable about. <u>Next,</u> . . .

   _____

6. Following a high protein diet may be rewarding because it often produces quick weight loss. <u>On the other hand,</u> . . .

_____

7. The iris is a doughnut-shaped portion of the eyeball. <u>In the center</u> . . .

_____

8. Price is not the only factor consumers consider when making a major purchase. They also . . .

_____

9. Cholesterol, commonly found in many fast foods, is associated with heart disease. <u>Consequently,</u> . . .

_____

10. Many Web sites provide valuable links to related sites. <u>To illustrate,</u> visit . . .

_____

WORKING TOGETHER

Directions: Locate and mark five paragraphs in one of your textbooks or in Part Six of this text that are clear examples of the thought patterns discussed in this chapter. Write the topic sentence of each paragraph on a separate index card. Once your instructor has formed small groups, choose a group "reader" who will collect all the cards and read each sentence aloud. Groups should discuss each and predict the pattern of the paragraph from which the sentence was taken. The "finder" of the topic sentence then confirms or rejects the choice, quoting sections of the paragraph if necessary.

Learning Style Tips

If you tend to be a . . .	Then identify thought patterns by . . .
Spatial learner	Drawing a diagram of the ideas in the passage
Verbal learner	Outlining the passage

MASTERING VOCABULARY

Directions: Match each word in Column A with its meaning in Column B. Determine the meaning from its context in this chapter, its word parts, or use a dictionary, if necessary.

Column A

_____ 1. nonverbal (p. 266)

_____ 2. preliterate (p. 266)

_____ 3. interact (p. 272)

_____ 4. disorders (p. 276)

_____ 5. imbalances (p. 276)

_____ 6. erupting (p. 283)

_____ 7. coeducational (p. 284)

_____ 8. antisocial (p. 288)

_____ 9. uncertainty (p. 291)

_____ 10. superhighway (p. 292)

Column B

a. disparities

b. doubt

c. exploding

d. both sexes learning together

e. unspoken

f. communicate and cooperate

g. against what society expects

h. illnesses

i. before reading existed

j. broad, multi-lane highway

SELF-TEST SUMMARY

How can I better comprehend and recall paragraphs I read?	Recognizing the author's thought pattern will improve comprehension and recall.
What is a thought pattern?	A thought pattern is the way in which an author organizes ideas.

What are the six common thought patterns?

The six common thought patterns are:

1. Illustration/Example—an idea is explained by providing specific instances or experiences that illustrate it.
2. Definition—an object or idea is explained by describing the general class or group to which it belongs and how the item differs from others in the same group (distinguishing features).
3. Comparison/Contrast—a new or unfamiliar idea is explained by showing how it is similar to or different from a more familiar idea.
4. Cause/Effect—connections between events are explained by showing what caused an event or what happened as a result of a particular event.
5. Classification—an object or idea is explained by dividing it into parts and describing or explaining each.
6. Chronological Order/Process—events or procedures are described in the order in which they occur in time.

What other thought patterns are used in academic writing?

1. Statement and Clarification—an explanation will follow.
2. Summary—a condensed view of the subject will be presented.
3. Addition—additional information will follow.
4. Spatial order—physical location or position will be described.

How can transitional words and phrases help you understand thought patterns?

Transitional words and phrases emphasize the connection and relationship among ideas in a paragraph or passage.

Name _____

Section _____ Date _____

Number right _____ x 20 points = Score _____

Directions: For each of the following topic sentences, predict what pattern the paragraph is likely to follow.

_____ 1. Exposing children to music at an early age appears to have several positive effects.
    a. classification
    b. definition
    c. cause/effect
    d. comparison/contrast

_____ 2. Depending on how you plan to use the Internet at home, you may select either dial-up Internet service, cable modem service, or a digital subscriber line (DSL).
    a. definition
    b. summary
    c. chronological order
    d. comparison/contrast

_____ 3. Organisms can be grouped into three domains: Bacteria, Archaea, and Eukarya.
    a. classification
    b. cause/effect
    c. summary
    d. spatial order

_____ 4. According to psychiatrist Elisabeth Kübler-Ross, terminally ill patients go through five stages as they face death.
    a. comparison/contrast
    b. chronological order
    c. cause/effect
    d. spatial order

_____ 5. In conclusion, it is simply too soon to tell what President Clinton's legacy will be.
    a. enumeration
    b. summary
    c. comparison/contrast
    d. definition

**CHAPTER 9
MASTERY TEST 2:
Paragraph Skills**

Name _____
Section _____ Date _____
Number right _____ x 20 points = Score _____

Directions: Read the passage below and then answer the questions that follow.

Companies need to be sensitive to the concerns of consumer groups. Building good relationships with these groups benefits an organization in two ways. First, by understanding the concerns of these groups, the firm is able to develop its own socially responsible programs and practices that will gain the favor of the groups and others in the community. Second, when problems arise such as a potentially dangerous product design flaw, activist groups are more likely to work with the firm to make changes and less likely to organize some form of public protest against it.

Adolph Coors, the beer manufacturer, developed good relationships with several consumer groups when it promoted a romance novel as part of a $40 million, five-year marketing program against illiteracy. The book, titled *Perfect,* reached the *New York Times'* best-seller list. Coors's literacy program campaign drew thousands of inquiries, improved Coors's reputation in the community, and favorably influenced Coors's other important relationships with customers, employees, and shareholders.

To review, evaluating a firm's internal environment includes assessing corporate resources and competencies, understanding the corporate environment, and looking at the relationships a firm has with various groups. In this way the firm can identify the strengths and weaknesses that can create (or not create) both economic and social profit.[37]

_____ 1. The pattern that the authors use to organize their ideas in the first paragraph is
a. definition.
b. comparison/contrast.
c. cause/effect.
d. enumeration.

_____ 2. The transitional words that signal the authors' thought pattern in the first paragraph are
a. *companies* and *consumer groups.*
b. *programs* and *practices.*
c. *first* and *second.*
d. *more likely* and *less likely.*

_____ 3. The pattern that the authors use to organize their ideas in the second paragraph is
a. chronological order.
b. illustration/example.
c. classification.
d. addition.

_____ 4. The pattern that the authors use to organize their ideas in the third paragraph is
a. comparison/contrast.
b. summary.
c. spatial order.
d. illustration/example.

_____ 5. The transitional words that signal the authors' thought pattern in the third paragraph are
a. *evaluating includes.*
b. *in this way.*
c. *to review.*
d. *strengths* and *weaknesses.*

Name _____

Section _____ Date _____

Number right _____ x 10 points = Score _____

Directions: Read each of the following paragraphs. Write the letter of the main thought pattern used in the blank provided.

    a. definition

    b. comparison/contrast

    c. illustration/example

    d. cause/effect

    e. classification

    f. chronological order/process

_F_ 1. You need to take a few steps to prepare to become a better note-taker. First, get organized. It's easiest to take useful notes if you have a system. A loose leaf notebook works best because you can add, rearrange, or remove notes for review. If you use spiral or other permanently bound notebooks, use a separate notebook for each subject to avoid confusion and to allow for expansion. Second, set aside a few minutes each day to review the syllabus for your course, to scan the assigned readings, and to review your notes from the previous class period. If you do this just before each lecture, you'll be ready to take notes and practice critical thinking. Finally, prepare your pages by drawing a line down the left margin approximately two inches from the edge of the paper. Leave this margin blank while you take notes so that later you can use it to practice critical thinking.[38]

_A_ 2. Genetics is the scientific study of heredity, the transmission of characteristics from parents to offspring. Genetics explains why offspring resemble their parents and also why they are not identical to them. Genetics is a subject that has considerable economic, medical, and social significance, and is partly the basis for the modern theory of evolution. Because of its importance, genetics has been a topic of central interest in the study of life for centuries. Modern concepts in genetics are fundamentally different, however, from earlier ones.[39]

_C_ 3. Colors surely influence our perceptions and our behaviors. People's acceptance of a product, for example, is largely determined by its package. The very same coffee taken from a yellow can was described as weak, from a dark brown can too strong, from a red can rich, and from a blue can mild. Even our acceptance of a person may depend on the colors worn. Consider, for example, the comments of one color expert: "If you have to pick the wardrobe for your defense lawyer in court and choose anything but blue, you deserve to lose the case. . . ." Black is so powerful it could work against a lawyer with the jury. Brown lacks sufficient authority. Green would probably elicit a negative response.[40]

(continued)

B

4. France and the United States present an interesting contrast of cultural factors that affect the push-pull mix. U.S. homemakers spend more time watching television and reading magazines, and they rely more on friends and advertising before purchasing a new product. In contrast, French homemakers spend more time shopping, examining items on shelves, and listening to the opinions of retailers. Therefore, it has been easier to presell U.S. homemakers, whereas in France discounts to distributors and point-of purchase displays have been more effective.[41]

F

5. In 1980, the Asian children far outperformed the American children on a broad battery of mathematical tests. On computation and word problems, there was virtually no overlap between schools, with the lowest-scoring Beijing schools doing better than the highest-scoring Chicago schools. By 1990, the gap between the Asian and American children had grown ever greater. Only 4 percent of the Chinese children and 10 percent of the Japanese children had scores as lows as those of the average American child. These differences could not be accounted for by educational resources: the Chinese had worse facilities and larger classes than the Americans. On the average, the American children's parents were far better-off financially and were better educated than the parents of the Chinese children. Nor could the test differences be accounted for by differ-

ences in the children's fondness for math: 85 percent of the Chinese kids said they like math, but so did almost 75 percent of the American children. Not did it have anything to do with intellectual ability in general, because the American children were just as knowledgeable and capable as the Asian children on tests of general information.[42]

A

6. Convenience goods are products bought with a minimum of time and effort. Little forethought or planning occurs prior to the purchase of a convenience good. Convenience goods can be further categorized into three subtypes: staples, emergency goods, and impulse goods. Staples are convenience goods that consumers have purchased many times before. This means the consumer already has a high level of knowledge about the product and does not need to do a great deal of shopping. Emergency goods are convenience goods that consumers purchase with little forethought, planning, or effort because a situation arises that requires immediate possession of the item. If you are caught in a rainstorm while out of town you might purchase an umbrella even if you have one at home. Impulse goods are convenience goods that consumers purchase with no preplanning or thought. Seeing the item offered for sale is the stimulus that motivates the purchase. For example, have you ever stood in line at the checkout in a grocery store and added a candy bar, some gum, a magazine, or some batteries to your purchases?

If so, you have bought impulse goods.[43]

E 7. The next step is to install browser software on your computer. You can purchase a browser in your local software retail outlet or, if you have some other online access vehicle, possibly download it free from the browser vendor's web site. As you are installing the browser, you will be asked for information about your ISP, for which your ISP will have prepared you. (An ISP typically furnishes several pages of detailed instructions.) Once you are set up, you invoke the browser as you would any software on your computer, and it will begin by dialing the Internet service provider for you. You are on your way to the Internet experience.[44]

D 8. The effects of alcohol on the fetus are different at different stages of pregnancy; the most dangerous stage is the first trimester (12 weeks), but a little alcohol later in pregnancy is sometimes recommended as a way to prevent premature contractions. In a longitudinal British study, the children of mothers who did not drink at all during pregnancy were not different from those of mothers who had had fewer than 10 drinks a week during pregnancy. In contrast, a similar American study, in which more than 500 children have been followed from birth to age 14, found small but significant differences in the children's intellectual performance when the mother had a drink or two of alcohol per day during their

pregnancies. So most American researchers conclude that the safest course of action for pregnant women is to abstain entirely.[45]

A 9. Pitch is the dimension of auditory experience related to the frequency of the sound wave and, to some extent, its intensity. Frequency refers to how rapidly the air (or other medium) vibrates—that is, the number of times per second the wave cycles through a peak and a low point. One cycle per second is known as 1 hertz (Hz). The healthy ear of a young person normally detects frequencies in the range of 16 Hz (the lowest note on a pipe organ) to 20,000 Hz (the scraping of a grasshopper's legs).[46]

A 10. Culture change can originate from two sources: innovation and borrowing. *Innovation* is the invention of new forms. It involves the recombination of what people already know into something different. For example, Canadian Joseph-Armand Bombardier became an innovator when he added tracks, designed to propel earth-moving equipment, to a small bus that originally ran on tires, producing the first snowmobile in the 1950s. Later the Skolt Lapps of Finland joined him as innovators when they adapted his now smaller, more refined snowmobile for herding reindeer in 1961. The Lapp innovation was not the vehicle itself. That was borrowed. What was new was the use of the vehicle in herding, something usually done by men on skis.[47]

**CHAPTER 9
MASTERY TEST 4:
Reading Selection**

Name _____
Section _____ Date _____
Number right _____ x 10 points = Score _____

Right Place, Wrong Face

Alton Fitzgerald White

In this selection, the author describes what it was like to be treated as a criminal on the basis of nothing more than having the "wrong face."

Vocabulary Preview

ovation (par. 3) enthusiastic, prolonged applause

overt (par. 4) not secret, obvious

splurged (par. 5) indulged in a luxury

vestibule (par. 5) a small entrance hall or passage into the interior of a building

residue (par. 9) something that remains after a substance is taken away

violation (par. 14) the condition of being treated unfairly or offended

1   As the youngest of five girls and two boys growing up in Cincinnati, I was raised to believe that if I worked hard, was a good person, and always told the truth, the world would be my oyster. I was raised to be a gentleman and learned that these qualities would bring me respect.

2   While one has to earn respect, consideration is something owed to every human being. On Friday, June 16, 1999, when I was wrongfully arrested at my Harlem apartment building, my perception of everything I had learned as a young man was forever changed—not only because I wasn't given even a second to use the manners my parents taught me, but mostly because the police, whom I'd always naively thought were sup-

posed to serve and protect me, were actually hunting me.

3   I had planned a pleasant day. The night before was payday, plus I had received a standing ovation after portraying the starring role of Coalhouse Walker Jr. in the Broadway musical *Ragtime*. It is a role that requires not only talent but also an honest emotional investment of the morals and lessons I learned as a child.

4   Coalhouse Walker Jr. is a victim (an often misused word, but in this case true) of overt racism. His story is every black man's nightmare. He is hard-working, successful, talented, charismatic, friendly, and polite. Perfect prey for someone with authority and not even a fraction of those qualities. On that Friday afternoon, I became a real-life Coalhouse Walker. Nothing could have prepared me for it. Not even stories told to me

by other black men who had suffered similar injustices.

5   Friday for me usually means a trip to the bank, errands, the gym, dinner, and then off to the theater. On this particular day, I decided to break my pattern of getting up and running right out of the house. Instead, I took my time, slowed my pace, and splurged by making strawberry pancakes. Before I knew it, it was 2:45; my bank closes at 3:30, leaving me less than 45 minutes to get to midtown Manhattan on the train. I was pressed for time but in a relaxed, blessed state of mind. When I walked through the lobby of my building, I noticed two light-skinned Hispanic men I'd never seen before. Not thinking much of it, I continued on to the vestibule, which is separated from the lobby by a locked door.

6   As I approached the exit, I saw people in uniforms rushing toward the door. I sped up to open it for them. I thought they might be paramedics, since many of the building's occupants are elderly. It wasn't until I had opened the door and greeted them that I recognized that they were police officers. Within seconds, I was told to "hold it"' they had received a call about young Hispanics with guns. I was told to get against the wall. I was searched, stripped of my backpack, put on my knees, handcuffed, and told to be quiet when I tried to ask questions.

7   With me were three other innocent black men who had been on their way to their U-Haul. They were moving into the apartment beneath mine, and I had just bragged to them about how safe the building was. One of these gentlemen got off his knees, still handcuffed, and unlocked the door for the officers to get into the lobby where the two strangers were standing. Instead of thanking or even acknowledging us, they led us out the door past our neighbors, who were all but begging the police in our defense.

8   The four of us were put into cars with the two strangers and taken to the precinct station at 165th and Amsterdam. The police automatically linked us, with no questions and no regard for our character or our lives. No consideration was given to where we were going or why. Suppose an ailing relative was waiting upstairs, while I ran out for her medication? Or young children, who'd been told that Daddy was running to the corner store for milk and would be right back? My new neighbors weren't even allowed to lock their apartment or check on the U-Haul.

9   After we were lined up in the station, the younger of the two Hispanic men was identified as an experienced criminal, and drug residue was found in a pocket of the other. I now realize how naive I was to think that the police would then uncuff me, apologize for their mistake, and let me go. Instead, they continued to search my backpack, questioned me, and put me in jail with the criminals.

10   The rest of the nearly five-hour ordeal was like a horrible dream. I was handcuffed, strip-searched, taken in and out for questioning. The officers told me that they knew exactly who I was, knew I was in *Ragtime*, and that in fact they already had the men they wanted.

11   How then could they keep me there, or have brought me there in the first place? I was told it was standard procedure. As if the average law-abiding citizen knows what that is and can dispute it. From what I now know, "standard procedure" is something that every citizen, black and white, needs to learn, and fast.

12   I felt completely powerless. Why, do you think? Here I was, young, pleasant, and

successful, in good physical shape, dressed in clean athletic attire. I was carrying a backpack containing a substantial paycheck and a deposit slip, on my way to the bank. Yet after hours and hours I was sitting at a desk with two officers who not only couldn't tell me why I was there but seemed determined to find something on me, to the point of making me miss my performance.

13   It was because I am a black man!

14   I sat in that cell crying silent tears of disappointment and injustice with the realization of how many innocent black men are convicted for no reason. When I was handcuffed, my first instinct had been to pull away out of pure insult and violation as a human being. Thank God I was calm enough to do what they said. When I was thrown in jail with the criminals and strip-searched, I somehow knew to put my pride aside, be quiet, and do exactly what I was told, hating it but coming to terms with the fact that in this situation I was a victim. They had guns!

15   Before I was finally let go, exhausted, humiliated, embarrassed, and still in shock, I was led to a room and given a pseudo-apology. I was told that I was at the wrong place at the wrong time. My reply? "I was where I live."

16   Everything I learned growing up in Cincinnati has been shattered. Life will never be the same.

Directions: Choose the letter that best answers each of the following questions.

CHECKING YOUR COMPREHENSION

_____ 1. The author's main purpose in this selection is to
   a. describe his recent experience with racism.
   b. discuss the effects of racism on young people.
   c. criticize the New York police department.
   d. contrast Cincinnati with New York.

_____ 2. Coalhouse Walker Jr. is the name of
   a. the author of the article.
   b. a black actor in New York.
   c. the main character in a Broadway play.
   d. a racist police officer.

_____ 3. The main idea of paragraph 5 is that the author
   a. had errands to take care of.
   b. was making strawberry pancakes.
   c. lives 45 minutes from midtown Manhattan.
   d. changed his routine and was enjoying a leisurely day.

_____ 4. The two strangers in the lobby of the building were
   a. friends of the author.
   b. new residents of the building.
   c. undercover police officers.
   d. suspected criminals.

_____ 5. After opening the door for the police, the author was
   a. thanked by the police and released to go.
   b. assaulted by criminals.
   c. handcuffed and taken away by the police.
   d. harassed by his neighbors.

_____ 6. In paragraph 2, the word "naively" means
   a. innocently.
   b. negatively.
   c. purposely.
   d. unfortunately.

APPLYING YOUR SKILLS

_____ 7. The main thought pattern used in this selection is
   a. definition.
   b. chronological order.
   c. enumeration.
   d. classification.

_____ 8. In paragraph 2, the transitional word or phrase that indicates the chronological order thought pattern is
   a. while.
   b. On Friday.
   c. because.
   d. but.

_____ 9. In paragraph 9, all of the following transitional words indicate the chronological order thought pattern *except*
   a. after.
   b. now.
   c. instead.
   d. then.

_____ 10. The main thought pattern used in paragraphs 12 and 13 is
   a. cause/effect.
   b. summary.
   c. enumeration.
   d. definition.

Go Electronic!

For additional readings and exercises, and Internet activities, visit the book's Web site at:

http://www.ablongman.com/mcwhorter

If you need a username and password, please see your instructor.

Take a Road Trip to Ellis Island and the Statue of Liberty!

Be sure to visit the Patterns of Organization module in your Reading Road Trip CD-ROM for multimedia tutorials, exercises, and tests.

10

Reading Textbook Chapters

THIS CHAPTER WILL SHOW YOU HOW TO

1. Use textbook learning aids
2. Follow the organization of textbook chapters
3. Read technical material

Do you ever wonder how you will be able to learn the vast amounts of information contained in each of your textbooks? Fortunately, nearly all textbook authors are college instructors. They work with students daily and understand students' difficulties. Therefore, they include in their textbooks numerous features or aids to make learning easier. They also organize chapters in ways that express their ideas as clearly as possible. This chapter will discuss textbook learning aids and the organization of textbook chapters. It will also suggest special approaches to use when reading technical material.

TEXTBOOK LEARNING AIDS

While textbooks may seem long, difficult, and impersonal, they do contain numerous features that are intended to help you learn. By taking advantage of these features, you can make textbook reading easier.

The Preface

The **preface** is the author's introduction to the text. The preface presents basic information about the text you should know before you begin reading. It may contain such information as:

311

- Why and for whom the author wrote the text
- How the text is organized
- Purpose of the text
- References and authorities consulted
- Major points of emphasis
- Learning aids included and how to use them
- Special features of the text

The following is an excerpt from the preface of a computer science text. Read the excerpt, noting the type of information it provides.

Preface

theme and
purpose

Computers: Tools for an Information Age, Brief Edition, is up-to-date in every respect, from DVDs to MMX chips to cookies to push technology. The connectivity theme is integrated into several aspects of the book. In particular, we make it easy for students to explore the Internet.

Focus on the Internet

The Internet is close to center stage here. Notable features are as follows:

primary
focus of
the text

- **Quick start in Chapter 1.** The Internet is introduced in Chapter 1, in a section that gives basic information about the Web, browsers, servers, and Internet protocol.
- **New Internet chapter.** Chapter 7, "The Internet: A Resource for All of Us," focuses on the important aspects of Internet technology, from URLs to links to search engines. This chapter may be used independently of other chapters if students want information early on. Chapter 7 begins on page 195.
- **Planet Internet.** In this edition, Planet Internet has been expanded to a two-page spread at the end of each chapter. Without being technically oriented, each introduces students to some aspect of the World Wide Web. Topics include places to start, global aspects of the Internet, FAQs, business, entrepreneurs, shopping, careers, entertainment, and resources . . .

division of
text into
parts

Organization of the Text

The text is divided into an introductory photo essay and three parts, followed by one appendix:

- The opening Photo Essay gives students a feeling for the exciting world of computers and shows the diverse ways that people use them.
- Part 1, "An Overview of Computers," has two chapters, one to introduce hardware and another to introduce software, including home and business applications and brief coverage of operating systems.
- Part 2, "Hardware Tools," explores computer hardware including coverage of the central processing unit, input/output, and storage. . . .

features of
the text

Special Features

We have already described the new features called Getting Practical and New Directions, the two-page Planet Internet, and the Visual Internet gallery. In addition, the book offers:

- **Making the Right Connections.** Each chapter includes a feature article on linking people to computers. Topics range from the connectivity of workers in remote regions of Alaska (Chapter 2, page 56) to computers that can notify police if they are stolen (Chapter 4, page 96).
- **Margin notes.** To further engage the student, margin notes are placed throughout the text. The margin notes extend the text material by providing additional information and highlighting interesting applications of computers. . . .

learning
aids

In-Text Learning Aids

Each chapter includes the following pedagogical support:

- At the beginning of each chapter, **learning objectives** provide key concepts for students.
- **Key terms** are boldfaced throughout the text.
- A **Chapter Review** offers a summary of core concepts and boldfaced key terms.
- A **Quick Poll** offers ideas to generate class discussion. . . .

Service

Addison Wesley Longman is committed to providing you with service that is second to none. We would like to thank you for your interest in this textbook, and encourage you to contact us with your questions and comments. Please write to:

is@awl.com if the Information Systems team can be of assistance. We welcome any and all feedback about our company and products.

capron@awl.com if you have questions for the author about the material in this book.[1]

resources, questions and support

To the Student

Some textbooks contain a section titled "To the Student." This section is written specifically for you. It contains practical introductory information about the text. It may, for example, explain features of the book and how to use them, or it may offer suggestions for learning and studying the text. Often, a "To the Instructor" section precedes or follows "To the Student" and contains information useful to your instructor.

EXERCISE 10-1	**Directions:** Read or reread To the Student on p. xxvii of this book. Then answer the following questions.

1. How will this book help you become a successful student?

_____

_____

2. Place brackets around the sections that list the parts of the book.

_____

_____

3. Describe the mastery tests included at the end of each chapter.

_____

_____

4. What features (learning aids) does each chapter contain to help you learn?

   _____

   _____

5. How can you make rapid progress in this course?

   _____

   _____

Table of Contents

The **table of contents** is an outline of the text. It lists all the important topics and subtopics covered. Glancing through a table of contents will give you an overview of the text and suggest its organization.

Before beginning to read a particular chapter in a textbook, refer to the table of contents again. Although chapters are intended to be separate parts of a book, it is important to see how they fit together as parts of the whole—the textbook itself.

The Opening Chapter

The first chapter of a textbook is one of the most important. Here the author sets the stage for what is to follow. At first glance, the first chapter may not seem to say much, and you may be tempted to skip it. Actually, the opening chapter deserves close attention. More important, it introduces the important terminology used throughout the text.

Typically you can expect to find as many as 40 to 60 new words introduced and defined in the first chapter. These words are the language of the course, so to speak. To be successful in any new subject area, it is essential to learn to read and speak its language.

Typographical Aids

Textbooks contain various typographical aids (arrangements or types of print) that make it easy to pick out what is important to learn and remember. These include the following:

1. **Italic type** (slanted print) is often used to call attention to a particular word or phrase. Often new terms are printed in italics in the sentence in which they are defined.

   The term *drive* is used to refer to internal conditions that force an individual to work toward some goal.

2. **Enumeration** refers to the numbering or lettering of facts and ideas within a paragraph. It is used to emphasize key ideas and to make them easy to locate.

> Consumer behavior and the buying process involve five mental states: (1) awareness of the product, (2) interest in acquiring it, (3) desire or perceived need, (4) action, and (5) reaction or evaluation of the product.

3. **Headings and subheadings** divide the chapters into sections and label the major topic of each section. Basically, they tell in advance what each section will be about. When read in order, the headings and subheadings form a brief outline of the chapter.

4. **Colored print** is used in some texts to emphasize important ideas or definitions.

Chapter Questions

Many textbooks include discussion and/or review questions at the end of each chapter. Try to read these through when you preread the chapter (see Chapter 5). Then, after you have read the chapter, use the questions to review and test yourself. Since the review questions cover the factual content of the chapter, they can help you prepare for objective exams. Discussion questions often deal with interpretations or applications of the content. Use these in preparing for essay exams. Math, science, or technical courses may have problems instead of questions (see p. 329 of this chapter). Here are a few sample review and discussion questions taken from a business marketing textbook:

Review Questions

1. List some product characteristics that are of concern to marketers.
2. Distinguish between a trademark and a brand name.
3. What are some characteristics of good brand names?
4. Describe the three kinds of labels.

Discussion Questions

1. What do you think is the future of generic products?
2. Go to your local food store and look at the ways the products are packaged. Find three examples of packages that have value in themselves. Find three examples of packages that promote the products' effectiveness.
3. There is much controversy about the use of warning labels on products. Outline the pros and cons of this issue.
4. How would you go about developing a brand name for a new type of bread?

Did you notice that the review questions check your knowledge of factual information? These questions ask you to list, describe, or explain. To answer them, you have to recall the information contained in the chapter. The discussion questions, on the other hand, cannot be answered simply by looking up information in the text. Instead, you have to apply the information in the text to a practical situation or pull together and organize information.

Vocabulary List

Textbooks often contain a list of new terms introduced in the book. This list may appear at the beginning or end of individual chapters or at the back of the book. In some texts new terms are printed in the margin next to the portion of the text in which the term is introduced. Regardless of where they appear, vocabulary lists are a valuable study and review aid. Many instructors include on exams items that test mastery of new terms. Here is a sample vocabulary list taken from a financial management textbook.

Key Terms

assets
budget
cash flow statement
fixed disbursements
liabilities
money market fund
net worth
net worth statement
occasional disbursements

Notice that the author identifies the terms but does not define them. In such cases, mark new terms as you come across them in a chapter. After you have finished the chapter, review each marked term and its definition. To learn the terms, use the index card system suggested in Chapter 4.

Glossary

A **glossary** is a mini-dictionary that lists alphabetically the important vocabulary used in a book. A glossary is faster and more convenient to use than a dictionary. It does not list all the common meanings of a word, as a dictionary does, but instead gives only the meaning used in the text. Here is an excerpt from the glossary of a health textbook:

> **continuum** a progression of infinite degrees of some characteristic between two extremes
>
> **contraception** the prevention of conception
>
> **contraceptive** any technique, drug, or device that prevents conception
>
> **control** in an experiment, the standard against which observations or conclusions must be checked in order to establish their validity; for example, a person who or animal that has not been exposed to the treatment or condition being studied in the other people or animals
>
> **convalescence** the period of recovery after a disease
>
> **convulsion** sudden and repeated involuntary contraction of all of the body's muscles.[2]

Look at the entry for the word *control*. First, you can see that *control* is defined only as the term is used in the field of health science. The word *control* has many other meanings (see the section on multiple-meaning words in Chapter 4). Compare the glossary definition with the collegiate dictionary definition of the same word shown below.

con•trol (kən-trōl′) *tr. v.* **-trolled, -trol•ling, -trols. 1.** To exercise authoritative or dominating influence over; direct. See Synonyms at **conduct. 2.** To hold in restraint; check: *struggled to control my temper; regulations intended to control prices.* **3.a.** To verify or regulate (a scientific experiment) by conducting a parallel experiment or by comparing with another standard. **b.** To verify (an account, for example) by using a duplicate register for comparison.—**control** *n.* **1.** Authority or ability to manage or direct: *lost control of the skidding car; the leaders in control of the country.* **2.** Abbrev. **cont., contr. a.** One that controls; a controlling agent, device, or organization. **b.** Often **controls.** An instrument or set of instruments used to operate, regulate, or guide a machine or vehicle. **3.** A restraining device, measure, or limit; a curb: *a control on prices; price controls.* **4.a.** A standard of comparison for checking or verifying the results of an experiment. **b.** An individual or group used as a standard of comparison in a control experiment. **5.** An intelligence agent who supervises or instructs another agent. **6.** A spirit presumed to speak or act through a medium. [Middle English *controllen,* from Anglo-Norman *contreroller,* from Medieval Latin *contrā/rotulā/re,* to check by duplicate register, from *contrā/rotulus,* duplicate register: Latin *contrā/,* contra- + Latin *rotulus,* roll, diminutive of *rota,* wheel; see **ret-** in Appendix.]—**con•trol′la•bil′i•ty** *n.* **con•trol′la•ble** *adj.*[3]

Try to pick out the definition of *control* that is closest to the one given in the glossary. Did it take time to find the right definition? You can see that a glossary is a time-saving device.

At the end of a course, a glossary can serve as a useful study aid, since it lists the important terminology introduced throughout the text. Review the glossary and test your recall of the meaning of each entry.

| EXERCISE 10-2 | **Directions:** Choose a textbook from one of your other courses. (Do not choose a workbook or book of readings.) If you do not have a textbook, use a friend's or borrow one from the library. Answer each of the following questions by referring to the textbook. |

Textbook title: _____

1. What learning aids does the book contain?

   _____

   _____

   _____

2. Of what importance is the information given in the preface?

   _____

   _____

3. Preread the opening chapter. What is its function?

   _____

   _____

4. Review the table of contents. How is the subject divided?

   _____

   _____

HOW TEXTBOOK CHAPTERS ARE ORGANIZED

Have you ever walked into an unfamiliar supermarket and felt lost and confused? You did not know where anything was located and thought you would never find the items you needed. How did you finally locate what you needed? You probably found that signs hanging over the aisles indicated the types of products shelved in each section, which enabled you to find the right aisle. Then you no doubt found that similar products were grouped together; for example, all the cereal was in one place, all the meat was in another, and so forth.

You can easily feel lost and confused when reading textbook chapters, too. A chapter can seem like a huge, disorganized collection of facts, ideas, numbers, dates, and events to be memorized. Actually, a textbook chapter is, in one respect, much like a large supermarket. It, too, has signs that identify what is located in each section. These signs are the headings that divide the chapter into topics. Underneath each heading, similar ideas are grouped together, just as similar products are grouped together in a supermarket. Sometimes a group of similar or related ideas is labeled by a subheading (usually set in smaller type than the heading and/or indented differently). In most cases, several paragraphs come under one heading. In this way chapters take a major idea, break it into its important parts, and then break those parts into smaller parts.

You could picture the organization of the present chapter as shown in the diagram below.

Notice that this chapter has three major headings and that the first major heading is divided into eight subheadings. Since the chapter is divided into three major headings, you know that it covers three major topics. You can also tell that the first major heading discusses eight types of textbook aids. Of

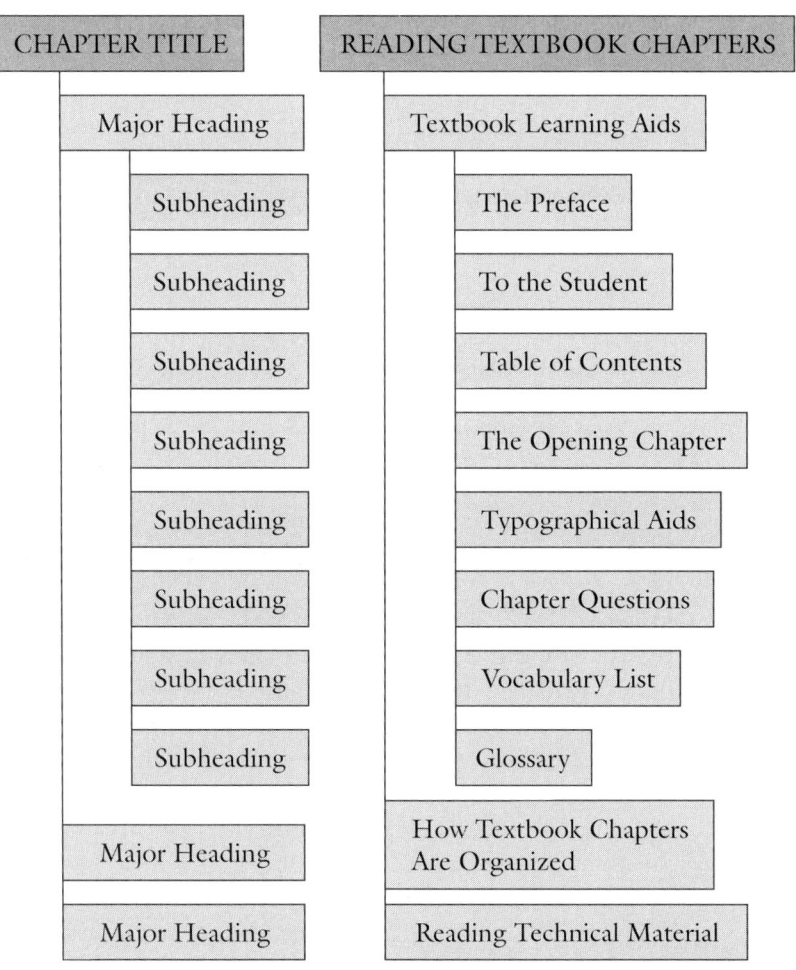

course, the number of major headings, subheadings, and paragraphs under each will vary from chapter to chapter in a book.

When you know how a chapter is organized, you can use this knowledge to guide your reading. Once you are familiar with the structure, you will also begin to see how ideas are connected. The chapter will then seem orderly, moving from one idea to the next in a logical fashion.

Look at the following partial listing of headings and subheadings from a chapter of a sociology textbook.

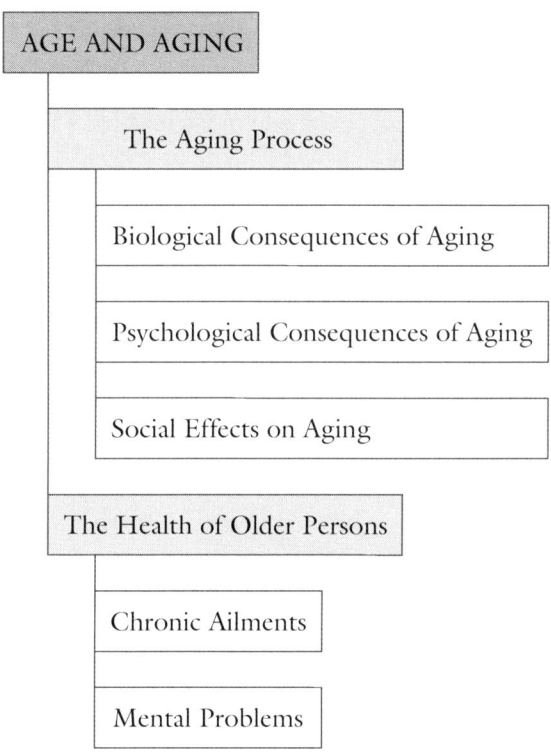

In this chapter on age and aging, "The Aging Process" and "The Health of Older Persons" are the first two major topics. The topic "The Aging Process" is broken into three parts: biological consequences, psychological consequences, and social effects. Although not shown on the diagram, each of these subtopics is further divided into paragraphs that list and describe, respectively, biological consequences, psychological consequences, and the social effects of aging. If there were four paragraphs under the subheading "Biological Consequences of Aging," it would be reasonable to expect that four main points will be presented about these consequences.

You are probably beginning to see that titles and headings, taken together, form a brief outline of a chapter. Later, in Chapter 12, you will see how these headings can help you make a more complete outline of a chapter. For now, think of headings as a guide to reading that directs you through a chapter point by point.

EXERCISE 10-3   **Directions:** On a separate sheet, draw a diagram that shows the organization of Chapter 4 of this book.

EXERCISE 10-4   **Directions:** Choose one of the textbooks that you are using for another course. Select a chapter you have already read and, on a separate sheet, draw an organizational diagram of its contents. Use the diagram on p. 320 as a guide.

READING TECHNICAL MATERIAL

If you are taking courses in the sciences, technologies, engineering, data processing, or health-related fields, you are working with a specialized type of textbook. This type of textbook is also used in courses that prepare students for specialized careers, such as food service, air conditioning and refrigeration repair, lab technology, and so forth.

In this section you will see how technical textbooks differ from those used in other classes. You will also learn several specific approaches to reading technical material.

Each of the following paragraphs describes a spice called nutmeg. Read each and decide how they differ.

Nutmeg is a spice derived by grating the kernel of the fruit produced by the nutmeg tree. This tree belongs to the nutmeg family, Myristicacae, genus Myristica, species M. fragrans. The tree grows to a height of seventy feet and is an evergreen. As the fruit of the tree ripens, it hardens and splits open at the top, showing a bright scarlet membrane. The spice called mace is made from this membrane.

Nutmeg is a pungent, aromatic spice often added to foods to give them a delicious tang and perfume. It adds a subtle spiciness to desserts and perks up the flavor of such bland dishes as potatoes. Nutmeg comes from a tree grown in warm climates. The nutmeg tree is tall and gracious, with long, pale leaves and beautiful yellow flowers.

Did you notice that the first paragraph presented only precise, factual information? The words used have exact meanings. Some words have technical meanings (*genus, species, Myristica*). Others are everyday words used in a special way (*evergreen, membrane*). An abbreviation, *M.*, was also used. Because of its language, the paragraph does not allow for interpretation or expression of opinion. In fact, you cannot tell whether the writer likes or has ever tasted nutmeg. The purpose of the paragraph is to give clear, detailed information about nutmeg.

The second paragraph is written quite differently. It presents fewer facts and more description. Many words—such as *delicious, beautiful, gracious,* and *subtle*— do not have a precise meaning. They allow room for interpretation and judgment. This paragraph is written to help you imagine how nutmeg tastes as well as to tell where it comes from.

The first paragraph is an example of technical writing. You can see that technical writing is a precise, exact, factual type of writing. This section will discuss particular features of technical writing and suggest approaches to reading technical material.

Fact Density

Technical writing is highly factual and dense (packed with ideas). A large number of facts are closely fitted together in each paragraph. Compared to other types of writing, technical writing may seem crowded with information and difficult to read. Here are a few suggestions on how to handle densely written material:

1. **Read technical material more slowly and carefully than other textbooks.** Allow more time for a technical reading assignment than for other assignments.

2. **Plan on reviewing various sections several times.** Sometimes it is useful to read a section once rather quickly to learn what key ideas it contains. Then read it a second time carefully, fitting together all the facts that explain the key ideas.

3. **Keep a notebook of important information.** In some textbooks, you can underline what is important to remember. (This method is discussed in Chapter 13.) However, since technical books are so highly factual, underlining may not work well—it may seem that everything is important, and you will end up with most of a page underlined. Instead, try using a notebook to record information you need to remember. Writing information in your own words is a good way to check whether you really understand it.

EXERCISE 10-5	**Directions:** Refer to the two paragraphs about nutmeg on p. 322. Count how many facts (separate pieces of information) each paragraph contains. Write the number in the space provided. Then list several facts as examples.

	Paragraph 1	**Paragraph 2**
Number of facts:	1. _____	1. _____
Examples of facts:	1. _____	1. _____
	2. _____	2. _____
	3. _____	3. _____

The Vocabulary of Technical Writing

Reading a technical book is in some ways like visiting a foreign country where an unfamiliar language is spoken. You hear an occasional word you know, but, for the most part, the people are communicating in a way you cannot understand.

Technical writing is built upon a set of precise, exact word meanings in each subject area. Since each field has its own language, you must learn the language in order to understand the material. Here are a few sentences taken from several technical textbooks. As you read each sentence, note the large number of technical words used.

Engineering Materials

If the polymer is a mixture of polymers, the component homopolymers (polymers of a single monomer species) and their percentages should be stated.[4]

Auto Mechanics

Each free end of the three stator windings is connected to the leads of one negative diode and one positive diode.[5]

Data Processing

Another advantage of the PERFORM/VARYING statement is that the FROM value and the BY value may be any numeric value (except that the BY value may not be zero).[6]

In the above examples, some words are familiar ones with new, unfamiliar meanings (*FROM, BY*). Others are words you may never have seen before (*monomer, stator*).

TABLE 10-1 Examples of Specialized Vocabulary in Technical Writing

Field	Word	Technical Meaning
Familiar words		
chemistry	base	a chemical compound that reacts with an acid to form a salt
electrical engineering	ground	a conductor that makes an electrical connection with the earth
nursing	murmur	an abnormal sound heard from a body organ (especially the heart)
Specialized terms		
computer science	modem	an interface (connector) that allows the computer to send and receive digital signals over telephone lines or through satellites
astronomy	magnetosphere	the magnetic field that surrounds the earth or other magnetized planet
biology	cocci	spherically shaped bacteria

In technical writing, there are two types of specialized vocabulary: (1) familiar words with new technical meanings, and (2) specialized terms.

Examples of each are given in Table 10-1.

Tips for Learning Technical Vocabulary

Many of the techniques you have already learned for developing your general vocabulary also work with technical vocabulary. Here are some ways to apply these techniques:

1. **Context clues (see Chapter 2) are commonly included in technical writing.** A definition clue is most frequently used when a word is introduced for the first time. As each new word is introduced, mark it in your text and later transfer it to your notebook. Organize this section of your notebook by chapter. Use the card system described in Chapter 4 to learn words you are having trouble remembering.

2. **Analyzing parts (see Chapter 3) is a particularly useful approach for developing technical vocabulary.** The technical words in many fields are created from particular sets of prefixes, roots, and suffixes. Here are several examples from the field of medicine.

Prefix	Meaning	Example	Definition
cardi	heart	cardiogram	test that measures contractions of the heart
		cardiology	medical study of diseases and functioning of the heart
		cardiologist	physician who specializes in heart problems
hem/hema/hemo	blood	hematology	study of the blood
		hemophilia	disease in which blood fails to clot properly
		hemoglobin	protein contained in the red blood cells

Most technical fields have a core of commonly used prefixes, roots, and suffixes. As you read technical material, keep a list of common word parts in your notebook. Add to the list throughout the course. For those you have difficulty remembering, use a variation of the word card system suggested in Chapter 4. Write the word on the front and its meaning, its pronunciation, and a sample sentence on the back.

3. **Learn to pronounce each new term you come across.** Pronouncing a word is a good way to fix it in your memory and will also help you remember its spelling.

4. **Make use of the glossary in the back of the textbook, if it has one.** (See p. 317 in this chapter for further information on using a glossary.)

5. **If you are majoring in a technical field, it may be worthwhile to buy a subject area dictionary (see Chapter 4).** Nursing students, for example, often buy a copy of Taber's *Cyclopedic Medical Dictionary.*

Abbreviations and Notations

In many technical fields, sets of abbreviations and notations (signs and symbols) provide shortcuts to writing out complete words or meanings.

Examples:

Field	Symbol	Meaning
Chemistry	Al	aluminum
	F	fluorine
	Fe	iron
Biology	X	crossed with
	♀	female organism
	♂	male organism
Physics	M	mass
Astronomy	D	diameter
	Δ	distance

To understand technical material, you must learn the abbreviations and notation systems that are used in a specific field. Check to see whether lists of abbreviations and symbols are included in the appendix (reference section) in the back of the textbook. Make a list in your notebook of those you need to learn. Make a point of using these symbols in your class notes whenever possible. Putting them to use regularly is an excellent way to learn them.

Graphic Aids

Most technical books contain numerous drawings, charts, tables, and diagrams. These may make the text look difficult and complicated, but such graphic aids actually help explain and make the text easier to understand. Illustrations, for example, give a visual picture of the idea or process being explained. An example of a diagram taken from a computer programming text appears below. The text to which the diagram refers is included below. Would you find the text easy to understand without the diagram?

An *input device* is a mechanism that accepts data from outside the computer and converts it into an electronic form understandable to the computer. The data that is accepted is called *input data,* or simply *input.* For example, one common way of entering input into a computer is to type it with a typewriter-like *keyboard.*

An *output device* performs the opposite function of an input device. An output device converts data from its electronic form inside the computer to a form that can be used outside. The converted data is called *output data,* or simply *output.* . . .

Between the input devices and the output devices is the component of the computer that does the actual computing or processing. This is the *central processing unit,* or CPU. Input data is converted into an electronic form by an input device and sent to the central processing unit where the data is stored. In the CPU the data is used in calculations or other types of processing to produce the solution to the desired problem. The central processing unit contains two basic units: the internal storage and the processor. The *internal storage* is the "memory" of the computer. The *processor* is the unit that executes instructions to the program. Among other things, the processor contains electronic circuits that do arithmetic and perform logical operations. The final component of a computer is the auxiliary storage. This component stores data that is not currently being processed by the computer and programs that are not currently in use.[7]

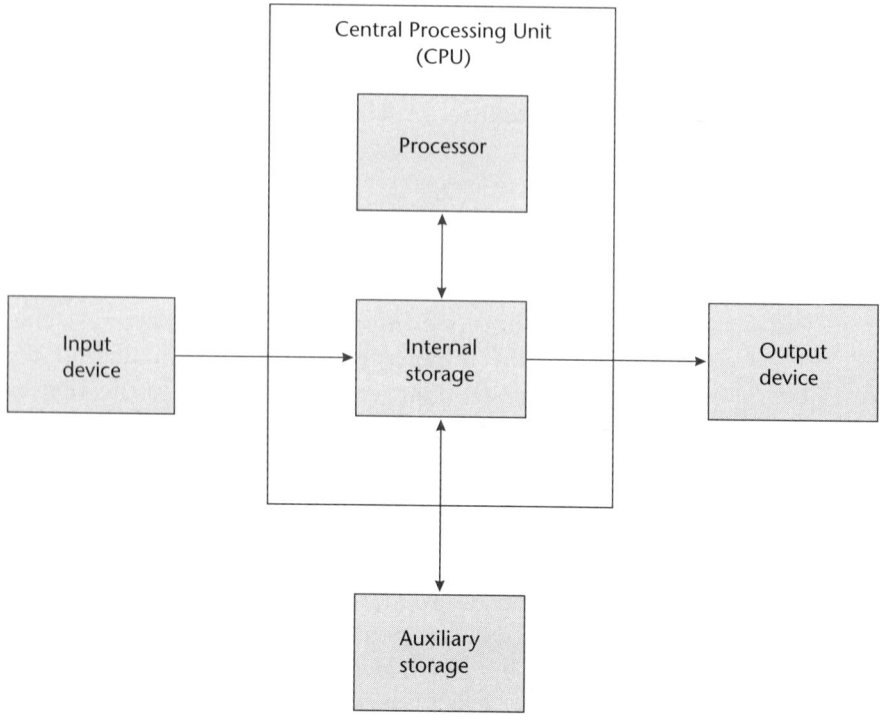

Figure 10-1 The Organization of a Computer.

Here are a few suggestions on how to use illustrations:

1. **Go back and forth between the text and the illustrations.** Illustrations are intended to be used together with the paragraphs that refer to them. You may have to stop reading several times to refer to an illustration. For example, when *input device* is mentioned in the preceding example, stop reading and find where the input device is located on the diagram. You may also have to reread parts of the explanation several times.

2. **Study each illustration carefully.** First, read the title or caption. These tell what the illustration is intended to show. Then look at each part of the illustration and try to see how they are connected. Notice any abbreviations, symbols, arrows, or labels. In the example given, the arrows are important. They suggest the direction or order in which the parts of the computer operate.

3. **Test your understanding of illustrations by drawing and labeling an illustration of your own without looking at the one in the text.** Then compare your drawing with the text. Notice whether anything is left out. If

so, continue drawing and checking until your drawing is complete and correct. Include these drawings in your notebook and use them for review and study.

Examples and Sample Problems

Technical books include numerous examples and sample problems. Use the following suggestions when working with these:

1. **Pay more attention to examples than you normally do in other textbooks.** Examples and sample problems will often help you understand how rules, principles, theories, or formulas are actually used. Think of examples as connections between ideas on paper and practical, everyday use of those ideas.

2. **Be sure to work through sample problems.** Make sure you understand what was done in each step and why. For particularly difficult problems, try writing in your notebook a step-by-step list of how to solve that type of problem. Refer to sample problems as guides or models when doing problems at the end of the chapter or others assigned by the instructor.

3. **Use the problems at the end of the chapter as a self-test.** As you work through each problem, keep track of rules and formulas that you did not know and had to look up. Make note of the types of problems you could not solve without referring to the sample problems. You will need to do more work with each of these types.

EXERCISE 10-6	**Directions:** Read the following excerpt from a textbook chapter titled "Mechanics" and answer the questions that follow.

Mechanics

Potential Energy

An object may store energy by virtue of its position. Such stored energy is called *potential energy,* for in the stored state an object has the potential for doing work. A stretched or compressed spring, for example, has potential energy. When a BB gun is cocked, energy is stored in the spring. A stretched rubber band has potential energy because of its position, for if it is part of a slingshot it is capable of doing work.

The chemical energy in fuels is potential energy, for it is actually energy of position when looked at from a microscopic point of view. This energy is available when the positions of electrical charges within and between molecules are altered, that is, when a chemical change takes place. Potential energy is possessed by any substance that

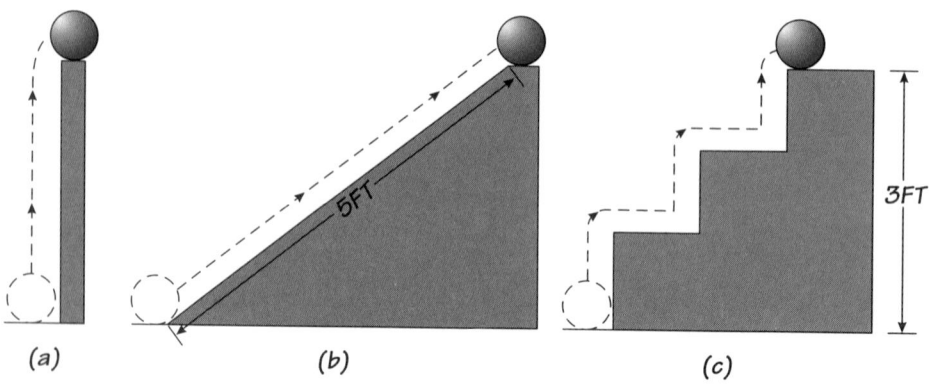

(a)   (b)   (c)

Figure A
The potential energy of the 10-lb ball is the same in each case because the work done in elevating its 3 feet is the same whether it is (a) lifted with a 10 lb of force, or (b) pushed with 6 lb of force up the 5-foot incline, or (c) lifted with 10 lb up each 1-foot stair—no work is done in moving it horizontally (neglecting friction).

can do work through chemical action. The energy of coal, gas, electric batteries, and foods is potential energy. Potential energy may be due to an elevated position of a body. Water in an elevated reservoir and the heavy ram of a pile driver when lifted have energy because of position. The energy of elevated positions is usually called *gravitational potential energy.*

The measure of the gravitational potential energy that an elevated body has is the work done against gravity in lifting it. The upward force required is equal to the weight of the body W, and the work done in lifting it through a height h is given by the product Wh; so we say

Gravitational potential energy = Wh

The potential energy of an elevated body depends only on its weight and vertical displacement h and is independent of the path taken to raise it (Figure A).

Kinetic Energy

If we push on an object, we can set it in motion. More specifically, if we do work on an object, we can change the energy of motion of that object. If an object is in motion, by virtue of that motion it is capable of doing work. We call energy of motion *kinetic energy* (Figure B). The kinetic energy of an object is equal to half its mass [m] multiplied by its velocity [v] squared.

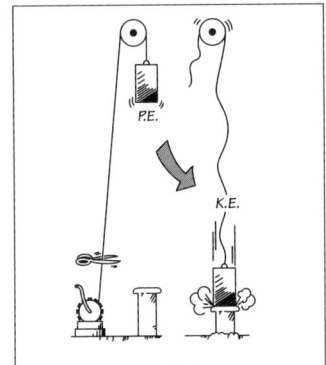

Figure B
The potential energy of the elevated ram is converted to kinetic energy when released.

Kinetic energy = $\frac{1}{2}mv^2$

It can be shown that the kinetic energy of a moving body is equal to the work it can do in being brought to rest.[*]

Net force [F] 3 distance [d] = kinetic energy

or, in shorthand notation,

$Fd = \frac{1}{2}mv^2$

Accident investigators are well aware that an automobile traveling at 60 miles per hour has four times as much kinetic energy as an automobile traveling 30 miles per hour. This means that a car traveling at 60 miles per hour will skid four times as far when its brakes are locked as a car traveling 30 miles per hour. This is because the velocity is squared for kinetic energy.

Question
When the brakes of a car traveling at 90 miles per hour are locked, how much farther will the car skid compared to locking the brakes at 30 miles per hour?[8]

[*]If we multiply both sides of $F = ma$ (Newton's second law) by d, we get $Fd = mad$; since $d = 1/2$ at 2, we can say $Fd = ma$ $(1/2$ at 2$) = 1/2$ $m(at)2$; and substituting $v = at$, we get $Fd = 1/2$ mv^2.

1. Underline the sentences that best define the terms *potential energy* and *kinetic energy.*

2. List the technical or specialized terms used in this selection. Define as many as possible.

   _____

   _____

3. List the abbreviations (notations) used in the article and give their meanings.

   _____

   _____

4. The writer uses examples as a means of explaining various ideas. List four of these examples and tell what each explains.

   a. _____

   b. _____

   c. _____

   d. _____

5. This excerpt contains two illustrations (Figures A and B). The author does not discuss either in the text itself. Their use is left up to the reader. Describe when and how often you referred to each diagram.

   _____

   _____

6. What is Figure A intended to show?

   _____

7. What is Figure B intended to show?

_____

8. What is the purpose of the question at the end of the article? To what type of energy does this question refer?

_____

_____

9. In your own words, explain the difference between potential energy and kinetic energy.

_____

_____

WORKING TOGETHER

Directions: Bring one of your textbooks to class. You may bring a textbook from another course or obtain one from the library. After your instructor forms groups, exchange texts with group members and review the learning aids in each text. Each student should evaluate the learning aid in each. Then, through discussion, make a list of the learning aids contained in each text and select the textbook that provides the "best" learning assistance. Groups may compare "winning" textbooks and choose an overall winner. Class members or the instructor may notify the course instructor(s) using the winning textbook that theirs was chosen.

Learning Style Tips

If you tend to be a(n) . . .	Then grasp textbook organization by . . .
Applied learner	Writing a list of what you expect to learn from the chapter in the order in which you expect it to be presented.
Conceptual learner	Studying the headings in the table of contents and discovering how they fit together.

MASTERING VOCABULARY

Directions: Determine the meaning of each of the following words used in this chapter. Then insert each one in the sentence in which it makes most sense.

integrated (p. 312)	converts (p. 327)
global (p. 312)	component (p. 327)
diverse (p. 313)	executes (p. 327)
derived (p. 322)	auxiliary (p. 327)
subtle (p. 322)	altered (p. 329)

1. A generator _____ mechanical power into electrical power.

2. Congress makes laws and the president _____ them.

3. The committee _____ many different ideas into its final plan.

4. By examining it closely, they determined that the document had been _____.

5. She _____ great pleasure from her walk in the park.

6. The use of satellites has made instantaneous _____ communication possible.

7. To upgrade your stereo system, first you will need to install a new amplifier _____.

8. The town meeting provided an opportunity for _____ ideas to be expressed.

9. It is wise to have _____ engines on a sailboat.

10. A _____ joke may be hard to understand at first.

SELF-TEST SUMMARY

What types of learning aids do textbooks contain?	At the beginning of a textbook, the table of contents and opening chapter provide information on the scope and focus of the book. Within each chapter, typographical aids—italic type, enumeration, headings and subheadings, and colored print—call attention to key information. At the end of each chapter, discussion questions and vocabulary lists provide an outline of important information and key words presented in the chapter. At the end of the textbook, the glossary provides a quick reference for important vocabulary presented in the book.
How are textbooks organized?	Textbooks are also organized so as to express ideas as clearly as possible. Through the use of headings and subheadings, chapters are divided into a number of sections that deal with different aspects of the subject covered in the chapter.
What features distinguish technical material?	The distinguishing features of technical material include fact density, specialized vocabulary, abbreviations and notations, drawings and illustrations, and examples and sample problems.

**CHAPTER 10
MASTERY TEST 1:
Technical Writing Skills**

Name _____

Section _____ Date _____

Number right _____ x 20 points = Score _____

Directions: Read each of the examples of technical writing below and answer the multiple choice item that follows it.

____ 1. **Light energy that has traveled millions of miles from the sun is captured by the chloroplasts of plant cells and converted into chemical energy.** Of the following words from this sentence, the one that is an example of specialized vocabulary is
  a. light.
  b. millions.
  c. chloroplasts.
  d. converted.

____ 2. **When an endotherm goes into the state of reduced activity known as torpor, its metabolic rate, body temperature, heart rate, and respiration rate decrease, thereby reducing its consumption of energy.** Of the following words from this sentence, the only one that can be defined using context clues is
  a. endotherm.
  b. torpor.
  c. metabolic.
  d. respiration.

____ 3. **Over 30 different substances enhance the clotting of blood, also known as coagulation; numerous factors can contribute to anticoagulation, some of them producing life-threatening effects.** Of the following words from this sentence, the only one that can be defined by analyzing word parts is
  a. substance.
  b. anticoagulation.
  c. enhance.
  d. clotting.

____ 4. Of the following sentences, choose the one that is most factually dense.
  a. In the world of biology, it is typical for plants to obtain most of the nitrogen they require from various nitrates that have been dissolved in water in the soil.
  b. Not to be confused with meiosis, the remarkably accurate mechanism known as mitosis consists of a multi-stage process of cell division in plants and animals.
  c. Bacteria and other prokaryotes reproduce most commonly by a specific type of cell division called binary fission, meaning "dividing in half" or "splitting."
  d. When a semipermeable membrane, such as a cell wall, divides two levels of a solvent, the molecules from the greater concentration of solvent will pass through the membrane until equilibrium is reached.

_____ 5. Of the following sentences, choose the one that contains notations that would be most important to learn in a chemistry course.

    a. Sodium (Na) and chlorine (Cl) can be combined to form salt.

    b. The Perseids meteor shower is typically most visible between 1 and 4 a.m. EDT (Eastern Daylight Time).

    c. Nitrogen makes up over 78 percent of the Earth's atmosphere.

    d. X-rays are electromagnetic waves that can penetrate thick materials.

Name _____
Section _____ Date _____
Number right _____ x 20 points = Score _____

Directions: For questions 1–3 below, use the portion of the table of contents from an economics textbook shown here.

> **Chapter 16 Government Spending, Taxation, and Deficits**
>
> **Government Spending**
> Majority Rule: The Power of the
> Median Voter
> Logrolling
> Rational Ignorance
>
> **Taxation**
> Principles of Taxation
> Taxes and Private Decision Making
> Figure 16.1: Supply-Side Economics
>
> **The Federal Budget**
> Deficits and Debt
> Problems of Deficit Reduction
> The Case for a Balanced Budget
>
> **Summary**
>
> **Questions and Problems**
>
> **Key Terms**

_____ 1. To find out what the term *logrolling* means, you should look under the heading
   a. Government Spending.
   b. Taxation.
   c. The Federal Budget.
   d. Summary.

_____ 2. The heading "The Federal Budget" includes all of the following subtopics except
   a. Majority Rule: The Power of the Median Voter.
   b. Deficits and Debt.
   c. Problems of Deficit Reduction.
   d. The Case for a Balanced Budget.

_____ 3. The textbook learning aids featured in the table of contents include
   a. examples and figures.
   b. a vocabulary list.
   c. chapter questions.
   d. all of the above.

Directions: For questions 4 and 5, refer to the following excerpt from the preface of a health textbook.

As we enter a new millennium, health challenges once considered unimaginable have emerged. Needless to say, writing an introductory health text presents an interesting challenge. As quickly as the last words are written for one edition, a new discovery is announced that probably should have been included in the book. So today's text has gone high tech, linking you to the latest developments in disease prevention, health promotion, and policy change through the *Access to Health* companion Web site at **www.abacon.com** and the interactive CD-ROM you received along with this text.

Access to Health is designed not just to help teach you health facts, but to help you think of health as a broader concept. Many chapters include special feature boxes designed to help you build health behavior skills as well as think about and apply the concepts: **"Reality Check"** boxes focus attention on potential risks and safety issues, often as they relate to college-age students; **"Health in a Diverse World"** boxes promote acceptance of diversity on college campuses and assist you in adjusting to an increasingly diverse world; **"Consumer Health"** boxes focus on health issues as they relate to consumer skills; and, **"Assess Yourself"** boxes allow you the chance to examine your behaviors and determine ways to improve your health.[9]

_____ 4. According to the preface, this textbook provides access to the latest health information through
   a. its companion Web site.
   b. "Assess Yourself" boxes.
   c. including new discoveries in each new edition.
   d. "Reality Check" boxes.

_____ 5. The special feature box intended to help you find ways to improve your own health is called
   a. "Reality Check."
   b. "Health in a Diverse World."
   c. "Consumer Health."
   d. "Assess Yourself."

**CHAPTER 10
MASTERY TEST 3:
Textbook Skills**

Name _____

Section _____ Date _____

Number right _____ x 10 points = Score _____

Directions: Read the selection and answer the following questions by writing the letter of the best choice in the space provided.

The Physiology of Stress

1   In his 1956 book *The Stress of Life,* Canadian physician Hans Selye (1907–1982) greatly advanced the study of stress. Selye noted that many environmental factors—heat, cold, pain, toxins, viruses, and so on—can throw the body out of balance. These factors, called *stressors,* force the body to respond by mobilizing its resources and preparing the individual to fight or flee. Using data from many animal studies, Selye concluded that "stress" consists of a series of physiological reactions that occur in three phases:

1. *The alarm phase,* in which the organism mobilizes to meet the threat with a package of biological responses that allow the person or animal to escape from danger no matter what the stressor is: crossing a busy street or having deadline pressures at work.
2. *The resistance phase,* in which the organism attempts to resist or cope with a threat that cannot be avoided. During this phase, the body's physiological responses are in high gear—a response to the original stressor—but this very mechanism makes the body more susceptible to other stressors. For example, when your body has mobilized to fight off the flu, you may find that you are more easily annoyed by minor frustrations. In most cases, the body will eventually adapt to the stressor and return to normal.

3. *The exhaustion phase,* which occurs if the stressor persists. Over time, the body's resources may be overwhelmed. Depleted of energy, the body becomes vulnerable to fatigue, physical problems, and eventually illness.

2   Not all stress is bad, however. Some stress, which Selye called *eustress* (YOO-stress), is positive and feels good, even if it also requires the body to produce short-term energy: competing in an athletic event, falling in love, working hard on a project you enjoy. Selye did not believe that all stress could be avoided or that people should aim for a stress-free life, which is an impossible goal anyway. The goal is to minimize wear and tear on the system.

3   Selye recognized that psychological stressors, such as fighting with a loved one or grief over loss, can have as great an impact on health as do physical stressors, such as heat, crowds, or noise. He also observed that some factors *mediate,* or act as buffers, between the stressor and the stress. A comfortable climate or a nutritious diet, for example, can soften the impact of an environmental stressor such as pollution. Conversely, a harsh climate or a poor diet can make such stressors worse. But by and large, Selye concentrated on the biological responses that result from a person's or animal's attempt to adapt to environmental demands. A diagram of his view would look like this:

Chronic stressors ⟶ Physiological alarm and exhaustion ⟶ Illness

4   Health psychologists have since expanded on Selye's model of stressors and illness, hoping to find out why individuals differ so much in their susceptibility to stress and vulnerability to disease. They want to know why, of two people who are exposed to a flu virus, one is sick all winter and the other doesn't even get the sniffles; or why, of two people who have high-pressure jobs, one gets heart disease and the other doesn't. They want to know how external stressors "get under the skin" and make trouble for some people but not others.

5   One of the most intensively studied bodily systems in relation to stress is the immune system. In the 1980's, scientists created an interdisciplinary field with the cumbersome name **psychoneuroimmunology**, or *PNI* for short: "psycho" for psychological processes such as emotions and perceptions, "neuro" for the nervous and endocrine systems, and "immunology" for the immune system. The white blood cells of the immune system are designed to do two things: (1) recognize foreign substances (antigens), such as flu viruses, bacteria, and tumor cells; and (2) destroy or deactivate them. When an antigen invades the body, white blood cells called *phagocytes* are dispatched to ingest and eliminate the intruder. If this effort is unsuccessful, other white blood cells, called *lymphocytes,* and other processes of the immune system are summoned. To defend the body against antigens, the immune system deploys different cells as weapons, depending on the nature of the enemy.

6   Prolonged stress can suppress some or many of these cells that fight disease and infection. For instance, in one study 420 people heroically volunteered to fight in the war against the common cold. Some were given nose drops containing viruses known to cause a cold's miserable symptoms and others received uncontaminated nose drops. Everyone was then quarantined for a week. The results: contaminated people who were under high stress, who felt their lives were "unpredictable, uncontrollable, and overwhelming," were twice as likely to develop colds as those reporting low levels of stress.

7   A second approach to studying individual vulnerability to stress focuses on *psychological factors,* such as personality traits, perceptions, and emotions. An event that is stressful or enraging for one person may be challenging for another and boring for a third. Likewise, losing a job, traveling to China, or having "too much" work is stressful to some people and not to others.

8   A third approach focuses on *how the individual behaves when under stress* and how he or she manages it. Not all individuals who are under stress behave in the same way. Some drink too much, drive recklessly, or fail to take care of themselves, all of which increases their risk of illness or accident. Others, in contrast, cope constructively and thereby reduce the effects of stress.

9   Thus, unlike Selye, who defined stress narrowly as the body's response to any environmental threat, health psychologists now define stress to include qualities of the individual (e.g., how the person perceives the stressor) and whether the individual feels able to cope with the stressor:

Chronic stressors → Physiological reactions → Health or illness

↑ Physiological traits and perceptions   ↑ Coping skills

10   **Psychological stress** is caused by an interaction of the person and the environment, in which the person believes that the situation strains or overwhelms his or her resources and is endangering his or her ability to cope.

_____ 1. Which of the following is the best definition of the word "stressors" as it is used in the selection?
a. psychological reactions to the world
b. how an individual copes with the environment
c. germs or bacteria which cause illness
d. environmental factors that throw the body out of balance

_____ 2. The abbreviation PNI stands for which of the following?
a. psychoneuroimmunology
b. physiology and neurological institute
c. the three phases of stress
d. psychological factors

_____ 3. Selye defined "eustress" as stress which
a. keeps one from acting.
b. lasts a long time.
c. is helpful.
d. someone else has.

_____ 4. The selection uses _all_ of the following learning aids _except_
a. bold face.
b. diagrams.
c. enumeration.
d. marginal notations.

_____ 5. Which of the following is a type of white blood cell mentioned in the selection?
a. phagocytes
b. antigens
c. bacteria
d. viruses

_____ 6. The experiment with the common cold was done to show the relationship between
a. loneliness and tension.
b. stress and physical illness.
c. quarantine and stress.
d. coping skills and emotions.

_____ 7. If you are easily annoyed when you have the flu, you are in which of the following phases of stress?
a. chronic
b. resistance
c. alarm
d. exhaustion

_____ 8. Health psychologists recently have added which of the following to Selye's model of stressors and illness?
a. illness
b. stressors
c. individual differences in response to stressors
d. physiological alarm

_____ 9. Which of the following best describes the purpose of the diagrams?
  a. to analyze a debate
  b. to outline a problem
  c. to classify an example
  d. to show a process

_____ 10. The selection would best fit as part of which of the following larger textbook sections?
  a. Stress and the Body
  b. Avoiding Illnesses
  c. Coping with Stress
  d. The Sense of Control

**CHAPTER 10
MASTERY TEST 4:
Reading Selection**

Name _____

Section _____ Date _____

Number right _____ x 10 points = Score _____

Legible Clothing

Joseph A. DeVito

What do the clothes you wear reveal about you? In this article, taken from a book titled *Human Communication*, the author discusses the messages that clothing sends about the wearer.

Vocabulary Preview

status (par. 1) social standing or position

paraphrase (par. 3) explain in other words

affiliation (par. 4) association or connection with a group

metaphorical (par. 4) one thing representing another

satirizing (par. 4) making fun of

insignia (par. 5) a distinguishing sign

1   Legible clothing is anything that you wear which contains some verbal message; such clothing can literally be read. In some instances it says status; it tells others that you are, for example, rich or stylish or youthful. The Gucci or Louis Vuitton logos on your luggage communicate your status and financial position. In a similar way your sweatshirt saying Bulls or Pirates communicates your interest in sports and perhaps your favorite team.

2   John Molloy, in *Molloy's Live for Success*, advises you to avoid legible clothing except the kind that says rich. Legible clothing, argues Molloy, communicates lower

status and lack of power. Humorist Fran Lebowitz says that legible clothes "are an unpleasant indication of the general state of things. I mean, be realistic. If people don't want to listen to you, what makes you think they want to hear from your sweater?"

3 Yet legible clothing is being bought and worn in record numbers. Many designers and manufacturers have their names integrated into the design of the clothing: DKNY, Calvin Klein, L.L. Bean, and Levi's are just a few examples. At the same time that you are paying extra to buy the brand name, you also provide free advertising for the designer and manufacturer. To paraphrase Vidal Sassoon, "As long as you look good, so does the advertiser. And, when you look bad, the advertiser looks bad." Imitators—the cheap knock-offs you see on the street—are resisted by the original manufacturers not only because these impact on their own sales. In fact, the impact is probably minimal since the person who would pay $6,000 for a Rolex would not buy a $10 imitation on the street. Rather, such knock-offs are resisted because they are perceived to be worn by the wrong people— people who would destroy the image the manufacturer wishes to communicate.

4 T-shirts and sweatshirts are especially popular as message senders. In one study, the types of t-shirt messages were classified into four main categories. The order in which these are presented reflects the shirts the subjects (600 male and female college students) considered their favorites. Thirty-three percent, for example, considered affiliation message shirts their favorites while 17 percent considered those with personal messages their favorites. The order from most favorite down, was:

1. Affiliation messages, for example, a club or school name. It communicates that you are a part of a larger group.
2. Trophy, for example, a shirt from a high-status event such as a concert or perhaps a ski lodge. This is a way of saying that the wearer was in the right place.
3. Metaphorical expressions, for example, pictures of rock groups or famous athletes.
4. Personal messages, for example, "beliefs, philosophies and causes as well as satirizing current events."

5 Another important dimension of clothing, currently being debated in educational and legal circles, is the use of gang clothing. Some argue that gang clothing and gang colors contribute to violence in the schools and should therefore be prohibited. Others argue that gang clothing—or any clothing— is covered by the first amendment to the Constitution. Consider a specific case. In Harvard, Illinois, you can be arrested for wearing a Star of David in public—not because it's a religious symbol, but because certain gangs use it as a gang symbol. In 1993, Harvard passed a law that makes it illegal "for any person within the city to knowingly use, display or wear colors, emblems, or insignia" that would communicate their membership in (or sympathy for) gangs.

6 Consider your own use of legible clothing. Do you wear legible clothing? What messages do you wish to communicate? Are you successful in communicating the messages you want? Do labels influence your perceptions of others? How do you feel about the law in Harvard, Illinois? Would

you support such a law in your own community?

Directions: Choose the letter of the choice that best answers each of the following questions.

CHECKING YOUR COMPREHENSION

_____ 1. The main point of the reading is that legible clothing
   a. is only worn by members of the lower class.
   b. has a negative effect on sales of higher-priced clothing.
   c. says something about the wearer.
   d. is often banned in high schools.

_____ 2. The main idea of paragraph 4 is that
   a. many people wear personal messages on shirts.
   b. college students are the most likely group to wear legible clothing.
   c. sports sweatshirts indicate your favorite team.
   d. messages on shirts fit into four categories.

_____ 3. Which of the following statements best summarizes the main point of paragraph 5?
   a. Legible clothing is a form of free speech protected by the U.S. Constitution.
   b. The role of gang-related clothing is being discussed by both lawyers and teachers.
   c. The Star of David has become a gang symbol in Illinois.
   d. Gang violence in schools is increasing.

_____ 4. According to the passage, manufacturers are mainly against name brand knock-offs because
   a. knock-offs destroy the image the manufacturer wants to communicate.
   b. the profits of the manufacturers are effectively cut in half by knock-offs.
   c. knock-offs do not provide free advertising for the manufacturers.
   d. the brand name products generally cost more than the knock-offs.

_____ 5. According to the passage, which of the following examples of t-shirt messages is in the most popular category for wearers?
   a. Rolling Stones Spring 1995 tour
   b. a Michael Jordan picture
   c. "Life, liberty, and the pursuit of chocolate"
   d. Howard University

_____ 6. The word "status" in paragraph 1 is best defined as
   a. situation.
   b. legal condition.
   c. powerless.
   d. rank or position.

APPLYING YOUR SKILLS

_____ 7. The learning aid contained in this selection is
a. enumeration.
b. subheadings.
c. italics.
d. vocabulary lists.

_____ 8. The main purpose of the questions at the end of this selection is to
a. review the main points.
b. emphasize technical vocabulary.
c. make you think about yourself.
d. solve problems.

_____ 9. In paragraph 4, "affiliation" is used to mean
a. dependent.
b. connection.
c. personal.
d. negative.

_____ 10. The dictionary defines "legible" as "able to be read." As used in the selection, "legible" includes all of the following _except_
a. pictures.
b. words and numbers.
c. shape of a shirt.
d. logos and labels.

Go Electronic!
For additional readings and exercises, and Internet activities, visit the book's Web site at:

http://www.ablongman.com/mcwhorter

If you need a username and password, please see your instructor.

Take a Road Trip to the Grand Canyon!
Be sure to visit the Reading Textbooks module in your Reading Road Trip CD-ROM for multimedia tutorials, exercises, and tests.

11

Reading Graphic and Electronic Information

THIS CHAPTER WILL SHOW YOU HOW TO

1. Approach graphic information
2. Use and interpret electronic information

One student was talking with a friend about her biology textbook. She said, "It's difficult enough to read the chapters, but then you have to figure out all the diagrams and tables, too. And those things take time. Besides, my instructor wants us to visit several Web sites, too!" This student does not realize that graphic aids are designed to make the chapter itself easier to read and understand. Graphics and visuals summarize and condense information and actually save you time. Web sites and other electronic sources provide access to current, up-to-date information.

Try reading the following paragraph *without* looking at the diagram shown in Figure 11-1.

> Our generalized flower is composed of four regions, each a **whorl** (or circle) of highly modified leaves. The whorls arise from a widened area, the **receptacle**, at the base of the flower. The whorl closest to the stem is the **calyx**, formed from leaflike **sepals** that were once the protective covering over the developing bud. The second whorl is the **corolla**, composed of the **petals**. In species that must attract animal pollinators (such as insects, birds, or even bats), the petals may be very bright and attractive, some with just the qualities to particularly attract certain species of pollinators. The third and fourth whorls contain the reproductive organs. The male part is the **stamen**, the female part, the **carpel**. Sometimes a carpel, or group of fused

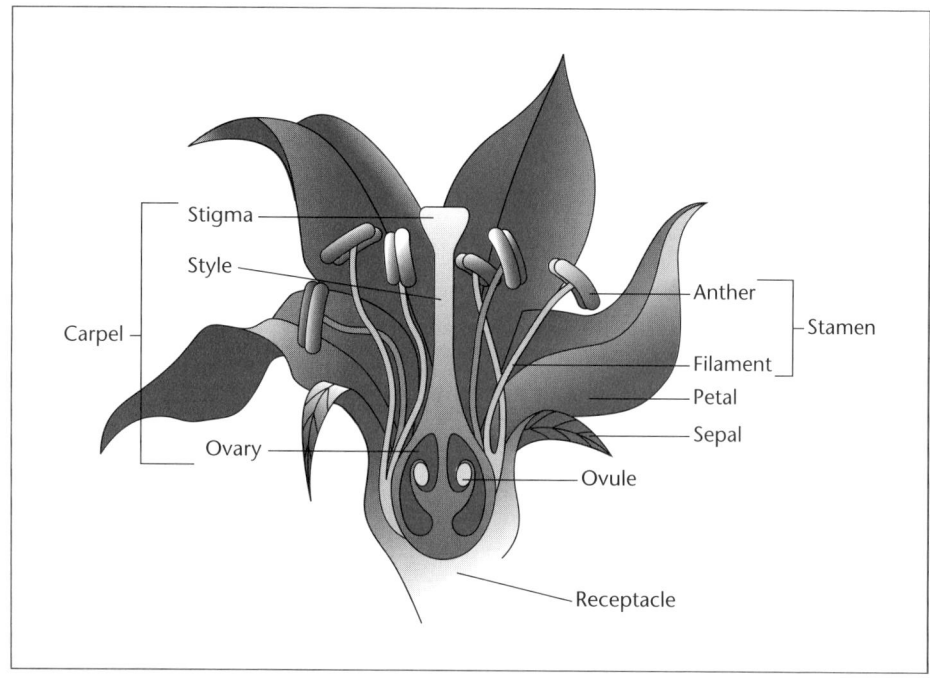

Figure 11-1 Diagram of a flower.[2]

carpels (as they often appear) is called a **pistil**. Each stamen consists of a slender **filament** capped by an **anther** where, following meiosis, the male gametophyte is produced and released as **pollen**. Each carpel has three parts: the **ovary, style,** and **stigma**.[1]

Did you find the paragraph difficult and confusing? Now study Figure 11-1 and then reread the above paragraph.

Now the paragraph is easier to understand. You can see that graphics are a valuable aid, not a hindrance. This chapter will describe the various types of graphics commonly included in college textbooks. You will learn how to approach and interpret each kind. You will also learn about various types of electronic learning aids.

A GENERAL APPROACH TO GRAPHICS

Graphics include tables, charts, graphs, diagrams, photographs, and maps. Here is a general step-by-step approach to reading graphics. As you read, apply each step to the graph shown in Figure 11-2 (Step 7 does not apply to this example).

1. **Read the title or caption.** The title will identify the subject and may suggest the relationship being described.
2. **Discover how the graphic is organized.** Read the column headings or labels on the horizontal and vertical axes.
3. **Identify the variables.** Decide what comparisons are being made or what relationship is being described.
4. **Analyze the purpose.** Based on what you have seen, predict what the graphic is intended to show. Is its purpose to show change over time, describe a process, compare costs, or present statistics?
5. **Determine scale, values, or units of measurement.** The scale is the ratio that a graphic has to the thing it represents. For example, a map may be scaled so that one inch on the map represents one mile.
6. **Study the data to identify trends or patterns.** Note changes, unusual statistics, or unexplained variations.
7. **Read the graphic along with corresponding text.** Refer to the paragraphs that discuss the graphic. These paragraphs may explain certain features of the graphic and identify trends or patterns.
8. **Make a brief summary note.** In the margin, jot a brief note summarizing the trend or pattern the graphic emphasizes. Writing will crystallize the idea in your mind and your note will be useful for reviewing.

In Figure 11-2 the title indicates the purpose of the graph: to compare the availability of jobs in various fast growth areas in 1990 and 2005. The vertical axis lists the number of jobs available. The horizontal axis lists the types of jobs. The graph compares the number of jobs available in 1990 with those projected for 2005. The unit of comparison is percentage of increase. The graph arranges the fastest growing jobs from highest to lowest percentage of increase. Each of the ten job areas examined is projected to show more than a 60 percent increase in employment by 2005. The top five areas project at least a 70 percent increase by 2005. The majority of these occupations are involved with human and medical support and services. A summary note might read "fastest growing jobs over the period of 1990–2005 will revolve around human health and well-being."

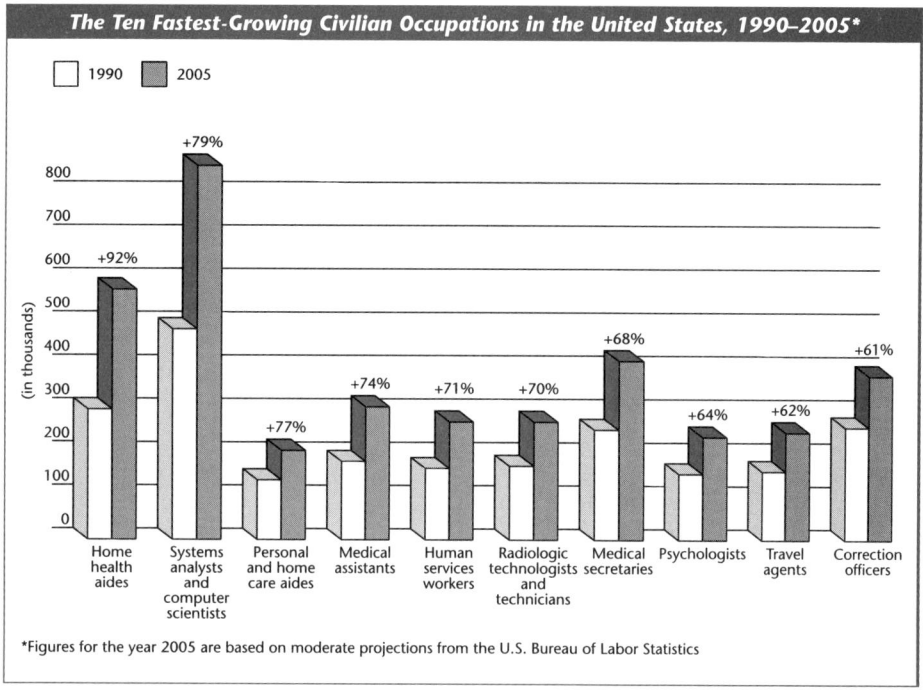

Figure 11-2 A sample graph.[3]

TYPES OF GRAPHICS

This section will describe six types of graphics: tables, graphs, charts, diagrams, maps, and photographs.

Tables

A table is an organized arrangement of facts, usually numbers or statistics. A table condenses large amounts of data to allow you to read and interpret it easily. Use the steps listed below as well as those listed on p. 350 to read the table in Figure 11-3.

1. **Determine how the information is divided and arranged.** The table in Figure 11-3 is divided into three columns: date, estimated world population, and time required for population to double.

2. **Make comparisons and look for trends.** Do this by surveying rows and columns, noting how each compares with the others. Look for similarities, differences, or sudden or unexpected variations. Underline or highlight

Doubling Times of the Human Population*

Date	Estimated World Population	Time Required for Population to Double
8000 B.C.	5 million	1,500 years
A.D. 1650	500 million	200 years
A.D. 1850	1,000 million (1 billion)	80 years
A.D. 1930	2,000 million (2 billion)	45 years
A.D. 1990	5,300 million (5.3 billion)	40 years
A.D. 2010	8,000 million (8 billion)	?

*Doubling times can roughly be calculated from annual percentage growth rate by simply dividing the growth rate into 70. The growth rate of MDCs is 0.6 percent; of LDCs, it's 2.1 percent. Do the arithmetic.

Figure 11-3 A sample table.[4]

unusual or outstanding figures. For Figure 11-3, note that from 1650 on dramatically less time has been required for each doubling of the world population—from 200 years in 1650 to only 40 years in 1990.

3. **Draw conclusions.** Decide what the numbers mean and what they suggest about the subject. This table appeared in a section of a biology textbook dealing with the growth of human population. You can conclude that since the world population will have doubled in less than 40 more years, in 40 years we also will need to double our material goods just to maintain present living standards.

4. **Look for clues in corresponding text.** The textbook paragraph that corresponds to the table in Figure 11-3 is reprinted below.

> Some countries have a much firmer grip on their population problems than others, as evidenced by their doubling times (see table). To go from five million people on earth (the present number in only three of New York City's five boroughs) in 8000 B.C. to 500 million in A.D. 1650 took six or seven doublings over a period of 9,000 to 10,000 years. During that time, the human population doubled on an average of about every 1,500 years. A glance at the table will show that, all other things being equal, in only about 40 years, we will need two cars, two schools, two roads, two wells, two houses, and two cities throughout the world for every one that presently exists. And that will only maintain our status quo as far as material goods are concerned.[5]

Notice the author explains and interprets the data presented in the table. He provides real-life examples (two cars, two schools, two wells) of what doubling the population means. Also, at the end of the paragraph, he interprets the data, questioning whether there are enough natural resources to support continued population growth.

<table>
<tr><td>**EXERCISE 11-1**</td><td>**Directions:** The table in Figure 11-4 lists the fitness potential for many popular sports. Study the table and answer the questions that follow.</td></tr>
</table>

Fitness Potential for Popular Sports

Sport	Cardiorespiratory Endurance	Muscular Strength and Endurance		Flexibility	Caloric Range	
		Upper Body	Lower Body		Calories per Minute	Calories per Hour
Back packing[a]	2–3	2	3	2	5–10	300–600
Badminton	2–3	2	2	2	5–10	300–600
Baseball/Softball	1–2	2	2	2	4–7.5	240–450
Basketball	3	2	3	2	10–12.5	600–750
Bowling	1	2	1	1	2.5–4	150–240
Canoeing	2–3	3	1	1	4–10	240–600
Football (touch)	1–2	2	2	2	5–10	300–600
Golf	1	2	3	2	4–5	240–300
Handball	3	3	3	2	10–12.5	600–750
Karate	2	3	3	4	7.5–10	450–600
Racquetball	4	3	3	2	7.5–12.5	450–750
Scuba diving	1	2	2	2	5–7.5	300–450
Skating (ice)	4	1	2–3	2	5–10	300–600
Skating (roller)	2–3	1	2–3	2	5–10	300–600
Skiing (alpine)	2	3	3	3	6–10	360–600
Skiing (nordic)	4–5	3	4	3	7.5–15	450–900
Soccer	3–4	2	3–4	3	7.5–15	450–900
Surfing[b]	2	3	3	3	5–12.5	300–750
Tennis	2–3	2-3	3	2	5–10	300–600
Volleyball	2–3	2	2-3	2	5–10	300–600
Waterskiing	1	3	3	2	5–7.5	300–450

[a]Benefits depend on walking terrain and weight of pack.
[b]Paddling the board out beyond the breaking waves can be demanding.
1 = poor, 2 = fair, 3 = good, 4 = excellent.

Figure 11-4 A table for use in Exercise 11.1.[6]

1. How is the table arranged?

_____

2. Which sport is rated highest for cardiorespiratory endurance?

_____

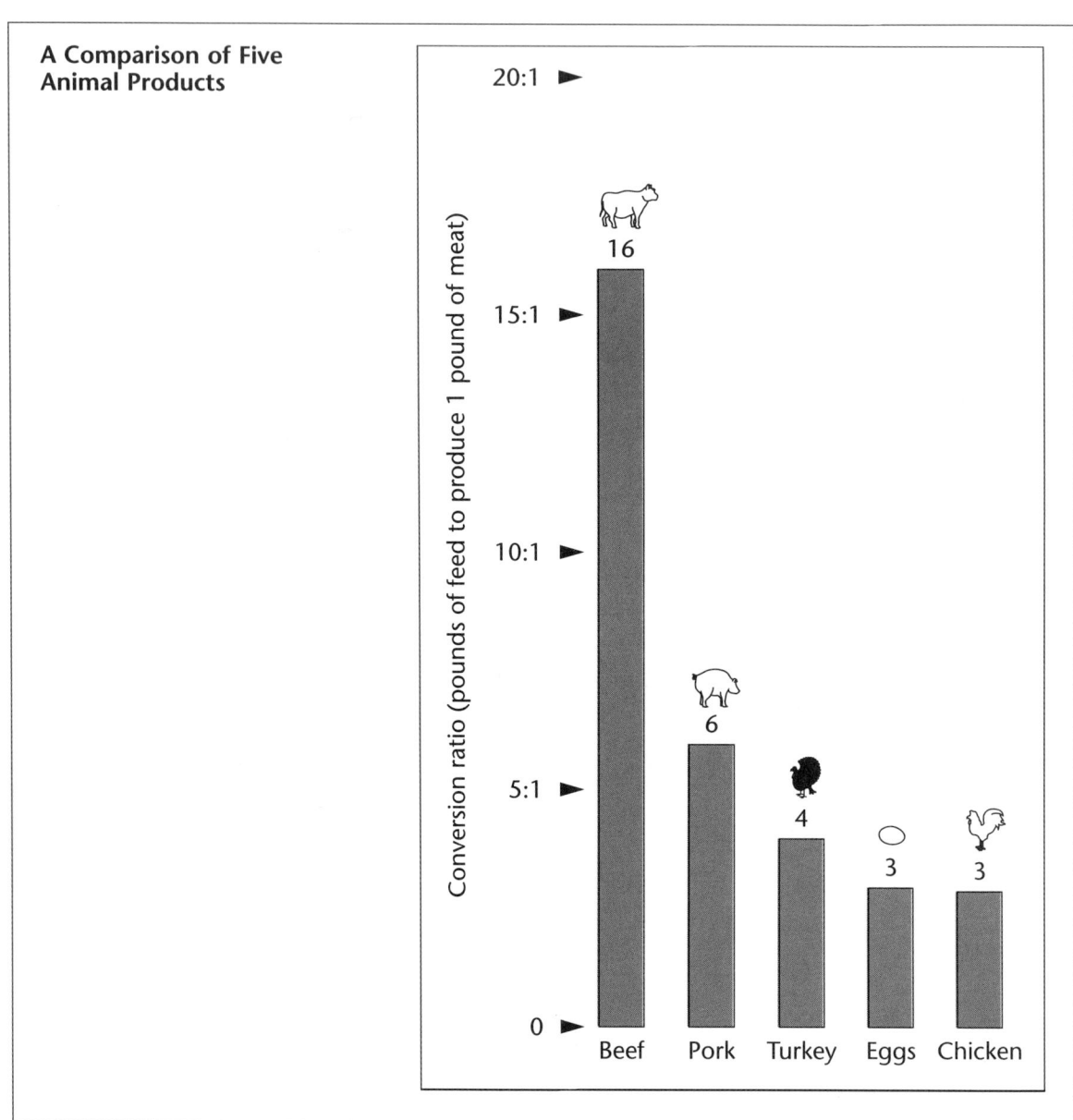

A Comparison of Five Animal Products

Figure 11-5 A sample bar graph.[7]

3. Which sport uses the least number of calories per hour?

_____

4. Which sport is rated highest for flexibility?

_____

Graphs

There are four types of graphs: bar, multiple bar, stacked bar, and linear. Each plots a set of points on a set of axes.

Bar Graphs   A bar graph is often used to make comparisons between quantities or amounts, and is particularly useful in showing changes that occur with passing time. Bar graphs usually are constructed to emphasize differences. The graph shown in Figure 11-5 compares the efficiency of producing five common types of animal products. You can readily see that beef, which requires 16 pounds of feed to produce 1 pound of meat, is by far the least efficient.

Multiple Bar Graphs   A multiple bar graph makes at least two or three comparisons simultaneously. As you read them, be sure to identify exactly what comparisons are being made. Figure 11-6 compares the number of communication appliances owned per 1000 people in five different countries.

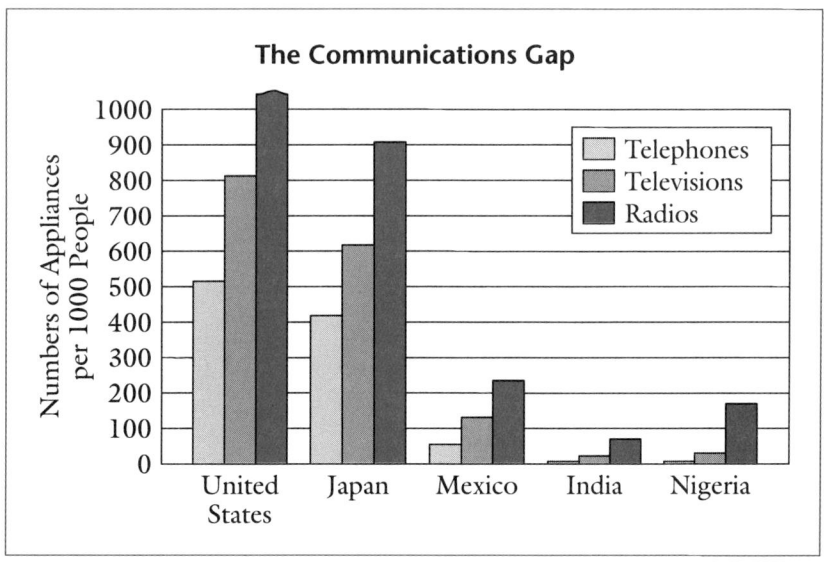

Figure 11-6 A sample multiple bar graph.[8]

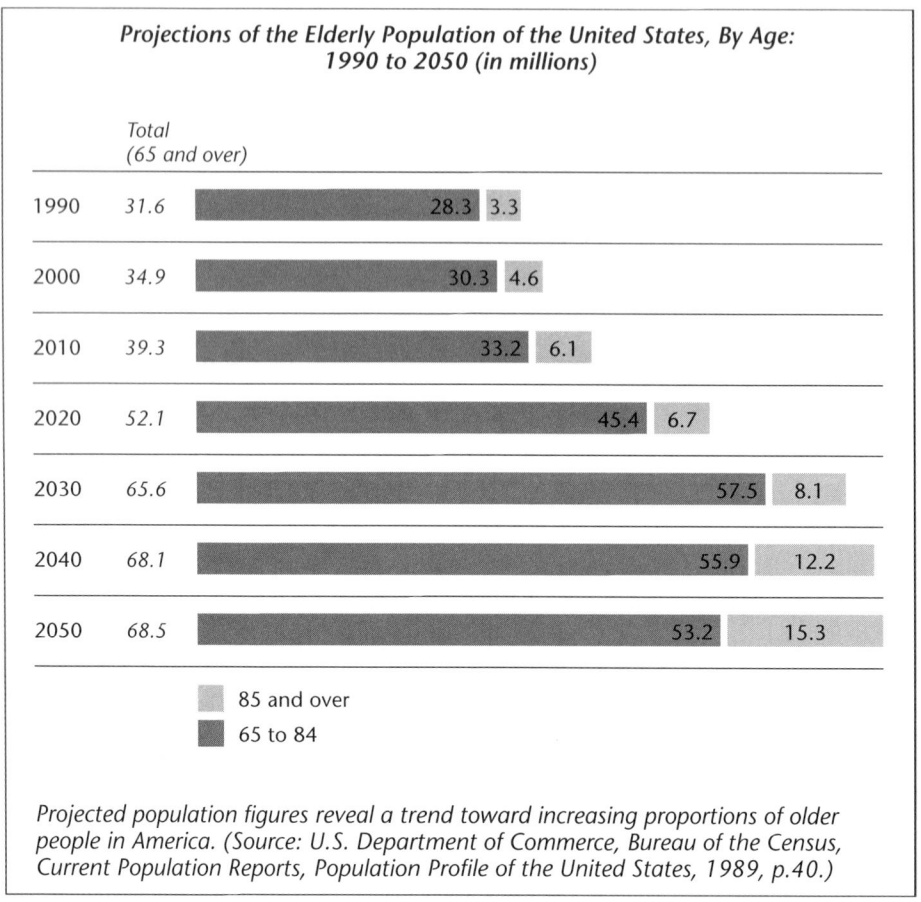

Figure 11-7 A sample stacked bar graph.[9]

Stacked Bar Graphs   A stacked bar graph is an arrangement of data in which bars are placed one on top of another rather than side by side. This variation is often used to emphasize whole/part relationships. Stacked bar graphs show the relationship of a part to an entire group or class. The graph in Figure 11-7 shows projected population figures for those over age 65 and those over age 85. Stacked bar graphs also allow numerous comparisons. The graph in Figure 11-7 compares the projected number of elderly people under and over 85 at seven time periods.

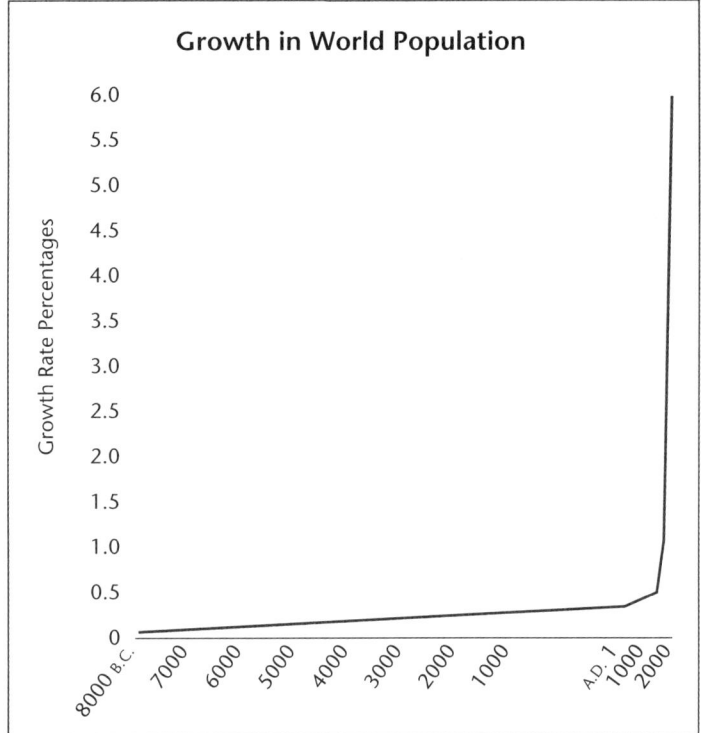

Figure 11-8 A sample linear graph.[10]

Linear Graphs   A linear, or line, graph plots and connects points along a vertical and a horizontal axis. A linear graph allows more data points than a bar graph. Consequently, it is used to present more detailed and/or larger quantities of information. A linear graph may compare two variables; if so, then it consists of a single line. More often, however, linear graphs are used to compare relationships among several sets of variables and multiple lines are included. The graph shown in Figure 11-8 compares world population in billions of people every thousand years.

Linear graphs are usually used to display continuous data—data connected in time or events occurring in sequence. The data in Figure 11-8 are continuous, as they move from 8000 B.C. to A.D. 2000.

EXERCISE 11-2	Directions: Study the graphs shown in Figures 11-9 through 11-11 and answer the corresponding questions.

Figure 11-9   Marriage and Increasing Life Expectancies

1. What is the purpose of the graph?

   _____

   _____

2. About how many years earlier did couples marry in the early 1900s than they do to-day?

   _____

   _____

3. Approximately how long were couples in the early 1900s married before they died? What about couples of today?

   _____

   _____

4. About how much longer do married couples of today live compared to couples of the early 1900s?

   _____

   _____

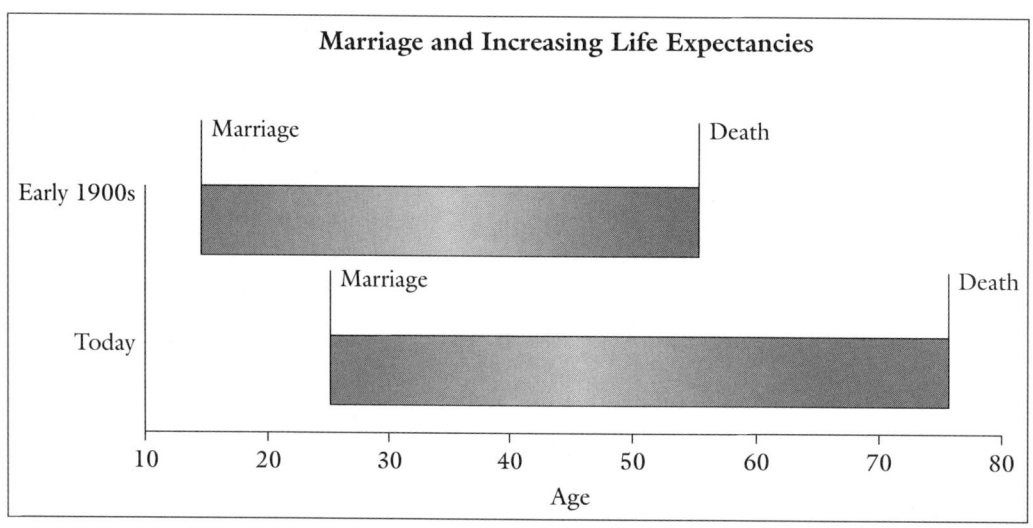

Figure 11-9 A bar graph for use in Exercise 11-2.[11]

Figure 11-10   Unequal Pay for Equal Education

1. What comparisons does this graph allow you to make?

_____

_____

2. How is this graph organized?

_____

_____

3. What patterns are evident?

_____

_____

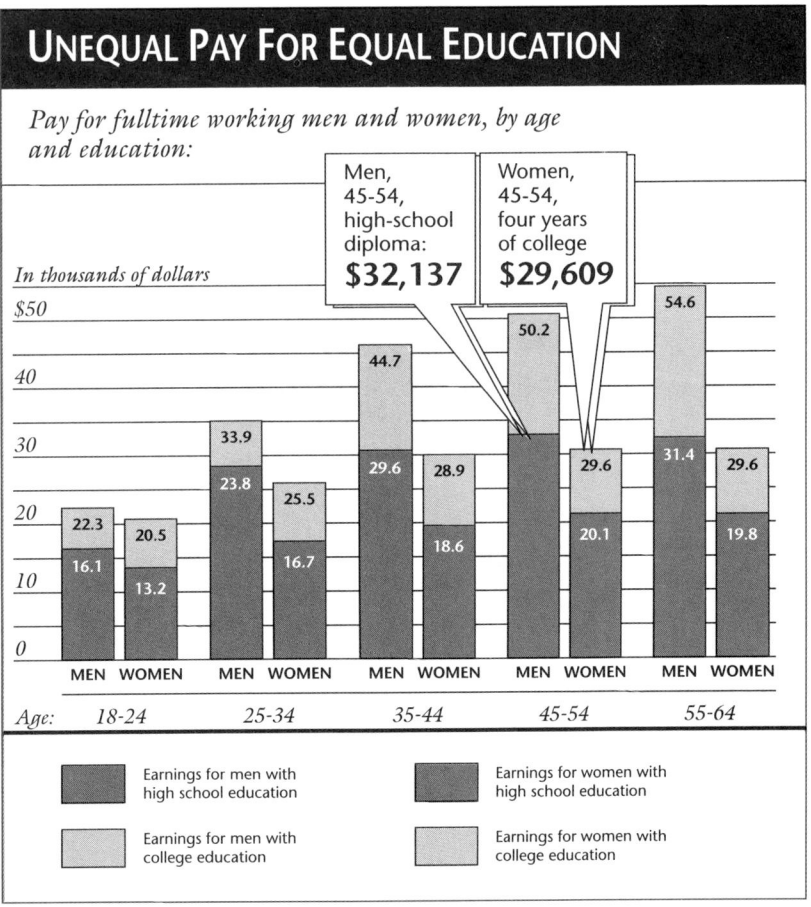

Figure 11-10 A multiple bar graph for use in Exercise 11-2.[12]

Figure 11-11   Rate of Technological Change

1. Describe the purpose of the graph.

_____

_____

2. What trend is evident?

_____

_____

3. Think of some examples of technological changes that have occurred over the
   past 50 years that may account for the dramatic upswing near the year 2000.

_____

_____

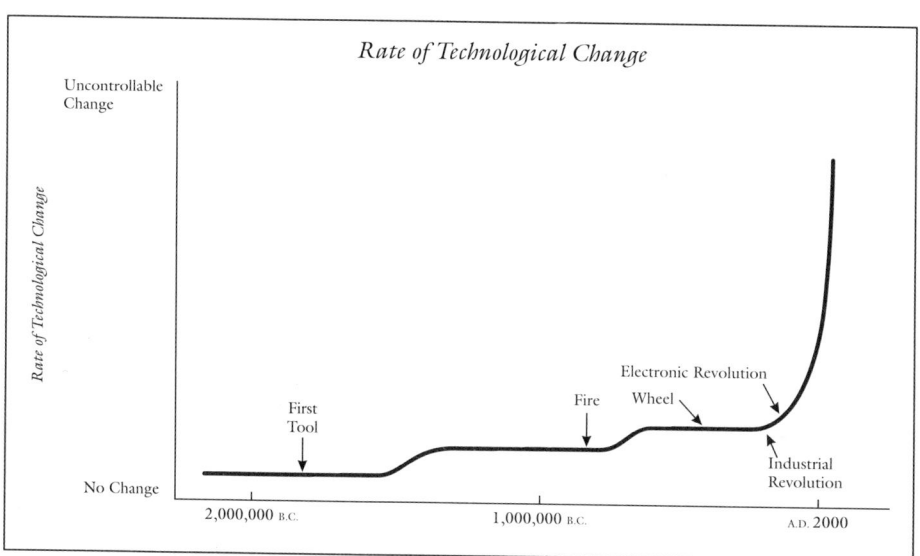

Figure 11-11 A linear graph for use in Exercise 11-2.[13]

CHARTS

Four types of charts are commonly used in college textbooks: pie charts, organizational charts, flowcharts, and pictograms.

Pie Charts   Pie charts, sometimes called circle graphs, are used to show whole/part relationships or to depict how given parts of a unit have been divided or classified. They enable the reader to compare the parts to each other as well as to compare each part to the whole. The chart in Figure 11-12 indicates the types of jobs women hold, and the percentage who holds each.

Organizational Charts   An organizational chart divides an organization, such as a corporation, a hospital, or a university, into its administrative parts, staff positions, or lines of authority. Figure 11-13 shows the organization of the American political party. It reveals that party members belong to precinct and ward organizations. From these organizations county committees are formed. County committee members are represented on state committees and state delegates are chosen for national positions.

Flowcharts   A flowchart is a specialized type of chart that shows how a process or procedure works. Lines or arrows are used to indicate the direction (route or routes) through the procedure. Various shapes (boxes, circles, rectangles) enclose what is done at each stage or step. You could draw, for exam-

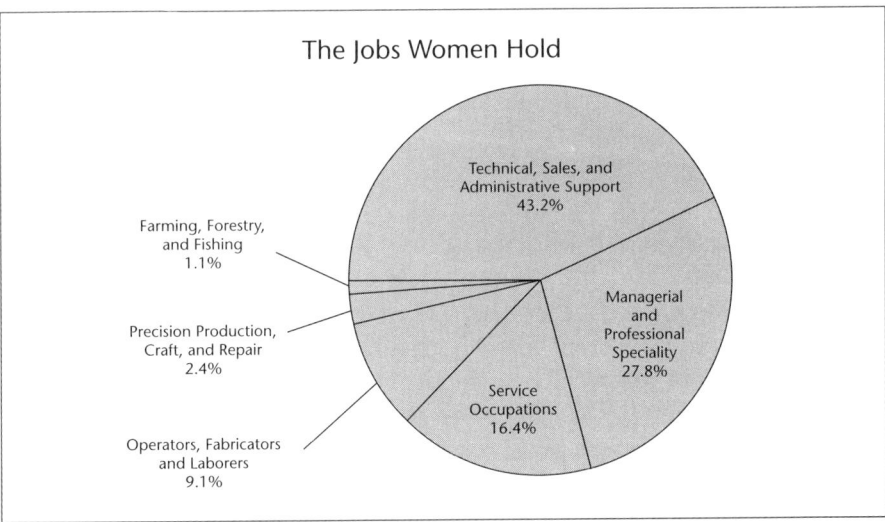

Figure 11-12 A sample pie chart.[14]

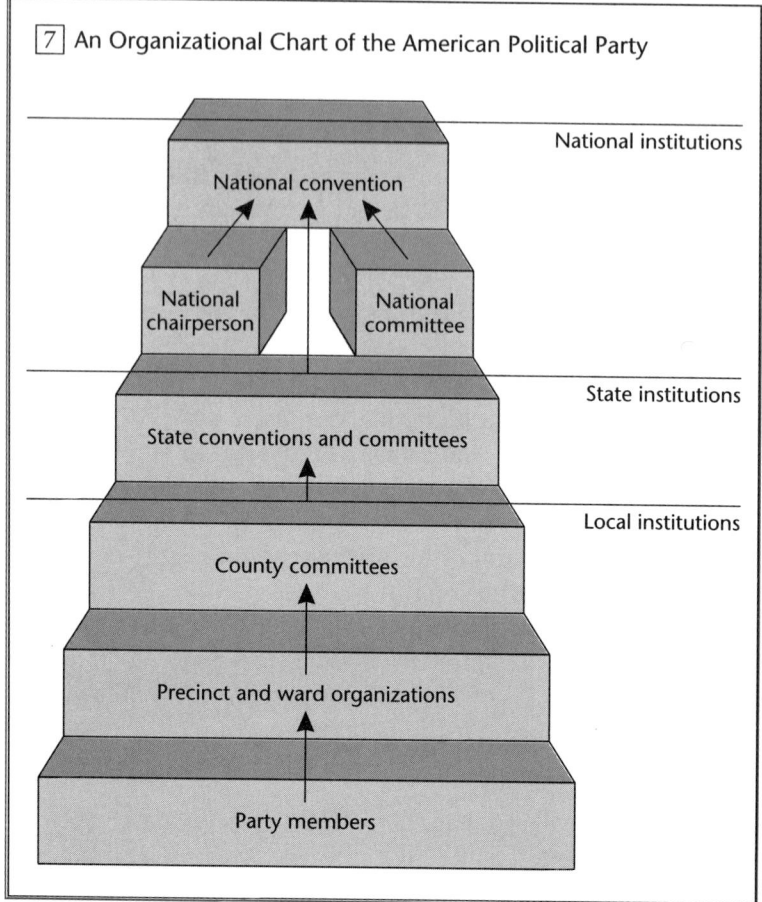

7 An Organizational Chart of the American Political Party

National institutions

National convention

National chairperson

National committee

State institutions

State conventions and committees

Local institutions

County committees

Precinct and ward organizations

Party members

Figure 11-13 A sample organizational chart.[15]

ple, a flowchart to describe how to apply for and obtain a student loan or how to locate a malfunction in your car's electrical system. Refer to the flowchart shown in Figure 11-14, taken from a business management textbook. It describes the steps in the decision-making process.

To read flowcharts effectively, use the following suggestions:

1. **Decide what process the flowchart shows.**
2. **Next, follow the chart, using the arrows and reading each step.** Start at the top or far left of the chart.

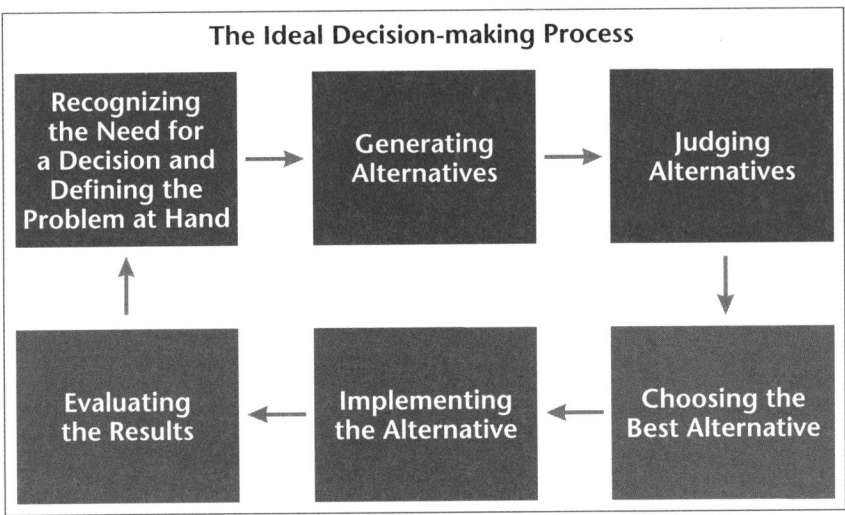

Figure 11-14 A sample flowchart.[16]

3. **When you've finished, summarize the process in your own words.** Try to draw the chart from memory without referring to the text. Compare your drawing with the chart and note discrepancies.

    Now study the flowchart shown in Figure 11-14 and try to express each step in your own words. You might have said something like: (1) Know what has to be decided; (2) Think of all possibilities; (3) Weigh each possibility; (4) Select one; (5) Try it out; and (6) Decide if it worked.

Pictograms   A pictogram uses symbols or drawings (such as books, cars, or buildings), instead of numbers, to represent specified quantities or amounts. This type of chart tends to be visually appealing, makes statistics seem realistic, and may carry an emotional impact. For example, a chart that uses knives to indicate the number of stabbing deaths each year per state may have a more significant impact than statistics presented in table form. A sample pictogram is shown in Figure 11-15. This pictogram uses human figures to represent seventh- to twelfth-grade students. The pictogram compares the number of drinkers with nondrinkers. It indicates the number who drink weekly and the number who purchase alcohol themselves. Patterns of drinking are described.

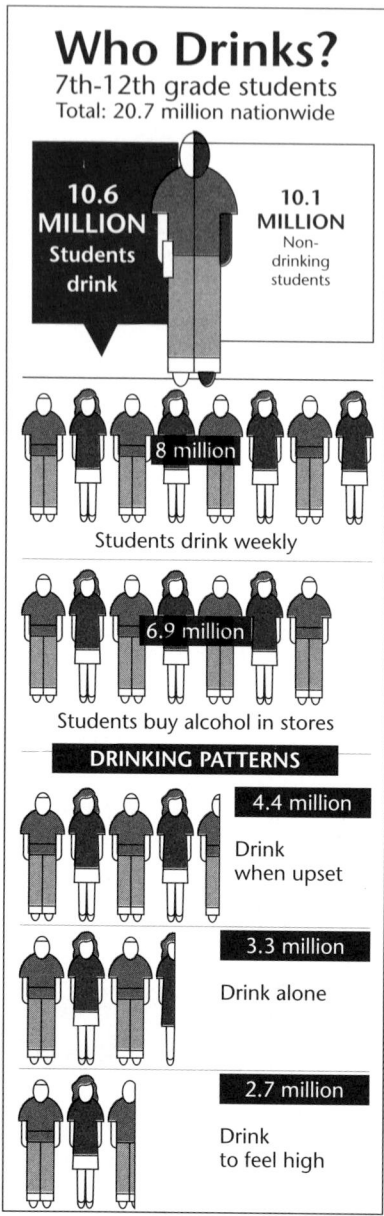

Figure 11-15 A sample pictogram.[17]

**EXERCISE
11-3**

Directions: Study the charts shown in Figures 11-16 through 11-18 and answer the corresponding questions.

Figure 11-16   Race and Ethnicity Origin for the United States

1. What is the purpose of these charts?

_____

_____

2. What patterns are evident?

_____

_____

_____

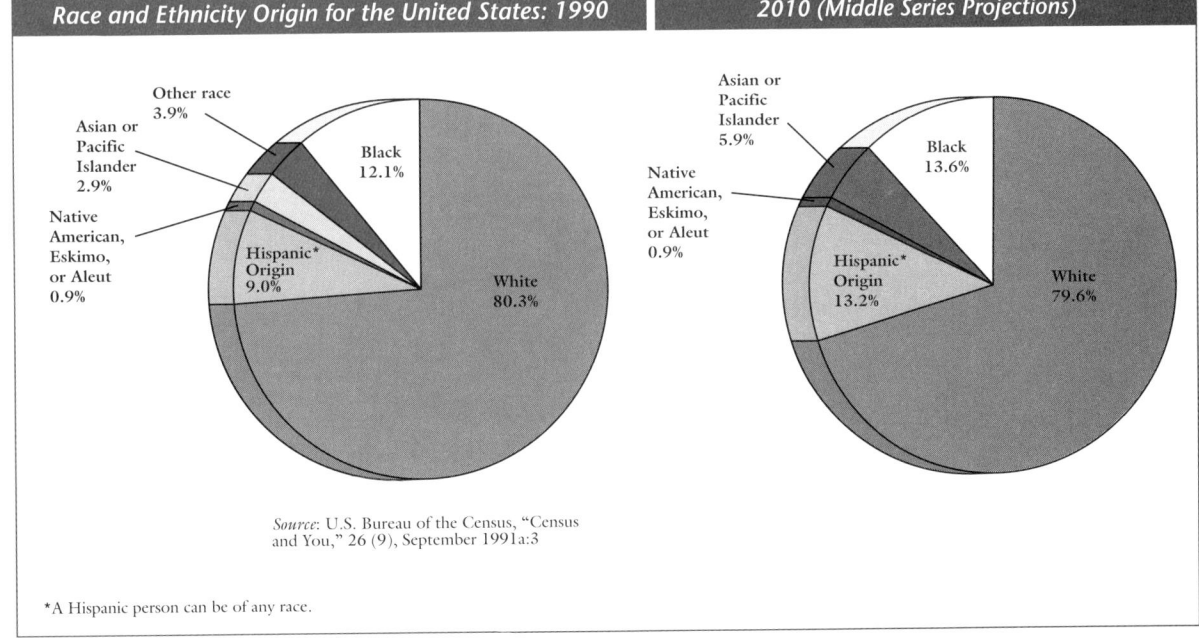

Race and Ethnicity Origin for the United States: 1990   2010 (Middle Series Projections)

Other race 3.9%
Asian or Pacific Islander 2.9%
Native American, Eskimo, or Aleut 0.9%
Hispanic* Origin 9.0%
Black 12.1%
White 80.3%

Asian or Pacific Islander 5.9%
Native American, Eskimo, or Aleut 0.9%
Hispanic* Origin 13.2%
Black 13.6%
White 79.6%

Source: U.S. Bureau of the Census, "Census and You," 26 (9), September 1991a:3

*A Hispanic person can be of any race.

Figure 11-16 Pie charts for use in Exercise 11-3.[18]

Figure 11-17 The Organization of a Medium Market Television Station

1. What is the purpose of the chart?

_____

_____

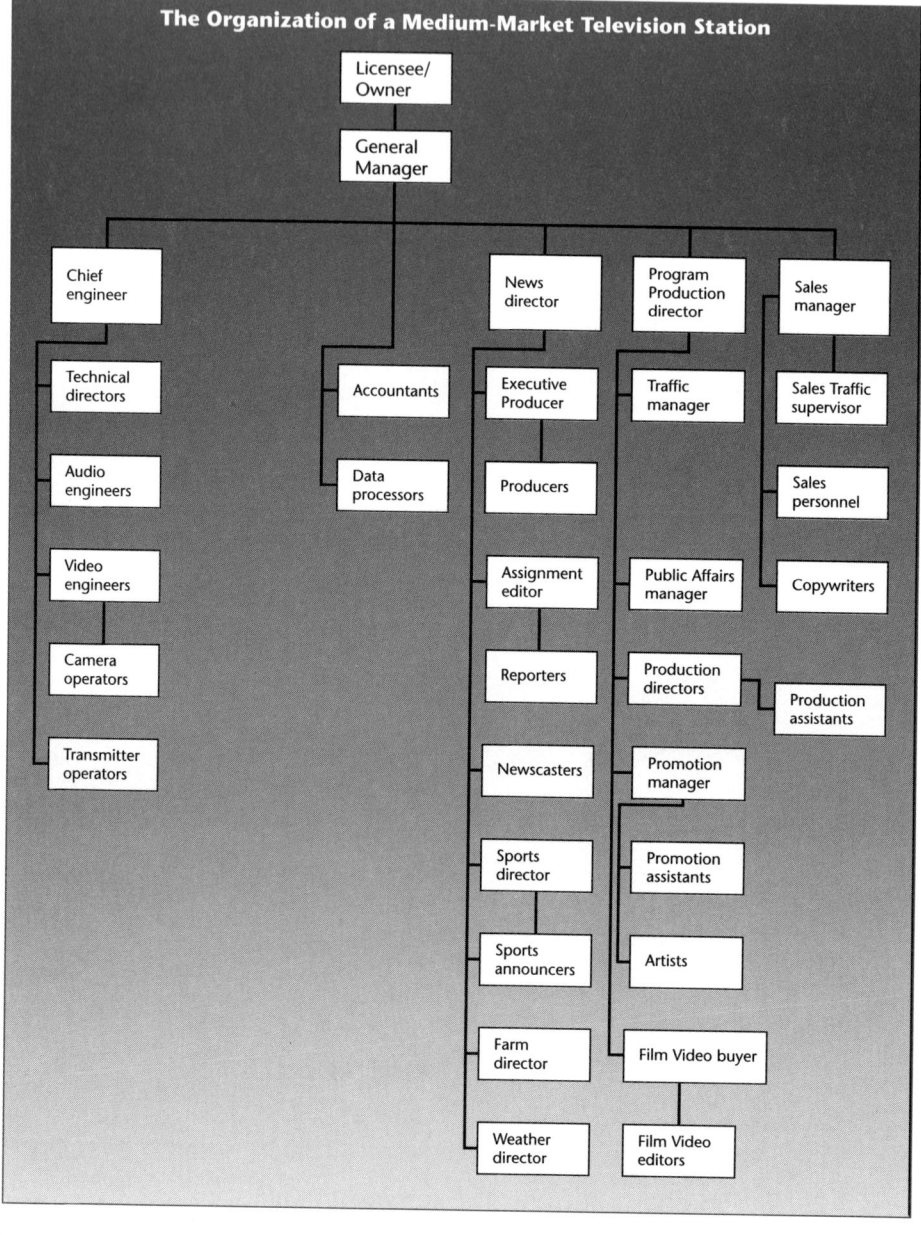

Figure 11-17 An organizational chart for use in Exercise 11-3.[19]

2. To which person or office would the artists report directly?

_____

_____

3. Who is in charge of the department in which sports announcers and newscasters work?

_____

_____

Figure 11-18   The Components of the Criminal Justice System (see page 368 for figure 11-18)

1. What is the purpose of the chart?

_____

_____

2. Summarize its organization.

_____

_____

3. After a person's "Initial Appearance" what happens next if the charges against him are not dropped or dismissed?

_____

_____

Diagrams

Diagrams often are included in technical and scientific as well as many other college texts to explain processes. Diagrams are intended to help you visualize relationships between parts and understand sequences. They may also be used to illustrate ideas or concepts. Figure 11-19, taken from a biology textbook, shows the respiratory (breathing) system of an insect.

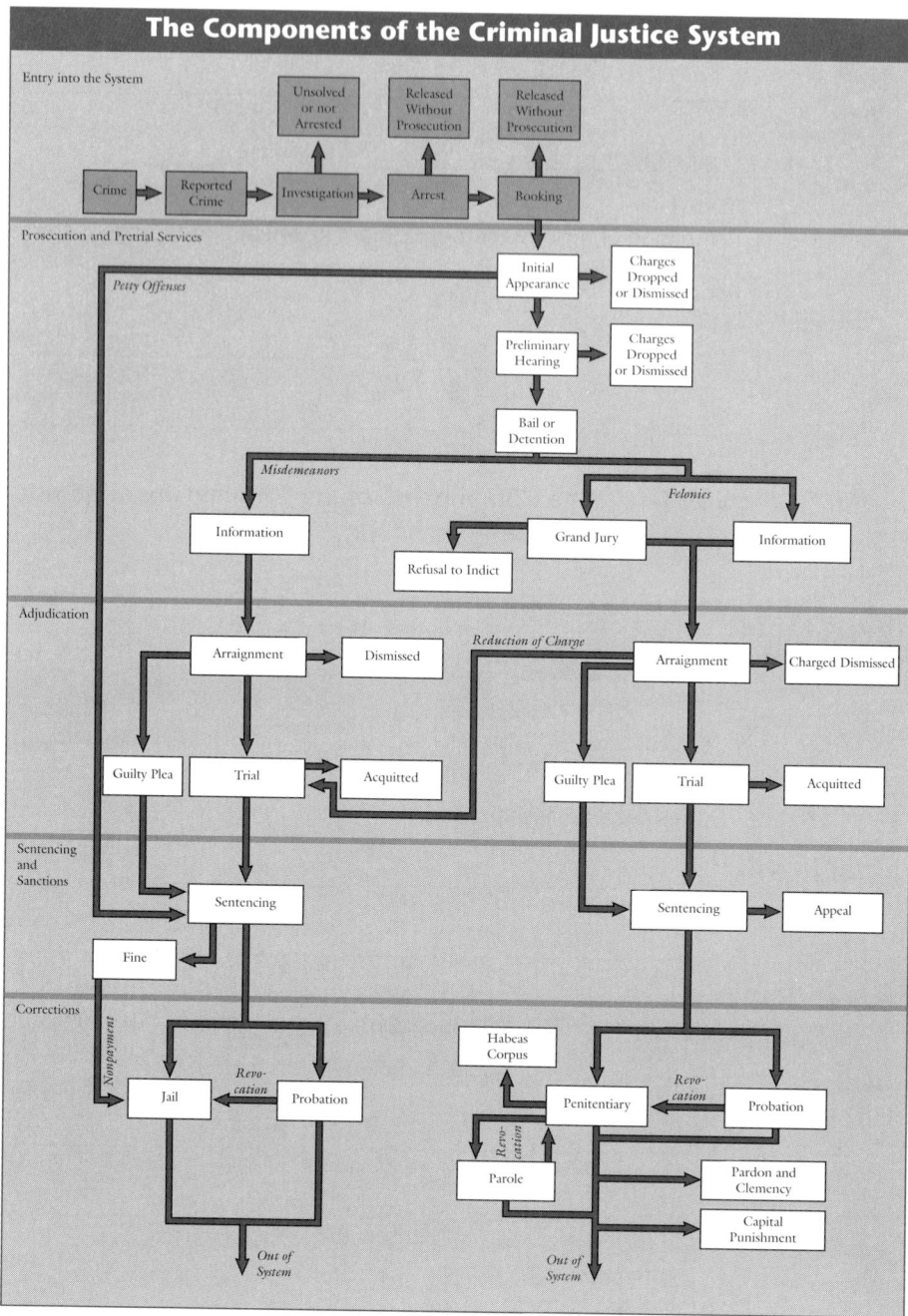

Figure 11-18 A flowchart for use in Exercise 11-3.[20]

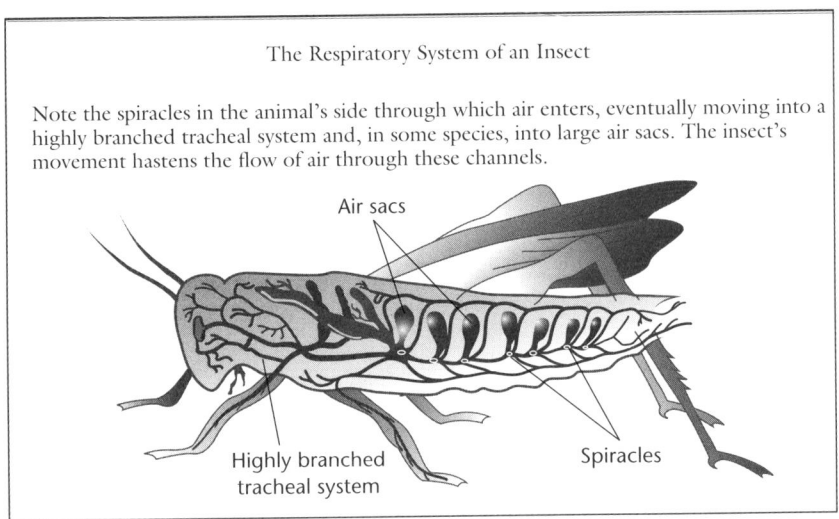

The Respiratory System of an Insect

Note the spiracles in the animal's side through which air enters, eventually moving into a highly branched tracheal system and, in some species, into large air sacs. The insect's movement hastens the flow of air through these channels.

Air sacs

Highly branched
tracheal system

Spiracles

Figure 11-19 A sample diagram.[21]

Accompanying Text

Terrestrial insects generally solve the oxygen problem by breathing through a tracheal system. The system is comprised of tiny tubes that open to the air and permeate their body tissue. The openings to the system are called spiracles. As shown in Figure 19-6, oxygen enters the tracheal system directly from the air and, aided by the insect's bodily movement, moves through the tracheae (plural) deep into the body tissue. Each trachea ends amidst groups of cells or in expanded air sacs. The tracheal network is so extensive that no cell lies far from an oxygen source.[22]

Reading diagrams differs from reading other types of graphics in that diagrams often correspond to fairly large segments of text, requiring you to switch back and forth frequently between the text and the diagram to determine which part of the process each paragraph refers to. Figure 11-19 includes the text that accompanies the diagram.

Because diagrams of processes and their corresponding text are often difficult, complicated, or highly technical, plan on reading these sections more than once. Read first to grasp the overall process. In subsequent readings, focus on the details of the process, examining each step and understanding its progression.

One of the best ways to study a diagram is to redraw it in as much detail as possible without referring to the original. Or, test your understanding and recall of the process outlined in a diagram by explaining it, step by step in writing, using your own words.

EXERCISE 11-4	**Directions:** Study the diagram and accompanying text shown in Figure 11-20 and answer the following questions.

1. What is the purpose of the diagram?

_____

_____

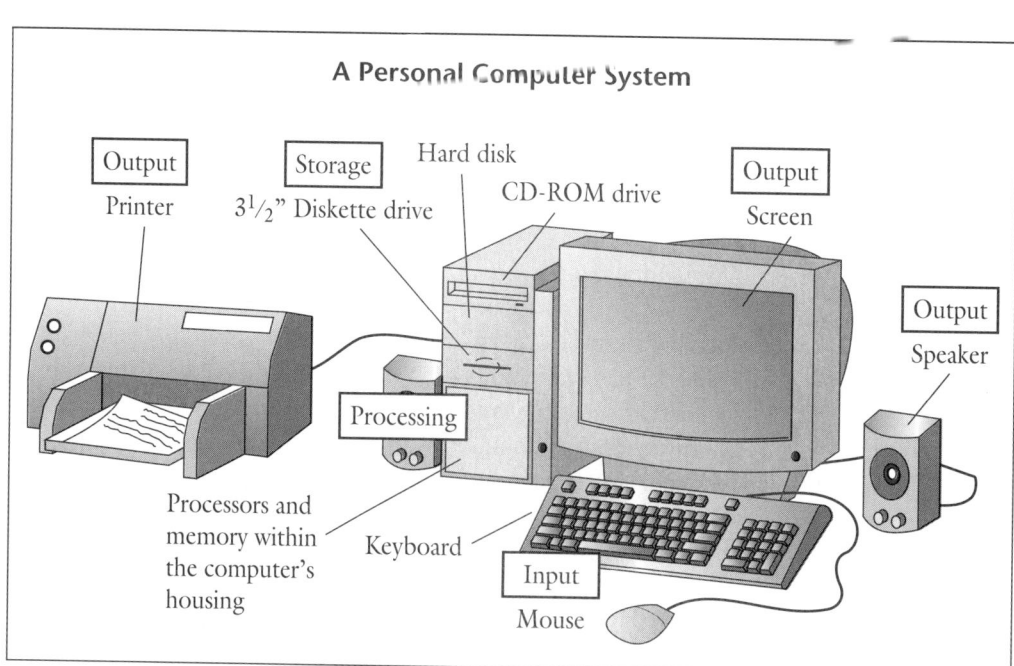

A Personal Computer System

Output — Printer

Storage — 3½" Diskette drive

Hard disk

CD-ROM drive

Output — Screen

Output — Speaker

Processing

Processors and memory within the computer's housing

Keyboard

Input — Mouse

Figure 11-20 A diagram for use in Exercise 11-4.[23] In this personal computer system, the input device is a keyboard or a mouse. The input device feeds data to the central processing unit, which is inside the computer housing, the vertical box to the left of the screen. The output devices in this example are the screen, the printer, and the speakers. The secondary storage devices are hard drive, a 3½-inch disk drive, and a CD-ROM drive, all within the computer housing. This popular configuration, with the housing standing on end, is called a minitower.

2. Which parts of personal computers are considered input devices?

_____

_____

3. What type of devices are printers, screens, and speakers?

_____

_____

4. Where is data from input devices sent next?

_____

_____

Maps

Maps describe relationships and provide information about location and direction. They are commonly found in geography and history texts, and also appear in ecology, biology, and anthropology texts. While most of us think of maps as describing distances and locations, maps also are used to describe the placement of geographical and ecological features such as areas of pollution, areas of population concentration, or political data (voting districts).

When reading maps, use the following steps:

1. **Read the caption.** This identifies the subject of the map.
2. **Use the legend or key to identify the symbols or codes used.**
3. **Note distance scales.**
4. **Study the map, looking for trends or key points.** Often the text that accompanies the map states the key points the map illustrates.
5. **Try to visualize, or create a mental picture of, the map.**
6. **As a learning and study aid, write, in your own words, a statement of what the map shows.**

The map in Figure 11-21 shows new countries that have emerged since World War II.

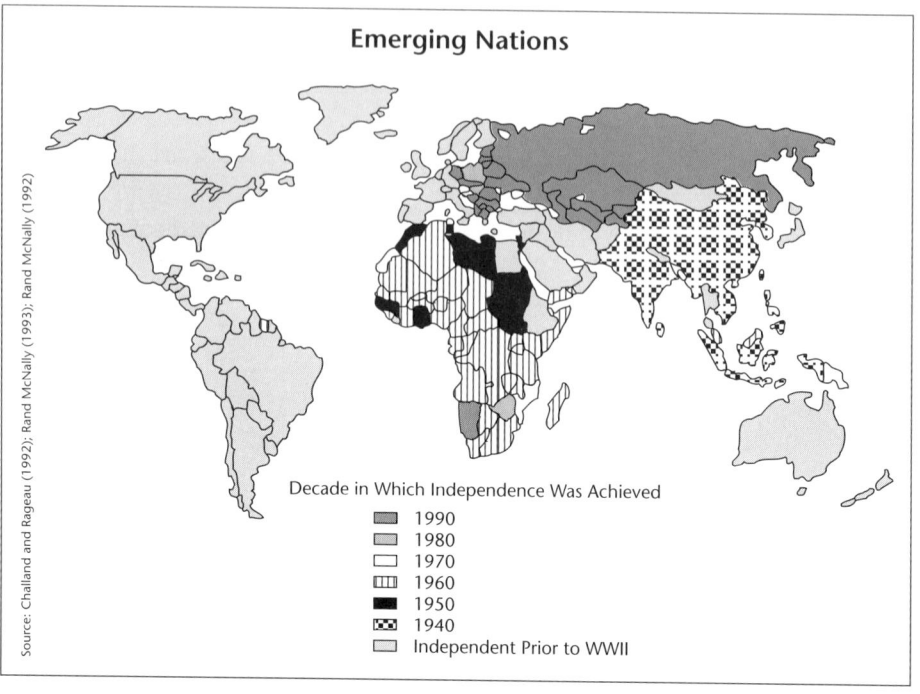

Figure 11-21 A sample map.[24]

Photographs

Although sometimes considered an art form instead of a graphic, photographs are used in place of words. Their purpose is similar to other graphics—to replace verbal descriptions in presenting information. Photographs also are used to spark interest, and, often, to draw out an emotional response or feeling. Use these suggestions when studying a photograph:

1. **Read the caption.** It often provides a clue to the photographer's intended meaning.

2. **Ask: What is my first overall impression?** What details did I notice first? These questions will lead you to discover the purpose of the photograph.

EXERCISE 11-5	**Directions:** Study the photograph in Figure 11-22 and answer the questions that follow.

1. Describe what is happening in the picture.

   _____

   _____

2. Describe the feeling of each person.

   _____

   _____

3. What does this picture reveal about the relationship between these two people?

   _____

   _____

Figure 11-22 A photograph for use in Exercise 11-5.

TYPES OF ELECTRONIC LEARNING AIDS

College instructors are increasingly using a variety of instructional media to supplement their textbook and lecture material. Two forms of electronic learning aids are becoming common: CD-ROM and computerized tutorials.

Learning Style Tips

If you tend to be a . . .	Then study graphics by . . .
Spatial learner	Studying the graphic so that you can visualize it.
Verbal learner	Write sentences that summarize what the graphic shows.

CD-ROMs That Accompany Textbooks

A CD-ROM may be included with the textbook when you purchase it or it may be available in your college's academic computer labs. (Not all textbooks have CD-ROM accompaniments.) A CD-ROM contains a wealth of information, activities, and learning resources. Here is an example of what a CD-ROM that accompanies a psychology text might contain:

- review of key topics
- "click here" function for more information on terms, concepts, etc.
- demonstrations and experiments
- matching games and other learning activities
- review quizzes
- glossary of key terms
- student notepad (for recording your own ideas)
- reference sources

The best part of CD-ROMs is that they are interactive and engaging. The sound, dialogue, and visuals hold your interest and are well suited if you tend to be an auditory, spatial, or pragmatic learner. Many of the activities are interactive—you get involved with the material by responding, rather than just reading it.

Here are a few guidelines for using CD-ROMs that accompany textbooks:

1. **Use them with, but *not in place of,* your text.** CD-ROMs are supplements. Although they are fun to use, you must still read your textbook.

2. **Use the CD-ROM as a chapter preview.** View the CD-ROM on a particular topic to get an overview of it before reading the corresponding text material.

3. **Use the CD-ROM for review and practice.** After you have read the text, use the CD-ROM to help you learn the material.

4. **Use the quiz or self-test modules when studying for an exam.** Use the quizzes to discover which topics you need to study further.

5. **If the CD-ROM has a notepad (a place where you can write your own notes), use it.** You will learn more efficiently if you express what you have learned in your own words.

Computer Tutorials

Computer tutorials accompany some textbooks (for example, the Reading Road Trip CD-ROM accompanies this book). This software is usually available from your instructor or the college's academic computer lab. Their main purpose is often to provide practice and application of skills or concepts taught in the textbook. For example, a physiology textbook may have software that helps you learn the functions and parts of each of the body's systems (circulatory, digestive, immune, and so forth). Software for an algebra text may contain review of various algebraic functions, activities and games, and review quizzes. Here are some suggestions for making the best use of available software:

1. **Try whatever is available.** Even if you've never used a computer before, if software is available, try it out. College computer labs are usually staffed with friendly, helpful people (sometimes other students) who can show you how to get started.

2. **Keep a record of your progress on quizzes.** Many programs will do this for you and allow you to print a progress report. This record will enable you to see your strengths and weaknesses, plan further study, and review troublesome topics.

3. **Space out your practice.** Because many software programs are fun and engaging, some students work on them for hours at a time. To get maximum benefit from the time you are spending, limit your work to an hour or so. Beyond that, many activities become routine, your mind switches to "automatic pilot," and learning ceases to occur.

4. **Consolidate your learning.** When you finish a module or program segment, do not just exit and shut the machine off. Stop and reflect on what you have learned. If you worked on an algebra module about the multiplication of polynomials, then stop and recall the techniques you've learned. Write notes or summarize the process in a separate section of your course notebook reserved for this purpose.

INTERNET SOURCES

The Internet is a worldwide network of computers through which you can access a wide variety of information and services. Through the Internet, you can access the World Wide Web (a network of networks), a service that connects this vast array of resources. Many instructors use the Internet and have begun requiring their students to do so. In many cases, the Internet has become a visual medium. Many sources use graphics and photographs to present and display information. Here is an overview of the services your instructor may ask you to access.

E-Mail (Electronic Mail)

E-mail (electronic mail) enables you to send messages from one person or place to another by using your computer. A variety of computer programs are available that allow you to send and receive messages electronically, as well as to print them for future reference. There are many academic uses for e-mail. Students in a class may collaborate on a project or critique each others' papers using e-mail. Other times, instructors and students may communicate through e-mail. In completing a research paper, it is possible to contact professors or other students doing research on the topic you are studying. It is also possible to transmit word processing files by attaching them to an e-mail message.

Subj: Research on learning styles
Date: 98-02-23 11:49:34 EST
From: Maryrod@daemon.edu   (Mary Rodriguez)
Reply to: Maryrod@daemon.edu
To: KateApp@ncc.edu

Dear Kate,
In response to your request for recent research on the learning styles of university versus community college students, I do know of one article that may be useful as a starting point:
Henson, Mark and Schemeck, R.R. "Learning Styles of Community College Versus University Students." Perceptual Motor Skills, 76(1), 118.
Good luck on your research project.
Mary

Figure 11-23 A sample e-mail message.

Most e-mail follows a consistent format and, consequently, is easy to read. Figure 11-23 shows a sample e-mail message. Messages begin with a memo format in which the topic of the message, date the message was sent, sender, and receiver are identified as "Subject" or "Re," "Date," "From," and "To." The message follows this introductory identifying information. Following the message is transmittal information that tracks the electronic path through which the message was sent. This information can be ignored unless you wish to verify the source of the sender.

Web Sites

A Web site is a location on the World Wide Web where you can obtain information on a particular subject. It is a collection of related pages stored together. You can move around the site from page to page by clicking on specially marked words or images on the screen called *links*. Each page is called a *Web page* and stands for a set of information. (It can be any length and is not restricted to a single screen or printed page.) The first page you see when you access a Web site is called its home page.

Major corporations such as Hertz, Burger King, and General Motors have Web sites, as do many universities, government agencies, and local businesses. A sample home page for Nike footwear is shown in Figure 11-24. Notice that this site offers information as well as product descriptions.

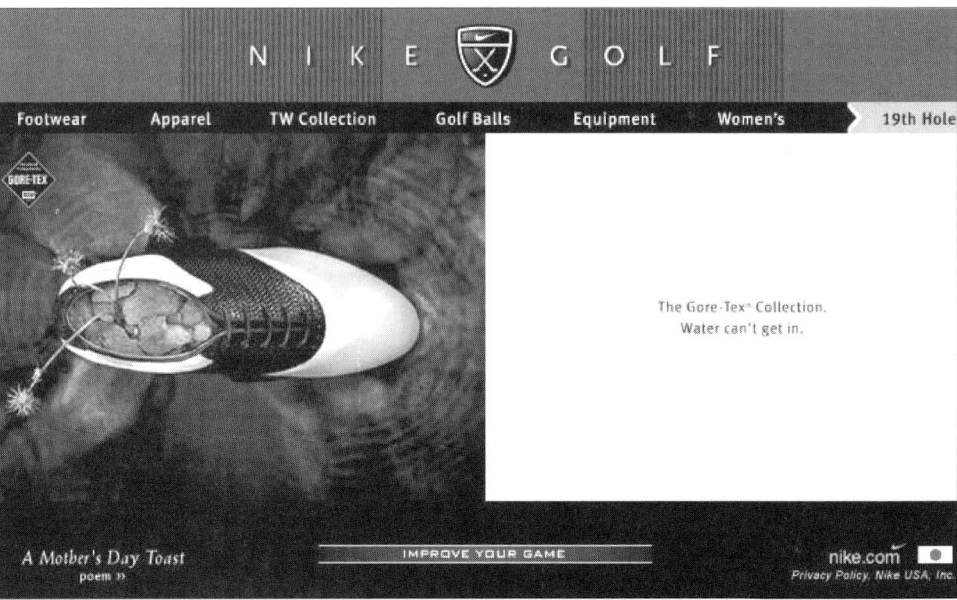

Figure 11-24 A sample home page.

Faculty and Academics — Saint Mary's College

Sociology

"The focus of sociology is the structure and the process of social life in contemporary American society. It addresses pressing social issues such as race, gender, age, and poverty, and examines the impact that cultural, structural, and socio-historical forces have on society, the group, and the individual". Saint Mary's College 1995-1997 Catalog.

Saint Mary's College Library Resources

- Albert - search for book, periodical, video, & multimedia holdings at Saint Mary's College Library
- Infotrac - search for articles in periodicals at Saint Mary's College Library
- Information available at saint Mary's College Library
  - Sociology

Internet Resources

- General Resources
- Journals
- Statistics, Polls, and Social Science Date Sets
- Special Topics
  - Aging
  - Crime
  - Demography and Population
  - Family and Children

General

- A Sociological Tour Through Cyperspace - a web document with information and many links to WWW resources in Sociology. Created by Michael Kearl, Professor of Sociology, Trinity University, TX. A great starting point!
- SocioSite - (Sociological Institute, University of Amsterdam) A comprehensive collection of WWW Sociology Links. Select "Subject Areas" for links to resources in a broad array of subjects related to Soc iology.
- SocioWeb - also provides access to many useful Sociology sites.
- Sociologists Page - Links to information about major sociological thinkers including excerpts from their writings. (Sociological Institute of the University of Amsterdam). . . .

Figure 11-25 A sample Web site.

Web sites have recently been established by textbook publishers and authors to provide information and activities that supplement the text. A Web site for a biology text, for example, may contain reviews of recent research and discoveries not included in the text. A Web site for an English composition textbook may contain additional current readings or up-to-date information on using and evaluating electronic sources or exercises that relate to specific portions of the textbook. Web sites also provide interesting links, or connections, that direct you to other Web sites that offer related information. Web sites are useful sources of information when researching a topic. An excerpt from a Web site sponsored by Saint Mary's College is shown in Figure 11-25. It is intended as a resource for students to help them locate library resources in the field of sociology.

EXERCISE 11-6	**Directions:** Visit a Web site sponsored by an educational institution and a Web site sponsored by a corporation. Then answer the following questions.

1. What is the purpose of each site? _____

   _____

2. In what ways are they similar and in what ways do they differ? _____

   _____

Web Site Addresses

Each Web site has its own address, known as its URL (Uniform Resource Locator). Here's how to read a URL for the *San Francisco Chronicle:*

transfer format   host computer   directory path   file name

http://www.sfgate.com/chronicle/index.shtml

The transfer format identifies the type of server the document is located on and indicates the type of transfer format that is to be used. The second part names the host computer. The directory path is the "address" part of the Web site. The last part is the document, or file, name.

Many sites can be contacted using only the transfer format and the host computer address. Then once you've contacted the site, you can move to different files within the Web site.

Anyone can place a Web site on the Internet. Consequently, you must be cautious and verify that the sources are reliable. See "Is an Internet Source Reliable?," on page 474.

Examining a Web site address can help you evaluate the source. Commercial sources usually have < .com > as part of the host computer address; colleges and universities and other educational institutions are labeled < .edu >, government agencies are identified by < .gov >, < .net > refers to a network, and < .org > refers to an organization. Thus the URL can help you distinguish educational, governmental and commercial success.

Reading a Web Site

The home page, which is the master directory of the Web site, is the key to reading and using the site effectively. It may contain an identifying logo and will offer an overview of what you will find on other connected pages at the site and may suggest links to other Web sites.

A Web page usually contains a heading, called a header, that serves as a title for the information on that page. It usually appears in bigger, bolder type than the rest of the text on the page. These headers serve as valuable, concise descriptions of the contents of the page. Use them to decide whether the page contains the information you need and if it is worth reading.

Newsgroups

Newsgroups are collections of people interested in a particular topic or issue and who correspond to discuss it. Participants post messages on a given topic; other participants read and respond. Read postings with a critical mind-set. Most postings are written by average people expressing their opinions; their ideas may be informative, but they may also contain incorrect information, bias, and unsubstantiated opinion. You should verify any information you get from a newsgroup with a second source.

EXERCISE 11-7

Directions: Visit a newsgroup and either lurk or participate in the discussion. Then answer the following questions.

1. What was the topic of discussion? _____

_____

2. Were the postings largely fact or opinion? _____

_____

3. Did you detect bias or prejudice? _____

_____

4. How useful is the newsgroup as a source of information? _____

_____

WORKING TOGETHER

Directions: Bring a copy of your local newspaper or of *USA Today* to class. After your instructor forms groups, each group should select and tear out four to five graphics. For each graphic, the group should identify the type of graphic, analyze its purpose, and identify the trend or pattern it reveals. Groups should then discuss what other types of graphics could be used to accomplish the author's purpose. Each group should submit one graphic to the instructor along with a brief summary of the members' analysis.

SELF-TEST SUMMARY

How do I read a graphic?

To read a graphic, follow these eight steps:

1. Read the title.
2. Discover how the graphic is organized.
3. Identify variables.
4. Analyze its purpose.
5. Determine the scale of measurement.
6. Identify trends and patterns.
7. Read corresponding text.
8. Write a summary note.

How many types of graphics are there, what are they, and how are they used?

There are six major types of graphics:

1. Tables—used to arrange and organize facts
2. Graphs—including bar, multiple bar, stacked bar, and linear graphs—are used to make comparisons between or among sets of information
3. Charts—including pie charts, organizational charts, flowcharts, and pictograms present visual displays of information
4. Diagrams—demonstrate physical relationships between parts and display sequences
5. Maps—describe information about location and direction
6. Photographs—used to spark interest or to draw out an emotional response

What are two types of electronic learning aids? Explain the function of each.

1. CD-ROMs review and/or expand chapter content.
2. Computer tutorials provide practice and application of textbook material.

List three sources of information available through the Internet.

1. e-mail
2. Web sites
3. newsgroups

Name _____

Section _____ Date _____

Number right _____ x 20 points = Score _____

Directions: Use the graphic below to answer the following questions.

Ancestry of U.S. Residents (1990 U.S. Census)

Percentage of the total population	Group	Number in millions
23.3%	German	57.95
15.6	Irish	38.74
13.1	English	32.68
9.6	African American	23.77
5.9	Italian	14.66
5.0	American	12.4
4.7	Mexican	11.6
4.1	French	10.32
3.8	Polish	9.37
3.5	American Indian	8.71

Source: adapted from *Messages*, p. 30

_____ 1. This type of graph is known as
   a. an organizational chart.
   b. a pie chart.
   c. a bar graph.
   d. a flowchart.

(continued)

_____ 2. The purpose of this graph is to
   a. compare the ancestry groups of
      United States residents to other
      ancestry groups and to the total
      U.S. population.
   b. present changes in the ancestry
      groups of U.S. residents over time.
   c. compare the income levels of vari-
      ous ancestry groups in the U.S.
   d. predict the immigration patterns of
      various groups over the next ten
      years.

_____ 3. According to the graph, the ancestry
      group with the largest percentage of
      the total U.S. population is
   a. German.
   b. Irish.
   c. American.
   d. American Indian.

_____ 4. The number of people who claimed
      Italian ancestry was
   a. 5.9 million.
   b. 14.66 million.
   c. 59 million.
   d. 146 million.

_____ 5. Each of the following ancestry groups
      represented less than 10 percent of the
      total population in 1990 *except*
   a. African American.
   b. Mexican.
   c. American Indian.
   d. English.

Name _____

Section _____ Date _____

Number right _____ x 20 points = Score _____

Directions: Use the text and graph below to answer the questions that follow.

How many teenagers smoke? In 1991, the Youth Risk Behavior Survey (YRBS) indicated that 27.5 percent of teenagers smoked; by 1997, 36.4 percent were current cigarette smokers. Overall, since 1991 cigarette smoking has increased at each grade level surveyed, as shown in the figure below. The number of teenagers who become daily smokers before the age of 18 is estimated to be more than 3,000 per day. Every day another 6,000 teens under the age of 18 smoke their first cigarette. The increase in cigarette use is attributed in part to the ready availability of tobacco products through vending machines and the aggressive drive by tobacco companies to entice young people to smoke.[25]

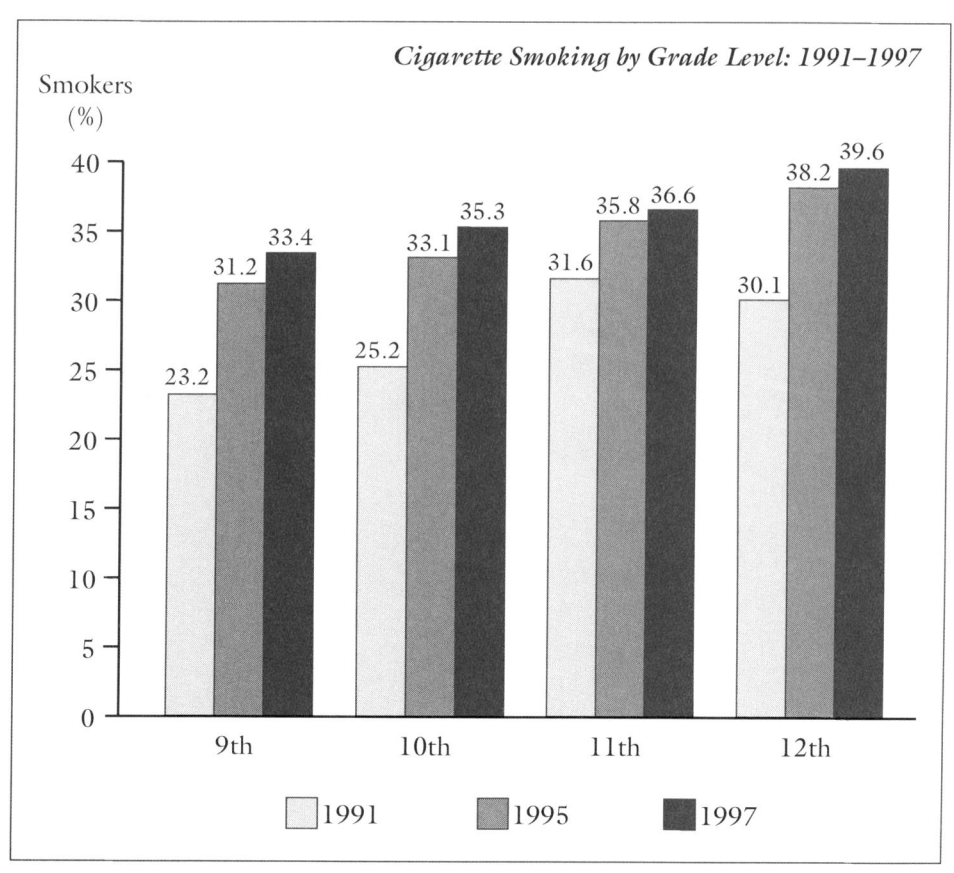

Cigarette Smoking by Grade Level: 1991–1997

Source: CDC, Youth Risk Behavior Surveillance System.

(continued)

——— 1. The purpose of the graph is to show the
   a. percentage of the United States population that smokes.
   b. increase in the percentage of smokers in grades 9–12 during the years 1991–1997.
   c. number of teenagers who become smokers in grades 9–12.
   d. amount of money the tobacco companies spent on smokers in grades 9–12 during the years 1991–1997.

——— 2. According to the graph, the grade with the *highest* percentage of smokers in 1991 was
   a. 9th.
   b. 10th.
   c. 11th.
   d. 12th.

——— 3. The percentage of 9th graders who smoked in 1997 was
   a. 23.2.
   b. 25.2.
   c. 31.2.
   d. 33.4.

——— 4. From 1991 to 1997, the grade which experienced the *greatest increase* in the percentage of smokers was
   a. 9th.
   b. 10th.
   c. 11th.
   d. 12th.

——— 5. Of the following facts, the only one that appears *both* in the text and in the graphic is:
   a. In 1997, 39.6 percent of 12th graders were smokers.
   b. It is estimated that more than 3,000 teenagers a day become daily smokers before the age of 18.
   c. Cigarette smoking has increased at each of the grades 9–12 since 1991.
   d. Every day 6,000 teenagers under the age of 18 smoke their first cigarette.

Name _____
Section _____ Date _____
Number right _____ x 10 points = Score _____

Directions: Study the graph below and choose the letter that best answers each of the questions that follow.

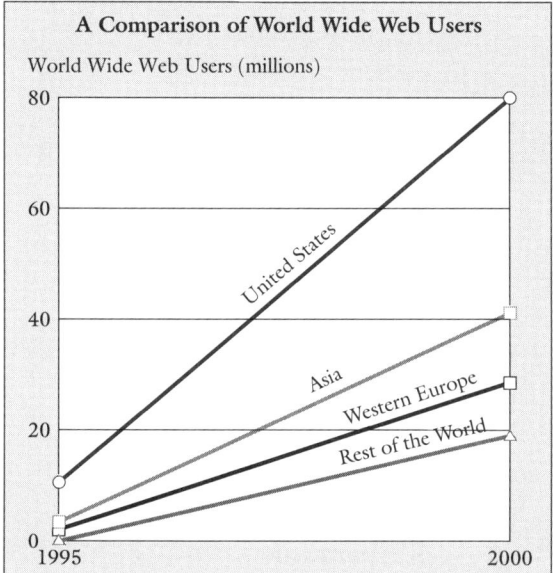

A Comparison of World Wide Web Users

_____ 1. In 1995, which of the following two areas of the world had almost the same number of World Wide Web users?
   a. Western Europe and the rest of the world
   b. Western Europe and the U.S.
   c. Asia and the U.S.
   d. rest of the world and the U.S.

_____ 2. In 2000, which of the following areas of the world had the most World Wide Web users?
   a. U.S.
   b. Asia
   c. rest of the world
   d. Western Europe

_____ 3. Approximately how many World Wide Web users were in Western Europe in 2000?
   a. 35 million
   b. 28 million
   c. 15 million
   d. 80 million

_____ 4. Which area of the world showed the largest increase in World Wide Web users?
   a. U.S.
   b. Europe
   c. Asia
   d. rest of the world

Directions: Study the pie chart below and choose the letter that best answers each of the questions that follow.

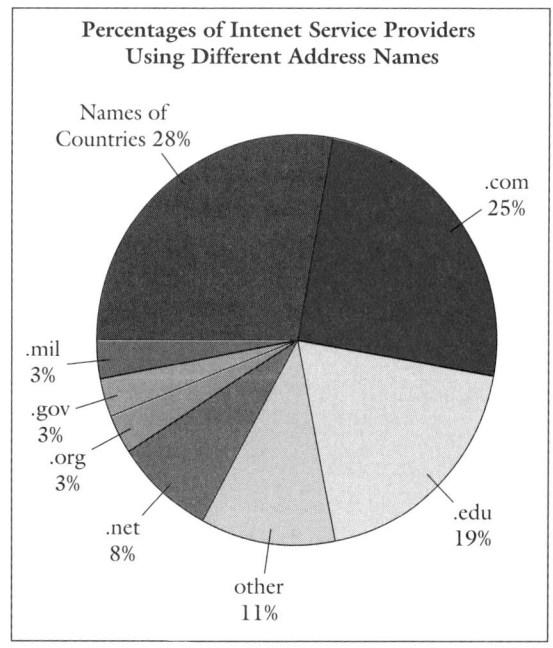

Percentages of Intenet Service Providers Using Different Address Names

(*continued*)

_____ 5. Which of the following address names is used by the second largest percentage of Internet service providers?
   a. edu
   b. other
   c. com
   d. names of countries

_____ 6. Which of the following address names contain the same percentages of Internet service providers?
   a. mil and net
   b. edu and com
   c. gov and org
   d. com and names of countries

_____ 7. What percentage of Internet service providers use the name of a country in their addresses?
   a. 25 percent
   b. 8 percent
   c. 11 percent
   d. 28 percent

Directions: Study the following chart and answer the following questions.

_____ 8. The brain is part of the
   a. spinal cord.
   b. autonomic nervous system.
   c. peripheral nervous system.
   d. central nervous system.

_____ 9. Which of the following nervous systems controls muscles?
   a. somatic nervous system
   b. autonomic nervous system
   c. brain
   d. central nervous system

_____ 10. Which of the following nervous systems has the greatest number of divisions?
   a. autonomic
   b. spinal cord
   c. peripheral
   d. sympathetic

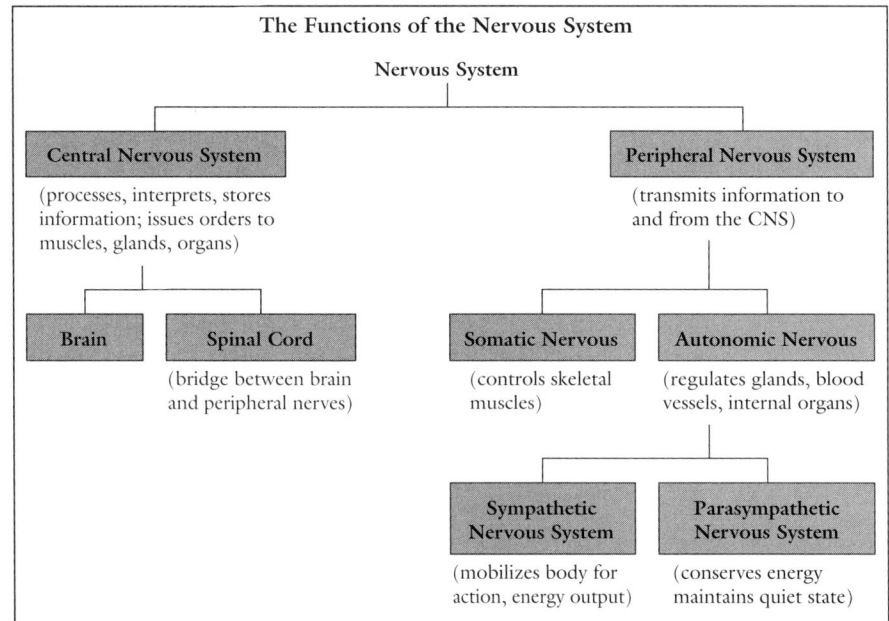

Name _____

Section _____ Date _____

Number right _____ x 10 points = Score _____

School's Out? But This Is Only April

USA Today

Have you wondered why college semesters are so short? In this argumentative essay, the author argues that shorter semesters are cheating students.

Vocabulary Preview

elite (par. 4) superior group or class

abbreviated (par. 5) shortened

depreciated (par. 7) lessened in value

rigor (par. 9) strictness

comprehensive (exams) (par. 9) exams covering the entire course

glean (par. 10) gather, collect

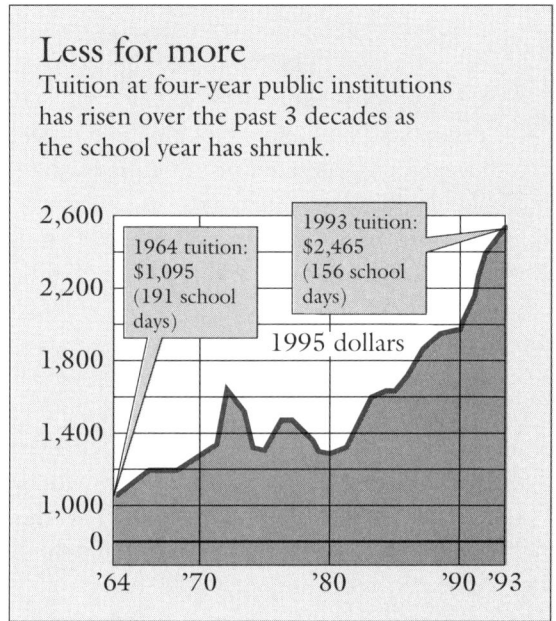

Less for more
Tuition at four-year public institutions has risen over the past 3 decades as the school year has shrunk.

1964 tuition:
$1,095
(191 school days)

1993 tuition:
$2,465
(156 school days)

1995 dollars

Source: USA TODAY research

1   Students at the University of Pittsburgh finish their classes Friday. Rice University's course work wraps up next week. And at Tulane, the last day of classes is April 29.

2   The calendar says it is springtime. But for college students, summer is here.

3   These early vacation breaks are part of a shortening of the school year at colleges nationwide. Data collected by the National Association of Scholars shows that the length of the average college year has shrunk 35 days since 1964. Yet over the same period, inflation-adjusted college costs have doubled.

4   The result: Students and their families are paying more for less. In fact, at the nation's elite universities, the combination of higher tuition and condensed class time means an education prices out at about $1,000 a week.

5   The reason for the abbreviated academic calendar is largely economic. Universities discovered they can save money on operating expenses by shortening the school year.

6   Teachers like it because they have more time for research. Students don't complain because they can earn more in their summer jobs. And the practice of trimming away a class day here, while tacking on another holiday there, is less obvious—and controversial—than other cost-cutting strategies.

7   So who's hurt? The student earning a depreciated diploma, for starters.

8 During the same period that colleges sliced away one-fifth of their academic calendars, they also shortened the length of the standard class by 3.5 minutes. As a result of this double decrease, educators teach less and students are given a shorter time to absorb class material.

9 Researchers who track the trend see it as part of the overall decline in rigor at American universities. They say it is no coincidence that the shorter school year has been phased in at the same time colleges have lightened academic demands on students by dropping thesis requirements, abolishing comprehensive exams and reducing scientific lab work.

10 Yet by reducing class time, colleges aren't cutting students any breaks in the long run. The complex subject matter covered in many university courses is best learned through repeated, long-term exposure. And because students are spending less time in class, they have fewer opportunities to glean knowledge and expertise from their professors.

11 Researchers also believe the pressures of the compressed schedule contribute to the growing number of students unable to complete their degree requirements within the traditional four years. This month, the American College Testing program reported a record low for students earning their bachelor's degrees on schedule. Even within five years of college enrollment, only 52.8% of college students earn a degree.

12 That may not be a problem for universities. After all, they save money by shortening the school year and then collect extra tuition from students who can't finish their course work during the shrunken semester.

13 Yet the students getting a college education—and the families who are funding it—are investing more and getting less.

14 For them, summer has arrived. But that's no reason to celebrate.

Directions: Choose the letter that best answers each of the following questions.

CHECKING YOUR COMPREHENSION

_____ 1. The main point of the selection is that
   a. shortened school years are cheating college students.
   b. students learn as much as they need to in shorter classes.
   c. universities have found a way to cut costs harmlessly.
   d. a shorter school year is beneficial to students who need summer jobs to earn tuition money.

_____ 2. The main idea of paragraph 11 is that because of shorter schedules
   a. students are not motivated to study as hard.
   b. more students are attending college.
   c. colleges are costing more and becoming more self-sufficient.
   d. students need more than four years to get their degrees.

_____ 3. The main point of paragraph 6 is
   a. most students are now able to begin their summer jobs sooner.
   b. a shorter school year has some advantages for teachers, students, and universities.
   c. universities need to find less obvious and controversial ways to save money.
   d. shorter classes mean more classes can be offered in a day.

_____ 4. Since 1964, the average class length has become shorter by
   a. 3.5 minutes.
   b. 7 minutes.
   c. 35 days.
   d. half.

_____ 5. According to this selection, college subject matter is best learned through
   a. taking comprehensive exams each term.
   b. writing a thesis.
   c. repetition over a long period of time.
   d. studying during the summer.

_____ 6. In paragraph 9, the word "rigor" means
   a. quality.
   b. time.
   c. teachers.
   d. demands.

APPLYING YOUR SKILLS

_____ 7. According to the graph, in which of the following years was college tuition the highest?
   a. 1970
   b. 1972
   c. 1977
   d. 1982

_____ 8. The overall trend shown on the graph is that
   a. school days were shorter in 1993 than they were in 1980.
   b. tuition is more expensive at private schools than at public schools.
   c. tuition has risen since 1964.
   d. tuition in 1995 is about the same as in 1993.

_____ 9. Tuition seems to have decreased the most between which of the following years?
   a. 1972–1975
   b. 1977–1980
   c. 1981–1983
   d. 1990–1992

_____ 10. Which of the following questions cannot be answered by the information found in the graph?
   a. What is the difference in the cost of tuition in 1964 and 1993?
   b. What was the average number of school days in 1964?
   c. Does the chart account for inflation in its tuition figures?
   d. What is the difference in number of school days in 1993 and 1964?

12

Organizing and Remembering Information

THIS CHAPTER WILL SHOW YOU HOW TO

1. Highlight and mark important information in textbook chapters
2. Outline information to show its organization
3. Draw maps to organize information
4. Summarize ideas for review purposes
5. Review for maximum retention

Suppose you are planning a cross-country trip next summer. To get ready you begin to collect all kinds of information: maps, newspaper articles on various cities, places to visit, names of friends' friends, and so forth. After a while, you find that you have a great deal of information and that it is difficult to locate any one item. You begin to realize that the information you have collected will be of little or no use unless you organize it in some way. You decide to buy large envelopes and put different kinds of information into separate envelopes, such as information on individual states.

In this case, you found a practical, commonsensical solution to a problem. The rule or principle that you applied was this: When something gets confusing, organize it.

This rule also works well when applied to college textbooks. Each text contains thousands of pieces of information—facts, names, dates, theories, principles. This information quickly becomes confusing unless it is organized. Once you have organized it, you will be able to find and remember what you need more easily than if your text were still an unassorted heap of facts.

Organizing information requires sifting, sorting, and in some cases rearranging important facts and ideas. There are five common methods of organizing textbook materials:

- Highlighting
- Marking
- Outlining
- Mapping
- Summarizing

In this chapter you will learn techniques for doing each. You will also see how to study and review more effectively.

HIGHLIGHTING AND MARKING

Highlighting and marking important facts and ideas as you read are effective methods of identifying and organizing information. They are also the biggest time-savers known to college students. Suppose it took you four hours to read an assigned chapter in sociology. One month later you need to review that chapter to prepare for an exam. If you did not highlight or mark as you read the first time, then, in order to review the chapter once, you would have to spend another four hours rereading it. However, if you had highlighted and marked as you read, you could review the chapter in an hour or less—a savings of 300 percent. This means you can save many hours each semester. More important, the less time you spend identifying what to learn, the more thoroughly you can learn the necessary information. This strategy can help improve your grades.

Highlighting Effectively

Here are a few basic suggestions for highlighting effectively:

1. **Read a paragraph or section first.** Then go back and highlight what is important.
2. **Highlight important portions of the topic sentence.** Also highlight any supporting details you want to remember (see Chapters 7 and 8).
3. **Be accurate.** Make sure your highlighting reflects the content of the passage. Incomplete or hasty highlighting can mislead you as you review the passage and may cause you to miss the main point.
4. **Use a system for highlighting.** There are several from which to choose: for instance, using two or more different colors of highlighters to distinguish between main ideas and details, or placing a bracket around the

main idea and using highlighter to mark important details. No one system is more effective than another. Try to develop a system that works well for you.

5. **Highlight as few words as possible in a sentence.** Seldom should you highlight an entire sentence. Usually highlighting the key idea along with an additional phrase or two is sufficient. Read the following paragraph. Notice that you can understand its meaning from the highlighted parts alone.

> Obviously, everybody spends part of his or her life as a single person. Traditionally, it was common that as adolescents entered adulthood, they felt compelled to find both jobs and marriage partners. Today, expectations and goals are changing. As an adolescent moves through high school, and perhaps college, he or she faces a number of decisions regarding the future. Marrying right after school is no longer a top priority for many, and the social stigma against remaining single is rapidly disappearing. In fact, single adults are now one of the fastest-growing factions in the United States; in the past two decades, the number of singles has more than doubled, and now represents more than one-fourth of all households.

6. **Use headings to guide your highlighting** (see Chapter 10). Use the headings to form questions that you expect to be answered in the section (see Chapter 5). Then highlight the answer to each question.

Highlighting the Right Amount

If you highlight either too much or too little, you defeat the purpose. By highlighting too little, you miss valuable information, and your review and study of the material will be incomplete. On the other hand, if you highlight too much, you are not identifying the most important ideas and eliminating less important facts. The more you highlight, the more you will have to reread when studying and the less of a time-saver the procedure will prove to be. As a general rule of thumb, highlight no more than 20 to 30 percent of the material.

Here is a paragraph highlighted in three different ways. First read the paragraph that has not been highlighted; then look at each highlighted version. Try to decide which version would be most useful if you were rereading it for study purposes.

> Money (or actually the lack of it) is a major source of stress for many people. In a sense, this is one of the most "valid" stressors because so many of our basic survival needs require money. Anyone struggling to survive on a small income is likely to feel plenty of stress. But money has significance beyond its obvious value as a medium of exchange. Even some of the wealthiest people become stressed

over money-related issues. To some people, wealth is a measurement of human value and their self-esteem is based on their material assets. Stress management for such people requires taking an objective look at the role money plays for them.[1]

Example 1:

Money (or actually the lack of it) is a major source of stress for many people. In a sense, this is one of the most "valid" stressors because so many of our basic survival needs require money. Anyone struggling to survive on a small income is likely to feel plenty of stress. But money has significance beyond its obvious value as a medium of exchange. Even some of the wealthiest people become stressed over money-related issues. To some people, wealth is a measurement of human value and their self-esteem is based on their material assets. Stress management for such people requires taking an objective look at the role money plays for them.

Example 2:

Money (or actually the lack of it) is a major source of stress for many people. In a sense, this is one of the most "valid" stressors because so many of our basic survival needs require money. Anyone struggling to survive on a small income is likely to feel plenty of stress. But money has significance beyond its obvious value as a medium of exchange. Even some of the wealthiest people become stressed over money-related issues. To some people, wealth is a measurement of human value and their self-esteem is based on their material assets. Stress management for such people requires taking an objective look at the role money plays for them.

Example 3:

Money (or actually the lack of it) is a major source of stress for many people. In a sense, this is one of the most "valid" stressors because so many of our basic survival needs require money. Anyone struggling to survive on a small income is likely to feel plenty of stress. But money has significance beyond its obvious value as a medium of exchange. Even some of the wealthiest people become stressed over money-related issues. To some people, wealth is a measurement of human value and their self-esteem is based on their material assets. Stress management for such people requires taking an objective look at the role money plays for them.

The last example is the best example of effective highlighting. Only the most important information has been highlighted. In the first example, too little of the important information has been highlighted while what *has* been highlighted is either unnecessary or incomplete. The second example, on the other hand, has too much highlighting to be useful for review.

<table>
<tr><td>**EXERCISE 12-1**</td><td>**Directions:** Read and highlight the following selection using the guidelines presented in this section.</td></tr>
</table>

Tailoring the Marketing Mix for Global Markets

Marketers have several options as to the products they present in the global arena. They can sell the same product abroad that they sell at home, they can modify the product for foreign markets, or they can develop an entirely new product for foreign markets.

The simplest strategy is product extension, which involves offering the same product in all markets, domestic and foreign. This approach has worked successfully for companies including Pepsico, Coca-Cola, Kentucky Fried Chicken, and Levis. Pepsi and Coke are currently battling for market share in both Russia and Vietnam, countries with small but growing soft-drink markets. Both firms are producing and selling the same cola to the Russian and Vietnamese markets that they sell to other markets around the world. Not all companies that have attempted it, however, have found success with product extension. When Duncan Hines introduced its rich, moist American cakes to England, the British found them too messy to hold while sipping tea. Japanese consumers disliked the coleslaw produced by Kentucky Fried Chicken; it was too sweet for their tastes. KFC responded by cutting the sugar in half.

The strategy of modifying a product to meet local preferences or conditions is product adaptation. Cosmetics companies produce different colors to meet the differing preferences of European consumers. French women like bold reds while British and German women prefer pearly pink shades of lipstick and nail color. Nestle's sells varieties of coffee to suit local tastes worldwide. Unilever produces frozen versions of local delicacies such as Bami Goreng and Madras Curry for markets in Indonesia and India.

Product invention consists of developing a new product to meet a market's needs and preferences. The opportunities that exist with this strategy are great since many unmet needs exist worldwide, particularly in developing and less-developed economies. Marketers have not been quick, however, to attempt product invention. For example, despite the fact that an estimated 600 million people worldwide still scrub clothes by hand, it was the early 1980s before a company (Colgate-Palmolive) developed an inexpensive, all plastic, manual washing machine with the tumbling action of an automatic washer for use in homes without electricity.[2]

EXERCISE 12-2   **Directions:** Read or reread and highlight Chapter 5 in this book. Follow the guidelines suggested in this chapter.

Testing Your Highlighting

As you highlight, check to be certain your highlighting is effective and will be helpful for review purposes. To test the effectiveness of your highlighting, take any passage and reread only the highlighted portions. Then ask yourself the following questions:

- Does the highlighting tell what the passage is about?
- Does it make sense?
- Does it indicate the most important idea in the passage?

EXERCISE 12-3   **Directions:** Test the effectiveness of your highlighting for the material you highlighted in Exercises 12-1 and 12-2. Make changes, if necessary.

Marking

When reading many types of textbooks, highlighting alone will not clearly identify and organize information. Also, highlighting does not allow you to react to or sort ideas. Try making notes in the margin in addition to highlighting. Notice how the marginal notes in the following passage organize the information in a way that highlighting cannot.

4 forms of energy
1. hydraulic
2. electrical
3. geothermal
4. sun

The Source of Energy

Within the biosphere itself several forms of energy are produced: hydraulic energy, created by water in motion (a river pouring over a dam, storm waves striking a shoreline); electrical energy (lightning); and geothermal energy (underground water converted to steam by hot rock formations). Powerful as these sources of energy can be, they are insignificant compared with the huge flow of energy that comes to earth from the sun.

Radiation
↓
light
↓
energy

The sun's energy begins with reactions like that of a hydrogen bomb. Nuclear fusion deep in the sun's core creates radiation, which makes its way to the sun's surface and is then radiated away—most of it as visible light, some as ultraviolet light and infrared light and X rays (see Figure 1.3). This sunlight is the dominant form of energy in our world, one that primitive peoples recognized eons ago as the giver of life. All the energy humans produce in a single year from our many energy sources—coal, oil, hydraulic power, nuclear power—amounts, according to our present estimates, to only two ten-thousandths of the total energy coming to us each day from the sun.[3]

Here are a few examples of useful types of marking:

1. **Circle words you do not know.**

   Sulfur is a yellow, solid substance that has several allotropic forms.

2. **Mark definitions with an asterisk.**

   *Chemical reactivity is the tendency of an element to participate in chemical reactions.

3. **Write summary words or phrases in the margin.**

   reaction w/air

   Some elements, such as aluminum (Al) or Copper (Cu), tarnish just from sitting around in the air. They react with oxygen (O_2) in the air.

4. **Number lists of ideas, causes, and reasons.**

   ① ② ③
   Metallic properties include conductivity, luster, and ductility.

5. **Place brackets around important passages.**

   In Group IVA, carbon (C) is a nonmetal, silicon (Si) and germanium (Ge) are metaloids, and tin (Sn) and lead (Pb) are metals.

6. **Draw arrows or diagrams to show relationships or to clarify information.**

   graphite

   Graphite is made up of a lot of carbon layers stacked on top of one another, like sheets of paper. The layers slide over one another, which makes it a good lubricant.

7. **Make notes to yourself, such as "good test question," "reread," or "ask instructor."**

   Test!

   Carbon is most important to us because it is a basic element in all plant and animal structures.

8. **Put question marks next to confusing passages or when you want more information.**

   why?

   Sometimes an element reacts so violently with air, water, or other substances that an explosion occurs.

Try to develop your own code or set of abbreviations. Here are a few examples:

Types of Marking	Examples
ex	example
T	good test question
sum	good summary
def	important definition
RR	reread later

EXERCISE 12-4

Directions: Read each of the following passages and then highlight and mark each. Try various ways of highlighting and marking.

Passage 1:

Dieting

1   Millions of people in the United States want to lose weight without sacrificing their favorite foods, without pain, and without great effort. If only we could be thin and firm by waving a magic wand!

2   It's very popular to resort to well-publicized weight-loss programs that involve special food requirements such as high-fat, high-protein, low-carbohydrate, or liquid protein. There are hundreds of such programs that continue to come and go; many of them are reported as "breakthroughs," but if this were the case, even newer break-throughs would not be needed. The problem is that most diet plans focus on short-term (and often futile) weight loss which results in weight cycling, or "yo-yo" dieting and psychological problems that result from repeated failures to keep weight off. Only 5 percent of people who try are able to maintain their weight losses. Much better is a program of lifetime weight management, which involves learning new eating and exercise habits.

3   Unwilling or unable to lose weight through diet and exercise, many people in the United States pour over $5 billion each year into diet pills, water pills, diet drugs, hormones, health spas, surgery, and fad diets. Many of these products and procedures, if they work at all, may commit a person to a cycle of quick weight loss, rebound weight gain when normal eating is resumed, then greater difficulty with weight loss in the next diet attempt. Weight loss has become a fertile field for quick-fix methods, gimmicks, and quackery. We will discuss fad diets, chemical strategies, and surgical procedures in the following sections.

Fad Diets

4   There is usually at least one fad diet book on the best-seller list in any given week. Some fad diets are simple variations of a basic 1000–1200-calorie balanced diet. Others may be dangerous because they emphasize one food or food group and the elimination of others, and advise people to follow diets low in energy and nutrients. Some fad diets are more hazardous to a person's health than the obesity they propose to cure, creating adverse reactions ranging from headaches to death. Of 29,000 claims, treatments, and therapies for losing weight, fewer than 6 percent are effective, and 13 percent are downright dangerous.

Diet Books

5   Fad diet books are long on advertising and packaging and short on unique approaches. Many of them are products of advertising specialists, not of scientists who are experts in dietetics. Although they list "degrees" after their names, the writers/practitioners sometimes have no training in nutrition or food science, or have credentials from unaccredited schools. "Doctor" Robert Hass, author of *Eat to Win*, was awarded a Ph.D. by Columbia Pacific University, in San Rafael, California, from which students could earn degrees in one year or less. "Doctor" Harry Diamond, author of *Fit for Life*, was a graduate of the former American College of Health Science in Austin, Texas, which stopped awarding degrees after the State of Texas said it was not qualified to operate as a college. Even a legitimate degree may not prevent a person from authoring scientifically inaccurate advice. Such was the case with Robert Atkins, a medical doctor, who authored *Diet Revolution*, which advised meals rich in animal fats and cholesterol and almost devoid of carbohydrates. Fad diets may be neither dangerous nor beneficial to a person's health, although this is not always the case.[4]

Passage 2:

Melting Point

1   The particles (atoms or molecules) of a solid are held together by attractive forces. . . . Heating up a solid, such as a piece of ice, gives its molecules more energy and makes them move. Pretty soon they are moving fast enough to overcome the attractive forces that were holding them rigidly together in the solid. The temperature at which this happens is the *melting point* of the solid. When a liquid, such as water, is cooled, the reverse process happens. We take energy away from the molecules, and pretty soon the molecules are moving slowly enough for their attractive forces to hold them rigidly together again and form a solid. The temperature at which this happens is the *freezing point* of the liquid. Melting point and freezing point are really the

same thing, approached from opposite directions. To melt a substance, we supply heat; to freeze it, we remove heat.

2   While a solid is melting, its temperature stays constant at its melting point. Even though we keep heating a solid as it melts, we won't increase its temperature until all of the solid has changed to liquid. When a solid starts to melt, all of the heat that is put into it from then on goes into breaking up the attractive forces that hold the atoms or molecules together in the solid. When the solid is all melted, then the heat that is put in can once more go into increasing the temperature of the substance. The amount of heat that it takes to melt one gram of any substance at its melting point is called the *heat of fusion*. If we let the substance freeze, then it will give off heat in the amount of the heat of fusion. Freezing is a process that releases energy.

3   Every substance has a melting (or freezing) point except diamond, which no one has been able to melt yet. The stronger the attractive forces that hold atoms or molecules together in the solid, the higher its melting (or freezing) point will be. The forces holding a diamond together in the solid state are so strong that they can't be overcome by heating. Most elements are solids at "room temperature," a vague term meaning a range of about 20°C to 30°C. A substance that's a solid at room temperature has a melting point higher than room temperature. Some substances are borderline, and they can be either liquids or solids depending on the weather: we've all seen tar melt on a hot day. Olive oil will solidify (freeze) on a cold day. . . .[5]

OUTLINING

Outlining is a good way to create a visual picture of what you have read. In making an outline, you record the writer's organization and show the relative importance of and connection between ideas.

Outlining has a number of advantages:

- It gives an overview of the topic and enables you to see how various subtopics relate to one another.
- Recording the information in your own words tests your understanding of what you read.
- It is an effective way to record needed information from reference books you do not own.

How to Outline

Generally, an outline follows a format like the one below.

I. First major idea
  A. First supporting detail
    1. Detail
    2. Detail
  B. Second supporting detail
    1. Detail
      a. Minor detail or example
      b. Minor detail or example
II. Second major idea
  A. First supporting idea

Notice that the most important ideas are closer to the left margin. Less important ideas are indented toward the middle of the page. A quick glance at an outline shows what is most important, what is less important, and how ideas support or explain one another.

Here are a few suggestions for using the outline format:

1. **Do not be overly concerned with following the outline format exactly.** As long as your outline shows an organization of ideas, it will work for you.

2. **Write words and phrases rather than complete sentences.**

3. **Use your own words.** Do not lift words from the text.

4. **Do not write too much.** If you need to record numerous facts and details, underlining rather than outlining might be more effective.

5. **Pay attention to headings.** Be sure that all the information you place underneath a heading explains or supports that heading. Every heading indented the same amount on the page should be of equal importance.

Now read the following passage on franchising and then study its outline.

Franchising

Franchising is an arrangement whereby a supplier, or franchiser, grants a dealer, or franchisee, the right to sell products in exchange for some type of consideration. For example, the franchiser may receive some percentage of total sales in exchange for furnishing equipment, buildings, management know-how, and marketing assistance to the franchisee. The franchisee supplies labor and capital, operates the franchised business, and agrees to abide by the provisions of the franchise agreement. In the next section we look at the major types of retail franchises, the advantages and disadvantages of franchising, and trends in retailing.

Major Types of Retail Franchises

Retail franchise arrangements can generally be classified as one of three general types. In the first arrangement, a manufacturer authorizes a number of retail stores to sell a certain brand-name item. This franchise arrangement, one of the oldest, is common in the sales of passenger cars and trucks, farm equipment, shoes, paint, earth-moving equipment, and petroleum. About 90 percent of all gasoline is sold through franchised independent retail service stations, and franchised dealers handle virtually all sales of new cars and trucks. The second type of retail franchise occurs when a producer licenses distributors to sell a given product to retailers. This franchising arrangement is common in the soft-drink industry. Most national manufacturers of soft-drink syrups—Coca-Cola, Dr Pepper, Pepsi-Cola—franchise independent bottlers, which then serve retailers. In the third type of retail franchise, a franchiser supplies brand names, techniques, or other services, instead of a complete product. The franchiser may provide certain production and distribution services, but its primary role in the arrangement is the careful development and control of marketing strategies. This approach to franchising, which is the most typical today, is used by many organizations, including Holiday Inn, AAMCO, McDonald's, Dairy Queen, Avis, Hertz, Kentucky Fried Chicken, and H&R Block.[6]

I. Franchising

    A. Arrangement betw. franchiser (supplier) and franchisee (dealer)

        1. Right to sell products exchanged for type of consideration

        2. Franchiser may receive percentage of sales for supplying equip., building, or services

        3. Franchisee supplies labor and capital, and operates business

    B. Types

        1. Manufacturer authorizes stores to sell brand-name items

            a. Ex: cars, shoes, gasoline

        2. Producer licenses distributors to sell product to retailers

            a. Ex: soft-drink industry

        3. Franchiser supplies brand-names or services but not complete product

            a. Primary role is marketing

            b. Ex: Hertz, McDonald's

            c. Most commonly used type of franchise

EXERCISE 12-5

Directions: Read the following passage and the incomplete outline that follows. Fill in the missing information in the outline.

Changing Makeup of Families and Households

The traditional definition of a typical U.S. household was one that contained a husband, a nonworking wife, and two or more children. That type of household accounts for only about nine percent of households today. In its place we see many single-parent households, households without children, households of one person, and other nontraditional households. A number of trends have combined to create these changes in families and households. Americans are staying single longer—more than one-half of the women and three-quarters of the men between 20 and 24 years old in the United States are still single. Divorce rates are at an all-time high. It is predicted that almost two-thirds of first marriages may end up in divorce. There is a widening gap between the life expectancy of males and females. Currently average life expectancy in the United States is 74 years for men and 78 years for women. Widows now make up more than one-third of one-person households in the United States. These trends have produced a declining average size of household.

The impact of all these changes is significant for marketers. Nontraditional households have different needs for goods and services than do traditional households. Smaller households often have more income per person than larger households, and require smaller houses, smaller cars, and smaller package sizes for food products. Households without children often spend more on personal entertainment and respond more to fads than do traditional households. More money may be spent on travel as well.[7]

   I. Typical U.S. household has changed

      A. Used to consist of

          1. husband

          2. nonworking wife

          3. two or more children

      B. _____

          1. _____

2. _____

3. _____

II. Trends that created this change

A. _____

1. _____

2. _____

B. Divorce rates higher

1. maybe two-thirds of marriages

C. _____

1. _____

2. _____

III. _____

A. Different goods and services needed

B. _____

C. _____

D. _____

E. _____

MAPPING

Mapping is a visual method of organizing information. It involves drawing diagrams to show how ideas in an article or chapter are related. Some students prefer mapping to outlining because they feel it is freer and less tightly structured.

Maps can take numerous forms. You can draw them in any way that shows the relationships of ideas. Figure 12-1 shows two sample maps. Each was drawn to show the overall organization of Chapter 7 in this book. First refer back to Chapter 7, then study each map.

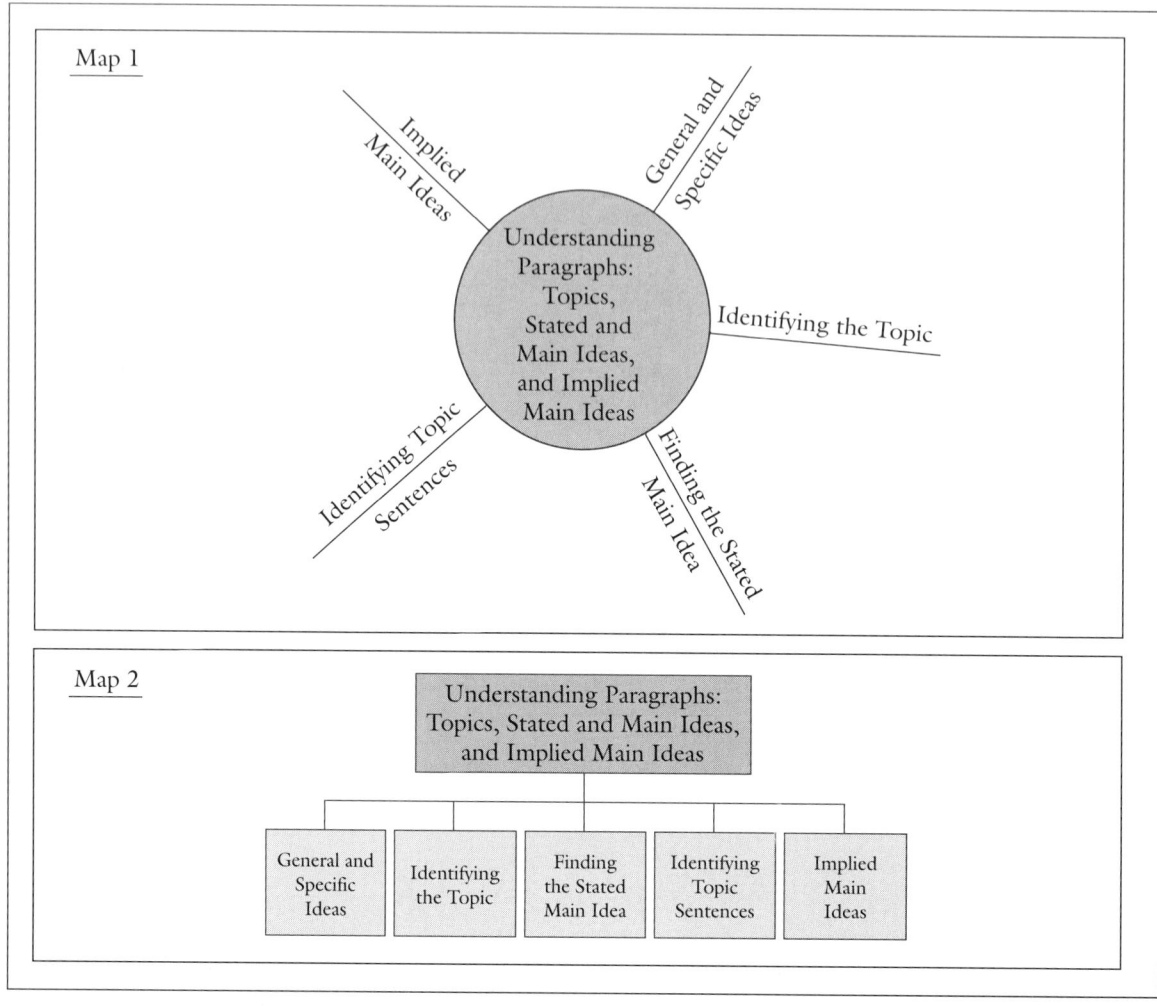

Figure 12-1 Sample maps.

How to Draw Maps

Think of a map as a picture or diagram that shows how ideas are connected. Use the following steps in drawing a map.

1. **Identify the overall topic or subject.** Write it in the center or top of the page.

2. **Identify major supporting information that relates to the topic.** Draw each piece of information on a line connected to the central topic.

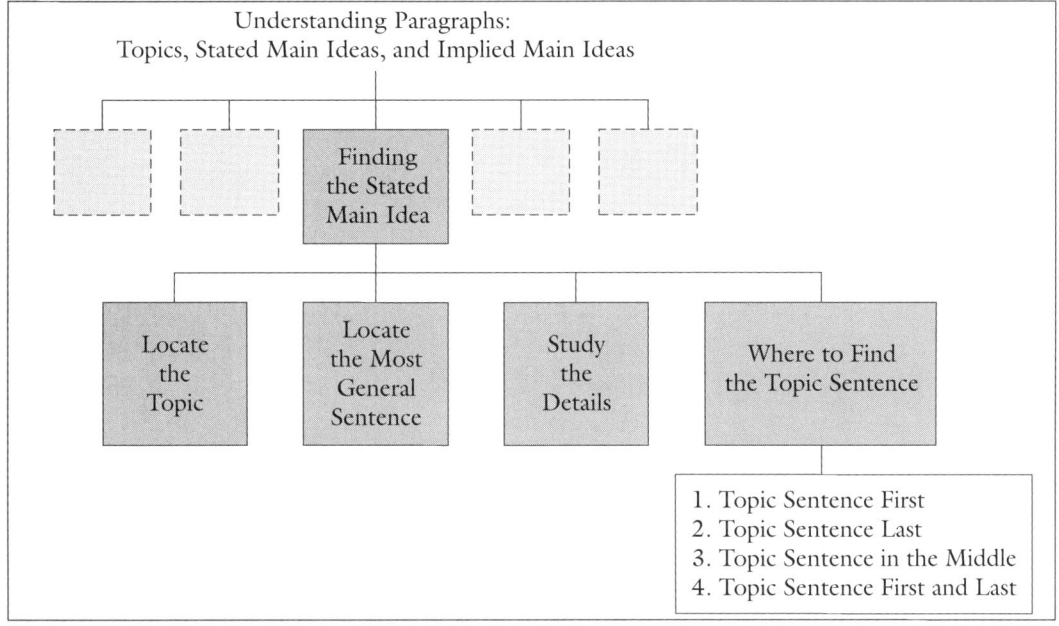

Figure 12-2 Map with greater detail.

3. **As you discover details that further explain an idea already mapped, draw a new line branching from the idea it explains.**

How you arrange your map will depend on the subject matter and how it is organized. Like an outline, it can be quite detailed or very brief, depending on your purpose. A portion of a more detailed map of Chapter 7 is shown in Figure 12-2.

Once you are skilled at drawing maps, you can become more creative, drawing different types of maps to fit what you are reading. For example, you can draw a time line (see Figure 12-3) that shows historical events, or a process diagram to show processes and procedures (see Figure 12-4).

| EXERCISE 12-6 | **Directions:** Draw a map of the excerpt "Tailoring the Marketing Mix for Global Markets" on p. 396. |

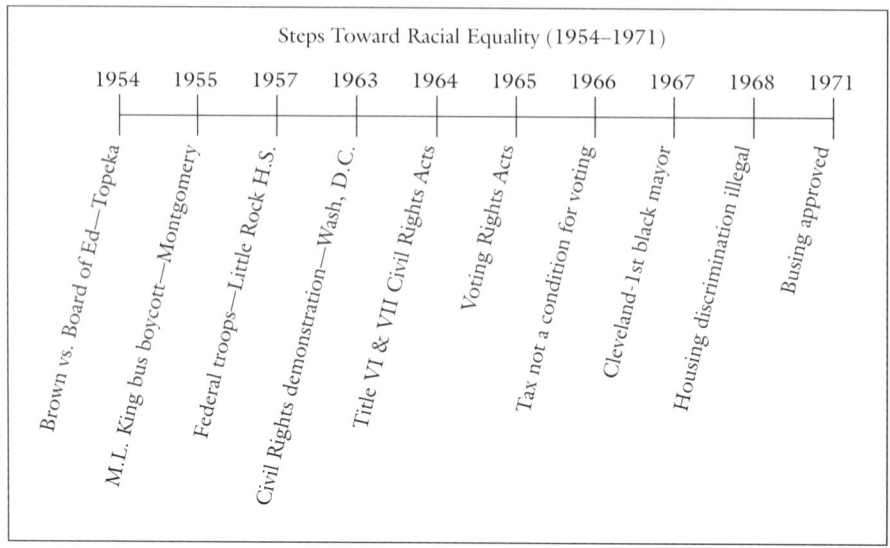

Figure 12-3 Sample time line.

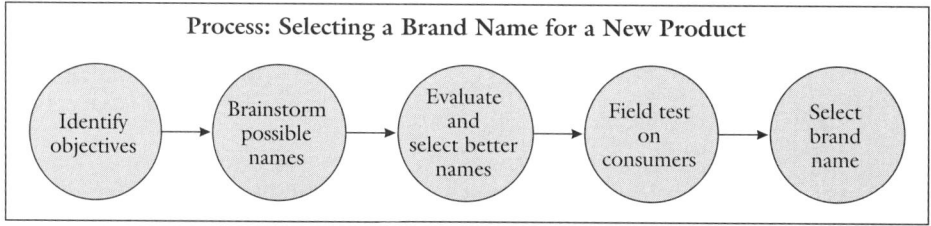

Figure 12-4 Sample process map.

EXERCISE 12-7

Directions: Draw a map of Chapter 6 in this book.

SUMMARIZING

A summary is a brief statement that reviews the major idea of something you have read. Its purpose is to make a record of the most important ideas in condensed form. A summary is much shorter than an outline and contains less detailed information.

A summary goes one step beyond recording what the writer says. It pulls together the writer's ideas by condensing and grouping them. Numerous situations in college courses require the ability to summarize, such as:

- Answering an essay question
- Reviewing a film or videotape
- Writing a term paper
- Recording results of a laboratory experiment or demonstration
- Summarizing the plot (main events) of a short story before analyzing it
- Quickly reviewing large amounts of information

How to Write a Summary

Before writing a summary, be sure you understand the material and have identified the writer's major points.

1. **Write a brief outline of the material or underline each major idea.**

2. **Write one sentence that states the writer's overall concern or most important idea.** To do this, ask yourself what one topic the material is about. Then ask what point the writer is trying to make about that topic. This sentence will be the topic sentence of your summary.

3. **Be sure to use your own words rather than those of the author.**

4. **Review the major supporting information that the author gives to explain the major ideas.** See Chapters 7 and 8 for further information.

5. **Decide on the level of detail you need.** The amount of detail you include, if any, will depend on your purpose for writing the summary.

6. **Normally, present ideas in the summary in the same order in which they appeared in the original materials.**

7. **For other than textbook material, if the writer presents a clear opinion or expresses an attitude toward the subject matter, include it in your summary.**

8. **Do not concentrate on correctness when writing summaries for your own use.** Some students prefer to write summaries using words and phrases rather than complete sentences.

Read the following summary of "Changing Makeup of Families and Households," which appeared on p. 404.

Notice that this summary contains only the broadest, most important ideas. Details are not included. The first sentence shows how the typical household has changed, the second sentence lists the three trends that are causing this change, and the last sentence details the implications for marketers.

The typical U.S. household has changed from a husband, nonworking wife, and two or more children to a smaller sized unit that might contain a single parent, no children, or even only one person. Three trends that have caused this change are: people are staying single longer, divorce rates are higher, and women are outliving men by more. Because of these changes, marketers have found that the current, smaller household needs different goods and services, has more income per person, tends to purchase smaller items, and spends more on entertainment, fads, and travel than the typical household of the past.

EXERCISE 12-8	**Directions:** On a separate sheet, write a summary of a television show you recently viewed.

EXERCISE 12-9	**Directions:** On a separate sheet, write a summary of one of the reading selections in Part Five of this text.

EXERCISE 12-10	**Directions:** Write a summary of the article "Franchising" on p. 402. When you have finished, compare it with the sample summary shown in Figure 12-5 on p. 411. Then answer the following questions.

1. How does your summary differ from the sample?
2. Did your summary begin with a topic sentence? How does it compare with the one in the sample?
3. Did your summary include ideas in the order they were given in the article?

IMMEDIATE AND PERIODIC REVIEW

Once you have read and organized information, the last step is to learn it. Fortunately, this is not a difficult task if you have organized the information effectively. In fact, through underlining, outlining, and/or summarizing, you have already learned a large portion of the material. Review, then, is a way to fix, or store, information in your memory for later recall. There are two types of review, immediate and periodic.

Franchising is an arrangement between a supplier (franchisor) and a dealer (franchisee). The franchiser supplies products or services and receives a percentage of the profits. The franchisee supplies labor and capital, and operates the business. There are three types of franchises: 1) authorized stores sell brand-name products, 2) distributors are licensed by producer to sell product to retailers, and 3) franchisor supplies brand name and/or services but does not supply the product.

Figure 12-5 Sample summary: "Franchising."

How Immediate Review Works

Immediate review is done right after you have finished reading an assignment or writing an outline or summary. When you finish any of these, you may feel like breathing a sigh of relief and taking a break. However, it is worth the time and effort to spend another five minutes reviewing what you just read and refreshing your memory. The best way to do this is to go back through the chapter and reread the headings, graphic material, introduction, summary, and any underlining or marginal notes.

Immediate review works because it consolidates, or draws together, the material just read. It also gives a final, lasting impression of the content. Considerable research has been done on the effectiveness of immediate review. Results indicate that review done immediately rather than delayed until a later time makes a large difference in the amount remembered.

How Periodic Review Works

Although immediate review will increase your recall of information, it won't help you retain information for long periods of time. To remember information over time, periodically refresh your memory. This is known as **periodic review**. Go back over the material on a regular basis. Do this by looking again at those sections that carry the basic meaning and reviewing your underlining, outlining, and/or summaries. Here is an example of a schedule one student set up to periodically review assigned chapters in a psychology textbook. You can see that this student reviewed each chapter the week after reading it and again two weeks later. This schedule is only an example. You'll need to make a schedule for each course that fits the course requirements. For math and science courses, for example, you may need to include a review of previous homework assignments and laboratory work. In other courses, less or more frequent review of previous material may be needed.

```
Week 1—Read ch. 1
Week 2—Review ch. 1
          Read ch. 2
Week 3—Review ch. 1 & 2
          Read ch. 3
Week 4—Review ch. 3
          Review ch. 1
          Read ch. 4
Week 5—Review ch. 4
          Review ch. 2
          Read ch. 5
```

EXERCISE 12-11

Directions: Choose one of your courses that involves regular textbook reading assignments. Plan a reading and periodic review schedule for the next three weeks. Assume that new chapters will be assigned as frequently as in previous weeks and that you want to review whatever has been covered over the past three weeks.

WORKING TOGETHER

Directions: Your instructor will choose a reading from Part Five and will then divide the class into three groups. Members of one group should outline the material, another group should draw maps, and the third should write summaries. When the groups have completed their tasks, the class members should review each other's work. Several students can read their summaries, draw maps, and write outlines on the chalkboard. Discuss which of the three methods seemed most effective for the material and how well prepared each group feels for (a) an essay exam, (b) a multiple-choice exam, and (c) a class discussion.

Learning Style Tips

If you tend to be a . . .	Strengthen your review strategies by . . .
Creative learner	Brainstorming before and after each assignment to discover new ways to tie the material together
Pragmatic learner	Creating, writing, and answering review questions; prepare and take self-tests.

MASTERING VOCABULARY

Directions: Select the choice that best provides the meaning of each word as it was used in this chapter. Use context clues, word parts, and a dictionary, if necessary.

_____ 1. sacrificing (p. 399)
   a. buying
   b. eating
   c. giving up
   d. saving

_____ 2. futile (p. 399)
   a. routine
   b. ineffective
   c. extreme
   d. careful

_____ 3. maintain (p. 399)
   a. keep
   b. change
   c. show off
   d. slow down

_____ 4. fertile (p. 399)
   a. academic
   b. challenging
   c. new
   d. productive

_____ 5. variations (p. 400)
   a. alternatives
   b. changes
   c. diets
   d. charts

_____ 6. adverse (p. 400)
   a. changing
   b. uplifting
   c. bad
   d. helpful

_____ 7. unique (p. 400)
   a. technical
   b. nutritional
   c. difficult
   d. new

_____ 8. unaccredited (p. 400)
   a. not appreciated
   b. not approved
   c. unstructured
   d. nonexistent

_____ 9. legitimate (p. 400)
   a. genuine
   b. medical
   c. college
   d. useful

_____ 10. devoid (p. 400)
   a. built on
   b. afraid
   c. lacking
   d. full

SELF-TEST SUMMARY

There is so much information in textbooks. How can I organize it all?

Five methods for organizing textbook information are:

1. Highlighting—a way of sorting important information from less important information. It eliminates the need to reread entire textbook chapters in order to review their major content. It also has the advantage of helping you stay active and involved with what you are reading.
2. Marking—involves using signs, symbols, and marginal notes to react to, summarize, or comment on the material.
3. Outlining—a method of recording the most important information and showing the organization and relative importance of ideas. It is particularly useful when you need to see how ideas relate to one another or when you want to get an overview of the subject.
4. Mapping—a visual method of organizing information. It involves drawing diagrams to show how ideas in an article or chapter are related.
5. Summarizing—a way to pull together the most important ideas in condensed form. It provides a quick review of the material and forces you to explain the writer's ideas in your own words.

Name _____
Section _____ Date _____
Number right _____ x 20 points = Score _____

Directions: Read each of the following sentences, then choose the answer that indicates the most important words to highlight in each sentence.

_____ 1. Unlike group therapies, which are usually supervised by a licensed therapist, self-help groups are not regulated by law or by professional standards, and they vary widely in their philosophies and methods.[8]
   a. Unlike/therapies/usually/supervised regulated/vary widely
   b. self-help groups/not regulated by law or/professional standards/vary/in/philosophies and methods
   c. unlike group therapies/usually supervised/licensed therapist self-help groups/not regulated/law/professional standards/vary/in philosophies and methods
   d. self-help groups/not/law/standards/philosophies/methods

_____ 2. In 1629 a number of English Puritans formed the Massachusetts Bay Company and settled near Boston, where their charter gave them the rights to virtual self-government.[9]
   a. In 1629/number of English Puritans formed/Massachusetts Bay Company/settled/Boston where/charter gave/rights to/self-government
   b. 1629/Puritans/Massachusetts Bay Company/Boston/charter/self-government

   c. In 1629/English Puritans formed Massachusetts Bay Company/near Boston/charter gave/rights to/self-government
   d. In 1629 a number/formed Massachusetts Bay Company/settled near Boston/gave them/self-government

_____ 3. Since that landmark opening of the first true theme park (Disneyland) in 1955, the operations of amusement parks have become more sophisticated, with technology playing a far more important role.[10]
   a. landmark opening of/true theme park Disneyland/operations of amusement parks have become more sophisticated with technology playing/role
   b. Since/opening/Disneyland in 1955/operations of amusement parks/more sophisticated/technology/more important
   c. landmark opening/first/Disneyland in 1955/amusement parks/become more sophisticated/with technology/more important role
   d. theme park/Disneyland in 1955/amusement parks/sophisticated/technology/role

(*continued*)

____ 4. The primary reason that it is important to understand the underlying
source of stress and to come to grips
with it is that there is a well-established scientific connection between
too much stress and the incidence of
disease.[11]

 a. primary reason/it is important/
understand/underlying source of
stress and/come to grips with it
is/well-established scientific connection between/much stress and/inci-
dence of disease

 b. reason/important/source of stress/
scientific connection/stress/inci-
dence of disease

 c. important to understand/stress/
come to grips/there is/well-estab-
lished scientific connection/stress
and/incidence of disease

 d. important to understand/underlying
source of stress and come to grips
with it/scientific connection
between/stress and/disease

____ 5. The best ways to avoid inconsiderate
behavior are to try to see the other
person's point of view; listen actively;
avoid interrupting the other person;
and avoid making any gestures, such
as head shaking or finger pointing,
that indicate disagreement or that are
threatening in nature.[12]

 a. avoid inconsiderate behavior/try to
see the other person's point of
view/listen actively avoid interrupt-
ing/avoid/gestures/that indicate disagreement or/are threatening

 b. best ways to avoid inconsiderate
behavior/to try to see other person's
point of view/listen actively/avoid
interrupting/other person/avoid
making any gestures/head shak-
ing/finger pointing/indicate dis-
agreement/threatening in nature

 c. avoid inconsiderate behavior/point
of view/listen/avoid interrupting/
avoid gestures

 d. best ways/inconsiderate behavior/
other/point of view/listen/interrupt-
ing/making any gestures/head shak-
ing/finger pointing/indicate disa-
greement/threatening in nature

Name _____

Section _____ Date _____

Number right _____ x 20 points = Score _____

Directions: Read the passage below and then complete the map and the summary by answering the questions that follow each of them.

1   The first thing good listeners must do is figure out why they're listening. Researchers have identified five kinds of listening that reflect purposes you may have when communicating with others: appreciative, discriminative, empathic, comprehension, and critical.

2   **Appreciative listening** focuses on something other than the primary message. Some listeners enjoy seeing a famous speaker. Others relish a good speech, a classic movie, or a brilliant performance. On these occasions, you listen primarily to entertain yourself.

3   **Discriminative listening** requires listeners to draw conclusions from the way a message is presented rather than from what is said. In discriminative listening, people seek to understand the meaning behind the message. You're interested in what the speaker really thinks, believes, or feels. You're engaging in discriminative listening when you draw conclusions about how angry your parents are with you, based not on what they say but on how they say it. You draw inferences from the presentation of the message rather than from the message itself.

4   **Empathic or therapeutic listening** is intended to provide emotional support for the speaker. Although it is more typical of interpersonal than public communication, empathic listening does occur in public

speaking situations, for example, when you hear an athlete apologize for unprofessional behavior or a classmate reveal a personal problem to illustrate a speech. In each case, your role is supportive.

5   **Listening for comprehension** occurs when you want to gain additional information or insights from the speaker. You are probably most familiar with this form of listening because you've relied heavily on it for your education. When you listen to a radio newscast, to a classroom lecture on marketing strategies, or to an elections official explaining new registration procedures, you're listening to understand—to comprehend information, ideas, and processes.

6   **Critical listening** is the most difficult kind of listening because it requires you to both interpret and evaluate the message. It demands that you go beyond understanding the message to interpreting it and evaluating its strengths and weaknesses. You'll practice this sort of listening in class. A careful consumer also uses critical listening to evaluate television commercials, political campaign speeches, or arguments offered by salespeople. When you are listening critically, you decide whether to accept or reject ideas and whether to act on the message.[13]

(continued)

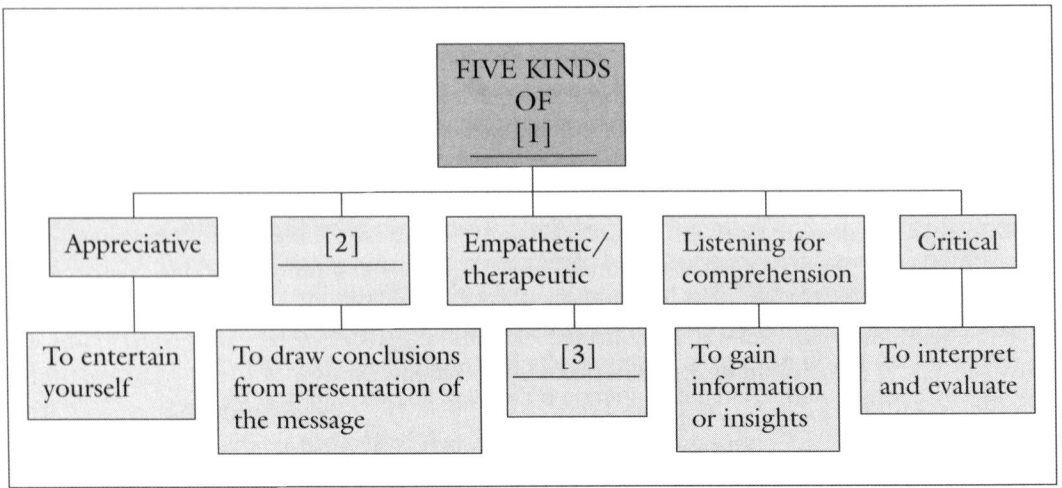

Refer to the map to answer questions 1–3.

_____ 1. The word that correctly fills in blank
[1] is
a. purposes.
b. listening.
c. communicating.
d. responding.

_____ 2. The word that correctly fills in blank
[2] is
a. conclusive.
b. emotional.
c. comprehensive.
d. discriminative.

_____ 3. The phrase that correctly fills in blank
[3] is
a. to apologize for behavior.
b. to reveal a personal problem.
c. to illustrate a speech.
d. to provide emotional support.

Refer to the following summary of the passage to
answer questions 4 and 5.

Summary: In communication, there are
five types of listening. Appreciative listening
is mainly for your own entertainment.
Discriminative listening is when you have to
figure out what the speaker means by
_____[4]_____. Empathic or therapeutic
listening requires you to give emotional support to the speaker; it happens more in interpersonal communication than in public
speaking situations. Listening for comprehension is when you are trying to learn information or gain understanding. Critical
listening is the most difficult because you
have to interpret and then _____[5]_____.

_____ 4. The phrase that correctly fills in blank
[4] is
a. how the message is presented.
b. what the speaker says.
c. how you feel about the speaker.
d. what you want to hear.

_____ 5. The phrase that correctly fills in blank
[5] is
a. understand it.
b. repeat it.
c. evaluate it.
d. respond to it.

Name _____

Section _____ Date _____

Number right _____ x 10 points = Score _____

Directions: Read the following selection and choose the letter that best answers each of the questions that follow.

Participatory and Passive Listening

The general key to effective listening in interpersonal situations is active participation. Perhaps the best preparation for participatory listening is to act (physically and mentally) like a participant. For many people, this may be the most abused rule of effective listening. Recall, for example, how your body almost automatically reacts to important news: Almost immediately, you assume an upright posture, cock your head to the speaker, and remain relatively still and quiet. You do this almost reflexively because this is the way you listen most effectively. Even more important than this physical alertness is mental alertness. As a listener, participate in the communication interaction as an equal partner with the speaker, as one who is emotionally and intellectually ready to engage in the sharing of meaning.

Effective participatory listening is expressive. Let the listener know that you are participating in the communication interaction. Nonverbally, maintain eye contact, focus your concentration on the speaker rather than on others present, and express your feelings facially. Verbally, ask appropriate questions, signal understanding with "I see" or "yes," and express agreement or disagreement as appropriate.

Passive listening is, however, not without merit and some recognition of its value is warranted. Passive listening—listening without talking or directing the speaker in any obvious way—is a powerful means of communicating acceptance. This is the kind of listening that people ask for when they say, "Just listen to me." They are essentially asking you to suspend your judgment and "just listen." Passive listening allows the speaker to develop his or her thoughts and ideas in the presence of another person who accepts but does not evaluate, who supports but does not intrude. By listening passively, you provide a supportive and receptive environment. Once that has been established, you may wish to participate in a more active way, verbally and nonverbally.

_____ 1. Which of the following is the best outline for paragraph 1?
  a. A. Actions of a participant
       1. physical
       2. interaction
  b. A. Actions of a participant
       1. sit straight
       2. be quiet
       3. head cocked
       4. be alert
  c. A. Physical actions
       1. sit straight
       2. be quiet
      B. mental actions
  d. A. Active participation in listening
       1. physical alertness
          a. sit straight
          b. quiet
          c. head cocked
       2. mental alertness

(continued)

_____ 2. Which of the following is the best outline for paragraph 2?
   a. B. Listening is expressive
        1. eye contact—maintain
        2. facial expressions verbally
        3. ask questions
   b. B. Communication interaction
        1. nonverbal
             a. agree/disagree
             b. signal understanding
        2. verbal
             a. eye contact
             b. facial expression
             c. ask questions
   c. B. Expressive participation
        1. nonverbal
             a. eye contact
             b. focus on speaker
             c. facial expressions
        2. verbal
             a. ask questions
             b. signal understanding
             c. agree/disagree
   d. B. Expressions of a participant
       C. Nonverbal expressions
       D. Verbal expressions

_____ 3. Which of the following is the best outline for paragraph 3?
   a. C. Active listening
        1. definition
        2. reasons
   b. C. Reasons for passive listening
       D. Definition of passive listening
   c. C. Meaning of passive listening
        1. no talking or directing of
           speaker
        2. communicates acceptance
        3. suspend judgment and "just
           listen"

   D. Results of passive listening
        1. speaker can develop
           thoughts and ideas
        2. you provide supportive,
           receptive environment
   d. C. Passive listening
        1. judgmental
        2. supportive
        3. definition

_____ 4. Which group of words is best to highlight in the first sentence of the selection?
   a. key / effective listening / active par-
      ticipation
   b. general / interpersonal / participa-
      tion
   c. general / key / situations / active
   d. key / interpersonal situations / is

_____ 5. Which of the following phrases from
the first paragraph would be most
important to highlight?
   a. cock your head
   b. for many people
   c. Recall, for example
   d. active participation

_____ 6. Which group of words is best to highlight in the last sentence of paragraph
2?
   a. ask / questions / disagreement / as /
      appropriate
   b. verbally / questions / signal / under-
      standing / express / agreement / dis-
      agreement
   c. ask / questions / signal / agreement
      / appropriate
   d. verbally / I see / yes

_____ 7. Which of the following sentences from the last paragraph defines passive listening?
a. first
b. second
c. third
d. last

_____ 8. Which of the following marginal notations would be most useful for paragraph 1?
a. alert vs. engaged
b. still and quiet
c. physical actions/mental actions
d. physically alert

_____ 9. Which of the following marginal notations would be the best for paragraph 3?
a. passive listening = non-judgmental & supportive
b. just listen = nonverbal
c. passive vs. active listening
d. listening vs. hearing

_____ 10. Which of the following maps best presents the ideas in the selection?

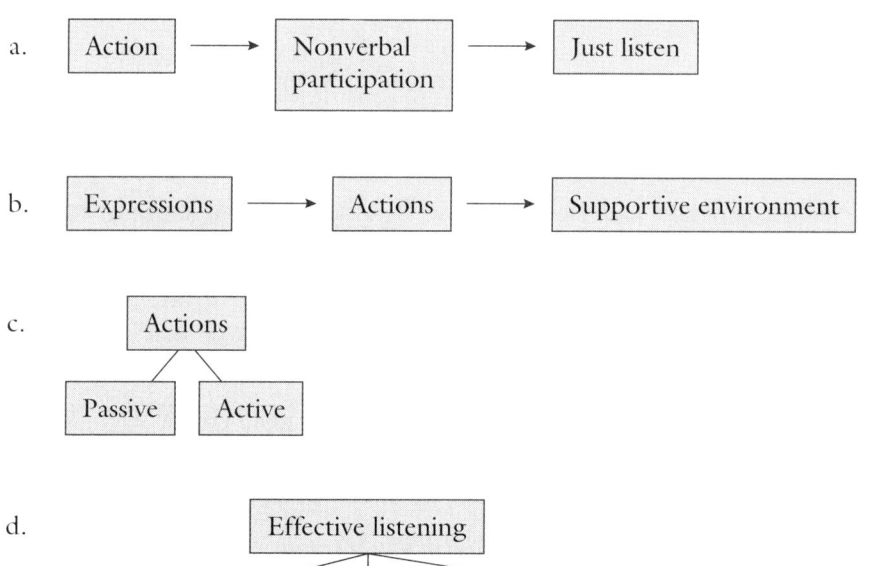

Name _____

Section _____ Date _____

Number right _____ x 10 points = Score _____

Planning a Fitness Program

Rebecca J. Donatelle

This article discusses the benefits of exercise and the importance of creating a fitness program that suits your needs. The article was taken from a health textbook titled *Access to Health*.

Vocabulary Preview

sedentary (par. 1) characterized by sitting; not physically active

sporadically (par. 1) occurring now and then; infrequently

rigorously (par. 1 in box) characterized by difficulty or strictness

reneging (par. 6 in box) going back on a commitment

chronicle (par. 8 in box) keep a record

prudent (par. 2) sensible

debilitating (par. 2) causing disability

monotonous (par. 6) boringly repetitive

1   Regular physical activity and exercise can help you avoid preventable diseases and add to both the quality and length of your life. If you are currently active, you are aware of the benefits of regular physical activity and should be motivated to continue your efforts. If you are sedentary or sporadically active, you realize that you should not delay one day longer in making the behavior changes necessary to improve your fitness. You should also be aware of the importance of creating a program you love and motivat-ing yourself through positive self-talk. (See the Skills for Behavior Change box.)

Identifying Fitness Goals

2   Before you initiate a fitness program, analyze your personal needs, limitations, physical activity likes and dislikes, and daily schedule. Your primary reason for exercis-ing may be to lower your risks for health problems. This goal is prudent, particularly for those who have a family history of car-diovascular diseases (heart attack, stroke, high blood pressure), diabetes, obesity, and/or substance abuse. If you have inherit-ed no major risks for fatal or debilitating diseases, then your primary reason for exer-cising may be to improve the quality of your life. Your specific goal may be to achieve (or maintain) healthy levels of body fat, car-diovascular fitness, muscular strength and endurance, or flexibility and mobility.

3   Once you become committed to regular physical activity and exercise, you will observe gradual changes in your functional abilities and note progress toward your goals. Unfortunately, all the benefits gained through regular physical activity will be lost if you stop exercising. You can't get fit for a couple of years while you're young and expect the positive changes to last the rest of your life. Perhaps your most vital goal will be to become committed to fitness for the long haul—to establish a realistic schedule of

diverse exercise activities that you can maintain and enjoy throughout your life.

Designing the Program

4 Once you commit yourself to becoming physically active, you must decide what type of fitness program is best suited to your needs. The amounts and types of exercises required to yield beneficial results vary with the age and physical condition of the exerciser. Men over age 40 and women over age 50 should consult their physicians before beginning a fitness program.

5 Good fitness programs are designed to improve or maintain cardiorespiratory fitness, flexibility, muscular strength and endurance, and body composition. A comprehensive program could include a warm-up period of easy walking followed by stretching activities to improve flexibility, then selected strength development exercises, followed by performance of an aerobic activity for 20 minutes or more, and concluding with a cool-down period of gentle flexibility exercises.

6 The greatest proportion of exercise time should be spent developing cardiovascular fitness, but you should not exclude the other components. Choose an aerobic activity you think you will like. Many people find cross training—alternate-day participation in two or more aerobic activities (i.e., jogging and swimming)—less monotonous and more enjoyable than long-term participation in only one aerobic activity. Cross training is also beneficial because it strengthens a variety of muscles, thus helping you avoid overuse injuries to muscles and joints.

7 Jogging, walking, cycling, rowing, step aerobics, and cross- country skiing are all excellent activities for developing cardiovascular fitness. Responding to the exercise boom, fitness equipment manufacturers have made it easy for you to participate in these activities. Most colleges and universities now have recreation centers where students can use stair-climbing machines, stationary bicycles, treadmills, rowing machines, and ski-simulators.

What Do You Think?

8 You now have the ability to design your own fitness program. Which two activities would you select for a cross-training program? Do the activities you selected exercise different major muscle groups? What may happen to you if they don't?

Skills for Behavior Change

Starting an Exercise Routine

Beginners often start their exercise programs too rigorously. The most successful exercise program is one that is realistic and appropriate for your skill level and needs. Be realistic about the amount of time you will need to get into good physical condition. Perhaps the most significant factor early on in an exercise program is personal comfort. You'll need to experiment to find an activity that you truly enjoy. Be open to exploring new activities and new exercise equipment.

• *Start slow as a beginning exerciser.* For the sedentary, first-time exerciser, any type and amount of physical activity will be a step in the right direction. If you are extremely overweight or out of condition, you might only be able to walk for five minutes at a time. Don't be discouraged; you're on your way!

- *Make only one life change at a time.* Success at one major behavioral change will encourage you to make other positive changes.

- *Have reasonable expectations for yourself and your fitness program.* Many people become exercise dropouts because their expectations were too high to begin with. Allow sufficient time to reach your fitness goals.

- *Choose a specific time to exercise and stick with it.* Learning to establish priorities and keeping to a schedule are vital steps toward improved fitness. Experiment by exercising at different times of the day to learn what schedule works best for you.

- *Exercise with a friend.* Reneging on an exercise commitment is much more difficult if you exercise with someone else. Partners can motivate and encourage each other, provided they remember that the rate of progress will not be the same for them both.

- *Make exercise a positive habit.* Usually, if you are able to practice a desired activity for three weeks, you will be able to incorporate it into your lifestyle.

- *Keep a record of your progress.* Include various facts about your physical activities (duration, intensity) and chronicle your emotions and personal achievements as you progress.

- *Take lapses in stride.* Physical deconditioning—a decline in fitness level—occurs at about the same rate as physical conditioning. First, renew your commitment to fitness, and then restart your exercise program.

Directions: Choose the letter that best answers each of the following questions.

CHECKING YOUR COMPREHENSION

_____ 1. The main point of the selection is that people
   a. do not exercise enough.
   b. have unrealistic fitness goals.
   c. are unaware of the benefits of exercise.
   d. should have a regular exercise program.

_____ 2. The main idea of paragraph 2 is that
   a. people should identify their exercise goals before beginning a fitness program.
   b. the most important goal of exercise should be to increase endurance.
   c. people who have inherited health risks should see a doctor before beginning a fitness program.
   d. the most common fitness goal is to achieve healthy levels of body fat.

_____ 3. According to the article, the greatest proportion of exercise time should be spent
   a. strengthening muscles.
   b. improving flexibility.
   c. developing cardiovascular fitness.
   d. maintaining body composition.

_____ 4. Cross training is defined in the article as
    a. a warm-up period followed by aerobic activity.
    b. aerobic activity followed by a cooldown period.
    c. participation in two or more aerobic activities on alternate days.
    d. participation in one aerobic activity in the morning and a different one in the evening.

_____ 5. According to the information in the Behavior Change box, beginning exercisers should do all of the following _except_
    a. start slowly.
    b. always exercise alone.
    c. keep a record of their progress.
    d. establish an exercise schedule.

_____ 6. The best definition of the word "boom" in paragraph 7 is
    a. a loud noise.
    b. a rapid increase in activity or popularity.
    c. to grow in value.
    d. to make a deep hollow sound.

APPLYING YOUR SKILLS

_____ 7. The most useful summary marginal notation for paragraph 2 would be
    a. analyze life style and set goals.
    b. identify family patterns of illness.
    c. cardiovascular diseases, diabetes, obesity, substance abuse.
    d. body fat, cardiovascular fitness, muscle strength & endurance, flexibility & mobility

_____ 8. The following is an outline off the section titled "Identifying Fitness Goals" (paragraphs 2 and 3). The phrase that belongs in the blank line is

> I. Identifying fitness goals
>   A. Before you begin
>   1. Analyze your needs, preferences, limitations, and schedule
>   2. Primary reason may be to lower health risks
>   3. If no family history of illness goal may be to improve quality of life
>   B. Once you are committed
>   1. observe gradual changes and note progress
>   2. _____
>   3. build a fitness program that will last a lifetime

    a. All benefits are lost if you stop.
    b. Try to get fit for at least a couple of years.
    c. Expect positive changes.
    d. Positive changes are easy to achieve.

(continued)

_____ 9. The best paraphrase of paragraph 4 is
  a. Men over age 40 and women over age 50 should consult their doctors before beginning an exercise program.
  b. When you have decided to begin an exercise program, you need to figure out what type would suit you best. Your age and physical condition affect the type and amount of exercise you need in order to get good results. Before starting an exercise program, women older than 50 and men older than 40 should consult their doctors.
  c. Once you commit yourself to physical activity, you have to decide what type of fitness program is best for you. Men and women over age 40 should talk to their physicians before beginning a fitness program.
  d. After you have decided to become physically active, you must decide which fitness program you will be able to stick with. The age and physical condition of the exerciser is not as important as the type of exercise chosen.

_____ 10. The phrase that belongs in place of [A] in the following map of paragraph 5 is
  a. Improve cardiorespiratory fitness.
  b. Cross training.
  c. Twenty minutes of aerobic activity.
  d. Avoid overuse injuries.

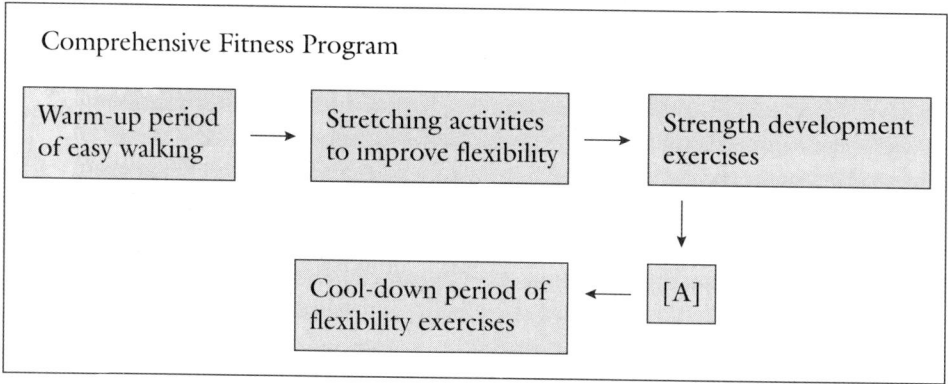

13

Interpreting the Writer's Message and Purpose

THIS CHAPTER WILL SHOW YOU HOW TO

1. Recognize words that suggest positive or negative attitudes
2. Make inferences about what you read
3. Understand figurative language
4. Discover the author's purpose
5. Recognize tone

Up to this point, we have been primarily concerned with building vocabulary, understanding a writer's basic organizational patterns, acquiring factual information, and organizing that information for learning and recall. So far, each chapter has been concerned with understanding what the author *says*, with factual content. Now our focus must change. To read well, you must go beyond what the author says and also consider what he or she *means*.

Many writers directly state some ideas but hint at others. It is left to the reader to pick up the clues or suggestions and use logic and reasoning skills to figure out the writer's unstated message. This chapter will explain several features of writing that suggest meanings. Once you are familiar with these, you will better understand the writer's unstated message. This chapter will also discuss how to discover the author's purpose, recognize tone, and understand context.

427

CONNOTATIVE MEANINGS

Which of the following would you like to be a part of: a crowd, mob, gang, audience, congregation, or class? Each of these words has the same basic meaning: "an assembled group of people." But each has a different *shade* of meaning. *Crowd* suggests a large, disorganized group. *Audience,* on the other hand, suggests a quiet, controlled group. Try to decide what meaning each of the other words in the list suggests.

This example shows that words have two levels of meaning—a literal meaning and an additional shade of meaning. These two levels of meaning are called denotative and connotative. A word's **denotative meaning** is the meaning stated in the dictionary—its literal meaning. A word's **connotative meaning** is the additional implied meanings, or nuances, that a word may take on. Often the connotative meaning carries either a positive or negative, favorable or unfavorable impression. The words *mob* and *gang* have a negative connotation because they imply a disorderly, disorganized group. *Congregation, audience,* and *class* have a positive connotation because they suggest an orderly, organized group.

Here are a few more examples. Would you prefer to be described as "slim" or "skinny"? As "intelligent" or "brainy"? As "heavy" or "fat"? As "particular" or "picky"? Notice that each pair of words has a similar literal meaning, but that each word within the pair has a different connotation.

Depending on the words they choose, writers can suggest favorable or unfavorable impressions of the person, object, or event they are describing. For example, through the writer's choice of words, the two sentences below create two entirely different impressions. As you read them, underline words that have a positive or negative connotation.

> The unruly crowd forced its way through the restraint barriers and ruthlessly attacked the rock star.

> The enthusiastic group of fans burst through the fence and rushed toward the rock star.

When reading any type of informative or persuasive material, pay attention to the writer's choice of words. Often a writer may communicate subtle or hidden messages, or he or she may encourage the reader to feel positively or negatively toward the subject.

Read the following paragraph on violence in sports and, as you read, underline words that have a strong positive or negative connotation.

> So it goes. Knifings, shootings, beatings, muggings, paralysis, and death become part of our play. Women baseball fans are warned to walk with friends and

avoid taking their handbags to games because of strong-arm robberies and purse snatchings at San Francisco's Candlestick Park. A professional football coach, under oath in a slander case, describes some of his own players as part of a "criminal element" in his sport. The commissioner of football proclaims that playing field outlaws and bullies will be punished, but to anybody with normal eyesight and a working television set the action looks rougher than ever. In Europe and South America—and, chillingly, for the first time in the United States—authorities turn to snarling attack dogs to control unruly mobs at athletic events.[1]

EXERCISE 13-1	**Directions:** For each of the following pairs of words, underline the word with the more positive connotation.

1. request   demand
2. overlook   neglect
3. ridicule   tease
4. glance   stare
5. display   expose
6. garment   gown
7. gaudy   showy
8. clumsy   awkward
9. artificial fake
10. token   keepsake

EXERCISE 13-2	**Directions:** For each word listed below, write a word that has a similar denotative meaning but a negative connotation. Then write a word that has a positive connotation. Use your dictionary or thesaurus, if necessary.

	Negative	*Positive*
Example: eat	gobble	dine
1. take	_____	_____
2. ask	_____	_____
3. look at	_____	_____

4. walk   _____   _____

5. dress   _____   _____

6. music   _____   _____

7. car   _____   _____

8. laugh   _____   _____

9. large   _____   _____

10. woman   _____   _____

IMPLIED MEANINGS

An **inference** is an educated guess or prediction about something unknown based on available facts and information. It is the logical connection that you draw between what you observe or know and what you do not know.

Suppose that you arrive ten minutes late for your sociology class. All the students have papers in front of them, and everyone is busily writing. Some students have worried or concerned looks on their faces. The instructor is seated and is reading a book. What is happening? From the known information you can make an inference about what you do not know. Did you figure out that the instructor had given the class a surprise quiz? If so, then you made a logical inference.

While the inference you made is probably correct, you cannot be sure until you speak with the instructor. Occasionally a logical inference can be wrong. Although it is unlikely, perhaps the instructor has laryngitis and has written notes on the board for the students to copy. Some students may look worried because they do not understand what the notes mean.

Here are a few more everyday situations. Make an inference for each.

> You are driving on an expressway and you notice a police car with flashing red lights behind you. You check your speedometer and notice that you are going ten miles over the speed limit.

> A woman seated alone in a bar nervously glances at everyone who enters. Every few minutes she checks her watch.

In the first situation, a good inference might be that you are going to be stopped for speeding. However, it is possible that the officer only wants to pass you to get to an accident ahead or to stop someone driving faster than you. In the second situation, one inference is that the woman is waiting to meet someone who is late.

The following paragraphs are taken from a book by Bill Cosby titled *Time Flies*. First, read them for factual content.

When I was twenty-five, I saw a movie called *The Loneliness of the Long Distance Runner,* in which a young man running for a reform school was far ahead in a cross-country race and then suddenly stopped as an act of rebellion. That young runner had been struck by the feeling that he had to go his own way and not the way demanded by society.

That young runner was me.

I hadn't been doing time, of course, just *marking* time at Temple, where my mind was not on books but bookings; and so, I had dropped out to go into show business, a career move as sound as seeking my future as a designer of dirigibles. Although my mother and father kept telling me that I should finish college before I flopped in show business, I felt that only I, with the full wisdom of a north Philadelphia jock, knew what was best for me. I empathized with the hero of *The Loneliness of the Long Distance Runner,* who had said about his race, "You have to run, run, run without knowing *why.*"[2]

These paragraphs are primarily factual—they tell who did what, when, and where. However, some ideas are not directly stated and must be inferred from the information given. Here are a few examples. Some are fairly obvious inferences; others are less obvious.

1. The runner did not finish the race.
2. The runner could have won the race.
3. Cosby was *not* the young runner from reform school.
4. Cosby thought he was like the runner.
5. Temple is a university or college.
6. Cosby did not do well academically at Temple.
7. A career in show business is impractical.
8. Cosby's parents thought he would fail in show business.
9. Cosby felt it was acceptable to act without having specific reasons.
10. Cosby now realizes that he wasn't as wise as he thought he was at the time.

Although none of the above ideas are directly stated, they can be inferred from clues provided in the passage. Some of the statements could be inferred from actions, others by adding facts together, and still others by the writer's choice of words.

Now read the following passage to find out why Cindy Kane is standing on the corner of Sheridan and Sunnyside.

An oily midnight mist had settled on the city streets . . . asphalt mirrors from a ten-o'clock rain now past . . . a sleazy street-corner reflection of smog-smudged neon . . . the corner of Sheridan and, incongruously, Sunnyside . . . Chicago.

A lone lady lingers at the curb . . . but no bus will come.

She is Cindy Kane, twenty-eight. Twenty-eight hard years old. Her iridescent dress clings to her slender body. Her face is buried under a technicolor avalanche of makeup.

She is Cindy Kane.

And she has a date.

With someone she has never met . . . and may never meet again.

Minutes have turned to timelessness . . . and a green Chevy four-door pulls slowly around the corner.

The driver's window rolls down. A voice comes from the shadow . . .

"Are you working?"

Cindy nods . . . regards him with vacant eyes.

He beckons.

She approaches the passenger side. Gets in. And the whole forlorn, unromantic ritual begins all over again. With another stranger.[3]

If you made the right inferences, you realized that Cindy Kane is a prostitute and that she is standing on the corner waiting for a customer. Let us look at the kinds of clues the writer gave that led to this inference.

1. DESCRIPTION. By the way the writer describes Cindy Kane, you begin to suspect that she is a prostitute. She is described as "hard." She is wearing an iridescent, clinging dress and "a technicolor avalanche of makeup." These descriptive details convey an image of a gaudy, unconventional appearance.

2. ACTION. The actions, although few, also provide clues about what is happening. The woman is lingering on the corner. When the car approaches, she gets in.

3. CONVERSATION. The only piece of conversation, the question, "Are you working?" is one of the strongest clues the writer provides.

4. WRITER'S COMMENTARY/DETAILS. As the writer describes the situation, he slips in numerous clues. He establishes the time as around midnight ("An oily midnight mist"). His reference to a "reflection of smog-smudged neon" suggests an area of bars or night clubs. The woman's face is "buried under . . . makeup." Covering or hiding one's face is usually associated with shame or embarrassment. In the last paragraph, the reference to a "forlorn, unromantic ritual" provides a final clue.

How to Make Inferences

Making an inference is a thinking process. As you read, you are following the author's thoughts. You are also alert for ideas that are suggested but not directly stated. Because inference is a logical thought process, there is no simple, step-by-step procedure to follow. Each inference depends entirely on the situation, the facts provided, and the reader's knowledge and experience.

However, here are a few guidelines to keep in mind as you read. These will help you get in the habit of looking beyond the factual level to the inferential.

1. **Be sure you understand the literal meaning.** You should have a clear grasp of the key idea and supporting details of each paragraph.

2. **Notice details.** Often a detail provides a clue that will help you make an inference. When you spot a striking or unusual detail, ask yourself: Why did the writer include this piece of information?

3. **Add up the facts.** Consider all the facts taken together. Ask yourself: What is the writer trying to suggest from this set of facts? What do all these facts and ideas point toward?

4. **Watch for clues.** The writer's choice of words and detail often suggest his or her attitude toward the subject. Notice, in particular, descriptive words, emotionally charged words, and words with strong positive or negative connotations.

5. **Be sure your inference is supportable.** An inference must be based on fact. Make sure there is sufficient evidence to justify any inference you make.

EXERCISE 13-3	**Directions:** Read each of the following passages. Then answer the questions that follow. You will need to reason out, or infer, the answers.

Passage A:

Eye-to-eye contact and response are important in real-life relationships. The nature of a person's eye contact patterns, whether he or she looks another squarely in the eye or looks to the side or shifts his gaze from side to side, tells a lot about the person. These patterns also play a significant role in success or failure in human relationships. Despite its importance, eye contact is not involved in television watching. Yet children spend several hours a day in front of the television set. Certain children's programs pretend to speak directly to each individual child. (Mr. Rogers is an example, telling the child "I like you, you're special," etc.) However, this is still one-way communication and no response is required of the child. How might such a distortion of real-life relationships affect a child's development of trust, or openness, of an ability to relate well to other people?[4]

1. How would the author answer the question asked in the last sentence of the paragraph?

   _____

2. What is the author's attitude toward television?

   _____

3. To develop a strong relationship with someone should you look directly at him or her or shift your gaze?

   _____

4. What activities, other than television, do you think this author would recommend for children?

   _____

Passage B:

There is little the police or other governmental agencies can't find out about you these days.

For starters, the police can hire an airplane and fly over your backyard filming you sunbathing and whatever else is visible from above. A mail cover allows the post office, at the request of another government or police agency, to keep track of people sending you mail and organizations sending you literature through the mail. A pen register at the phone company may be installed at police request to collect the numbers dialed to and from your home telephone. Police or other governmental agencies may have access to your canceled checks and deposit records to find out who is writing checks to you and to whom you are writing checks. Library and film rental records disclose what you are reading and what you are watching. Even the trash you discard may be examined to see what you are throwing away.

No doubt by now you've realized that the accumulation of this information provides a fairly complete and accurate picture about a person, including her health, friends, lovers, political and religious activities, and even beliefs. Figure that, if the Gillette razor company knows when it's your eighteenth birthday to send you a sample razor, your government, with its super, interconnecting computers, knows much more about you.[5]

1. What is the author's attitude toward government agencies?

   _____

2. For what reason might a police agency request a pen register?

_____

3. Where do you think the author stands on the issue of right to privacy? (What rights to privacy do we or should we have?)

_____

Passage C:

George Washington is remembered not for what he was but for what he should have been. It doesn't do any good to point out that he was an "inveterate landgrabber," and that as a young man he illegally had a surveyor stake out some prize territory west of the Alleghenies in an area decreed off limits to settlers. Washington is considered a saint, and nothing one says is likely to make him seem anything less. Though he was a wily businessman and accumulated a fortune speculating in frontier lands, he will always be remembered as a farmer—and a "simple farmer" at that.

Even his personal life is misremembered. While Washington admitted despising his mother and in her dying years saw her infrequently, others remembered his mother fondly and considered him a devoted son. While his own records show he was something of a dandy and paid close attention to the latest clothing designs, ordering "fashionable" hose, the "neatest shoes," and coats with "silver trimmings," practically no one thinks he was vain. Though he loved to drink and dance and encouraged others to join him, the first President is believed to have been something of a prude.[6]

1. Describe how Washington is usually remembered.

_____

_____

2. Describe the author's attitude toward Washington.

_____

3. Does the author think attitudes toward Washington are likely to change?

_____

4. Explain the term "inveterate landgrabber."

_____

_____

5. Why do you think there is such a discrepancy between what Washington did and how he is remembered?

_____

Passage D:

I am a peace-loving woman. But several events in the past 10 years have convinced me I'm safer when I carry a pistol. This was a personal decision, but because handgun possession is a controversial subject, perhaps my reasoning will interest others.

I live in western South Dakota on a ranch 25 miles from the nearest large town; for several years I spent winters alone here. As a free-lance writer, I travel alone a lot—more than 100,000 miles by car in the last four years. With women freer than ever before to travel alone, the odds of our encountering trouble seem to have risen. And help, in the West, can be hours away. Distances are great, roads are deserted, and the terrain is often too exposed to offer hiding places.

A woman who travels alone is advised, usually by men, to protect herself by avoiding bars and other "dangerous situations," by approaching her car like an Indian scout, by locking doors and windows. But these precautions aren't always enough. I spent years following them and still found myself in dangerous situations. I began to resent the idea that just because I am female, I have to be extra careful. . . .

When I got my pistol, I told my husband, revising the old Colt slogan, "God made men *and women,* but Sam Colt made them equal." Recently I have seen a gunmaker's ad with a similar sentiment. Perhaps this is an idea whose time has come, though the pacifist inside me will be saddened if the only way women can achieve equality is by carrying weapons.

We must treat a firearm's power with caution. "Power tends to corrupt, and absolute power corrupts absolutely," as a man (Lord Acton) once said. A pistol is not the only way to avoid being raped or murdered in today's world, but, intelligently wielded, it can shift the balance of power and provide a measure of safety.[7]

1. Predict the author's position on the issue of gun control.

_____

_____

2. What does the author think of the advice that women should avoid dangerous situations?

_____

3. The author lives on a ranch in South Dakota and describes the particular problems she faces there. What problems might a resident of a large city describe to justify carrying a gun?

_____

4. What was the original Colt slogan?

_____

EXERCISE 13-4

Directions: Read each of the following selections and answer the questions that follow.

Selection 1:

The Lion's Share

The lion, the jackal, the wolf, and the hyena had a meeting and agreed that they would hunt together in one party and share equally among them whatever game they caught.

They went out and killed an antelope. The four animals then discussed which one of them would divide the meat. The lion said, "Whoever divides the meat must know how to count."

Immediately the wolf volunteered, saying, "Indeed, I know how to count." He began to divide the meat. He cut off four pieces of equal size and placed one before each of the hunters.

The lion was angered. He said, "Is this the way to count?" And he struck the wolf across the eyes, so that his eyes swelled up and he could not see.

The jackal said, "The wolf does not know how to count. I will divide the meat." He cut three portions that were small and a fourth portion that was very large. The three small portions he placed before the hyena, the wolf, and himself. The large portion he put in front of the lion, who took his meat and went away.

"Why was it necessary to give the lion such a large piece?" the hyena said. "Our agreement was to divide and share equally. Where did you ever learn how to divide?"

"I learned from the wolf," the jackal answered.

"Wolf? How can anyone learn from the wolf? He is stupid," the hyena said.

"The jackal was right," the wolf said. "He knows how to count. Before, when my eyes were open, I did not see it. Now, though my eyes are wounded, I see it clearly."

—Dresser, *The Rainmaker's Dog,* pp. 110–11

1. Why was the lion angry?

   _____

2. How did the jackal learn from the experience?

   _____

3. What did the wolf mean when he said, "though my eyes are wounded, I see it clearly"?

   _____

4. What lesson can be learned from the story?

   _____

   _____

Selection 2:

Private Pains

The damnedest thing happened while I was driving down Pioneer Avenue last week. I was passing an intersection and noticed a middle-aged lady stopped in her car waiting to enter the road. There was nothing remarkable about the car, but I happened to look at just the right time and saw she was crying.

Her cheeks were wet and her mouth was sort of twisted in that sorrowful half-smile people sometimes get when they cry. She didn't seem to be in any kind of predicament, and I'd never seen her before, so I did what we usually do when we see people crying; I looked away and drove on.

I kept thinking about it as I drove down the road. What could have driven this woman to tears in the middle of the day while waiting at a stop sign? Maybe she'd just gotten some terrible news about something. Maybe a parent had died or her husband left her. Perhaps a child was hurt at school and she was panicked and on her way there at that very moment. It could have been her birthday or anniversary, and her family had gone off to work and school without saying anything about it. Who could tell?

It might even have been something rather silly. She may have been coming from her hairdresser, who'd done an absolutely horrible job on her, and she didn't know how she'd face people. Or found that she'd inadvertently *not* been invited to her club luncheon that day. Maybe she was just having one of those days we all have from time to time, and trying to make a left turn onto Pioneer Avenue in lunch-hour traffic was the last straw this poor woman could bear.

I wanted to turn around and go ask her what was wrong, but I knew she'd be gone by then. Even if she wasn't, I didn't think she'd talk to a stranger about it. I had a brief vision of opening her car door and holding her, telling her it would be all right. But I knew I would never do that, and would probably get arrested if I did.

It bugged the heck outa me. [I kept] Wondering what kind of tragedy this woman was carrying with her and enduring by herself. I thought about the sadness we all carry with us every day, and take to bed with us at night. The small pains and disappointments that keep us off our mark a little. They make us snap at store clerks without meaning to, or beep our horns at a slowpoke even when we're in no particular hurry. The sadness that sits like a chip on our shoulders, daring anyone to touch it. It makes our mouths taut and our eyes steely. We move stiffly, looking at our feet when we walk, lost in our own little worlds.

This woman, all alone in her car and for no apparent reason, had let her taut mouth fold and her steely eyes fill with tears. The tears came easier with every car that rolled by and left her there, myself included.

Possibly she was the store clerk someone had snapped at, or the slowpoke that got honked at. I don't know, I'm just guessing. It seems we spend so much time torturing each other to get to the head of the line or maneuver into that last parking space. Maybe we should forget about all that stuff every once in a while and just keep our eyes peeled for the tears of a stranger.[9]

1. What inferences did the author make about the woman who was crying?

   _____

2. Which inferences seem least plausible?

   _____

3. Does the author regret not stopping to comfort the woman? Justify your answer.

   _____

4. Explain the meaning of the last line of the selection.

   _____

FIGURATIVE LANGUAGE

Read each of the following statements:

The cake tasted like a moist sponge.

The wilted plants begged for water.

Jean wore her heart on her sleeve.

You know that a cake cannot really have the same taste as a sponge, that plants do not actually request water, and that a person's heart cannot really be attached to her or his sleeve. However, you know what message the writer is communicating in each sentence. The cake was soggy and tasteless, the plants were extremely dry, and Jean revealed her feelings to everyone around her.

Each of these sentences is an example of figurative language. **Figurative language** is a way of describing something that makes sense on an imaginative level but not on a factual or literal level. Notice that while none of the above expressions is literally true, each is meaningful. In many figurative expressions, one thing is compared with another for some quality they have in common. Take, for example, the familiar expression in the following sentence:

Sam eats like a horse.

The diagram below shows the comparison being made in this figurative expression:

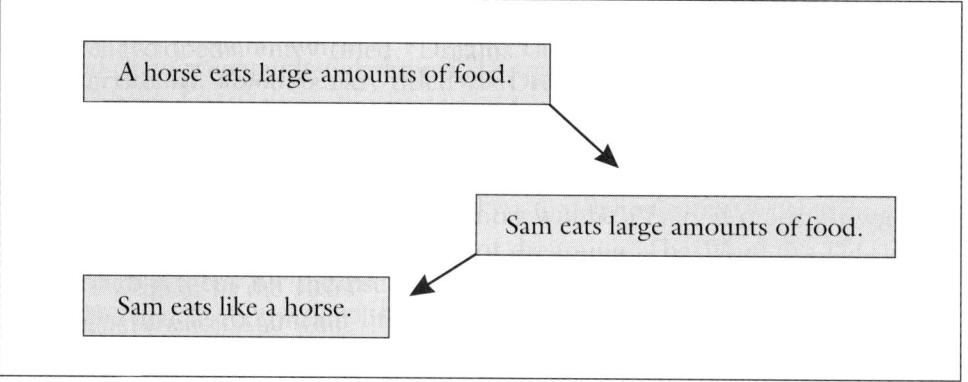

You can see that two unlike things—Sam and a horse—are compared because they are alike in one particular way—the amount they eat.

The purpose of figurative language is to paint a word picture—to help you visualize how something looks, feels, or smells. Figurative language is a device writers use to express an idea or feeling and, at the same time, allow the reader the freedom of imagination. Since it is not factual, figurative language allows the writer to express attitudes and opinions without directly stating them. Depending on the figurative expression chosen, a writer can create a variety of impressions.

When reading an article that contains figurative language, be sure to pay close attention to the images and feelings created. Be sure you recognize that the writer is shaping your response to the topic or subject.

Figurative language is used in many types of articles and essays. It is also used in everyday speech and in slang expressions. Various types of literature, especially poetry, also use figurative language. Notice its use in the following excerpt from a poem by Emily Dickinson.

> My Life has stood—a Loaded Gun—
> In Corners—till a Day
> The Owner passed—identified—
> And carried Me away—[10]

In the opening stanza of this poem, Dickinson compares her life to a loaded gun.

Here are a few more examples from other sources. Notice how each creates a visual image of the person, object, or quality being described.

> The red sun was pasted in the sky like a wafer.
>   (Stephen Crane, *The Red Badge of Courage*)

> In plucking the fruit of memory,
> one runs the risk of spoiling its bloom.
>   (Joseph Conrad)

> "I will speak daggers to her, but use none."
>   (Shakespeare, *Hamlet*)

> Life, like a dome of many-colored glass,
> Stains the white radiance of Eternity.
>   (Shelley, "Adonais")

> Float like a butterfly, sting like a bee.
>   (Muhammad Ali)

EXERCISE 13-5	**Directions:** Each of the following sentences includes a figurative expression. Read each sentence and explain in your own words what the expression means.

1. My psychology quiz was a piece of cake.

   _____

2. My life is a junkyard of broken dreams.

   _____

3. "Life is as tedious as a twice-told tale." (Shakespeare, *King John III*)

   _____

4. "A sleeping child gives me the impression of a traveler in a very far country." (Ralph Waldo Emerson)

   _____

5. "I refuse to accept the notion that nation after nation must spiral down a militaristic stairway into the hell of nuclear war." (Martin Luther King, Jr.)

   _____

EXERCISE 13-6	**Directions:** Read each of the following articles and answer the questions that follow.

Article 1:

Love In The Afternoon—In A Crowded Prison Hall

1   Each time I visit my man in prison, I relive the joy of reunion—and the anguish of separation.

2   We meet at the big glass door at the entrance to the small visitors' hall at Lompoc Federal Correctional Institution. We look at each other silently, then turn and walk into a room jammed with hundreds of molded fiberglass chairs lined up side by side. Finding a place in the crowded hall, we sit down, appalled that we're

actually in a prison. Even now, after four months of such clocked, supervised, regulated visits, we still can't get used to the frustrations.

3   Yet, as John presses me gently to his heart, I feel warm and tender, and tears well up inside me, as they do each weekend. I have seven hours to spend with the man I love—all too brief a time for sharing a lifetime of emotion: love and longing, sympathy and tenderness, resentment and anger.

4   The guard's voice jars us: "Please keep the chairs in order!"

5   We can't keep from laughing, for we're struck by the absurdity of the scene: 60 couples, some with families, packed in a single room—each trying, somehow, to create an atmosphere of intimacy. And what's demanded by the single guard who's assigned to oversee us? *Chairs in a straight line.*

6   Nevertheless, John and I abide by the rules, holding each other as close as we can—without moving our chairs—and the loneliness of the past week gradually subsides.

7   We break our silent communion with small talk much like the kind we shared at home for the past three years. Like: *Should we have the van repaired, or sell it?*

8   Then we speak of our separate needs and fears. He feels defeated—by confinement, by prison life, by the 20 months left to serve on a two-year sentence for a drug-related charge that we think should never have come to trial. He feels deeply insecure, too, doubting my fidelity and hating himself for doubting me. He wants support and reassurance.

9   But what about me? *Doesn't he understand that this has been an ordeal for me, too?* My whole life fell apart when he went to prison. Our wedding plans were canceled; I had to quit school, sell everything, find a job, and move in with relatives.

10   Prison has become my second full-time occupation. Each weekend I spend 10 hours traveling. Always I must save money—money for my motel room in Lompoc, money for his collect phone calls to supplement the letters we write, money for his supplies at the prison commissary.

11   Worst of all, there's the almost unbearable burden of conducting my home life alone. At least in prison he has no decisions to make, no meals to worry about, no rent. So I, too, need reassurance and emotional support.[11]

1. Answer each of the following questions by making an inference.

   a. Who is visiting the man in prison?

   _____

   b. Why is she there?

   _____

      c. Does she go there often? How do you know?

      _____

      d. Why do they break the silence with small talk?

      _____

      e. Why does the guard insist that the chairs be kept in a straight line?

      _____

      f. Why did the woman have to quit school?

      _____

      g. Does the writer feel sorry for herself? How do you know?

      _____

2. List several words with negative connotations that suggest how the writer feels about the prison.

    _____

3. List several words with positive connotations that suggest how the woman feels about the man she is visiting.

    _____

    _____

4. What main point do you think the writer is trying to make?

    _____

    _____

Article 2:

Stop Junk Mail Forever

1   Every American, on average, receives 677 sales pitches in his or her mailbox every year—thanks to low-cost, third-class postal rates. While the direct mailers who produce and distribute those 40 million tons of sales pitches take in

over $200 billion annually, taxpayers bear the burden of some $320 million to cart their unsolicited promos, pleas, and promises to and from incinerators, garbage dumps (on land and sea), and recycling centers. Sixty-eight million trees and 28 billion gallons of water (and the animals who lived there) are used to produce each year's crop of catalogs and come-ons. Nearly half get trashed unopened.

2   Many of the environmental organizations that you'd expect to speak up for the trees, rivers, and wildlife are silent about junk mail. Why? Because they support themselves just like the other mailbox fishermen do . . . by casting an extremely wide net to catch a couple of fish. A "response rate" of 1% or 2%— that's 1 or 2 of every 100 pieces mailed—is considered typical, no matter if the mailer is a worthy charity . . . or the distributor of yet one more vegetable slicer.

3   There's another issue of great concern to us: Privacy. We think Americans should have the right to choose how personal information about them is marked, if at all. What follows are some clear instructions on how to keep your name, business, address, and other personal information private—off of those thousands upon thousands of mailing lists that are regularly bought and sold, without our approval, for pennies a name.[12]

1. Underline three words in the article that carry positive or negative connotative meanings.

   _____

2. What is the author's attitude toward environmental organizations?

   _____

3. What is the author's attitude toward vegetable slicers? Why does he or she use them as an example?

   _____

4. Explain why the phrase "mailbox fishermen" is an example of figurative language.

   _____

UNDERSTANDING THE AUTHOR'S PURPOSE

Writers have many different reasons or purposes for writing. Read the statements on the next page and try to decide why each was written:

1. About 14,000 ocean-going ships pass through the Panama Canal each year. This averages about three ships per day.

2. *New Unsalted Dry Roasted Almonds.* Finally, a snack with a natural flavor and without salt. We simply shell the nuts and dry-roast them until they're crispy and crunchy. Try a jar this week.

3. Man is the only animal that blushes or has a need to.

4. If a choking person has fallen down, first turn him or her face up. Then knit together the fingers of both your hands and apply pressure with the heel of your bottom hand to the victim's abdomen.

5. If your boat capsizes, it is usually safer to cling to the boat than to try to swim ashore.

Statement 1 was written to give information, 2 to persuade you to buy almonds, 3 to amuse you and make a comment on human behavior, 4 to explain, and 5 to give advice.

In each of the examples, the writer's purpose was fairly clear, as it will be in most textbooks (to present information), newspaper articles (to communicate daily events), and reference books (to compile facts). However, in many other types of writing, authors have varied, sometimes less obvious, purposes. In these cases, an author's purpose must be inferred.

Often a writer's purpose is to express an opinion indirectly. Or the writer may want to encourage the reader to think about a particular issue or problem. Writers achieve their purposes by manipulating and controlling what they say and how they say it. This section will focus on techniques writers use and features of language that writers control to achieve the results they want.

Style and Intended Audience

Are you able to recognize a friend just by his or her voice? Can you identify family members by their footsteps? You are able to do so because each person's voice and footsteps are unique. Have you noticed that writers have unique characteristics as well? One author may use many examples; another may use few. One author may use relatively short sentences, another may use long, complicated ones. The characteristics that make a writer unique are known as **style.** By changing style, writers can create different effects.

Writers may vary their styles to suit their intended audiences. A writer may write for a general-interest audience (anyone who is interested in the subject but is not considered an expert). Most newspapers and periodicals, such as *Time* and *Newsweek,* appeal to a general-interest audience. On the other hand, a writer may have a particular interest group in mind. A writer may write for medical doctors in the *Journal of American Medicine,* for skiing enthusiasts in

Skiing Today, or for antique collectors in *The World of Antiques.* A writer may also target his or her writing for an audience with particular political, moral, or religious attitudes. Articles in the *New Republic* often appeal to a particular political viewpoint, whereas the *Catholic Digest* appeals to a specific religious group.

Depending on the group of people for whom the author is writing, he or she will change the level of language, choice of words, and method of presentation. One step toward identifying an author's purpose, then, is to ask yourself the question: Who is the intended audience? Your response will be your first clue to determining why the author wrote the article.

EXERCISE 13-7

Directions: Read each of the following statements and decide for whom each was written. Write a sentence that describes the intended audience.

---

1. Chances are you're going to be putting money away over the next five years or so. You are hoping for the right things in life. Right now, a smart place to put your money is in mutual funds or bonds.

_____

2. Think about all the places your drinking water has been before you drink another drop. Most likely it has been chemically treated to remove bacteria and chemical pollutants. Soon you may begin to feel the side effects of these treatments. Consider switching to filtered, distilled water today.

_____

3. Introducing the new, high-powered Supertuner III, a stereo system guaranteed to keep your mother out of your car.

_____

4. Bright and White laundry detergent removes dirt and stains faster than any other brand.

_____

5. As a driver, you're ahead if you can learn to spot car trouble before it's too late. If you can learn the difference between drips and squeaks that occur

under normal conditions and those that mean big trouble is just down the road, then you'll be ahead of expensive repair bills and won't find yourself stranded on a lonely road.

Tone

The tone of a speaker's voice helps you interpret what he or she is saying. If the following sentence were read aloud, the speaker's voice would tell you how to interpret it: "Would you mind closing the door?" In print you cannot tell whether the speaker is polite, insistent, or angry. In speech you could tell by whether the speaker emphasized the word *would, door,* or *mind.*

Just as a speaker's tone of voice tells how the speaker feels, so does a writer convey a tone, or feeling, through his or her writing. Tone refers to the attitude or feeling a writer expresses about his or her subject. A writer may adopt a sentimental tone, an angry tone, a humorous tone, a sympathetic tone, an instructive tone, a persuasive tone, and so forth. Here are a few examples of different tones. How does each make you feel?

- Instructive

    When purchasing a piece of clothing, one must be concerned with quality as well as with price. Be certain to check for the following: double-stitched seams, matched patterns, and ample linings.

- Sympathetic

    The forlorn, frightened-looking child wandered through the streets alone, searching for someone who would show an interest in helping her find her parents.

- Persuasive

    Child abuse is a tragic occurrence in our society. Strong legislation is needed to control the abuse of innocent victims and to punish those who are insensitive to the rights and feelings of others.

- Humorous

    "Those people who study animal behavior professionally must dread those times when their cover is blown at a dinner party. The unfortunate souls are sure to be seated next to someone with animal stories. The conversation will invariably be about some pet that did this or that, and nonsense is the polite word for it. The worst stories are about cats. The proud owners like to talk about their ingenuity, what they are thinking, and how they 'miss' them while they're at the party. Those cats would rub the leg of a burglar if he rattled the Friskies box."[13]

- Nostalgic

> "Things change, times change, but when school starts, my little granddaughter will run up the same wooden stairs that creaked for all of the previous generations and I will still hate it when the summer ends."[14]

In the first example, the writer offers advice in a straightforward, informative style. In the second, the writer wants you to feel sorry for the child. This is done through description. In the third example, the writer tries to convince the reader that action must be taken to prevent child abuse. The use of such words as *tragic, innocent,* and *insensitive* establish this tone.

The tone of an article directly affects how the reader interprets and responds to it. If, as in the fourth example, the writer's tone is humorous and you do not recognize this, you will miss the point of the entire selection. If the writer's tone is sympathetic, it is important to know that an appeal to your feelings is being made. You can begin to suspect, then, that you may not receive an objective, unbiased treatment of the subject.

The author's tone is intended to rub off on you, so to speak. If a writer's tone is humorous, the writer hopes you will be amused. If a writer's tone is persuasive, the writer hopes you will accept his or her viewpoint. You can see how tone can be important in determining an author's purpose. Therefore, a second question to ask when trying to determine an author's purpose is: What tone does the writer use? Or: How is the writer trying to make me feel about the subject?

EXERCISE 13-8	**Directions:** Read each of the following statements, paying particular attention to the tone. Then write a sentence that describes the tone. Prove your point by listing some of the words that reveal the author's feelings.

1. No one says that nuclear power is risk-free. There are risks involved in all methods of producing energy. However, the scientific evidence is clear and obvious. Nuclear power is at least as safe as any other means used to generate electricity.

_____

_____

2. The condition of our city streets is outrageous. The sidewalks are littered with paper and other garbage—you could trip while walking to the store. The

streets themselves are in even worse condition. Deep potholes and crumbling curbs make it unsafe to drive. Where are our city tax dollars going if not to correct these problems?

_____

_____

3. I am a tired American. I am tired of watching criminals walk free while they wait for their day in court. I'm tired of hearing about victims getting as much as or more hassle than criminals. I'm tired of reading about courts of law that even accept a lawsuit in which a criminal sues his or her intended victim.

_____

_____

4. Cross-country skis have heel plates of different shapes and materials. They may be made of metal, plastic, or rubber. Be sure that they are tacked on the ski right where the heel of your boot will fall. They will keep snow from collecting under your foot and offer some stability.

_____

_____

5. We in the United States have made great progress in lowering our birth rates. But now, because we have been responsible, it seems to some that we have a great surplus. There is, indeed, waste that should be eliminated, but there is not as much fat in our system as most people think. Yet we are being asked to share our resources with the hungry peoples of the world. But why should we share? The nations having the greatest needs are those that have been the least responsible in cutting down on births. Famine is one of nature's ways of telling profligate peoples that they have been irresponsible in their breeding habits.[15]

_____

_____

_____

6. In July of 1986 my daughter, Lucy, was born with an underdeveloped brain. She was a beautiful little girl—at least to me and my husband—but her dis-

abilities were severe. By the time she was two weeks old we knew that she would never walk, talk, feed herself, or even understand the concept of mother and father. It's impossible to describe the effect that her five-and-a-half-month life had on us; suffice it to say that she was the purest experience of love and pain that we will ever have, that she changed us forever, and that we will never cease to mourn her death, even though we know that for her it was a triumphant passing.[16]

_____

_____

_____

Language

One important feature that writers adjust to suit their purpose is the kind of language they use. There are two basic types of language: objective and subjective.

Objective and Subjective Language **Objective language** is factual, whereas **subjective language** expresses attitudes and feelings.

Read each of the following descriptions of the death penalty. As you read, decide how they differ.

> The death penalty is one of the most ancient of all types of formal punishment for crime. In early criminal codes, death was the penalty for a wide range of offenses, such as kidnapping, certain types of theft, and witchcraft. Today, in the United States, the death penalty is reserved for only the most serious of crimes—murder, kidnapping, and treason.

> The death penalty is a prime example of man's inhumanity to man. The death penalty violates the Eighth Amendment to the Constitution, which prohibits cruel and unusual punishment.

You probably noticed that the first paragraph gave facts about the death penalty and that the second paragraph seemed to state a case against it. These two paragraphs are examples of two different types of writing.

The first paragraph is an example of objective language. The writer reported information without showing feelings. You cannot tell whether the writer favors or is opposed to the death penalty.

The second paragraph is an example of subjective language. Here, the writer expresses freely his or her own attitudes and feelings. You know exactly how the author feels about the death penalty. Through choice of words and selection of facts, a tone of moral disapproval is evident. Such words as *inhumanity, violates,* and *cruel* have negative connotations.

<table>
<tr>
<td>

EXERCISE

13-9

</td>
<td>

Directions: Choose a topic that interests you or use one of the topics listed below. On a separate sheet, write two brief paragraphs. In the first, use only objective, factual information. In the second, try to show your feelings about the topic by using subjective language.

</td>
</tr>
</table>

---

1. One of your college instructors
2. Managing your time
3. Current fashion fads

Descriptive Language   **Descriptive language** is a particular type of subjective language. It is the use of words that appeal to one or more of the reader's senses. Descriptive words help the reader create an imaginary picture of the object, person, or event being described. Here is a paragraph that contains numerous descriptive words and phrases. As you read, underline words and phrases that help you to imagine what the Oregon desert is like.

> You can camp in the Oregon desert for a week and see no one at all, no more than the glow of headlights hovering over a dirt road miles distant, disappearing soundlessly over the curve of the Earth. You can see, as you wander over those dry flats, that man has been there, that vast stretches of sagebrush have replaced the bunchgrass grazed off by his cattle and sheep. Against a hill you can find the dry-rotting foundation of a scuttled homestead. But the desert is not scarred by man's presence. It is still possible to be alone out there, to stare at your hands for an hour and have no one ask why. It is possible to feel the cracks in the earth, to sense the enormity of space, to roll, between the tips of your fingers, the dust of boulders gone to pieces.[17]

Through descriptive language, a writer often makes you feel a certain way about the topic. In the preceding paragraph, the writer is trying to suggest that the desert is lonely, peaceful, and a good place to think or relax. Did you notice such words and phrases as *soundlessly, enormity of space, distant, wander, vast stretches?*

Directions: Read each of the following articles and answer the questions that follow.

Article 1:

Americans and the Land

I have often wondered at the savagery and thoughtlessness with which our early settlers approached this rich continent. They came at it as though it were an enemy, which of course it was. They burned the forests and changed the rainfall; they swept the buffalo from the plains, blasted the streams, set fire to the grass, and ran a reckless scythe through the virgin and noble timber. Perhaps they felt that it was limitless and could never be exhausted and that a man could move on to new wonders endlessly. Certainly there are many examples to the contrary, but to a large extent the early people pillaged the country as though they hated it, as though they held it temporarily and might be driven off at any time.[18]

1. Is this selection an objective or subjective account of the early settlement of America? Give examples to support your choice.

   _____

   _____

2. Describe the writer's tone. How does it make you feel?

   _____

   _____

3. Why do you think the author wrote this selection?

   _____

   _____

Article 2:

A Day in the Life of a Lab Rat:
At Least the Human Kind Get Paid

1   It is 6:35 Friday morning and I'm watching cartoons with 31 other men. Some of them are still in their underwear, alternately gazing up at the television and down at their bare feet, muttering, "Coffee, coffee . . ." Others have already showered and combed their hair and are now sitting up straight, with their backs to the television, watching the clock across the room as if it were a descending deity. The rest of us are hunched over, glaring at Muppet Babies through half-closed eyes. I look down at the piece of paper in my hands. My gaze rests on the third line [of the questionnaire].
Item #3. I wake up fresh and rested most mornings.

2   A voice crackles over the loudspeaker: "Number One—Rupert. Lab." This is the first thing the voice has said since it told us to wake up, to get out of bed, to sit in these chairs. And now everyone glances over at Rupert as he stands and makes his way past the pool table, past the Super Nintendo station, past the dining tables, across the gray room lit by fluorescent bulbs.
Item #9. My daily life is full of things that keep me interested.
Item #10. I am afraid of losing my mind.

3   It's 6:42. None of us has had much sleep, and now the door to the sleeping room is locked. We won't be given any food until noon. I decide not to look at the clock anymore. Without it, however, it could be any time of day; heavy venetian blinds close out the world. The only way out is a door on the far side of the room. But if anyone tries to open it a siren will sound.

4   "Number Five—Jesus. Lab." Jesus is a big smiley guy from Colombia who punches me in the arm when I beat him at pool and lifts me off the ground in a bear hug when I lose. The voice over the loudspeaker does not pronounce his name with the Latin accent, Hey-Zeus, or even with the French one: Jay-Zoo. Here he is just plain "Jesus."

5   Jesus mutters something in Spanish as he pushes himself out of his chair.

6   "What did he say?" asks Number Four, sitting down.

7   "Think of the money," I say.

8   Number Four nods. It has become a sort of materialistic mantra around here—"Think of the money." This is not, after all, a jail, nor rehab, nor some Orwellian summer camp. This is Phoenix International Life Sciences Inc.—the Rolls Royce of clinical testing. And we're all in it for the money.

9   If you want to make some cash as a human lab rat, this is the place to be. According to the company's prospectus, it is "the world's fifth-largest contract research organization serving the pharmaceutical, generic drug, and biotech-nology industries." With net revenues of $171 million in 1998, Phoenix pays top dollar to healthy males for the right to test drugs on their bodies. And although

it now has clinics across the United States and Europe, Phoenix is wisely based in Montreal, a city overflowing with poor young men.

10 "Number Six—Sauganee. Lab." This is actually as close as they've come to my name so far.

11 I am here because my money ran out before my school term, my lease, and my need for food. And although I've had no trouble finding work in cities all over the world, from Veracruz to Venice, Montreal is different, especially if your French is about on a par with Andrew Dice Clay's. So, after a long desperate job search (which included applying for such positions as "promotional swordfighter" and "Jewish homemaker"), I finally decided to answer a long-running ad in HOUR magazine for "participants in a study," promising "compensatory indemnity of up to $1,000."

12 I signed myself up for the first available study and had only to pass the medical exam and screening process. Phoenix took samples of my blood and urine, measured my height and weight and EKG levels, asked a bunch of questions, then sent me home. I felt pretty confident. After all, I was young and resilient—a perfect specimen.[19]

1. Where do the events in this article take place?

   _____

2. Why did the author volunteer to participate in the lab program?

   _____

3. What is the author's purpose in writing?

   _____

3. Describe the tone of the article.

   _____

   _____

4. Explain the figurative expression "watching the clock as if it were a descending diety." (paragraph 1)

   _____

   _____

5. What is on the paper that the author is holding?

_____

_____

6. List several examples of descriptive language.

_____

_____

_____

WORKING TOGETHER

Directions: Bring a magazine ad to class. Working in groups of three or four students, make as many inferences as possible about each ad. For example, answer questions such as "What is happening?" "How does each person feel?" and "How will this ad sell the product?" Group members who differ in their opinions should present evidence to support their own inferences. Each group should then state to the class, as specifically as possible, the purpose of each ad. Be specific; try to say more than "To sell the product."

Learning Style Tips

If you tend to be a(n) . . .	Then build your interpretive reading skills by . . .
Applied learner	Asking the questions: How can I use this information? Of what value is this information?
Conceptual learner	Studying to see how the ideas fit together, looking for connections and relationships, as well as inconsistencies

MASTERING VOCABULARY

Directions: Determine the meaning of each of the following words used in this chapter. Then insert each one in the sentence in which it makes most sense.

proclaims (p. 429)
empathized (p. 431)
distortion (p. 433)
accumulation (p. 434)
precautions (p. 436)
abide (p. 443)
unsolicited (p. 445)
enormity (p. 452)
prospectus (p. 454)
generic (p. 454)

1. There was a great _____ of trash in the vacant lot.

2. We receive a pile of _____ mail every day.

3. They were surprised at the _____ of the Grand Canyon.

4. The store clerk _____ with the crying, lost child.

5. _____ food products are often chapter than brand name products.

6. The sales manager rewrote the _____ for her proposed new product line four times.

7. You should take a number of _____ before lighting a barbecue grill.

8. After the election board _____ a winner, there will be a press conference.

9. Both teams must _____ by the referee's decision.

10. The defendant's story was filled with _____

SELF-TEST SUMMARY

How do authors suggest their ideas without directly stating them?	Authors use three features to state their ideas indirectly. These three features are: 1. Connotative meaning—the shades of meaning a word may have in addition to its literal meaning. 2. Implied meaning—ideas suggested based on facts and information given by the author. 3. Figurative language—a way of describing things that make sense on an imaginative level, but not on a factual level.
How can I identify the author's purpose?	There are four ways to identify the author's purpose. These are: 1. Style A—writer will change his or her style (level of language, choice of words, and method of presentation) to suit the intended audience. 2. Audience—Analyzing the style and identifying the intended audience are the first steps toward identifying an author's purpose. 3. Tone—A writer's tone (serious, humorous, angry, sympathetic) is a clue to how the writer wants you to feel about the topic. 4. Language—A writer's language may be objective or subjective, depending on whether the writer is simply presenting facts or expressing an opinion or feelings. This language presents one or more clues to the writer's purpose.

Name _____

Section _____ Date _____

Number right _____ x 20 points = Score _____

Directions: Read each statement and answer the questions that follow.

_____ 1. "Before the meeting began, several staff members stood in a corner of the room and **chatted** about the new organizational chart." Replace the bold-faced word in this sentence with one of the words below that has a *negative* connotative meaning.
   a. conversed
   b. wondered
   c. gossiped
   d. talked

_____ 2. "Gordon is so **cheap** that he always uses coupons at the grocery store and only dines out once a year." Replace the boldfaced word in this sentence with one of the words below that has a *positive* connotative meaning.
   a. stingy
   b. miserly
   c. tightfisted
   d. thrifty

_____ 3. Of the following sentences, the only one that does *not* contain figurative language is
   a. I worked my fingers to the bone on this project.
   b. I stayed up past midnight in order to finish the project on time.
   c. The project took on a life of its own.
   d. My professor said the project looked like a million bucks.

_____ 4. "When you are hitting a baseball, it's important to see the ball as soon as it leaves the pitcher's hand." The tone in this sentence can best be described as
   a. sympathetic.
   b. sentimental.
   c. instructive.
   d. persuasive.

_____ 5. "Even though I grew up in the Midwest, to me Christmas will always mean bright sunshine, warm breezes, and the thrill of splashing in the ocean near my grandparents' house in San Diego." The tone in this sentence can best be described as
   a. sympathetic.
   b. humorous.
   c. persuasive.
   d. nostalgic.

**CHAPTER 13
MASTERY TEST 2:
Interpretative Skills**

Name _____

Section _____ Date _____

Number right _____ x 20 points = Score _____

Directions: Read each of the following paragraphs and answer the questions that follow.

Paragraph 1: Over the past 20 years, psychologists have made a science of the joys and devastations of couples' relationships. They've come to understand, at least in part, why some relationships happily endure and what contributes to the hellhole interactions that claim over half of all first marriages, usually within the first 7 years. Although these same psychologists note that most marriages start with great optimism and true love, they get into trouble for a very humbling reason: we just don't know how to handle the negative feelings that are a result of the differences between two people, the very differences that formed the basis for attraction in the first place.[20]

____ 1. One inference that can be made from this paragraph is that
  a. the author disapproves of divorce.
  b. more than half of all first marriages end in divorce.
  c. the author is a marriage counselor.
  d. all divorces occur within the first seven years of marriage.

Paragraph 2: Alas, all is not perfect in the virtual world. E-commerce does have its limitations. Security is one important concern. We hear horror stories of consumers whose credit cards and other identity information have been stolen. While an individual's financial liability in most theft cases is limited to $50, the damage to one's credit rating can last for years. Some shady companies are making money by prying and then selling personal information to others.

Pretty scary. Almost daily we hear of hackers getting into a business or even a government Web site and causing havoc. Businesses risk the loss of trade secrets and other proprietary information. Many must spend significant amounts to maintain security and conduct regular audits to ensure the integrity of their sites.[21]

____ 2. In this paragraph, an example of *objective* language is
  a. "horror stories."
  b. "individual liability."
  c. "shady companies."
  d. "Pretty scary."

Paragraph 3: If we want to create safe classrooms in which teachers and students have the right to question existing knowledge and produce new knowledge, we must prepare you, who are planning to teach, for the problems you will face. One of your most frustrating problems will revolve around your discovery that power can shape and even dominate your life and your school. Power is a basic reality of human existence, present in all human relationships, including those of lovers, business partners, basketball teams, teachers and students, college faculties, courts, government bodies and so on.[22]

____ 3. For this paragraph, the authors' intended audience is
  a. parents of school-age children.
  b. people who work in positions of power.
  c. college professors.
  d. people who are planning to become teachers.

Paragraph 4: Computer games are big business, but many of the best-sellers are filled with gore and violence that are not the best things for children to see. Is there an alternative? A company formed by five young people in Sweden thinks so, and they're succeeding by offering product alternatives that prove you don't need to be bloody to be the best. The company, called Daydream Software, got its start when one of the programmers gave a computer to his little sister for Christmas. He had a hard time finding appropriate games she could play, however. This frustrating discovery led to discussions with friends about finding methods to push players' thrill buttons other than endless blood and splatter. All of Daydream's founders have children, and they design games they would want their own kids to play. They want the player to come away with more than just the echo of machine guns and a sore trigger finger.[23]

_____ 4. One inference that can be made from this paragraph is that
    a. Daydream's computer games are nonviolent.
    b. Daydream's computer games are more expensive than other computer games.
    c. the people who produce violent computer games do not have children.
    d. violent computer games are always more exciting than nonviolent games.

Paragraph 5: Another shameful abandonment of human rights affected Native Americans. Between 1700 and 1763, thousands of white settlers poured into Indian lands west of the mountains. The result was bloody warfare, marked by barbarous atrocities on both sides. Looking to the British for protection, most of the tribes fought against Americans during the Revolution, only to have their territories put under control of their enemies in the peace of 1783. Protracted negotiations with the American government led to more surrenders and numerous treaties, all of which were broken as the flood of white land speculators and settlers moved westward. In desperation, the Indians attempted unification and a hopeless resistance. By 1800 enforced living on land set aside for Indians was already promoting the disintegration of Native American cultures.[24]

_____ 5. The authors' purpose in this paragraph is to
    a. explain the role of Native Americans in the settling of the west.
    b. describe the effect of westward expansion on Native Americans.
    c. criticize Native Americans for their treatment of whites in the 18th century.
    d. defend the actions of whites against Native Americans in the 18th century.

Name _____

Section _____ Date _____

Number right _____ x 10 points = Score _____

Directions: After reading the selection, choose the letter that best answers each of the questions that follow.

Hidden Treasures: Unlocking Strengths in the Public Social Services

1   In January 1964, fresh out of college with a B.A. in English, I began my social work career as a social investigator with the New York Department of Welfare. At that time, we were implementing the 1962 Defined Service Amendments to the Social Security Act. The plan was to "casework" everybody out of poverty—or at least those who were "willing to help themselves." We were to emphasize the social rather than the investigative part of our roles. Having just completed my training week, I made an appointment with Matilda Jones for her quarterly recertification visit.

2   Matilda had four children. Two were literally lost in the foster care system. Following agency advice, Matilda had voluntarily placed her children during a time of family crisis. Also at our urging, she had not visited them for a long time; the practice wisdom of the time suggested that Matilda should not visit in order to give everyone "time to adjust." Now we were unable to locate the children in the labyrinthine* maze of contract agencies to whom we had entrusted their care. Matilda's third child had already been labeled "high risk" at his school—a school he attended when Matilda was able to get him there, which was not very often. Matilda had just brought her

newborn home from the hospital; he had several conditions that reflected poor prenatal care and marginal obstetrical services.

3   These were the days before the separation of income maintenance and services, so I went prepared by my training to recertify the family's eligibility for AFDC as well as to offer social services. I could see Matilda in the window of her tenement as I turned off Broadway and walked cautiously through the rubble of the West Side Urban Renewal District. From her observation post at the front end of her railroad apartment, she signaled to the men hanging out on the street below to give me safe passage. It was 10:00 A.M. and she was having her breakfast: a piece of toast and a can of beer.

4   Matilda had learned the system when I was still in grade school. She was ready for me. She had her rent receipt, her electric bill, her clothing inventory, her list of clothing and furniture needs for the baby, and the baby's health department card. She was prepared to discuss the baby's paternity. I made the requisite† notes in my little caseworker's book, then closed it and invoked‡ my training. I said, "Mrs. Jones, you know all of this paperwork is very important, but there are other important things we could do together. I really want to work with you on problems and issues and concerns that are important to you. Now I'm going to leave my book closed, and I'd really like to talk with you, just talk about stuff together, and about things we could do together that'll result in better things happening in your life."

*confusing and complicated

†required, necessary

‡remembered, recalled

5   Matilda studied me for a very long moment before she leaned into the space between us and said, "Look, white girl, I wanna tell you something. I got to document my life to you—because I'm poor. I got to show you all my papers, prove I paid my bills, take my baby to your pig doctor, and show you this card that says I take care of my baby—all because I'm poor. I even have to talk about my sex life with you—because I'm poor. I gotta do all that—but I don't have to take your social workin'.

6   "Now I'm gonna tell you three things about your social workin'," she continued. "Number one, it ain't got nothin' to do with my life. Number two, I can't eat it. And number three, it don't dull the pain like my Pabst Blue Ribbon. Now you get along, white girl—and you think about that."

7   I have thought about that for 30 years. One of the results has been my participation in efforts to build a strengths-oriented practice in the public social services. Two components of that effort in which I have been involved included designing a statewide competency-based training program and conducting field research on the characteristics and activities of effective workers in that state.[25]

_____ 1. The article was written by a
   a. welfare recipient.
   b. social worker.
   c. a novelist.
   d. a lawyer.

_____ 2. The tone of the author toward herself and the social welfare system is
   a. concerned and critical.
   b. light and humorous.
   c. angry and resentful.
   d. positive and admiring.

_____ 3. The author's main purpose for writing this selection is to
   a. analyze the causes of poverty.
   b. show problems with earlier approaches to social work.
   c. show the good methods of casework she used in 1964.
   d. report on a client's recertification visit.

_____ 4. The main point the author makes is that
   a. welfare recipients hate social workers.
   b. social workers know more than their clients.
   c. the standard approach to social work must be changed.
   d. social work is only useful to those "willing to help themselves."

_____ 5. To support her main point, the author
   a. explains a process.
   b. presents statistics.
   c. uses humor.
   d. tells a story.

_____ 6. The author implies that Matilda's first two children could no longer be located due to the fault of
   a. their mother.
   b. their foster parents.
   c. the Department of Welfare.
   d. the New York public schools.

(continued)

_____ 7. Which of the following details best supports the inference that Matilda lived in a dangerous neighborhood?

a. "She signaled to the men hanging out on the street below to give me safe passage."

b. "I could see Matilda in the window of her tenement as I turned off Broadway . . ."

c. "Matilda studied me for a long time before she leaned into the space between . . ."

d. "It was 10:00 A.M. and she was having her breakfast: a piece of toast and a can of beer."

_____ 8. Which of the following statements best reveals Matilda's attitude toward the social worker?

a. "Look, white girl, I wanna tell you something."

b. "I gotta do all that—but I don't have to take any of your social workin'."

c. She was ready for me.

d. She was having her breakfast: a piece of toast and a can of beer.

_____ 9. Which of the following phrases from the selection has a negative connotation?

a. . . . emphasize the social rather than the investigative part . . .

b. . . . studied me for a very long moment . . .

c. . . . designing a statewide competency-based training program . . .

d. . . . walked cautiously through the rubble . . .

_____ 10. The audience that the author most likely intended this selection for is

a. social workers.

b. welfare recipients.

c. medical doctors.

d. religious leaders.

Name _____ _____

Section _____ Date _____ __

Number right _____ x 10 points = Score _____

Dreams for Sale

Kenneth R. Weiss

In order to have children, some couples are paying thousands of dollars to egg donors. This article, which originally appeared in the *Los Angeles Times*, describes the thriving egg-donation industry.

Vocabulary Preview

tryst (par. 1) an appointed meeting

pedigree (par. 1) background; credentials

ubiquitous (par. 4) seeming to be everywhere at the same time

brokers (par. 5) agents who arrange sales

brash (par. 5) lacking in sensitivity or tact

invasive (par. 5) a medical procedure involving entry into the body, as by puncture or incision

entrepreneur (par. 10) one who organizes, operates, and assumes the risk for a business venture

brazen (par. 10) shamelessly bold

altruism (par. 12) an unselfish interest in the welfare of others; selflessness

narcissism (par. 12) excessive love or admiration of oneself

rendezvous (par. 14) to come together or meet

synchronized (par. 14) occurring at the same time

coercive (par. 16) forceful

1   Slipping away from Harvard for a week last June, a Ph.D. candidate named Rachel, a tall strawberry-blonde with a creamy com-

plexion and blue-green eyes, jetted to San Francisco for an unusual tryst. Awaiting her was a wealthy Bay Area couple, desperate for a baby, willing to pay Rachel thousands of dollars to help them realize their dream. The middle-aged husband and wife, who found Rachel through a San Diego broker, were attracted as much to her slender 5-foot-11 frame and Norwegian ancestry as they were to her Ivy League pedigree. "You look even more gorgeous than the pictures," she recalled one of the pair saying.

2   The next morning, with Rachel under general anesthesia, a needle poked into her ovaries and harvested 17 eggs ripened by weeks of hormone shots. They were then fertilized with the husband's sperm and implanted into the wife's womb.

3   For her donation, Rachel made about $18,000, just enough to cover a semester at an Ivy League school. She was back in California again in February—this time in San Diego to do business with another couple. "I asked for a little more this time," she said, "and they agreed to it."

4   California has become the center of a flourishing egg-donation industry that increasingly recruits women from university campuses nationwide. "Pay your tuition with eggs," reads one of the ubiquitous advertisements in college newspapers. California brokers now recruit heavily from the nation's top academic institutions—Harvard, Yale and Stanford—promoting their donors' eggs

on Web sites and in brochures as name-brand genetic material.

5   With the number of egg transplants—each usually involving multiple eggs—surpassing 7,000 in 1998 and doubling every two to three years, the fierce competition has forced brokers to offer even larger financial enticements. Ads promising payments as high as six figures have created a split in the once low-profile industry, raising ethical concerns about targeting young women who are struggling with the cost of higher education. More established egg brokers accuse brash newcomers of crude recruiting tactics that stress short-term gain and downplay the risks of hormone treatments and invasive surgery.

6   Rachel, at first, was thinking only about the money when she spotted an ad in her college newspaper seeking a tall woman with at least 1400 out of a possible 1600 SAT score. Then 23, she was pursuing a master's degree at Yale, piling on debt from student loans. "It was the dollar figure that attracted me," said Rachel, who like most donors, asked that only her first name be used. "It was a full-page ad. I opened it up and saw that it was $50,000 and said, 'All right!'"

7   Although she was turned down by the first couple when she answered the $50,000 ad, Rachel was eventually selected by the childless pair in San Francisco. "Once you meet them and you see how excited they are, you say, 'Wow, it's more than just the money,'" she said. There was something satisfying, too, in getting chosen after nearly a year of being sized up by couples who did everything from quiz her about her tennis game to measure her shoulders. "It's neat to be picked," she said. "Someone actually wants you."

. . .

8   *Egg Donor Needed. Large Financial Incentive. Intelligent, athletic egg donor needed for loving family. You must be at least 5'10". Have a 1400+ SAT score. Possess no major family medical issues. $50,000. Free medical screening. All Expenses Paid.*

. . .

9   The ad above, answered by Rachel and about 200 other young women, was placed by broker Darlene Pinkerton in campus newspapers at Ivy League schools, as well as the Massachusetts Institute of Technology, Stanford and the California Institute of Technology, two years ago. As the first ad offering such an extravagant sum, it opened the egg-brokerage business to a whole new breed of start-up companies. Since then, others have bid up the price. An agency in Newport Beach, Calif., holds the record with its Stanford Daily ad in March 2000 offering $100,000 for eggs of a white woman younger than 30 with "proven college-level athletic ability preferred."

10   Businesses that don't handle big-money donors often make up for it in volume. Options, the National Fertility Registry, which generally limits donor fees to $5,000, advertises regularly in 60 campus newspapers. Rory McGlynn, Options assistant director, said his brokerage coordinates 1,000 egg transfers a year from its office in Los Angeles. Brokers typically collect commissions of $3,000 to $5,000 or more for each match. All that cash has attracted a new sort of aggressive entrepreneur with brazen marketing and sales tactics. "It has moved from a gentlemanly marketplace of insiders to a more open, flamboyant marketplace," said Arthur Caplan, director of the University of

Pennsylvania's Center for Bioethics. "There is not much difference between those ads and what goes on with prize breeding of animals." The newer brokers run eye-grabbing ads that offer $25,000, $50,000 or more for women with the right combination of beauty and brains.

Bait and Switch

11   Longtime broker Karen Synesiou, director of Egg Donation Inc. in Beverly Hills, Calif., who no longer advertises in campus newspapers because she believes that most undergraduates are too young to provide the service, is critical of such ads. "They are fake ads to attract media attention and a lot of donors. Believe me, the donors are going to be told, 'You don't qualify for the $80,000, but I have another couple. You would get $5,000.'" At Pinkerton's agency, A Perfect Match, which ran the nation's first $50,000 ad, only two donors have made that amount, Pinkerton said. Rachel and many other respondents ended up settling for less. The average donor fee, she said, runs about $10,000.

12   The motivations of donors—and recipient couples—are complex. And they are made much more so by the infusion of big money into the transaction. Helen Rosenberg, a Rutgers University professor, has not only published studies on the motives of egg donors, she has given birth to two children from donated eggs and is an active broker. "The motivating force is not just altruism: it's narcissism," she said. "I've interviewed 1,100 college girls, and they all say, 'My genes are wonderful, and my eggs should be out there.'"

13   Some of the issues raised in egg donation are similar to those that arise in donation of sperm—but there are big differences: Men's sperm is far more plentiful than women's eggs, the medical risks of egg donation are greater and—perhaps most important—there is a lot more money involved.

14   Unlike sperm, which can be frozen and banked until needed, eggs must be fresh to be viable. So college women fly into Los Angeles or other cities to rendezvous with older women, their cycles chemically synchronized so they can transfer eggs at just the right moment.

15   With so many dollars at stake, Caplan and others worry about donors' behavior. A $50,000 fee could seduce a college donor into discounting the rare, but very real, risks of infection, infertility and even death. A cash-strapped donor might neglect to disclose a family history of cancer. Or she might gloss over the possibility of her child's someday knocking on her door, seeking his biological mother.

16   After months of debate, fertility doctors and other members of the American Society of Reproductive Medicine recommended last year that donor fees be limited to $5,000. Anything more, the society determined, could be coercive. Lawmakers, however, have been reluctant to set down rules in the fast-changing field.

Improving on Nature

17   By far, the questions surrounding gene-shopping are most troubling to ethicists. Bioethics expert Alex Capron of the University of Southern California says parents who have to give up on genetic offspring

sometimes hunt for a child who satisfies other ego needs: better looks, athletic ability or whatever would make them prouder parents. Their attitude, he said, is: "I want the best child, the way I want the best car, and I'm willing to pay for it."

18   Pinkerton, however, said that was the last thing on the minds of the highly educated couple who inspired the ad that kicked off the craze for higher-priced eggs. Sure, the couple sought a donor who was at least 5-foot-10, she said. "What people don't understand is that the woman is 5-foot-11 and the husband is 6-foot-5. "They want a tall child," she said. "People are not trying to create a super-athlete or super-intelligent being. They are trying to match themselves."

19   It is true, brokers say, that women of Asian descent look for donors with similar heritage, and Jewish families want Jewish donors. Most women seek to match their height, hair and eye color, and most brokers encourage parents to pick donors who resemble them. Still, agencies report a steady stream of would-be parents smitten by the human tendency to want to improve on nature.

Genetic Crapshoot

20   For recipient couples, beauty often plays as large a role as any other characteristic, brokers say. That reflects a broad misunderstanding of the genetics Mixmaster—a beautiful mother, as many a homely child knows, does not guarantee beautiful offspring.

21   "It's a crap shoot," Rosenberg tells prospective parents. In fact, no characteristic can be guaranteed—or guaranteed against.

That "raises the questions of disappointment and false promises, scamming and product liability," Caplan said. He predicts lawsuits claiming, "You told me I'd get a Grade A egg and I got a child with a genetic defect." He and others fear that egg-selling has become a business fraught with moral—and perhaps legal—peril. "There is all this talk of donation, helping another couple," Caplan said. "But clearly it's a business, selling the best available stock that money can buy."

Directions: Choose the letter that best answers each of the following questions.

CHECKING YOUR COMPREHENSION

_____ 1. The main purpose of this selection is to
a. compare sperm donation to egg donation.
b. present options for couples who are unable to have children.
c. criticize women who would sell their eggs.
d. describe egg donors and the egg donation market.

_____ 2. The woman named Rachel in the article is
a. an egg donor.
b. an egg broker.
c. the recipient of an egg.
d. an ethicist.

_____ 3. The main idea of paragraph 4 is that
   a. many egg donors are being recruited from college campuses.
   b. the egg-donation industry is located in California.
   c. egg donors earn enough money to pay for their college tuition.
   d. the nation's top universities use Web sites to promote egg donation.

_____ 4. The main idea of paragraph 7 is that Rachel thinks egg donation is
   a. satisfying as well as profitable.
   b. an easy way to make money.
   c. unrealistic for most young women.
   d. a matter of selecting the right characteristics.

_____ 5. According to egg broker Darlene Pinkerton, the couple who placed the ad shown in the article sought a tall donor because they
   a. are very short.
   b. believe tall people are more intelligent.
   c. are also tall and want the child to match them.
   d. believe tall people are more athletic.

_____ 6. In paragraph 14, the word "banked" means
   a. financed.
   b. stored.
   c. arranged.
   d. counted.

APPLYING YOUR SKILLS

_____ 7. The article includes comments from ethics expert Arthur Caplan in order to illustrate the
   a. medical procedure for extracting eggs from donors.
   b. moral and legal issues associated with the egg-selling industry.
   c. higher quality of eggs from students at Ivy League universities.
   d. advantages of sperm donation over egg donation.

_____ 8. The main audience this article is intended for is
   a. college students.
   b. medical professionals, especially physicians.
   c. egg donors.
   d. the general public who knows little about the subject.

_____ 9. The overall tone of this article is
   a. sad.
   b. informative.
   c. humorous.
   d. disgusted.

(continued)

_____ 10. The figurative expression "genetics Mixmaster" in paragraph 20 refers to the
  a. medical equipment that is used during the egg donation process.
  b. inability of some couples to have children without medical intervention.
  c. ongoing debate among fertility doctors and other members of the American Society of Reproductive Medicine.
  d. wide and unpredictable variety of genes that make up each person.

Go Electronic!
For additional readings, exercises, and Internet activities, visit this book's Web site at:

http://www.ablongman.com/mcwhorter

If you need a user name and password, please see your instructor.

Take a Road Trip to the Great Lakes!
Be sure to visit the Inference module in your Reading Road Trip CD-ROM for multimedia tutorials, exercises, and tests.

14

Evaluating: Asking Critical Questions

THIS CHAPTER WILL SHOW YOU HOW TO

1. Judge the accuracy and value of what you read
2. Ask questions to evaluate what you read

If you were thinking of purchasing a used car from a private owner, you would ask questions before deciding whether to buy it. You would ask about repairs, maintenance, gas mileage, and so forth. When it comes to buying something, most of us have learned the motto "Buyer beware." We have learned to be critical, sometimes suspicious, of a product and its seller. We realize that salespeople will often tell us only what will make us want to buy the item. They will not tell what is wrong with the item or whether it compares unfavorably with a competitor's product.

Although many of us have become wise consumers, few of us have become wise, critical readers. We need to adopt a new motto: Reader beware. You can think of some writers as sellers and their written material as the product to be sold. Just as you would ask questions about a car before buying it, so should you ask questions about what you read before you accept what is said. You should ask questions about who wrote the material and where it came from. You need to decide whether the writer is selling you a one-sided, biased viewpoint. You should evaluate whether the writer provides sufficient support for his or her ideas to allow you to accept them. This chapter will discuss these critical issues and show you how to apply them to articles and essays.

WHAT IS THE SOURCE OF THE MATERIAL?

Just as you might check the brand label on an item of clothing before you buy it, so should you check to see where an article or essay comes from before you read it. You will often be asked to read material that is not in its original form. Many textbooks, such as this one, include excerpts or entire selections borrowed from other authors. Instructors often photocopy articles or essays and distribute them or place them on reserve in the library for students to read.

A first question to ask before you even begin to read is: What is the source; from what book, magazine, or newspaper was this taken? Knowledge of the source will help you judge the accuracy and soundness of what you read. For example, in which of the following sources would you expect to find the most accurate and up-to-date information about computer software?

- An advertisement in *Time*
- An article in *Reader's Digest*
- An article in *Software Review*

The article in *Software Review* would be the best source. This is a magazine devoted to the subject of computers and computer software. *Reader's Digest*, on the other hand, does not specialize in any one topic and often reprints or condenses articles from other sources. *Time*, a weekly newsmagazine, does contain information, but a paid advertisement is likely to provide information on only one line of software.

Knowing the source of an article will give clues to the kind of information the article will contain. For instance, suppose you went to the library to locate information for a research paper on the interpretation of dreams. You found the following sources of information. What do you expect each to contain?

- An encyclopedia entry titled "Dreams"
- An article in *Woman's Day* titled "A Dreamy Way to Predict the Future"
- An article in *Psychological Review* titled "An Examination of Research on Dreams"

You can predict that the encyclopedia entry will be a factual report. It will provide a general overview of the process of dreaming. The *Woman's Day* article will probably focus on the use of dreams to predict future events. You can expect the article to contain little research. Most likely, it will be concerned largely with individual reports of people who accurately dreamt about the future. The article from *Psychological Review*, a journal that reports research in psychology, will present a primarily factual, research-oriented discussion of dreams.

As part of evaluating a source or selecting an appropriate source, be sure to check the date of publication. For many topics, it is essential that you work with current, up-to-date information. For example, suppose you've found an article on the safety of over-the-counter (nonprescription) drugs. If the article was written four or five years ago, it is already outdated. New drugs have been approved and released; new regulations have been put into effect; packaging requirements have changed. The year a book was published can be found on the copyright page. If the book has been reprinted by another publisher or has been reissued in paperback, look to see when it was first published and check the year(s) in the copyright notice.

EXERCISE 14-1

Directions: For each set of sources listed below, choose the one that would be most useful for finding information on the stated topic. Then, in the space provided, give a reason for your choice.

_____ 1. **Topic:** gas mileage of American-made cars
   Sources:
   a. A newspaper article titled "Gas-Eating American Cars"
   b. An encyclopedia article on "Gas Consumption of Automobile Engines"
   c. A research report in *Car and Driver* magazine on American car performance

   Reason: _____

_____ 2. **Topic:** viruses as a cause of cancer
   Sources:
   a. A textbook titled *Well-Being: An Introduction to Health*
   b. An article in *Scientific American* magazine on controlling viruses
   c. An issue of the *Journal of the American Medical Association* devoted to a review of current research findings on the causes of cancer

   Reason: _____

_____ 3. **Topic:** the effects of aging on learning and memory
   Sources:
   a. An article in *Reader's Digest* titled "Older Means Better"
   b. A psychology textbook titled *A General Introduction to Psychology*
   c. A textbook titled *Adult Development and Aging*

   Reason: _____

IS AN INTERNET SOURCE RELIABLE?

While the Internet contains a great deal of valuable information and resources, it also contains rumor, gossip, hoaxes, and misinformation. In other words, not all Internet sources are trustworthy. You must evaluate a source before accepting it. Unlike print sources, the Internet has no editors or publishers to verify the accuracy of the information presented. As explained in Chapter 11, any individual, company, or organization can put information on a Web site or in a newsgroup posting. Here are some guidelines to follow when evaluating Internet sources.

1. **Check the author.** For Web sites, look for professional credentials or affiliations. If no author is listed, you should be skeptical. For newsgroups or discussion groups, check to see if the author has given his or her name and a signature (a short biographical description included at the end of messages).

2. **Discover the purpose of the posting.** Many Web sites have an agenda such as to sell a product, promote a cause, advocate a position, and so forth. Look for bias in the reporting of information.

3. **Check the date of the posting.** Be sure you are obtaining current information. A Web site usually includes the date on which it was last updated.

4. **Check the sponsoring organization of the site.** If a site is sponsored or provided by a well-known organization, such as a reputable newspaper such as the *New York Times,* the information is apt to be reliable.

5. **Check links (addresses of other sources suggested by the Web site).** If these links are no longer working, the Web site you are visiting may be outdated or not reputable.

6. **Cross-check your information.** Try to find the same information in, ideally, two other sources, especially if the information is vitally important (issues dealing with health, financial discussion, etc.) or if it is at odds with what seems logical or correct.

EXERCISE 14-2	**Directions:** Visit a Web site and become familiar with its organization and content. Evaluate it using the suggested criteria. Then write a brief paragraph explaining why the Web site is or is not a reliable source.

WHAT IS THE AUTHORITY OF THE AUTHOR?

Another clue to the reliability of the information is the author's qualifications. If the author lacks expertise in or experience with a subject, the material may not be accurate or worthwhile reading.

In textbooks, the author's credentials may appear on the title page or in the preface. In nonfiction books and general market paperbacks, a summary of the author's life and credentials may be included on the book jacket or back cover. In many other cases, however, the author's credentials are not given. You are left to rely on the judgment of the editors or publishers about an author's authority.

If you are familiar with an author's work, then you can anticipate the type of material you will be reading and predict the writer's approach and attitude toward the subject. If, for example, you found an article on world banking written by former President Carter, you could predict it will have a political point of view. If you were about to read an article on John Lennon written by Ringo Starr, one of the other Beatles, you could predict the article might possibly include details of their working relationship from Ringo's point of view.

EXERCISE 14-3	**Directions:** Read each statement and choose the individual who would seem to be the best authority on the subject.

_____ 1. *General Hospital* is one of the best soap operas on TV.
    a. Rick Levine, a former producer of *General Hospital*
    b. Sally Hastings, a soap-opera fan for 2 years
    c. Frances Hailey, a TV critic for the *New York Times*

_____ 2. The president's recent news conference was a success.
    a. Peter Jennings, a well-known news commentator
    b. Janet Ferrick, one of the president's advisors
    c. Howard Summers, a professor of economics

_____ 3. Kurt Vonnegut is one of the most important modern American novelists.
    a. James Toth, producer of a TV documentary on Vonnegut's life
    b. John Vilardo, a *Time* magazine columnist
    c. Cynthia Weinstein, a professor of twentieth-century literature at Georgetown University

DOES THE WRITER MAKE ASSUMPTIONS?

An assumption is an idea, theory, or principle that the writer believes to be true. The writer then develops his or her ideas based on that assumption. Of course, if the assumption is not true or is one you disagree with, then the ideas that depend on that assumption are of questionable value. For instance, an author may believe that the death penalty is immoral and, beginning with that assumption, develop an argument for different ways to prevent crime. However, if you believe that the death penalty *is* moral, then from your viewpoint, the writer's argument is invalid.

Read the following paragraph. Identify the assumption the writer makes, and write it in the space provided.

> The evil of athletic violence touches nearly everyone. It tarnishes what may be our only religion. Brutality in games blasphemes play, perhaps our purest form of free expression. It blurs the clarity of open competition, obscuring our joy in victory as well as our dignity in defeat. It robs us of innocence, surprise, and self-respect. It spoils our fun.[1]

Assumption: _____

Here the assumption is stated in the first sentence—the writer assumes that athletic violence exists. He makes no attempt to prove or explain that sports are violent. He assumes this and goes on to discuss its effects. You may agree or disagree with this assumption.

EXERCISE 14-4	**Directions:** For each of the following paragraphs, identify the assumption that is made by the writer and write it in the space provided.

1. Do you have any effective techniques that you use regularly to reduce your level of stress? If not, you may be among the many people who intellectually recognize the dangers of chronic stress—perhaps even have benefited from relaxation exercises—but somehow haven't made stress reduction part of their daily schedule. And you may be especially fascinated by a unique six-second exercise conceived and developed by Charles F. Stroebel, M.D., Ph.D., director of research at The Institute of Living in Hartford, Connecticut, and professor of psychiatry at the University of Connecticut Medical School.[2]

    Assumption: _____

2. Do boys need to rely on heroes more than girls do as sources of identity while growing up? While no one has gathered statistics, it is true that boys are more often called upon to prove themselves through performance. For example, even today, they're often still judged by how well they can kick and throw a ball. So they may have a greater *dependence* on athletes, if only as models to imitate. The baseball/football trading card ritual is still very common among elementary school-age boys; girls, however, have no equivalent for this practice, nor are they rated for their physical accomplishments the same way. Despite today's increasingly "nonsexist" child rearing, girls are still evaluated more on the basis of how they relate to other people than as solitary, achieving individuals.[3]

Assumption: _____

IS THE AUTHOR BIASED?

As you evaluate any piece of writing, always try to decide whether the author is objective or one-sided (biased). Does the author present an objective view of the subject or is a particular viewpoint favored? An objective article presents all sides of an issue, while a biased one presents only one side.

You can decide whether a writer is biased by asking yourself these questions:

1. **Is the writer acting as a reporter—presenting facts—or as a salesperson—providing only favorable information?**
2. **Are there other views toward the subject that the writer does not discuss?**

Use these questions to determine whether the author of the following selection is biased:

Teachers, schools, and parent associations have become increasingly concerned about the effects of television on school performance. Based on their classroom experiences, many teachers have reported mounting incidences of fatigue, tension, and aggressive behavior, as well as lessened spontaneity and imagination.

So what have schools been doing? At Kimberton Farms School in Phoenixville, Pennsylvania, parents and teachers have been following written guidelines for five years which include no television *at all* for children through the first grade. Children in second grade through high school are encouraged to watch no television on school nights and to restrict viewing to a total of three to four hours on weekends. According to Harry Blanchard, head of the faculty, "You can observe the effects with some youngsters almost immediately. . . . Three days after they turn off the set you see a marked improvement in their behavior. They concentrate better, and are more able to follow directions and get along with their neighbors. If they go back to the set you notice it right away."

As Fiske has pointed out, In the final analysis, the success of schools in minimizing the negative effects of television on their (children's) academic progress depends almost entirely on whether the parents share this goal.[4]

The subject of this passage is children's television viewing. It expresses concern and gives evidence that television has a negative effect on children. The other side of the issue—the positive effects or benefits—is not mentioned. There is no discussion of such positive effects as the information to be learned from educational television programs or the use of television in increasing a child's awareness of different ideas, people, and places. The author is biased and expresses only a negative attitude toward television.

Occasionally, you may come upon unintentional bias—bias that the writer is not aware of. A writer may not recognize his or her own bias on cultural, religious, or sexual issues.

IS THE WRITING SLANTED?

Slanting refers to the inclusion of details that suit the author's purpose and the omission of those that do not. Suppose you were asked to write a description of a person you know. If you wanted a reader to respond favorably to the person, you might write something like this:

> Alex is tall, muscular, and well-built. He is a friendly person and seldom becomes angry or upset. He enjoys sharing jokes and stories with his friends.

On the other hand, if you wanted to create a less positive image of Alex, you could omit the above information and emphasize these facts instead:

> Alex has a long nose and his teeth are crooked. He talks about himself a lot and doesn't seem to listen to what others are saying. Alex wears rumpled clothes that are too big for him.

While all of these facts about Alex may be true, the writer decides which to include, and which to omit.

Much of what you read is slanted. For instance, advertisers tell only what is good about a product, not what is wrong with it. In the newspaper advice column, Dear Abby gives her opinion on how to solve a reader's problem, but she does not discuss all the possible solutions.

As you read material that is slanted, keep these questions in mind:

1. What types of facts has the author omitted?
2. How would the inclusion of these facts change your reaction or impression?

EXERCISE 14-5

Directions: Below is a list of different types of writing. For each item, decide whether it has little slant (L), is moderately slanted (M), or is very slanted (V). Write L, M, or V in the space provided.

_____ 1. Help-wanted ads

_____ 2. An encyclopedia entry

_____ 3. A newspaper editorial

_____ 4. A biology textbook

_____ 5. A letter inviting you to apply for a charge account

_____ 6. A college catalog

_____ 7. An autobiography of a famous person

_____ 8. An insurance policy

_____ 9. *Time* magazine

_____ 10. *Catholic Digest* magazine

HOW DOES THE WRITER SUPPORT HIS OR HER IDEAS?

Suppose a friend said he thought you should quit your part-time job immediately. What would you do? Would you automatically accept his advice, or would you ask him why? No doubt you would not blindly accept the advice but would inquire why. Then, having heard his reasons, you would decide whether they made sense.

Similarly, when you read, you should not blindly accept a writer's ideas. Instead, you should ask why by checking to see how the writer supports or explains his or her ideas. Then, once you have examined the supporting information, decide whether you accept the idea.

Evaluating the supporting evidence a writer provides involves using your judgment. The evidence you accept as conclusive may be regarded by someone else as insufficient. The judgment you make depends on your purpose and background knowledge, among other things. In judging the quality of supporting information a writer provides, you should watch for the use of (1) generalizations, (2) personal experience, and (3) statistics as evidence.

Generalizations

What do the following statements have in common?

Dogs are vicious and nasty.

College students are more interested in having fun than in learning.

Parents want their children to grow up to be just like them.

These sentences seem to have little in common. Although the subjects are different, the sentences do have one thing in common: each is a generalization. Each makes a broad statement about a group—dogs, college students, parents. The first statement says that dogs are vicious and nasty. Yet the writer could not be certain that this statement is true unless he or she had seen *every* existing dog. No doubt the writer felt this statement was true based on his or her observation of and experience with dogs.

A generalization is a statement that is made about an entire group or class of individuals or items based on experience with some members of that group. It necessarily involves the writer's judgment.

The question that must be asked about all generalizations is whether they are accurate. How many dogs did the writer observe and how much research did he or she do to justify the generalization? Try to think of exceptions to the generalization; in this instance, a dog that is neither vicious nor nasty.

As you evaluate the supporting evidence a writer uses, be alert for generalizations that are presented as facts. A writer may, on occasion, support a statement by offering unsupported generalizations. When this occurs, treat the writer's ideas with a critical, questioning attitude.

EXERCISE 14-6	**Directions:** Read each of the following statements and decide whether it is a generalization. Place a checkmark next to the statements that are generalizations.

_____ 1. My sister wants to attend the University of Chicago.

_____ 2. Most engaged couples regard their wedding as one of the most important occasions in their lives.

_____ 3. Senior citizens are a cynical and self-interested group.

_____ 4. People do not use drugs unless they perceive them to be beneficial.

_____ 5. Warning signals of a heart attack include pain or pressure in the left side of the chest.

EXERCISE 14-7	**Directions:** Read the following paragraphs and underline each generalization.

1. Teenagers need privacy; it allows them to have a life of their own. By providing privacy, we demonstrate respect. We help them disengage themselves from us and grow up. Some parents pry too much. They read their teenagers' mail and listen in on their telephone calls. Such violations may cause permanent resentment. Teenagers feel cheated and enraged. In their eyes, invasion of privacy is a dishonorable offense. As one girl said: "I am going to sue my mother for malpractice of parenthood. She unlocked my desk and read my diary."[5]

2. Farmers are interested in science, in modern methods, and in theory, but they are not easily thrown off balance and they maintain a healthy suspicion of book learning and of the shenanigans of biologists, chemists, geneticists, and other late-rising students of farm practice and management. They are, I think, impressed by education, but they have seen too many examples of the helplessness and the impracticality of educated persons to be either envious or easily budged from their position.[6]

3. Although the most commonplace reason women marry young is to "complete" themselves, a good many spirited young women gave another reason: "I did it to get away from my parents." Particularly for girls whose educations and privileges are limited, a _jailbreak marriage_ is the usual thing. What might appear to be an act of rebellion usually turns out to be a transfer of dependence.[7]

Personal Experience

Writers often support their ideas by describing their own personal experiences. Although a writer's experiences may be interesting and reveal a perspective on an issue, do not accept them as proof. Suppose you are reading an article on drug use and the writer uses his or her personal experience with particular drugs to prove a point. There are several reasons why you should not accept the writer's conclusions about the drugs' effects as fact. First, the effects of a drug may vary from person to person. The drugs' effects on the writer may be unusual. Second, unless the writer kept careful records about times, dosages, surrounding circumstances, and so on, he or she is describing events from memory. Over time, the writer may have forgotten or exaggerated some of the effects. As you read, treat ideas supported only through personal experience as *one person's experience*. Do not make the error of generalizing the experience.

Statistics

People are often impressed by **statistics**— figures, percentages, averages, and so forth. They accept these as absolute proof. Actually, statistics can be misused, misinterpreted, or used selectively to give other than the most objective, accurate picture of a situation.

Here is an example of how statistics can be misused. Suppose you read that magazine *A* increased its readership by 50 percent, while magazine *B* had only a 10 percent increase. From this statistic, some readers might assume that magazine *A* has a wider readership than magazine *B*. The missing but crucial statistic is the total readership of each magazine prior to the increase. If magazine *A* had a readership of 20,000 and this increased by 50 percent, its readership would total 30,000. If magazine *B*'s readership was already 50,000, a 10 percent increase, bringing the new total to 55,000, would still give it the larger readership despite the smaller increase. Even statistics, then, must be read with a critical, questioning mind.

Here is another example:

> Americans in the workforce are better off than ever before. The average salary of the American worker is $23,000.

At first the above statement may seem convincing. However, a closer look reveals that the statistic given does not really support the statement. The term *average* is the key to how the statistic is misused. An average includes all salaries, both high and low. It is possible that some Americans earn $4,000 while others earn $250,000. Although the average salary may be $23,000, this does not mean that everyone earns $23,000.

EXERCISE 14-8	**Directions:** Read each of the following statements and decide how the statistic is misused. Write your explanation in the space provided.

1. Classrooms on our campus are not overcrowded. There are ten square feet of floor space for every student, faculty member, and staff member on campus.

2. More than 12,000 people have bought Lincoln Town Cars this year, so it is a popular car.

3. The average water pollution by our local industries is well below the hazardous level established by the Environmental Protection Agency.

IS IT FACT OR OPINION?

Facts are statements that can be verified. They can be proven true or false. **Opinions** are statements that express a writer's feelings, attitudes, or beliefs. They are neither true nor false. Here are a few examples of each:

Facts
1. My car insurance costs $1500.
2. The theory of instinct was formulated by Konrad Lorenz.
3. Greenpeace is an organization dedicated to preserving the sea and its animals.

Opinions

1. My car insurance is too expensive.
2. The slaughter of baby seals for their pelts should be outlawed.
3. Population growth should be regulated through mandatory birth control.

The ability to distinguish between fact and opinion is an essential part of evaluating an author's supporting information. Factual statements from reliable sources can usually be accepted as correct. Opinions, however, must be considered as one person's viewpoint that you are free to accept or reject.

EXERCISE 14-9

Directions: Identify and mark each of the following statements as either fact or opinion.

_____ 1. Alligators provide no physical care for their young.

_____ 2. Humans should be concerned about the use of pesticides that kill insects at the bottom of the food chain.

_____ 3. There are 28 more humans living on the earth now than there were ten seconds ago.

_____ 4. We must bear greater responsibility for the environment than our ancestors did.

_____ 5. Nuclear power is the only viable solution to our dwindling natural resources.

_____ 6. Between 1850 and 1900 the death rate in Europe decreased due to industrial growth and advances in medicine.

_____ 7. Dogs make the best pets because they can be trained to obey.

_____ 8. Solar energy is available wherever sunlight reaches the earth.

_____ 9. By the year 2010, many diseases, including cancer, will be preventable.

_____ 10. Hormones are produced in one part of the body and carried by the blood to another part of the body where they influence some process or activity.

Judgment Words

When a writer or speaker expresses an opinion he or she often uses words or phrases that can tip you off that a judgment or opinion is being offered. Here are a few examples.

Professor Rodriguez is a *better* teacher than Professor Harrigan.

My sister's behavior at the party was *disgusting*.

Here is a list of words that often suggests that the writer is interpreting, judging or evaluating, or expressing feelings.

bad	good	worthless	amazing	frightening
worse	better	worthwhile	wonderful	
worst	best	disgusting	lovely	

EXERCISE 14-10

Directions: For each of the following statements underline the word or phrases that suggest the statement is an opinion.

1. Purchasing a brand new car is a terrible waste of money.

2. Many wonderful vegetarian cookbooks are available in bookstores.

3. Of all the film versions of Victor Hugo's novel *Les Miserables,* the 1935 version starring Charles Laughton is the best.

4. The introductory biology textbook comes with an amazing CD-ROM.

5. Volunteers for Habitat for Humanity are engaged in a worthwhile activity.

Informed Opinion

The opinion of experts is known as **informed opinion.** For example, the Surgeon General is regarded as an authority on the health of Americans and his or her opinion on this subject is more trustworthy than casual observers or non-professionals.

Here are a few examples of expert opinions.

- Diana Baumrind, a psychologist at the University of California at Berkeley: "*Occasional spankings do not damage a child's social or emotional development.*"
- Alan Greenspan, Chair of the Federal Reserve Board: "*The period of sub-par economic performance is not yet over.*"
- Jane Goodall, primate expert and ethologist: "*Chimps are in massive danger of extinction from dwindling habitats—forests are being cut down at an alarming rate.*"

Textbook authors, too, often offer informed opinion. As experts in their fields, they may make observations and offer comments that are not strictly factual. Instead, they are based on years of study and research. Here is an example from an American government textbook:

> The United States is a place where the pursuit of private, particular, and narrow interests is honored. In our culture, following the teachings of Adam Smith, the pursuit of self-interest is not only permitted but actually celebrated as the basis of the good and prosperous society.[8]

The author of this statement has reviewed the available evidence and is providing his expert opinion on what the evidence indicates about American political culture. The reader, then, is free to disagree and offer evidence to support an opposing view.

Some authors are careful to signal the reader when they are presenting an opinion. Watch for words and phrases such as:

apparently	this suggests	in my view	one explanation is
presumably	possibly	it is likely that	according to
in my opinion	it is believed	seemingly	

Other authors do just the opposite; they try to make opinions sound like facts.

In the following excerpt from a social problems textbook, notice how the author carefully distinguishes factual statements from opinion by using qualifying words and phrases (underlined here for easy identification).

Economic Change, Ideology, and Private Life

It seems clear that there has been a major change in attitudes and feelings about family relationships since the eighteenth century. It is less clear how and why the change came about. One question debated by researchers is: In what social class did the new family pattern originate—in the aristocracy, as Trumbach (1978) believes, or in the upper gentry, as Stone (1977) argued, or in the working class, as Shorter (1975) contended? Or was the rise of the new domesticity a cultural phenomenon that affected people in all social categories at roughly the same time? Carole Shammas (1980) <u>has found evidence</u> of such a widespread cultural change by looking at the kinds of things people had in their homes at various times in the past, as recorded in probate inventories. She found that in the middle of the eighteenth century all social classes experienced a change in living habits; even working-class households now contained expensive tools of domesticity, such as crockery, teapots, eating utensils, and so on. Thus, <u>according to Shammas</u>, the home was becoming an important center for social interaction, and family meals had come to occupy an important place in people's lives.[9]

EXERCISE 14-11

Directions: Read each of the following statements. In each, underline the word or phrase that suggests that the author is offering an informed opinion.

---

1. It seems clear that parents who would bring a young child to an R-rated movie are putting their own interests ahead of what's best for the child.

2. Voters rejected the proposed rapid transit system connecting the southern and northern suburbs, possibly because of racial issues.

3. According to the city superintendent of schools, school uniforms lead to improved behavior and fewer disruptions in the classroom.

4. One explanation for low attendance at professional sporting events is the high price of tickets.

5. It is believed that most people practice some form of recycling in their daily lives.

EXERCISE 14-12

Directions: Each of the following paragraphs contains both fact and opinion. Read each paragraph and label each sentence as fact or opinion.

Paragraph 1. [1]Flowering plants that are native to the South include purple coneflower and rose verbena. [2]In the view of many longtime gardeners, these two plants are an essential part of the Southern landscape. [3]Trees that are native to the South include a variety of oaks, as well as flowering dogwoods and redbuds. [4]Dogwoods are especially lovely, with their white, pink, or coral blossoms announcing the arrival of spring. ^{5}For fall color, the deep red of Virginia willow makes a spectacular show in the native Southern garden.

Sentences:

1. _____

2. _____

3. _____

4. _____

5. _____

Paragraph 2. ^{1}Today, many companies provide child care assistance, either on- or off-site, for their employees. ^{2}This suggests that employers are becoming aware that their workers' family concerns can affect the company's bottom line. ^{3}The Eli Lilly pharmaceutical company, for example, has built two child-development centers with a total capacity of more than 400 children. ^{4}In addition to assistance with daily child care, Bank of America reimburses employees for child-care expenses related to business travel. ^{5}It seems clear that other, less progressive employers will have to follow these companies' leads in order to attract and retain the best employees.

Sentences:

1. _____

2. _____

3. _____

4. _____

5. _____

Paragraph 3. ^{1}Preparing a will is an important task that millions of people ignore, presumably because they prefer not to think about their own death. ^{2}However, if you die without a will, the courts will determine how your assets should be distributed, as directed by state law. ^{3}Even more important than establishing a will, in my opinion, is expressing your willingness to be an organ donor upon your death. ^{4}Each year, 25,000 new patients are added to the waiting list for organ transplants. [5]The legacy of an organ donor is far more valuable than any material assets put in a will.

Sentences:

1. _____

2. _____

3. _____

4. _____

5. _____

DOES THE WRITER MAKE VALUE JUDGMENTS?

A writer who states that an idea or action is right or wrong, good or bad, desirable or undesirable is making a **value judgment.** That is, the writer is imposing his or her own judgment on the worth of an idea or action. Here are a few examples of value judgments:

Divorces should be restricted to couples who can prove incompatibility.

Abortion is wrong.

Welfare applicants should be forced to apply for any job they are capable of performing.

Premarital sex is acceptable.

You will notice that each statement is controversial. Each involves some type of conflict or idea over which there is disagreement:

1. Restriction versus freedom
2. Right versus wrong
3. Force versus choice
4. Acceptability versus nonacceptability

You may know of some people who would agree and others who might disagree with each statement. A writer who takes a position or side on a conflict is making a value judgment.

As you read, be alert for value judgments. They represent one person's view *only* and there are most likely many other views on the same topic. When you identify a value judgment, try to determine whether the author offers any evidence in support of the position.

EXERCISE 14-13	**Directions:** Read the following selection and answer the questions that follow.

A Welfare Mother

1   I start my day here at five o'clock. I get up and prepare all the children's clothes. If there's shoes to shine, I do it in the morning. About seven o'clock I bathe the children. I leave the baby with the baby sitter and I go to work at the settlement house. I work until twelve o'clock. Sometimes I'll work longer if I have to go to welfare and get a check for somebody. When I get back, I try to make hot food for the kids to eat. In the afternoon it's pretty well on my own. I scrub and clean and cook and do whatever I have to do.

2   Welfare makes you feel like you're nothing. Like you're laying back and not doing anything and it's falling in your lap. But you must understand, mothers, too, work. My house is clean. I've been scrubbing since this morning. You could check my clothes, all washed and ironed. I'm home and I'm working. I am a working mother.

3   A job that a woman in a house is doing is a tedious job—especially if you want to do it right. If you do it slipshod, then it's not so bad. I'm pretty much of a perfectionist. I tell my kids, hang a towel. I don't want it thrown away. That is very hard. It's a constant game of picking up this, picking up that. And putting this away, so the house'll be clean.

4   Some men work eight hours a day. There are mothers that work eleven, twelve hours a day. We get up at night, a baby vomits, you have to be calling the doctor, you have to be changing the baby. When do you get a break, really? You don't. This is an all-around job, day and night. Why do they say it's charity? We're working for our money. I am working for this check. It is not charity. We are giving some kind of home to these children.

5   I'm so busy all day I don't have time to daydream. I pray a lot. I pray to God to give me strength. If He should take a child away from me, to have the strength to accept it. It's His kid. He just borrowed him to me.

6   I used to get in and close the door. Now I speak up for my right. I walk with my head up. If I want to wear big earrings, I do. If I'm overweight, that's too bad. I've gotten completely over feeling where I'm little. I'm working now, I'm pulling my weight. I'm gonna get off welfare in time, that's my goal—get off.

7   It's living off welfare and feeling that you're taking something for nothing the way people have said. You get to think maybe you are. You get to think, Why am I so stupid? Why can't I work? Why do I have to live this way? It's not enough to live on anyway. You feel degraded.

8   The other day I was at the hospital and I went to pay my bill. This nurse came and gave me the green card. Green card is for welfare. She went right in front of me and gave it to the cashier. She said, "I wish I could stay home and let the money fall in my lap." I felt rotten. I was just burning inside. You hear this all the way around you. The doctor doesn't even look at you. People are ashamed to show that green card. Why can't a woman just get a check in the mail: Here, this check is for you. Forget welfare. You're a mother who works.

9   This nurse, to her way of thinking, she represents the working people. The ones with the green card, we represent the lazy no-goods. This is what she was saying. They're the good ones and we're the bad guys.[10]

1. What do you think is the source of this selection?

    _____

    _____

2. Do you consider this welfare mother to be an authority? Why or why not?

    _____

3. What assumptions does this welfare mother make? Do you agree or disagree? Why?

    _____

    _____

4. Do you think this view of a welfare mother is biased? Why or why not?

    _____

5. Is the writing in this article slanted? If so, give some examples.

    _____

6. How does this welfare mother support her ideas?

    _____

7. Does this welfare mother make any value judgments? If so, what are they?

_____

8. Does this welfare mother make any generalizations? If so, underline them.

_____

EXERCISE 14-14	**Directions:** Read the following article and answer the questions that follow.

The War on Children's Culture

1 My 9-year-old daughter, Emma, and her friends have recently developed an inverse rating system. If grown-ups don't like a children's movie or TV show, it's worth considering. Anything adult critics absolutely hate is a must-see.

2 In recent years, as children's culture has become enormously diverse and lucrative, movie and television critics have become the disapproving voice of the adult world, transmitting to Nintendo-playing, comic book-reading, video-game playing children an unrelenting barrage of contempt.

3 "We don't really care for what adults see, and they don't like what we see," says Emma's friend Ben, who is 12.

4 No. Kids wouldn't be caught dead showing interest in grown-up movies or programs. But the adult world takes its child-rearing responsibilities seriously and *does* pay attention to what kids do and watch. The result is an undeclared and, in some ways, disturbing war on broad aspects of children's culture. . . .

5 Some sort of truce seems in order. It feels inappropriate to be engaged in cultural warfare with our children. When we are so relentlessly contemptuous of their culture, the signals must seem especially confusing. If this stuff is so horrible, why do all their friends like it, and how come we let them watch it? If it isn't horrible, how come everyone says it is?

6 Television, perhaps because it's beamed right into our living rooms, and because parents fear their inability to control it, is the target of many of these assaults. TV is portrayed as the corrupting demon, munching away at young brain cells.

7 Often, the media seem to find it a primary function to warn children about the very things they most enjoy, rather than to explore or explain or defend it. Dozens of newspapers and magazines ran critical reviews of one or the other of the two "Turtles" movies and many more published articles or editorials deploring their violence. Yet both movies were instant hits, smashes, with the audiences they were intended—for the young. Kids I've asked about this disparity all have the same response: adults just don't get it. . . .

If You Hate It, They Love It

8   Meanwhile, the list of anti-kid-culture flashpoints is growing longer all the time. From the start, "The Simpsons" on the Fox network has been criticized by some educational and parent groups—even the former Secretary of Education, William Bennett—because of its often blistering portrayals of educators, schools and parental authority.

9   A number of schools have banned "Underachiever and Proud of It" T-shirts with Bart's likeness. It's a tactic that can backfire. When a middle-school student in the suburb I live in was sent home because of his "I'm Bart Simpson: Who the Hell Are You?" T-shirt, Simpson-watching by my daughter and her buddies went from an occasional amusement to an almost religious ritual.

10   This is familiar ground for my generation. After reading an article in the 1950's warning that Buddy Holly's songs fostered disrespect for authority, my father put the offending records aside until I was older and, presumably, less impressionable. I lost none of my enthusiasm for Buddy Holly. . . .

What's a Parent to Do?

11   Adults might stand a better chance of helping to define their children's values by making perhaps the ultimate sacrifice—watching with them. It goes against the grain: television is one of the few things small children are happy to do by themselves and for long periods, which encourages children being left alone with it.

12   But children's own critical instincts might grow if, rather than sneering, parents were sitting with them in front of the VCR, comparing differences in animation, plot, character development and humor. My wife changed my daughter's perception of the early Disney movies considerably when she pointed out that the women in them seemed to always need rescuing—something my daughter hadn't noticed and was not appreciative of once she did. The two are still fighting, in fact, about whether the Little Mermaid should have left her aquatic world behind for her One True Love or made the prince come to hers.

13   In subsequent movies, Emma has become especially conscious of how women are portrayed. One thing she strongly disliked about the first Turtle movie, in fact, was that April O'Neill, the female (human) reporter, also needed rescuing. Meanwhile, we've largely banned the purchase of toys and products related to TV or films, arguing that a story and its characters must be appreciated—or not—on its own merits, not because of the things you can buy.

14   The range and diversity of children's entertainment makes it difficult to control, especially for hard-pressed parents, more of whom are working longer hours all the time. Children, like their parents, have become little entertainment moguls with access to scores of choices. If they can't access the full range of choices at home, odds are they can down the street at their buddies' houses.

15   Children seem to be infinitely more accepting than adults of what they see, more inclined to like a movie or television program than not. They frequently

resent cultural offerings that seem preachy or stodgily educational. And they have keen noses for hypocrisy. "Makes the Turtles look like the Care Bears," sniffed Emma, when she saw a preview in a movie theater for "The Silence of the Lambs." It's not like their parents are listening to classical music all night, either. . . .

Here Today, Here Tomorrow

16   Whatever else happens to children's culture, parents and other adults can count on one thing: television—the things you can watch on it, the things you can plug into it, and all its other controversial offshoots—will continue to grow. Condemnation alone seems a poor strategy for responding to the technology that has given children more tantalizing choices to make than any generation in history.[11]

1. What is the main point of the article?

    _____

    _____

2. What is the author's attitude toward children's culture?

    _____

    _____

3. This article appeared in the *New York Times*. Evaluate it as source for:

    a.   a sociology term paper

    b.   parents who want to learn more about children's culture

    _____

    _____

4. Is the article biased? Explain your answer.

    _____

5. What types of supporting evidence does the author provide? Mark several examples of each type in the article.

_____

_____

6. What assumptions does the author make?

_____

_____

7. Describe the tone of the article.

_____

WORKING TOGETHER

Directions: Bring to class a brief (two- to three-paragraph) newspaper article, editorial, film review, etc. Working in groups of three to four students, each student should read his or her piece aloud. The group can then discuss and evaluate (1) assumptions, (2) bias, (3) slanted writing, (4) methods of support, and (5) value judgments for each article. Each group should choose one representative article and submit its findings to the class or instructor.

Learning Style Tips

If you tend to be a . . .	Then build your critical reading skills by . . .
Creative learner	Asking "What if . . .?" and "So what?" questions to free new ideas and new ways of looking at the subject
Pragmatic learner	Writing marginal notes, recording your thoughts, reactions, and impressions

MASTERING VOCABULARY

Directions: Match each word in Column A with its meaning in Column B. Determine the meaning from its context in this chapter, its word parts, or use a dictionary, if necessary.

	Column A		Column B
_____	1. diverse (p. 492)	a.	described
_____	2. lucrative (p. 492)	b.	easily influenced
_____	3. unrelenting (p. 492)	c.	varied
_____	4. contemptuous (p. 492)	d.	two-facedness
_____	5. portrayed (p. 492)	e.	profitable
_____	6. disparity (p. 492)	f.	hateful
_____	7. impressionable (p. 493)	g.	later
_____	8. appreciative (p. 493)	h.	difference
_____	9. subsequent (p. 493)	i.	constant
_____	10. hypocrisy (p. 494)	j.	grateful

SELF-TEST SUMMARY

How can I evaluate what I read?

In order to evaluate what you read, ask yourself nine questions:

1. What is the source of the material?
2. Is an Internet source reliable?
3. What is the authority of the author?
4. Does the author make assumptions?
5. Is the author biased?
6. Is the writing slanted?
7. How does the author support his or her ideas?
8. Is it fact or opinion?
9. Does the author make value judgments?

Name _____

Section _____ Date _____

Number right _____ x 20 points = Score _____

Directions: Read each sentence and decide whether it can best be described as a fact, an opinion, an informed opinion, or a generalization.

_____ 1. Although the President nominates individuals to fill positions on the Supreme Court, the nomination must be confirmed by a majority vote in the Senate.
a. fact
b. opinion
c. informed opinion
d. generalization

_____ 2. A five-ounce cup of regular brewed coffee contains almost twice as much caffeine as a six-ounce cup of hot steeped tea.
a. fact
b. opinion
c. informed opinion
d. generalization

_____ 3. There should be a law against using a cell phone while driving.
a. fact
b. opinion
c. informed opinion
d. generalization

_____ 4. Australians are friendly and gregarious people.
a. fact
b. opinion
c. informed opinion
d. generalization

_____ 5. According to child psychologist Lawrence Kohlberg, the moral development of children takes place in three stages: preconventional morality, conventional morality, and postconventional (or principled) morality.
a. fact
b. opinion
c. informed opinion
d. generalization

CHAPTER 14 MASTERY TEST 2: Critical Reading Skills

Name _____

Section _____ Date _____

Number right _____ x 20 points = Score _____

Directions: Read each of the passages below and answer the questions that follow.

Passage 1: Tuition vouchers have been proposed as a way to improve the quality of public schools. Under a tuition voucher program, the government gives parents of school-age children a set amount of money to pay for school tuition. Parents can use the money at either a public or private school. In order to attract students, public schools will have to improve their meager offerings dramatically; competition from more adaptive private schools will force public schools to wake up and pay better attention to the needs of students.[12]

_____ 1. The author's bias is revealed in the
   a. first sentence.
   b. second sentence.
   c. third sentence.
   d. last sentence.

Passage 2: Although the President's wife does not have an official government position, each First Lady of the past forty years has become known for her attention to a particular issue. For example, Lady Bird Johnson supported highway beautification, Rosalyn Carter was a mental health advocate, Barbara Bush promoted literacy, and Hillary Rodham Clinton was involved in health care reform during her husband's first term. During her husband's second term, however, Ms. Clinton took advantage of her position to launch her own political career as a U.S. senator. In doing so, Ms. Clinton became the first First Lady to run for political office.[13]

_____ 2. The only sentence in this paragraph that contains an opinion is the
   a. first sentence.
   b. second sentence.
   c. third sentence.
   d. last sentence.

Passage 3: Traveling through Europe presents countless opportunities to meet people from other countries. Unfortunately, many of them don't speak English. Of course, that's part of the fun, as I discovered when I went to Europe as a senior in high school. My efforts to communicate with a Greek sailor, an Italian bus driver, and an Austrian bank teller at various times during that trip convinced me that with persistence, and a sense of humor, you can usually make yourself understood. It's not so important to be able to say the words correctly or to say them with the right accent, and it truly does not help to say the same words slowly and loudly. What works best, both abroad *and* at home, is to say them with a smile.

_____ 3. The author supports the ideas in this paragraph primarily with
   a. statistics.
   b. personal experience.
   c. generalizations.
   d. facts.

Passage 4: Welfare and related programs are expensive. Our country has amassed a large public debt, partially due to past spending on social services. Each year, welfare spending continues to increase. Despite the costs of welfare, it is unfair to blame welfare recipients for the past debt problems welfare programs created.

_____ 4. The statement in this paragraph that is a value judgment is the
   a. first sentence.
   b. second sentence.
   c. third sentence.
   d. last sentence.

Passage 5: Most of us believe that racism is a bad thing. However, when we are at a party or in another social setting where someone tells a racist joke, we often find it difficult to voice our objections. Why is that? Are we against racism only when it is convenient or easy? Our dilemma is that we see ourselves two ways: as polite people who would never purposely embarrass a friend or even an acquaintance, and as socially aware individuals who know racist comments are wrong. This moral inconsistency is even more troubling when we become parents and must serve as role models for our children. How do we explain the difference between "right" and "polite"—or is there really a difference?

_____ 5. The assumption that the author makes in this paragraph is that most people
   a. would rather not embarrass another person.
   b. believe children know right from wrong.
   c. want their children to behave properly at parties.
   d. enjoy racist jokes.

**CHAPTER 14
MASTERY TEST 3:
Critical Reading Skills**

Name _____

Section _____ Date _____

Number right _____ x 10 points = Score _____

Selection 1

Directions: Read the passage below and choose the letter that best answers each of the questions that follow.

Having built four new elementary schools in the last five years, members of the Palmville School Board were convinced they had solved the problem with overcrowding that had plagued the public schools ever since the mid-1980s. As a result, they were disappointed when School Superintendent Marisa LaRoux made her mid-July Projected Enrollment Report. She pointed out that the town's population has expanded by several hundred more families than were projected because the good weather this year spurred home building and the low mortgage rates encouraged buyers. In addition, more families are deciding to have two or more children, bringing the average number of children per family to 1.9, much higher than the figure of 1.65 used in the past to calculate demands for school services. The superintendent also admitted that the decades-old policy of calculating a family of two as a family without children has proven to be a serious mistake because it ignored the many children growing up in single-parent families. Based on this information, the superintendent concluded that the overcrowding problem would continue this year and probably for many years in the future. Chairperson Clifton Washington summed up the school board's response this way: "The schools are overcrowded now and if more students are going to be coming to us asking for instruc-

tion, then we'd better get back into the school-building business."

_____ 1. Which of the following types of evidence does the school superintendent use in her report?
a. opinions
b. personal experiences
c. facts and statistics
d. generalizations

_____ 2. Which of the following is a value judgment that the school board seems to have made?
a. Public school boards should not study projected enrollments.
b. Previous enrollment studies were always wrong.
c. Overcrowding in schools helps education.
d. Education and schools are important.

_____ 3. Which of the following sentences is *not* an assumption used by the school board when they studied school enrollment in the past?
a. A household of two people does not have any children.
b. The average number of children per family was 1.9.
c. Low mortgage rates encourage home buying.
d. Good weather increased new home building.

_____ 4. Which of the following, if added to the evidence, would *not* support the author's ideas?
   a. Reducing overcrowding is a good idea because students usually learn better in less crowded classrooms.
   b. The recent plant closing in the area has forced many people to move away from Palmville.
   c. All the teachers support building new schools over expanding the school year.
   d. If we build new schools, the best teachers will apply for the new jobs.

_____ 5. Which of the following is a conclusion reached by the school board?
   a. They need to build more schools.
   b. Schools will always be overcrowded.
   c. Four new elementary schools would solve overcrowding.
   d. Most families in the area have more than two children.

Selection 2

Directions: Read the passage below and choose the letter that best answers the questions that follow.

The latest state proposal to divert more water from agricultural to residential uses might be expected to gain support from rapidly urbanizing Palmville. Speaking through their Town Meeting, however, the citizens of the town argue that the state should not meddle with arrangements that have con- tributed so much to the economic and social health of the region. The report of the Town Meeting contained these arguments: (1) Farming in the Palmville area constitutes an important element in the state's food supply, which would be expensive to replace. (2) Farms and support industries provide a large proportion of the jobs of Palmville residents. (3) The farms are an important part of the social fabric of the town and the region, pro- viding, among other things, healthful summer employment for many of the town's youth. (4) Diverting water from the farms would cause many to be sold to real estate developers, thus increasing the population *and* the demand for water. (5) The town's zoning plan will limit growth over the next decade and should slow the increasing demand for water. Whether state officials will be persuaded by these arguments remains to be seen, but Palmville residents hope to prevent changes that might threaten the community they have built so carefully.

_____ 1. Which of the following types of evidence do the town citizens rely on in their arguments?
   a. statistics
   b. personal experiences
   c. facts
   d. generalizations

(*continued*)

_____ 2. Which of the following value judgments seems to be the reason behind the arguments by the Palmville citizens?
a. Residential areas are more important than farm areas.
b. Proposals by the state should be supported.
c. Changes will destroy the community.
d. Water is not important to Palmville.

_____ 3. Which of the following sentences is an assumption (rather than an argument) made by the citizens?
a. Farms are important to the town.
b. The town's zoning plan will limit growth over the next decade.
c. Farms and support industries provide jobs for Palmville residents.
d. Farms provide summer employment for youths from Palmville.

_____ 4. Which of the following sentences would _not_ provide evidence for the Palmville citizens' ideas?
a. The state proposals should not be supported because this is a local issue.
b. Fewer farms will probably increase unemployment in the area.
c. Because farms are beautiful, they are productive.
d. Diverting the water will cause taxes to rise.

_____ 5. Which of the following is supported by the evidence presented by the citizens of Palmville?
a. State officials will be persuaded by the citizens' arguments.
b. Change will occur even if Palmville residents fight it.
c. Farming around Palmville is an important part of the economy of the region.
d. The town's zoning plan is worse than the state's latest proposal.

Name _____

Section _____ Date _____

Number right _____ x 10 points = Score _____

Arming Myself With a Gun Is Not the Answer

Bronwyn Jones

After a terrifying experience with a stalker, the author discusses why she chooses not to protect herself with a gun. This article first appeared in *Newsweek* magazine in 2000.

Vocabulary Preview

harried (par. 1) stressful, busy, rushed

idyllic (par. 1) simple and peaceful

incoherently (par. 3) not expressed clearly or logically

avid (par. 5) enthusiastic

paranoia (par. 8) feelings of persecution or extreme distrust of others

corrupt (par. 8) to ruin or spoil the integrity of something

deterrent (par. 9) something that prevents or discourages an action

incarcerated (par. 11) jailed or imprisoned

1   When my father died 15 years ago, my brother and I inherited the old Midwestern farmhouse our grandparents had purchased in the 1930s. I was the one who decided to give up my harried existence as a teacher in New York City and make a life in this idyllic village, population 350, in northern Michigan.

2   A full-time job in the English department of a nearby college quickly followed. I settled into small-town life, charmed by a community where your neighbors are also your friends and no one worries about locking a door. Eventually I forgot about the big-city stress of crowds, noise and crime.

3   I felt safe enough to keep my phone number listed so colleagues and students could reach me after hours. I was totally unprepared when I returned home one evening to an answering machine filled with incoherently and horribly threatening messages. I could identify the voice—it belonged to a former student of mine. Shocked and frightened I called 911, and an officer arrived in time to pick up the phone and hear the man threaten to rape and kill me. The cop recognized the caller as the stalker in a similar incident that had been reported a few years before, and immediately rushed me out of the house. I soon learned that my would-be assailant had been arrested, according to police, drunk, armed with a 19-inch double-edged knife and just minutes from my door.

4   It was revealed in court testimony that my stalker was a schizophrenic who had fallen through the cracks of the mental-health system. In spite of my 10-year personal-protection order, I live with the fear that he will return unsupervised to my community. Time and again, colleagues and friends have urged me to get a gun to protect myself.

5   And why shouldn't I? This part of rural Michigan is hometown to an avid gun culture. Nov. 15, the opening day of deer-hunting season, is all but an official holiday. It is

not uncommon to see the bumper sticker CHARLTON HESTON IS MY PRESIDENT displayed, along with a gun rack on the back of local pickup trucks.

6   A good friend recommended several different handguns. The assistant prosecutor on the case told me I'd have no problem getting a concealed-weapon permit. A female deputy offered to teach me how to shoot.

7   But I haven't gotten a gun, and I'm not going to. When I questioned them, my friends and colleagues had to admit that they've used guns only for recreational purposes, never for self-defense. The assistant prosecutor said that he would never carry a concealed weapon himself. And an ex-cop told me that no matter how much you train, the greatest danger is of hurting yourself.

8   The truth is when you keep a gun for self-protection, you live with constant paranoia. For me, owning a gun and practicing at a target range would be allowing my sense of victimization to corrupt my deepest values.

9   Contrary to all the pro-gun arguments, I don't believe guns are innocent objects. If they were, "gunnies" wouldn't display them as badges of security and freedom. When someone waves a gun around, he or she is advertising the power to snuff out life. But guns are no deterrent. Like nuclear weapons, they only ensure greater devastation when conflict breaks out or the inevitable human error occurs.

10   I never needed a weapon in the years prior to my terrifying experience. And while I learned not to flinch at the sight of men and women in fluorescent orange carrying rifles into the woods at the start of deer season, owning a gun for play or protection didn't occur to me. But I've learned firsthand that even small, close-knit communities are subject to the kind of social problems—like disintegrating families and substance abuse—that can propel a troubled person toward violence. So I now carry pepper spray and my cell phone at all times.

11   In Michigan—and elsewhere—as federal funding for state mental-health care continues to shrink and state psychiatric hospitals are forced to close, the numbers of untreated, incarcerated and homeless mentally ill are rising. People with serious mental illness and violent tendencies need 24-hour care. It costs less to house them in group homes with trained counselors than it does to keep them in prisons or hospitals. But until states fund more of this kind of care, people like my stalker will continue to return unsupervised to our communities.

12   And people like me will be forced to consider getting guns to protect ourselves. I am lucky. I survived, though not unchanged. I know my fear cannot be managed with a gun. The only reasonable response is to do what I can to help fix the mental-health system. Awareness, education and proper funding will save more lives and relieve more fears than all the guns we can buy.

Directions: Choose the letter that best answers each of the following questions.

CHECKING YOUR COMPREHENSION

_____ 1. The main point of this selection is that
  a. small towns are just as dangerous as big cities.
  b. mentally ill people belong in 24-hour care facilities.
  c. today's culture promotes gun ownership.
  d. keeping a gun for self-protection was not a solution for the author.

_____ 2. The main idea of paragraph 2 is that the author
  a. missed living in New York City.
  b. worked in the English department.
  c. felt safe living in the small town.
  d. made many new friends in the small town.

_____ 3. The person who threatened the author was
  a. a complete stranger.
  b. an ex-boyfriend from New York City.
  c. a former student.
  d. an escaped convict.

_____ 4. As a result of being threatened, the author decided to
  a. carry a gun for protection.
  b. move back to New York City.
  c. carry pepper spray and a cell phone at all times.
  d. take shooting lessons from a female deputy.

_____ 5. The main idea of paragraph 11 is that
  a. group homes, not prisons, are the proper place for mentally ill people.
  b. communities are endangered by the lack of funding for mental-health care.
  c. states should enact stricter laws against stalking.
  d. even small towns are subject to violence.

_____ 6. The term "gunnies" in paragraph 9 refers to
  a. hunters.
  b. criminals.
  c. police officers.
  d. gun owners.

APPLYING YOUR SKILLS

_____ 7. The author's bias is revealed in the statement
  a. "A good friend recommended several different handguns."
  b. "This part of Michigan is home to an avid gun culture."
  c. "Time and again, colleagues and friends have urged me to get a gun to protect myself."
  d. "Contrary to all the pro-gun arguments, I don't believe guns are innocent objects."

_____ 8. The author supports her ideas primarily through
  a. facts.
  b. personal experience.
  c. statistics.
  d. generalizations.

(continued)

_____ 9. Of the following sentences from the selection, the only one that is a *fact* is
   a. "When my father died 15 years ago, my brother and I inherited the old Midwestern farmhouse our grandparents had purchased in the 1930s."
   b. "And why should I?"
   c. "I know my fear cannot be managed with a gun."
   d. "The truth is when you keep a gun for self-protection, you live with constant paranoia."

_____ 10. Of the following sentences from the selection, the only one that is an *opinion* is
   a. "But guns are no deterrent."
   b. "The cop recognized the caller as the stalker in a similar incident that had been reported a few years before."
   c. "It was revealed in court testimony that my stalker was a schizophrenic."
   d. "November 15 [is] the opening day of deer-hunting season."

Go Electronic!
For additional readings, exercises, and Internet activities, visit this book's Web site at:

http://www.awlonline.com/mcwhorter

If you need a user name and password, please see your instructor.

Take a Road Trip to the American Southwest!
Be sure to visit the Inference module in your Reading Road Trip CD-ROM for multimedia tutorials, exercises, and tests.

READING AND INTERPRETING SHORT STORIES

A short story is a creative or imaginative work describing a series of events for the purpose of entertainment and/or communicating a serious message. It has six basic elements. The next section describes each. But first, read the following short story, "The Story of an Hour," and then refer back to it as you read about each of the six elements.

The Story of an Hour

Kate Chopin

1   Knowing that Mrs. Mallard was afflicted with heart trouble, great care was taken to break to her as gently as possible the news of her husband's death.

2   It was her sister Josephine who told her, in broken sentences; veiled hints that revealed in half concealing. Her husband's friend Richards was there, too, near her. It was he who had been in the newspaper office when intelligence of the railroad

disaster was received, with Brently Mallard's name leading the list of "killed." He had only taken the time to assure himself of its truth by a second telegram, and had hastened to forestall any less careful, less tender friend in bearing the sad message.

3   She did not hear the story as many women have heard the same, with a paralyzed inability to accept its significance. She wept at once, with sudden, wild abandonment, in her sister's arms. When the storm of grief had spent itself she went away to her room alone. She would have no one follow her.

4   There stood, facing the open window, a comfortable, roomy armchair. Into this she sank, pressed down by a physical exhaustion that haunted her body and seemed to reach into her soul.

5   She could see in the open square before her house the tops of trees that were all aquiver with the new spring life. The delicious breath of rain was in the air. In the street below a peddler was crying his wares. The notes of a distant song which someone was singing reached her faintly, and countless sparrows were twittering in the eaves.

6   There were patches of blue sky showing here and there through the clouds that had met and piled one above the other in the west facing her window.

7   She sat with her head thrown back upon the cushion of the chair, quite motionless, except when a sob came up into her throat and shook her, as a child who has cried itself to sleep continues to sob in its dreams.

8   She was young, with a fair, calm face, whose lines bespoke repression and even a certain strength. But now there was a dull stare in her eyes, whose gaze was fixed away off yonder on one of those patches of blue sky. It was not a glance of reflection, but rather indicated a suspension of intelligent thought.

9   There was something coming to her and she was waiting for it, fearfully. What was it? She did not know; it was too subtle and elusive to name. But she felt it, creeping out of the sky, reaching toward her through the sounds, the scents, the color that filled the air.

10   Now her bosom rose and fell tumultuously. She was beginning to recognize this thing that was approaching to possess her, and she was striving to beat it back with her will—as powerless as her two white slender hands would have been.

11   When she abandoned herself a little whispered word escaped her slightly parted lips. She said it over and over under her breath: "free, free, free!" The vacant stare and the look of terror that had followed it went from her eyes. They stayed keen and bright. Her pulses beat fast, and the coursing blood warmed and relaxed every inch of her body.

12   She did not stop to ask if it were or were not a monstrous joy that held her. A clear and exalted perception enabled her to dismiss the suggestion as trivial.

13   She knew that she would weep again when she saw the kind, tender hands folded in death; the face that had never looked save with love upon her, fixed and gray and dead. But she saw beyond that bitter moment a long procession of years to come that would belong to her absolutely. And she opened and spread her arms out to them in welcome.

14   There would be no one to live for her during those coming years; she would live for herself. There would be no powerful will bending hers in that blind persistence with which men and women believe they have a right to impose a private will upon a fellow-creature. A kind intention or a cruel intention made the act seem no less a crime as she looked upon it in that brief moment of illumination.

15   And yet she had loved him—sometimes. Often she had not. What did it matter! What could love, the unresolved mystery, count for in face of this possession of self-assertion which she suddenly recognized as the strongest impulse of her being!

16   "Free! Body and soul free!" she kept whispering.

17   Josephine was kneeling before the closed door with her lips to the keyhole, imploring for admission. "Louise, open the door! I beg; open the door—you will make yourself ill. What are you doing, Louise? For heaven's sake open the door."

18   "Go away. I am not making myself ill." No; she was drinking in a very elixir of life through that open window.

19   Her fancy was running riot along those days ahead of her. Spring days, and summer days, and all sorts of days that would be her own. She breathed a quick prayer that life might be long. It was only yesterday she had thought with a shudder that life might be long.

20   She arose at length and opened the door to her sister's importunities. There was a feverish triumph in her eyes, and she carried herself unwittingly like a goddess of Victory. She clasped her sister's waist, and together they descended the stairs. Richards stood waiting for them at the bottom.

21   Someone was opening the front door with a latchkey. It was Brently Mallard who entered, a little travel-stained, composedly carrying his grip-sack and umbrella. He had been far from the scene of the accident, and did not even know there had been one. He stood amazed at Josephine's piercing cry; at Richards' quick motion to screen him from the view of his wife.

22   But Richards was too late.

23   When the doctors came they said she had died of heart disease—of joy that kills.[1]

Plot

The plot is the basic story line—the sequence of events as they occur in the work. The plot focuses on conflict and often follows a predictable structure. The plot frequently begins by setting the scene, introducing the main characters, and providing the background information needed to follow the story. Next, there is often a complication or problem that arises. Suspense builds as the problem or conflict unfolds. Near the end of the story, events reach a climax—the point at which the outcome (resolution) of the conflict will be decided. A conclusion quickly follows as the story ends.

The plot of "The Story of an Hour" involves a surprise ending: Mrs. Mallard learns that her husband has been killed in an railroad disaster. She ponders his death and relishes the freedom it will bring. At the end of the story, when Mrs. Mallard discovers that her husband is not dead after all, she suffers a heart attack and dies.

Setting

The setting is the time, place, and circumstances under which the action occurs. The setting provides the mood or atmosphere in which the characters interact. The setting of "The Story of an Hour" is one hour in a time near the present in the Mallards' home.

Characterization

Characters are the actors in a narrative story. The characters reveal themselves by what they say—the dialogue—and by their actions, appearance, thoughts, and feelings. The narrator, or person who tells the story, may also comment on or reveal information about the characters. As you read, analyze the characters' traits and motives. Also analyze their personalities and watch for character changes. Study how the characters relate to one another.

In "The Story of an Hour" the main character is Mrs. Mallard; her thoughts and actions after learning of her husband's supposed death are the crux of the story.

Point of View

The point of view refers to the way the story is presented or the person from whose perspective the story is told. Often the story is not told from the narrator's perspective. The story may be told from the perspective of one of the characters, or that of an unknown narrator. In analyzing point of view, determine the role and function of the narrator. Is the narrator reliable and knowledgeable? Sometimes the narrator is able to enter the minds of some or all of the characters, knowing their thoughts and understanding their actions and motivations. In other stories, the narrator may not understand the actions or implications of the events in the story.

"The Story of an Hour" is told by a narrator not involved in the story. The story is told by a third-person narrator who is knowledgeable and understands the characters' actions and motives. In the story's last line, the narrator tells us that doctors assumed Mrs. Mallard died of "the joy that kills."

Tone

The tone or mood of a story reflects the author's attitude. Like a person's tone of voice, tone suggests feelings. Many ingredients contribute to tone, including the author's choice of detail (characters, setting, etc.) and the language that is used. The tone of a story may be, for example, humorous, ironic, or tragic. The author's feelings are not necessarily those of the characters or the narrator. Instead, it is through the narrator's description of the characters and their actions that we infer tone. In "The Story of an Hour," the tone might be described as serious. Serious events occur that dramatically affect Mrs. Mallard's life. The story also has an element of surprise and irony. We are surprised to learn that Mr. Mallard is not dead after all, and it is ironic, or the opposite of what we expect, to learn that Mrs.Mallard dies "of the joy that kills."

Theme

The theme of the story is its meaning or message. The theme of a work may also be considered its main idea or main point. Themes are often large, universal ideas dealing with life and death, human values, or existence. To establish the theme, ask yourself, "What is the author trying to say about life by telling the story?" Try to explain it in a single sentence. One theme of "The Story of an Hour" is freedom. Mrs. Mallard experiences a sense of freedom upon learning of her husband's supposed death. She sees "a long procession of years to come that would belong to her absolutely." There is also a theme of rebirth, suggested by references to springtime; her life without her husband was just beginning. The author also may be commenting on the restrictive or repressive nature of marriage during the time the story was written. After Mr. Mallard's death, "There will be no powerful will bending hers. . . ." Mrs. Mallard, after all, dies not from losing her husband but from the thought of losing her newly found freedom.

If you are having difficulty stating the theme, try the following suggestions:

1. **Study the title.** Now that you have read the story, does it take on any new meanings?
2. **Analyze the main characters.** Do they change? If so, how and in reaction to what?
3. **Look for broad general statements.** What do the characters or the narrator say about life or the problems they face?
4. **Look for symbols, figurative expressions, meaningful names (example: Mrs. Goodheart), or objects that hint at larger ideas.**

The Chief's Knife

A Yoruba Folk Tale

This story is a folk tale from the Yoruba people of western Nigeria. The Yorubas are traditionally urban dwellers who consider their proverbs an important source of information and conversation. They believe in magic spells and witchcraft as well as spirits that can cause good or bad things to happen.

Vocabulary Preview

inlaid (par. 1) set into the surface

bush (par. 7) wild, uncultivated land

1   In a certain village there was a chief. He owned a beautiful forged knife made by a celebrated ironworker in the kingdom of Benin. Its designs were inlaid with copper and brass, and the chief valued it highly. There was a great dance in the village one time in the chief's honor. People came from everywhere. The chief gave out gifts. When the dancing was ended, the people went away. The next day the chief could not find his knife. He sent servants to look for it. They could not find it. He said at last: "My knife inlaid with copper and brass, it was given to me by my uncle. Yesterday I had it in my hand. Today it is gone. Someone has stolen it. Therefore, let the countryside be searched. He who has taken this thing, he will be punished."

2   People said: "Whoever could have had so much foolishness in him to let him steal a thing belonging to the chief?" Word was carried here and there that the knife must be found. Word came to the village of Gbo. The people looked around. Their eyes fell upon a young hunter. They said to him: "Were you not in the chief's village at the celebration?"

3   He said: "Yes, I was there. I ate. I danced."

4   They said: "Does not a hunter need a knife?"

5   He replied: "I have weapons already. I would not skin game with a knife belonging to a chief."

6   They said: "He answers too sharply. He is not respectful. His eyes are too angry. If he is innocent, why does he speak in this fashion?"

7   The hunter went away. People said: "Did you notice how he said just so much, then no more? He broke off speaking. He turned his back. He is surely the thief." The days came and the nights came. When the hunter went out of his house, they watched him. When he returned with his meat from the forest, they watched him. They began to comment. "See how suspiciously he walks," one man said. "He has something to hide." Another said: "Yes, and he spends much time in the bush. What can he be doing there?" And yet another: "He speaks little. He avoids us. Surely he is the one who took the chief's knife."

8   Wherever he went, he was noticed. The days went by. And now when he spoke, people answered roughly, not wanting to be seen talking to the hunter. He had to take his leopard skins to another village to sell them, for in the village of Gbo no one

would buy. It was clear to all that the hunter was not a good man. "See how he comes out of his house in the early dawn, before the village is awake," some said. "This is the mark of a man who has offended the community." "Yes, and notice how he returns to his house in the darkness, when his face can't be seen," others said. Someone suggested that the chief be told that the thief was in their village. Others said: "No, it would only bring shame on the village, and the chief would be hard on us." As for the hunter, he was alone, and now sometimes he stayed at night in the forest instead of coming home.

9   Then one day a messenger from the chief reported that the forged knife inlaid with brass and copper had been found. The chief himself had placed it in the rafters of his house, and it had fallen into the grass wall. The people of Gbo were pleased. They went about their affairs. When the hunter came out of his house in the early dawn, someone said: "See how hard the hunter works, how long his days are." When the hunter returned late at night, someone said: "See how determined he is. He will not return home without game." Someone greeted the hunter, and he answered with only a few words. "See how it is with him," someone said. "He does not talk too much like some people do. He is not vain like other hunters." When they saw him walking across the fields, they said: "See how he walks, afraid of nothing, full of courage." They admired the hunter in every way. They said: "One need only look at him to see that he is an honest man."

10   So it came to be said:

> "When the chief's knife is stolen,
> The hunter walks like a thief,
> When the chief's knife is found,
> The hunter is praised."[2]

Directions: Choose the letter that best answers each of the following questions.

Checking Your Comprehension

_____ 1. The knife in this story belongs to
   a. a young hunter from the village of Gbo.
   b. a famous ironworker in Benin.
   c. the chief's cook.
   d. the chief.

_____ 2. The knife was discovered missing after
   a. a dance to honor the chief.
   b. a terrible storm.
   c. the chief's uncle came to visit.
   d. a battle between the villages.

_____ 3. The villagers suspected the young hunter of stealing the knife because
    a. they knew that he had stolen things before.
    b. he was seen hiding something in the forest.
    c. they thought he spoke and acted as if he were guilty.
    d. he was seen using a knife just like the chief's.

_____ 4. Because of the villager's suspicions, all of the following happened _except_
    a. no one would buy the hunter's skins.
    b. the hunter was criticized for everything he did.
    c. the villagers told the chief that the hunter stole his knife.
    d. no one wanted to be seen talking to the hunter.

_____ 5. At the end of the story, we find out that the
    a. hunter was guilty of stealing the knife.
    b. knife had been hidden by the chief.
    c. chief's cook had stolen the knife.
    d. chief never really had a knife.

The Elements of a Short Story

_____ 1. The story is told from the perspective of
    a. the hunter.
    b. the chief.
    c. the ironworker who made the knife.
    d. a narrator not involved in the story.

_____ 2. The story was probably told in order to
    a. warn against hunters.
    b. amuse listeners or readers.
    c. teach a lesson.
    d. criticize the villagers.

_____ 3. The climax of the story occurs when the
    a. knife is first given to the chief by his uncle.
    b. chief declares that his knife has been stolen.
    c. hunter is suspected of stealing the knife.
    d. knife is found.

_____ 4. The most important change that takes place in the story is in the way the
   a. hunter behaves.
   b. villagers perceive the hunter.
   c. chief treats the villagers.
   d. villagers treat each other.

_____ 5. Of the following statements, the one that best expresses the message of the story is:
   a. A person is innocent until proven guilty.
   b. Guard valuable possessions carefully.
   c. Look at yourself before blaming others.
   d. Suspicion can make an innocent person appear guilty.

Discussion Questions

1. Have you ever had a suspicion about someone? Explain what you did about your suspicion and whether or not it turned out to be accurate.

2. Have you ever been the victim of an inaccurate suspicion? Describe how you reacted and whether your behavior helped or hurt your situation.

3. How would the story be different if told from another perspective, say, from the hunter's point of view?

4. Create your own modern American version of this folk tale.

The Chaser

John Collier

Born in London, England in 1901, this writer was first published at the age of 19. He started out as a poet and then moved on to write short stories and novels in the fantasy genre. In 1935 Collier moved to Hollywood and wrote for movies and television until his death from a stroke in 1980.

Vocabulary Preview

chaser (title) a mild drink taken after hard liquor; one who chases or pursues another

obscurely (par. 1) not clearly or distinctly; difficult to see

imperceptible (par. 7) impossible to detect

autopsy (par. 7) examination of a dead body to determine the cause of death

confidential (par. 17) showing trust or confidence in another

bountifully (par. 19) generously or abundantly

516 Part 5 ◆ A Fiction Mini Reader

detachment (par. 20) objectivity or indifference

rapture (par. 26) great joy or pleasure

draught (par. 33) variation of the word "draft," meaning a current of air

siren (par. 33) a seductive woman

phial (par. 41) a small bottle for liquids; a vial

au revoir (par. 45) a French phrase meaning "until we meet again"

1   Alan Austen, as nervous as a kitten, went up certain dark and creaky stairs in the neighborhood of Pell Street, and peered about for a long time on the dim landing before he found the name he wanted written obscurely on one of the doors.

2   He pushed open this door, as he had been told to do, and found himself in a tiny room, which contained no furniture but a plain kitchen table, a rocking-chair, and an ordinary chair. On one of the dirty buff-colored walls were a couple of shelves, containing in all perhaps a dozen bottles and jars.

3   An old man sat in the rocking-chair, reading a newspaper. Alan, without a word, handed him the card he had been given. "Sit down, Mr. Austen," said the man very politely. "I am glad to make your acquaintance."

4   "Is it true," asked Alan, "that you have a certain mixture that has—er—quite extraordinary effects?"

5   "My dear sir," replied the old man, "my stock in trade is not very large—but I don't deal in laxatives and teething mixtures—but such as it is, it is varied. I think nothing I sell has effects which could be precisely described as ordinary."

6   "Well, the fact is—" began Alan.

7   "Here, for example," interrupted the old man, reaching for a bottle from the shelf. "Here is a liquid as colorless as water, almost tasteless, quite imperceptible in coffee, milk, wine, or any other beverage. It is also quite imperceptible to any known method of autopsy."

8   "Do you mean it is a poison?" cried Alan, very much horrified.

9   "Call it a glove-cleaner if you like," said the old man indifferently. "May it will clean gloves. I have never tried. One might call it a life-cleaner. Lives need cleaning sometimes."

10   "I want nothing of that sort," said Alan.

11   "Probably it is just as well," said the old man. "Do you know the price of this? For one teaspoonful, which is sufficient, I ask five thousand dollars. Never less. Not a penny less."

12   "I hope all your mixtures are not as expensive," said Alan apprehensively.

13   "Oh dear, no," said the old man. "It would be no good charging that sort of price for a love potion, for example. Young people who need a love potion very seldom have five thousand dollars. Otherwise they would not need a love potion."

14   "I am glad to hear that," said Alan.

15   "I look at it like this," said the old man. "Please a customer with one article, and he will come back when he needs another. Even if it is more costly. He will save up for it, if necessary."

16   "So," said Alan, "you really do sell love potions?"

17   "If I did not sell love potions," said the old man, reaching for another bottle, "I should not have mentioned the other matter to you. It is only when one is in a position to oblige that one can afford to be so confidential."

18   "And these potions," said Alan. "They are not just—just—er—"

19   "Oh, no," said the old man. "Their effects are permanent, and extend far beyond casual impulse. But they include it. Bountifully, insistently. Everlastingly."

20   "Dear me!" said Alan, attempting to look of scientific detachment. "How very interesting!"

21   "But consider the spiritual side," said the old man.

22   "I do, indeed," said Alan.

23   "For indifference," said the old man, "they substitute devotion. For scorn, adoration. Give one tiny measure of this to the young lady—its flavor is imperceptible in orange juice, soup, or cocktails—and however gay and giddy she is, she will change altogether. She will want nothing but solitude, and you."

24   "I can hardly believe it," said Alan. "She is so fond of parties."

25   "She will not like them any more," said the old man. "She will be afraid of the pretty girls you may meet."

26   "She will actually be jealous?" cried Alan in rapture. "Of me?"

27   "Yes, she will want to be everything to you."

28   "She is, already. Only she doesn't care about it."

29   "She will, when she has taken this. She will care intensely. You will be her sole interest in life."

30   "Wonderful!" cried Alan.

31   "She will want to know all you do," said the old man. "All that has happened to you during the day. Every word of it. She will want to know what you are thinking about, why you smile suddenly, why you are looking sad."

32   "That is love!" cried Alan.

33   "Yes," said the old man. "How carefully she will look after you! She will never allow you to be tired, sit in a draught, to neglect your food. If you are an hour late, she will be terrified. She will think you are killed, or that some siren has caught you."

34   "I can hardly imagine Diana like that!" cried Alan, overwhelmed with joy.

35   "You will not have to use your imagination," said the old man. "And, by the way, since there are always sirens, if by any chance you should, later on, slip a little, you need not worry. She will forgive you, in the end. She will be terribly hurt, of course, but she will forgive you—in the end."

36   "That will not happen," said Alan fervently.

37   "Of course not," said the old man. "But, if it did, you need not worry. She would never divorce you. Oh, no! And, of course, she herself will never give you the least, the very least, grounds for—uneasiness."

38   "And how much," said Alan, "Is this wonderful mixture?"

39   "It is not as dear," said the old man, "as the glove-cleaner, or life-cleaner, as I sometimes call it. No. That is five thousand dollars, never a penny less. One has to be older than you are, to indulge in that sort of thing. One has to save up for it."

40   "But the love potion?" said Alan.

41   "Oh, that," said the old man, opening the drawer in the kitchen table, and taking out a tiny, rather dirty-looking phial. "That is just a dollar."

42   "I can't tell you how grateful I am," said Alan, watching him fill it.

43   "I like to oblige," said the old man. "Then customers come back, later in life, when they are rather better off, and want more expensive things. Here you are. You will find it very effective."

44   "Thank you again," said Alan. "Good-bye."

45   "Au revoir," said the old man.[3]

Directions: Choose the letter that best answers each of the following questions:

Checking Your Comprehension

_____ 1. In the story, Alan Austen goes to see the old man in order to
   a. borrow money.
   b. buy poison.
   c. sell a valuable item.
   d. buy a love potion.

_____ 2. The main idea of paragraph 9 is that the old man
   a. sells practical mixtures, such as a glove-cleaner, as well as potions.
   b. offers a variety of multi-purpose mixtures.
   c. creates the potions because he wants to help people.
   d. feels no guilt about the poison he sells.

_____ 3. Love potions are inexpensive because the old man
   a. likes his young customers.
   b. believes that satisfied customers will come back when they can spend more.
   c. does not use expensive ingredients.
   d. wants to help his customers find true love.

_____ 4. The author uses the term "au revoir" in the final paragraph to imply that
   a. the old man expects to see Alan again.
   b. the old man is envious of the romance that Alan will achieve with the potion.
   c. Alan has indicated that he will be back to visit the old man.
   d. the story takes place in France.

_____ 5. According to the old man, if Alan were to be unfaithful to Diana, she would
a. divorce him immediately.
b. be unfaithful to him in return.
c. forgive him, eventually.
d. no longer be under the spell of the love potion.

The Elements of a Short Story

_____ 1. The setting of the story is
a. Alan Austen's apartment.
b. the old man's shop.
c. Diana's apartment.
d. a restaurant.

_____ 2. The tone of the story can best be described as
a. pleasant and hopeful.
b. sad and depressing.
c. cynical and "tongue-in-cheek."
d. suspenseful and frightening.

_____ 3. By the end of the story, the reader knows what the old man knows, which
is that
a. the love potion will make Alan very happy for the rest of his life.
b. Alan and Diana would have fallen in love without the potion.
c. the love potion is inexpensive because it is worthless.
d. Alan will regret creating the kind of love that he now believes he wants.

_____ 4. The theme of the story is that
a. absolute love, the kind the potion creates, is undesirable.
b. people should take drugs with care.
c. men should not attempt to alter a woman's affections.
d. women know better than to think potions are effective.

_____ 5. The story was told by
a. Alan Austen.
b. the old man.
c. a narrator who is not a character in the story.
d. another customer in the shop.

Discussion Questions

1. What do you think the word "chaser" refers to in the title? Did the author intend it to have more than one meaning?

2. What is your opinion of Alan's definition of love? Would you buy a potion that had the same effects?

3. Why was the "life-cleaner" potion so much more expensive than the love potion?

The Tell-Tale Heart

Edgar Allan Poe

Edgar Allan Poe was born in Boston in 1809 and was orphaned at the age of two. He was raised by wealthy foster parents who provided him with a privileged upbringing, including education and travel. He embarked upon a successful literary career as both editor and contributor to several major journals. However, after his wife died in 1847, Poe's personal problems and heavy drinking became worse. This lead to unemployment, poverty, and eventually to his death in Baltimore at the age of 40. Poe is most famous for his macabre poems and short stories, and he is considered by many to be the inventor of the modern detective story.

Vocabulary Preview

hearken (par. 1) listen or pay attention

dissimulation (par. 3) disguising one's true intentions

profound (par. 3) insightful

sagacity (par. 4) wisdom

suppositions (par. 7) assumptions or beliefs

crevice (par. 8) a narrow opening or crack

scantlings (par. 13) small pieces of lumber

suavity (par. 14) pleasantness; showing politeness and charm

deputed (par. 14) assigned or delegated

audacity (par. 15) boldness

gesticulations (par. 17) gestures or movements

derision (par. 17) ridicule or contempt

1 True!—nervous—very, very dreadfully nervous I had been and am; but why *will* you say that I am mad? The disease had sharpened my senses—not destroyed—not dulled them. Above all was the sense of hearing acute. I heard all things in the heaven and in the earth. I heard many things in hell. How, then, am I mad? Hearken! and observe how healthily—how calmly I can tell you the whole story.

2   It is impossible to say how first the idea entered my brain; but once conceived, it haunted me day and night. Object there was none. Passion there was none. I loved the old man. He had never wronged me. He had never given me insult. For his gold I had no desire. I think it was his eye! yes, it was this! One of his eyes resembled that of a vulture—a pale blue eye, with a film over it. Whenever it fell upon me, my blood ran cold; and so by degrees—very gradually—I made up my mind to take the life of the old man, and thus rid myself of the eye for ever.

3   Now this is the point. You fancy me mad. Madmen know nothing. But you should have seen *me*. You should have seen how wisely I proceeded—with what caution—with what foresight—with what dissimulation I went to work! I was never kinder to the old man than during the whole week before I killed him. And every night, about midnight, I turned the latch of his door and opened it—oh, so gently! And then, when I had made an opening sufficient for my head, I put in a dark lantern, all closed, closed, so that no light shone out, and then I thrust in my head. Oh, you would have laughed to see how cunningly I thrust it in! I moved it slowly—very, very slowly, so that I might not disturb the old man's sleep. It took me an hour to place my whole head within the opening so far that I could see him as he lay upon his bed. Ha!—would a madman have been so wise as this? And then, when my head was well in the room, I undid the lantern cautiously—oh, so cautiously—cautiously (for the hinges creaked)—I undid it just so much that a single thin ray fell upon the vulture eye. And this I did for seven long nights—every night just at midnight—but I found the eye always closed; and so it was impossible to do the work; for it was not the old man who vexed me, but his Evil Eye. And every morning, when the day broke, I went boldly into the chamber, and spoke courageously to him, calling him by name in a hearty tone, and inquiring how he had passed the night. So you see he would have been a very profound old man, indeed, to suspect that every night, just at twelve, I looked in upon him while he slept.

4   Upon the eighth night I was more than usually cautious in opening the door. A watch's minute hand moves more quickly than did mine. Never before that night had I *felt* the extent of my own powers—of my sagacity. I could scarcely contain my feelings of triumph. To think that there I was, opening the door, little by little, and he not even to dream of my secret deeds or thoughts. I fairly chuckled at the idea; and perhaps he heard me; for he moved on the bed suddenly, as if startled. Now you may think that I drew back—but no. His room was as black as pitch with the thick darkness, (for the shutters were close fastened, through fear of robbers), and so I knew that he could not see the opening of the door, and I kept pushing it on steadily, steadily.

5   I had my head in, and was about to open the lantern, when my thumb slipped upon the tin fastening, and the old man sprang up in bed, crying out—"Who's there?"

6   I kept quite still and said nothing. For a whole hour I did not move a muscle, and in the meantime I did not hear him lie down. He was still sitting up in the bed, listening;—just as I have done, night after night, hearkening to the death watches* in the wall.

death watches: beetles that infest timbers. Their clicking sound was thought to be an omen of death.

7   Presently I heard a slight groan, and I knew it was the groan of mortal terror. It was not a groan of pain or of grief—oh, no!—it was the low stifled sound that arises from the bottom of the soul when overcharged with awe. I knew the sound very well. Many a night, just at midnight, when all the world slept, it has welled up from my own bosom, deepening, with its dreadful echo, the terrors that distracted me. I say I knew it well. I knew what the old man felt, and pitied him, although I chuckled at heart. I knew that he had been lying awake ever since the first slight noise, when he had turned in the bed. His fears had been ever since growing upon him. He had been trying to fancy them causeless, but could not. He had been saying to himself—"It is nothing but the wind in the chimney—it is only a mouse crossing the floor," or "It is merely a cricket which has made a single chirp." Yes, he had been trying to comfort himself with these suppositions; but he had found all in vain. *All in vain;* because Death, in approaching him, had stalked with his black shadow before him, and enveloped the victim. And it was the mournful influence of the unperceived shadow that caused him to feel—although he neither saw nor heard—to *feel* the presence of my head within the room.

8   When I had waited a long time, very patiently, without hearing him lie down, I resolved to open a little—a very, very little crevice in the lantern. So I opened it—you cannot imagine how stealthily, stealthily—until, at length, a single dim ray, like the thread of the spider, shot from out the crevice and fell upon the vulture eye.

9   It was open—wide, wide open—and I grew furious as I gazed upon it. I saw it with perfect distinctness—all a dull blue, with a hideous veil over it that chilled the very marrow in my bones; but I could see nothing else of the old man's face or person: for I had directed the ray as if by instinct, precisely upon the damned spot.

10   And now have I not told you that what you mistake for madness is but over-acuteness of the senses?—now, I say, there came to my ears a low, dull, quick sound, such as a watch makes when enveloped in cotton. I knew *that* sound well, too. It was the beating of the old man's heart. It increased my fury, as the beating of a drug stimulates the soldier into courage.

11   But even yet I refrained and kept still. I scarcely breathed. I held the lantern motionless. I tried how steadily I could maintain the ray upon the eye. Meantime the hellish tattoo of the heart increased. It grew quicker and quicker, and louder and louder every instant. The old man's terror *must* have been extreme! It grew louder, I say, louder every moment!—do you mark me well? I have told you that I am nervous: so I am. And now at the dead hour of the night, amid the dreadful silence of that old house, so strange a noise as this excited me to uncontrollable terror. Yet, for some minutes longer I refrained and stood still. But the beating grew louder, louder! I thought the heart must burst. And now a new anxiety seized me—the sound would be heard by a neighbor! The old man's hour had come! With a loud yell, I threw open the lantern and leaped into the room. He shrieked once—once only. In an instant I dragged him to the floor, and pulled the heavy bed over him. I then smiled gaily, to find the deed so far done. But, for many minutes, the heart beat on with a muffled sound. This, however,

did not vex me; it would not be heard through the wall. At length it ceased. The old man was dead. I removed the bed and examined the corpse. Yes, he was stone, stone dead. I placed my hand upon the heart and held it there many minutes. There was no pulsation. He was stone dead. His eye would trouble me no more.

12   If still you think me mad, you will think so no longer when I describe the wise precautions I took for the concealment of the body. The night waned, and I worked hastily, but in silence. First of all I dismembered the corpse. I cut off the head and the arms and the legs.

13   I then took up three planks from the flooring of the chamber, and deposited all between the scantlings. I then replaced the boards so cleverly, so cunningly, that no human eye—not even *his*—could have detected anything wrong. There was nothing to wash out—no stain of any kind—no bloodspot whatever. I had been too wary for that. A tub had caught all—ha! ha!

14   When I had made an end of these labors, it was four o'clock—still dark as midnight. As the bell sounded the hour, there came a knocking at the street door. I went down to open it with a light heart,—for what had I *now* to fear? There entered three men, who introduced themselves, with perfect suavity, as officers of the police. A shriek had been heard by a neighbor during the night; suspicion of foul play had been aroused; information had been lodged at the police office, and they (the officers) had been deputed to search the premises.

15   I smiled,—for *what* had I to fear? I bade the gentlemen welcome. The shriek, I said, was my own in a dream. The old man, I mentioned, was absent in the country. I took my visitors all over the house. I bade them search—search *well*. I led them, at length, to *his* chamber. I showed them his treasures, secure, undisturbed. In the enthusiasm of my confidence, I brought chairs into the room, and desired them *here* to rest from their fatigues, while I myself, in the wild audacity of my perfect triumph, placed my own seat upon the very spot beneath which reposed the corpse of the victim.

16   The officers were satisfied. My *manner* had convinced them. I was singularly at ease. They sat, and while I answered cheerily, they chatted of familiar things, But, ere long, I felt myself getting pale and wished them gone. My head ached, and I fancied a ringing in my ears: but still they sat and still chatted. The ringing became more distinct:— it continued and became more distinct: I talked more freely to get rid of the feeling: but it continued and gained definitiveness—until, at length, I found that the noise was *not* within my ears.

17   No doubt I now grew *very* pale—but I talked more fluently, and with a heightened voice. Yet the sound increased—and what could I do? It was *a low, dull, quick sound— much such a sound as a watch makes when enveloped in cotton.* I gasped for breath— and yet the officers heard it not. I talked more quickly—more vehemently; but the noise steadily increased. I arose and argued about trifles, in a high key and with violent gesticulations; but the noise steadily increased. Why *would* they not be gone? I paced the floor to and fro with heavy strides, as if excited to fury by the observations of the men—but the noise steadily increased. Oh God! what *could* I do? I foamed—I

raved—I swore! I swung the chair upon which I had been sitting, and grated it upon the boards, but the noise arose over all and continually increased. It grew louder—louder—*louder!* And still the men chatted pleasantly and smiled. Was it possible they heard not? Almighty God!—no, no! They heard!—they suspected!—they *knew!*—they were making a mockery of my horror!—this I thought and this I think. But any thing was better than this agony! Anything was more tolerable than this derision! I could bear those hypocritical smiles no longer! I felt that I must scream or die!—and now—again!—hark! louder! louder! louder! *louder!*—

18   "Villains!" I shrieked, "dissemble no more! I admit the deed!—tear up the planks!—here, here!—it is the beating of his hideous heart!"

Directions: Choose the letter that best answers each of the following questions.

Checking Your Comprehension

   1. In this story, the main character describes how
   a. an old man tried to murder him.
   b. he prevented an old man's murder.
   c. he caught and arrested a murderer.
   d. he murdered an old man.

   2. The character was inspired to kill the old man because
   a. he wanted the old man's gold.
   b. the old man had wronged him.
   c. the old man had insulted him.
   d. he was disturbed by one of the old man's eyes.

   3. Once the character decided to kill the old man, he
   a. killed him later that day.
   b. waited until the next day to kill him.
   c. waited a whole week before killing him.
   d. waited almost a year and then changed his mind.

   4. The reason the killer waited was that he
   a. wanted to find someone to help him kill the old man.
   b. couldn't kill the old man unless the old man's eye was open.
   c. needed to find a weapon.
   d. was afraid of being caught.

   5. When the police came to the house, they
   a. immediately found the old man's body and arrested the killer.
   b. searched for clues but left without making an arrest.
   c. were suspicious of the man's story and took him in for questioning.
   d. were satisfied with the man's story.

The Elements of a Short Story

 1. The tone of the story can best be described as
   a. suspenseful.
   b. humorous.
   c. ironic.
   d. sad.

 2. The setting of the story is
   a. the old man's house.
   b. the police station.
   c. prison.
   d. an insane asylum.

 3. This story is told from the perspective of
   a. the old man.
   b. the police.
   c. the killer.
   d. a neighbor.

 4. The title is a reference to how the
   a. killer imagined the old man's heart beating so loudly that it gave him away.
   b. old man knew that he was going to be murdered.
   c. police officers found the old man's heart and knew he had been murdered.
   d. killer gave himself away by the loud beating of his own heart.

 5. Which statement best expresses the theme of the story?
   a. Murder is immoral.
   b. Madness is a social disease.
   c. Law enforcement personnel deserve respect.
   d. Guilt is powerful and self-destructive.

Discussion Questions

1. How does Poe create feelings of suspense in this story?
2. How does Poe convince us that the narrator is mad?
3. What do you think is the relationship between the old man and his killer?
4. Why do you think Poe chose to tell this story from the killer's point of view?

The Lady, or the Tiger?

Frank R. Stockton

Frank Stockon (1834–1902) worked as an engraver in Philadelphia after high school while writing on a freelance basis. His first short story was published in 1855. He went on to publish many books, short stories, poems, and articles for adults and children. Stockton also worked as an editor for various newspapers and magazines during his life.

Vocabulary Preview

barbaric (par. 1) cruel, primitive, uncivilized

fancy (par. 1) sudden liking or desire for something

emanated (par. 4) came out of

treading an epithalamic measure (par. 6) dancing to a poem or song performed at a wedding

courtiers (par. 9) members of a royal court who attend the king

tribunal (par. 10) court of justice

moiety (par. 13) one of two parts

devious (par. 20) rambling, roundabout

1   In the very olden time there lived a semi-barbaric king, whose ideas, though somewhat polished and sharpened by the progressiveness of distant Latin neighbors, were still large, florid, and untrammeled, as became the half of him which was barbaric. He was a man of exuberant fancy, and, withal, of an authority so irresistible that, at his will, he turned his varied fancies into facts. He was greatly given to self-communing, and, when he and himself agreed upon anything, the thing was done. When every member of his domestic and political systems moved smoothly in its appointed course, his nature was bland and genial; but, whenever there was a little hitch, and some of his orbs got out of their orbits, he was blander and more genial still, for nothing pleased him so much as to make the crooked straight and crush down uneven places.

2   Among the borrowed notions by which his barbarism had become semified was that of the public arena, in which, by exhibitions of manly and beastly valor, the minds of his subjects were refined and cultured.

3   But even here the exuberant and barbaric fancy asserted itself. The arena of the king was built, not to give the people an opportunity of hearing the rhapsodies of dying gladiators, nor to enable them to view the inevitable conclusion of a conflict between religious opinions and hungry jaws, but for purposes far better adapted to widen and develop the mental energies of the people. This vast amphitheater, with its encircling galleries, its mysterious vaults, and its unseen passages, was an agent of poetic justice, in which crime was punished, or virtue rewarded, by the decrees of an impartial and incorruptible chance.

4   When a subject was accused of a crime of sufficient importance to interest the king, public notice was given that on an appointed day the fate of the accused person would be decided in the king's arena, a structure which well deserved its name, for, although its form and plan were borrowed from afar, its purpose emanated solely from the brain of this man, who, every barleycorn a king, knew no tradition to which he owed more allegiance than pleased his fancy, and who ingrafted on every adopted form of human thought and action the rich growth of his barbaric idealism.

5   When all the people had assembled in the galleries, and the king, surrounded by his court, sat high up on his throne of royal state on one side of the arena, he gave a signal, a door beneath him opened, and the accused subject stepped out into the amphitheater. Directly opposite him, on the other side of the inclosed space, were two doors, exactly alike and side by side. It was the duty and the privilege of the person on trial to walk directly to these doors and open one of them. He could open either door he pleased; he was subject to no guidance or influence but that of the aforementioned impartial and incorruptible chance. If he opened the one, there came out of it a hungry tiger, the fiercest and most cruel that could be procured, which immediately sprang upon him and tore him to pieces as a punishment for his guilt. The moment that the case of the criminal was thus decided, doleful iron bells were clanged, great wails went up from the hired mourners posted on the outer rim of the arena, and the vast audience, with bowed heads and downcast hearts, wended slowly their homeward way, mourning greatly that one so young and fair, or so old and respected, should have merited so dire a fate.

6   But, if the accused person opened the other door, there came forth from it a lady, the most suitable to his years and station that his majesty could select among his fair subjects, and to this lady he was immediately married, as a reward of his innocence. It mattered not that he might already possess a wife and family, or that his affections might be engaged upon an object of his own selection; the king allowed no such subordinate arrangements to interfere with his great scheme of retribution and reward. The exercises, as in the other instance, took place immediately, and in the arena. Another door opened beneath the king, and a priest, followed by a band of choristers, and dancing maidens blowing joyous airs on golden horns and treading an epithalamic measure, advanced to where the pair stood, side by side, and the wedding was promptly and cheerily solemnized. Then the gay brass bells rang forth their merry peals, the people shouted glad hurrahs, and the innocent man, preceded by children strewing flowers on his path, led his bride to his home.

7   This was the king's semi-barbaric method of administering justice. Its perfect fairness is obvious. The criminal could not know out of which door would come the lady; he opened either he pleased, without having the slightest idea whether, in the next instant, he was to be devoured or married. On some occasions the tiger came out of one door, and on some out of the other. The decisions of this tribunal were not only fair, they were positively determinate: the accused person was instantly punished if he found himself guilty, and, if innocent, he was rewarded on the spot, whether he liked it or not. There was no escape from the judgments of the king's arena.

8   The institution was a very popular one. When the people gathered together on one of the great trial days, they never knew whether they were to witness a bloody slaughter or a hilarious wedding. This element of uncertainty lent an interest to the occasion which it could not otherwise have attained. Thus, the masses were entertained and pleased, and the thinking part of the community could bring no charge of unfairness against this plan, for did not the accused person have the whole matter in his own hands?

9   This semi-barbaric king had a daughter as blooming as his most florid fancies, and with a soul as fervent and imperious as his own. As is usual in such cases, she was the apple of his eye, and was loved by him above all humanity. Among his courtiers was a young man of that fineness of blood and lowness of station common to the conventional heroes of romance who love royal maidens. This royal maiden was well satisfied with her lover, for he was handsome and brave to a degree unsurpassed in all this kingdom, and she loved him with an ardor that had enough of barbarism in it to make it exceedingly warm and strong. This love affair moved on happily for many months, until one day the king happened to discover its existence. He did not hesitate nor waver in regard to his duty in the premises. The youth was immediately cast into prison, and a day was appointed for his trial in the king's arena. This, of course, was an especially important occasion, and his majesty, as well as all the people, was greatly interested in the workings and development of this trial. Never before had such a case occurred; never before had a subject dared to love the daughter of the king. In after years such things become commonplace enough, but then they were in no slight degree novel and startling.

10   The tiger-cages of the kingdom were searched for the most savage and relentless beasts, from which the fiercest monster might be selected for the arena; and the ranks of maiden youth and beauty throughout the land were carefully surveyed by competent judges in order that the young man might have a fitting bride in case fate did not determine for him a different destiny. Of course, everybody knew that the deed with which the accused was charged had been done. He had loved the princess, and neither he, she, nor any one else, thought of denying the fact; but the king would not think of allowing any fact of this kind to interfere with the workings of the tribunal, in which he took such great delight and satisfaction. No matter how the affair turned out, the youth would be disposed of, and the king would take an aesthetic pleasure in watching the course of events, which would determine whether or not the young man had done wrong in allowing himself to love the princess.

11   The appointed day arrived. From far and near the people gathered, and thronged the great galleries of the arena, and crowds, unable to gain admittance, massed themselves against its outside walls. The king and his court were in their places, opposite the twin doors, those fateful portals, so terrible in their similarity.

12   All was ready. The signal was given. A door beneath the royal party was opened, and the lover of the princess walked into the arena. Tall, beautiful, fair, his appearance was greeted with a low hum of admiration and anxiety. Half the audience had not

known so grand a youth had lived among them. No wonder the princess loved him! What a terrible thing for him to be there!

13   As the youth advanced into the arena, he turned, as the custom was, to bow to the king, but he did not think at all of that royal personage. His eyes were fixed upon the princess, who sat to the right of her father. Had it not been for the moiety of barbarism in her nature it is probable that lady would not have been there, but her intense and fervid soul would not allow her to be absent on an occasion in which she was so terribly interested. From the moment that the degree had gone forth that her lover should decide his fate in the king's arena, she had thought of nothing, night or day, but this great event and the various subjects connected with it. Possessed of more power, influence, and force of character than any one who had ever before been interested in such a case, she had done what no other person had done,—she had possessed herself of the secret of the doors. She knew in which of the two rooms, that lay behind those doors, stood the cage of the tiger, with its open front, and in which waited the lady. Through these thick doors, heavily curtained with skins on the inside, it was impossible that any noise or suggestions should come from within to the person who should approach to raise the latch of one of them. But gold, and the power of a woman's will, had brought the secret to the princess.

14   And not only did she know in which room stood the lady ready to emerge, all blushing and radiant, should her door be opened, but she knew who the lady was. It was one of the fairest and loveliest of the damsels of the court who had been selected as the reward of the accused youth, should he be proved innocent of the crime of aspiring to one so far above him; and the princess hated her. Often had she seen, or imagined that she had seen, this fair creature throwing glances of admiration upon the person of her lover, and sometimes she thought these glances were perceived, and even returned. Now and then she had seen them talking together; it was but for a moment or two, but much can be said in a brief space; it may have been on most unimportant topics, but how could she know that? The girl was lovely, but she had dared to raise her eyes to the loved one of the princess; and, with all the intensity of the savage blood transmitted to her through long lines of wholly barbaric ancestors, she hated the woman who blushed and trembled behind that silent door.

15   When her lover turned and looked at her, and his eye met hers as she sat there, paler and whiter than any one in the vast ocean of anxious faces about her, he saw, by that power of quick perception which is given to those whose souls are one, that she knew behind which door crouched the tiger, and behind which stood the lady. He had expected her to know it. He understood her nature, and his soul was assured that she would never rest until she had made plain to herself this thing, hidden to all other lookers-on, even to the king. The only hope for the youth in which there was any element of certainty was based upon the success of the princess in discovering this mystery; and the moment he looked upon her, he saw she had succeeded, as in his soul he knew she would succeed.

16   Then it was that his quick and anxious glance asked the question: "Which?" It was as plain to her as if he shouted it from where he stood. There was not an instant to be lost. The question was asked in a flash; it must be answered in another.

17   Her right arm lay on the cushioned parapet before her. She raised her hand, and made a slight, quick movement toward the right. No one but her lover saw her. Every eye but his was fixed on the man in the arena.

18   He turned, and with a firm and rapid step he walked across the empty space. Every heart stopped beating, every breath was held, every eye was fixed immovably upon that man. Without the slightest hesitation, he went to the door on the right, and opened it.

19   Now, the point of the story is this: Did the tiger come out of that door, or did the lady?

20   The more we reflect upon this question, the harder it is to answer. It involves a study of the human heart which leads us through devious mazes of passion, out of which it is difficult to find our way. Think of it, fair reader, not as if the decision of the question depended upon yourself, but upon that hot-blooded, semi-barbaric princess, her soul at a white heat beneath the combined fires of despair and jealousy. She had lost him, but who should have him?

21   How often, in her waking hours and in her dreams, had she started in wild horror, and covered her face with her hands as she thought of her lover opening the door on the other side of which waited the cruel fangs of the tiger!

22   But how much oftener had she seen him at the other door! How in her grievous reveries had she gnashed her teeth, and torn her hair, when she saw his start of rapturous delight as he opened the door of the lady! How her soul had burned in agony when she had seen him rush to meet that woman, with her flushing cheek and sparkling eye of triumph; when she had seen him lead her forth, his whole frame kindled with the joy of recovered life; when she had heard the glad shouts from the multitude, and the wild ringing of the happy bells; when she had seen the priest, with his joyous followers, advance to the couple, and make them man and wife before her very eyes; and when she had seen them walk away together upon their path of flowers, followed by the tremendous shouts of the hilarious multitude, in which her one despairing shriek was lost and drowned!

23   Would it not be better for him to die at once, and go to wait for her in the blessed regions of semi-barbaric futurity?

24   And yet, that awful tiger, those shrieks, that blood!

25   Her decision had been indicated in an instant, but it had been made after days and nights of anguished deliberation. She had known she would be asked, she had decided what she would answer, and, without the slightest hesitation, she had moved her hand to the right.

26   The question of her decision is one not to be lightly considered, and it is not for me to presume to set myself up as the one person able to answer it. And so I leave it with all of you: Which came out of the opened door,—the lady, or the tiger?

Directions: Choose the letter that best answers each of the following questions.

Checking Your Comprehension

____ 1. The princess's lover was put in the arena because
   a. he failed to ask the king's permission to marry his daughter.
   b. he was unfaithful to the princess.
   c. his relationship with the princess had been discovered.
   d. he hated the king.

____ 2. How did the princess find out behind which door the tiger was placed?
   a. Her father told her.
   b. She asked the maiden to signal her.
   c. She placed the tiger there herself.
   d. She paid to find out.

____ 3. If the accused person in the arena opens the door to find the lady, he
   a. could decide whether to marry her.
   b. was married to her immediately.
   c. was set free and had to remain unmarried.
   d. was obligated to serve the king as a servant and was not allowed to marry.

____ 4. How did the princess tell her lover which door to open?
   a. She gestured with her hand.
   b. She used a code the couple had previously agreed upon.
   c. She told her lover before he entered the arena.
   d. She sent a message to him through another prisoner.

____ 5. The king's system of justice relied on
   a. intelligence.
   b. guilt.
   c. evidence.
   d. chance.

The Elements of a Short Story

____ 1. The narrator of the story is
   a. the king.
   b. the princess.
   c. the princess's lover.
   d. an unknown person.

_____ 2. The climax of the story occurs when
   a. the lover's relationship is discovered.
   b. the lover's eyes meet those of the princess.
   c. the lover opens a door in the arena.
   d. the lady behind the door is revealed.

_____ 3. The character of the princess's lover can best be described as
   a. evil.
   b. trusting.
   c. bold.
   d. insensitive.

_____ 4. The king can most accurately be described as
   a. powerful and vain.
   b. sensitive and caring.
   c. reasonable and logical.
   d. alert and open.

_____ 5. One theme of the story is
   a. people should avoid taking lovers.
   b. love and passion are complex emotions.
   c. justice is difficult to define.
   d. barbarians have unfair laws.

Discussion Questions

1. Describe the princess's dilemma. Why did she have difficulty deciding which door to tell her lover to choose?

2. Did the princess tell her lover to choose the lady or the tiger? Justify your answer.

3. How would the story be different if told by the princess? Would it be as exciting?

4. Why do you think Stockton left the outcome of the story unresolved?

Practice is an important part of most types of learning—whether training for a sport or learning to type, cook, change a tire, or solve a math problem. The same is true of reading: *practice is important.* To read well, you must apply and practice the skills you have learned. You must try out these skills on a variety of types of reading materials.

The purpose of Part Six is to give you practice in applying the reading skills presented in Parts One through Four. Each selection gives you the opportunity to use your skills in a slightly different way on a new topic written by a different author. A set of exercises accompanies each selection. These exercises are organized in the same way. Each set has nine parts. The following is a brief introduction to each of these parts that provides some advice on how to use them to learn as much as possible.

- **Introduction.** Each selection begins with a brief introduction. This acquaints you with the topic of the selection and provides any background information you may need to know before you read the selection.
- **Vocabulary Preview.** Each selection contains some difficult words or phrases. This section lists some of them and gives a brief definition of each as used in the selection. (Words may have other meanings that are not listed.) Before you read the selection, be sure to go through this word list, noticing words you do not know and studying their meanings. Later, as you read the selection, refer back to this list to check meanings as you need them. The paragraph in which the word appears is given in parentheses following the word.
- **Prereading.** Prereading (see Chapter 5) is a way of getting ready to read. This portion of the exercise directs you to preview the selection and then asks questions that are intended to focus your attention on the article and help you discover what you already know about the subject.
- **Checking Your Comprehension.** This exercise gives you a chance to see whether you have understood what you have read. You will notice that the type of questions differ for each selection. Some are true-false questions, while others may require you to write an outline or summary. Regardless of the type, each question checks your ability to understand the writer's basic message. Specifically, the questions in this section test your ability to apply the skills taught in Chapters 5–12. Often, in order to answer the question or complete the directed activity, you will apply several skills discussed in these chapters.
- **Critical Reading and Thinking.** In this exercise you are asked to interpret and react to the author's ideas. You will find a variety of questions that give you the opportunity to apply the skills taught in Part Four. Each of these questions is open-ended and requires an explanation. Always answer in complete sentences. That way, you will be certain you have expressed a complete idea in a clear, understandable form.

- **Words in Context.** Although each selection has difficult words, you can figure some of them out using context clues (see Chapter 2). This exercise contains a list of words, along with the paragraph number in which they appear. You are asked to write a brief definition of each word. To do this, go back to the paragraph in which the word is used and reread, looking for meaning clues.
- **Vocabulary Review.** This exercise gives you practice with all or most of the words contained in the Vocabulary Preview section. It is an opportunity to work with these words in contexts other than those used in the selection.
- **Summarizing the Reading Selection.** In this section you will polish your summary writing skills. In the first four readings, you will be asked to fill in missing information in a summary that is already written. Then, once you are more familiar with the format and structure of a summary, you will be asked to write your own summary for the remaining four readings.
- **Writing Exercises.** These exercises give you practice expressing your own ideas in written form. Each exercise provides an opportunity for you to write about ideas discussed in the selection.

Selection 1
Living Life to the Fullest

Maya Angelou

Are you living your life to its fullest? Read this selection to find out. Maya Angelou, a famous poet and writer, tells a story that will help you answer this question.

Vocabulary Preview

sinewy (par. 1) lean and muscular

incurred (par. 1) brought on; met with

tautly (par. 2) tightly

meticulous (par. 3) extremely careful

maven (par. 6) expert

comradery (par. 14) friendship

founts (par. 14) sources

convivial (par. 14) agreeable; cheerful

scenarios (par. 16) plans; expected events

Prereading

Directions: Preview the selection and answer the following questions.

1. What do you already know about Aunt Tee?

   _____

   _____

   _____

2. What important issues do you think this reading will be concerned with?

   _____

   _____

   _____

1   Aunt Tee was a Los Angeles member of our extended family. She was seventy-nine when I met her, sinewy, strong, and the color of old lemons. She wore her coarse, straight hair, which was slightly streaked with gray, in a long braided rope across the top of her head. With her high cheekbones, old gold skin, and almond eyes, she looked more like an Indian chief than an old black woman. (Aunt Tee described herself and any favored member of her race as Negroes. *Black* was saved for those who had incurred her disapproval.)

2   She had retired and lived alone in a dead, neat ground-floor apartment. Wax flowers and china figurines sat on elaborately embroidered and heavily starched doilies. Sofas and chairs were tautly upholstered. The only thing at ease in Aunt Tee's apartment was Aunt Tee.

3   I used to visit her often and perch on her uncomfortable sofa just to hear her stories. She was proud that after working thirty years as a maid, she spent the next thirty years as a live-in housekeeper, carrying the keys to rich houses and keeping meticulous accounts.

4   "Living in lets the white folks know Negroes are as neat and clean as they are, sometimes more so. And it gives the Negro maid a chance to see white folks ain't no smarter than Negroes. Just luckier. Sometimes."

5   Aunt Tee told me that once she was housekeeper for a couple in Bel Air, California, lived with them in a fourteen-room ranch house. There was a day maid who cleaned, and a gardener who daily tended the lush gardens. Aunt Tee oversaw the workers. When she had begun the job, she had cooked and served a light breakfast, a good

lunch, and a full three- or four-course dinner to her employers and their guests. Aunt Tee said she watched them grow older and leaner. After a few years they stopped entertaining and ate dinner hardly seeing each other at the table. Finally, they sat in a dry silence as they ate evening meals of soft scrambled eggs, melba toast, and weak tea. Aunt Tee said she saw them growing old but didn't see herself aging at all.

6   She became the social maven. She started "keeping company" (her phrase) with a chauffeur down the street. Her best friend and her friend's husband worked in service only a few blocks away.

7   On Saturdays Aunt Tee would cook a pot of pigs' feet, a pot of greens, fry chicken, make potato salad, and bake a banana pudding. Then, that evening, her friends—the chauffeur, the other housekeeper, and her husband—would come to Aunt Tee's commodious live-in quarters. There the four would eat and drink, play records and dance. As the evening wore on, they would settle down to a serious game of bid whist.

8   Naturally, during this revelry jokes were told, fingers snapped, feet were patted, and there was a great deal of laughter.

9   Aunt Tee said that what occurred during every Saturday party startled her and her friends the first time it happened. They had been playing cards, and Aunt Tee, who had just won the bid, held a handful of trumps. She felt a cool breeze on her back and sat upright and turned around. Her employers had cracked her door open and beckoned to her. Aunt Tee, a little peeved, laid down her cards and went to the door. The couple backed away and asked her to come into the hall, and there they both spoke and won Aunt Tee's sympathy forever.

10   "Theresa, we don't mean to disturb you . . ." the man whispered, "but you all seem to be having such a good time . . ."

11   The woman added, "We hear you and your friends laughing every Saturday night, and we'd just like to watch you. We don't want to bother you. We'll be quiet and just watch."

12   The man said, "If you'll just leave your door ajar, your friends don't need to know. We'll never make a sound." Aunt Tee said she saw no harm in agreeing, and she talked it over with her company. They said it was OK with them, but it was sad that the employers owned the gracious house, the swimming pool, three cars, and numberless palm trees, but had no joy. Aunt Tee told me that laughter and relaxation had left the house; she agreed it was sad.

13   That story has stayed with me for nearly thirty years, and when a tale remains fresh in my mind, it almost always contains a lesson which will benefit me.

14   My dears, I draw the picture of the wealthy couple standing in a darkened hallway, peering into a lighted room where black servants were lifting their voices in merriment and comradery, and I realize that living well is an art which can be developed. Of course, you will need the basic talents to build upon: They are a love of life and ability to take great pleasure from small offerings, an assurance that the world owes you nothing and that every gift is exactly that, a gift. That people who may differ from you in political stance, sexual persuasion, and racial inheritance can be founts of fun, and if you are lucky, they can become even convivial comrades.

15   Living life as art requires a readiness to forgive. I do not mean that you should suffer fools gladly, but rather remember your own shortcomings, and when you encounter another with flaws, don't be eager to righteously seal yourself away from the offender forever. Take a few breaths and imagine yourself having just committed the action which has set you at odds.

16   Because of the routines we follow, we often forget that life is an ongoing adventure. We leave our homes for work, acting and even believing that we will reach our destinations with no unusual event startling us out of our set expectations. The truth is we know nothing, not where our cars will fail or when our buses will stall, whether our places of employment will be there when we arrive, or whether, in fact, we ourselves will arrive whole and alive at the end of our journeys. Life is pure adventure, and the sooner we realize that, the quicker we will be able to treat life as art: to bring all our energies to each encounter, to remain flexible enough to notice and admit when what we expected to happen did not happen. We need to remember that we are created creative and can invent new scenarios as frequently as they are needed.

17   Life seems to love the liver of it. Money and power can liberate only if they are used to do so. They can imprison and inhibit more finally than barred windows and iron chains.

Checking Your Comprehension

1. What term did Aunt Tee use to describe African Americans? Why did she prefer it?

_____

_____

2. What did her employers say that "won Aunt Tee's sympathy forever"?

_____

_____

3. How did the rich couple that Aunt Tee lived with change over the years?

_____

_____

4. According to the author, what are the basic talents for living well?

_____

_____

Critical Reading and Thinking

1. What kind of a person do you think Aunt Tee was? Point out passages that support this.

   _____

   _____

2. What is the author's attitude toward Aunt Tee and her lifestyle? How can you tell?

   _____

   _____

3. The author stated that "living is an art which can be developed." Do you agree or disagree? Justify your answer.

   _____

   _____

4. Is the last paragraph of this selection a summary or a conclusion? Why?

   _____

   _____

   _____

Words in Context

Directions: Locate each word in the paragraph indicated and reread that paragraph. Then, based on the way the word is used, write a synonym or brief definition. You may use a dictionary, if necessary.

1. revelry (par. 8)   _____

2. beckoned (par. 9)   _____

Vocabulary Review

Directions: Match each word in Column A with its meaning in Column B.

	Column A		Column B
_____	1. comradery	a.	tightly
_____	2. meticulous	b.	expert
_____	3. scenarios	c.	sources
_____	4. incurred	d.	friendship
_____	5. maven	e.	plans; expected events
_____	6. convivial	f.	brought on; met with
_____	7. sinewy	g.	extremely careful
_____	8. tautly	h.	agreeable; cheerful
_____	9. founts	i	lean and muscular

Summarizing the Reading Selection

Directions: Read the following incomplete summary. Then fill in the missing information.

The author describes her _____, a retired domestic servant living in Los Angeles. A woman of color, Aunt Tee worked for _____ as a maid and then live-in housekeeper for various white families in California.

One particular family was the subject of a _____ told by Aunt Tee. This family, a husband and wife, lived in a large house and employed several servants. Aunt Tee noticed the couple aging rapidly, eating less, and becoming more isolated from their friends and even each other. By contrast, she started socializing more and hosted regular Saturday night get-togethers with _____. On one of these Saturday nights, Aunt Tee's employers asked if they could stand _____ and just watch all the fun. They had everything money could buy, but not true happiness.

Aunt Tee's story made a great _____ on the author. She believes it has taught her about living a happy and full life using love, forgiveness, acceptance, flexibility, and creativity.

Writing Exercises

1. Write a paragraph describing your "requirements for good living."

2. Write a paragraph on a favorite relative or friend and explain his or her outlook on life.

3. Maya Angelou says that "life is pure adventure." Do you agree with this? Why or why not?

Selection 2
The Meaning of Work

Rodrigo Joseph Rodriguez

Work means different things to different people. In this selection, the author describes how his father's work experience has inspired him to pursue a different kind of work for himself. It first appeared in the October 1999 issue of *Hispanic Magazine*.

Vocabulary Preview

pursuit (par. 1) the act of striving to accomplish

immeasurable (par. 2) without limits

circuit (par. 2) a regular route from place to place within a territory

refinery (par. 3) an industrial plant for purifying products such as metals, oil, or sugar

diligent (par. 4) characterized by steady, earnest, and energetic effort

muffle (par. 5) something that dulls sound

Prereading

Directions: Preview the selection and answer the following questions.

1. What is the ethnic background of the author and his family?

    _____

2. Who are the two people whose work is described in this selection?

    _____

1   "Had you been born during the day, you would have known the meaning of work," my father says, in Spanish. He looks at my hands and arms. "Had you not gone to college," he says, "you would be working." Perhaps I would have never boxed my books and said goodbye in the pursuit of academic success. Moreover, I would not spend so

much time in libraries, universities, and museums. Instead, I would think of the more familiar life: marriage, family, a steady salary.

2   To papi, after all, this was the dream that founded the United States, a country with immeasurable opportunity—opportunities he hardly ever had, since he worked and lived in the shadows, speaking Spanish and following the cotton circuit. For papi, doing work means doing physical labor, not sitting before a computer screen or curled on the foldout recliner with a book. It means using arm and muscle, putting your hands to everyday use. I remember papi would always arrive from the refinery with dusty hair and an aching body, after the rest of us had finished our homework and had our dinner. His lunch box often held a treat for the first child who'd greet him as he entered the house. Work, work, work. He did not want his children to lead such a life. "If you study hard, you won't have to work like me," he'd warn us in Spanish. "Use this," he'd say, while pointing to his head. Then, he'd offer his hands and arms.

3   The only life he knew was that of a pipefitter at the refinery in Pasadena, Texas. Before a holiday, a bonus from the refinery's payroll office usually awaited him. On such occasions, I looked forward to a father-and-son stroll. Once, while waiting in line, one of papi's co-workers commented that I'd be a good worker when I grew older. "He'll work in air conditioning," my father retorted in English. That's what you should have said, he later told me. At the age of eight, what did I know?

4   Now that I am pursuing graduate study, I reflect on this academically privileged life, and life that has taken me throughout the United States and to other countries. Who would have thought? I wasn't always a bright student. Every grading period, the Cs and Ds told me otherwise. I remember those who hardly believed in me. It was an interior voice, a haunting voice that led me to the world of books. As a diligent student of letters, I read until my eyes squinted; I wrote until my arms ached. While still in high school, I remember sitting, looking out the window and wondering if I would ever receive my diploma to begin my collegiate studies. I was not sure I could do it, but I did. This is not to say everything happened all at once, but I always knew what I wanted: University Avenue. Maybe papi's voice and mami's hopes swirled in the back room of my brain. I like to think that everything was leading to this moment—now.

5   In May, 1997, my father attended my commencement in the rural quiet of Ohio— far away from our native Texas. I earned a bachelor's degree in liberal arts from Kenyon College. And, here I am, as Abraham once said in the Bible, far from that time and place, yet so close. Soon, I will lead two discussions in a class entitled "Masterworks of American Literature." I will ask my students, "What is American literature?" For the sake of hearing our nation's voices, I will speak of American literatures. I shall raise my voice against the muffle of the air conditioner.

6   Unlike family members who entered through the back doors of public institutions in Texas, performing manual labor, I enter academic institutions through the front door. I am reminded of their spirit and physical labor, how they paved the way for me to one day open the pages of books they hardly ever had the time, and, much less, leisure to read. Like the journeys of my forefathers and foremothers who forged paths across borders, I must shape my space in the pursuit of academic success.

Checking Your Comprehension

1. What was the father's definition of work?

   _____

   _____

   _____

2. What did the father want for his son?

   _____

   _____

   _____

3. Why didn't the father have the same opportunities as the son?

   _____

   _____

   _____

4. What clues indicate how the author performed in school?

   _____

   _____

   _____

5. To what does the author attribute his academic motivation?

   _____

   _____

   _____

6. What was the author's college degree?

_____

_____

_____

7. What does the author do now?

_____

_____

_____

Critical Reading and Thinking

1. How would you describe the author's attitude toward his father?

_____

_____

_____

2. Do you think the father is sorry that his son has not chosen "the more familiar life" of marriage, family, and a steady paycheck?

_____

_____

_____

3. What hints does the author give about his relationship with his father?

_____

_____

_____

4. What is the author's purpose? (See Chapter 13.)

_____

_____

_____

5. What does the author mean when he says "Who would have thought?" (par. 4)

_____

_____

_____

6. Explain the phrase "University Avenue" (par. 5).

_____

_____

_____

7. What can you infer from the author's statement that "For the sake of hearing our nation's voices, I will speak of American literatures"? (par. 5)

_____

_____

_____

8. How did his family members "pave the way" for the author? (par. 6)

_____

_____

_____

Words in Context

Directions: Locate each word in the paragraph indicated and reread that paragraph. Then, based on the way the word is used, write a synonym or brief definition. You may use a dictionary, if necessary.

1. boxed (par. 1)   _____

2. privileged (par. 4)   _____

3. interior (par. 4)   _____

Vocabulary Review

Directions: Match each word in Column A with its meaning in Column B.

	Column A		Column B
_____	1. pursuit	a.	an industrial plant for purifying metals, oil, or sugar
_____	2. immeasurable	b.	something that dulls sound
_____	3. circuit	c.	characterized by steady, earnest, and energetic effort
_____	4. refinery	d.	without limits
_____	5. diligent	e.	a regular route from place to place within a territory
_____	6. muffle	f.	the act of striving to accomplish

Summarizing the Reading Selection

Directions: Read the following incomplete summary. Then fill in the missing information.

A son recalls his _____ attitudes toward "work" and how they were shaped by his experiences. Papi, as he was called, held jobs which involved _____ and this is what he considered to be "work." These jobs left him exhausted and in pain at the end of the day. In his native Spanish, he would encourage his children _____ so they would not have _____ as he did.

The author took his father's advice and pushed himself to attend

_____ and then _____. Now his "work" involves

reading and writing, but he does not forget how Papi's _____ in

the fields and factories opened the classroom door for him.

Writing Exercises

1. Write a paragraph describing your own family background. How did family members "pave the way" for you?
2. What is the most difficult job you have ever had? Write a paragraph describing the job and why it was so difficult, and explain whether you would want your own son or daughter to do the same job.

Selection 3
How to Ace a Job Interview

Richard Koonce

There are many ways to handle yourself during a job interview, but some are better than others. Koonce offers a number of helpful suggestions.

Vocabulary Preview

quibble (par. 1) argue; find fault

prospective (par. 2) possible

refinement (par. 5) improvement

concise (par. 5) brief and meaningful

vignettes (par. 5) descriptions

emphasize (par. 10) stress; highlight

etiquette (par. 11) acceptable behavior; manners

Prereading

Directions: Preview the selection and answer the following questions.

1. Did your last job interview go well or poorly? Why?

    _____

    _____

2. Do you consider job interviews to be stressful? Why do you think this is?

_____

_____

1   Next to public speaking, most people think that enduring a job interview is one of the most stressful human experiences. I wouldn't quibble with that. However, a lot of people not only manage to master the art of effective interviewing as they go about job searches, but actually grow to enjoy the interview experience.

2   Good thing! Job interviews are something we all have to deal with from time to time in our careers. So, it pays to know how to handle yourself effectively when you're sitting across the desk from a prospective employer. Indeed, knowing how to navigate the terrain of job interviews can pay off big time for your career, land you a better job than the one you initially interview for, and position you for the job success and satisfaction you deserve.

3   How do you ace a job interview? Here are some tips. Recognize that when you interview for a job, employers are looking for evidence of four things: your ability to do the job, your motivation, your compatibility with the rest of the organization, and your self-confidence. If you understand how all those things play into an interviewer's questions (and an employer's hiring decisions), you'll have a better chance of getting hired.

4   Often the first thing an employer wants to know is, "Will you fit in?" Presuming a company has seen your resume ahead of time and invited you for an interview, it may assume you have certain skills. Now they want to know, "Will you be compatible with everyone else that works here?" Fitting in is a real hot button for employers. That's because it's expensive to go through the rehiring process if someone doesn't work out.

5   Along with determining compatibility, employers want to know that you're motivated to do a job. And, they want to know why you want to work for their organization. So be ready with career highlights that illustrate why hiring you would be a good decision for the organization. Showcase your talents as an instructional designer for example, or tell the interviewer about the process improvement efforts you've put in place in your current job that ensure continuous refinement of training courses. Concise oral vignettes like these can make a great impression on interviewers.

6   Throughout the interview, breathe deeply, speak slowly, and focus on projecting yourself confidently. This is important. Employers want to see self-confidence in job seekers. A lot of job seekers are too modest. They downplay their accomplishments. Don't embellish or exaggerate, but don't be a shrinking violet either. Rehearse ahead of time the answers to key questions that you expect to be asked, especially that all-time favorite: "Tell me about yourself."

7   Some other points to keep in mind:

8   Before the interview, do some research on the company you're interviewing with. That will enable you to demonstrate knowledge of the company when you meet the interviewer. It may also prompt questions that you'll want to get answers to, even as

questions are being asked of you. There are lots of research options. You can tap into the Internet and pull down everything from company profiles to Dun and Bradstreet financial reports. You can talk to friends or co-workers that may know something about the organization. And don't forget to watch the paper for late-breaking developments about the company. (If you read in the paper the day of your interview that your prospective employer is about to file Chapter 11, you may want to think twice about working there!) Arrive for the interview early enough to go to the restroom to check yourself out. The last thing you want is to arrive for your interview beaded with sweat, having just sprinted there from the subway stop two blocks away.

9 Once in the interview, concentrate on making a pleasant and strong first impression. Eighty percent of the first impression an interviewer gets of you is visual—and it's formed in the first two minutes of the meeting! So, men, wear a well-made suit, crisply starched white or blue shirt, and polished shoes. Women, you can get away with more color than men, but dress conservatively in dresses, or jacket and skirt combinations. Wearing a colorful scarf is a good way to weave in color, but keep jewelry to a minimum.

10 As you answer questions, be sure to emphasize as often as you can the reasons why your skills, background, and experience make you a good fit for the job that you're interviewing for.

11 After the interview, immediately send a thank-you note to the interviewer. This is a critical point of interview etiquette. Many job candidates eliminate themselves from competition for a job because they don't do this.

12 Finally, learn from every job interview you have. Don't be hard on yourself if things don't go your way. Even job interviews that don't go well can be great

learning experiences. And in my own life, I can look back on interviews where I'm glad I didn't get the job!

Checking Your Comprehension

1. Employers look for evidence of what four things in job applicants?

   _____

   _____

2. What is often the first thing a prospective employer wants to know about you?

   _____

   _____

3. How can you show a prospective employer that you're motivated to do a job?

   _____

   _____

4. According to the selection, what is the "all-time favorite" thing a prospective employer asks of you?

   _____

   _____

5. The author suggests that you do research on the company you're interviewing with. Name two ways you can do this.

   _____

   _____

6. What accounts most for an employer's first impression of you in a job interview?

   _____

   _____

Critical Reading and Thinking

1. The author states some people "actually grow to enjoy the interview experience." How do you suppose this happens?

   _____

   _____

2. Describe in your own words what a woman should wear to a job interview according to the author.

   _____

   _____

3. The author suggests you breathe deeply and speak slowly. Why should you do this?

   _____

   _____

4. Why do you think it would be wise not to exaggerate your accomplishments during an interview?

   _____

   _____

5. Why do you think it is important to concentrate on making a strong first impression?

   _____

   _____

Words in Context

Directions: Locate each word in the paragraph indicated and reread that paragraph. Then, based on the way the word is used, write a synonym or brief definition. You may use a dictionary, if necessary.

1. navigate (par. 2)   _____

2. compatibility (par. 3)   _____

3. ensure (par. 5)   _____

4. embellish (par. 6)   _____

Vocabulary Review

Directions: Match each word in Column A with its meaning in Column B.

	Column A		Column B
_____	1. etiquette	a.	brief and meaningful
_____	2. vignettes	b.	possible
_____	3. refinement	c.	acceptable behavior; manners
_____	4. emphasize	d.	argue; find fault
_____	5. concise	e.	improvement
_____	6. prospective	f.	descriptions
_____	7. quibble	g.	stress; highlight

Summarizing the Reading Selection

Directions: Read the following incomplete summary. Then fill in the missing information.

Almost everyone goes through a _____ at some point in their life. These interviews can be _____, but preparation and rehearsal can help reduce that stress, and improve your chances of reaching your career goals. Employers want to assess four things during an interview; they are your _____ and _____.

Throughout the interview, candidates should _____

_____

Before the interview, candidates should _____

_____

Once in the interview, candidates should _____

_____

After the interview, candidates should _____

_____

Writing Exercises

1. Write a paragraph describing a job interview you've had.
2. Imagine you've just had the "perfect" job interview. Describe how things went, what you said, and what kind of an impression you made.

Selection 4
Hispanic, USA: The Conveyor-Belt Ladies

Rose Del Castillo Guilbault

An important part of many jobs is getting along with co-workers, as well as working with supervisors and customers. In this article a young woman describes her experiences working in a vegetable packing plant. Read the article to find out how she came to be respected by her older co-workers.

Vocabulary Preview

tedious (par. 4) tiresome, dull

strenuous (par. 4) requiring great physical effort or energy

sorority (par. 5) an organization of women

irrevocably (par. 10) impossible to change

stigmatize (par. 10) to brand or label

gregarious (par. 12) sociable

dyspeptic (par. 12) having a bad disposition, grouchy

pragmatic (par. 17) practical

melancholic (par. 18) sad, gloomy

fatalism (par. 19) the belief that events in life are determined by fate and cannot be changed

crescendo (par. 29) a steady increase in volume or force

anti-climactic (par. 30) an ordinary or commonplace event that concludes a series of important events

Prereading

Directions: Preview the selection and answer the following question.

1. What did you learn about the author's co-workers?

<hr>

1   The conveyor-belt ladies were the migrant women, mostly from Texas, I worked with during the summers of my teenage years. I call them conveyor-belt ladies because our entire relationship took place while sorting tomatoes on a conveyor belt.

2   We were like a cast in a play where all the action occurs on one set. We'd return day after day to perform the same roles, only this stage was a vegetable-packing shed, and at the end of the season there was no applause. The players could look forward only to the same uninspiring parts on a string of grim real-life stages.

3   The women and their families arrived in May for the carrot season, spent the summer in the tomato sheds and stayed through October for the bean harvest. After that, they emptied the town, some returning to their homes in Texas (cities like McAllen, Douglas, Brownsville), while others continued on the migrant trail, picking cotton in the San Joaquin Valley or grapefruits and oranges in the Imperial Valley.

4   Most of these women had started in the fields. The vegetable packing sheds were a step up, easier than the back-breaking, grueling work the field demanded. The work was more tedious than strenuous, paid better, provided fairly steady hours and clean bathrooms. Best of all, you weren't subjected to the elements.

5   The summer I was 16, my mother got jobs for both of us as tomato sorters. That's how I came to be included in the seasonal sorority of the conveyor belt.

6   The work consisted of standing and picking flawed tomatoes off the conveyor belt before they rolled off into the shipping boxes at the end of the line. These boxes were immediately loaded onto waiting delivery trucks, so it was crucial not to let imperfect tomatoes through.

7   The work could be slow or intense, depending on the quality of the tomatoes and how many there were. Work increased when the company's deliveries got backlogged or after rainy weather had delayed picking.

8   During those times, it was not unusual to work from 7 A.M. to midnight, playing catch-up. I never heard anyone complain about the overtime. Overtime meant desperately needed extra money.

9   I was not happy to be part of the agricultural work force. I would have preferred working in a dress shop or baby-sitting, like my friends. But I had a dream that would cost a lot of money—college. And the fact was, this was the highest-paying work I could do.

10 But it wasn't so much the work that bothered me. I was embarrassed because only Mexicans worked at packing sheds. I had heard my schoolmates joke about the "ugly, fat Mexican women" at the sheds. They ridiculed the way they dressed and laughed at the "funny way" they talked. I feared working with them would irrevocably stigmatize me, setting me further apart from my Anglo classmates.

11   At 16 I was more American than Mexican and, with adolescent arrogance, felt superior to these "uneducated" women. I might be one of them, I reasoned, but I was not like them.

12   But it was difficult not to like the women. They were a gregarious, entertaining group, easing the long, monotonous hours with bawdy humor, spicy gossip and inventive laments. They poked fun at all the male workers and did hysterical impersonations of a dyspeptic Anglo supervisor. Although he didn't speak Spanish (other than "*Mujeres, trabajo, trabajo!*"), he seemed to sense he was being laughed at. That would account for the sudden rages when he would stamp his foot and forbid us to talk until break time.

13   "I bet he understands Spanish and just pretends so he can hear what we say," I whispered to Rosa.

14   "*Ay, no hija*, it's all the buzzing in his ears that alerts him that these *viejas* (old women) are bad-mouthing him!" Rosa giggled.

15   But it would have been easier to tie the women's tongues in a knot than to keep them quiet. Eventually the ladies had their way and their fun, and the men learned to ignore them.

16   We were often shifted around, another strategy to keep us quiet. This gave me ample opportunity to get to know everyone, listen to their life stories and absorb the gossip.

17   Pretty Rosa described her romances and her impending wedding to a handsome field worker. Bertha, a heavy-set, dark-skinned woman, told me that Rosa's marriage would cause nothing but headaches because the man was younger and too handsome. Maria, large, moon-faced and placid, described the births of each of her nine children, warning me about the horrors of childbirth. Pragmatic Minnie, a tiny woman who always wore printed cotton dresses, scoffed at Maria's stupidity, telling me she wouldn't have so many kids if she had ignored that good-for-nothing priest and gotten her tubes tied!

18   In unexpected moments, they could turn melancholic: recounting the babies who died because their mothers couldn't afford medical care; the alcoholic, abusive husbands who were their "cross to bear"; the racism they experienced in Texas, where they were branded "dirty Mexicans" or "Mexican dogs" and not allowed in certain restaurants.

19   They spoke with the detached fatalism of people with limited choices and alternatives. Their lives were as raw and brutal as ghetto streets—something they accepted with an odd grace and resignation.

20   I was appalled and deeply affected by these confidences. The injustices they endured enraged me; their personal struggles overwhelmed me. I knew I could do little but sympathize.

21   My mother, no stranger to suffering, suggested I was too impressionable when I emotionally told her the women's stories. "That's nothing," she'd say lightly. "If they were in Mexico, life would be even harder. At least there's opportunities here, you can work."

22   My icy arrogance quickly thawed, that first summer, as my respect for the conveyor-belt ladies grew.

23   I worked in the packing sheds for several summers. The last season also turned out to be the last time I lived at home. It was the end of a chapter in my life, but I didn't know it then. I had just finished junior college and was transferring to the university. I was already over-educated for seasonal work, but if you counted the overtime, no other jobs came close to paying so well, so I went back one last time.

24   The ladies treated me with warmth and respect. I was a college student, deserving of special treatment.

25   Aguedia, the crew chief, moved me to softer and better-paying jobs within the plant. I went from the conveyor belt to shoving boxes down a chute and finally to weighing boxes of tomatoes on a scale—the highest-paying position for a woman.

26   When the union's dues collector showed up, the women hid me in the bathroom. They had decided it was unfair for me to have to join the union and pay dues, since I worked only during the summer.

27   "Where's the student?" the union rep would ask, opening the door to a barrage of complaints about the union's unfairness.

28   Maria (of the nine children) tried to feed me all summer, bringing extra tortillas, which were delicious. I accepted them guiltily, always wondering if I was taking food away from her children. Others would bring rental contracts or other documents for me to explain and translate.

29   The last day of work was splendidly beautiful, warm and sunny. If this had been a movie, these last scenes would have been shot in soft focus, with a crescendo of music in the background.

30   But real life is anti-climactic. As it was, nothing unusual happened. The conveyor belt's loud humming was turned off, silenced for the season. The women sighed as they removed their aprons. Some of them just walked off, calling *Hasta la próxima!* Until next time!

31   But most of the conveyor-belt ladies shook my hand, gave me a blessing or a big hug.

32   "Make us proud!" they said.

33   I hope I have.

Checking Your Comprehension

1. Who were the "conveyor-belt ladies?" What did you discover about their lives?

_____

_____

2. Describe the primary job of the conveyor-belt ladies.

_____

_____

3. Why did the author choose to work at the packing shed?

_____

_____

4. Why was the author initially unhappy about working at the packing shed?

_____

_____

5. Why did the ladies hide the author when the union's dues collector arrived?

_____

_____

Critical Reading and Thinking

1. Since the author is of Mexican-American descent, why did she initially feel superior to her Mexican-American co-workers?

_____

_____

2. In what ways did the author's attitude change toward her co-workers?

_____

_____

3. Why did the author's attitude change toward her co-workers?

_____

_____

4. Describe the conveyor-belt ladies' attitude toward education.

_____

_____

5. Explain why the author's last day was anti-climactic.

_____

_____

Words in Context

Directions: Locate each word in the paragraph indicated and reread that paragraph. Then, based on the way the word is used, write a synonym or brief definition. You may use a dictionary, if necessary.

1. uninspiring (par. 2)   _____

2. grueling (par. 4)   _____

3. impending (par. 17)   _____

4. scoffed (par. 17)   _____

5. recounting (par. 18)   _____

Vocabulary Review

Directions: Match each word in Column A with its meaning in Column B.

Column A	Column B
_____ 1. gregarious	a. label
_____ 2. dyspeptic	b. unable to change
_____ 3. stigmatize	c. practical
_____ 4. sorority	d. sociable
_____ 5. pragmatic	e. grouchy
_____ 6. tedious	f. hard physical work
_____ 7. melancholic	g. gloomy
_____ 8. irrevocably	h. belief that life is controlled by fate
_____ 9. strenuous	i. tiresome
_____ 10. fatalism	j. steady increase in volume
_____ 11. anti-climactic	k. group of women
_____ 12. crescendo	l. commonplace event

Summarizing the Reading Selection

Directions: Read the following incomplete summary. Then fill in the missing information.

The author describes her experiences _____ along a

conveyor belt sorting _____. A teenager, she hoped for a

better future and was working at this relatively high-paying job to save

money for _____.

At first she felt ashamed to be _____

_____ She learned, however, that the

women were _____ She

also heard about _____

Every summer the author _____

_____ During her final months there, she _____

_____ On her last day, _____

_____

_____

Writing Exercises

1. Write a paragraph describing a situation or event that changed your attitude toward a person or group.

2. The author compares her job to performing in a play. Write a paragraph comparing a job you hold or have held to a play or some other event to which it is similar.

Selection 5
The Case for Selling Human Organs

Ronald Bailey

The need for human organs has reached a crisis. In this selection, the author (*Reason Magazine*'s science correspondent and the editor of *Earth Report 2000: Revisiting the True State of the Planet*) argues that one way to solve the organ shortage would be to pay organ donors or their families for their organs. This article first appeared on the Web site of *Reason* magazine in 2001.

Vocabulary Preview

cadaveric (par. 3) alive but with no brain function; brain-dead

salutary (par. 5) favorable or wholesome

durable (par. 7) long-lasting

euphemisms (par. 8) mild or pleasant expressions used in place of offensive or unpleasant terms

biotech (par. 10) biotechnology; the application of the principles of engineering and technology to the life sciences

surrogate (par. 11) a substitute; functioning in place of another

coercion (par. 13) forcing one to do something by use of pressure, threats or intimidation

dialysis (par. 14) a medical procedure in which blood is removed from an artery, purified, and returned to a vein

ethicists (par. 14) people who specialize in the rules or standards governing the moral conduct of individuals or members of a profession

Prereading

Directions: Preview the selection and answer the following questions.

1. How do you feel about organ donation?

   _____

   _____

2. Have you ever known someone who needed, received, or donated an organ?

   _____

   _____

1   National Organ and Tissue Donor Awareness Week is, by order of Congress, celebrated this week. It's been 34 years since Dr. Christian Bernard performed the world's first heart transplant in Cape Town, South Africa, but the modern era of organ transplantation essentially began when the anti-rejection drug cyclosporin was introduced in 1981.

2   In 2000, 22,827 organs were transplanted in the United States. Since 1990, a total of 185,347 organs have been transplanted into patients in the U.S. That's the good news.

3   The bad news is that, according to the nonprofit United Network for Organ Sharing (UNOS), there are now 75,863 men, women and children on the national organ transplantation waiting list. That's up from 20,481 a decade ago. Cadaveric donors—that is brain-dead donors—increased from 4,011 in 1989 to 5,984 in 2000, according to the U.S. Department of Health and Human Services (HHS). An average of 3.6 organs for transplant were taken from cadaveric donors. Meanwhile living donors surged from 1,918 in 1989 to 5,532 in 2000.

4   Despite these increases, an average of 15 people still die every day while waiting for an organ that could have saved their lives. "With the success and acceptance of organ transplantation, it has become routine therapy for many diseases," UNOS President Patricia Adams says. "We have the know-how to save tends of thousands of lives. What we don't have are enough donated organs to make it possible."

5   HHS Secretary Tommy Thompson announced plans to address the organ shortage by exploring the idea of creating a national online registry where people can officially record their desire to be organ donors after they die. Thompson has also launched a campaign to get corporations to discuss becoming donors with their employees. Finally, Thompson wants to create a national medal to honor the families of organ donors. All of these are decent, salutary goals. And they will do absolutely nothing to end the shortage.

6   The normal way to handle shortages is to let prices rise to the market-clearing price. With organs, it might work this way: A cadaveric donor's family might be able to sell their dear departed's organs to patients who need them. Better yet, consenting living donors would be able to bargain with transplantees or their insurance companies for the sale of, say, a kidney or a piece of liver (both can be surgically removed without causing much permanent harm to the seller). But there is nothing resembling a market in human organs in the United States.

7   Why? At the very beginning of the organ transplant era some people feared that their doctors might hasten their deaths in order to obtain transplantable organs. Others worried that people living in rich countries might pay poor people living in developing countries for their organs. These fears have given rise to one of the most durable urban legends of all time: the one about the guy who goes to Spring Break in Florida and wakes up 3 days later in a hotel room with a hole in his side through which someone has extracted one of his kidneys.

8   The taboo topic in the organ transplant community is payment for organs. When it is discussed, euphemisms like "rewarded gifting" or "compensated donation" are used.

9   In 1983, Dr. Barry Jacobs publicly suggested that the U.S. government consider setting up a fund to compensate the families of cadaveric donors. Dr. Jacobs also proposed to set up a business that would buy kidneys from living donors for transplantation in American patients. Spearheaded by U.S. Reps. Henry Waxman and Al Gore, Congress rushed the passage of the National Organ Transplantation Act in 1984 to ban the sale of human organs from either dead or living donors.

10 National Organ and Tissue Donor Awareness Week is an appropriate time to rethink this policy. In the long run, the organ shortage may be solved with biotech miracles like transplantable animal organs genetically tailored to match individual human immune systems, or by repairing damaged organs using human stem cells. But in the short run, monetary incentives will matter. As one transplant physician pointed out to me years ago, everybody else in the transplant business—from doctors to hospitals to pharmaceutical companies—gets paid. And, of course, the recipient gets something far more valuable than money. Given all that, it seemed reasonable to him that the bereaved families of brain-dead donors should be paid something, too.

11 But what about compensating living donors? It should be noted that in the United States we already have robust markets for blood, semen, human eggs, and surrogate wombs. Extending markets to include non-vital solid organs such as kidneys and pieces of liver, which can be obtained with reasonable safety from living donors, is not such a stretch. Keep in mind that of the more than 75,000 people on the waiting list for organs, 48,639 need kidneys and 17,413 need livers.

12 *The Journal of the American Medical Association* published its "Consensus Statement on the Live Organ Donor" in its December 13, 2000, issue which offers this guidance for determining when living organ donations are appropriate:

13 "The person who gives consent to be a live organ donor should be competent, willing to donate, free from coercion, medically and psychosocially suitable, fully informed of the risks and benefits as a donor, and fully informed of the risks, benefits, and alternative treatment available to the recipient. The benefits to both donor and recipient must outweigh the risks associated with the donation and transplantation of the living donor organ."

14 All of that is quite reasonable; the emphasis on true donor consent gets around the grisly reality in communist China, where organs are harvested from prisoners without consent. For the transplant recipient the hoped for benefits are clear—they are freed from dialysis, their health improves, they avoid dying. But how can doctors and ethicists be certain that the benefits outweigh the risks for the living donor? One good way to make sure that the "benefits to both the donor and the recipient must outweigh the risks" is to offer appropriate monetary compensation to a living donor for a kidney or a piece of liver.

15 When that happens, it will finally be time to celebrate National Organ and Tissue Donor Awareness Week.

Checking Your Comprehension

1. How does the author propose to address the organ shortage?

_____

_____

2. How does Health and Human Services Secretary Tommy Thompson propose to address the organ shortage?

_____

_____

3. According to the author, why isn't there a market in human organs in the United States?

_____

_____

4. What are the two organs mentioned by the author that can be removed without permanent harm to a living donor?

_____

_____

5. What happened as a result of Dr. Barry Jacobs' proposals regarding organ donation?

_____

_____

6. What guidelines currently exist for determining when living organ donations are appropriate?

_____

_____

7. How does China treat organ donation?

_____

_____

Critical Reading and Thinking

1. What types of information does the author use to support his argument?

   _____

   _____

2. What are the author's qualifications?

   _____

   _____

3. How can you tell that the writing in this article is slanted?

   _____

   _____

4. What is the author's purpose? (See Chapter 13.)

   _____

   _____

Words in Context

Directions: Locate each word in the paragraph indicated and reread that paragraph. Then, based on the way the word is used, write a synonym or brief definition. You may use a dictionary, if necessary.

1. launched (par. 5)   _____

2. hasten (par. 7)   _____

3. taboo (par. 8)   _____

4. incentives (par. 10)   _____

5. robust (par. 11)   _____

6. harvested (par. 14)   _____

Vocabulary Review

Directions: Match each word in Column A with its meaning in Column B.

Column A

1. cadaveric
2. salutary
3. durable
4. euphemisms
5. biotech
6. bereaved
7. surrogate
8. coercion
9. dialysis
10. ethicists

Column B

a. long-lasting

b. the application of the principles of engineering and technology to the life sciences

c. suffering the death of a loved one

d. forcing one to do something by use of pressure, threats or intimidation

e. alive but with no brain function

f. mild or pleasant expressions used in place of offensive or unpleasant terms

g. a medical procedure in which blood is removed from an artery, purified, and returned to a vein

h. a substitute; functioning in place of another

i. people who specialize in the rules or standards governing the moral conduct of individuals or members of a profession

j. favorable or wholesome

Summarizing the Reading Selection

Directions: On a separate sheet of paper, write a short summary (1–3 paragraphs) of the reading. Use your own words, but be concise and complete.

Writing Exercises

1. Do you plan to donate your organs? Write a paragraph explaining your decision.
2. What is your opinion of paying donors for their organs as a solution to the organ shortage? Write a paragraph explaining your view.
3. Why do you think payment for organs is a "taboo" topic in the organ transplant community? Explain your view.

Selection 6
A Guard's First Night on the Job

William Recktenwald

A prison is a separate society with its own set of rules and behaviors. This selection describes one evening in a prison from the viewpoint of a new guard.

Vocabulary Preview

rookie (par. 1) beginner or novice

cursory (par. 4) hastily done with little attention to detail

tiers (par. 5) groups of cells, rooms, or items arranged above or behind each other

apprehensive (par. 16) worried, anxious, or concerned

ruckus (par. 17) noisy confusion or disturbance

mace (par. 22) chemical with the combined effect of tear gas and nerve gas used
    to stun its victims

equivalent (par. 25) equal to

Prereading

Directions: Preview the selection and answer the following question.

> What fears and feelings would you have if you were just hired as a prison guard? What problems would you expect to face?

1   . . .When I arrived for my first shift, 3 to 11 P.M., I had not had a minute of training except for a one-hour orientation lecture the previous day. I was a "fish," a rookie guard, and very much out of my depth.

2   A veteran officer welcomed the "fish" and told us: "Remember, these guys don't have anything to do all day, 24 hours a day, but think of ways to make you mad. No matter what happens, don't lose your cool. Don't lose your cool!"

3   I had been assigned to the segregation unit, containing 215 inmates who are the most trouble. It was an assignment nobody wanted.

4   To get there, I passed through seven sets of bars. My uniform was my only ticket through each of them. Even on my first day, I was not asked for any identification, searched, or sent through a metal detector. I could have been carrying weapons, drugs, or any other contraband. I couldn't believe this was what's meant by a maximum-security institution. In the week I worked at Pontiac, I was subjected to only one check, and that one was cursory.

5   The segregation unit consists of five tiers, or galleries. Each is about 300 feet long and has 44 cells. The walkways are about 3½ feet wide, with the cells on one side and

a rail and cyclone fencing on the other. As I walked along one gallery, I noticed that my elbows could touch cell bars and fencing at the same time. That made me easy pickings for anybody reaching out of a cell.

6   The first thing (they) told me was that a guard must never go out on a gallery by himself. You've got no weapons with which to defend yourself, not even a radio to summon help. All you've got is the man with whom you're working.

7   My partner that first night was Bill Hill, a soft-spoken six-year veteran who immediately told me to take the cigarettes out of my shirt pocket because the inmates would steal them. Same for my pen, he said—or "They'll grab it and stab you."

8   We were told to serve dinner on the third tier, and Hill quickly tried to fill me in on the facts of prison life. That's when I learned about cookies and the importance they have to the inmates.

9   "They're going to try and grab them, they're going to try to steal them any way they can," he said. "Remember, you only have enough cookies for the gallery, and if you let them get away, you'll have to explain to the guys at the end why there weren't any for them."

10   Hill then checked out the meal, groaning when he saw the drippy ravioli and stewed tomatoes. "We're going to be wearing this," he remarked, before deciding to simply discard the tomatoes. We served nothing to drink. In my first six days at Pontiac, I never saw an inmate served a beverage.

11   Hill instructed me to put on plastic gloves before we served the meal. In view of the trash and waste through which we'd be wheeling the food cart, I thought he was joking. He wasn't.

12   "Some inmates don't like white hands touching their food," he explained.

13   Everything went routinely as we served the first 20 cells, and I wasn't surprised when every inmate asked for extra cookies.

14   Suddenly, a huge arm shot through the bars of one cell and began swinging a metal rod at Hill. As he ducked away, the inmate snared the cookie box.

15   From the other side of the cart, I lunged to grab the cookies—and was grabbed in turn. A powerful hand from the cell behind me was pulling my arm. As I jerked away, objects began crashing about, and a metal can struck me in the back.

16   Until that moment I had been apprehensive. Now I was scared. The food cart virtually trapped me, blocking my retreat.

17   Whirling around, I noticed that mirrors were being held out of every cell so the inmates could watch the ruckus. I didn't realize the mirrors were plastic and became terrified that the inmates would start smashing them to cut me up.

18   The ordinary din of the cell house had turned into a deafening roar. For the length of the tier, arms stretched into the walkway, making grabbing motions. Some of the inmates swung brooms about.

19   "Let's get out of here—now!" Hill barked. Wheeling the food cart between us, we made a hasty retreat.

20   Downstairs, we reported what had happened. My heart was thumping, my legs felt weak. Inside the plastic gloves, my hands were soaked with sweat. Yet the attack on

us wasn't considered unusual by the other guards, especially in segregation. That was strictly routine, and we didn't even file a report.

21   What was more shocking was to be sent immediately back to the same tier to pass out medication. But as I passed the cells from which we'd been attacked, the men in them simply requested their medicine. It was as if what had happened minutes before was already ancient history. From another cell, however, an inmate began raging at us. "Get my medication," he said. "Get it now, or I'm going to kill you." I was learning that whatever you're handing out, everybody wants it, and those who don't get it frequently respond by threatening to kill or maim you. Another fact of prison life.

22   Passing cell No. 632, I saw that a prisoner I had helped take to the hospital before dinner was back in his cell. When we took him out, he had been disabled by mace and was very wobbly. Hill and I had been extremely gentle, handcuffing him carefully, then practically carrying him down the stairs. As we went by his cell this time, he tossed a cup of liquid on us.

23   Back downstairs, I learned I would be going back to that tier for a third time, to finish serving dinner. This time, we planned to slip in the other side of the tier so we wouldn't have to pass the trouble cells. The plates were already prepared.

24   "Just get in there and give them their food and get out," Hill said. I could see he was nervous, which made me even more so. "Don't stop for anything. If you get hit, just back off, 'cause if they snare you or hook you some way and get you against the bars, they'll hurt you real bad."

25   Everything went smoothly. Inmates in the three most troublesome cells were not getting dinner, so they hurled some garbage at us. But that's something else I had learned: Getting no worse than garbage thrown at you is the prison equivalent of everything going smoothly.

Checking Your Comprehension

1. This selection describes the events that occurred during the guard's first night on the job. How is this selection organized?

   _____

   _____

2. What main point does the guard make? (See the Chapter 7 discussion of Main Ideas.)

   _____

   _____

3. Why did the guards wear gloves to serve the food?

_____

_____

4. Explain the prisoners' use of mirrors.

_____

_____

5. Write a summary of the guard's experiences. (See Chapter 12 discussion of Summarizing.)

_____

_____

Critical Reading and Thinking

1. Using evidence from the selection, show why the guard did not feel prepared to begin his first shift.

_____

_____

2. Do you think the new guard disagreed with how some things are done in a prison? If so, list the things with which the guard seemed dissatisfied.

_____

_____

3. Explain the figurative expression "I was a 'fish,' a rookie guard, and very much out of my depth." (See the Chapter 13 discussion of Figurative Language.)

_____

_____

4. What did you learn about life as a prisoner from this selection?

_____

_____

5. Why do you think the prisoner in Cell 632, whom the guards had treated gently on the way to the hospital, threw a cup of liquid at them later in the same evening?

_____

_____

6. Why are cookies so important to the prisoners? What might they represent?

_____

_____

7. This selection was reprinted in a textbook titled *Introduction to Criminology*. Why do you think the author of the textbook included this selection?

_____

_____

8. Decide whether this selection is a narrative or a descriptive essay. Defend your choice by referring to parts of the selection.

_____

_____

9. Based on his limited experience of one evening, the guard formed some generalizations about the prisoners and prison life. Underline several of these generalizations. (See the Chapter 14 discussion of Generalizations.)

_____

_____

Words in Context

Directions: Locate each word in the paragraph indicated and reread that paragraph. Then, based on the way the word is used, write a synonym or brief definition. You may use a dictionary, if necessary.

1. contraband (par. 4) _____

2. din (par. 18) _____

3. maim (par. 21) _____

Vocabulary Review

Directions: Use the words listed in the Vocabulary Preview to complete each of the following sentences.

1. A beginner on a professional hockey team is called a _____

2. An instructor who spent little time reading essay exams could be said to have read them in a _____ manner.

3. One kilometer is _____ to .62 miles.

4. The students were _____ about their final grades in chemistry.

5. The class of kindergarten children visiting the zoo created a _____

6. The police officer used _____ to stop the man who was attacking her.

7. The lobby of the new hotel had several _____

Summarizing the Reading Selection

Directions: On a separate sheet of paper, write a short summary (1–3 paragraphs) of the reading. Use your own words, but be concise and complete.

Writing Exercises

1. This selection was written from the perspective of the guard describing how he felt his first night on the job. Write a paragraph that describes the guard from

the perspective of one of the prisoners. (What do you think he looked like? How did he act? Was he nervous or frightened?)

2. Write a paragraph describing an experience for which you felt unprepared and how you handled it.

3. Write a paragraph explaining what you think is right or wrong with prisons today.

Selection 7
A Day on Wheels

Cheryl A. Davis

What should or shouldn't you say to a person who is disabled? This article describes some examples of rude behavior and the author's reactions to them.

Vocabulary Preview

meditation (par. 4) deep thought

gratuitous (par. 5) uncalled for

persistent (par. 5) unrelenting

unsolicited overture (par. 7) unasked-for response

apropos (par. 12) relevant

comme il faut (par. 16) as it should be, appropriate

dubious (par. 17) doubtful

mediating (par. 25) settling, conciliating

mortified (par. 27) shamed, humiliated

flagellated (par. 28) punished

adroit (par. 28) clever

paraplegic (par. 29) without use of the legs

haughtier (par. 31) more contemptful

civilities (par. 39) niceties, pleasantries

schizophrenia (par. 41) a mental illness

conciliatory (par. 45) soothing, friendly

Prereading

Directions: Preview the selection and answer the following questions.

1. What kinds of questions do people ask disabled people?

   _____

   _____

   _____

2. How would you react if you were disabled and were asked such questions?

   _____

   _____

   _____

1   "Man, if I was you, I'd shoot myself," said the man on the subway platform. No one else was standing near him. I realized he was talking to me.

2   "Luckily, you're not," I said, gliding gracefully away.

3   For me, this was not an unusual encounter; indeed, it was a typical episode in my continuing true-life sitcom, "Day on Wheels."

4   A train ride can be an occasion for silent meditation in the midst of mechanical commotion. Unfortunately, I rarely get to meditate.

5   I attract attention. I pretend to ignore them, the eyes that scrutinize me and then quickly glance away. I try to avoid the gratuitous chats with loosely wrapped passengers. Usually, I fail. They may be loosely wrapped, but they're a persistent lot.

6   I use a wheelchair; I am not "confined" to one. Actually, I get around well. I drive a van equipped with a wheelchair-lift to the train station. I use a powered wheelchair with high-amperage batteries to get to work. A manual chair, light enough to carry, enables me to visit the "walkies" who live upstairs and to ride in their Volkswagens.

7   My life has been rich and varied, but my fellow passengers assume that, as a disabled person, I must be horribly deprived and so lonely that I will appreciate any unsolicited overture.

8   "Do you work?" a woman on the train asked me recently.

9   I said I did.

10 "It's nice that you have something to keep you busy, isn't it?"

11 Since we are thought of as poor invalids in need of chatting up, people are not apt to think too hard about what they are saying to us. It seems odd, since they also worry about the "right" way to talk to disabled people.

12 "How do you take a bath?" another woman asked me, apropos of nothing.

13 One day, an elderly man was staring at me as I read the newspaper.

14 "Would you like to read the sports section?" I asked him.

15   "How many miles can that thing go before you need new batteries?" he responded.

16   When I was a little girl, I once saw a woman whose teeth looked strange. "Mommy, that lady has funny teeth," I said. My mother explained that it was not *comme il faut* to offer up personal observations about other people's appearances. I thought everyone's mommy taught that, but I was wrong.

17   For many years, I was in what some of us call "the phyz-diz-biz"—developing housing and educational programs for disabled people. I was active in the disability-rights movement. I went to "special" schools offering the dubious blessing of a segregated education. As a result, I have known several thousand disabled people, at one time or another, across the United States.

18   For those whose disablement is still recent, the gratuitous remarks and unsolicited contributions can be exceptionally hurtful. It takes time to learn how to protect yourself. To learn how to do it gracefully can take a lifetime.

19   Many of us take the position that the people who bother us are to be pitied for their ignorance. We take it upon ourselves to "educate" them. We forgive them their trespasses and answer their questions patiently and try to straighten them out.

20   Others prefer to ignore the rude remarks and questions altogether. I tried that, but it didn't work. There was one woman on the train who tipped the scales for me.

21   "You're much too pretty to be in a wheelchair," she said.

22   I stared straight ahead, utterly frozen in unanticipated rage.

23   Undaunted, she grabbed my left arm below the elbow to get my attention.

24   "I said, 'You're much too pretty to be in a wheelchair.'"

25   In my fury, I lost control. Between my brain and my mouth, the mediating force of acquired tact had vanished.

26   "What do you think?" I snapped. "That God holds a beauty contest and if you come in first, you don't have to be in one?"

27   She turned away and, a moment later, was chatting with an old woman beside her as if nothing had been said at all. But I was mortified, and I moved to the other end of the train car.

28   For that one lapse, I flagellated myself all afternoon. When I got home, I telephoned one of my more socially adroit disabled friends for advice.

29   Nick is a therapist, a Ph.D. from Stanford, and paraplegic. "How do you deal with the other bozos on the bus?" I asked him.

30   "I just say, 'Grow up,'" Nick answered.

31   That was a bit haughtier than I could pull off, I told him.

32   "Well, look," he said, "if those words don't do it, find something else. The main thing is to get them to stop bothering you, right?"

33   "Yes, but—"

34   "But what?"

35   "Nick, if I'm *too* rude, they won't learn a thing. They'll just tell themselves I'm maladjusted."

36   "Then tell them their behavior is inappropriate."

37   "Inappropriate. That's marvelous!" I decided to try it next time.

38   "Next time" arrived last week. I didn't see the man coming. I was on the train platform, and he approached me from behind and tapped me on the shoulder.

39   "What's your disability?" he asked, discarding civilities.

40   I turned and looked at him. "That is not an appropriate question to ask a stranger," I said quietly.

41   "Well, *I* have schizophrenia," he said proudly.

42   "I didn't ask you."

43   "I feel rejected," he said.

44   "Well, then don't say things like that to people you don't know."

45   The train came and we got on together. I offered him a conciliatory remark, and he quieted down. Clearly he was not the best person for my new approach, but I think I'm headed in the right direction.

Checking Your Comprehension

1. What kinds of assumptions do people make about disabled people?

    _____

    _____

2. What did the author's mother teach her?

    _____

    _____

3. How did the author feel after talking back to the people who asked her questions?

    _____

    _____

4. What happened when the author tried to ignore a rude remark?

    _____

    _____

5. What is the author's new approach to being asked rude questions? Has it worked so far?

_____

_____

Critical Reading and Thinking

1. What kind of generalizations does the author make about people who are not disabled? (See the Chapter 14 discussion of Generalizations.)

_____

_____

2. What is the author's purpose? (See the Chapter 13 discussion of the Author's Purpose.)

_____

_____

3. List five words the author uses that demonstrate her feelings about being asked inappropriate questions.

_____

_____

4. Why do you think people ask the kind of questions the author mentions?

_____

_____

5. Why does the author make a distinction between using a wheelchair and being confined to one? (par. 6) What are the connotations of these terms? (See the Chapter 13 discussion of Connotations.)

_____

_____

Words in Context

Directions: Locate each word in the paragraph indicated and reread that paragraph. Then, based on the way the word is used, write a synonym or brief definition. You may use a dictionary, if necessary.

1. commotion (par. 4)   _____

2. scrutinize (par. 5)   _____

3. high-amperage (par. 6) _____

4. undaunted (par. 23)   _____

Vocabulary Review

Directions: Use the words listed in the Vocabulary Preview to complete each of the following sentences.

1. Apologies are very _____ since they smooth things over.

2. She was _____ when her wig blew off.

3. The child's _____ comments interrupted serious adult conversation.

4. Because the attorney was very _____, the firm decided to hire her.

5. _____ are often exchanged when people run into old friends.

6. The contestant on the game show looked _____ as he gave his answer, but to his surprise, he learned it was correct.

7. Since the conversation was about museums, the comment about houseplants was not _____.

8. The child kept asking her father for candy; because she was so _____, he finally gave her some.

Summarizing the Reading Selection

Directions: On a separate sheet of paper, write a short summary (1–3 paragraphs) of the reading. Use your own words, but be concise and complete.

Writing Exercise

Describe an instance in which someone asked you an annoying, rude, or ignorant question about yourself and how you responded.

Selection 8
Learn to Handle Stress

David Mahoney and Richard Restak

Are you feeling stressed out? This selection offers some immediately useful, practical advice on how to deal with your stresses.

Vocabulary Preview

elaborate (par. 1) complicated

stressors (par. 3) sources of stress

prevailing (par. 5) overwhelming; overpowering

anticipated (par. 5) expected; looked forward to

cynical (par. 5) distrustful; disbelieving; suspicious

tangible (par. 6) real; clear-cut

diversify (par. 8) vary

centenarian (par. 9) a person who is at least 100 years old

Prereading

Directions: Preview the selection and answer the following questions.

1. What seems to cause the most stress for you? Why?

   _____

   _____

2. What do you usually do to help control the stress you feel?

_____

_____

1   Each of us is engaged in an elaborate juggling game involving work, family, intimate relationships, and self-interest. And managing these separate, interrelated areas of our lives creates stress.

2   Stress is best thought of as the way we respond to a physical or emotional demand. That demand may be something as unpleasant as the notification of a tax audit or as exciting as learning you've just won the lottery. In many instances stress is internally defined.

3   At this point, pause and consider: How do I regard stressors? As a loss of control? A punishment? How can we manage stress and maintain healthy functioning?

4   Let's remember that juggling act we are involved in. It's no longer sufficient to do well in two or three of those four areas (work, family, relationships, and self-interest); we have to master all four of them. Author and clinical psychologist Wayne M. Sotile believes that stress results when we concentrate on one area—usually work—and ignore the other three. We don't allow enough time for simple pleasures, thus forego-ing the key to managing stress: "resiliency—the ability to recover strength, spirit, and good humor quickly."

5   Sotile has identified a behavioral pattern he calls "hurry sickness," from which far too many of us suffer. Someone afflicted with "hurry sickness" experiences a prevail-ing sense of time urgency—there is never enough time to get things done. This leads to impatience with self and others; perfectionism, multi-tasking (doing too many things at one time), irritability, and temper tantrums when things don't come together as quickly or as easily as anticipated. Sufferers from "hurry sickness" are also competi-tive with others, controlling, hostile, cynical, and, most characteristic, totally involved in their work.

6   As an antidote to the stress of "hurry sickness" Sotile suggests we put our best efforts into maintaining our relationships. We need:

- *Tangible support:* someone to help us if we are sick or temporarily disabled.
- *Affectionate support:* someone to show love and affection, make us feel wanted.
- *Positive social interaction:* someone to have a good time with, get together with, and relax with.
- *Emotional/informational support:* someone to listen when we need to talk, give advice in times of crises.

7   Most people give and receive these supports in a marriage—one of the reasons we advise investing in your family dimension. A happy marriage is associated with a

decreased incidence of psychiatric illness, alcohol abuse, suicide, risk of death, and level of stress.

8   Other time-proven methods of reducing stress include:

1. Learn to "let go" of things that are outside of your control. Numerous studies on managing stress emphasize the importance of "accepting a stressful situation." That doesn't mean lying down and playing dead. It means you act like a boxer: You accept the challenge, don't give in to panic, put out your best shots, and stop worrying. If you're in over your head this time, there will be other fights in your future.

2. Learn to act when what you do can make a difference.

3. Balance work and recreation. Diversify your career from the beginning by taking up a serious avocation.

4. Work off the sense of stress by physical activity. A punching bag is a great means of keeping in shape and expressing hostility in a healthy way.

5. Take frequent breaks during the day. Not only does this create a change of pace, it also often leads to new outlooks or new attitudes.

6. Make yourself available to other people. When bored or lonely, call a friend and do something together. The best way of keeping ourselves in good repair is by tending and nourishing our relationships with others.

7. Get out of yourself by doing something for others. Most of us spend too much time inside our own heads. When we give our time to a person or a cause we believe in, stress disappears. It's amazing how difficult it is to put into practice this oldest and hardest rule: Only by giving do we receive.

8. Avoid the use of chemicals or food to alter your moods. Avoid sedatives and tranquilizers, limit caffeine, fats, sugar, and alcohol, and never smoke cigarettes.

9. Try to stay in tune with your moods and inner states. If your head aches or your stomach is churning, stop and try to figure out the stressor. If anxious or depressed, don't waste time denying your feelings. Do something physical as an antidote. At such times also move toward, not away from, other people.

10. Finally, when you're under stress, one of the best ways to stop the stress is to breathe slowly and deeply. Rapid, shallow breathing assisted our prehistoric ancestors to prepare for fighting or running.

9   Your chances of becoming a centenarian or of living a long and healthy life to whatever age depend on how successfully you manage stress in your daily life. Perhaps no area of brain-body interaction is as important as this, and perhaps no other is so much within your ability to influence.

Checking Your Comprehension

1. What does the author mean by a "juggling game" or "juggling act"?

_____

_____

2. When does psychologist Wayne Sotile believe stress results?

_____

_____

3. What does Sotile mean by "hurry sickness"?

_____

_____

4. What does he think is an antidote for "hurry sickness"?

_____

_____

5. How can learning how to handle stress affect your life?

_____

_____

Critical Reading and Thinking

1. What do you think is the major source of stress today? Why?

_____

_____

2. Do you think people are under more or less stress today than 100 years ago? Why?

_____

_____

3. Do you think it is true that people suffering from "hurry sickness" often become competitive, hostile, and cynical towards others? Why?

_____

_____

4. Which method of stress reduction do you think would work best for you? Why?

_____

_____

Words in Context

Directions: Locate each word in the paragraph indicated and reread that paragraph. Then, based on the way the word is used, write a synonym or brief definition. You may use a dictionary, if necessary.

1. afflicted (par. 5)   _____

2. antidote (par. 6)   _____

3. dimension (par. 7)   _____

4. avocation (par. 8)   _____

Vocabulary Review

Directions: Use the words listed in the Vocabulary Preview to complete each of the following sentences.

1. Rather than taking too many classes in one subject area, I tried to

_____ my course load.

2. After a hard week at work, he eagerly _____ the upcoming weekend.

3. My grandmother, who was born in 1896, is the honored _____ of our family.

4. Jennifer's painting took her weeks to complete, due to the _____ details she included.

5. Michael had been taken advantage of so many times by those he thought were his friends, that he developed a _____ opinion of people.

6. Money problems can become major _____ for many young couples.

7. The thought of seeing her old friends again after many years brought a _____ feeling of joy to Beth's life.

8. A student's midterm grades are a _____ indication of how well he or she is adjusting to college.

Summarizing the Reading Selection

Directions: On a separate sheet of paper, write a short summary (1–3 paragraphs) of the reading. Use your own words, but be concise and complete.

Writing Exercise

Describe a stressful situation you have experienced. How did you cope with the stress? After reading this article, how would you cope with it now?

PROGRESS CHARTS

Directions: As you complete each mastery test, record its chapter number, date and your percentage score.

Mastery Test 1

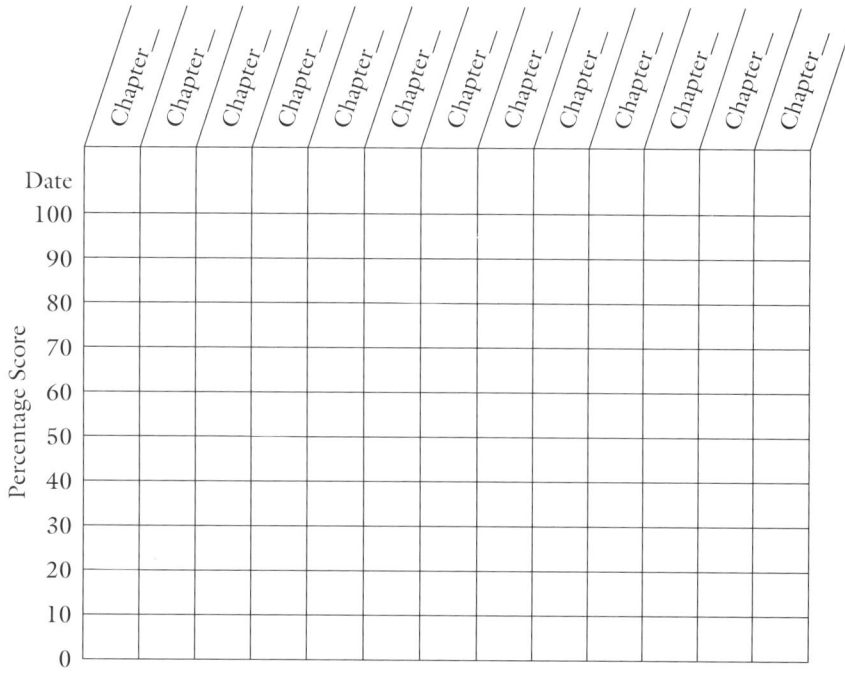

Mastery Test 2

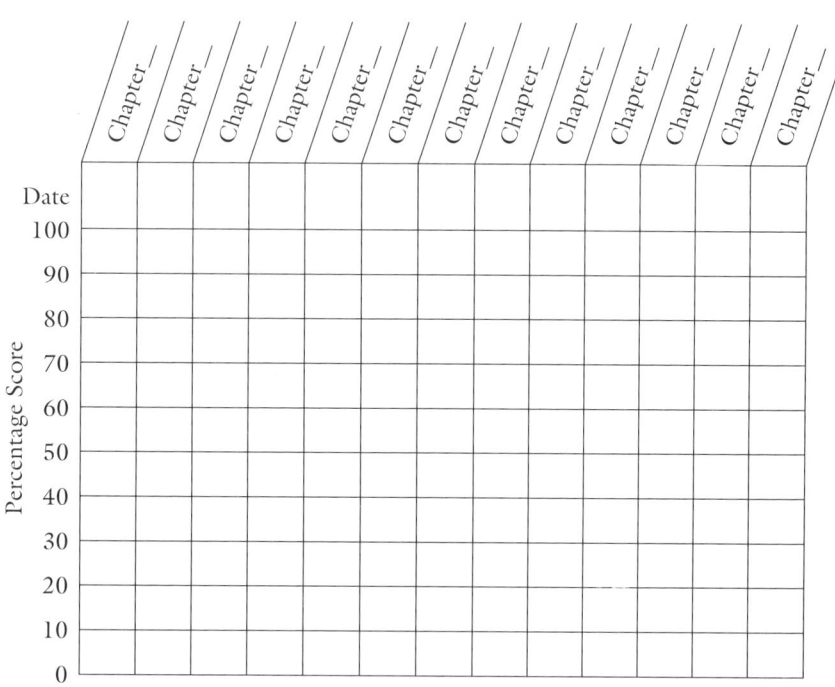

Mastery Test 3

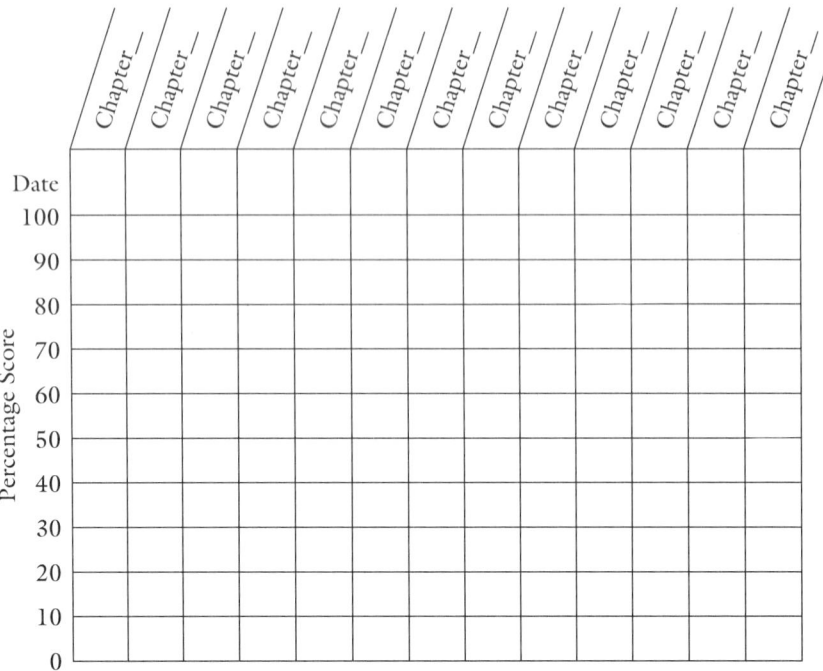

Mastery Test 4

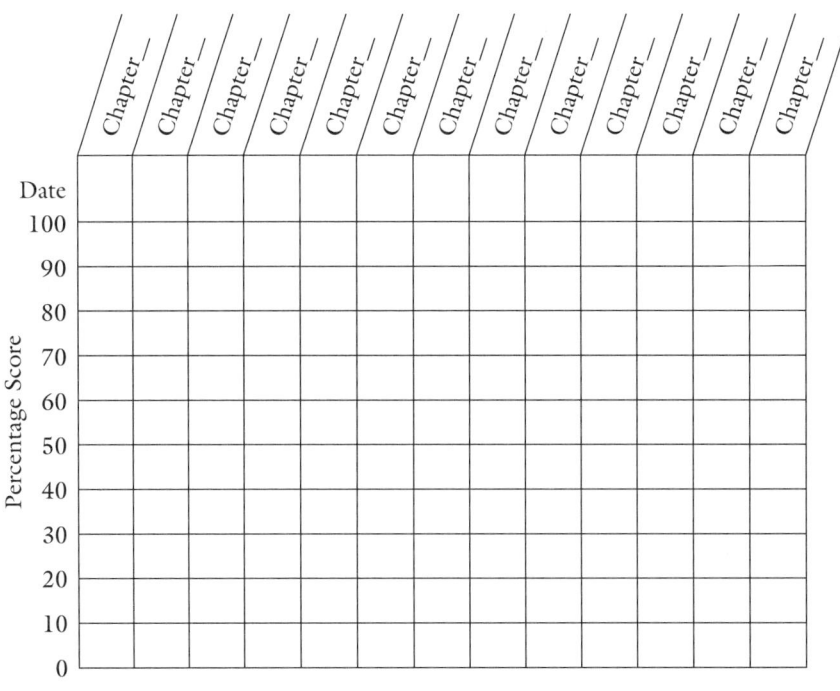

Endnotes

Chapter 1

1. Carol Wade and Carol Tavris, *Psychology,* 3rd ed. (New York: Harper & Row, 1993), p. 82.
2. James Trefil, "Greetings from the Antiworld," *Smithsonian,* June 1998, p. 62.
3. Robert Wallace, *Biology: The World of Life,* 5th ed. (Glenview, IL: Scott, Foresman, 1990), p. 185.
4. Knut Norstog and Andrew J. Meyerricks, *Biology* (Toronto: Charles E. Merrill, 1985), p. 193.
5. Ronald J. White, "Weightlessness and the Human Body," Scientific American Online, September 1998, p. 2.
6. Roger Chisholm and Mariln McCarty, *Principles of Economics* (Glenview, IL.: Scott, Foresman, 1981), p. 443.

Chapter 2

1. James Geiwitz, *Psychology,* 2nd ed. (Boston: Little, Brown, 1980) p. 189.
2. J. Ross Eschelman, Barbara G. Cushion, and Lawrence Basirico, *Sociology: An Introduction,* 4th ed. (New York: HarperCollins, 1993), p. 93.
3. Eschelman et al., pp. 98–99.
4. H. L. Capron, *Computers: Tools for an Information Age,* 5th ed. (New York: Addison Wesley Educational Publishers, Inc., 1998), p. 233.

Chapter 3

1. Curtis O. Byer and Louis W. Shainberg, *Living Well: Health in Your Own Hands,* 2nd ed. (New York: Addison Wesley Educational Publishers, Inc., 1995), p. 360.
2. Joseph A. DeVito, *Messages: Building Interpersonal Communication Skills,* 3rd ed. (New York: Addison Wesley Educational Publishers, Inc., 1996), pp. 22–23.
3. Byer and Shainberg, p. 67.
4. Robert Wallace, *Biology, The World of Life,* 6th ed. (New York: Addison Wesley Educational Publishers, Inc., 1992), p. 834.
5. Adapted from B. E. Pruitt and Jane J. Stein, *HealthStyles: Decisions for Living Well,* 2nd ed. (Needham Heights, MA: Allyn and Bacon, 1999), pp. 127–31.

Chapter 4

1. *American Heritage Dictionary of the English Language,* 3rd ed. (Boston: Houghton Mifflin, 1992), p. 104.
2. *American Heritage Dictionary,* p. 1308.

3. *American Heritage Dictionary*, p. 1981.
4. *American Heritage Dictionary*, p. 1093.
5. *American Heritage Dictionary*, p. 177.
6. *American Heritage Dictionary*, p. 653.

Chapter 5

1. Zena Block, *It's All on the Label* (Boston: Little, Brown, 1981), pp. 70–72.
2. Adapted from Rebecca J. Donatelle, *Access to Health*, 7th ed. (San Francisco: Benjamin Cummings, 2002), pp. 566–67.

Chapter 6

1. Richard P. Appelbaum and William J. Chambliss, *Sociology* (New York: HarperCollins, 1995), p. 540.
2. Edward S. Greenberg and Benjamin I. Page, *The Struggle for Democracy* (New York: HarperCollins, 1995), p. 446.
3. Greenberg and Page, p. 558.
4. Greenberg and Page, p. 540.
5. Alex Thio, *Sociology* (New York: HarperCollins, 1994), pp. 296–97.
6. Thio, p. 373.
7. Thio, p. 372.
8. From Roy A. Cook, Laura J. Yale, and Joseph J. Marqua, *Tourism: The Business of Travel* (Upper Saddle River, NJ: Prentice Hall, 1999), p. 135.
9. From Cook, Yale, and Marqua, p. 105.
10. From Hugh Barlow, *Criminal Justice in America* (Upper Saddle River, NJ: Prentice Hall, 2000), p. 569.

Chapter 7

1. Byer and Shainberg, p. 256.
2. Tim Curry, Robert Jiobu, and Kent Schwirian, *Sociology for the 21st Century* (Upper Saddle River, NJ: Prentice Hall, 2001), p. 356.
3. Adapted from Edward F. Bergman and William K. Renwick, *Introduction to Geography* (Upper Saddle River, NJ: Prentice Hall, 1999), pp. 343–44.
4. From Barlow, p. 290.
5. Stephen F. Davis and Joseph J. Palladino, *Psychology* (Upper Saddle River, N.J.: Prentice Hall, 2000), p. 190.
6. Rebecca J. Donatelle and Lorraine G. Davis, *Access to Health,* 6th ed. (Boston: Allyn and Bacon, 2000), p. 546.
7. Richard George, *The New Consumer Survival Kit* (Boston: Little, Brown, 1978), p. 212.
8. John Dorfman et al., *Well-Being: An Introduction to Health* (Glenview, IL: Scott, Foresman, 1980), p. 27.
9. Dorfman et al., p. 263.
10. K. Warner Schaie and James Geiwitz, *Adult Development and Aging* (Boston: Little, Brown, 1972), pp. 371–72.
11. Dorfman et al., p. 263.
12. Robert Wallace, *Biology: The World of Life*, 7th ed. (New York: Addison Wesley Educational Publishers, Inc., 1997), p. 497.
13. Richard Campbell, *Media and Culture* (Boston: St. Martin's Press, 1997), p. 196.
14. Byer and Shainberg, p. 289.
15. Bob Weinstein, *Jobs for the 21st Century* (New York: Macmillan, 1983), p. 118.
16. Edward S. Fox and Edward W. Wheatley, *Modern Marketing* (Glenview, IL: Scott, Foresman, 1978), p. 142.

17. William E. Thompson and Joseph V. Hickey, *Society in Focus* (New York: HarperCollins, 1994), p. 156.
18. Joyce Brothers, "What Dirty Words Really Mean," *Good Housekeeping*, May 1973.
19. Jean L. Weirich, *Personal Financial Management* (Boston: Little, Brown, 1983), p. 155.
20. William E. Smith and Raymond D. Liedlich, *From Thought to Theme* (New York: Harcourt Brace Jovanovich, 1983), pp. 281–82.
21. Adapted from Donatelle and Davis, p. 49.
22. Adapted from Joseph A. DeVito, *The Interpersonal Communication Book*, 9th ed. (Boston: Allyn & Bacon, 2001), p. 43.
23. Adapted from Cook, Yale, and Marqua, p. 151.
24. From Barlow, pp. 422–23.
25. Adapted from Wendy G. Lehnert, *Light on the Internet* (New York: Addison Wesley Longman, 1999), p. 44.
26. Adapted from Bergman and Renwick p. 365.
27. Adapted from Barlow, p. 271.
28. Adapted from Donatelle and Davis, pp. 285–86.
29. Adapted from Kathleen German, Bruce E. Gronbeck, Douglas Ehninger, and Alan H. Monroe, *Principles of Public Speaking*, 14th ed. (New York: Addison Wesley Longman, 2001), pp. 190–91.
30. Adapted from Curry et al., p. 138.
31. Adapted from Michael R. Solomon and Elnora W. Stuart, *Marketing.com: The Brave New World of E-Commerce* (Upper Saddle River, NJ: Prentice Hall, 2001) p. 13.
32. Adapted from German et al., p. 70.
33. Adapted from Michael R. Solomon, *Consumer Behavior*, 4th ed. (Upper Saddle River, NJ: Prentice Hall, 1999) p. 239.
34. Adapted from Donatelle and Davis, p. 40.
35. Adapted from Steven A. Beebe and John T. Masterson, *Communicating in Small Groups: Principles & Practice*, 6th ed. (New York: Addison Wesley Longman, 2000) p. 150.
36. Weinstein, pp. 110–11.
37. "Trees Talk to One Another," *Science Digest*, January 1984, p. 47.
38. John Neisbitt, *Megatrends* (New York: Warner Books, 1982), p. 23.
39. James Geiwitz, *Psychology*, 2nd ed. (Boston: Little, Brown, 1980), p. 276.
40. Frans Gerritsen, *Theory and Practice of Color* (New York: Van Nostrand, 1975), p. 9.
41. Adapted from Cook, Yale, and Marqua, pp. 246–47.
42. Adapted from Donatelle and Davis, pp. 289–90.
43. Adapted from Bergman and Renwick, pp. 384–85.
44. DeVito, *Messages*, pp. 224–25.
45. From Norstog and Meyerricks, p. 641.
46. From Solomon and Stuart, *Marketing.com*, p. 16.
47. Bergman and Renwick, p. 348.
48. DeVito, *Messages*, p. 140.
49. From Donatelle and Davis, p. 78.
50. From Cook, Yale, and Marqua, p. 86.

Chapter 8
1. Adapted from DeVito, *Messages*, p. 150.
2. Adapted from DeVito, *Messages*, p. 159.
3. From DeVito, *Messages*, p. 130.
4. Adapted from Pruitt and Stein, pp. 108, 110.
5. Adapted from Barlow, p. 238.

6. Geiwitz, p. 512.

7. Geiwitz, p. 513.

8. Geiwitz, p. 229.

9. George, p. 114.

10. "ABC's of How a President Is Chosen," *U.S. News & World Report,* February 18, 1980, p. 45.

11. Paul G. Hewitt, *Conceptual Physics* (Boston: Little, Brown, 1985), p. 15.

12. Ross J. Eshleman and Barbara G. Cashion, *Sociology: An Introduction,* 2nd ed. (Boston: Little, Brown, 1985), p. 88.

13. Hewitt, pp. 234–35.

14. Hewitt, p. 259.

15. From Solomon and Stuart, *Marketing.com,* p. 7.

16. Fact is from George Edwards III et al., *Government in America,* 9th ed. (New York: Addison Wesley Longman, 2000), pp. 458–59.

17. Facts from Davis and Palladino, pp. 563, 564, 566.

18. Facts from Donatelle and Davis, pp. 358, 371.

19. From John A. Garrity and Mark C. Carnes, *The American Nation,* 10th ed. (New York: Addison Wesley Longman, 2000), p. 706.

20. From Cook, Yale, and Marqua, pp. 150, 151.

21. From Lehnert, pp. 112, 131.

22. From Palmira Brummett, Robert B. Edgar, Neil Hackett, George F. Jewsbury, and Alastair M. Taylor, *Civilization Past & Present,* 9th ed. (New York: Addison Wesley Longman, 2000), p. 348.

23. Edward H. Reiley and Carroll L. Shry, *Introductory Horticulture* (Albany, NY: Delmar Publishers, 1979), p. 114.

24. Thio, p. 374.

25. DeVito, *Messages,* p. 284.

26. Adapted from Brummett et al., p. 919.

27. Adapted from Davis and Palladino , p. 609.

28. Adapted from Cook Yale, and Marqua, p. 156.

29. Adapted from Norstog and Meyerricks, p. 431.

30. Adapted from Stephen M. Kosslyn and Robin S. Rosenberg, *Psychology: The Brain, the Person, the World* (Boston: Allyn & Bacon, 2001), pp. 180–81.

Chapter 9

1. Sydney B. Newell, *Chemistry: An Introduction* (Boston: Little Brown,1980), p. 11.

2. Hewitt, p. 21.

3. Richard L. Weaver II, *Understanding Personal Communication* (Glenview, IL: Scott, Foresman and Company, 1987), p. 24.

4. Hewitt, p. 56.

5. Hewitt, p. 224.

6. *World Book* (Chicago: World Book, Inc., 2002), Vol. 14, p. 391.

7. Hal B. Pickle and Royce L. Abrahamson, *Introduction to Business* (Glenview, IL: Scott, Foresman and Company, 1987), p. 40.

8. Thompson and Hickey, p.70.

9. Pickel and Abrahamson, p. 119.

10. Hewitt, pp. 82–84.

11. *World Book,* Vol. 14, p. 332.

12. Robert C. Nickerson, *Fundamentals of Structured COBOL* (Glenview, IL: Scott, Foresman and Company, 1984), p. 2.

13. Weaver, p. 85.
14. Eshelman and Cashion, pp. 109–11.
15. Eshelman and Cashion, p. 583.
16. *World Book*, Vol. 14, p. 271.
17. Pickel and Abrahamson, p. 123.
18. Bowman O. Davis et al., *Conceptual Human Physiology* (Columbus, OH: Charles E. Merrill, 1985), p. 213.
19. Hewitt, p. 233.
20. Wade and Tavris, 3rd ed., p. 77.
21. Weaver, p. 24.
22. Weaver, p. 291.
23. Barlow, p.332.
24. Weaver, p. 123.
25. Hewitt, p. 252.
26. William M. Kephart and Davor Jedlicka, *The Family, Society, and the Individual* (New York: HarperCollins Publishers, 1991), p. 332.
27. *World Book*, Vol. 13, p. 221.
28. *World Book*, Vol. 13, p. 953.
29. Kephart and Jedlicka, pp. 332–33.
30. *World Book*, Vol. 13, p. 562.
31. *World Book*, Vol. 13, p. 672.
32. *World Book*, Vol. 13, pp. 795–96.
33. *World Book*, Vol. 13, p. 832.
34. Wade and Tavris, 3rd ed., p. 252.
35. *World Book*, Vol. 13, p. 46.
36. *World Book*, Vol. 13, p. 238.
37. Adapted from Michael R. Solomon and Elnora W. Stuart, *Marketing: Real People, Real Choices*, 2nd ed. (Upper Saddle River, NJ: Prentice Hall, 2000), p. 71.
38. Douglas Gronbeck, *Principles of Speech Communication* (New York: Addison Wesley Longman, Inc., 1988), pp. 32–33.
39. Michael C. Mix, Paul Farber, and Keith I. King, *Biology: the Network of Life* (New York: Addison Wesley Educational Publishers, Inc., 1996), p. 262.
40. DeVito, *The Interpersonal Communication Book*, 9th ed., pp. 219–220.
41. John D. Daniels and Lee H. Radebaugh, *International Business: Environments and Operations*, 8th ed. (New York: Addison Wesley Longman, Inc., 1995), p. 679.
42. Carole Wade and Carol Tavris, *Psychology*, 5th ed. (New York: Addison Wesley Educational Publishers, 1998), pp. 327–28.
43. Thomas Kinnear, Kenneth Bernhardt, and Kathlee Krentler, *Principles of Marketing*, 4th ed. (New York: Addison Wesley Longman, Inc., 1995), pp. 283–84.
44. Capron, p. 199.
45. Wade and Tavris, 5th ed. p. 494.
46. Wade and Tavris, 5th ed. p. 226.
47. James Spradley and David W. McCurdy, *Conformity and Conflict: Readings in Cultural Anthropology*, 9th ed. (New York: Addison Wesley Longman, Inc., 1997), p. 349.

Chapter 10
1. H. L. Capron, *Computers: Tools for an Information Age, Brief Edition* (New York: Addison Wesley Longman, Inc., 1998), pp. xxii, xxiv, xxv.
2. Byer and Shainberg, p. 311.

3. *American Heritage Dictionary of the English Language,* 3rd ed. (Boston: Houghton Mifflin Company, 1996), p. 410.
4. Kenneth Budinski, *Engineering Materials: Properties and Selection* (Reston, VA: Reston Publishing Co., 1979), p. 15.
5. Herbert E. Ellinger, *Auto-Mechanics,* 2nd ed. (Englewood Cliffs, NJ: Prentice Hall, 1977), p. 183.
6. Nickerson, p. 271.
7. Nickerson, p. 2.
8. Hewitt, pp. 54–56.
9. Adapted from Donatelle and Davis, pp. xix–xxi.

Chapter 11
1. Robert Wallace, *Biology: The World of Life,* 5th ed. (Glenview, IL: Scott Foresman, 1990), p. 314.
2. Wallace, 5th ed., p. 315.
3. Thompson and Hickey (front cover).
4. Wallace, 6th ed., p. 346.
5. Wallace, 6th ed., p. 346.
6. B. Getchell, *The Fitness Book* (Indianapolis: The Benchmark Press, 1987), p. 63.
7. Donald G. Kaufman and Cecilia M. Franz, *Biosphere 2000* (New York: HarperCollins, 1993), p. 172.
8. U.S. Bureau of the Census, *Statistical Abstract of the United States* (Washington, DC: U.S. Government Printing Office, 1993), p. 856.
9. William Pride, Robert J. Hughes, and Jack R. Kapoor, *Business* (Boston: Houghton Mifflin, 1991), p. 454.
10. Thompson and Hickey, p. 485.
11. Byer and Shainberg, p. G-5.
12. *Buffalo Evening News,* June 7, 1991.
13. Randall B. Dunham and Jon L. Pierce, *Management* (Glenview, IL: Scott, Foresman and Company, 1989), p. 721.
14. Neil J. Smelser, *Sociology* (Englewood Cliffs, NJ: Prentice-Hall, 1991), p. 218.
15. Robert L. Lineberry, *Government in America: People, Politics and Policy,* 2nd ed. (Glenview IL: Scott, Foresman and Company, 1983), p. 253.
16. David D. Van Fleet, *Contemporary Management* (Boston: Houghton Mifflin, 1991), p. 187.
17. Marge Thielman Hastreiter, "Not Every Mother Is Glad Kids Are Back in School," *Buffalo Evening News,* June 7, 1991, p. 1.
18. Thompson and Hickey (inside cover).
19. John C. Merrill, John Lee, and Edward Jay Friedlander, *Modern Mass Media* (New York: HarperCollins, 1994), p. 207.
20. Thompson and Hickey, p. 179.
21. Wallace, 5th ed., p. 427.
22. Wallace, 5th ed., p. 426.
23. Capron, 5th ed., p. 19.
24. Appelbaum and Chambliss, p. 552.
25. From Donatelle and Davis, pp. 272–73.

Chapter 12
1. Byer and Shainberg, pp. 78–79.
2. Kinnear, Bernhardt, and Krentler, p. 132.

3. Watson M. Laetsch, *Plants: Basic Concepts in Botany* (Boston: Little, Brown, 1979), p. 8.
4. Byer and Shainberg, p. 311.
5. Newell, pp. 47–48.
6. William M. Pride and O. C. Ferrell, *Marketing: Concepts and Strategies* (Boston: Houghton Mifflin, 1991) p. 380.
7. Kinnear, Bernhardt, and Krentler, pp. 39–40.
8. Carol Wade and Carol Tavris, *Invitation to Psychology,* 7th ed. (Upper Saddle River, NJ: Prentice Hall, 2002), p. 392.
9. Brummett et al., p. 446.
10. Cook, Yale, & Marqua, p. 156.
11. Pruit and Stein, p. 81.
12. Donatelle and Davis, p. 120.
13. Adapted from German et al., pp. 38–39.

Chapter 13
1. Robert C. Yeager, *Seasons of Shame: The New Violence in Sports* (New York: McGraw-Hill, 1979), p. 6.
2. Bill Cosby, *Time Flies* (New York: Doubleday, 1987), pp. 169–70.
3. Paul Arandt, *Paul Harvey's The Rest of the Story,* edited and compiled by Lynne Harvey (New York: Doubleday, 1977), p. 116.
4. Weaver, p. 291.
5. Lewis Katz, *Know Your Rights* (Cleveland: Banks Baldwin Law, 1993), p. 54.
6. Richard Shenkman, *Legends, Lies, and Myths of American History* (New York: William Morrow, 1988), pp. 37–38.
7. Linda M. Hasselstrom, "A Peaceful Woman Explains Why She Carries a Gun," *Utne Reader,* May/June 1991, pp. 88–91.
8. "The Lion's Share, A Somali Tale," from Cynthia Dresser, *The Rainmaker's Dog* (New York: St. Martin's Press, 1994), pp.110–11.
9. Tom Bodett, *As Far as You Can Go Without a Passport: The View from the End of the Road* (Reading, MA: Addison-Wesley, 1985), pp. 79–81.
10. Emily Dickenson, first stanza of poem #754, *The Complete Poems of Emily Dickenson,* edited by Thomas E. Johnson (Boston: Little, Brown, 1960), p. 369.
11. Sara King, "Love in the Afternoon—in a Crowded Prison Hall," *Los Angeles Times,* November 5, 1976.
12. "Stop Junk Mail Forever," *Mother Earth News,* August/September 1994, p. 18.
13. Wallace, 6th ed., p. 460.
14. Hastreiter, "Not Every Mother Is Glad Kids Are Back in School."
15. Johnson C. Montgomery, "The Island of Plenty," *The Norton Sampler: Short Essays for Composition,* Thomas Cooley, editor (New York: W.W. Norton, 1985), p. 310.
16. Bess Armstrong article, from *The Choices We Made,* edited by Angela Bonavoglia (New York: Random House, 1991), p. 165.
17. Barry Lopez, "Weekend," *Audubon,* July 1973.
18. John Steinbeck, *America and Americans* (New York: Viking Press, 1966), pp. 127–28.
19. Shaughnessy Bishop-Stall, "A Day in the Life of a Lab Rat," *Utne Reader Online: Technology,* June 16, 2001.
20. From Donatelle and Davis, p. 146.
21. From Solomon and Stuart, *Marketing.com,* p. 17.
22. From Joe L. Kincheloe et al., *Contextualizing Teaching* (Boston: Allyn & Bacon), pp. 90–91.
23. From Solomon and Stuart, *Marketing: Real People, Real Choices,* p. 59.

24. From Brummett et al., pp. 578–79.

25. Adapted from Mary Bricker-Jenkins, *The Strengths in Social Work Practice*, 2nd ed. (New York: Addison Wesley Longman Publishers, 1997), pp. 216–20.

Chapter 14

1. Yeager, p. 4.

2. Barbara Stern, "Calm Down in Six Seconds," *Vogue*, October 1981.

3. Denise Fortino, "Why Kids Need Heroes," from *Parents Magazine*, November 1984.

4. Mary Gander and Harry W. Gardiner, *Child and Adolescent Development* (Boston: Little, Brown, 1981), p. 384.

5. Haim Ginott, *Between Parent and Teenager* (New York: Macmillan, 1969), pp. 39–41.

6. E. B. White, *One Man's Meat* (New York: Harper & Row, 1944), pp. 305–6.

7. Gail Sheehy, *Passages* (New York: E. P. Dutton, 1976), p. 68.

8. Greenberg and Page, p. 186.

9. Skolnick, *The Intimate Environment: Exploring Marriage and the Family* (Boston: Allyn & Bacon, 1996) p. 96.

10. Studs Terkel, *Jesusita Novarro* (New York: Pantheon Books, 1974), pp. 303–4.

11. Jon Katz, "The War on Children's Culture," *New York Times*, August 4, 1991, pp. H-7, 15.

12. Adapted from Edwards et al., p. 685.

13. Adapted from Edwards et al., pp. 426–27.

14. Bronwyn Jones, "Arming Myself With a Gun Is Not the Answer," *Newsweek*, May 22, 2000.

Credits

Text and Figures

Copyright © 1996 by Houghton Mifflin Company. Reproduced by permission from *The American Heritage Dictionary of the English Language*, 3/e, pp. 104, 171, 653, 1093, 1308, 1981

Paul Arandt, *Paul Harvey's The Rest of the Story*, p. 116. © 1977 Doubleday.

Ronald Bailey, "The Case for Selling Human Organs." Reprinted with permission from Reason Online. Copyright © 2001 by Reason Foundation, 3415 S. Sepulveda Blvd., Suite 400, Los Angeles, CA 90034. www.reason.com.

Hugh D. Barlow, *Criminal Justice in America*, pp. 238, 271, 290, 422, 569. © 2000. Reprinted by permission of Pearson Education, Inc., Upper Saddle River, NJ.

Steven A. Beebe and John T. Masterson, *Communicating in Small Groups: Principles & Practice*, 6/e, p. 150. Copyright © 2000 by Allyn & Bacon. Reprinted by permission.

Bergman/Renwick, *Introduction to Geography*, 2/e, pp. 343–344, 348, 365, 384–385. Copyright © 2001. Reprinted by permission of Pearson Education, Inc., Upper Saddle River, NJ.

Shaughnessy Bishop-Stall, "A Day in the Life of a Lab Rat." Copyright © 2001. Reprinted by permission of the author.

Zenas Block, *It's All on the Label*, pp. 70–72. © 1981 Little, Brown.

Tom Bodett, excerpt from *As Far As You Can Go Without a Passport*, pp. 79–81. Copyright © 1985 by Tom Bodett. Reprinted by permission of Perseus Books Publishers, a member of Perseus Books, L.L.C.

Mary Bricker-Jenkins, *The Strengths in Social Work Practice*, 2/e. © 1997 Allyn & Bacon. Reprinted by permission of Pearson Education, Inc.

Joyce Brothers, M.D., excerpt from Dr. Joyce Brothers' column on "What Dirty Words Mean," from *Good Housekeeping*, May 1973. Reprinted by permission of the author.

Brummett et al., *Civilization: Past & Present*, 9/e, pp. 348, 446, 578–579, 919. Copyright © 2000. Reprinted by permission of Pearson Education, Inc.

Curtis Byer and Louis Shainberg, *Living Well: Health in Your Own Hands*, 2/e, pp. 67, 78–79, 256, 289, 311, 360, G-5. © 1995 Jones & Bartlett Publishers, Sudbury, MA. www.jbpub.com. Reprinted with permission.

H.L. Capron, *Computers: Tools for an Information Age*, Brief Edition, pp. xxiii, xxiv, xxv. © 1998. Reprinted by permission of Pearson Education, Inc., Upper Saddle River, NJ.

Pickle/Abrahamson, *Introduction to Business*, pp. 40, 119, 123. © 1987. Reprinted by permission of Pearson Education, Inc., Upper Saddle River, NJ.

Pride, William M. and O.C. Ferrell, *Marketing: Basic Concepts and Strategies*, Seventh Edition, p. 380. Copyright © 1991 by Houghton Mifflin Company. Used with permission.

Pruitt/Stein, *Health Styles: Decisions for Living Well*, 2/e, pp. 81, 108, 110, 127, 131. Copyright © 1999 Addison Wesley. Reprinted by permission of Pearson Education, Inc.

William Recktenwald, "A Guard's First Night on the Job." Copyrighted 2001 Chicago Tribune Company. All rights reserved. Used with permission.

Rodrigo Joseph Rodriguez, "The Meaning of Work," Hispanicmagazine.com, October 1999. Copyright © 1999 Hispanic Publishing Corporation. Used with permission.

Skolnick, *The Intimate Environment: Exploring Marriage and the Family*, p. 96. Copyright © 1996 by Allyn & Bacon. Reprinted with permission.

Solomon/Stuart, *Marketing: Real People, Real Choices*, 2/e, pp. 59, 71. © 2000. Reprinted by permission of Pearson Education, Inc., Upper Saddle River, NJ.

Deborah Tannen, "Don't Ask," from *You Just Don't Understand*. Copyright © 1990 by Deborah Tannen. By permission of HarperCollins Publishers, Inc. William Morrow Company, Inc.

Studs Terkel, "Jesusita Novarro," from *Working: People Talk About What They Do All Day*. Copyright © 1974 by Studs Terkel. Reprinted by permission of Donadio & Olson, Inc.

Alex Thio, *Sociology*, pp. 296–297, 372, 373, 374. © 1994 HarperCollins. Reprinted by permission of Pearson Education, Inc.

William Thompson and Joseph Hickey, *Society in Focus*, pp. front cover, 70, 156, 179, 451, 485. Copyright © 1994 by Allyn & Bacon. Reprinted by permission.

James Trefil "Greetings from the Antiworld," *Smithsonian*, June 1998, p. 62. Reprinted by permission.

USA Today, "School's Out for 98? But This is only April," *USA TODAY*, April 16, 1998. Copyright © 1998 USA Today. Reprinted with permission.

David D. Van Fleet, *Contemporary Management*, 2/e, p. 187. Copyright © 1991 by Houghton Mifflin Company. Used with permission.

Wade/Tavris, *Psychology*, 3/e, pp. 77, 82, 252. Copyright © 1993 Prentice Hall. Reprinted by permission of Pearson Education, Inc. Upper Saddle River, NJ.

Wallace, *Biology: The World of Life*, 5/e, excerpts taken from pp. 815, 209, 314, 315, 346, 426, 427, 460, 537, 585, 635, 674, 834. © 1990 Scott Foresman. Reprinted by permission of Pearson Education, Inc.

Seaborn "Beck" Weathers, "A Night Out in the Death Zone," from *Everest: Mountain without Mercy*. Copyright © National Geographic Society. Reprinted by permission.

Richard L. Weaver, *Understanding Interpersonal Communication*, pp. 24, 85, 123, 291. Copyright © 1987 by Allyn & Bacon. Reprinted by permission.

Kenneth Weiss, "Dreams for Sale," *Los Angeles Times*, June 17, 2001. Copyright © 2001 Los Angeles Times, Inc. All rights reserved.

Alton Fitzgerald White, "Ragtime, My Time," from *The Nation*, October 11, 1999. Reprinted with permission.

World Book, Vol. 13, pp. 46, 178, 238, 474, 672, 688, 795–796; Vol. 14, pp. 270, 271, 309. © 2002 World Book, Inc. Used with permission.

Robert C. Yeager, *Seasons of Shame: The New Violence in Sports*, pp. 4, 6. © 1979 McGraw Hill. Reprinted by permission of The McGraw Hill Companies, Inc.

Photographs

Index